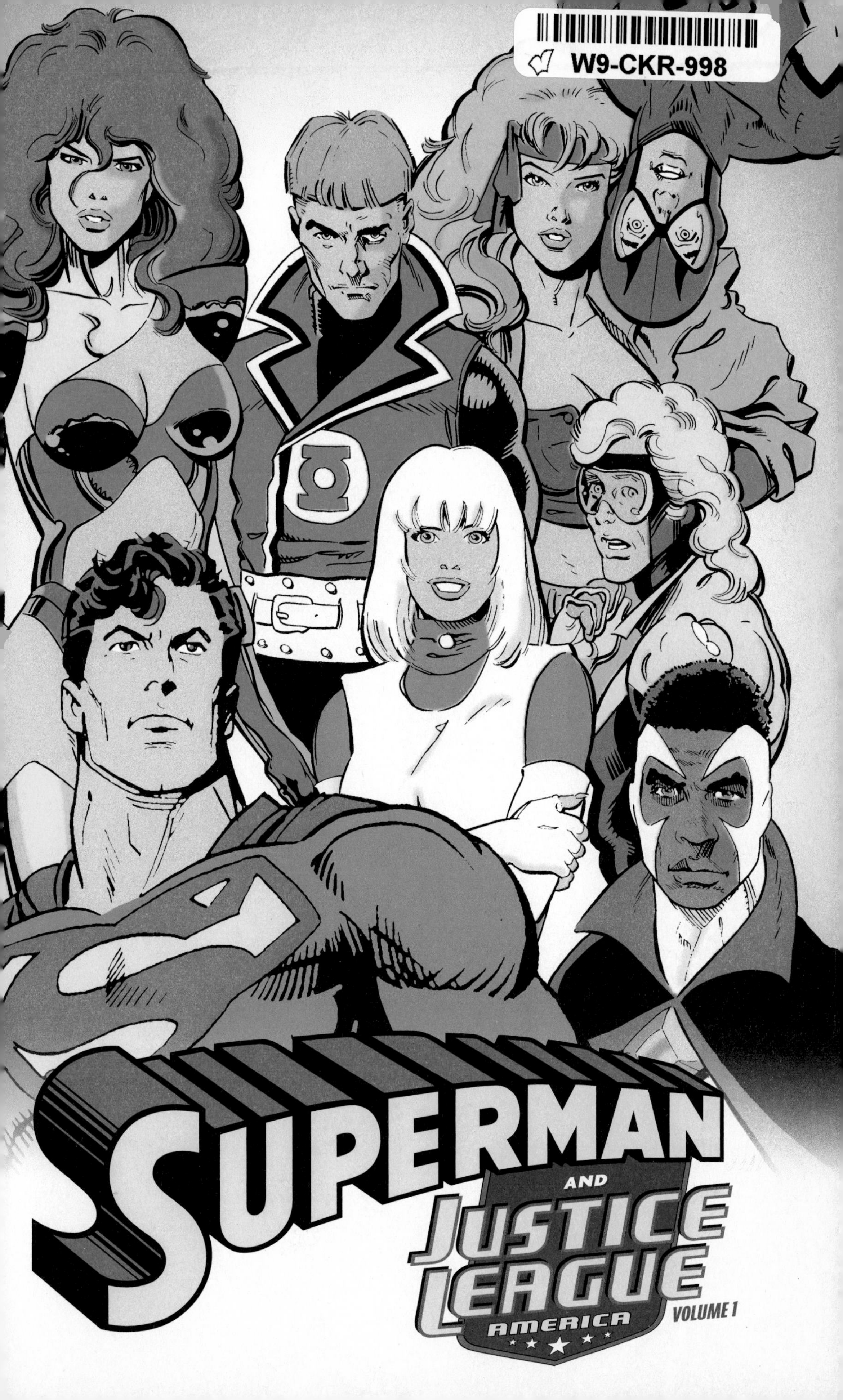
SUPERMAN
AND
JUSTICE LEAGUE AMERICA
VOLUME 1

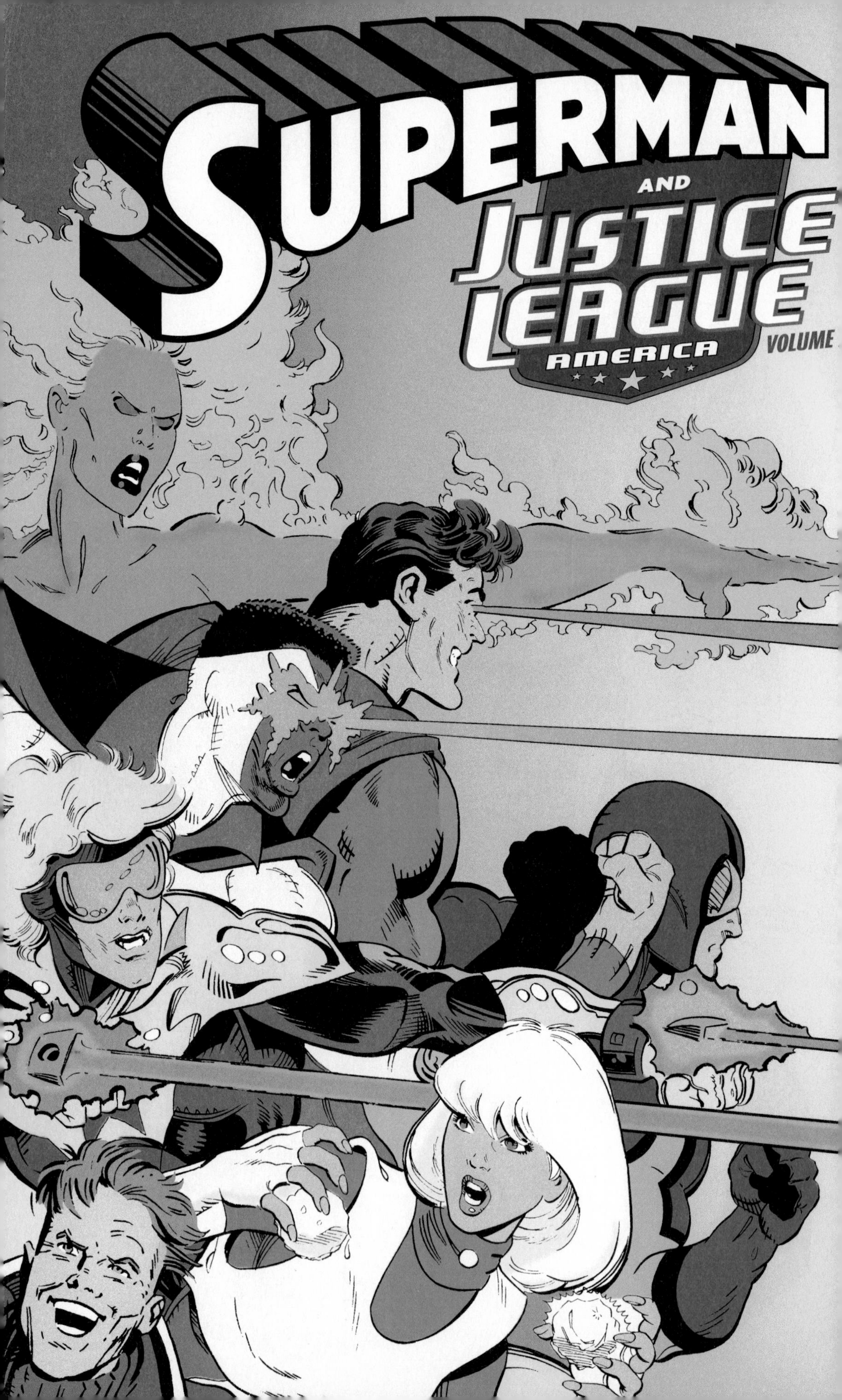
SUPERMAN
AND
JUSTICE LEAGUE AMERICA
VOLUME

DAN JURGENS
GERARD JONES
WRITERS

DAN JURGENS
RON RANDALL
PENCILLERS

RICK BURCHETT
RANDY ELLIOTT
JACKSON GUICE
JOSÉ MARZÁN JR.
INKERS

GENE D'ANGELO
JOHN CEBOLLERO
COLORISTS

BOB PINAHA
WILLIE SCHUBERT
LETTERERS

DAN JURGENS
RON RANDALL
COLLECTION COVER ART

SUPERMAN CREATED BY **JERRY SIEGEL** AND **JOE SHUSTER**.
BY SPECIAL ARRANGEMENT WITH THE JERRY SIEGEL FAMILY.

BRIAN AUGUSTYN Editor – Original Series
RUBEN DIAZ Assistant Editor – Original Series
JEB WOODARD Group Editor – Collected Editions
PAUL SANTOS Editor – Collected Edition
STEVE COOK Design Director – Books
CURTIS KING JR. Publication Design
BOB HARRAS Senior VP – Editor-in-Chief, DC Comics

DIANE NELSON President
DAN DiDIO and JIM LEE Co-Publishers
GEOFF JOHNS Chief Creative Officer
AMIT DESAI Senior VP – Marketing & Global Franchise Management
NAIRI GARDINER Senior VP – Finance
SAM ADES VP – Digital Marketing
BOBBIE CHASE VP – Talent Development
MARK CHIARELLO Senior VP – Art, Design & Collected Editions
JOHN CUNNINGHAM VP – Content Strategy
ANNE DEPIES VP – Strategy Planning & Reporting
DON FALLETTI VP – Manufacturing Operations
LAWRENCE GANEM VP – Editorial Administration & Talent Relations
ALISON GILL Senior VP – Manufacturing & Operations
HANK KANALZ Senior VP – Editorial Strategy & Administration
JAY KOGAN VP – Legal Affairs
DEREK MADDALENA Senior VP – Sales & Business Development
JACK MAHAN VP – Business Affairs
DAN MIRON VP – Sales Planning & Trade Development
NICK NAPOLITANO VP – Manufacturing Administration
CAROL ROEDER VP – Marketing
EDDIE SCANNELL VP – Mass Account & Digital Sales
COURTNEY SIMMONS Senior VP – Publicity & Communications
JIM (SKI) SOKOLOWSKI VP – Comic Book Specialty & Newsstand Sales
SANDY YI Senior VP – Global Franchise Management

SUPERMAN AND JUSTICE LEAGUE AMERICA VOL. 1
Published by DC Comics. Compilation Copyright © 2016 DC Comics. All Rights Reserved.
Originally published in single magazine form in JUSTICE LEAGUE SPECTACULAR 1 and
JUSTICE LEAGUE AMERICA 61-68. Copyright © 1992, DC Comics. All Rights Reserved. All
characters, their distinctive likenesses and related elements featured in this publication
are trademarks of DC Comics. The stories, characters and incidents featured in this
publication are entirely fictional. DC Comics does not read or accept unsolicited
submissions of ideas, stories or artwork.

DC Comics, 2900 West Alameda Avenue, Burbank, CA 91505
Printed by RR Donnelley, Salem, VA, USA. 2/19/16. First printing.
ISBN: 978-1-4012-6097-2

Library of Congress Cataloging-in-Publication Data is available.

MIX
Paper from
responsible sources
FSC® C101537

FSC
www.fsc.org

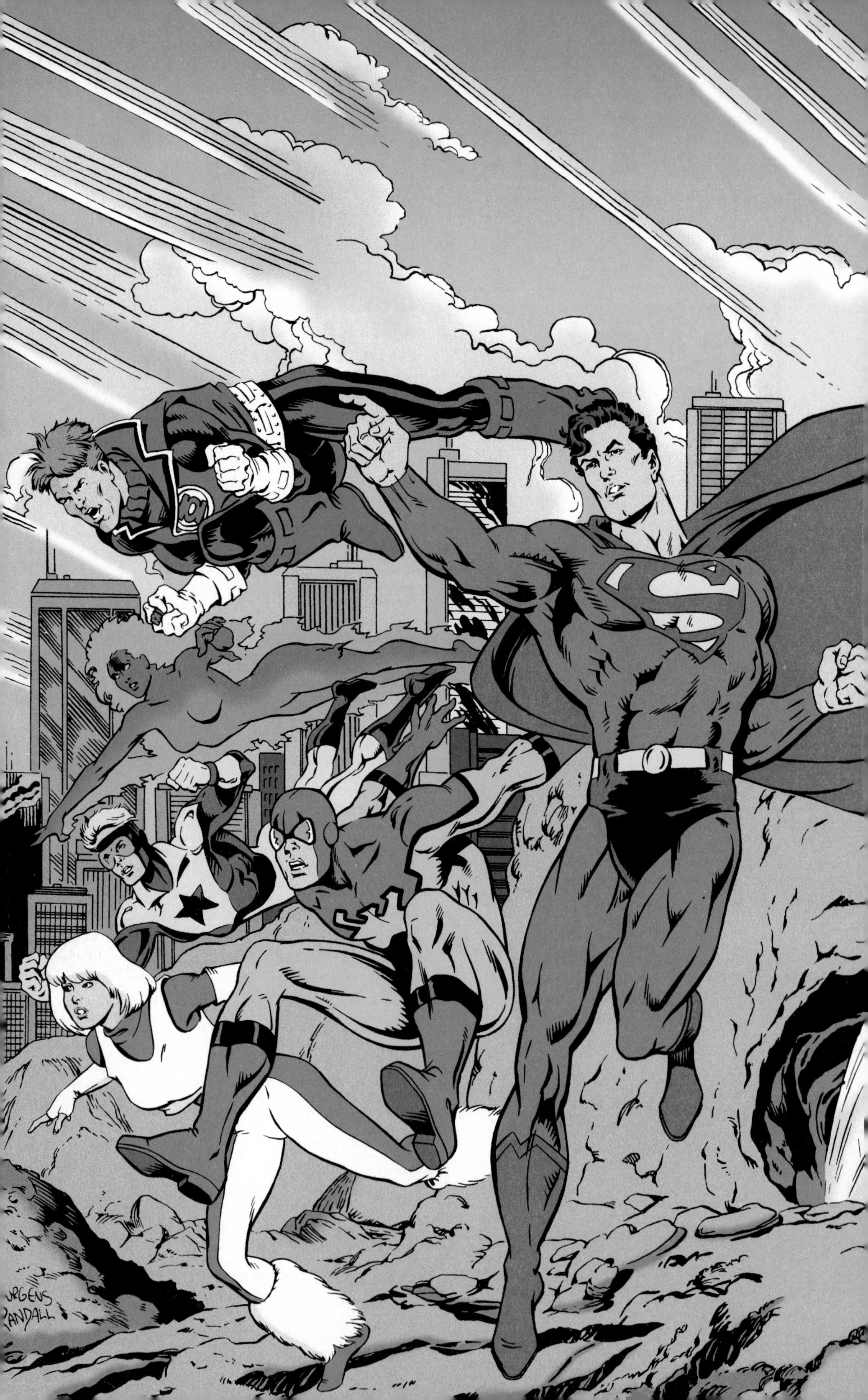

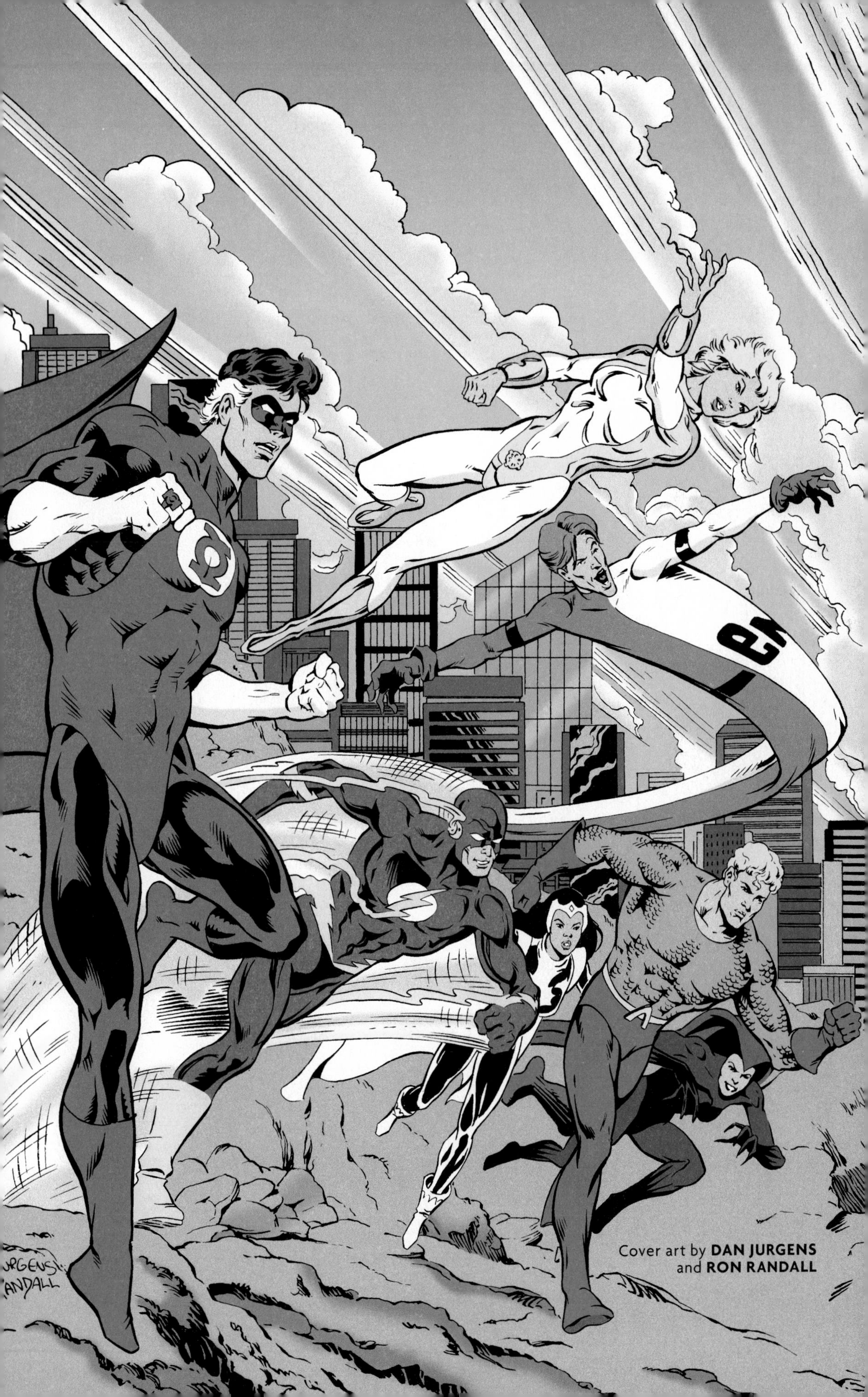

Cover art by **DAN JURGENS** and **RON RANDALL**

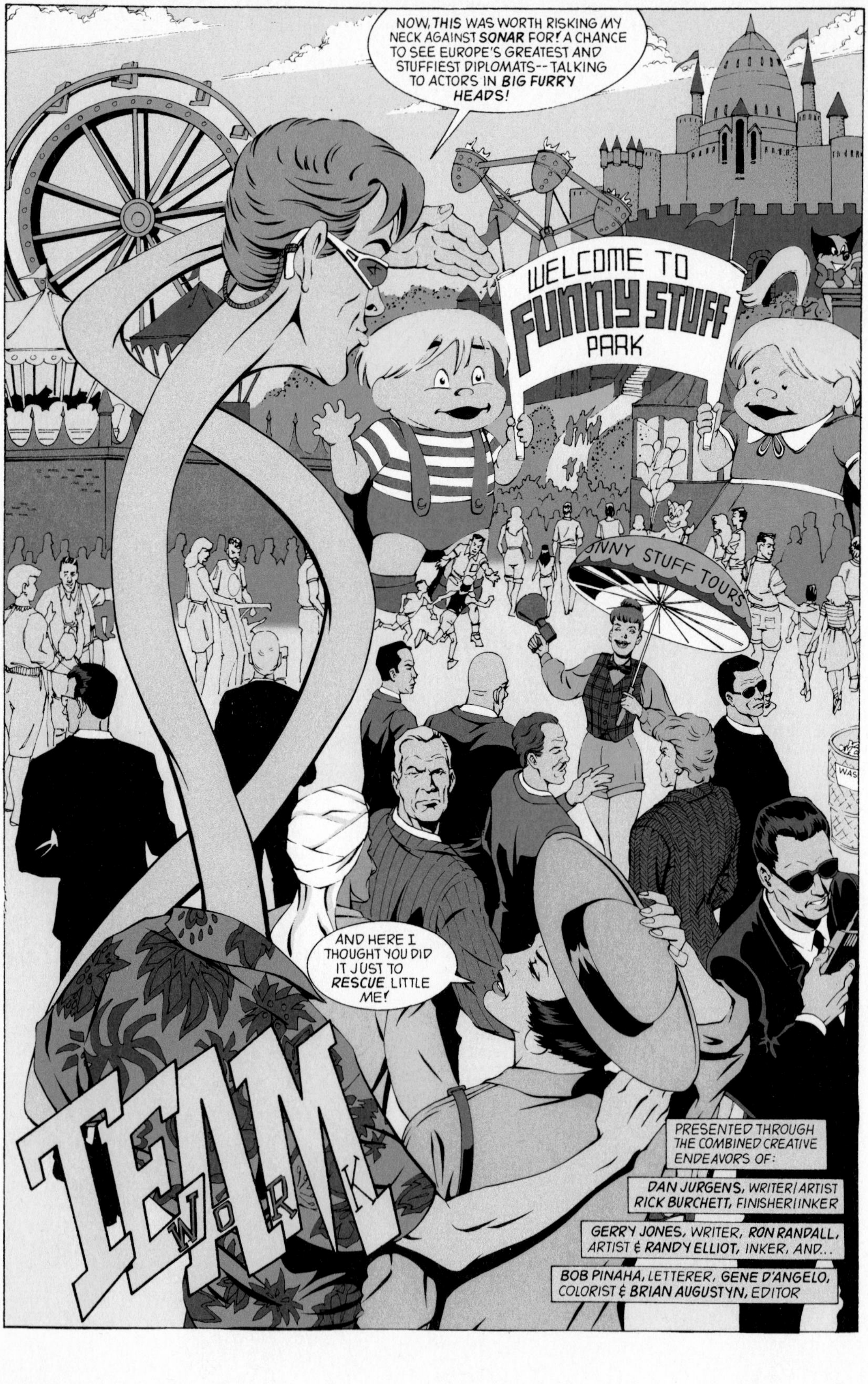
NOW, THIS WAS WORTH RISKING MY NECK AGAINST SONAR FOR! A CHANCE TO SEE EUROPE'S GREATEST AND STUFFIEST DIPLOMATS-- TALKING TO ACTORS IN BIG FURRY HEADS!
WELCOME TO FUNNY STUFF PARK
UNNY STUFF TOURS
AND HERE I THOUGHT YOU DID IT JUST TO RESCUE LITTLE ME!
TEAM WORK
PRESENTED THROUGH THE COMBINED CREATIVE ENDEAVORS OF:
DAN JURGENS, WRITER/ARTIST
RICK BURCHETT, FINISHER/INKER
GERRY JONES, WRITER, RON RANDALL, ARTIST & RANDY ELLIOT, INKER, AND..
BOB PINAHA, LETTERER, GENE D'ANGELO, COLORIST & BRIAN AUGUSTYN, EDITOR

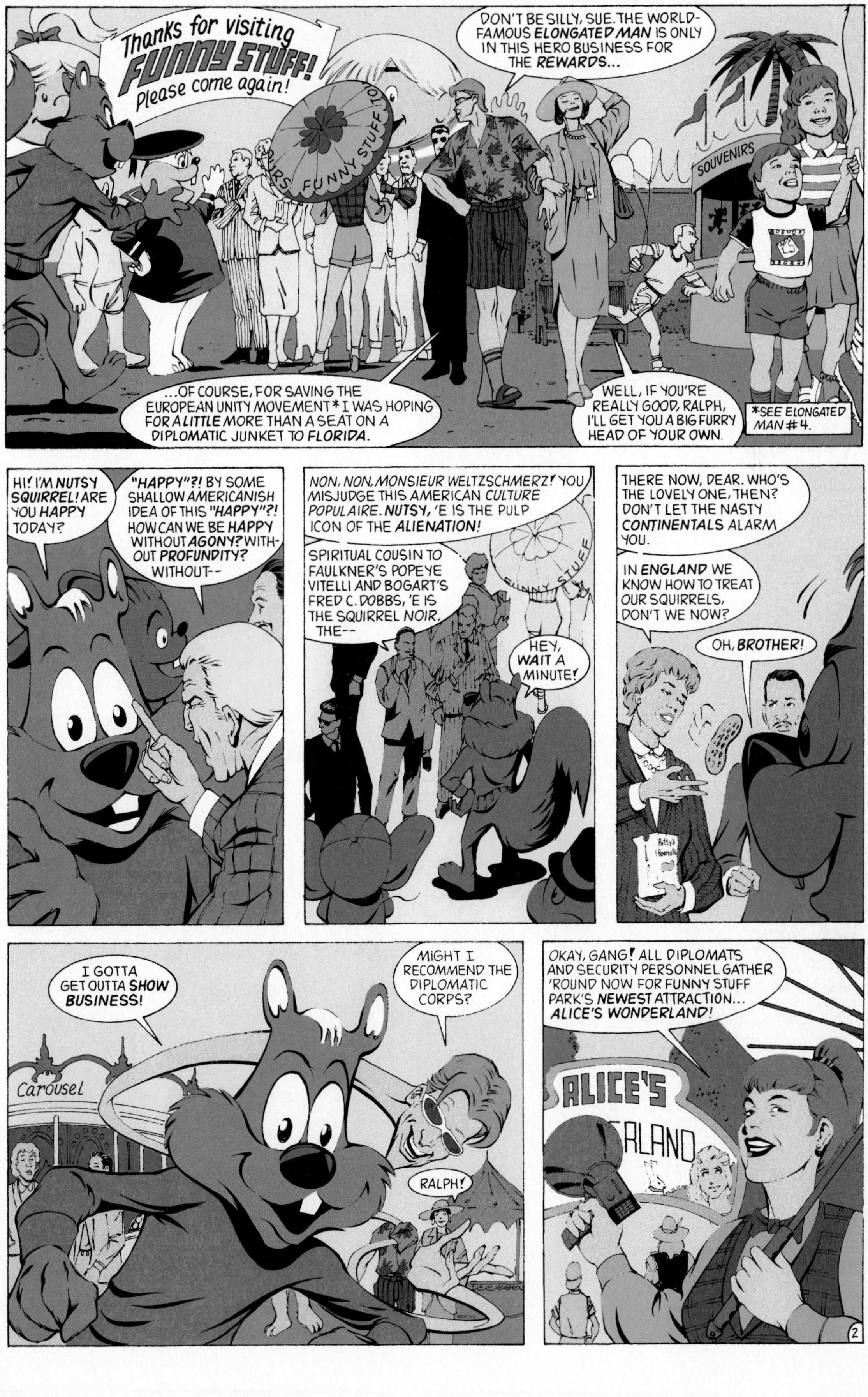

Thanks for visiting FUNNY STUFF! Please come again!
DON'T BE SILLY, SUE. THE WORLD-FAMOUS ELONGATED MAN IS ONLY IN THIS HERO BUSINESS FOR THE REWARDS...
...OF COURSE, FOR SAVING THE EUROPEAN UNITY MOVEMENT* I WAS HOPING FOR A LITTLE MORE THAN A SEAT ON A DIPLOMATIC JUNKET TO FLORIDA.
WELL, IF YOU'RE REALLY GOOD, RALPH, I'LL GET YOU A BIG FURRY HEAD OF YOUR OWN.
*SEE ELONGATED MAN #4.
SOUVENIRS
HI! I'M NUTSY SQUIRREL! ARE YOU HAPPY TODAY?
"HAPPY"?! BY SOME SHALLOW AMERICANISH IDEA OF THIS "HAPPY"?! HOW CAN WE BE HAPPY WITHOUT AGONY? WITHOUT PROFUNDITY? WITHOUT--
NON, NON, MONSIEUR WELTZSCHMERZ! YOU MISJUDGE THIS AMERICAN CULTURE POPULAIRE. NUTSY, 'E IS THE PULP ICON OF THE ALIENATION!
SPIRITUAL COUSIN TO FAULKNER'S POPEYE VITELLI AND BOGART'S FRED C. DOBBS, 'E IS THE SQUIRREL NOIR, THE--
HEY, WAIT A MINUTE!
THERE NOW, DEAR. WHO'S THE LOVELY ONE, THEN? DON'T LET THE NASTY CONTINENTALS ALARM YOU.
IN ENGLAND WE KNOW HOW TO TREAT OUR SQUIRRELS, DON'T WE NOW?
OH, BROTHER!
I GOTTA GET OUTTA SHOW BUSINESS!
MIGHT I RECOMMEND THE DIPLOMATIC CORPS?
Carousel
RALPH!
OKAY, GANG! ALL DIPLOMATS AND SECURITY PERSONNEL GATHER 'ROUND NOW FOR FUNNY STUFF PARK'S NEWEST ATTRACTION... ALICE'S WONDERLAND!
ALICE'S

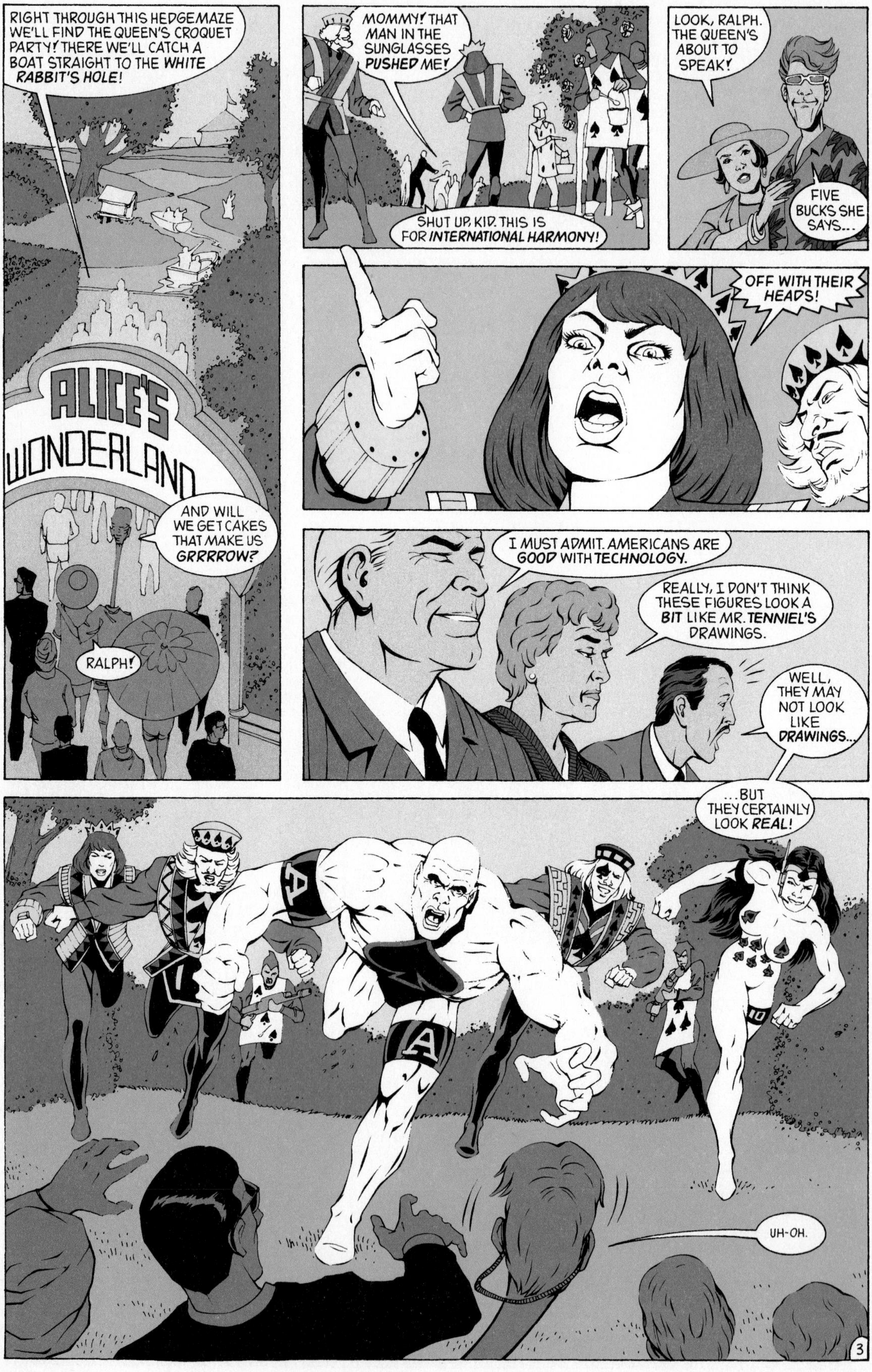
RIGHT THROUGH THIS HEDGEMAZE WE'LL FIND THE QUEEN'S CROQUET PARTY! THERE WE'LL CATCH A BOAT STRAIGHT TO THE WHITE RABBIT'S HOLE!
ALICE'S WONDERLAND
AND WILL WE GET CAKES THAT MAKE US GRRRROW?
RALPH!
MOMMY! THAT MAN IN THE SUNGLASSES PUSHED ME!
SHUT UP, KID. THIS IS FOR INTERNATIONAL HARMONY!
LOOK, RALPH. THE QUEEN'S ABOUT TO SPEAK!
FIVE BUCKS SHE SAYS...
OFF WITH THEIR HEADS!
I MUST ADMIT. AMERICANS ARE GOOD WITH TECHNOLOGY.
REALLY, I DON'T THINK THESE FIGURES LOOK A BIT LIKE MR. TENNIEL'S DRAWINGS.
WELL, THEY MAY NOT LOOK LIKE DRAWINGS...
...BUT THEY CERTAINLY LOOK REAL!
UH-OH.

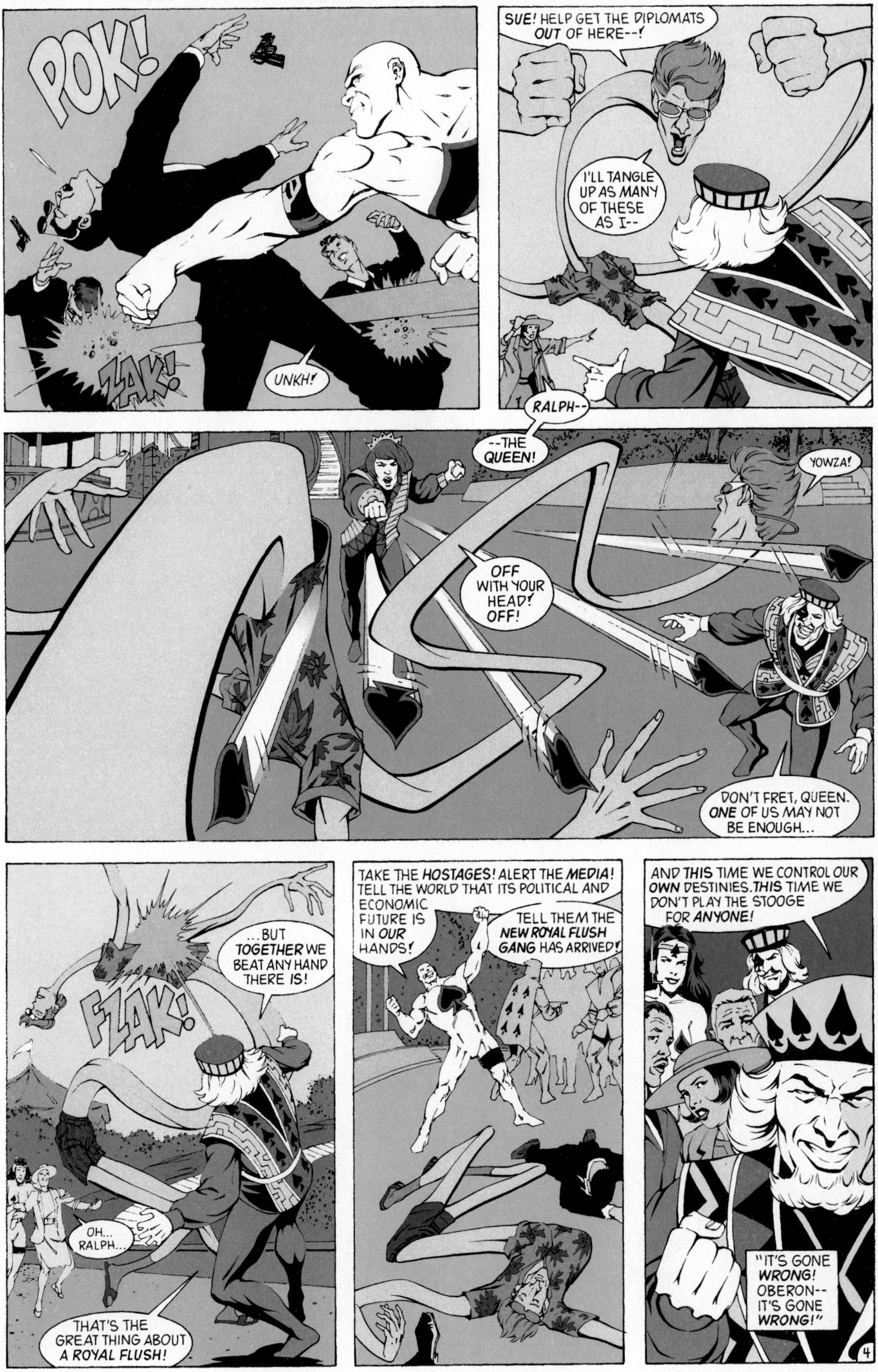
POK!
ZAK!
UNKH!
SUE! HELP GET THE DIPLOMATS OUT OF HERE--!
I'LL TANGLE UP AS MANY OF THESE AS I--
RALPH--
--THE QUEEN!
YOWZA!
OFF WITH YOUR HEAD! OFF!
DON'T FRET, QUEEN. ONE OF US MAY NOT BE ENOUGH...
FZAK!
...BUT TOGETHER WE BEAT ANY HAND THERE IS!
OH... RALPH...
THAT'S THE GREAT THING ABOUT A ROYAL FLUSH!
TAKE THE HOSTAGES! ALERT THE MEDIA! TELL THE WORLD THAT ITS POLITICAL AND ECONOMIC FUTURE IS IN OUR HANDS!
TELL THEM THE NEW ROYAL FLUSH GANG HAS ARRIVED!
AND THIS TIME WE CONTROL OUR OWN DESTINIES. THIS TIME WE DON'T PLAY THE STOOGE FOR ANYONE!
"IT'S GONE WRONG! OBERON-- IT'S GONE WRONG!"
4

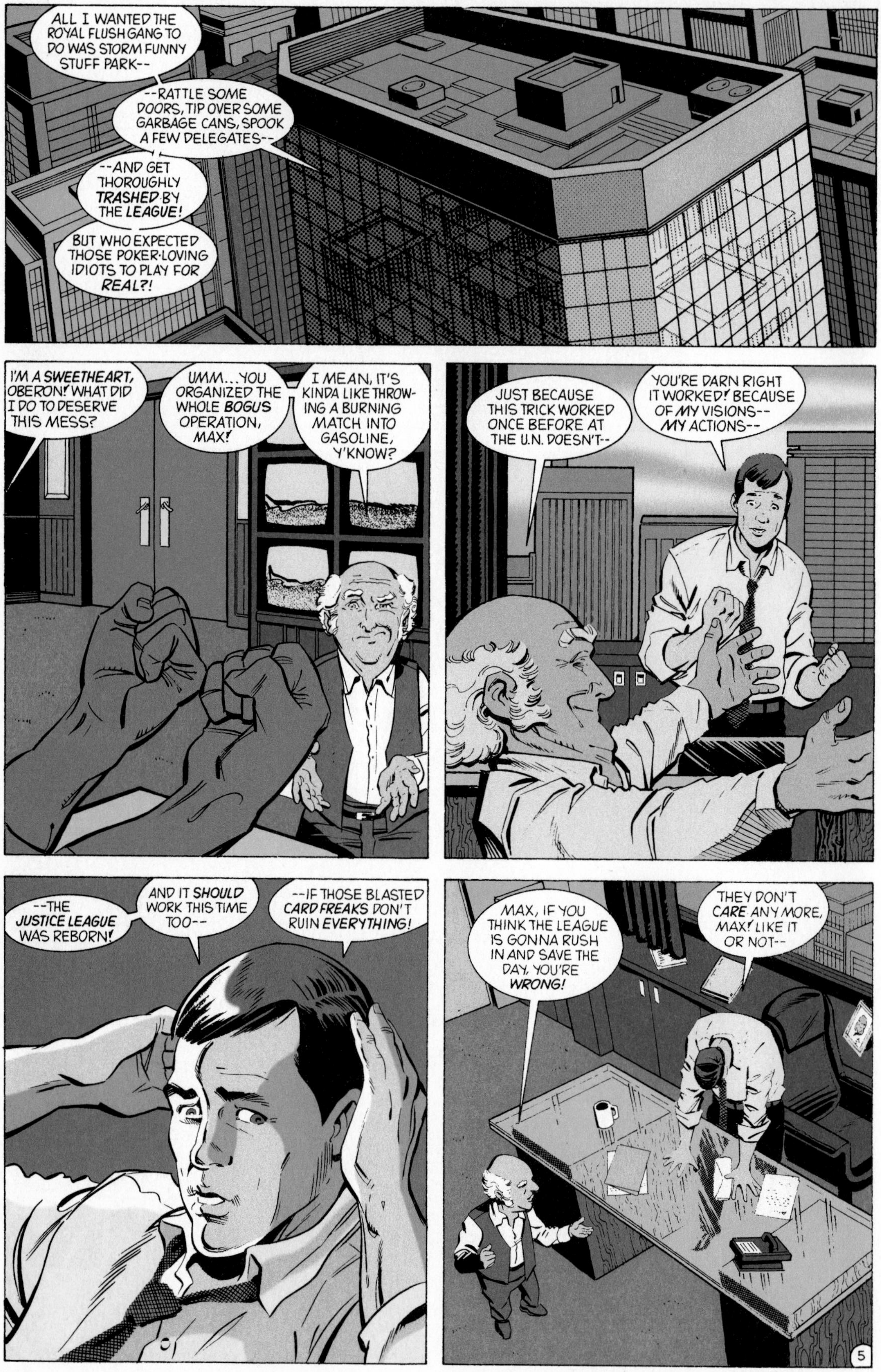
ALL I WANTED THE ROYAL FLUSH GANG TO DO WAS STORM FUNNY STUFF PARK--
--RATTLE SOME DOORS, TIP OVER SOME GARBAGE CANS, SPOOK A FEW DELEGATES--
--AND GET THOROUGHLY TRASHED BY THE LEAGUE!
BUT WHO EXPECTED THOSE POKER-LOVING IDIOTS TO PLAY FOR REAL?!
I'M A SWEETHEART, OBERON! WHAT DID I DO TO DESERVE THIS MESS?
UMM...YOU ORGANIZED THE WHOLE BOGUS OPERATION, MAX!
I MEAN, IT'S KINDA LIKE THROWING A BURNING MATCH INTO GASOLINE, Y'KNOW?
JUST BECAUSE THIS TRICK WORKED ONCE BEFORE AT THE U.N. DOESN'T--
YOU'RE DARN RIGHT IT WORKED! BECAUSE OF MY VISIONS--MY ACTIONS--
--THE JUSTICE LEAGUE WAS REBORN!
AND IT SHOULD WORK THIS TIME TOO--
--IF THOSE BLASTED CARD FREAKS DON'T RUIN EVERYTHING!
MAX, IF YOU THINK THE LEAGUE IS GONNA RUSH IN AND SAVE THE DAY, YOU'RE WRONG!
THEY DON'T CARE ANY MORE, MAX! LIKE IT OR NOT--

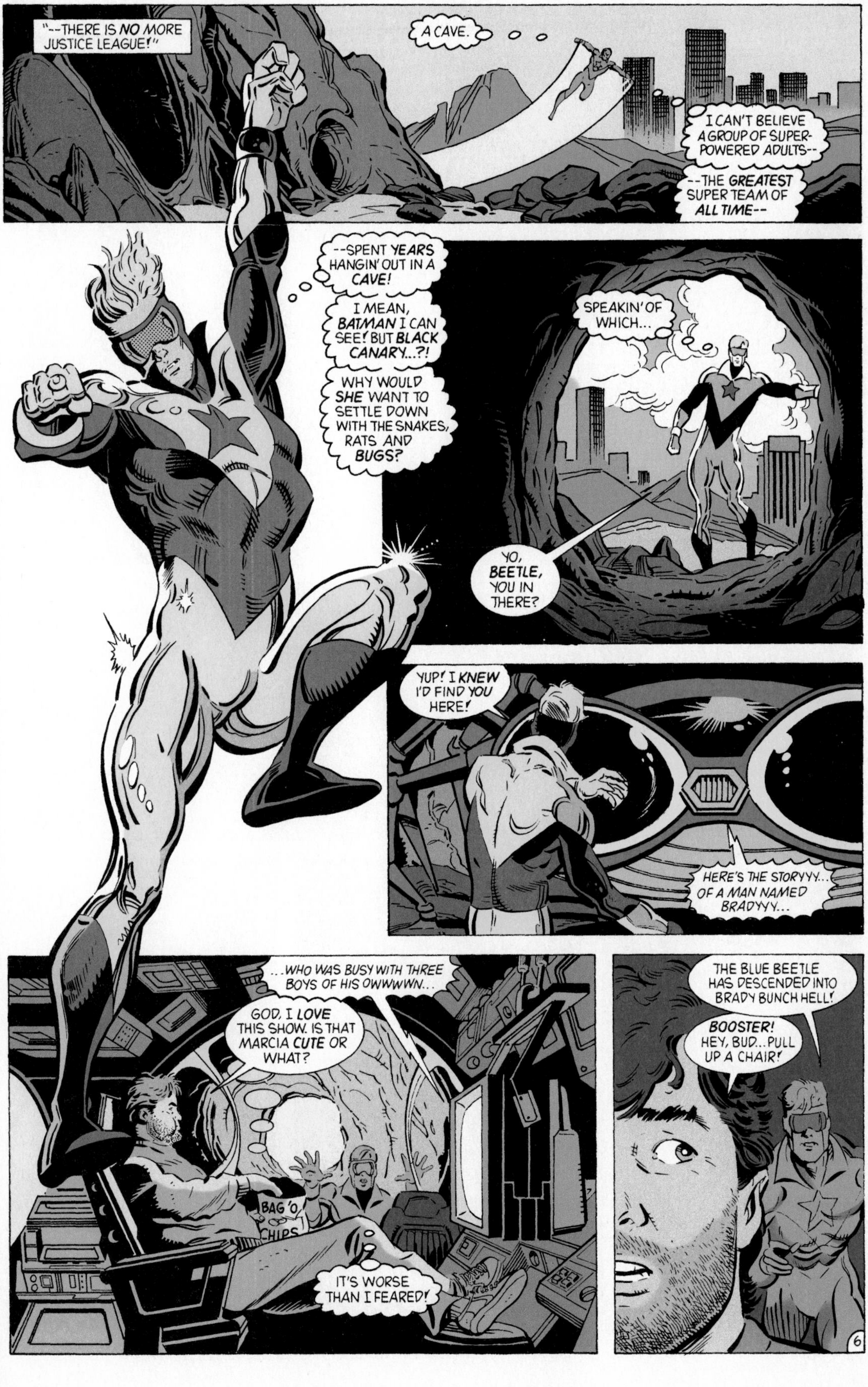

"--THERE IS NO MORE JUSTICE LEAGUE!"
A CAVE.
I CAN'T BELIEVE A GROUP OF SUPER-POWERED ADULTS--
--THE GREATEST SUPER TEAM OF ALL TIME--
--SPENT YEARS HANGIN' OUT IN A CAVE!
I MEAN, BATMAN I CAN SEE! BUT BLACK CANARY...?!
WHY WOULD SHE WANT TO SETTLE DOWN WITH THE SNAKES, RATS AND BUGS?
SPEAKIN' OF WHICH...
YO, BEETLE, YOU IN THERE?
YUP! I KNEW I'D FIND YOU HERE!
HERE'S THE STORYYY... OF A MAN NAMED BRADYYY...
...WHO WAS BUSY WITH THREE BOYS OF HIS OWWWWN...
GOD, I LOVE THIS SHOW. IS THAT MARCIA CUTE OR WHAT?
BAG 'O CHIPS
IT'S WORSE THAN I FEARED!
THE BLUE BEETLE HAS DESCENDED INTO BRADY BUNCH HELL!
BOOSTER! HEY, BUD... PULL UP A CHAIR!

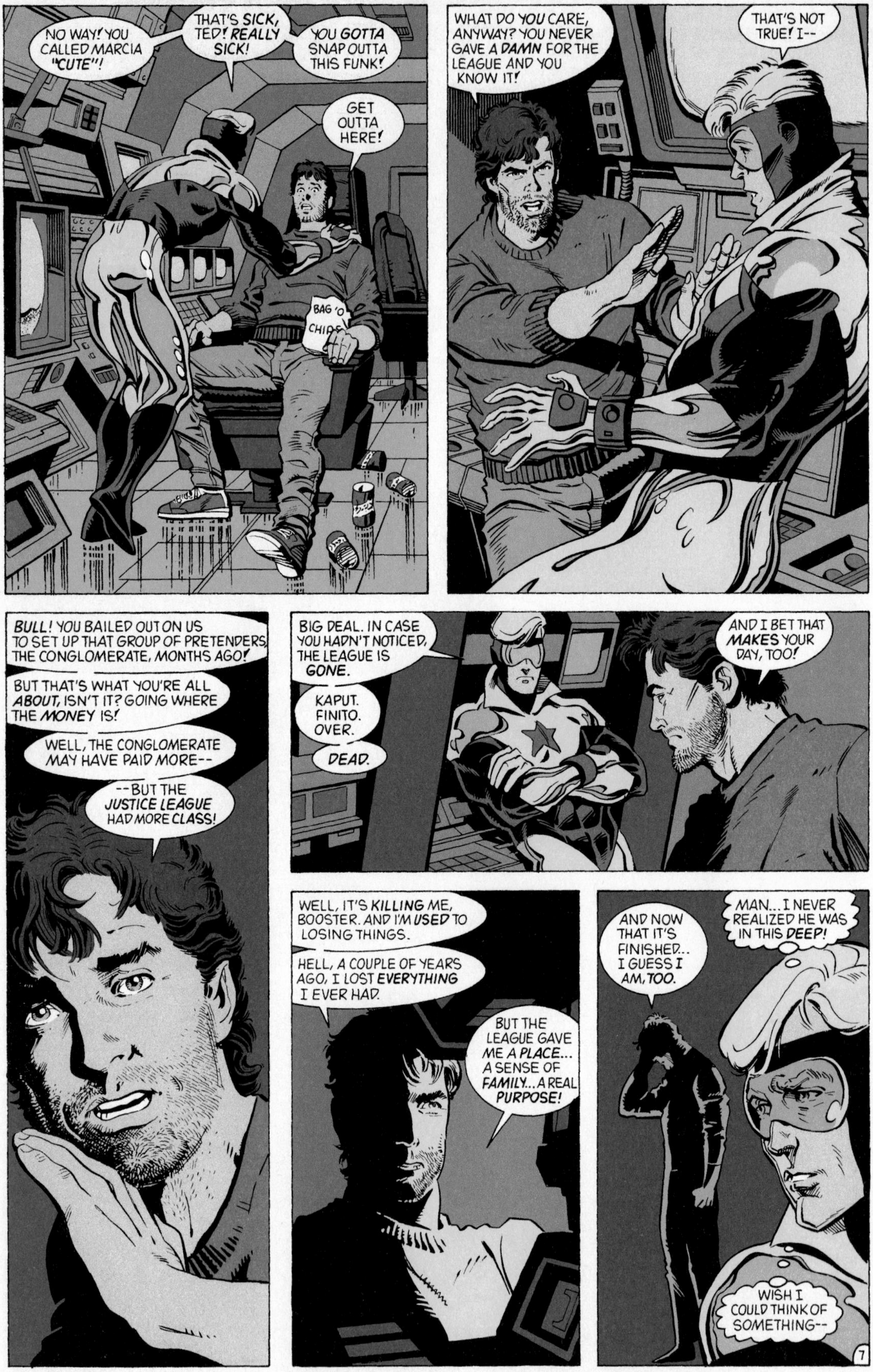
NO WAY! YOU CALLED MARCIA "CUTE"!
THAT'S SICK, TED! REALLY SICK!
YOU GOTTA SNAP OUTTA THIS FUNK!
GET OUTTA HERE!
BAG 'O CHIPS
WHAT DO YOU CARE, ANYWAY? YOU NEVER GAVE A DAMN FOR THE LEAGUE AND YOU KNOW IT!
THAT'S NOT TRUE! I--
BULL! YOU BAILED OUT ON US TO SET UP THAT GROUP OF PRETENDERS, THE CONGLOMERATE, MONTHS AGO!
BUT THAT'S WHAT YOU'RE ALL ABOUT, ISN'T IT? GOING WHERE THE MONEY IS!
WELL, THE CONGLOMERATE MAY HAVE PAID MORE--
--BUT THE JUSTICE LEAGUE HAD MORE CLASS!
BIG DEAL. IN CASE YOU HADN'T NOTICED, THE LEAGUE IS GONE.
KAPUT. FINITO. OVER.
DEAD.
AND I BET THAT MAKES YOUR DAY, TOO!
WELL, IT'S KILLING ME, BOOSTER. AND I'M USED TO LOSING THINGS.
HELL, A COUPLE OF YEARS AGO, I LOST EVERYTHING I EVER HAD.
BUT THE LEAGUE GAVE ME A PLACE... A SENSE OF FAMILY... A REAL PURPOSE!
AND NOW THAT IT'S FINISHED... I GUESS I AM, TOO.
MAN... I NEVER REALIZED HE WAS IN THIS DEEP!
WISH I COULD THINK OF SOMETHING--

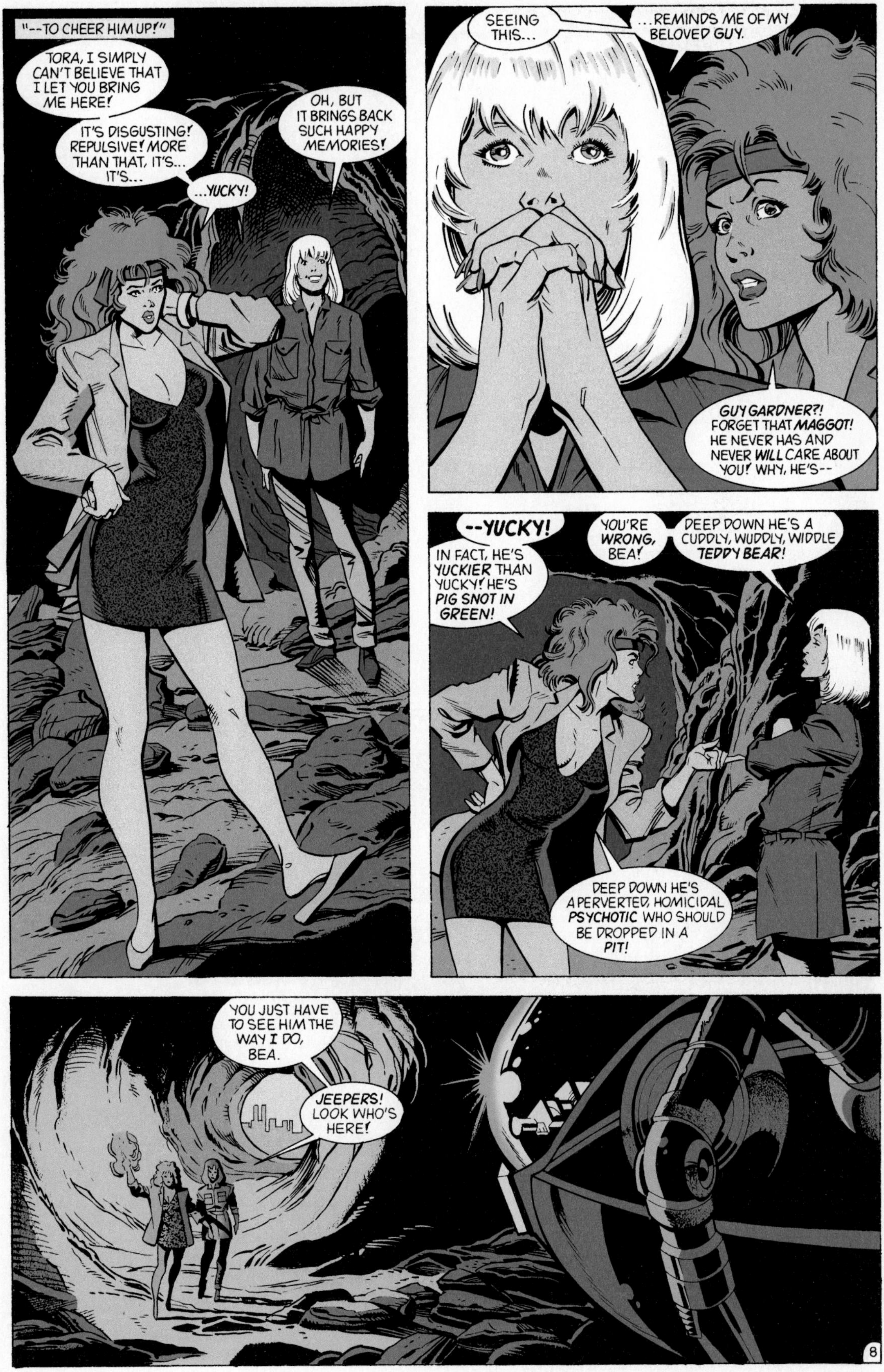

"--TO CHEER HIM UP!"
TORA, I SIMPLY CAN'T BELIEVE THAT I LET YOU BRING ME HERE!
IT'S DISGUSTING! REPULSIVE! MORE THAN THAT, IT'S... IT'S...
...YUCKY!
OH, BUT IT BRINGS BACK SUCH HAPPY MEMORIES!
SEEING THIS...
...REMINDS ME OF MY BELOVED GUY.
GUY GARDNER?! FORGET THAT MAGGOT! HE NEVER HAS AND NEVER WILL CARE ABOUT YOU! WHY, HE'S--
--YUCKY!
IN FACT, HE'S YUCKIER THAN YUCKY! HE'S PIG SNOT IN GREEN!
YOU'RE WRONG, BEA!
DEEP DOWN HE'S A CUDDLY, WUDDLY, WIDDLE TEDDY BEAR!
DEEP DOWN HE'S A PERVERTED, HOMICIDAL PSYCHOTIC WHO SHOULD BE DROPPED IN A PIT!
YOU JUST HAVE TO SEE HIM THE WAY I DO, BEA.
JEEPERS! LOOK WHO'S HERE!
8

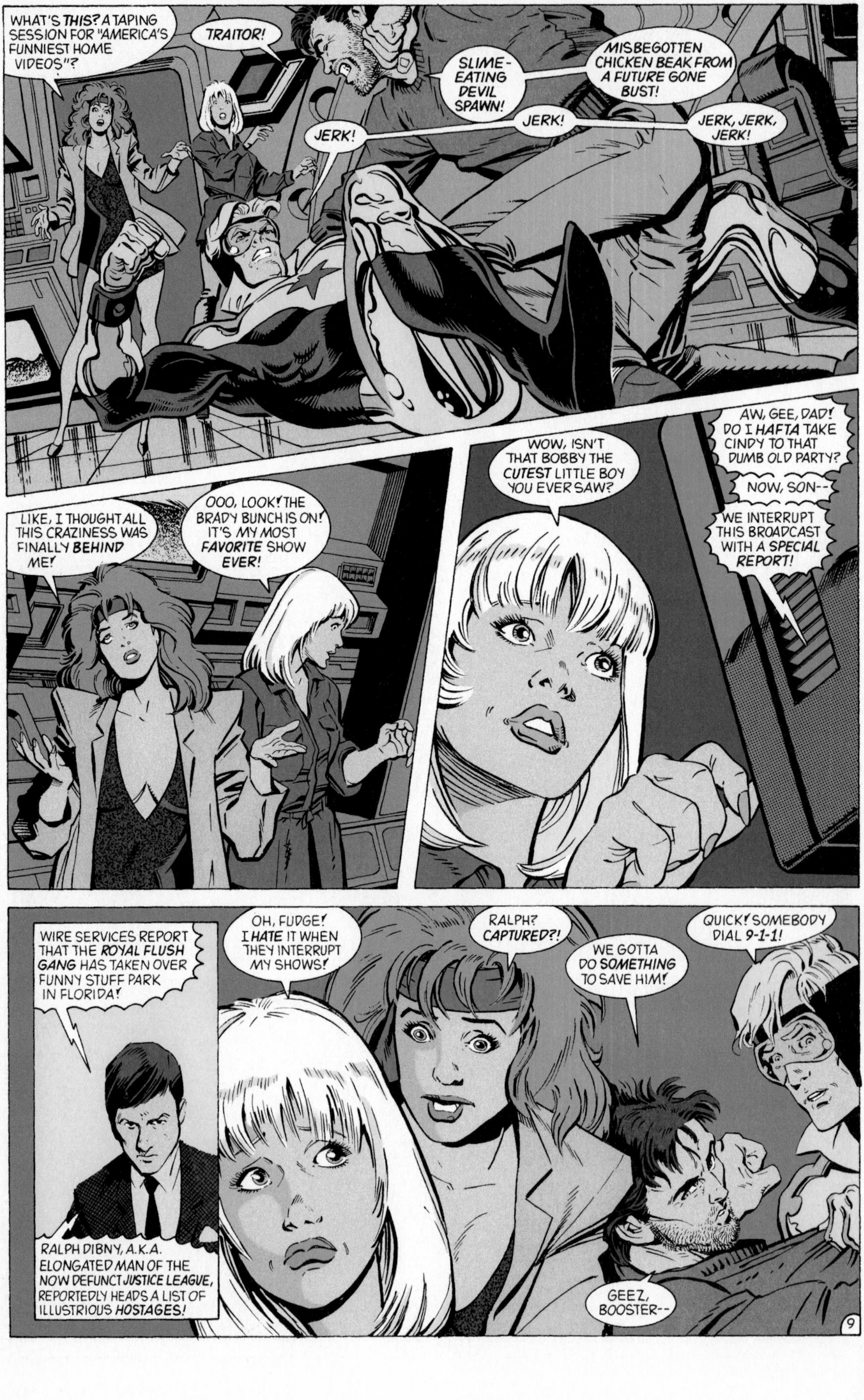
WHAT'S THIS? A TAPING SESSION FOR "AMERICA'S FUNNIEST HOME VIDEOS"?
TRAITOR!
SLIME-EATING DEVIL SPAWN!
MISBEGOTTEN CHICKEN BEAK FROM A FUTURE GONE BUST!
JERK!
JERK!
JERK, JERK, JERK!
LIKE, I THOUGHT ALL THIS CRAZINESS WAS FINALLY BEHIND ME!
OOO, LOOK! THE BRADY BUNCH IS ON! IT'S MY MOST FAVORITE SHOW EVER!
WOW, ISN'T THAT BOBBY THE CUTEST LITTLE BOY YOU EVER SAW?
AW, GEE, DAD! DO I HAFTA TAKE CINDY TO THAT DUMB OLD PARTY?
NOW, SON--
WE INTERRUPT THIS BROADCAST WITH A SPECIAL REPORT!
WIRE SERVICES REPORT THAT THE ROYAL FLUSH GANG HAS TAKEN OVER FUNNY STUFF PARK IN FLORIDA!
RALPH DIBNY, A.K.A. ELONGATED MAN OF THE NOW DEFUNCT JUSTICE LEAGUE, REPORTEDLY HEADS A LIST OF ILLUSTRIOUS HOSTAGES!
OH, FUDGE! I HATE IT WHEN THEY INTERRUPT MY SHOWS!
RALPH? CAPTURED?!
WE GOTTA DO SOMETHING TO SAVE HIM!
QUICK! SOMEBODY DIAL 9-1-1!
GEEZ, BOOSTER--
9

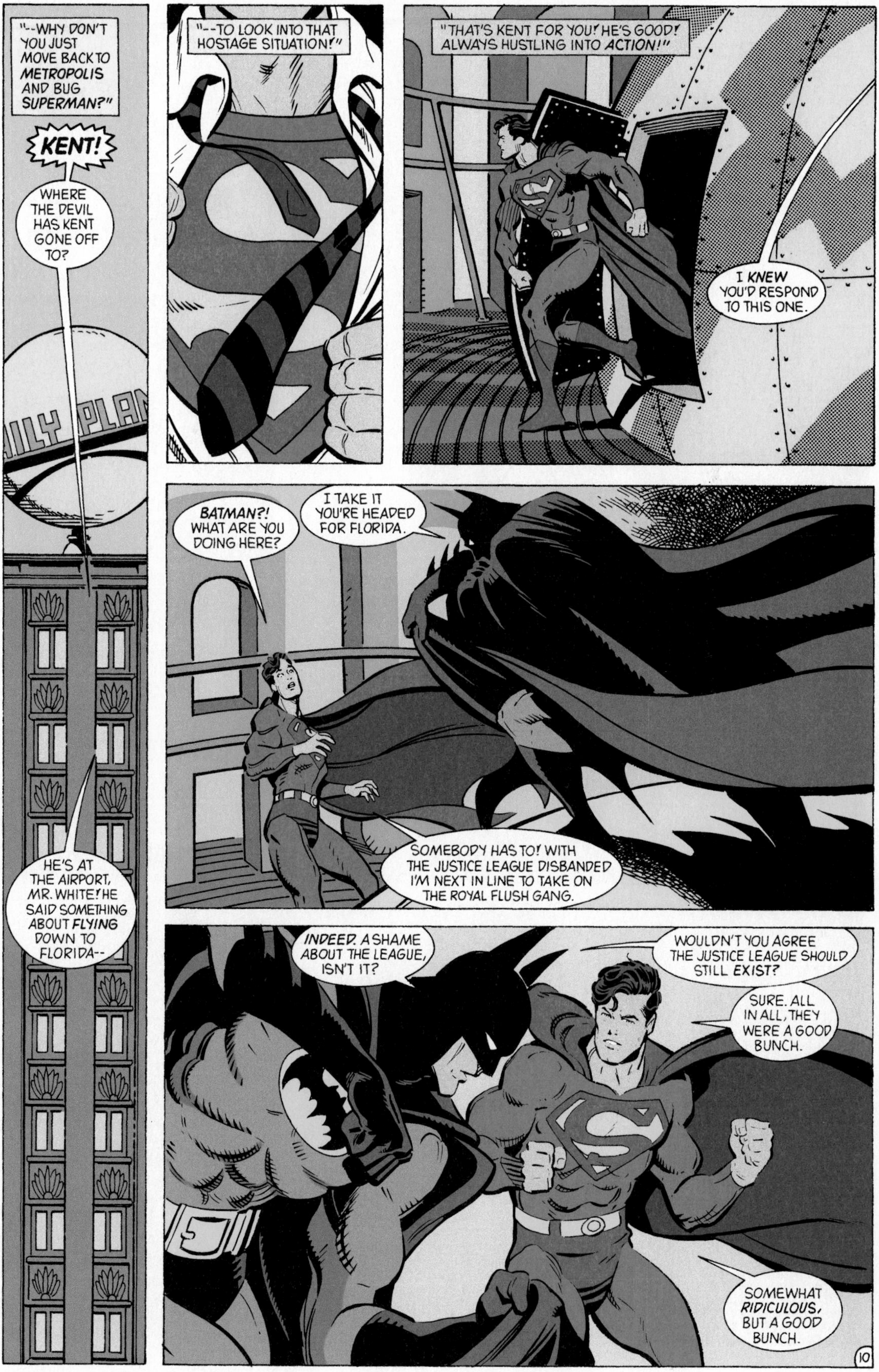
"--WHY DON'T YOU JUST MOVE BACK TO METROPOLIS AND BUG SUPERMAN?"
KENT!
WHERE THE DEVIL HAS KENT GONE OFF TO?
HE'S AT THE AIRPORT, MR. WHITE! HE SAID SOMETHING ABOUT FLYING DOWN TO FLORIDA--
"--TO LOOK INTO THAT HOSTAGE SITUATION!"
"THAT'S KENT FOR YOU! HE'S GOOD! ALWAYS HUSTLING INTO ACTION!"
I KNEW YOU'D RESPOND TO THIS ONE.
BATMAN?! WHAT ARE YOU DOING HERE?
I TAKE IT YOU'RE HEADED FOR FLORIDA.
SOMEBODY HAS TO! WITH THE JUSTICE LEAGUE DISBANDED I'M NEXT IN LINE TO TAKE ON THE ROYAL FLUSH GANG.
INDEED. A SHAME ABOUT THE LEAGUE, ISN'T IT?
WOULDN'T YOU AGREE THE JUSTICE LEAGUE SHOULD STILL EXIST?
SURE. ALL IN ALL, THEY WERE A GOOD BUNCH.
SOMEWHAT RIDICULOUS, BUT A GOOD BUNCH.
10

AGREED.

IN FACT, SEVERAL DAYS AGO, MAXWELL LORD CONTACTED ME TO *REBUILD* THE J.L.A.

NO WONDER YOU'RE HERE. BUT MY ANSWER IS STILL, "NO."

DON'T MISUNDERSTAND ME. I'M NOT *ASKING* YOU TO BE A MEMBER.

SOMEONE *SHOULD* TAKE CHARGE... BUT NOT *ME*--

--I THINK *YOU'RE* THAT SOMEONE.

ME... HEAD UP THE TEAM?!

FORGET IT! I WORK *ALONE!*

IT DOESN'T HAVE TO *STAY* THAT WAY. PEOPLE THINK OF ME AS A LONER YET I'VE OFTEN WORKED WITH OTHERS.

ROBIN, THE OUTSIDERS, THE LEAGUE--

--I'VE DONE MY BEST TO HELP THEM BE EFFECTIVE.

GREAT! YOU'VE DONE A GOOD JOB! BUT I'M MOST EFFECTIVE *SOLO!*

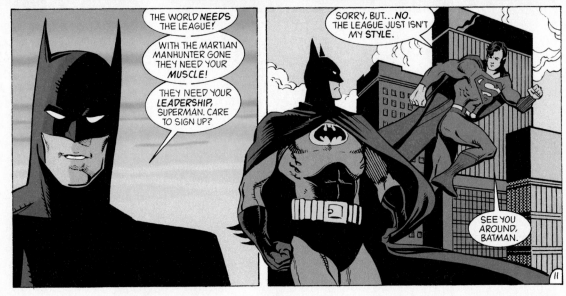

THE WORLD *NEEDS* THE LEAGUE!

WITH THE MARTIAN MANHUNTER GONE THEY NEED YOUR *MUSCLE!*

THEY NEED YOUR *LEADERSHIP,* SUPERMAN. CARE TO SIGN UP?

SORRY, BUT...*NO.* THE LEAGUE JUST ISN'T MY *STYLE.*

SEE YOU AROUND, BATMAN.

11

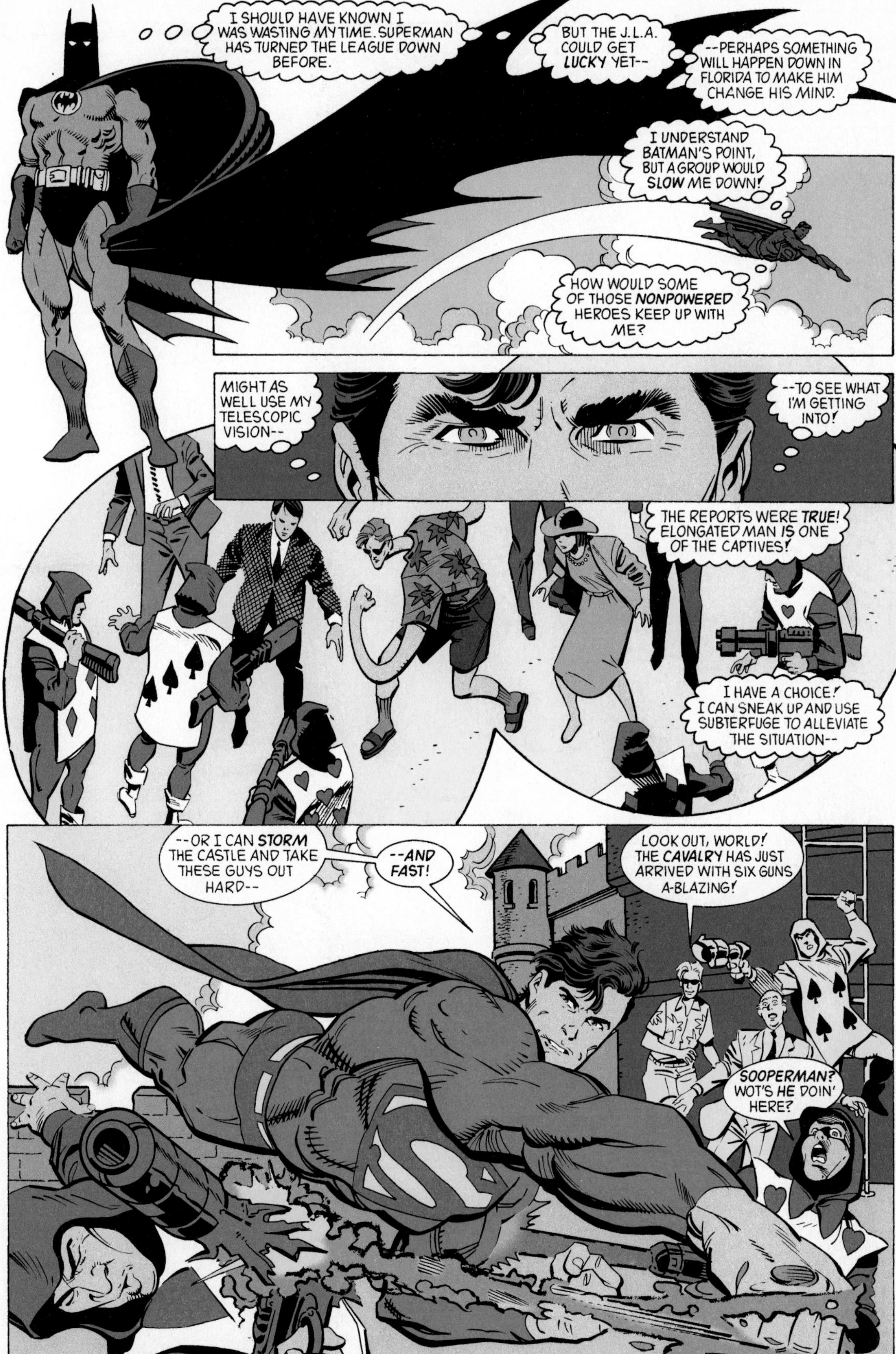
I SHOULD HAVE KNOWN I WAS WASTING MY TIME. SUPERMAN HAS TURNED THE LEAGUE DOWN BEFORE.
BUT THE J.L.A. COULD GET LUCKY YET--
--PERHAPS SOMETHING WILL HAPPEN DOWN IN FLORIDA TO MAKE HIM CHANGE HIS MIND.
I UNDERSTAND BATMAN'S POINT, BUT A GROUP WOULD SLOW ME DOWN!
HOW WOULD SOME OF THOSE NONPOWERED HEROES KEEP UP WITH ME?
MIGHT AS WELL USE MY TELESCOPIC VISION--
--TO SEE WHAT I'M GETTING INTO!
THE REPORTS WERE TRUE! ELONGATED MAN IS ONE OF THE CAPTIVES!
I HAVE A CHOICE! I CAN SNEAK UP AND USE SUBTERFUGE TO ALLEVIATE THE SITUATION--
--OR I CAN STORM THE CASTLE AND TAKE THESE GUYS OUT HARD--
--AND FAST!
LOOK OUT, WORLD! THE CAVALRY HAS JUST ARRIVED WITH SIX GUNS A-BLAZING!
SOOPERMAN? WOT'S HE DOIN' HERE?
12

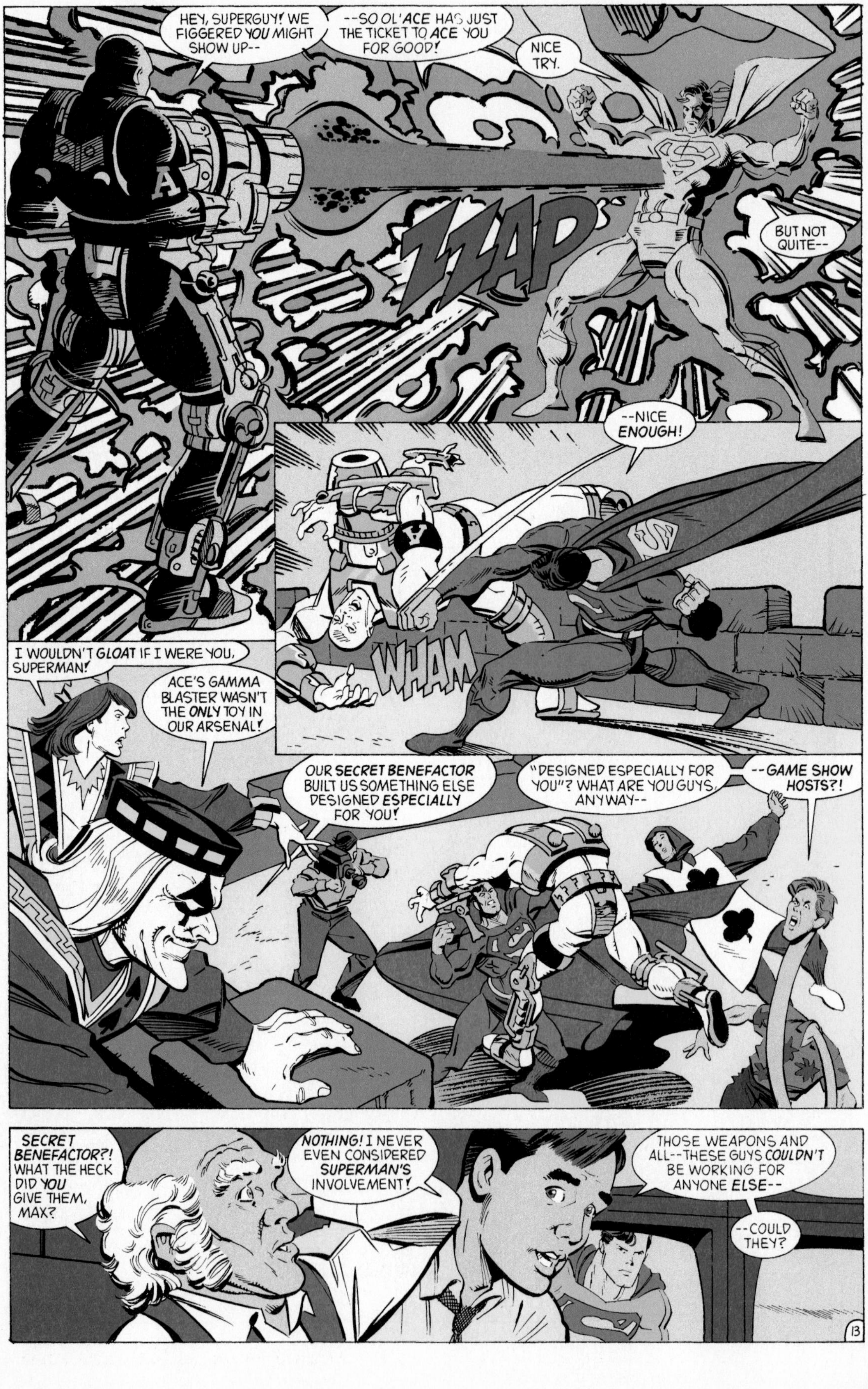
HEY, SUPERGUY! WE FIGGERED YOU MIGHT SHOW UP--
--SO OL' ACE HAS JUST THE TICKET TO ACE YOU FOR GOOD!
NICE TRY.
ZZAP
BUT NOT QUITE--
--NICE ENOUGH!
WHAM
I WOULDN'T GLOAT IF I WERE YOU, SUPERMAN!
ACE'S GAMMA BLASTER WASN'T THE ONLY TOY IN OUR ARSENAL!
OUR SECRET BENEFACTOR BUILT US SOMETHING ELSE DESIGNED ESPECIALLY FOR YOU!
"DESIGNED ESPECIALLY FOR YOU"? WHAT ARE YOU GUYS, ANYWAY--
--GAME SHOW HOSTS?!
SECRET BENEFACTOR?! WHAT THE HECK DID YOU GIVE THEM, MAX?
NOTHING! I NEVER EVEN CONSIDERED SUPERMAN'S INVOLVEMENT!
THOSE WEAPONS AND ALL--THESE GUYS COULDN'T BE WORKING FOR ANYONE ELSE--
--COULD THEY?
13

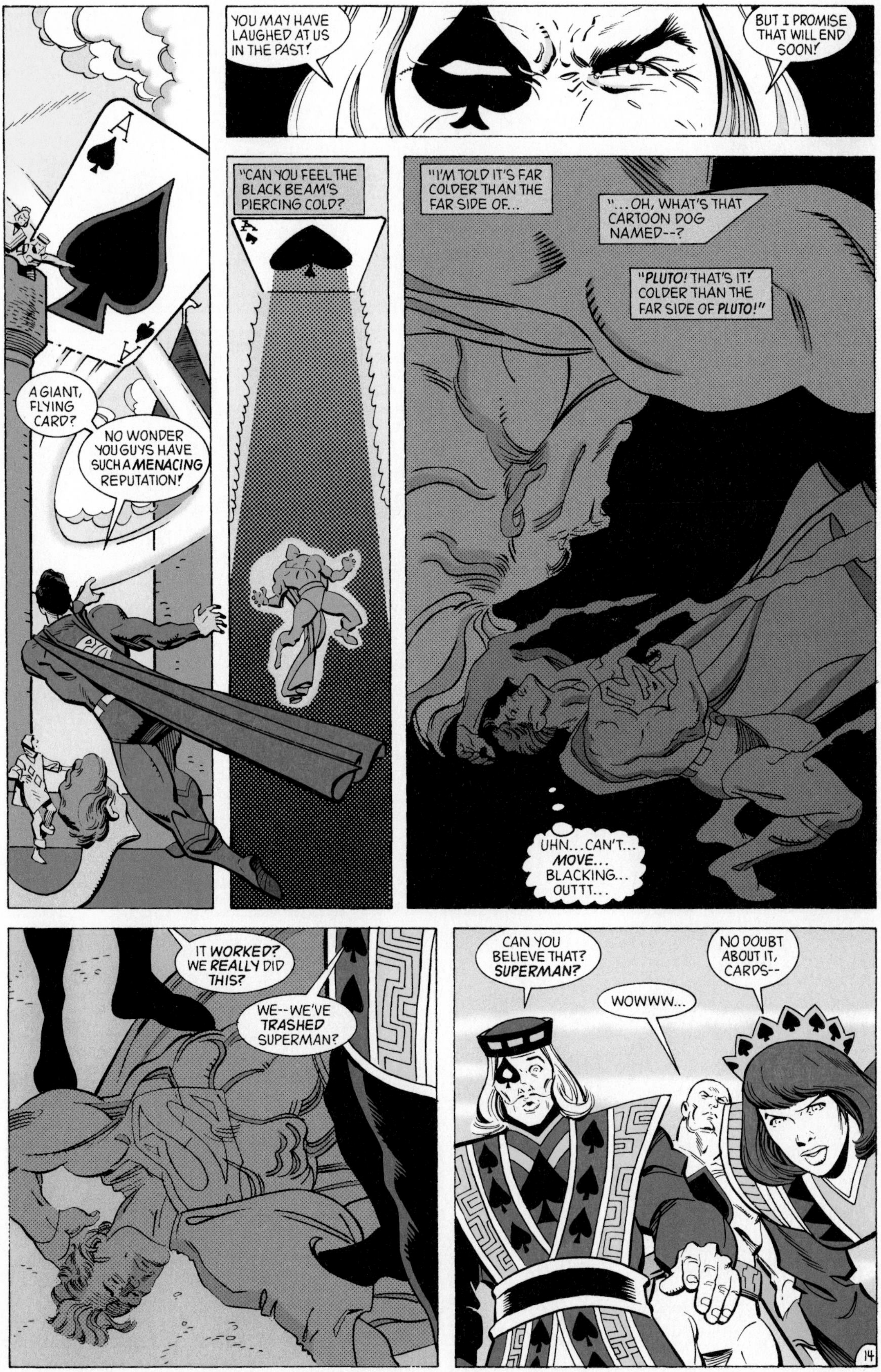
YOU MAY HAVE LAUGHED AT US IN THE PAST!
BUT I PROMISE THAT WILL END SOON!
A GIANT, FLYING CARD?
NO WONDER YOU GUYS HAVE SUCH A MENACING REPUTATION!
"CAN YOU FEEL THE BLACK BEAM'S PIERCING COLD?
"I'M TOLD IT'S FAR COLDER THAN THE FAR SIDE OF...
"...OH, WHAT'S THAT CARTOON DOG NAMED--?
"PLUTO! THAT'S IT! COLDER THAN THE FAR SIDE OF PLUTO!"
UHN...CAN'T... MOVE... BLACKING... OUTTT...
IT WORKED? WE REALLY DID THIS?
WE--WE'VE TRASHED SUPERMAN?
CAN YOU BELIEVE THAT? SUPERMAN?
WOWWW...
NO DOUBT ABOUT IT, CARDS--
14

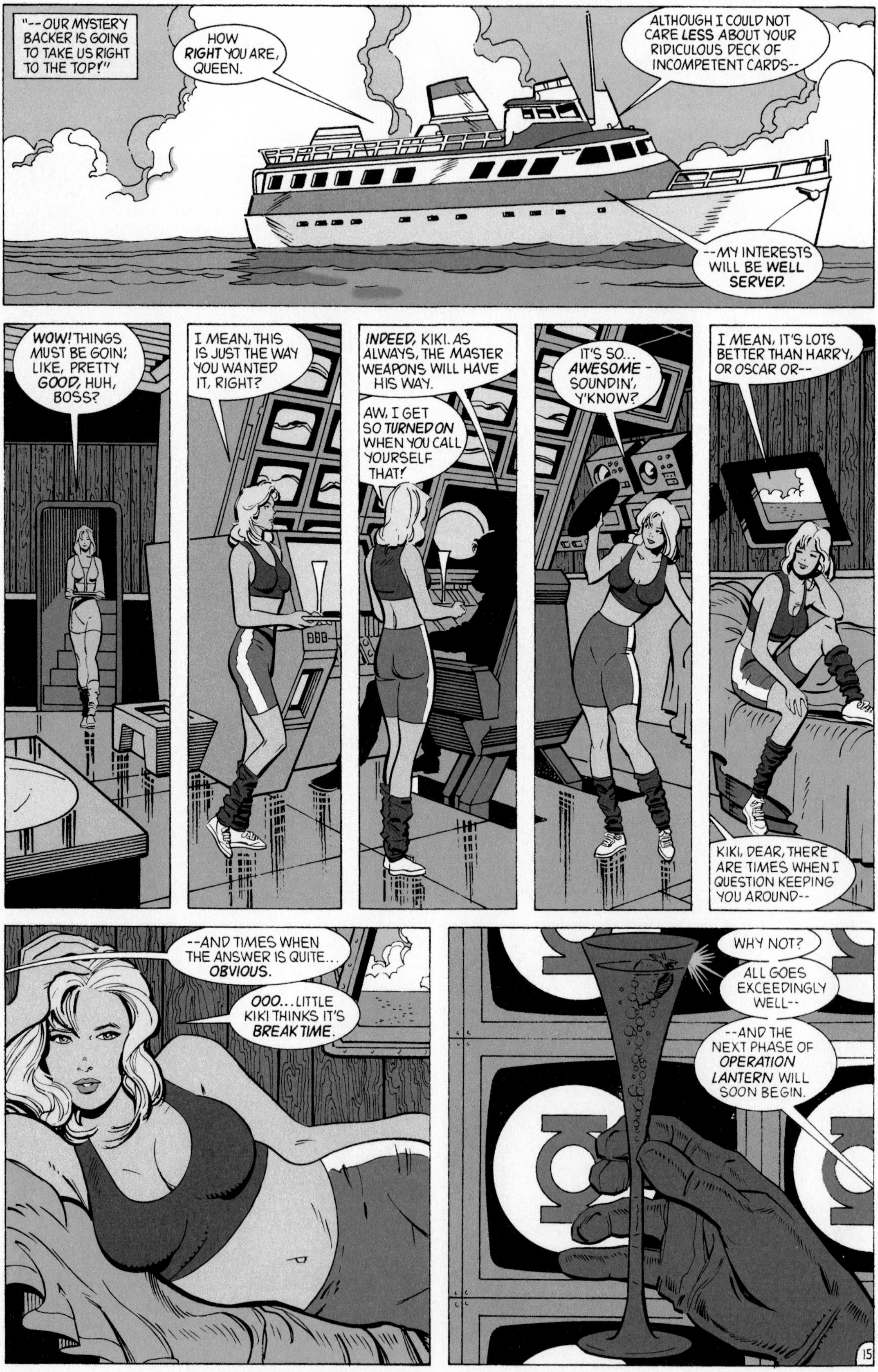
"--OUR MYSTERY BACKER IS GOING TO TAKE US RIGHT TO THE TOP!"
HOW RIGHT YOU ARE, QUEEN.
ALTHOUGH I COULD NOT CARE LESS ABOUT YOUR RIDICULOUS DECK OF INCOMPETENT CARDS--
--MY INTERESTS WILL BE WELL SERVED.
WOW! THINGS MUST BE GOIN', LIKE, PRETTY GOOD, HUH, BOSS?
I MEAN, THIS IS JUST THE WAY YOU WANTED IT, RIGHT?
INDEED, KIKI. AS ALWAYS, THE MASTER WEAPONS WILL HAVE HIS WAY.
AW, I GET SO TURNED ON WHEN YOU CALL YOURSELF THAT!
IT'S SO... AWESOME-SOUNDIN', Y'KNOW?
I MEAN, IT'S LOTS BETTER THAN HARRY, OR OSCAR OR--
KIKI, DEAR, THERE ARE TIMES WHEN I QUESTION KEEPING YOU AROUND--
--AND TIMES WHEN THE ANSWER IS QUITE... OBVIOUS.
OOO... LITTLE KIKI THINKS IT'S BREAK TIME.
WHY NOT?
ALL GOES EXCEEDINGLY WELL--
--AND THE NEXT PHASE OF OPERATION LANTERN WILL SOON BEGIN.
15

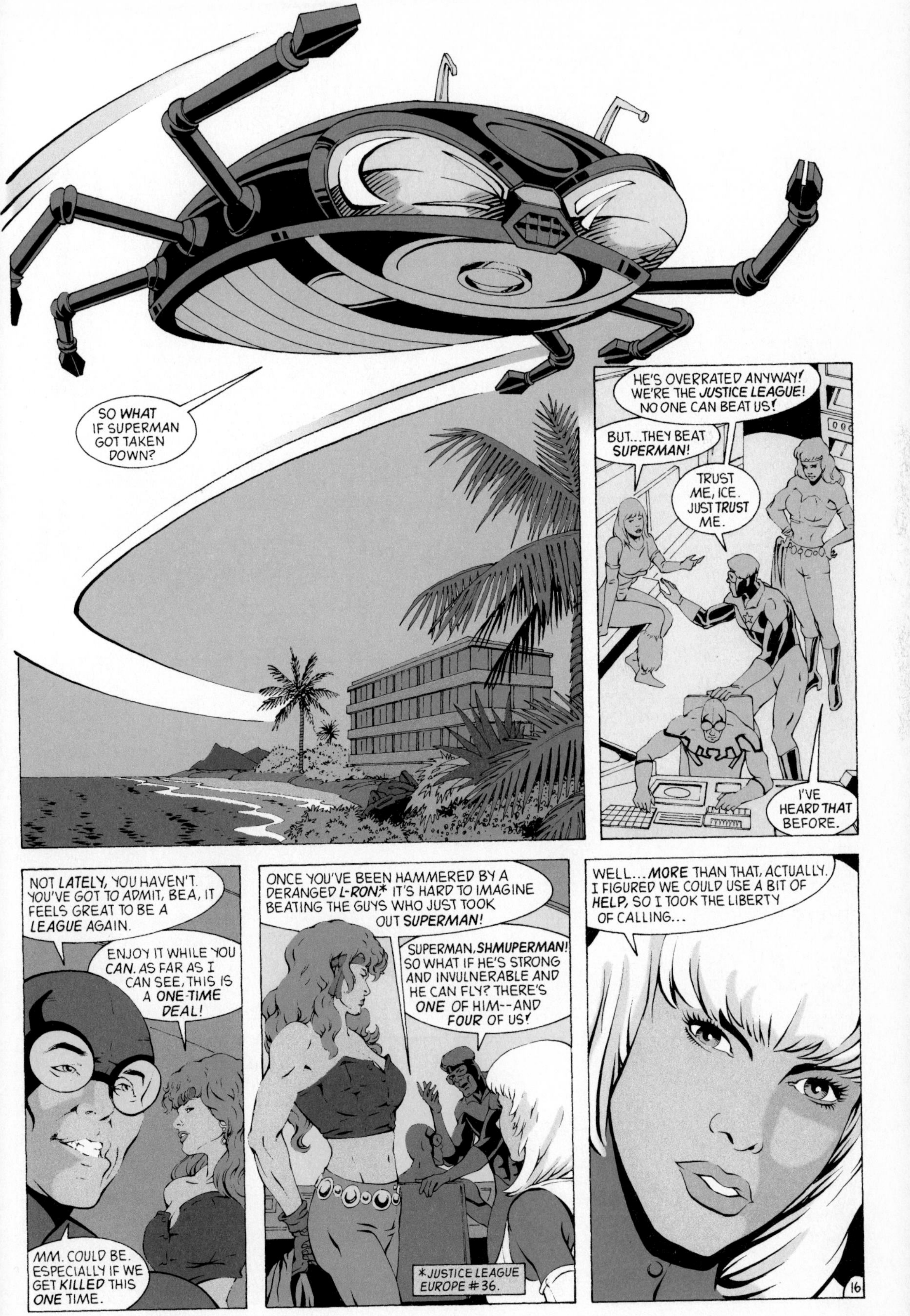
SO WHAT IF SUPERMAN GOT TAKEN DOWN?
HE'S OVERRATED ANYWAY! WE'RE THE JUSTICE LEAGUE! NO ONE CAN BEAT US!
BUT...THEY BEAT SUPERMAN!
TRUST ME, ICE. JUST TRUST ME.
I'VE HEARD THAT BEFORE.
NOT LATELY, YOU HAVEN'T. YOU'VE GOT TO ADMIT, BEA, IT FEELS GREAT TO BE A LEAGUE AGAIN.
ENJOY IT WHILE YOU CAN. AS FAR AS I CAN SEE, THIS IS A ONE-TIME DEAL!
MM. COULD BE. ESPECIALLY IF WE GET KILLED THIS ONE TIME.
ONCE YOU'VE BEEN HAMMERED BY A DERANGED L-RON,* IT'S HARD TO IMAGINE BEATING THE GUYS WHO JUST TOOK OUT SUPERMAN!
SUPERMAN, SHMUPERMAN! SO WHAT IF HE'S STRONG AND INVULNERABLE AND HE CAN FLY? THERE'S ONE OF HIM--AND FOUR OF US!
*JUSTICE LEAGUE EUROPE #36.
WELL... MORE THAN THAT, ACTUALLY. I FIGURED WE COULD USE A BIT OF HELP, SO I TOOK THE LIBERTY OF CALLING...
16

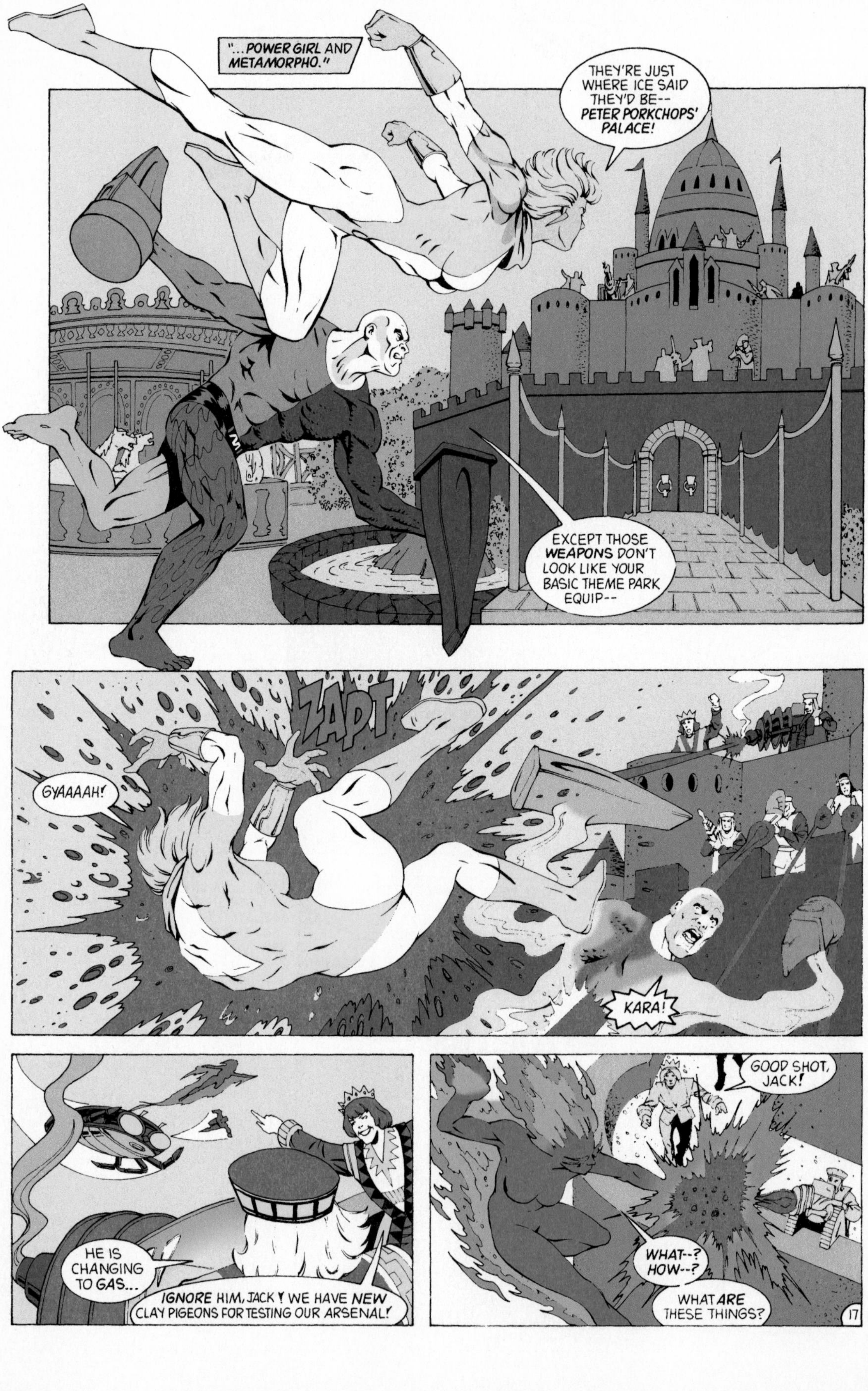
"...POWER GIRL AND METAMORPHO."
THEY'RE JUST WHERE ICE SAID THEY'D BE-- PETER PORKCHOPS' PALACE!
EXCEPT THOSE WEAPONS DON'T LOOK LIKE YOUR BASIC THEME PARK EQUIP--
ZAPT
GYAAAAH!
KARA!
HE IS CHANGING TO GAS...
IGNORE HIM, JACK! WE HAVE NEW CLAY PIGEONS FOR TESTING OUR ARSENAL!
GOOD SHOT, JACK!
WHAT--? HOW--?
WHAT ARE THESE THINGS?

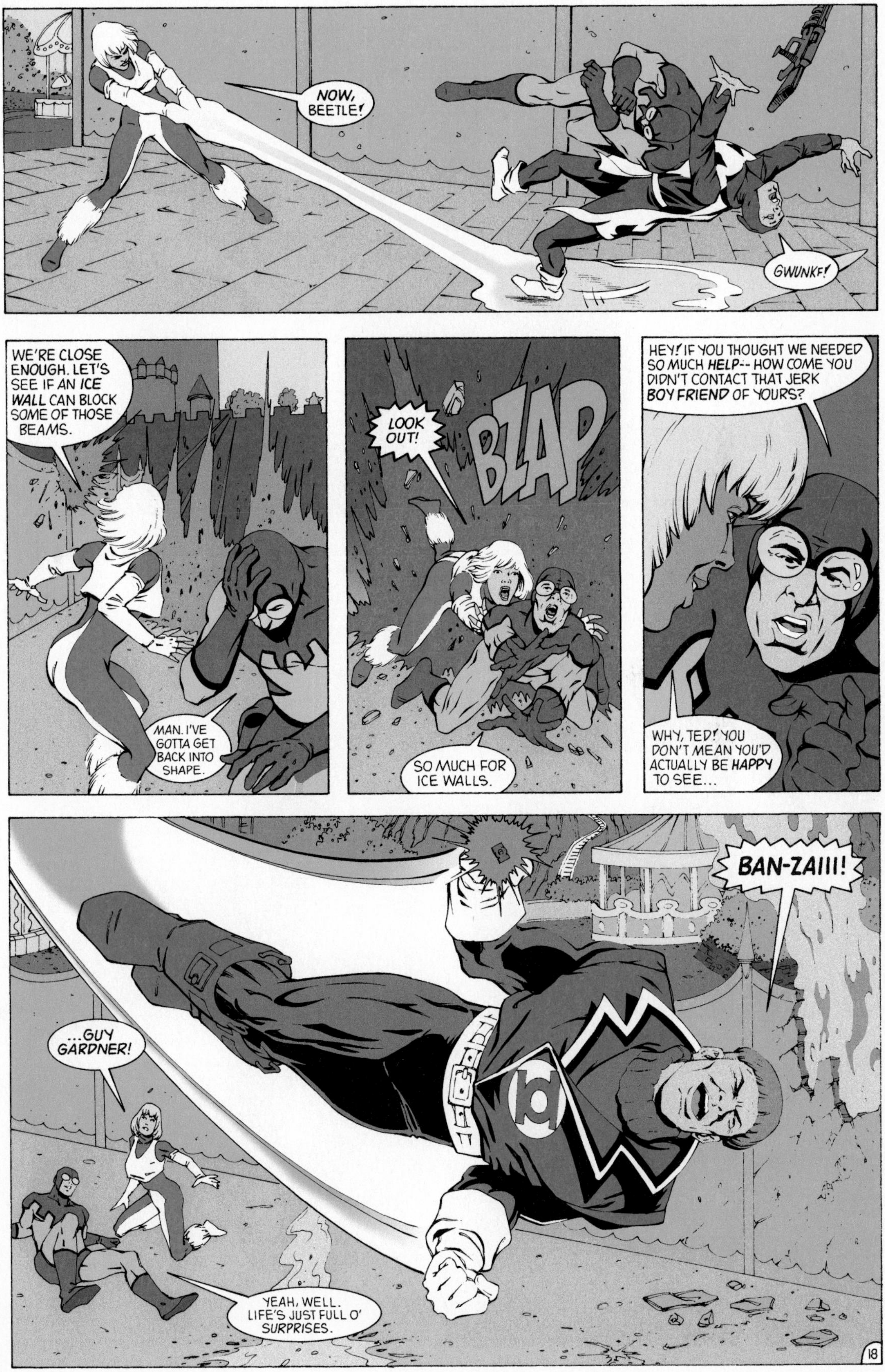
NOW, BEETLE!
GWUNKF!
WE'RE CLOSE ENOUGH. LET'S SEE IF AN ICE WALL CAN BLOCK SOME OF THOSE BEAMS.
MAN. I'VE GOTTA GET BACK INTO SHAPE.
LOOK OUT!
BZAP
SO MUCH FOR ICE WALLS.
HEY! IF YOU THOUGHT WE NEEDED SO MUCH HELP-- HOW COME YOU DIDN'T CONTACT THAT JERK BOY FRIEND OF YOURS?
WHY, TED! YOU DON'T MEAN YOU'D ACTUALLY BE HAPPY TO SEE...
BAN-ZAIII!
...GUY GARDNER!
YEAH, WELL. LIFE'S JUST FULL O' SURPRISES.
18

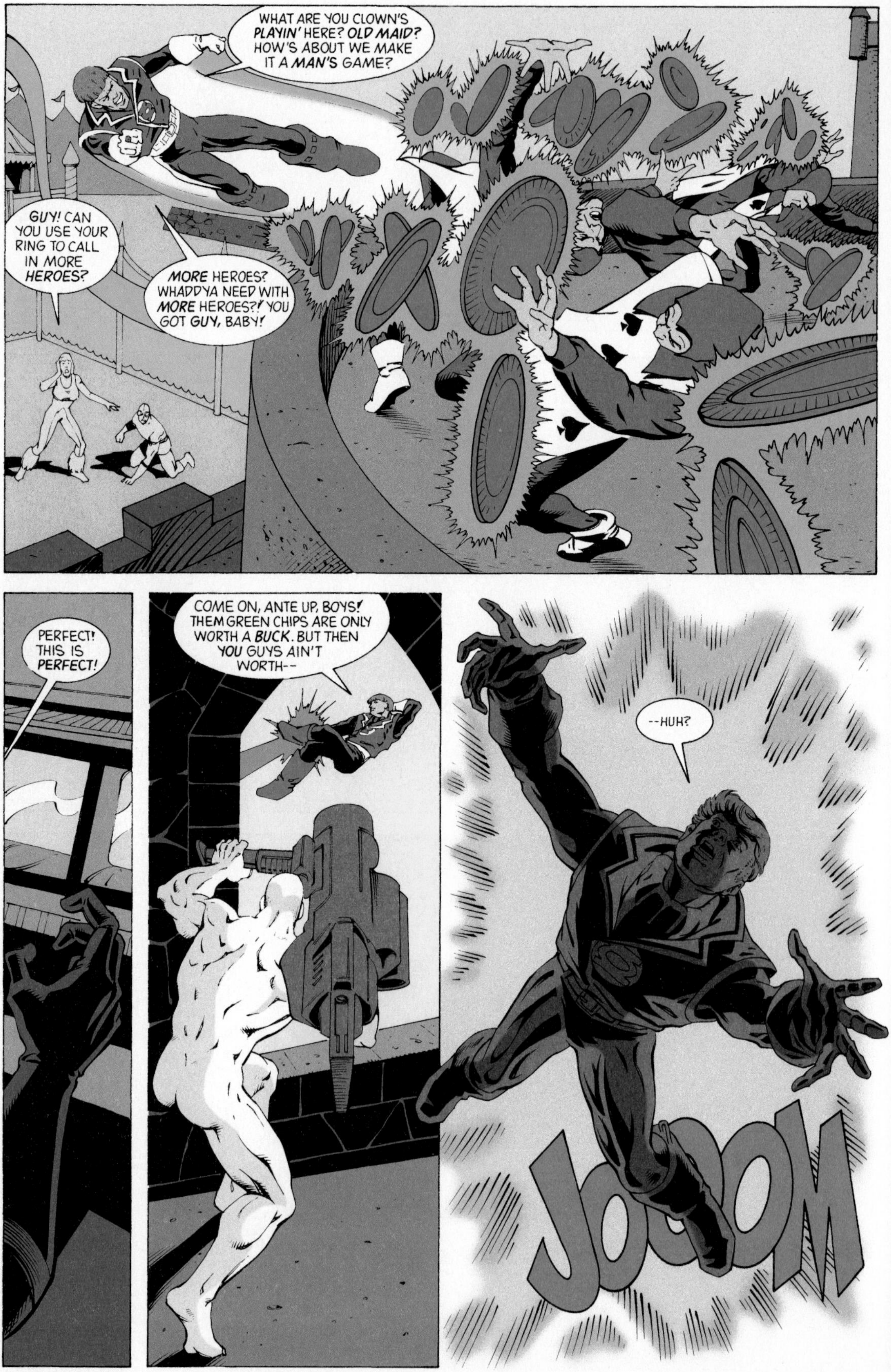
WHAT ARE YOU CLOWN'S PLAYIN' HERE? OLD MAID? HOW'S ABOUT WE MAKE IT A MAN'S GAME?
GUY! CAN YOU USE YOUR RING TO CALL IN MORE HEROES?
MORE HEROES? WHADDYA NEED WITH MORE HEROES?! YOU GOT GUY, BABY!
PERFECT! THIS IS PERFECT!
COME ON, ANTE UP, BOYS! THEM GREEN CHIPS ARE ONLY WORTH A BUCK. BUT THEN YOU GUYS AIN'T WORTH--
--HUH?
JOOOOM

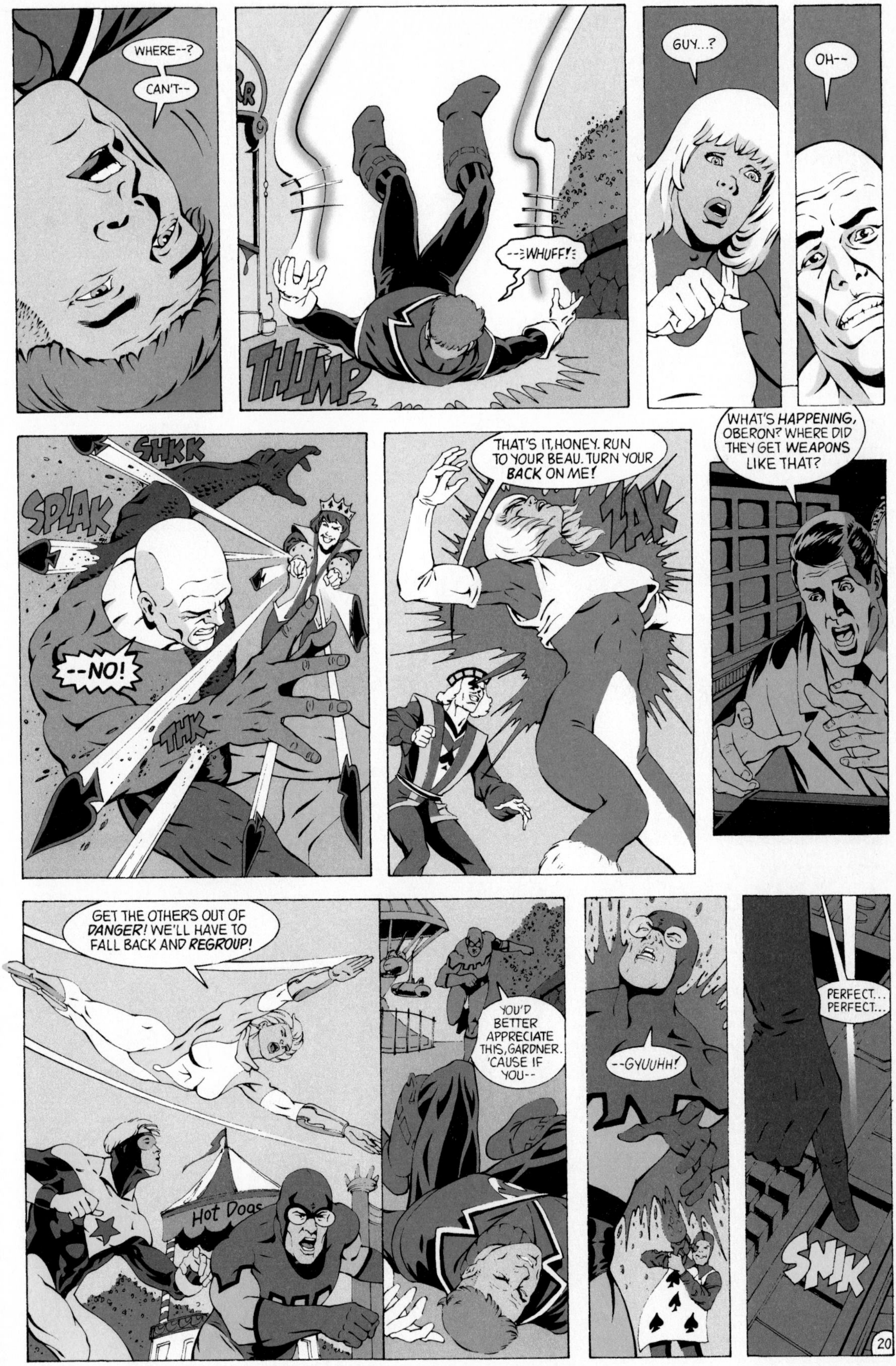

WHERE--?
CAN'T--
--WHUFF!
THUMP
GUY...?
OH--
SHKK
SPLAK
--NO!
THK
THAT'S IT, HONEY. RUN TO YOUR BEAU. TURN YOUR BACK ON ME!
ZAK
WHAT'S HAPPENING, OBERON? WHERE DID THEY GET WEAPONS LIKE THAT?
GET THE OTHERS OUT OF DANGER! WE'LL HAVE TO FALL BACK AND REGROUP!
Hot Dogs
YOU'D BETTER APPRECIATE THIS, GARDNER. 'CAUSE IF YOU--
--GYUUHH!
PERFECT... PERFECT...
SNIK

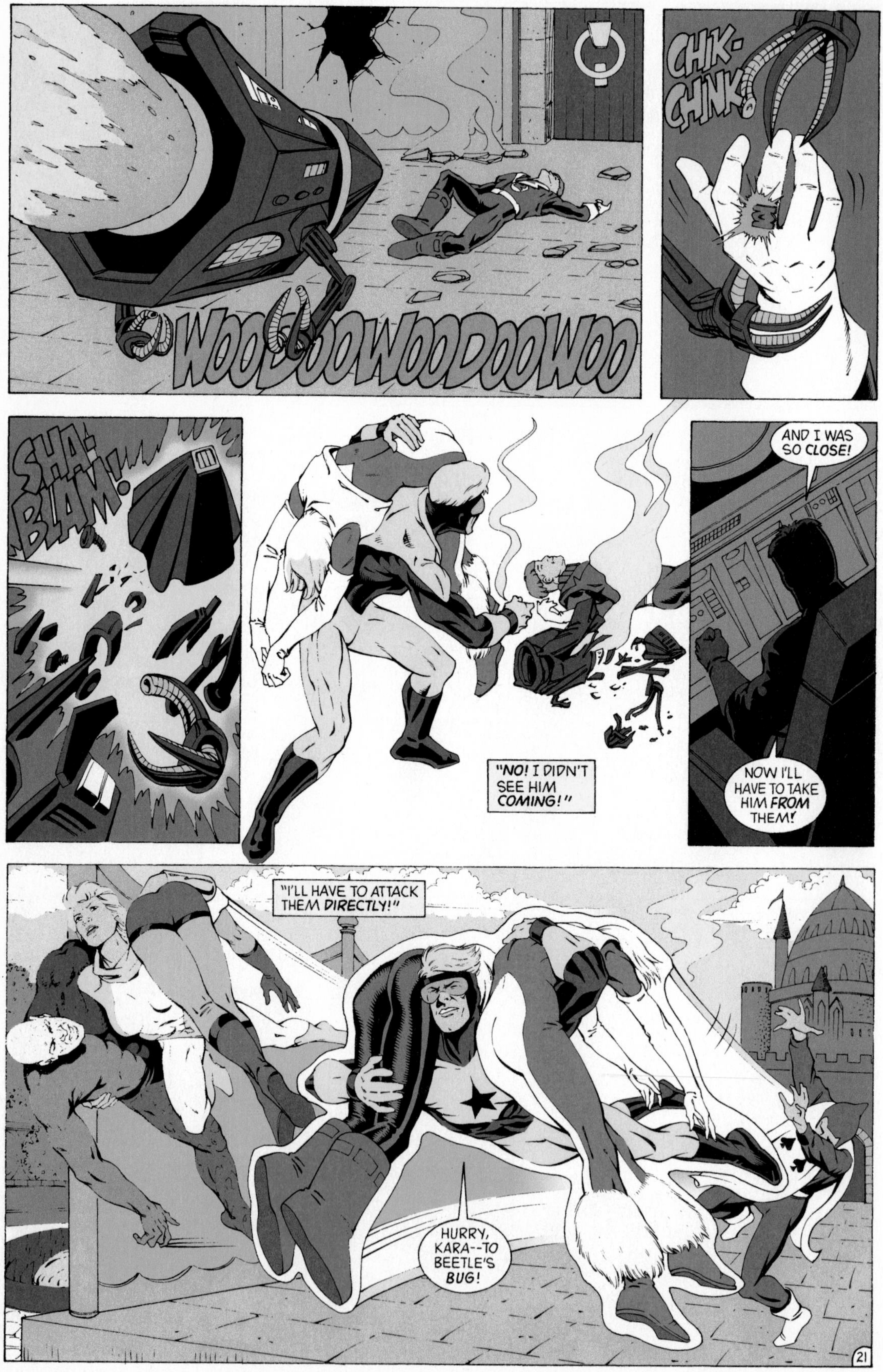
WOODOOWOODOOWOO
CHIK-CHINK!
SHA-BLAM!
AND I WAS SO CLOSE!
"NO! I DIDN'T SEE HIM COMING!"
NOW I'LL HAVE TO TAKE HIM FROM THEM!
"I'LL HAVE TO ATTACK THEM DIRECTLY!"
HURRY, KARA--TO BEETLE'S BUG!

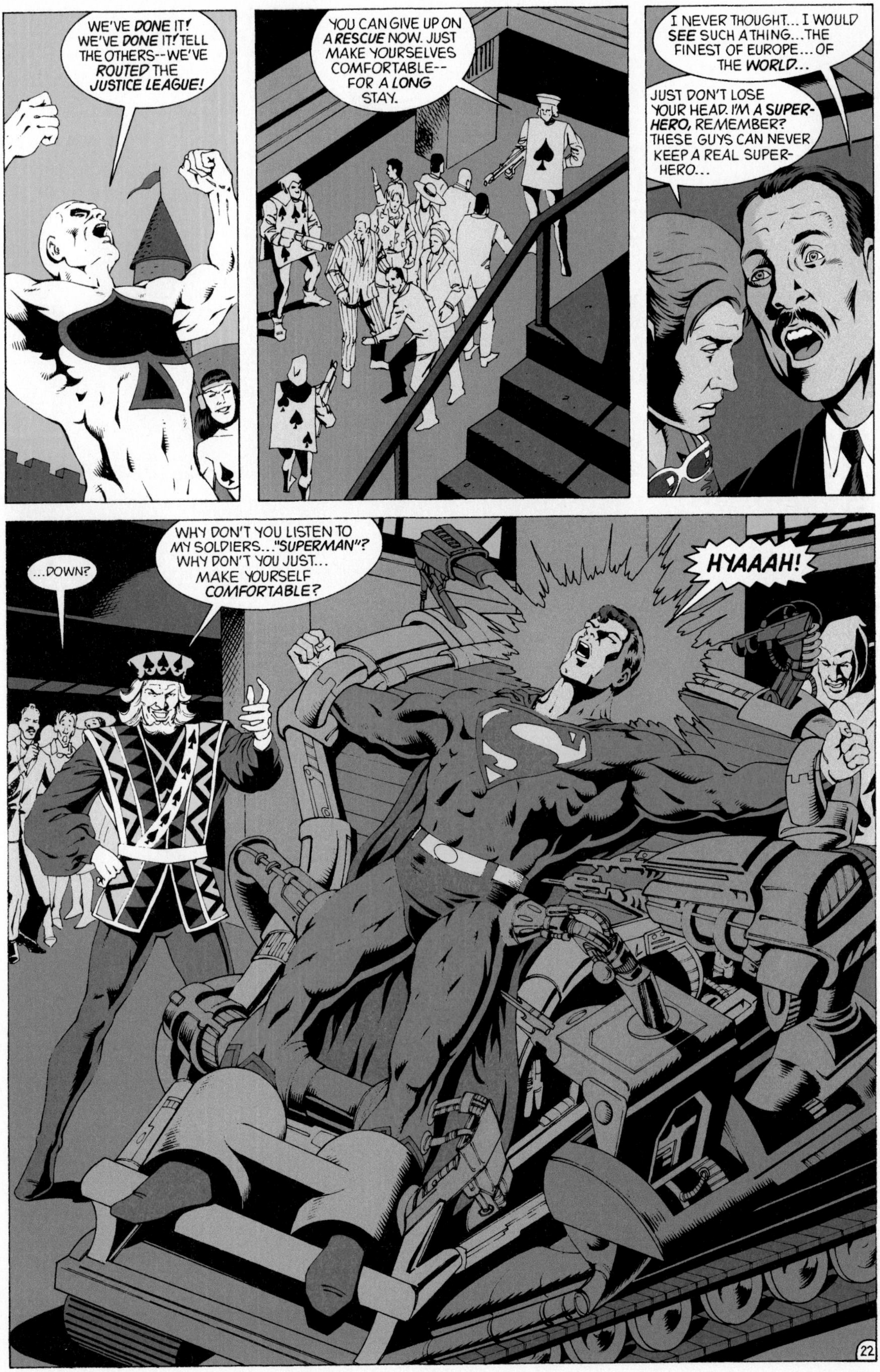
WE'VE DONE IT! WE'VE DONE IT! TELL THE OTHERS--WE'VE ROUTED THE JUSTICE LEAGUE!
YOU CAN GIVE UP ON A RESCUE NOW. JUST MAKE YOURSELVES COMFORTABLE-- FOR A LONG STAY.
I NEVER THOUGHT... I WOULD SEE SUCH A THING... THE FINEST OF EUROPE... OF THE WORLD...
JUST DON'T LOSE YOUR HEAD. I'M A SUPER-HERO, REMEMBER? THESE GUYS CAN NEVER KEEP A REAL SUPER-HERO...
...DOWN?
WHY DON'T YOU LISTEN TO MY SOLDIERS..."SUPERMAN"? WHY DON'T YOU JUST... MAKE YOURSELF COMFORTABLE?
HYAAAH!

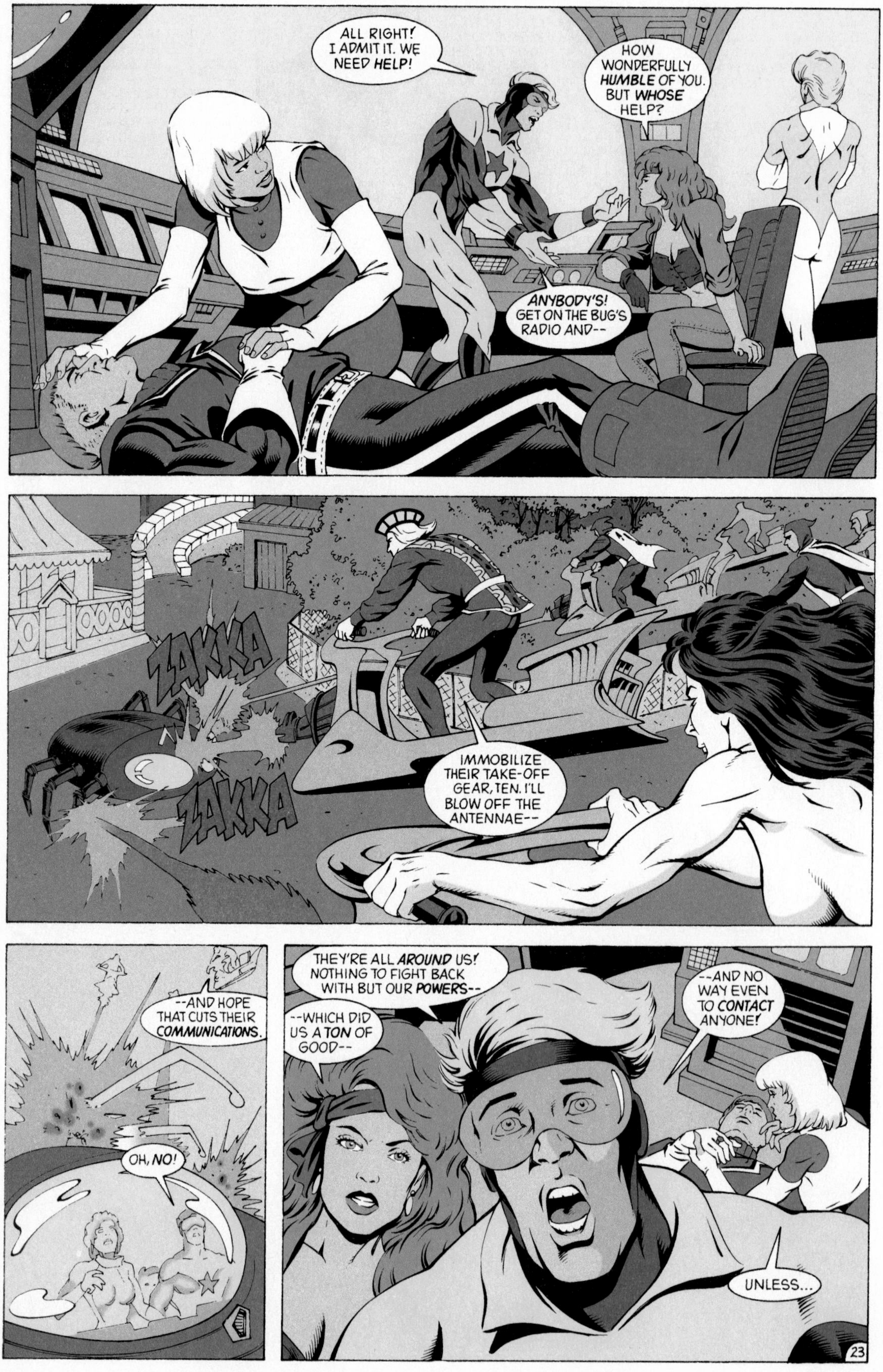

ALL RIGHT! I ADMIT IT. WE NEED HELP!
HOW WONDERFULLY HUMBLE OF YOU. BUT WHOSE HELP?
ANYBODY'S! GET ON THE BUG'S RADIO AND--
ZAKKA
ZAKKA
IMMOBILIZE THEIR TAKE-OFF GEAR, TEN. I'LL BLOW OFF THE ANTENNAE--
--AND HOPE THAT CUTS THEIR COMMUNICATIONS.
OH, NO!
THEY'RE ALL AROUND US! NOTHING TO FIGHT BACK WITH BUT OUR POWERS--
--WHICH DID US A TON OF GOOD--
--AND NO WAY EVEN TO CONTACT ANYONE!
UNLESS...
23

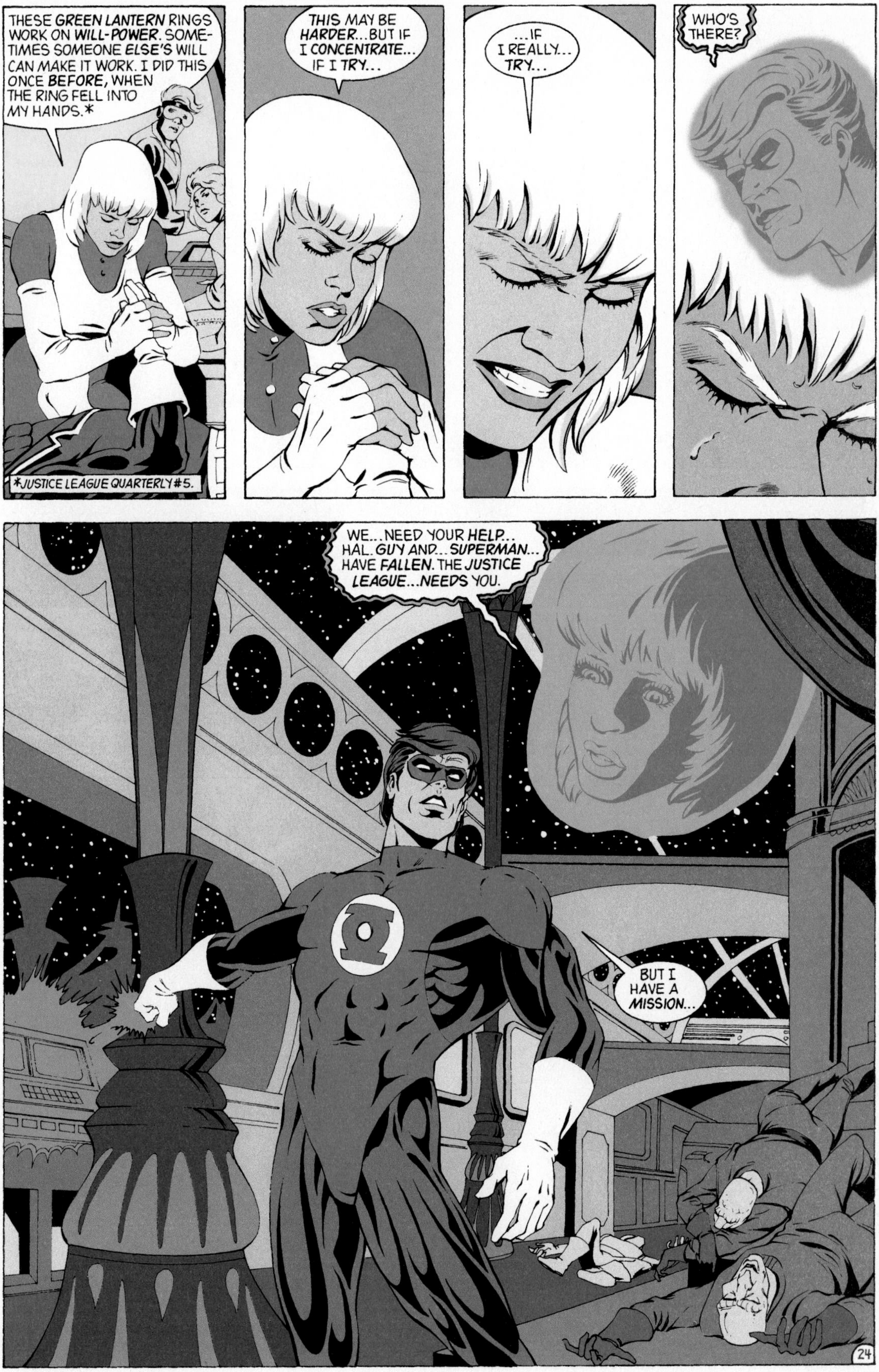
THESE GREEN LANTERN RINGS WORK ON WILL-POWER. SOMETIMES SOMEONE ELSE'S WILL CAN MAKE IT WORK. I DID THIS ONCE BEFORE, WHEN THE RING FELL INTO MY HANDS.*
*JUSTICE LEAGUE QUARTERLY #5.
THIS MAY BE HARDER... BUT IF I CONCENTRATE... IF I TRY...
...IF I REALLY... TRY...
WHO'S THERE?
WE... NEED YOUR HELP... HAL. GUY AND... SUPERMAN... HAVE FALLEN. THE JUSTICE LEAGUE... NEEDS YOU.
BUT I HAVE A MISSION...

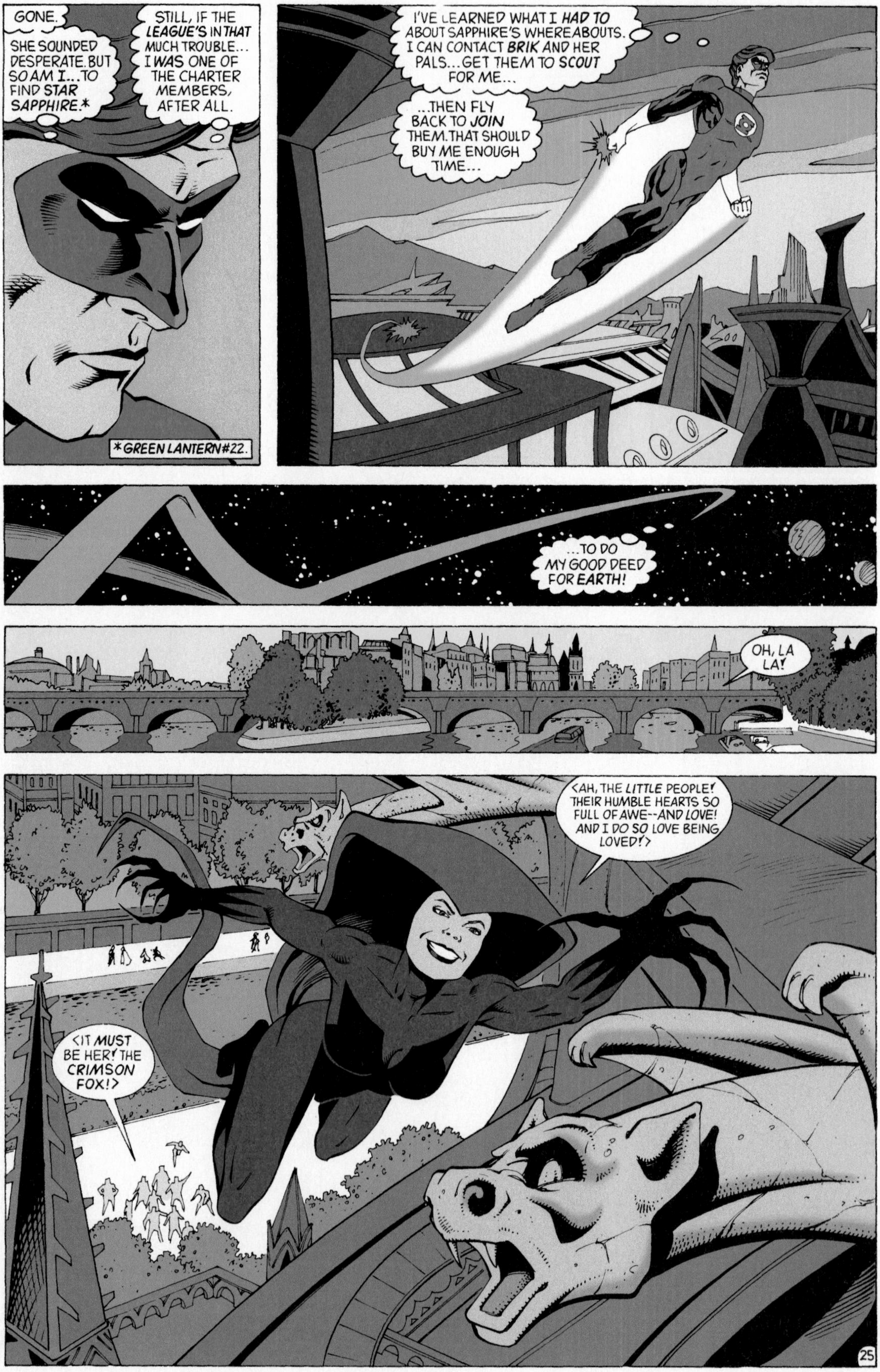
GONE.
SHE SOUNDED DESPERATE. BUT SO AM I...TO FIND STAR SAPPHIRE.*
STILL, IF THE LEAGUE'S IN THAT MUCH TROUBLE... I WAS ONE OF THE CHARTER MEMBERS, AFTER ALL.
*GREEN LANTERN #22.
I'VE LEARNED WHAT I HAD TO ABOUT SAPPHIRE'S WHEREABOUTS. I CAN CONTACT BRIK AND HER PALS...GET THEM TO SCOUT FOR ME...
...THEN FLY BACK TO JOIN THEM. THAT SHOULD BUY ME ENOUGH TIME...
...TO DO MY GOOD DEED FOR EARTH!
OH, LA LA!
<AH, THE LITTLE PEOPLE! THEIR HUMBLE HEARTS SO FULL OF AWE--AND LOVE! AND I DO SO LOVE BEING LOVED!>
<IT MUST BE HER! THE CRIMSON FOX!>

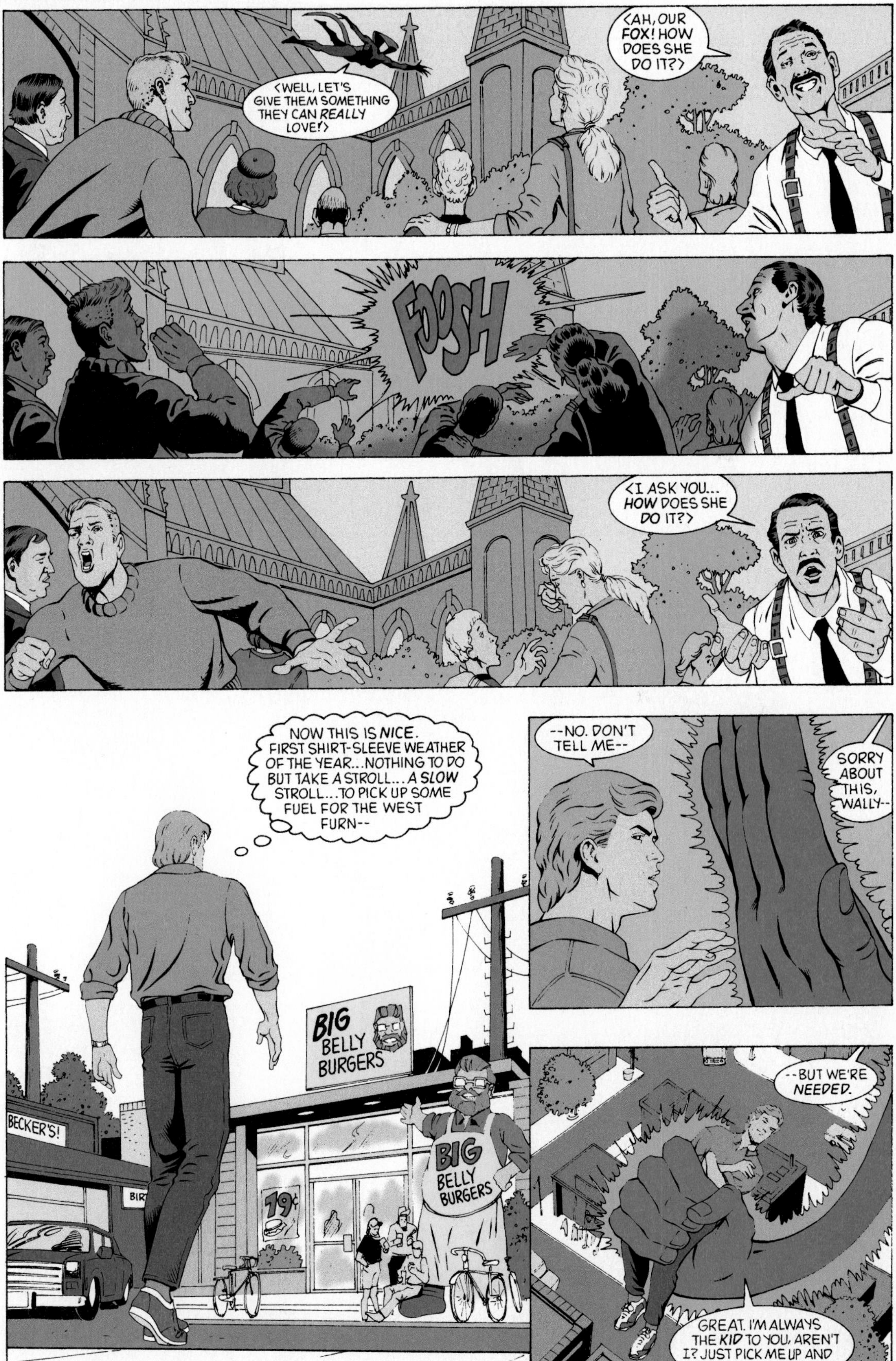
<WELL, LET'S GIVE THEM SOMETHING THEY CAN REALLY LOVE!>
<AH, OUR FOX! HOW DOES SHE DO IT?>
FOOSH
<I ASK YOU... HOW DOES SHE DO IT?>
NOW THIS IS NICE. FIRST SHIRT-SLEEVE WEATHER OF THE YEAR...NOTHING TO DO BUT TAKE A STROLL... A SLOW STROLL...TO PICK UP SOME FUEL FOR THE WEST FURN--
BIG BELLY BURGERS
BECKER'S!
BIG BELLY BURGERS
19¢
--NO. DON'T TELL ME--
SORRY ABOUT THIS, WALLY--
--BUT WE'RE NEEDED.
GREAT. I'M ALWAYS THE KID TO YOU, AREN'T I? JUST PICK ME UP AND SWING ME AROUND!

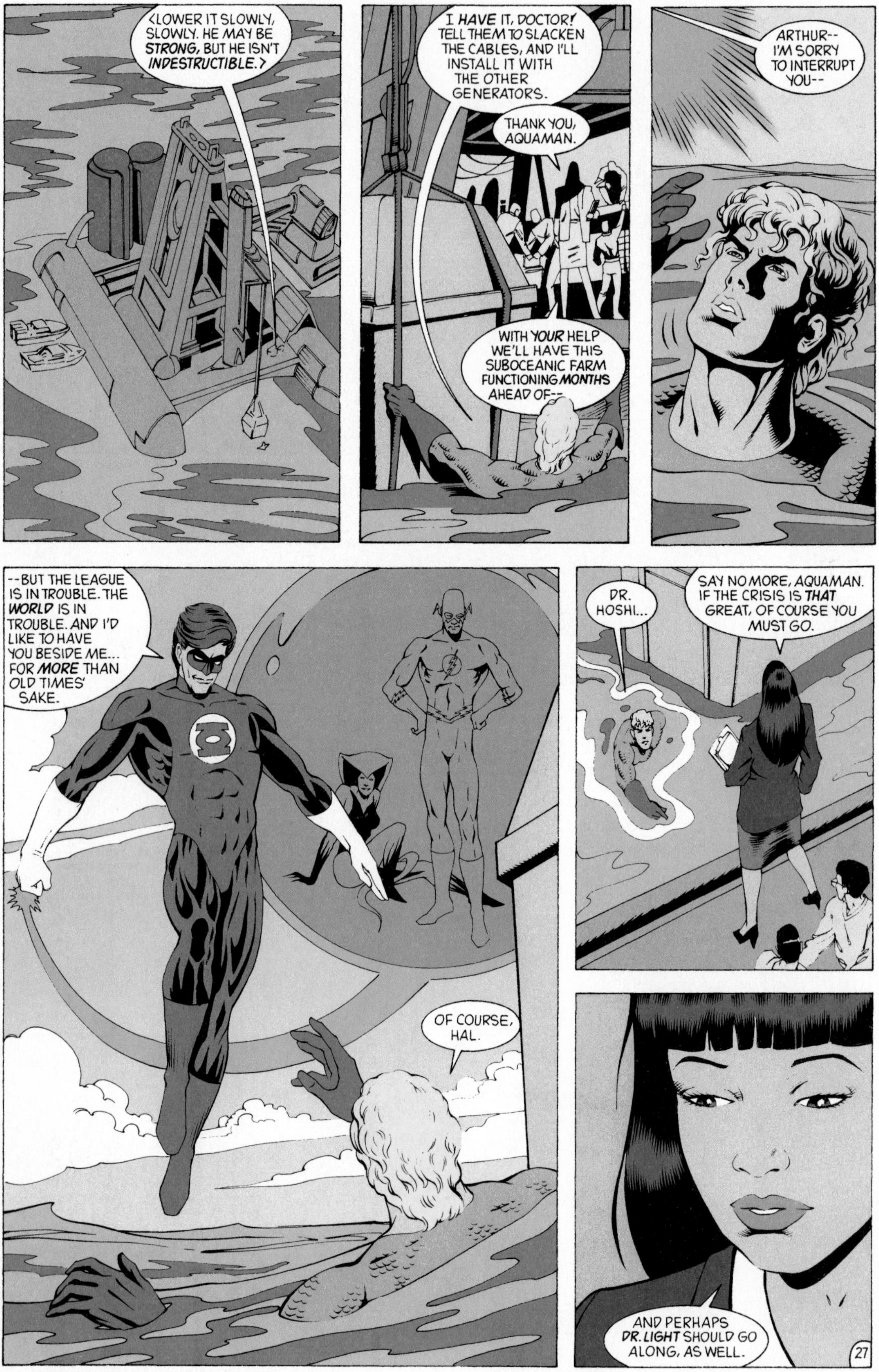
<LOWER IT SLOWLY, SLOWLY. HE MAY BE STRONG, BUT HE ISN'T INDESTRUCTIBLE.>
I HAVE IT, DOCTOR! TELL THEM TO SLACKEN THE CABLES, AND I'LL INSTALL IT WITH THE OTHER GENERATORS.
THANK YOU, AQUAMAN.
WITH YOUR HELP WE'LL HAVE THIS SUBOCEANIC FARM FUNCTIONING MONTHS AHEAD OF--
ARTHUR-- I'M SORRY TO INTERRUPT YOU--
--BUT THE LEAGUE IS IN TROUBLE. THE WORLD IS IN TROUBLE. AND I'D LIKE TO HAVE YOU BESIDE ME... FOR MORE THAN OLD TIMES' SAKE.
OF COURSE, HAL.
DR. HOSHI...
SAY NO MORE, AQUAMAN. IF THE CRISIS IS THAT GREAT, OF COURSE YOU MUST GO.
AND PERHAPS DR. LIGHT SHOULD GO ALONG, AS WELL.
27

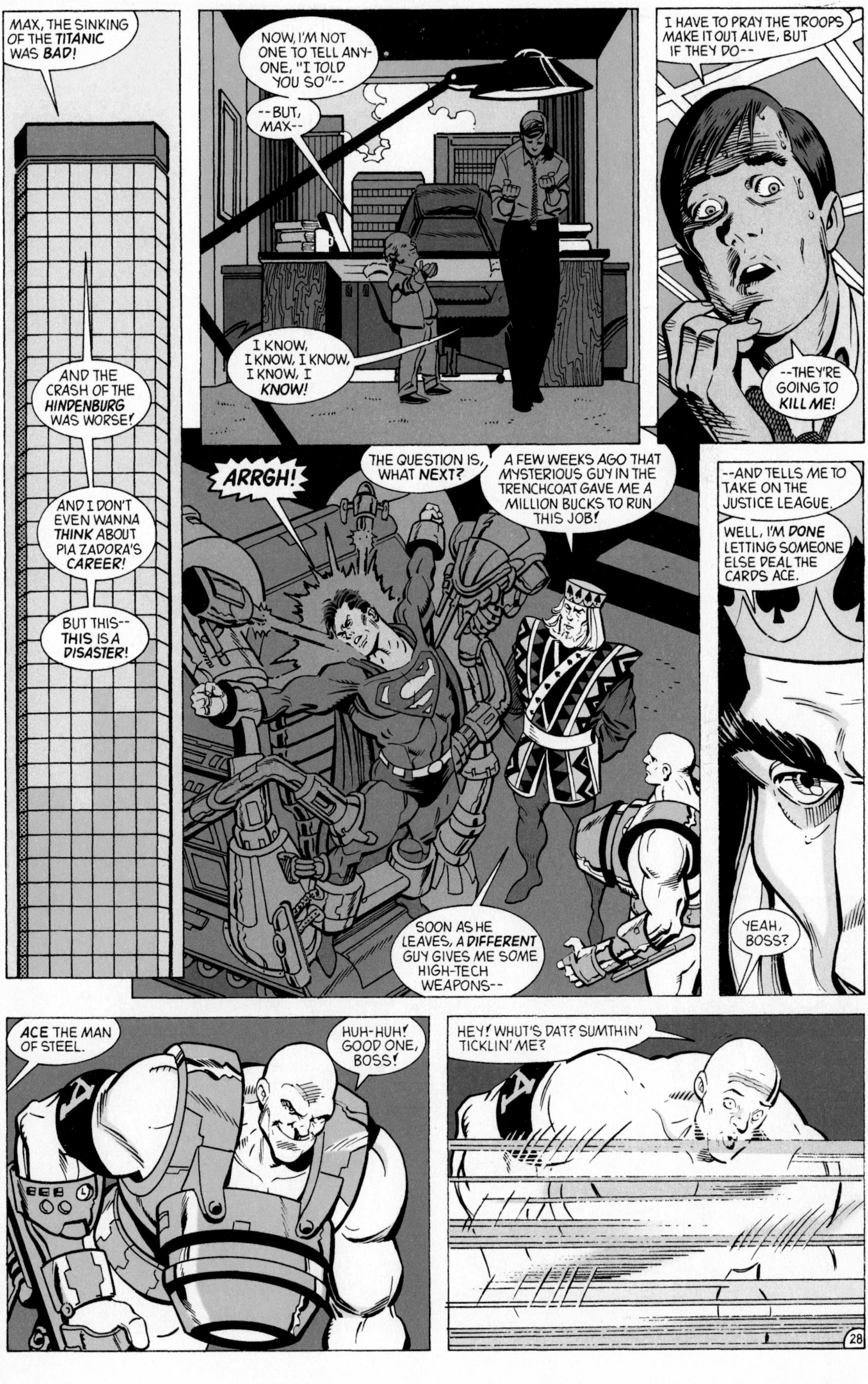

MAX, THE SINKING OF THE TITANIC WAS BAD!
NOW, I'M NOT ONE TO TELL ANY-ONE, "I TOLD YOU SO"--
--BUT, MAX--
I KNOW, I KNOW, I KNOW, I KNOW, I KNOW!
I HAVE TO PRAY THE TROOPS MAKE IT OUT ALIVE, BUT IF THEY DO--
--THEY'RE GOING TO KILL ME!
AND THE CRASH OF THE HINDENBURG WAS WORSE!
AND I DON'T EVEN WANNA THINK ABOUT PIA ZADORA'S CAREER!
BUT THIS-- THIS IS A DISASTER!
ARRGH!
THE QUESTION IS, WHAT NEXT?
A FEW WEEKS AGO THAT MYSTERIOUS GUY IN THE TRENCHCOAT GAVE ME A MILLION BUCKS TO RUN THIS JOB!
SOON AS HE LEAVES, A DIFFERENT GUY GIVES ME SOME HIGH-TECH WEAPONS--
--AND TELLS ME TO TAKE ON THE JUSTICE LEAGUE.
WELL, I'M DONE LETTING SOMEONE ELSE DEAL THE CARDS ACE.
YEAH, BOSS?
ACE THE MAN OF STEEL.
HUH-HUH! GOOD ONE, BOSS!
HEY! WHUT'S DAT? SUMTHIN' TICKLIN' ME?

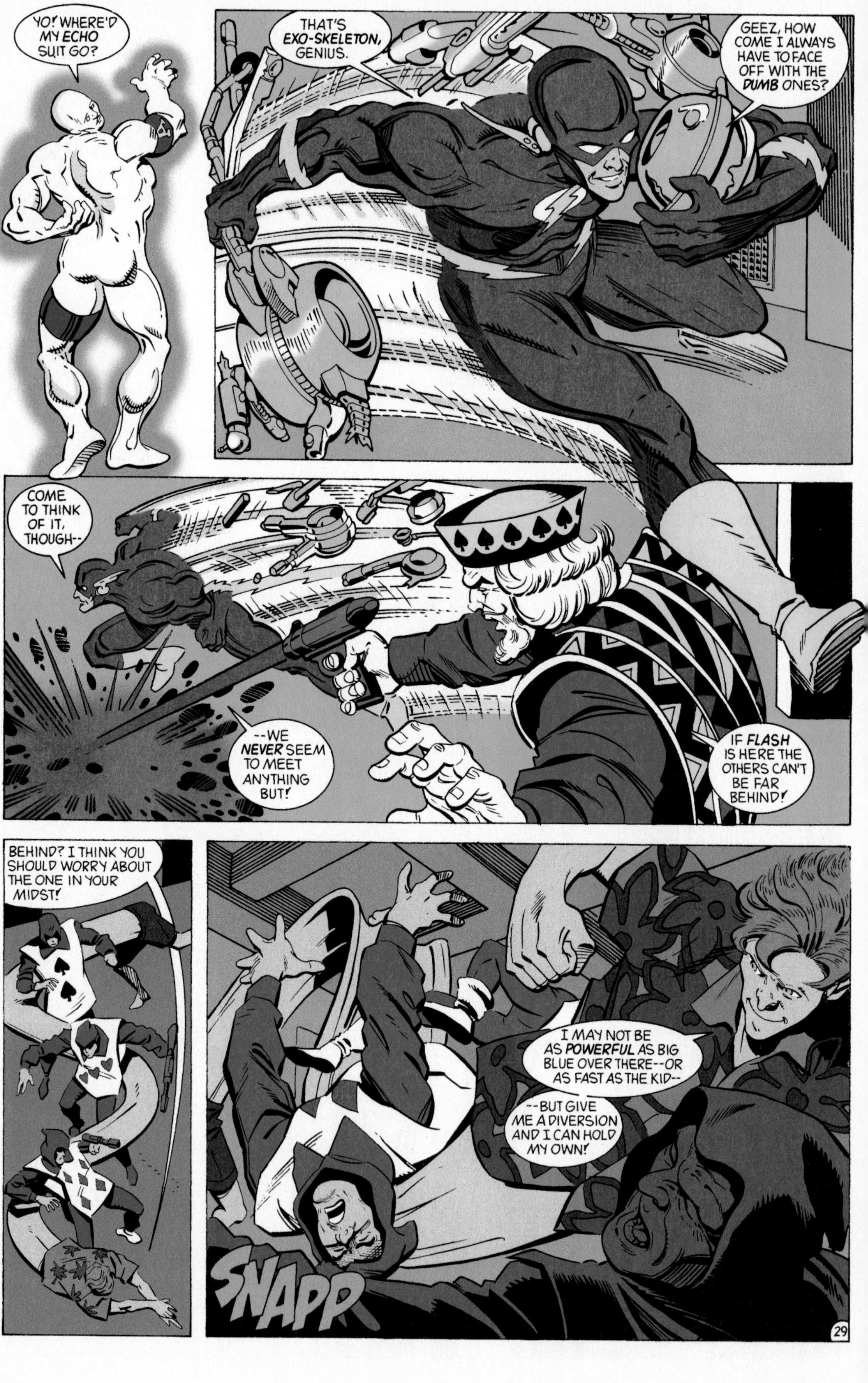
YO! WHERE'D MY ECHO SUIT GO?
THAT'S EXO-SKELETON, GENIUS.
GEEZ, HOW COME I ALWAYS HAVE TO FACE OFF WITH THE DUMB ONES?
COME TO THINK OF IT, THOUGH--
--WE NEVER SEEM TO MEET ANYTHING BUT!
IF FLASH IS HERE THE OTHERS CAN'T BE FAR BEHIND!
BEHIND? I THINK YOU SHOULD WORRY ABOUT THE ONE IN YOUR MIDST!
I MAY NOT BE AS POWERFUL AS BIG BLUE OVER THERE--OR AS FAST AS THE KID--
--BUT GIVE ME A DIVERSION AND I CAN HOLD MY OWN!
SNAPP

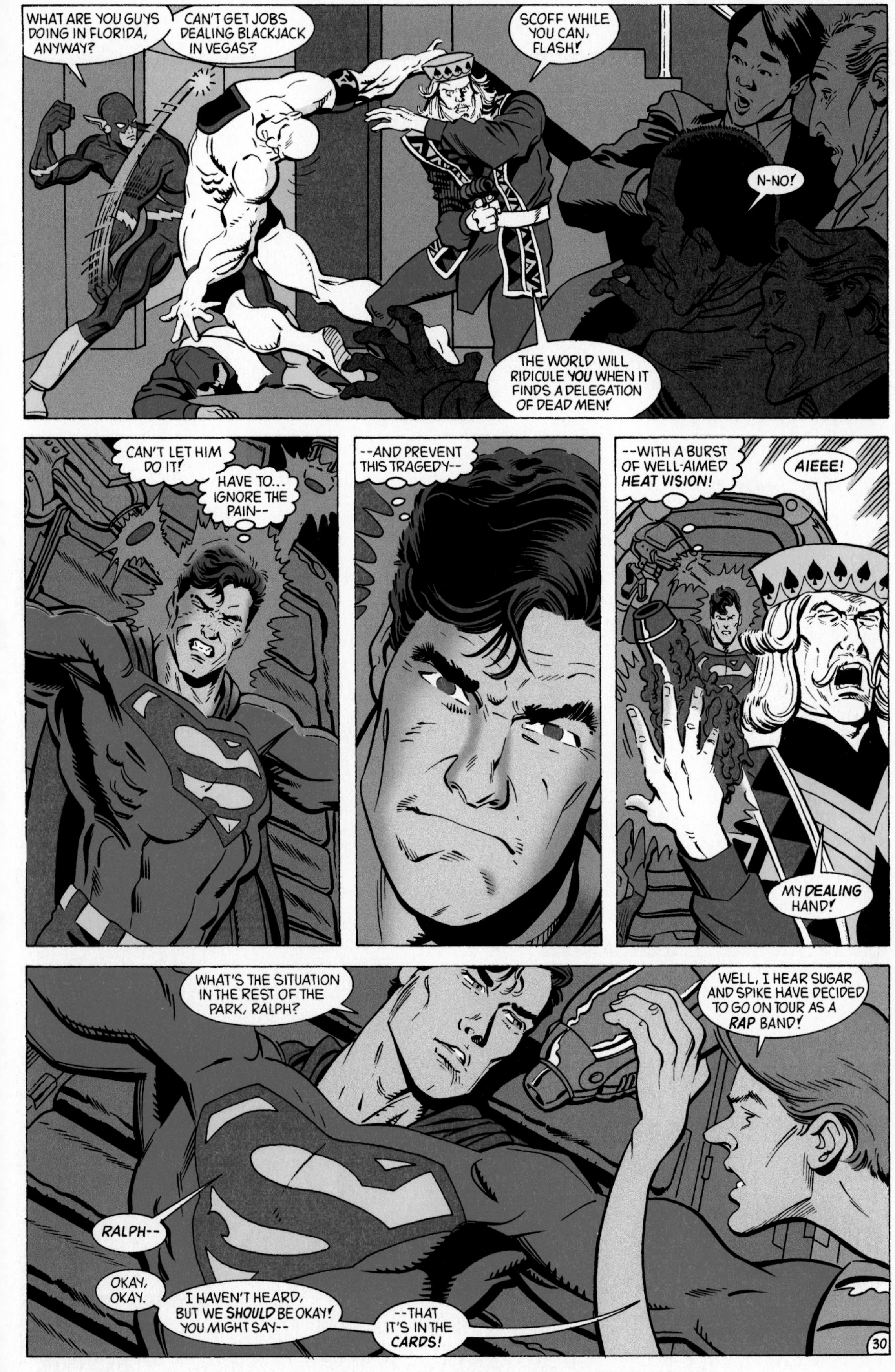
WHAT ARE YOU GUYS DOING IN FLORIDA, ANYWAY?
CAN'T GET JOBS DEALING BLACKJACK IN VEGAS?
SCOFF WHILE YOU CAN, FLASH!
N-NO!
THE WORLD WILL RIDICULE YOU WHEN IT FINDS A DELEGATION OF DEAD MEN!
CAN'T LET HIM DO IT!
HAVE TO... IGNORE THE PAIN--
--AND PREVENT THIS TRAGEDY--
--WITH A BURST OF WELL-AIMED HEAT VISION!
AIEEE!
MY DEALING HAND!
WHAT'S THE SITUATION IN THE REST OF THE PARK, RALPH?
WELL, I HEAR SUGAR AND SPIKE HAVE DECIDED TO GO ON TOUR AS A RAP BAND!
RALPH--
OKAY, OKAY.
I HAVEN'T HEARD, BUT WE SHOULD BE OKAY! YOU MIGHT SAY--
--THAT IT'S IN THE CARDS!

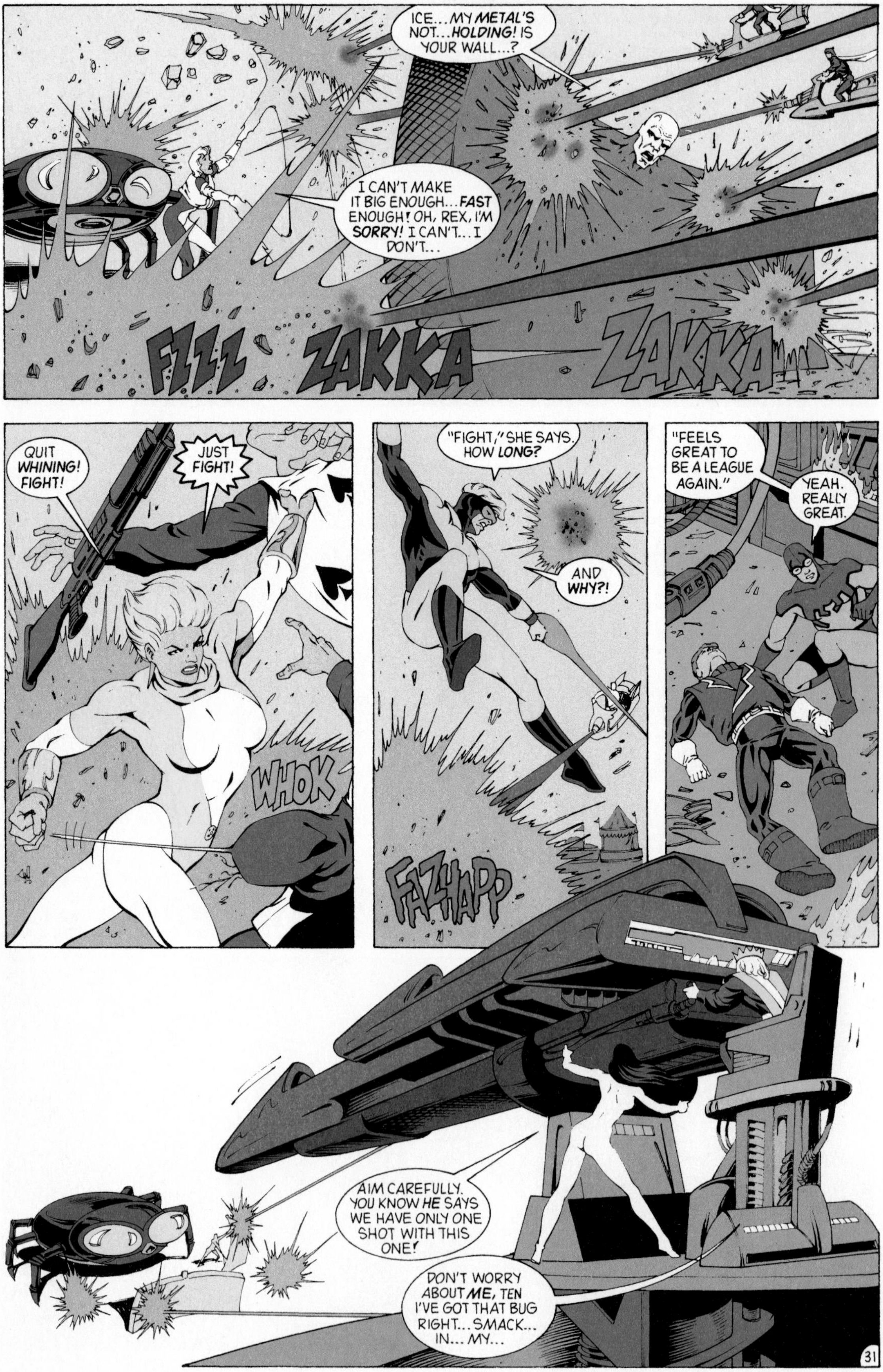
ICE... MY METAL'S NOT... HOLDING! IS YOUR WALL...?
I CAN'T MAKE IT BIG ENOUGH... FAST ENOUGH! OH, REX, I'M SORRY! I CAN'T... I DON'T...
FZZZ
ZAKKA
ZAKKA
QUIT WHINING! FIGHT!
JUST FIGHT!
WHOK
"FIGHT," SHE SAYS. HOW LONG?
AND WHY?!
FAZHAPP
"FEELS GREAT TO BE A LEAGUE AGAIN."
YEAH. REALLY GREAT.
AIM CAREFULLY. YOU KNOW HE SAYS WE HAVE ONLY ONE SHOT WITH THIS ONE!
DON'T WORRY ABOUT ME, TEN I'VE GOT THAT BUG RIGHT... SMACK... IN... MY...

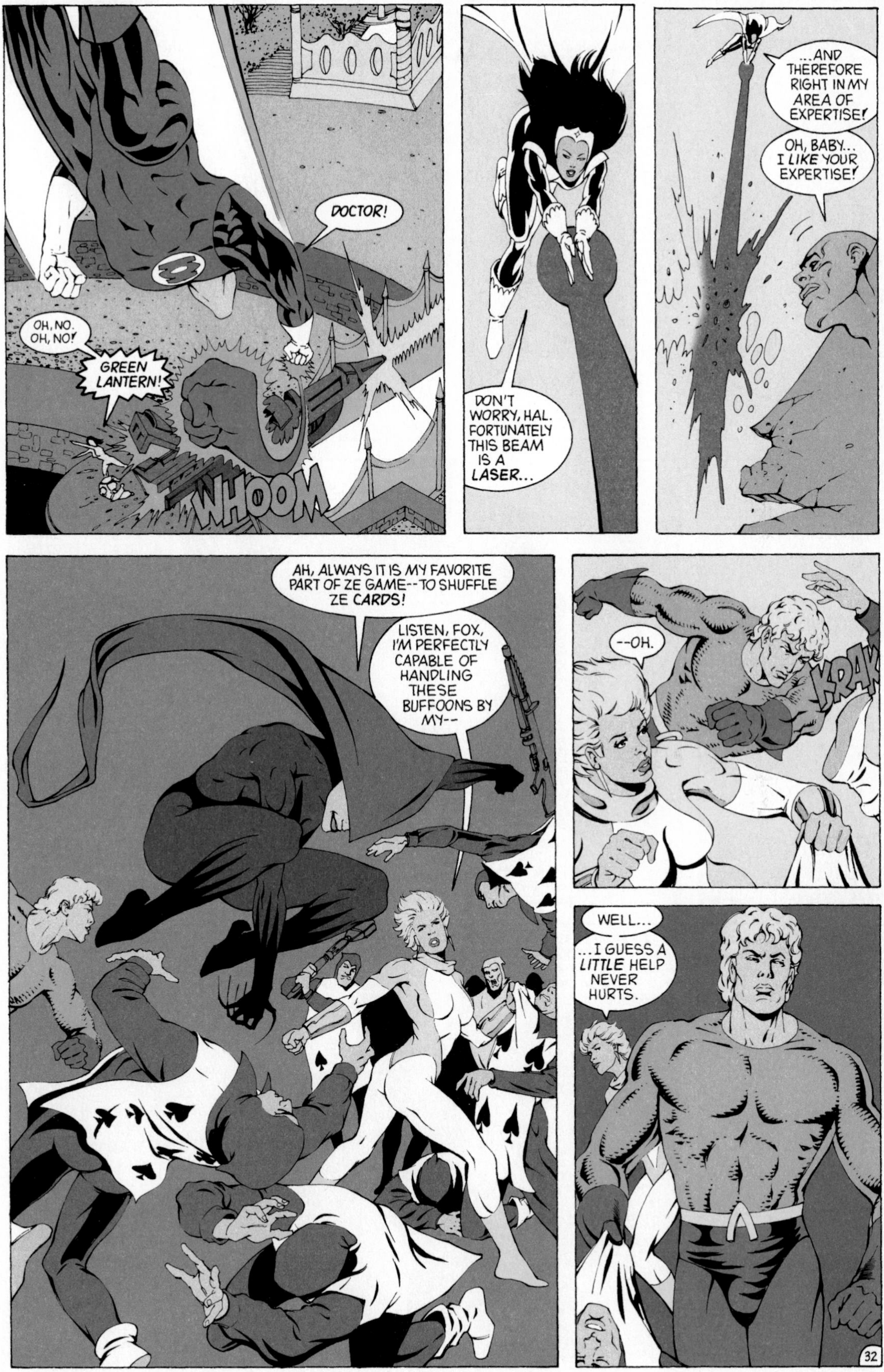
DOCTOR!
OH, NO. OH, NO!
GREEN LANTERN!
WHOOM
DON'T WORRY, HAL. FORTUNATELY THIS BEAM IS A LASER...
...AND THEREFORE RIGHT IN MY AREA OF EXPERTISE!
OH, BABY... I LIKE YOUR EXPERTISE!
AH, ALWAYS IT IS MY FAVORITE PART OF ZE GAME--TO SHUFFLE ZE CARDS!
LISTEN, FOX, I'M PERFECTLY CAPABLE OF HANDLING THESE BUFFOONS BY MY--
--OH.
WELL...
...I GUESS A LITTLE HELP NEVER HURTS.
32

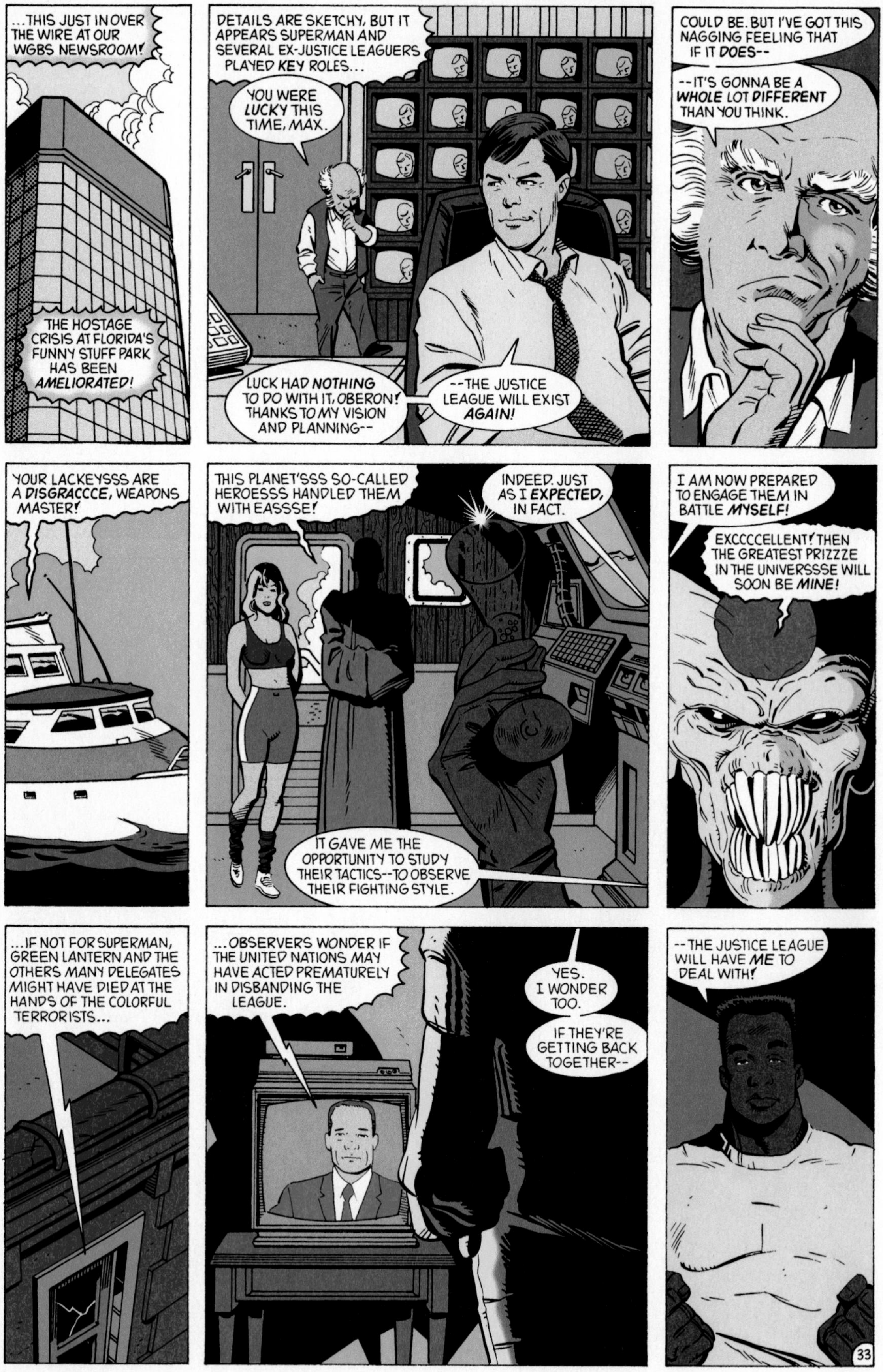

...THIS JUST IN OVER THE WIRE AT OUR WGBS NEWSROOM!
THE HOSTAGE CRISIS AT FLORIDA'S FUNNY STUFF PARK HAS BEEN AMELIORATED!
DETAILS ARE SKETCHY, BUT IT APPEARS SUPERMAN AND SEVERAL EX-JUSTICE LEAGUERS PLAYED KEY ROLES...
YOU WERE LUCKY THIS TIME, MAX.
LUCK HAD NOTHING TO DO WITH IT, OBERON! THANKS TO MY VISION AND PLANNING--
--THE JUSTICE LEAGUE WILL EXIST AGAIN!
COULD BE. BUT I'VE GOT THIS NAGGING FEELING THAT IF IT DOES--
--IT'S GONNA BE A WHOLE LOT DIFFERENT THAN YOU THINK.
YOUR LACKEYSSS ARE A DISGRACCCE, WEAPONS MASTER!
THIS PLANET'SSS SO-CALLED HEROESSS HANDLED THEM WITH EASSSE!
INDEED. JUST AS I EXPECTED, IN FACT.
IT GAVE ME THE OPPORTUNITY TO STUDY THEIR TACTICS--TO OBSERVE THEIR FIGHTING STYLE.
I AM NOW PREPARED TO ENGAGE THEM IN BATTLE MYSELF!
EXCCCCELLENT! THEN THE GREATEST PRIZZZE IN THE UNIVERSSSE WILL SOON BE MINE!
...IF NOT FOR SUPERMAN, GREEN LANTERN AND THE OTHERS MANY DELEGATES MIGHT HAVE DIED AT THE HANDS OF THE COLORFUL TERRORISTS...
...OBSERVERS WONDER IF THE UNITED NATIONS MAY HAVE ACTED PREMATURELY IN DISBANDING THE LEAGUE.
YES. I WONDER TOO.
IF THEY'RE GETTING BACK TOGETHER--
--THE JUSTICE LEAGUE WILL HAVE ME TO DEAL WITH!
33

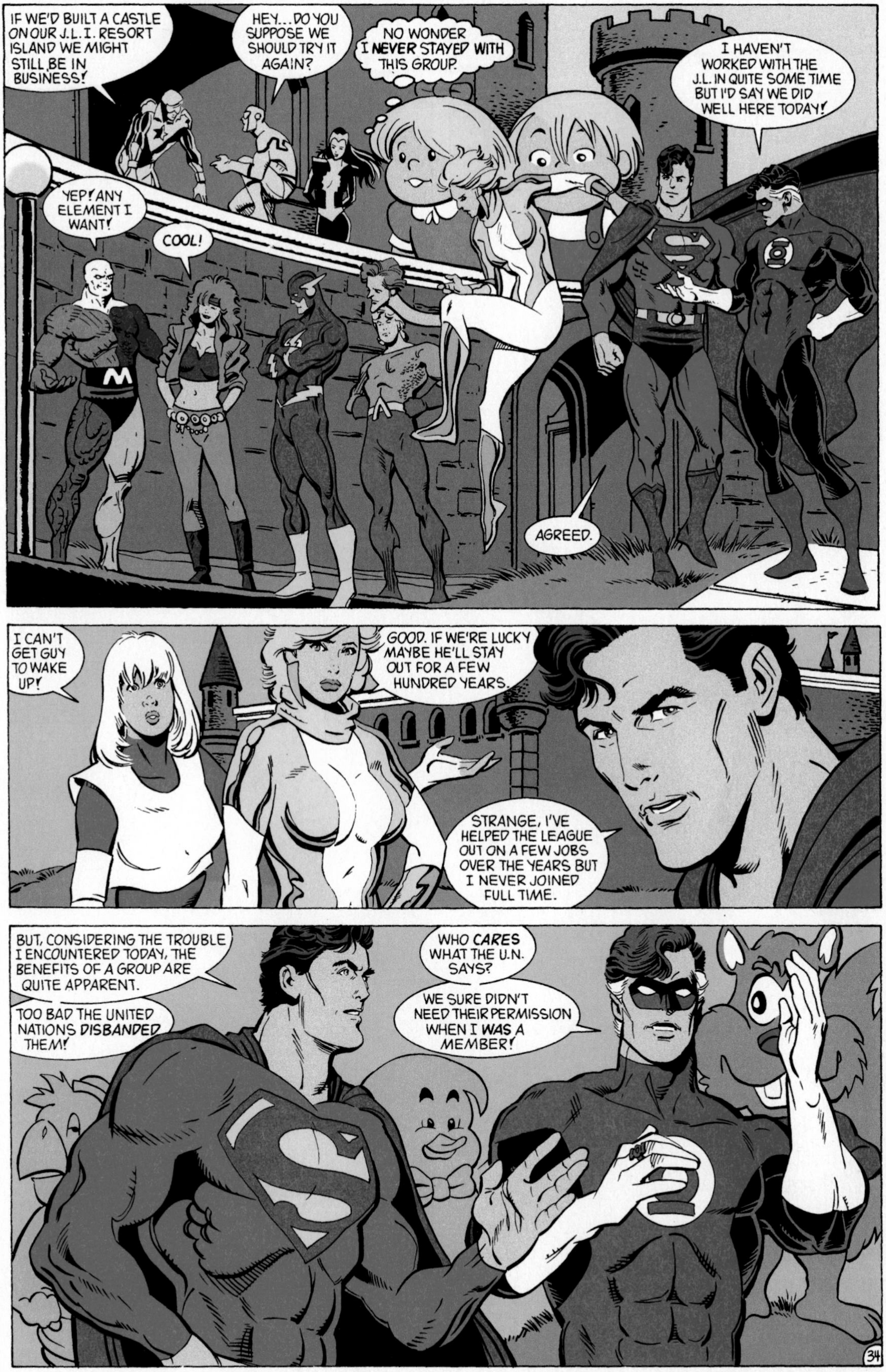
IF WE'D BUILT A CASTLE ON OUR J.L.I. RESORT ISLAND WE MIGHT STILL BE IN BUSINESS!
HEY... DO YOU SUPPOSE WE SHOULD TRY IT AGAIN?
NO WONDER I NEVER STAYED WITH THIS GROUP.
I HAVEN'T WORKED WITH THE J.L. IN QUITE SOME TIME BUT I'D SAY WE DID WELL HERE TODAY!
YEP! ANY ELEMENT I WANT!
COOL!
AGREED.
I CAN'T GET GUY TO WAKE UP!
GOOD. IF WE'RE LUCKY MAYBE HE'LL STAY OUT FOR A FEW HUNDRED YEARS.
STRANGE, I'VE HELPED THE LEAGUE OUT ON A FEW JOBS OVER THE YEARS BUT I NEVER JOINED FULL TIME.
BUT, CONSIDERING THE TROUBLE I ENCOUNTERED TODAY, THE BENEFITS OF A GROUP ARE QUITE APPARENT.
TOO BAD THE UNITED NATIONS DISBANDED THEM!
WHO CARES WHAT THE U.N. SAYS?
WE SURE DIDN'T NEED THEIR PERMISSION WHEN I WAS A MEMBER!
34

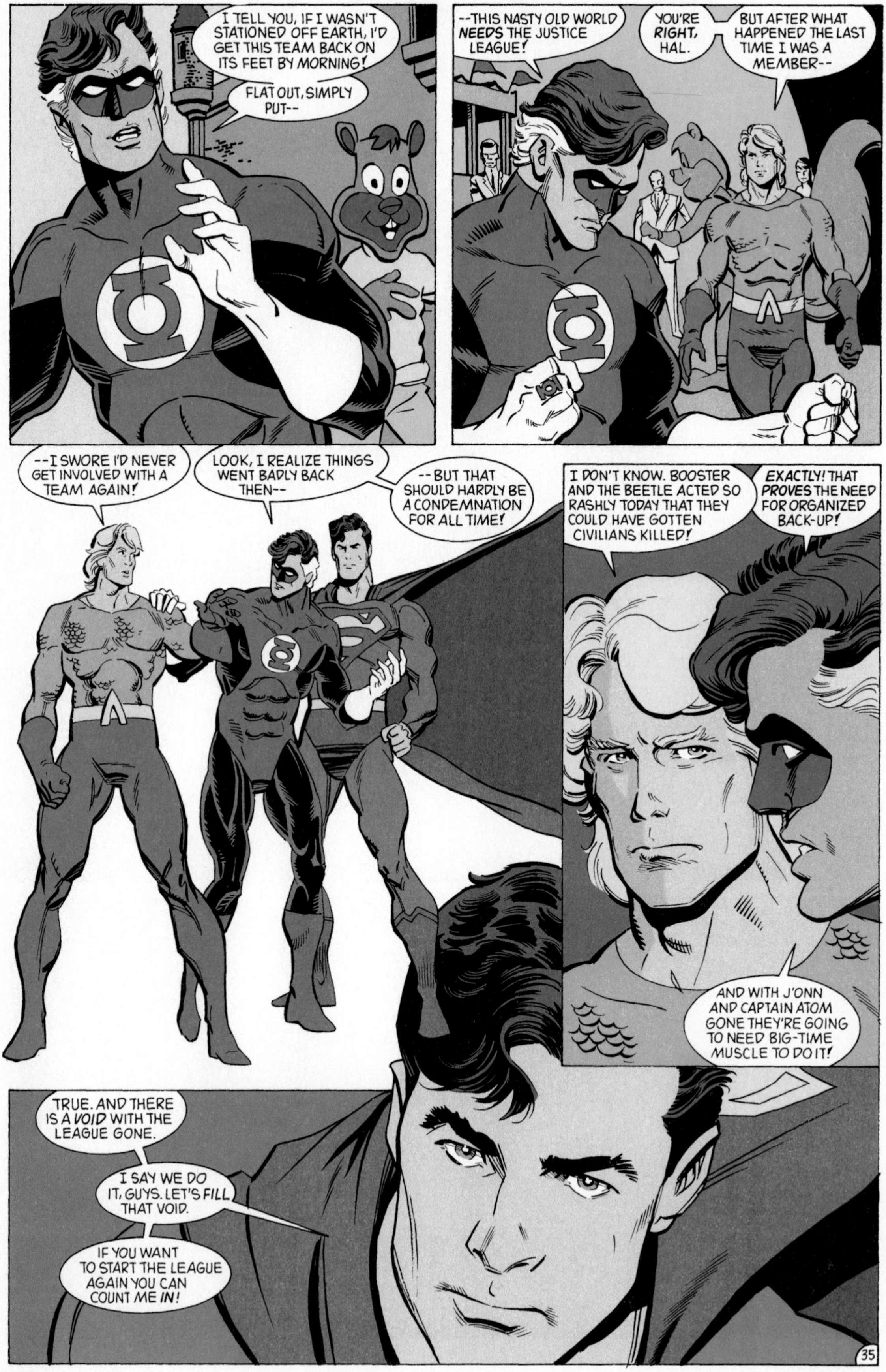

I TELL YOU, IF I WASN'T STATIONED OFF EARTH, I'D GET THIS TEAM BACK ON ITS FEET BY MORNING!
FLAT OUT, SIMPLY PUT--
--THIS NASTY OLD WORLD NEEDS THE JUSTICE LEAGUE!
YOU'RE RIGHT, HAL.
BUT AFTER WHAT HAPPENED THE LAST TIME I WAS A MEMBER--
--I SWORE I'D NEVER GET INVOLVED WITH A TEAM AGAIN!
LOOK, I REALIZE THINGS WENT BADLY BACK THEN--
--BUT THAT SHOULD HARDLY BE A CONDEMNATION FOR ALL TIME!
I DON'T KNOW. BOOSTER AND THE BEETLE ACTED SO RASHLY TODAY THAT THEY COULD HAVE GOTTEN CIVILIANS KILLED!
EXACTLY! THAT PROVES THE NEED FOR ORGANIZED BACK-UP!
AND WITH J'ONN AND CAPTAIN ATOM GONE THEY'RE GOING TO NEED BIG-TIME MUSCLE TO DO IT!
TRUE. AND THERE IS A VOID WITH THE LEAGUE GONE.
I SAY WE DO IT, GUYS. LET'S FILL THAT VOID.
IF YOU WANT TO START THE LEAGUE AGAIN YOU CAN COUNT ME IN!

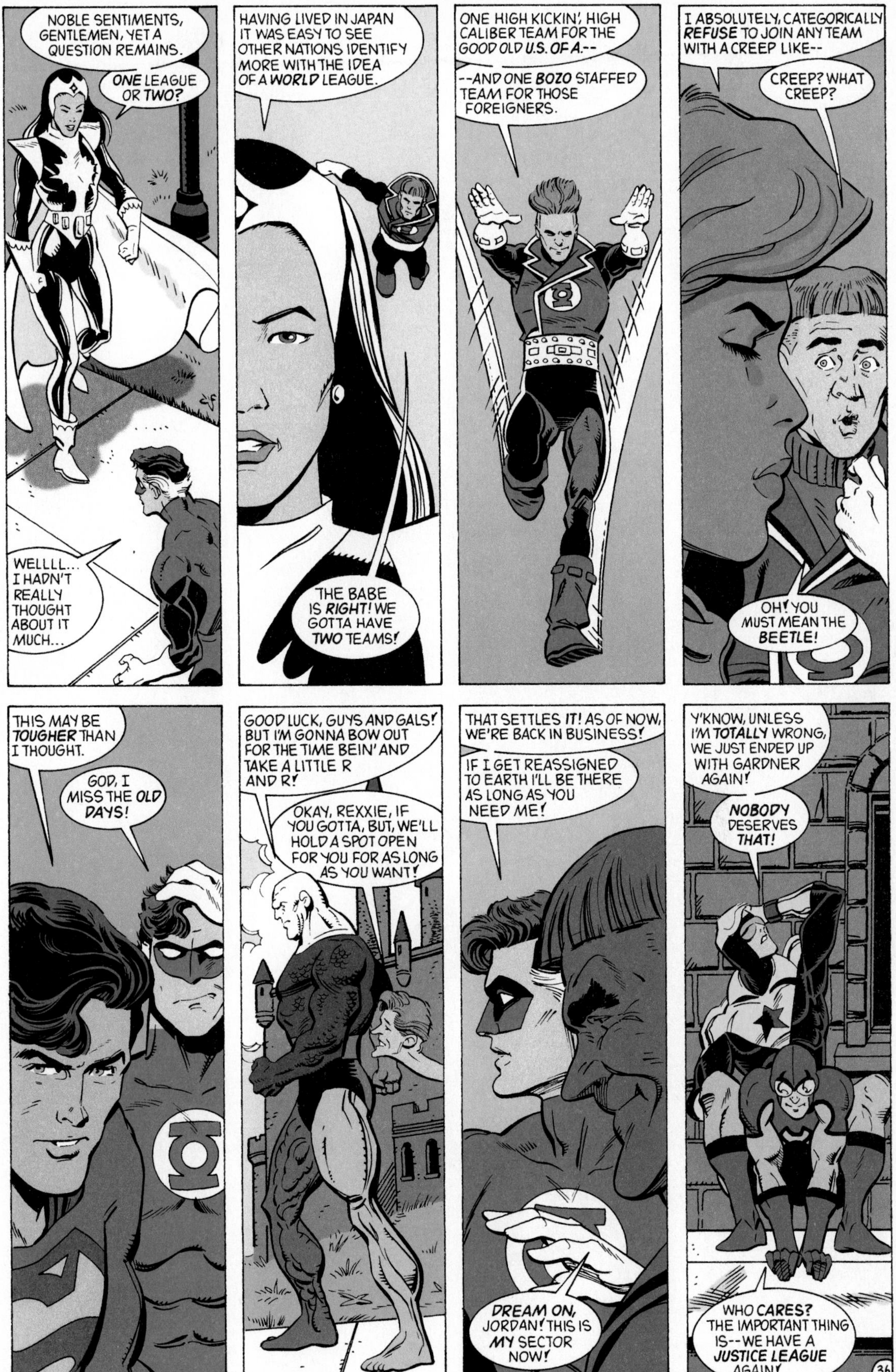
NOBLE SENTIMENTS, GENTLEMEN, YET A QUESTION REMAINS.
ONE LEAGUE OR TWO?
WELLLL... I HADN'T REALLY THOUGHT ABOUT IT MUCH...
HAVING LIVED IN JAPAN IT WAS EASY TO SEE OTHER NATIONS IDENTIFY MORE WITH THE IDEA OF A WORLD LEAGUE.
THE BABE IS RIGHT! WE GOTTA HAVE TWO TEAMS!
ONE HIGH KICKIN', HIGH CALIBER TEAM FOR THE GOOD OLD U.S. OF A.--
--AND ONE BOZO STAFFED TEAM FOR THOSE FOREIGNERS.
I ABSOLUTELY, CATEGORICALLY REFUSE TO JOIN ANY TEAM WITH A CREEP LIKE--
CREEP? WHAT CREEP?
OH! YOU MUST MEAN THE BEETLE!
THIS MAY BE TOUGHER THAN I THOUGHT.
GOD, I MISS THE OLD DAYS!
GOOD LUCK, GUYS AND GALS! BUT I'M GONNA BOW OUT FOR THE TIME BEIN' AND TAKE A LITTLE R AND R!
OKAY, REXXIE, IF YOU GOTTA, BUT, WE'LL HOLD A SPOT OPEN FOR YOU FOR AS LONG AS YOU WANT!
THAT SETTLES IT! AS OF NOW, WE'RE BACK IN BUSINESS!
IF I GET REASSIGNED TO EARTH I'LL BE THERE AS LONG AS YOU NEED ME!
DREAM ON, JORDAN! THIS IS MY SECTOR NOW!
Y'KNOW, UNLESS I'M TOTALLY WRONG, WE JUST ENDED UP WITH GARDNER AGAIN!
NOBODY DESERVES THAT!
WHO CARES? THE IMPORTANT THING IS--WE HAVE A JUSTICE LEAGUE AGAIN!
36

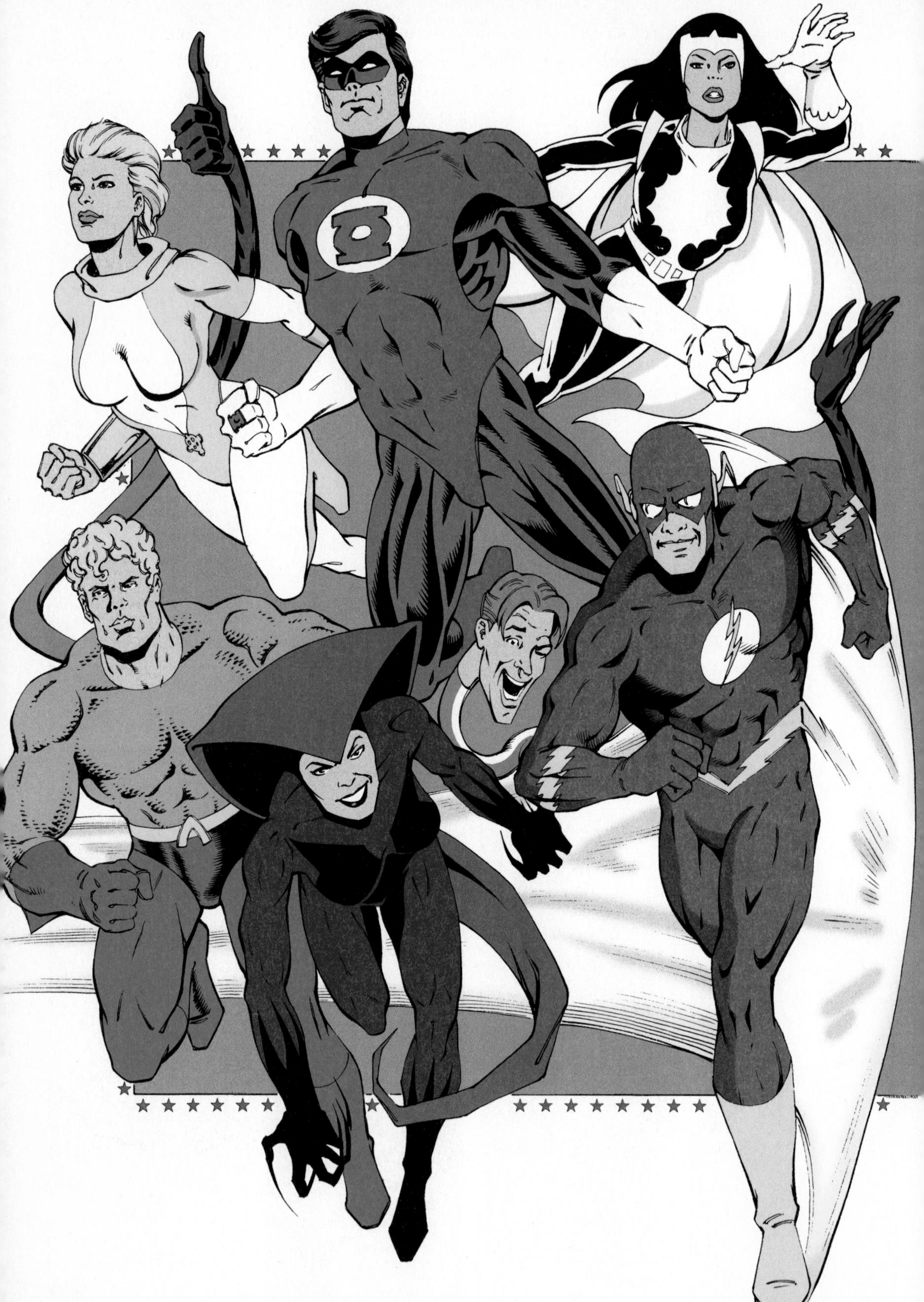

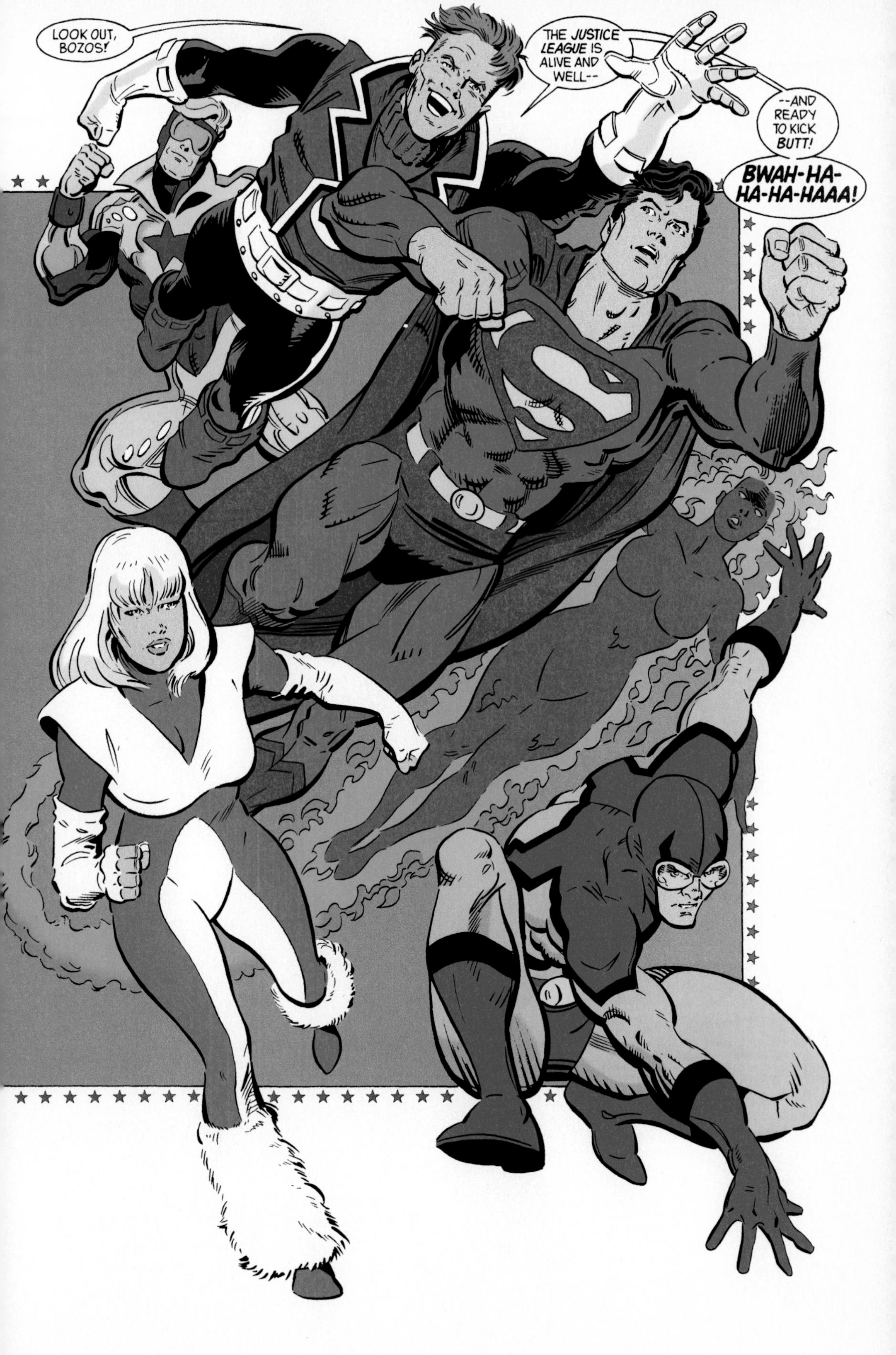

LOOK OUT, BOZOS!
THE JUSTICE LEAGUE IS ALIVE AND WELL--
--AND READY TO KICK BUTT!
BWAH-HA-HA-HA-HAAA!

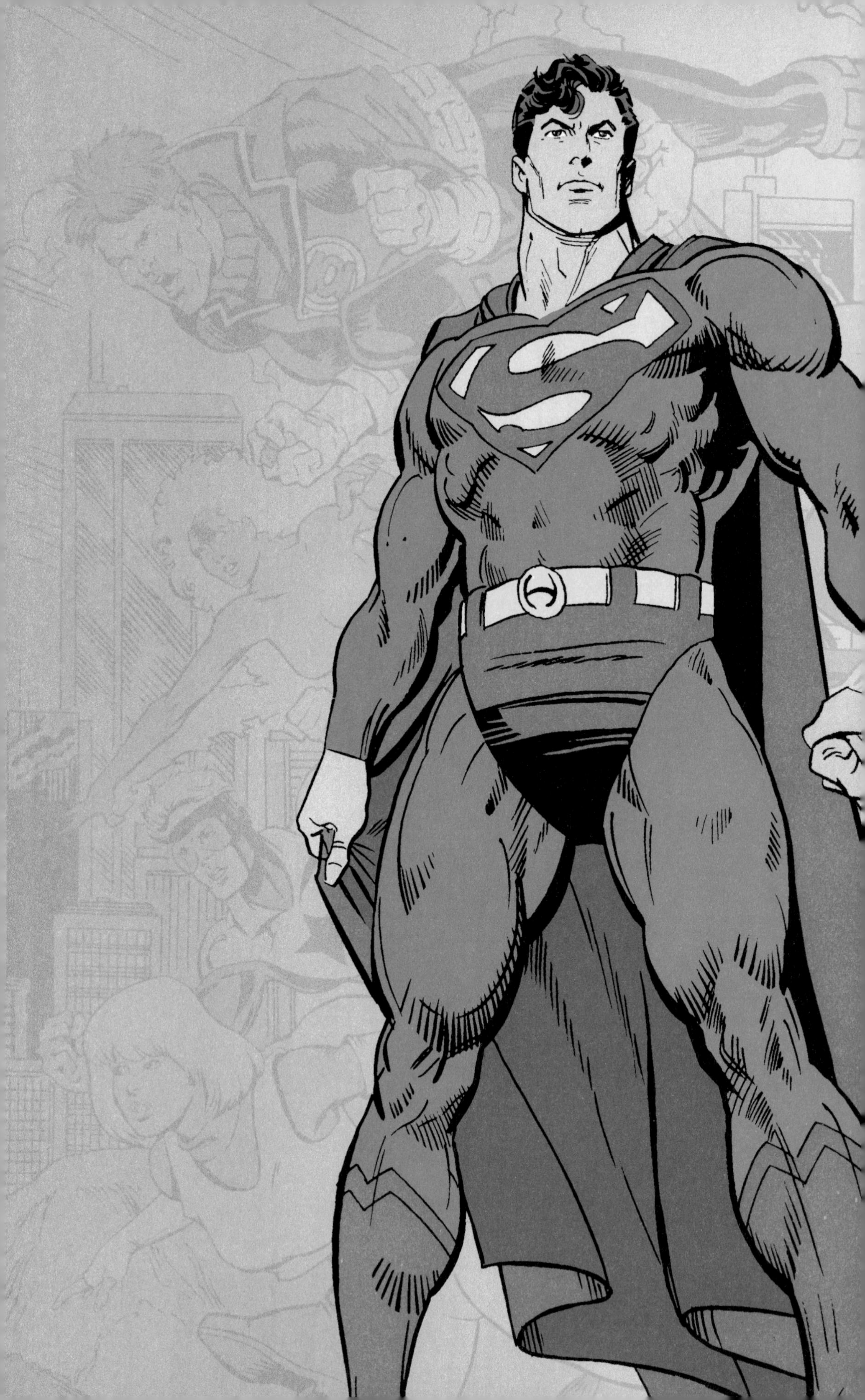

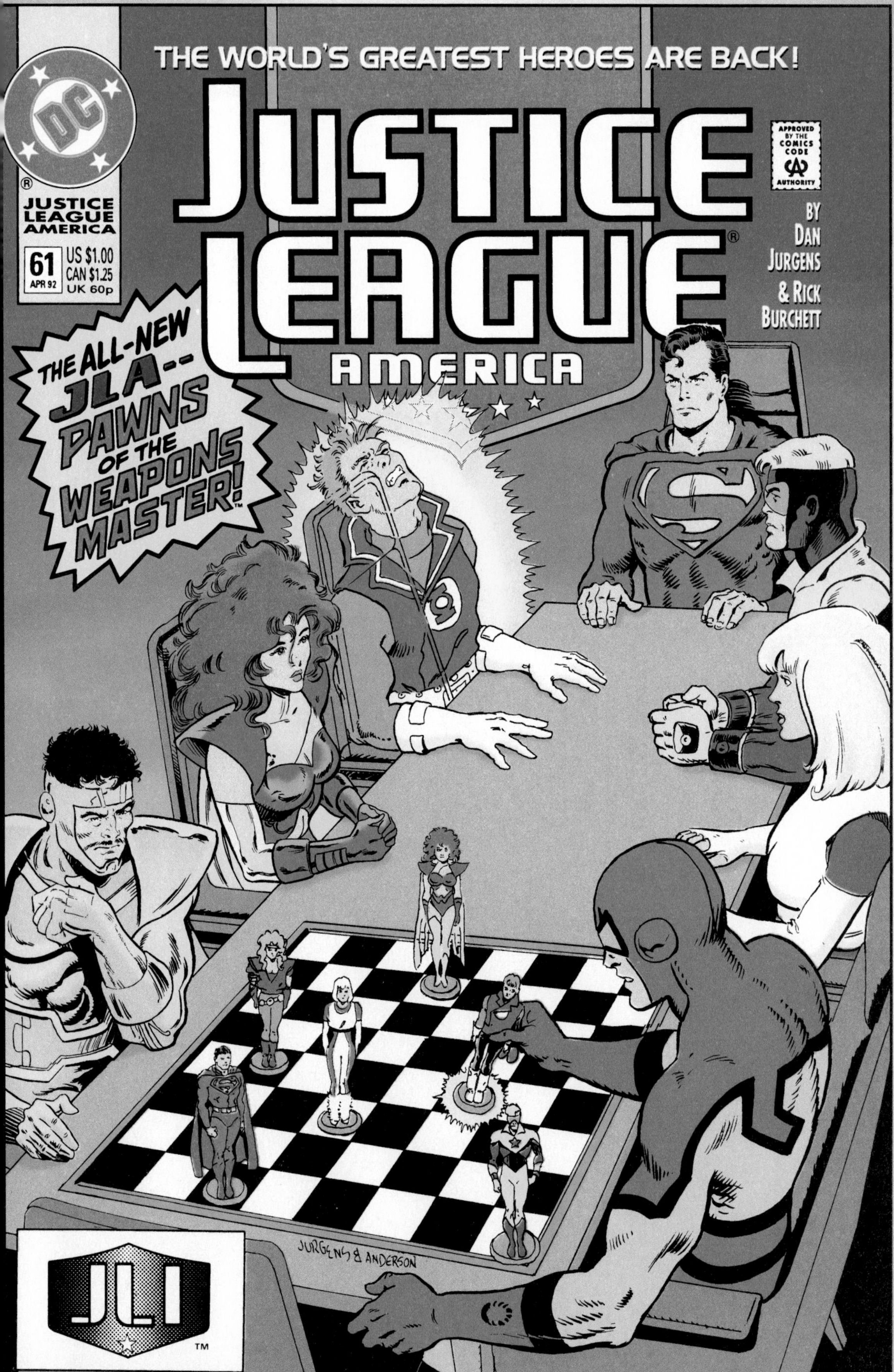
THE WORLD'S GREATEST HEROES ARE BACK!
JUSTICE LEAGUE AMERICA
61 APR 92
US $1.00 CAN $1.25 UK 60p
APPROVED BY THE COMICS CODE AUTHORITY
BY DAN JURGENS & RICK BURCHETT
THE ALL-NEW JLA-- PAWNS OF THE WEAPONS MASTER!
JURGENS & ANDERSON
JLI

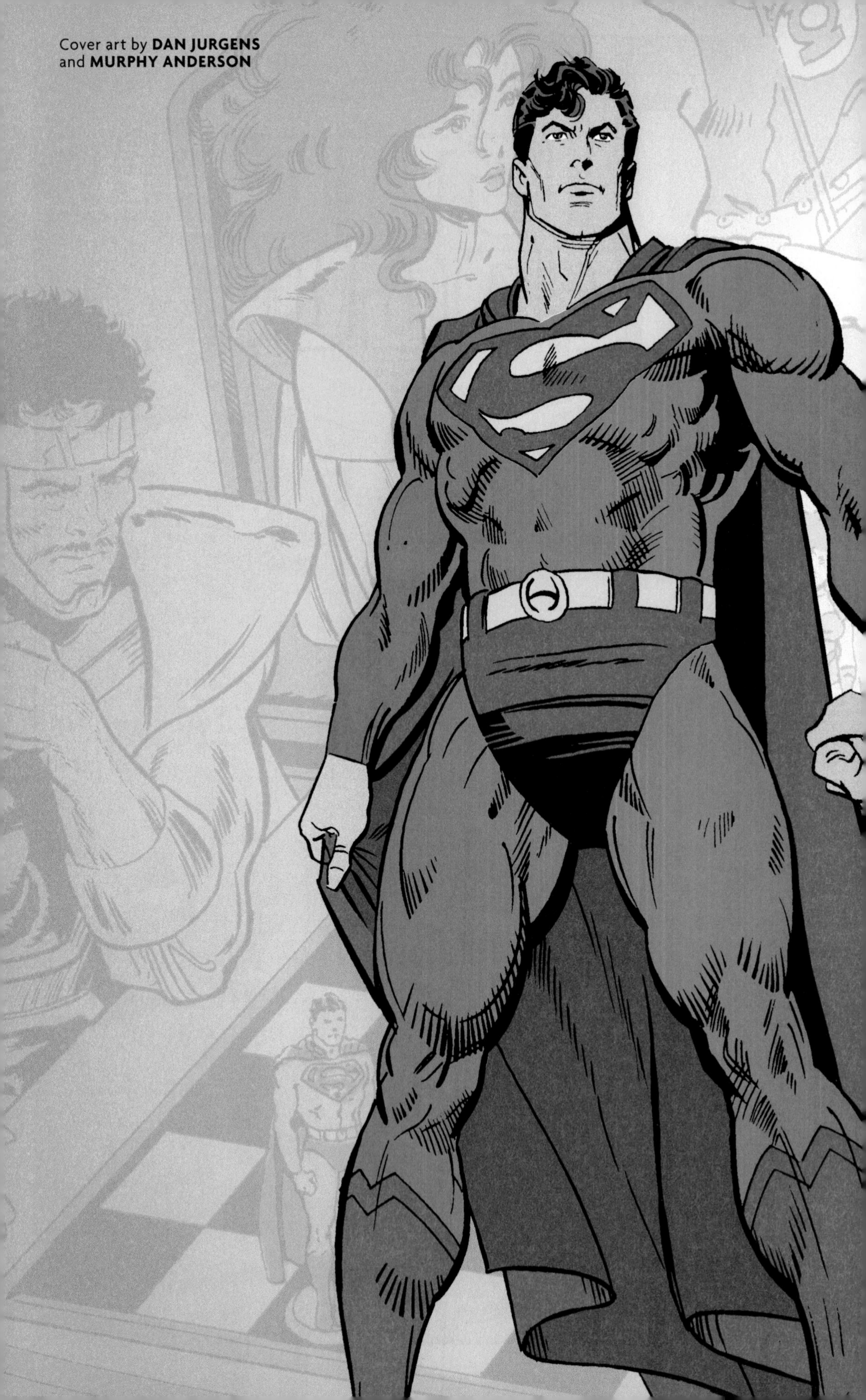

Cover art by **DAN JURGENS**
and **MURPHY ANDERSON**

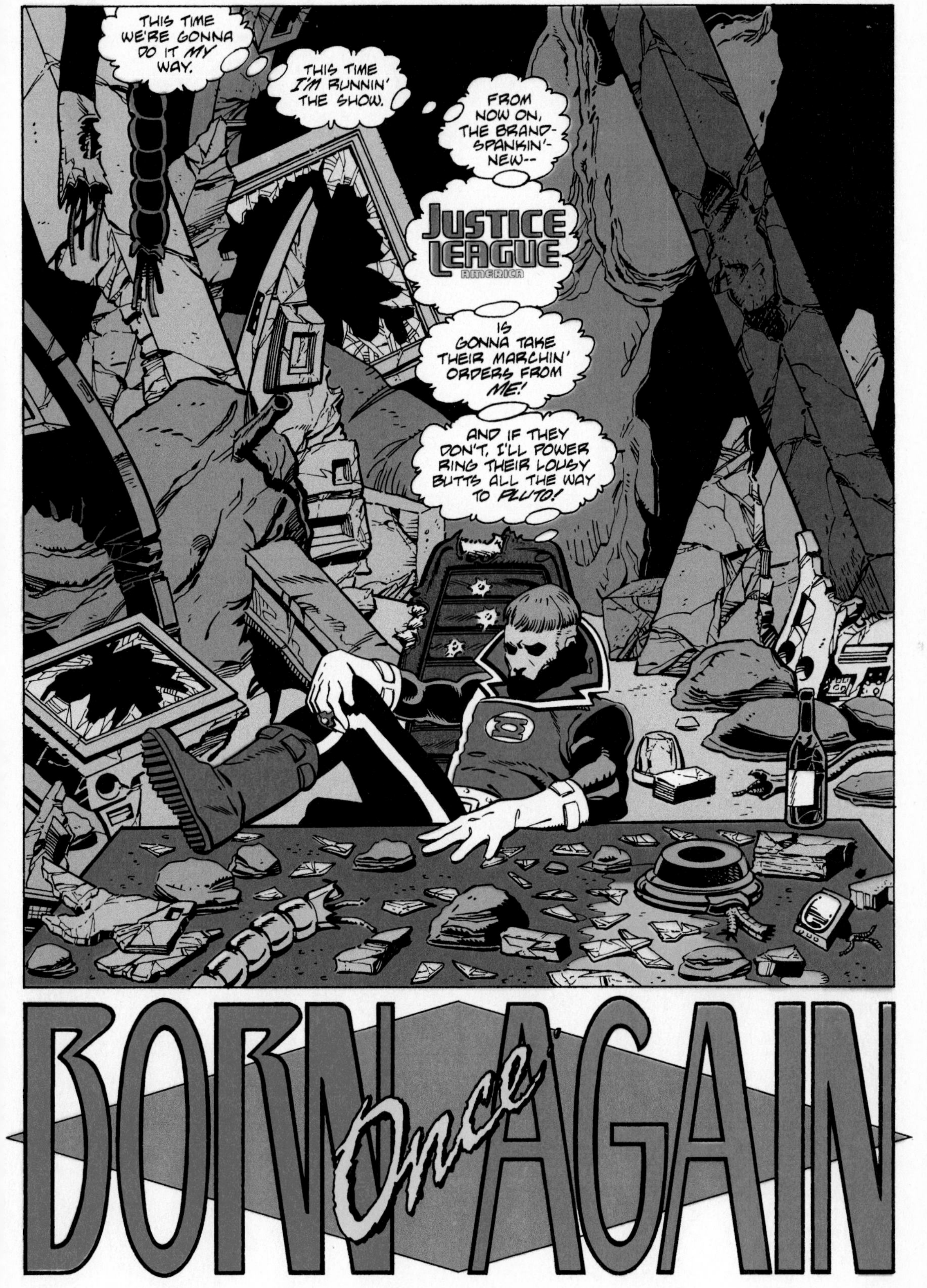
THIS TIME WE'RE GONNA DO IT MY WAY.
THIS TIME I'M RUNNIN' THE SHOW.
FROM NOW ON, THE BRAND-SPANKIN'-NEW--
JUSTICE LEAGUE AMERICA
IS GONNA TAKE THEIR MARCHIN' ORDERS FROM ME!
AND IF THEY DON'T, I'LL POWER RING THEIR LOUSY BUTTS ALL THE WAY TO PLUTO!

BORN *Once* AGAIN

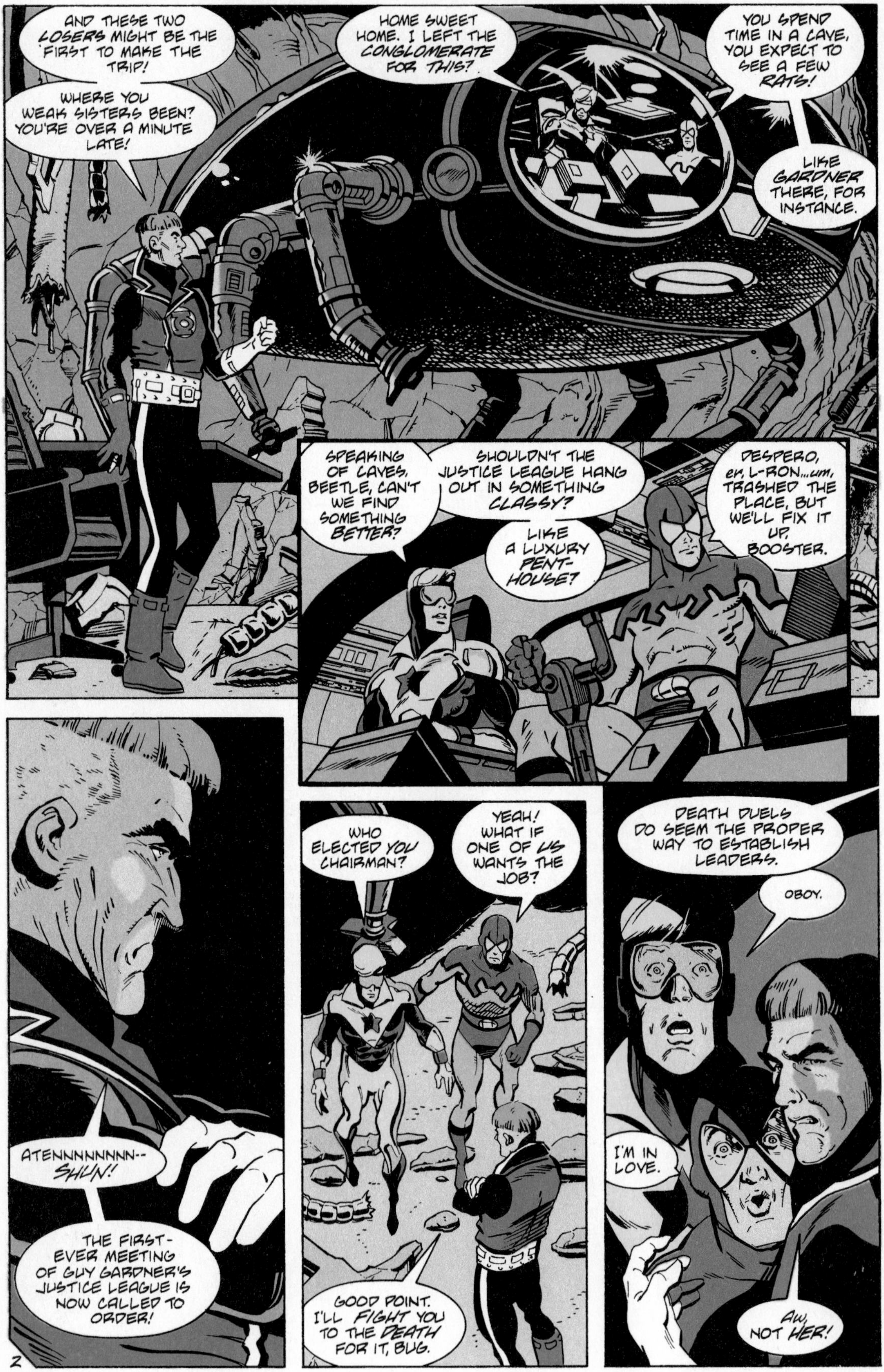

AND THESE TWO LOSERS MIGHT BE THE FIRST TO MAKE THE TRIP!
WHERE YOU WEAK SISTERS BEEN? YOU'RE OVER A MINUTE LATE!
HOME SWEET HOME. I LEFT THE CONGLOMERATE FOR THIS?
YOU SPEND TIME IN A CAVE, YOU EXPECT TO SEE A FEW RATS!
LIKE GARDNER THERE, FOR INSTANCE.
SPEAKING OF CAVES, BEETLE, CAN'T WE FIND SOMETHING BETTER?
SHOULDN'T THE JUSTICE LEAGUE HANG OUT IN SOMETHING CLASSY?
LIKE A LUXURY PENT-HOUSE?
DESPERO, er, L-RON...um, TRASHED THE PLACE, BUT WE'LL FIX IT UP, BOOSTER.
ATENNNNNNNN--SHUN!
THE FIRST-EVER MEETING OF GUY GARDNER'S JUSTICE LEAGUE IS NOW CALLED TO ORDER!
WHO ELECTED YOU CHAIRMAN?
YEAH! WHAT IF ONE OF US WANTS THE JOB?
GOOD POINT. I'LL FIGHT YOU TO THE DEATH FOR IT, BUG.
DEATH DUELS DO SEEM THE PROPER WAY TO ESTABLISH LEADERS.
OBOY.
I'M IN LOVE.
AW, NOT HER!

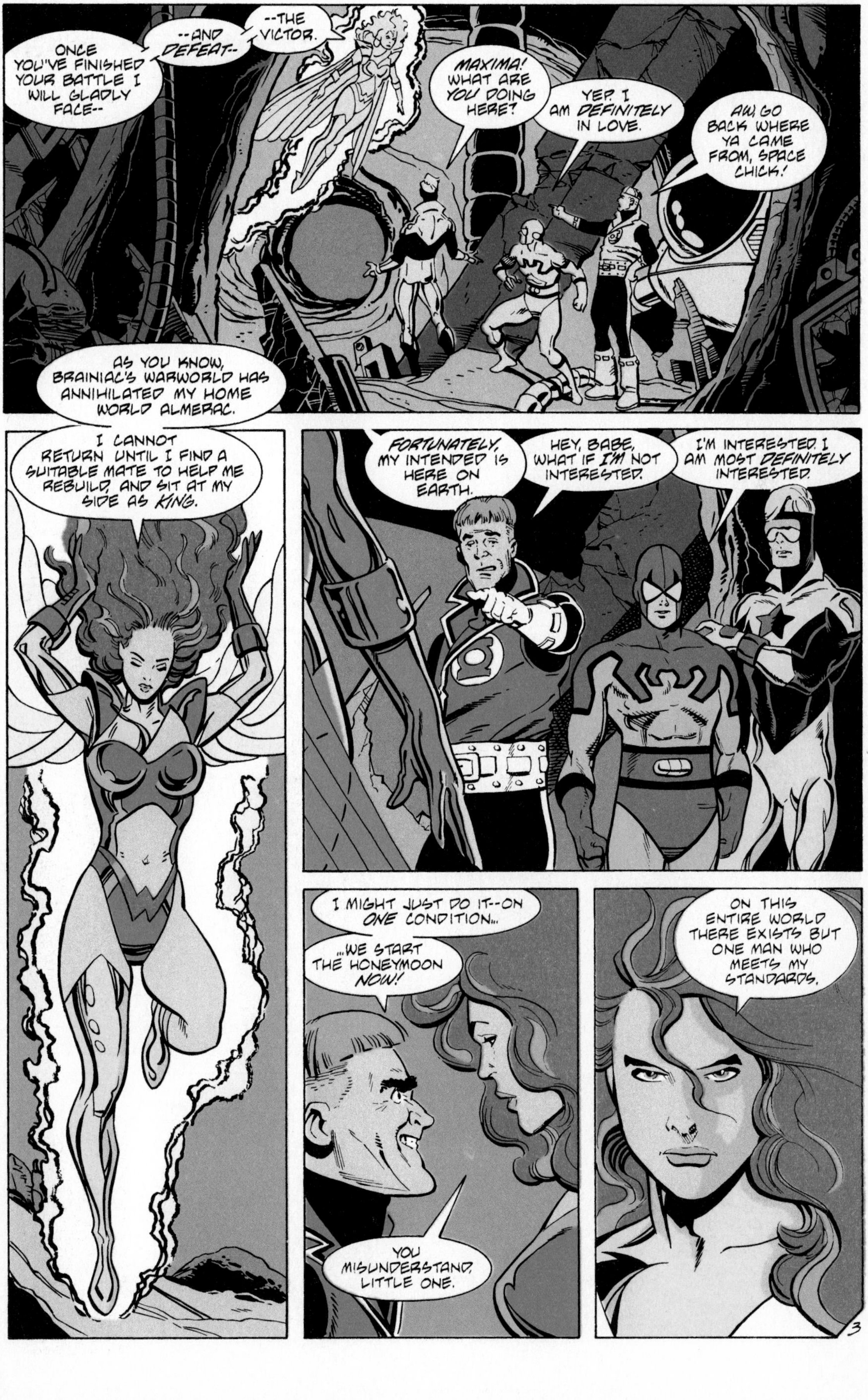

ONCE YOU'VE FINISHED YOUR BATTLE I WILL GLADLY FACE--
--AND DEFEAT--
--THE VICTOR.
MAXIMA! WHAT ARE YOU DOING HERE?
YEP. I AM DEFINITELY IN LOVE.
AW, GO BACK WHERE YA CAME FROM, SPACE CHICK!
AS YOU KNOW, BRAINIAC'S WARWORLD HAS ANNIHILATED MY HOME WORLD ALMERAC.
I CANNOT RETURN UNTIL I FIND A SUITABLE MATE TO HELP ME REBUILD, AND SIT AT MY SIDE AS KING.
FORTUNATELY, MY INTENDED IS HERE ON EARTH.
HEY, BABE, WHAT IF I'M NOT INTERESTED.
I'M INTERESTED. I AM MOST DEFINITELY INTERESTED.
I MIGHT JUST DO IT--ON ONE CONDITION...
...WE START THE HONEYMOON NOW!
YOU MISUNDERSTAND, LITTLE ONE.
ON THIS ENTIRE WORLD THERE EXISTS BUT ONE MAN WHO MEETS MY STANDARDS.

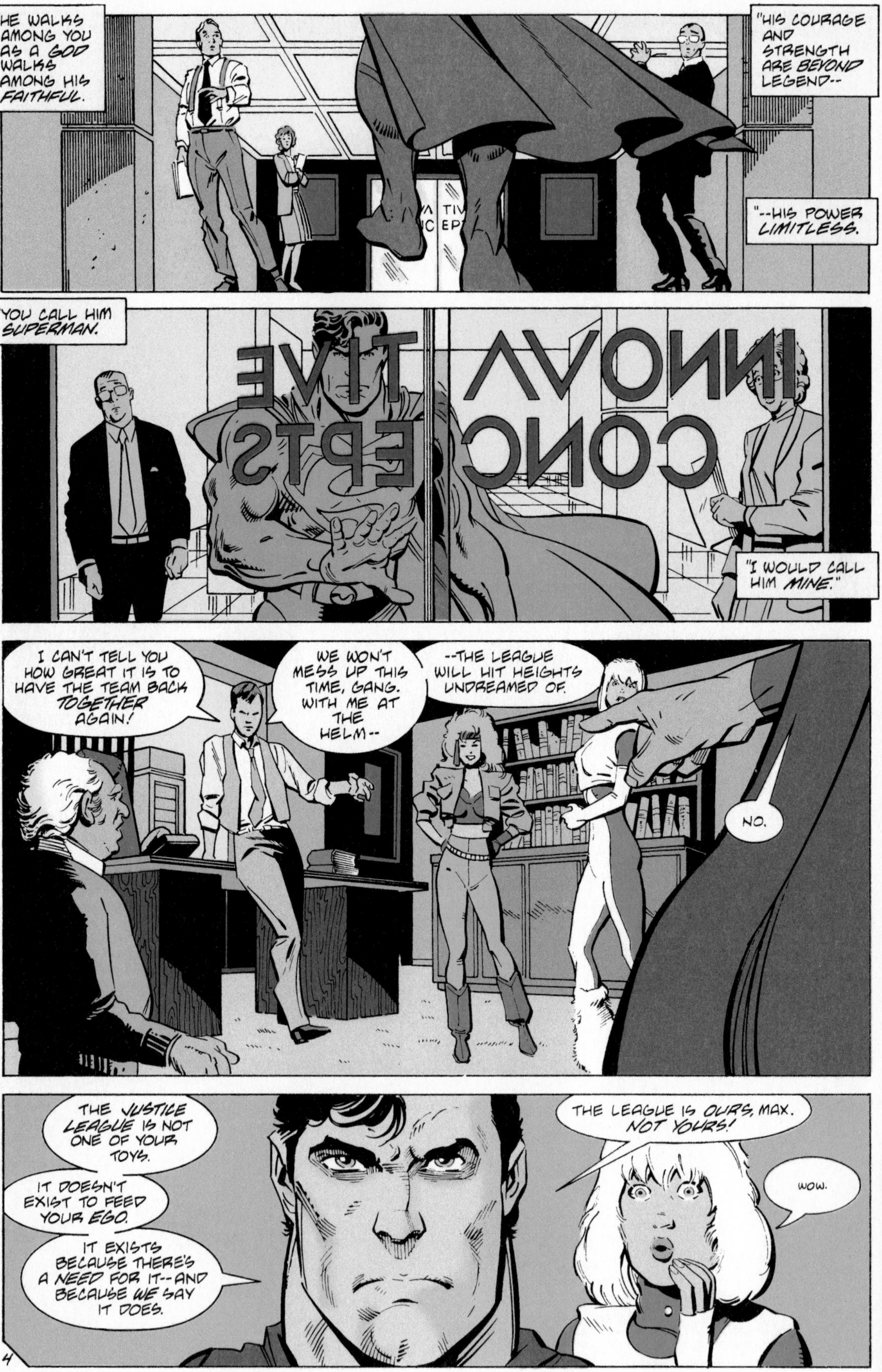
"HE WALKS AMONG YOU AS A GOD WALKS AMONG HIS FAITHFUL.
"HIS COURAGE AND STRENGTH ARE BEYOND LEGEND--
"--HIS POWER LIMITLESS.
"YOU CALL HIM SUPERMAN.
"I WOULD CALL HIM MINE."
I CAN'T TELL YOU HOW GREAT IT IS TO HAVE THE TEAM BACK TOGETHER AGAIN!
WE WON'T MESS UP THIS TIME, GANG. WITH ME AT THE HELM--
--THE LEAGUE WILL HIT HEIGHTS UNDREAMED OF.
NO.
THE JUSTICE LEAGUE IS NOT ONE OF YOUR TOYS.
IT DOESN'T EXIST TO FEED YOUR EGO.
IT EXISTS BECAUSE THERE'S A NEED FOR IT--AND BECAUSE WE SAY IT DOES.
THE LEAGUE IS OURS, MAX. NOT YOURS!
WOW.

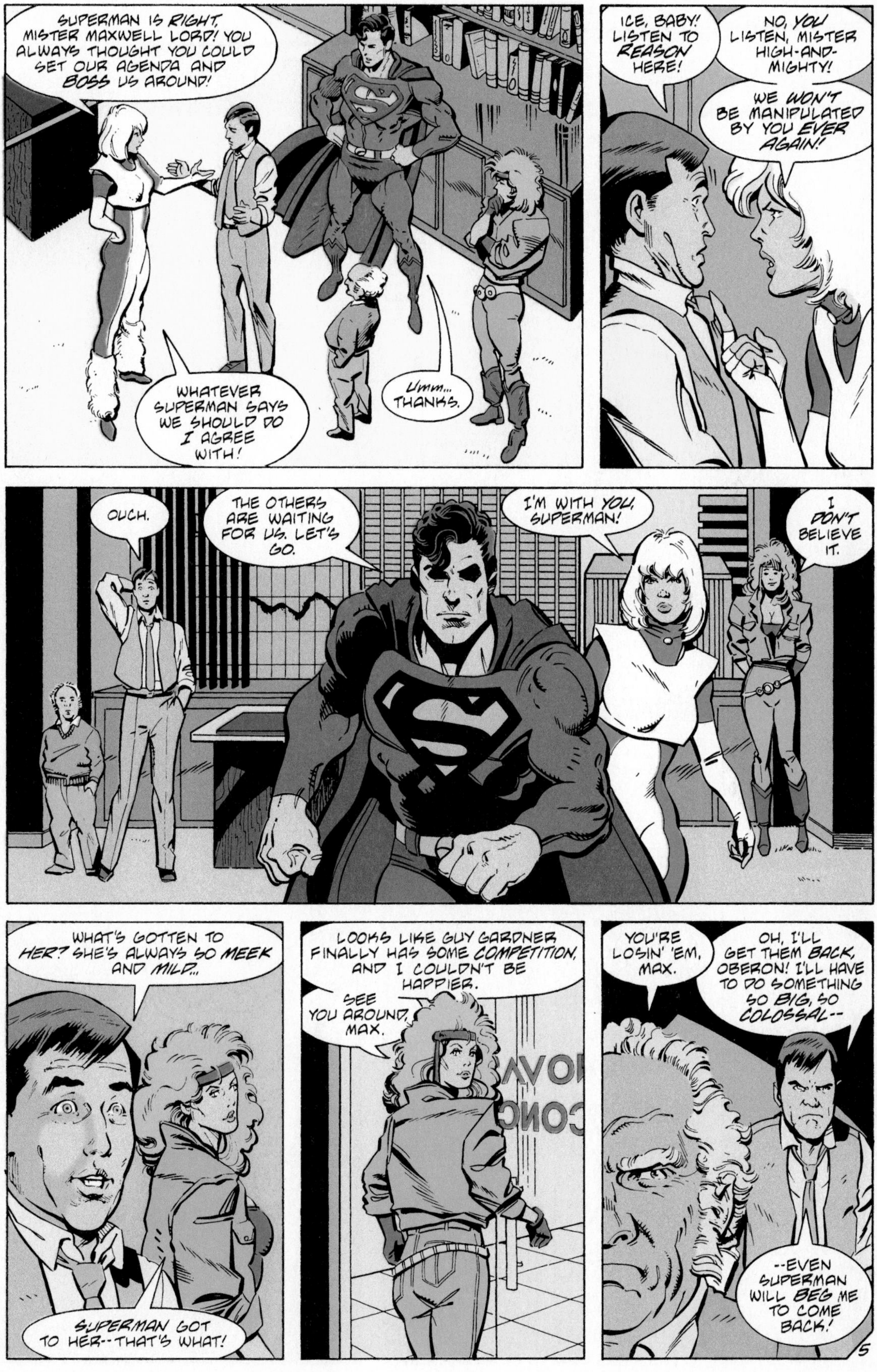

SUPERMAN IS RIGHT, MISTER MAXWELL LORD! YOU ALWAYS THOUGHT YOU COULD SET OUR AGENDA AND BOSS US AROUND!
WHATEVER SUPERMAN SAYS WE SHOULD DO I AGREE WITH!
Umm... THANKS.
ICE, BABY! LISTEN TO REASON HERE!
NO, YOU LISTEN, MISTER HIGH-AND-MIGHTY!
WE WON'T BE MANIPULATED BY YOU EVER AGAIN!
OUCH.
THE OTHERS ARE WAITING FOR US. LET'S GO.
I'M WITH YOU, SUPERMAN!
I DON'T BELIEVE IT.
WHAT'S GOTTEN TO HER? SHE'S ALWAYS SO MEEK AND MILD...
SUPERMAN GOT TO HER--THAT'S WHAT!
LOOKS LIKE GUY GARDNER FINALLY HAS SOME COMPETITION, AND I COULDN'T BE HAPPIER.
SEE YOU AROUND, MAX.
YOU'RE LOSIN' 'EM, MAX.
OH, I'LL GET THEM BACK, OBERON! I'LL HAVE TO DO SOMETHING SO BIG, SO COLOSSAL--
--EVEN SUPERMAN WILL BEG ME TO COME BACK!

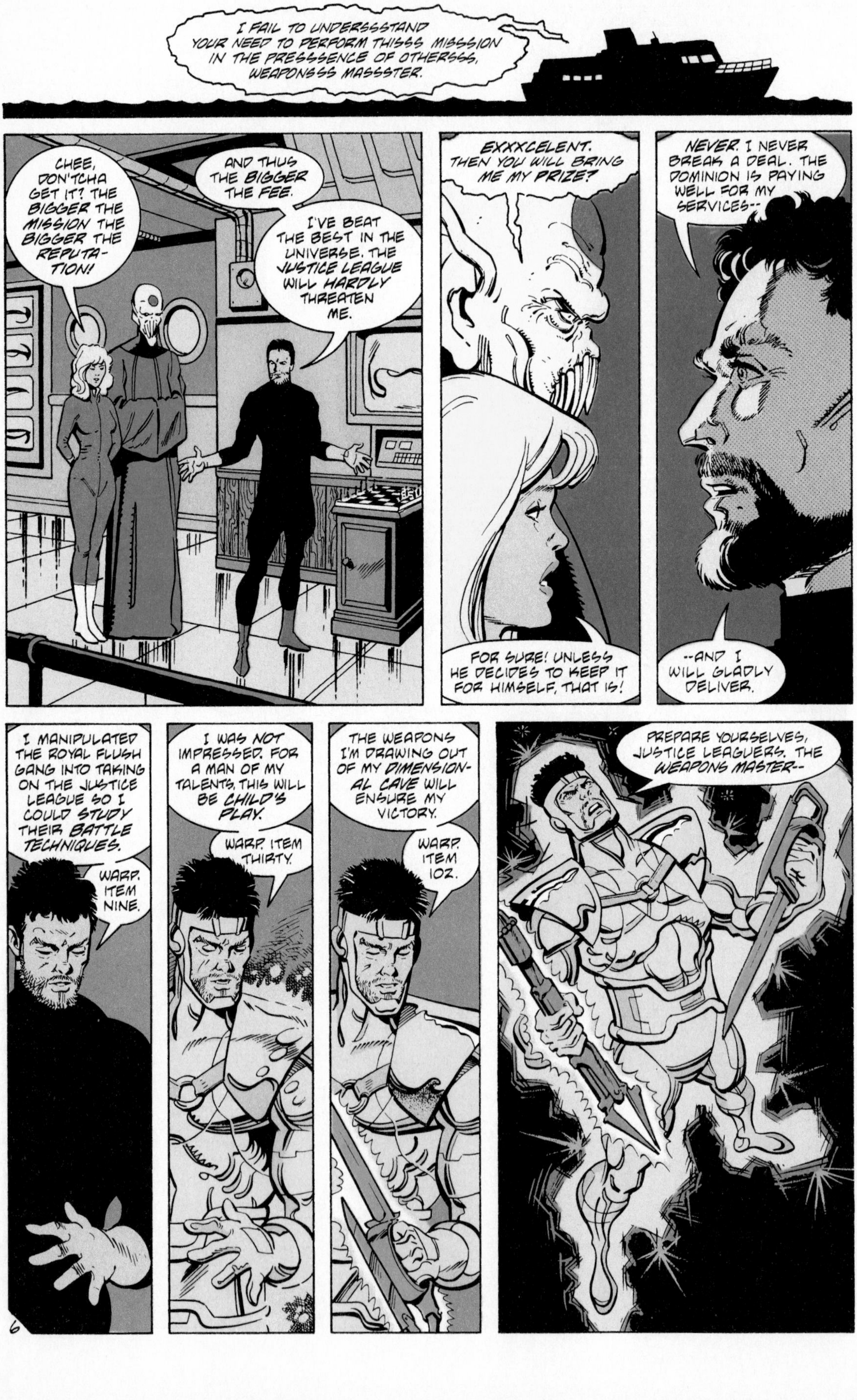
I FAIL TO UNDERSSSTAND YOUR NEED TO PERFORM THISSS MISSSION IN THE PRESSSENCE OF OTHERSSS, WEAPONSSS MASSSTER.
CHEE, DON'TCHA GET IT? THE BIGGER THE MISSION THE BIGGER THE REPUTATION!
AND THUS THE BIGGER THE FEE.
I'VE BEAT THE BEST IN THE UNIVERSE. THE JUSTICE LEAGUE WILL HARDLY THREATEN ME.
EXXXCELENT. THEN YOU WILL BRING ME MY PRIZE?
FOR SURE! UNLESS HE DECIDES TO KEEP IT FOR HIMSELF, THAT IS!
NEVER. I NEVER BREAK A DEAL. THE DOMINION IS PAYING WELL FOR MY SERVICES--
--AND I WILL GLADLY DELIVER.
I MANIPULATED THE ROYAL FLUSH GANG INTO TAKING ON THE JUSTICE LEAGUE SO I COULD STUDY THEIR BATTLE TECHNIQUES.
WARP. ITEM NINE.
I WAS NOT IMPRESSED. FOR A MAN OF MY TALENTS, THIS WILL BE CHILD'S PLAY.
WARP. ITEM THIRTY.
THE WEAPONS I'M DRAWING OUT OF MY DIMENSIONAL CAVE WILL ENSURE MY VICTORY.
WARP. ITEM 102.
PREPARE YOURSELVES, JUSTICE LEAGUERS. THE WEAPONS MASTER--

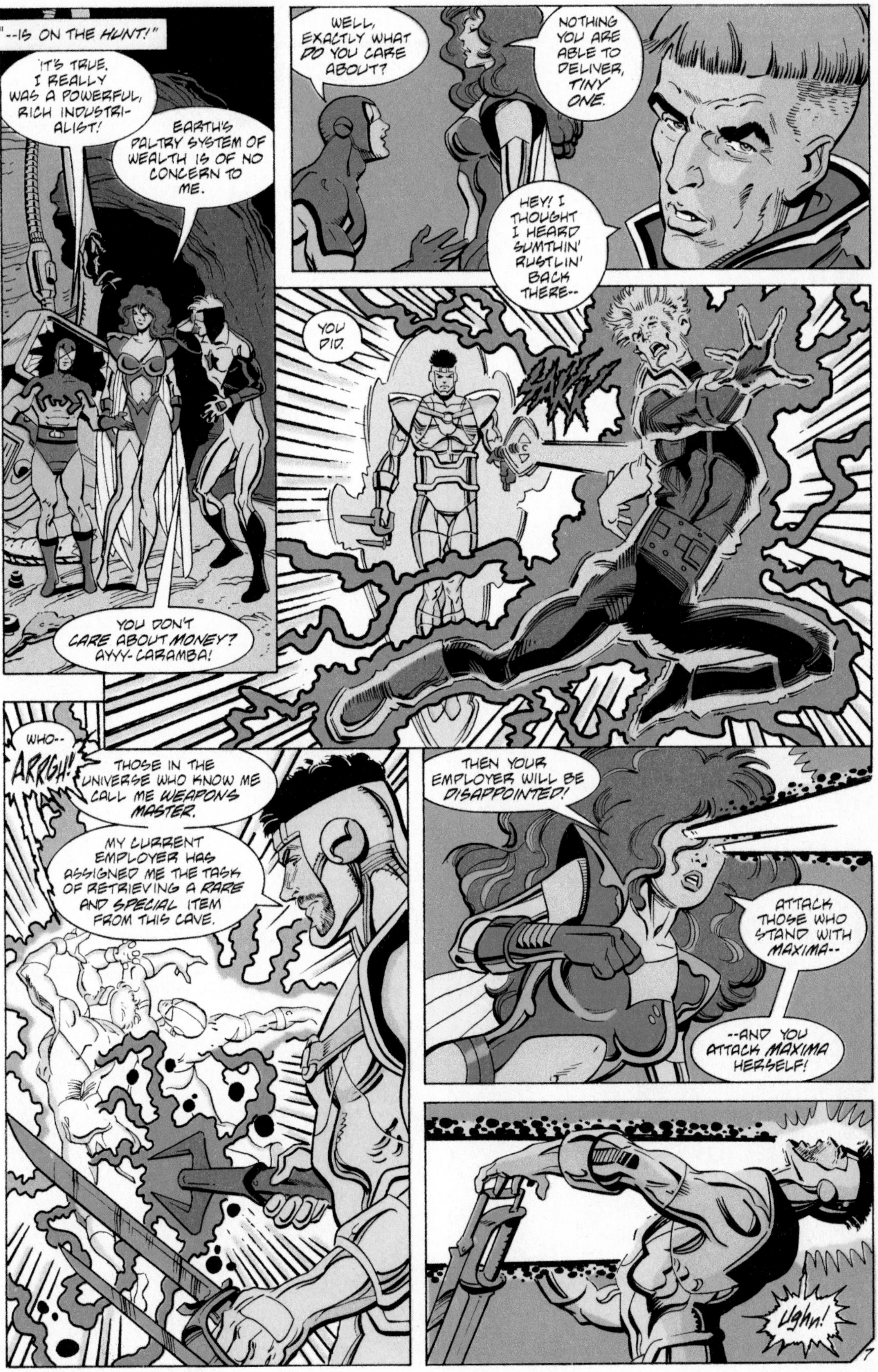
"--IS ON THE HUNT!"
IT'S TRUE. I REALLY WAS A POWERFUL, RICH INDUSTRI-ALIST!
EARTH'S PALTRY SYSTEM OF WEALTH IS OF NO CONCERN TO ME.
YOU DON'T CARE ABOUT MONEY? AYYY-CARAMBA!
WELL, EXACTLY WHAT DO YOU CARE ABOUT?
NOTHING YOU ARE ABLE TO DELIVER, TINY ONE.
HEY! I THOUGHT I HEARD SUMTHIN' RUSTLIN' BACK THERE--
YOU DID.
WHO--
ARRGH!
THOSE IN THE UNIVERSE WHO KNOW ME CALL ME WEAPONS MASTER.
MY CURRENT EMPLOYER HAS ASSIGNED ME THE TASK OF RETRIEVING A RARE AND SPECIAL ITEM FROM THIS CAVE.
THEN YOUR EMPLOYER WILL BE DISAPPOINTED!
ATTACK THOSE WHO STAND WITH MAXIMA--
--AND YOU ATTACK MAXIMA HERSELF!
Ughn!

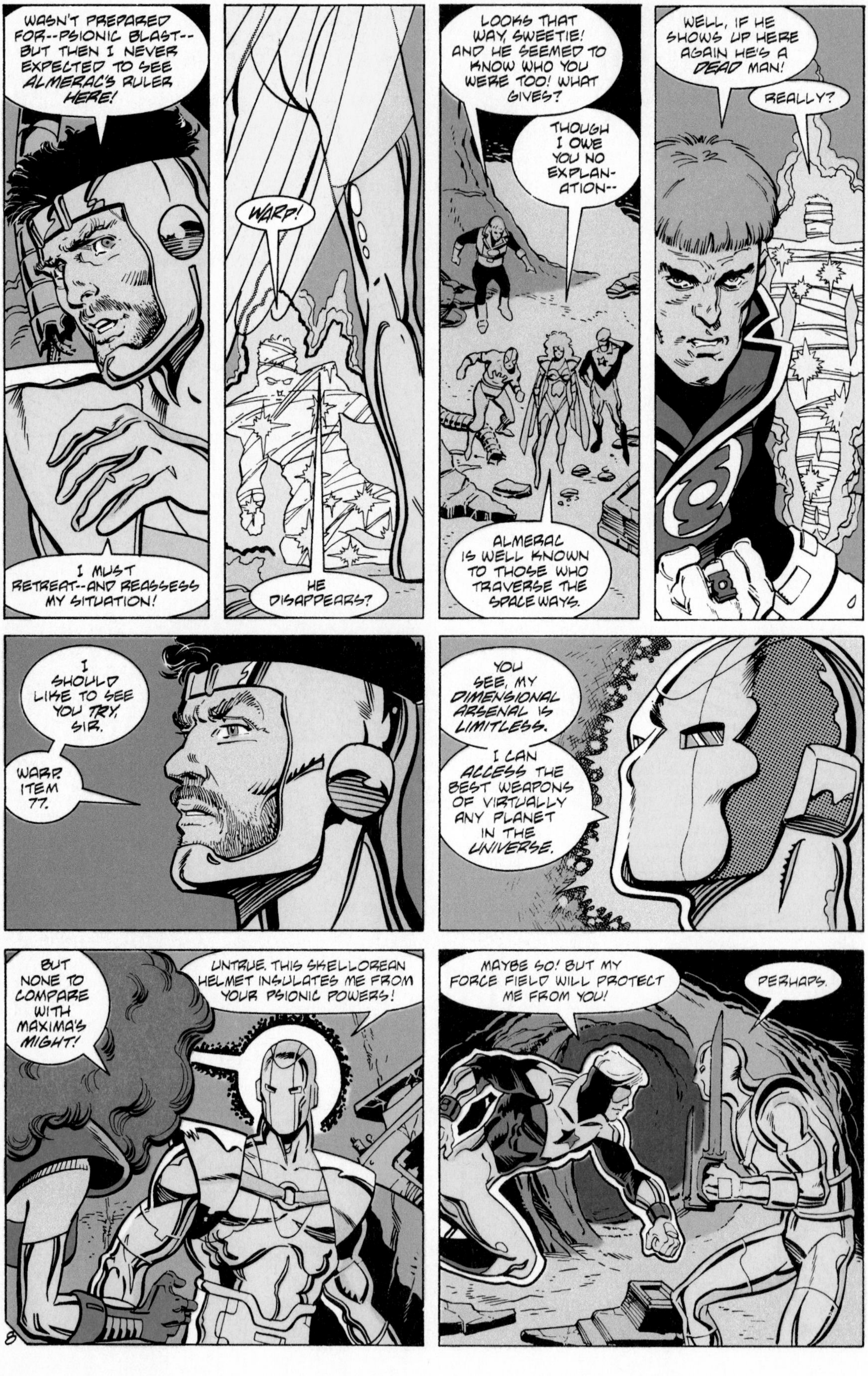
WASN'T PREPARED FOR--PSIONIC BLAST--BUT THEN I NEVER EXPECTED TO SEE ALMERAC'S RULER HERE!
I MUST RETREAT--AND REASSESS MY SITUATION!
WARP!
HE DISAPPEARS?
LOOKS THAT WAY, SWEETIE! AND HE SEEMED TO KNOW WHO YOU WERE TOO! WHAT GIVES?
THOUGH I OWE YOU NO EXPLANATION--
ALMERAC IS WELL KNOWN TO THOSE WHO TRAVERSE THE SPACE WAYS.
WELL, IF HE SHOWS UP HERE AGAIN HE'S A DEAD MAN!
REALLY?
I SHOULD LIKE TO SEE YOU TRY, SIR.
WARP. ITEM 77.
YOU SEE, MY DIMENSIONAL ARSENAL IS LIMITLESS.
I CAN ACCESS THE BEST WEAPONS OF VIRTUALLY ANY PLANET IN THE UNIVERSE.
BUT NONE TO COMPARE WITH MAXIMA'S MIGHT!
UNTRUE. THIS SKELLOREAN HELMET INSULATES ME FROM YOUR PSIONIC POWERS!
MAYBE SO! BUT MY FORCE FIELD WILL PROTECT ME FROM YOU!
PERHAPS.

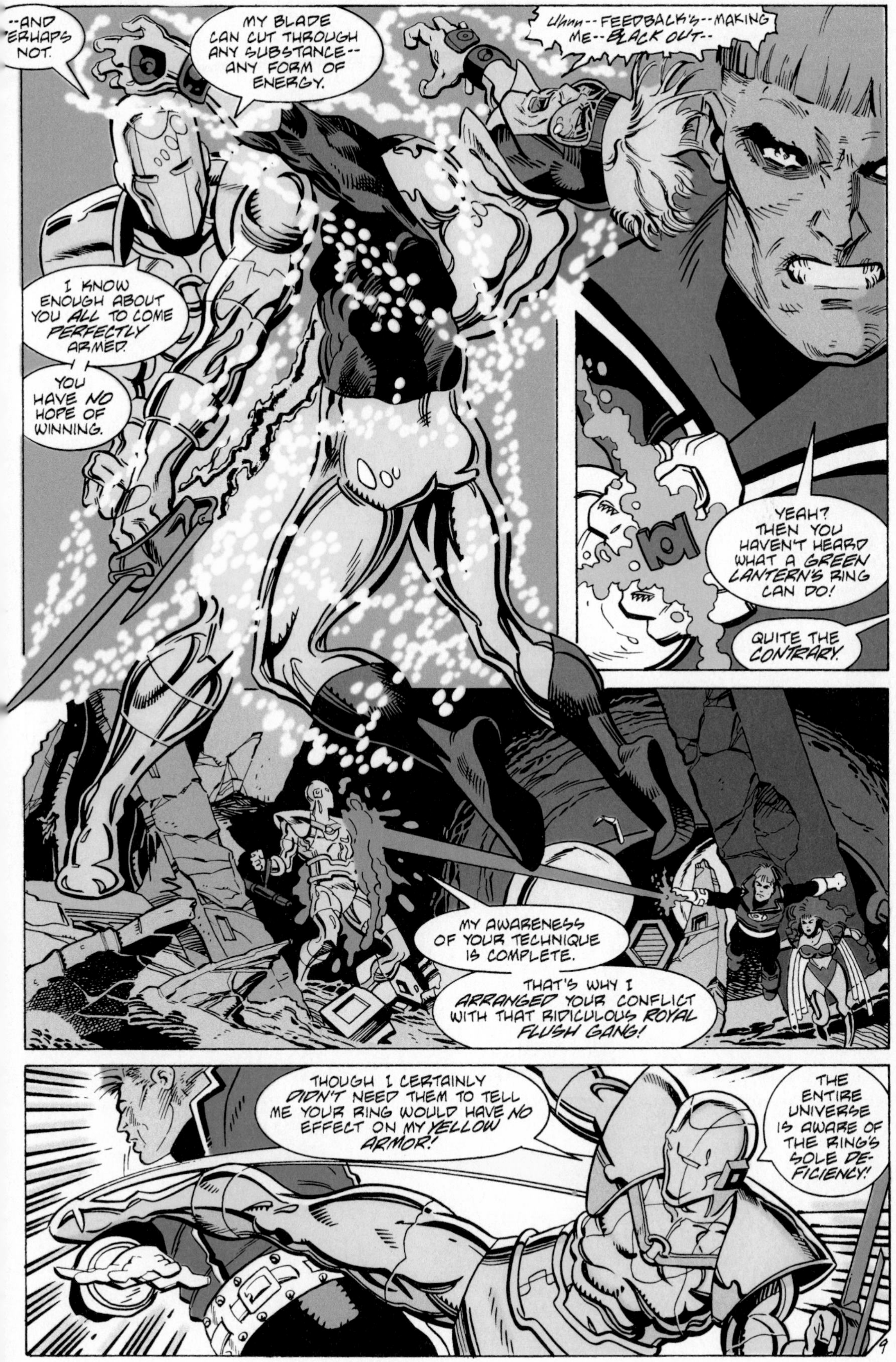
--AND PERHAPS NOT.
MY BLADE CAN CUT THROUGH ANY SUBSTANCE-- ANY FORM OF ENERGY.
UHNN--FEEDBACK'S--MAKING ME--BLACK OUT--
I KNOW ENOUGH ABOUT YOU ALL TO COME PERFECTLY ARMED.
YOU HAVE NO HOPE OF WINNING.
YEAH? THEN YOU HAVEN'T HEARD WHAT A GREEN LANTERN'S RING CAN DO!
QUITE THE CONTRARY.
MY AWARENESS OF YOUR TECHNIQUE IS COMPLETE.
THAT'S WHY I ARRANGED YOUR CONFLICT WITH THAT RIDICULOUS ROYAL FLUSH GANG!
THOUGH I CERTAINLY DIDN'T NEED THEM TO TELL ME YOUR RING WOULD HAVE NO EFFECT ON MY YELLOW ARMOR!
THE ENTIRE UNIVERSE IS AWARE OF THE RING'S SOLE DE-FICIENCY!
9

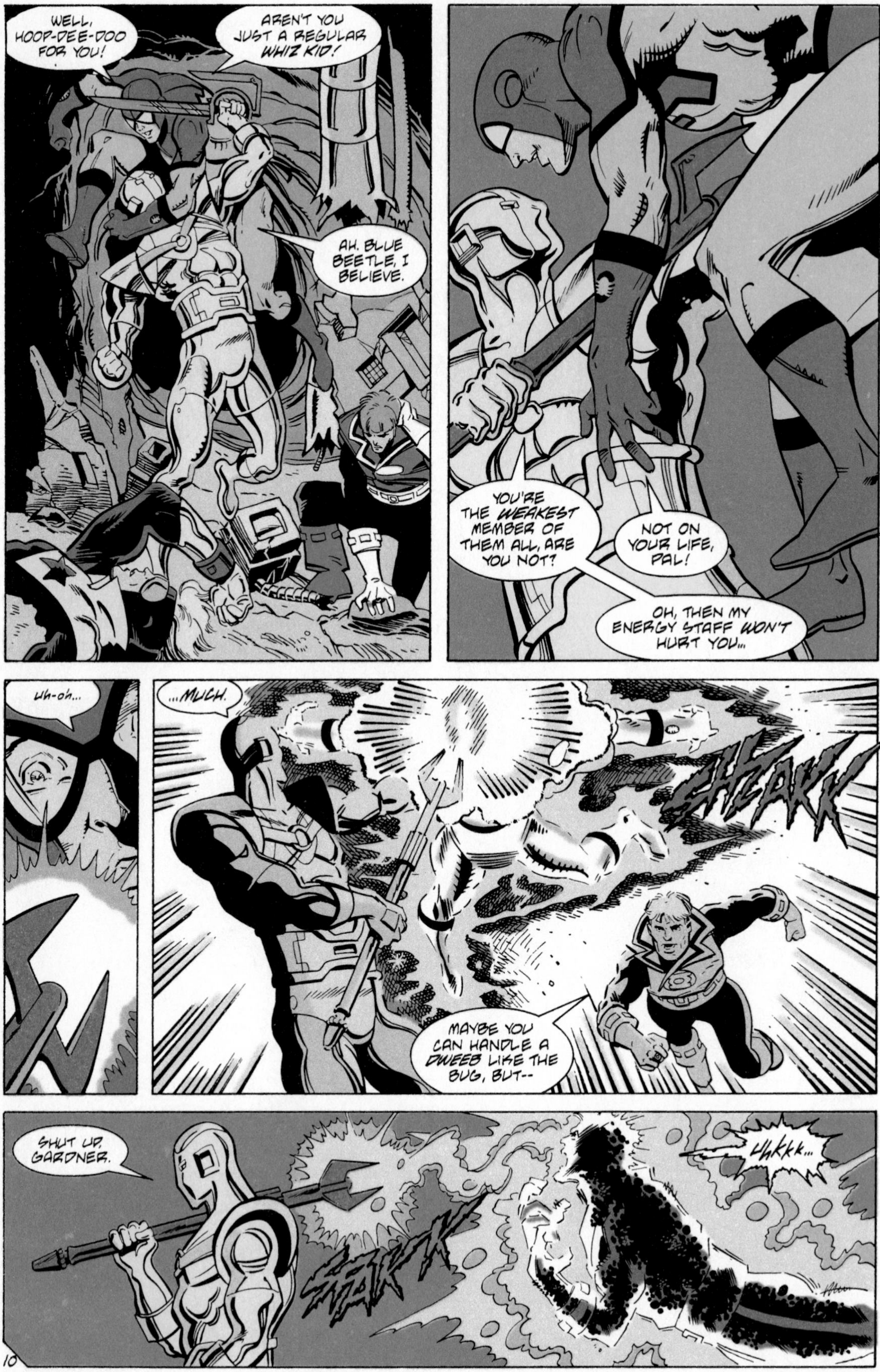

WELL, HOOP-DEE-DOO FOR YOU!
AREN'T YOU JUST A REGULAR WHIZ KID!
AH. BLUE BEETLE, I BELIEVE.
YOU'RE THE WEAKEST MEMBER OF THEM ALL, ARE YOU NOT?
NOT ON YOUR LIFE, PAL!
OH, THEN MY ENERGY STAFF WON'T HURT YOU...
uh-oh...
...MUCH.
MAYBE YOU CAN HANDLE A DWEEB LIKE THE BUG, BUT--
SHUT UP, GARDNER.
Uhkkk...

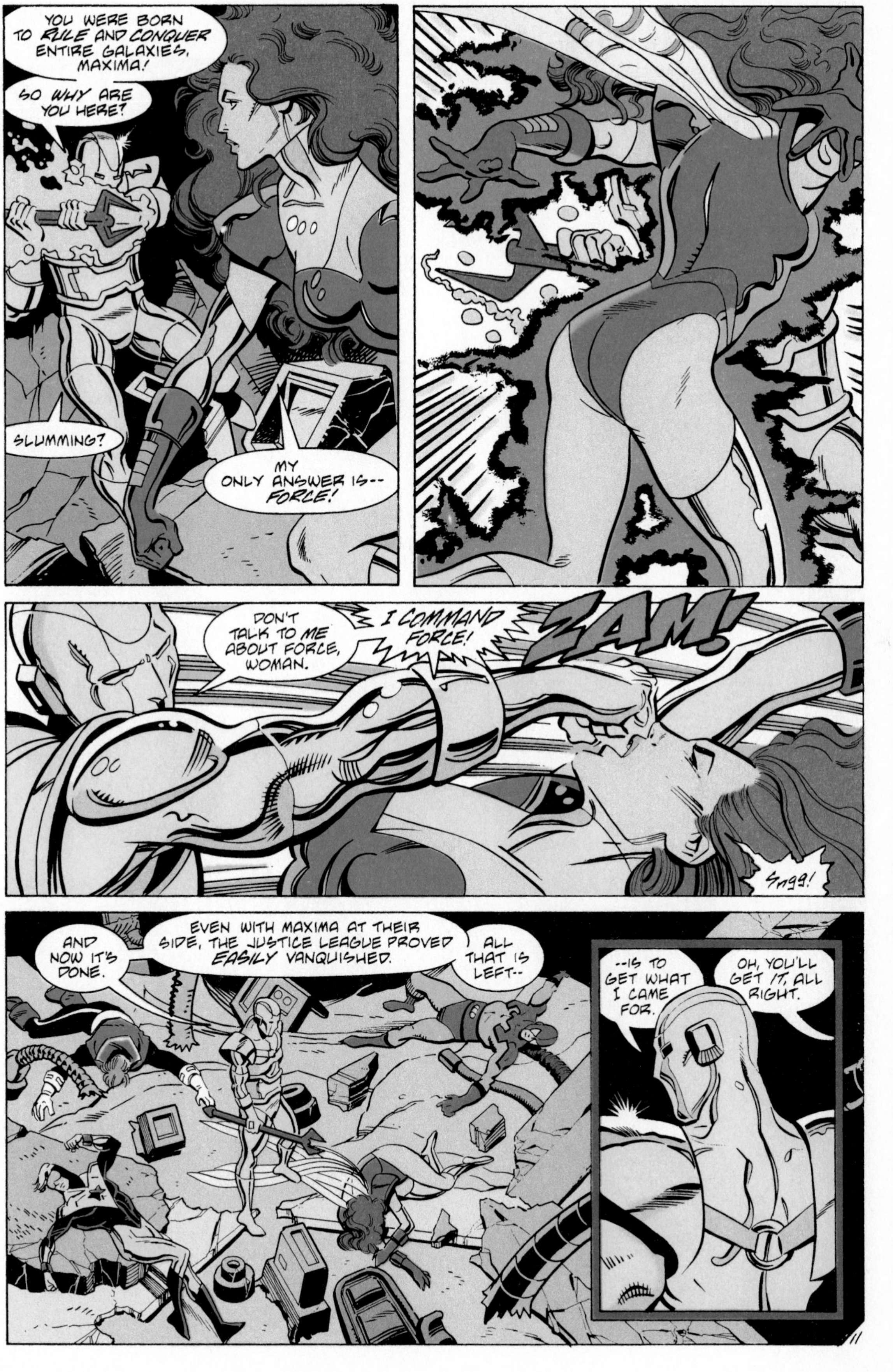
YOU WERE BORN TO RULE AND CONQUER ENTIRE GALAXIES, MAXIMA!
SO WHY ARE YOU HERE?
SLUMMING?
MY ONLY ANSWER IS-- FORCE!
DON'T TALK TO ME ABOUT FORCE, WOMAN.
I COMMAND FORCE!
ZAM!
Sngg!
AND NOW IT'S DONE.
EVEN WITH MAXIMA AT THEIR SIDE, THE JUSTICE LEAGUE PROVED EASILY VANQUISHED.
ALL THAT IS LEFT--
--IS TO GET WHAT I CAME FOR.
OH, YOU'LL GET IT, ALL RIGHT.

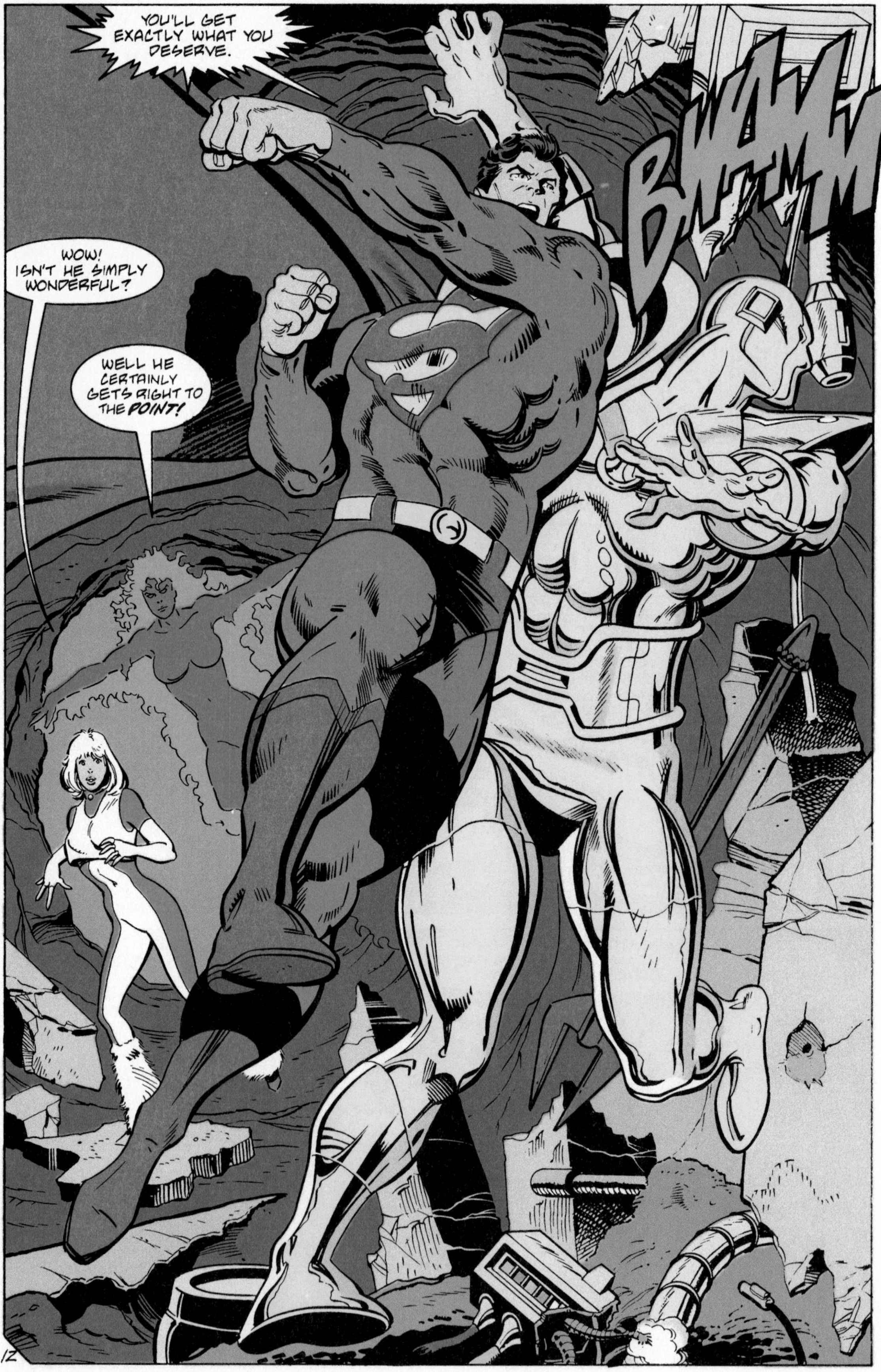
YOU'LL GET EXACTLY WHAT YOU DESERVE.
BWAM
WOW! ISN'T HE SIMPLY WONDERFUL?
WELL HE CERTAINLY GETS RIGHT TO THE POINT!

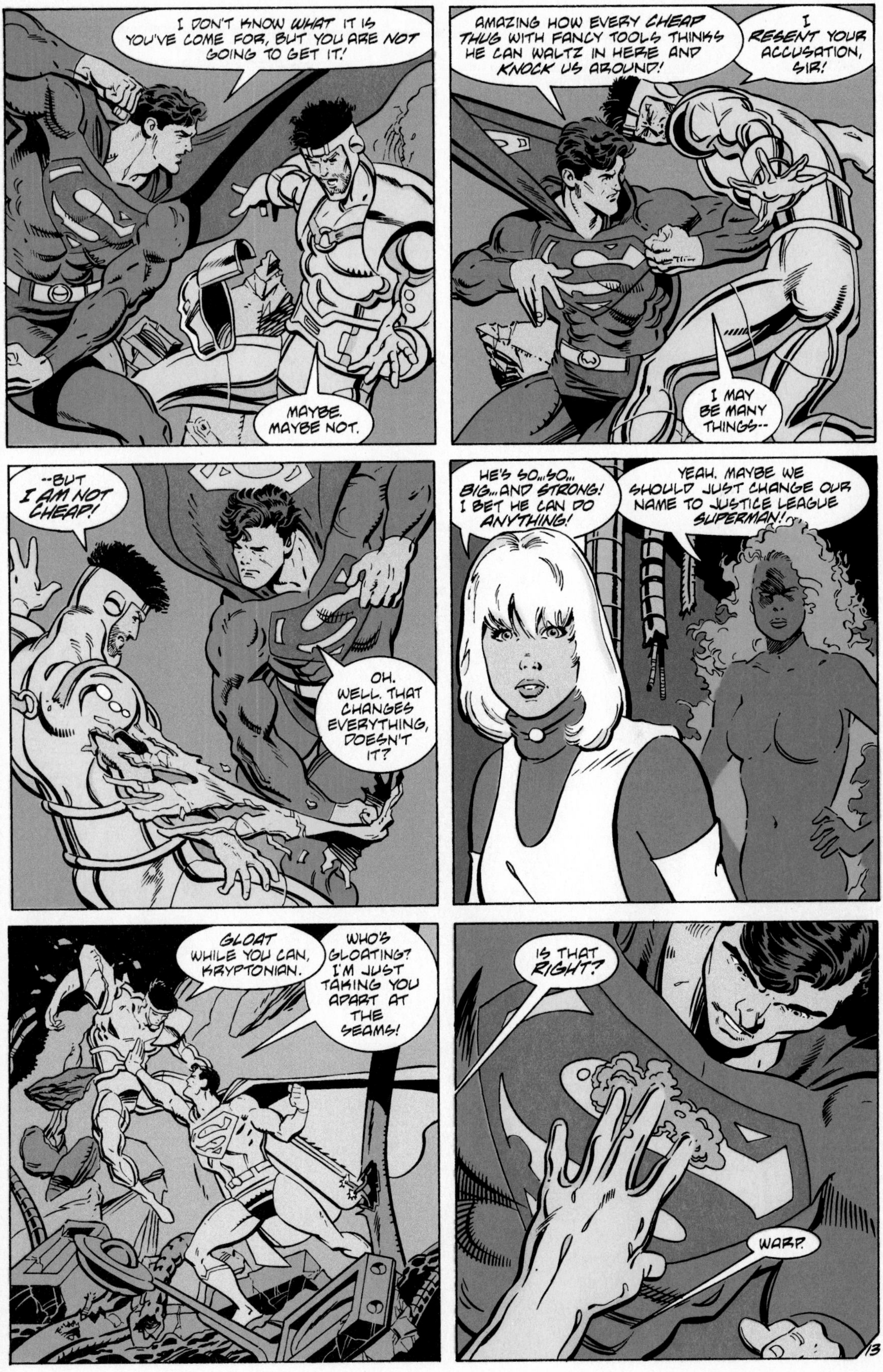
I DON'T KNOW WHAT IT IS YOU'VE COME FOR, BUT YOU ARE NOT GOING TO GET IT!
MAYBE. MAYBE NOT.
AMAZING HOW EVERY CHEAP THUG WITH FANCY TOOLS THINKS HE CAN WALTZ IN HERE AND KNOCK US AROUND!
I RESENT YOUR ACCUSATION, SIR!
I MAY BE MANY THINGS--
--BUT I AM NOT CHEAP!
OH. WELL. THAT CHANGES EVERYTHING, DOESN'T IT?
HE'S SO...SO... BIG...AND STRONG! I BET HE CAN DO ANYTHING!
YEAH. MAYBE WE SHOULD JUST CHANGE OUR NAME TO JUSTICE LEAGUE SUPERMAN!...
GLOAT WHILE YOU CAN, KRYPTONIAN.
WHO'S GLOATING? I'M JUST TAKING YOU APART AT THE SEAMS!
IS THAT RIGHT?
WARP.

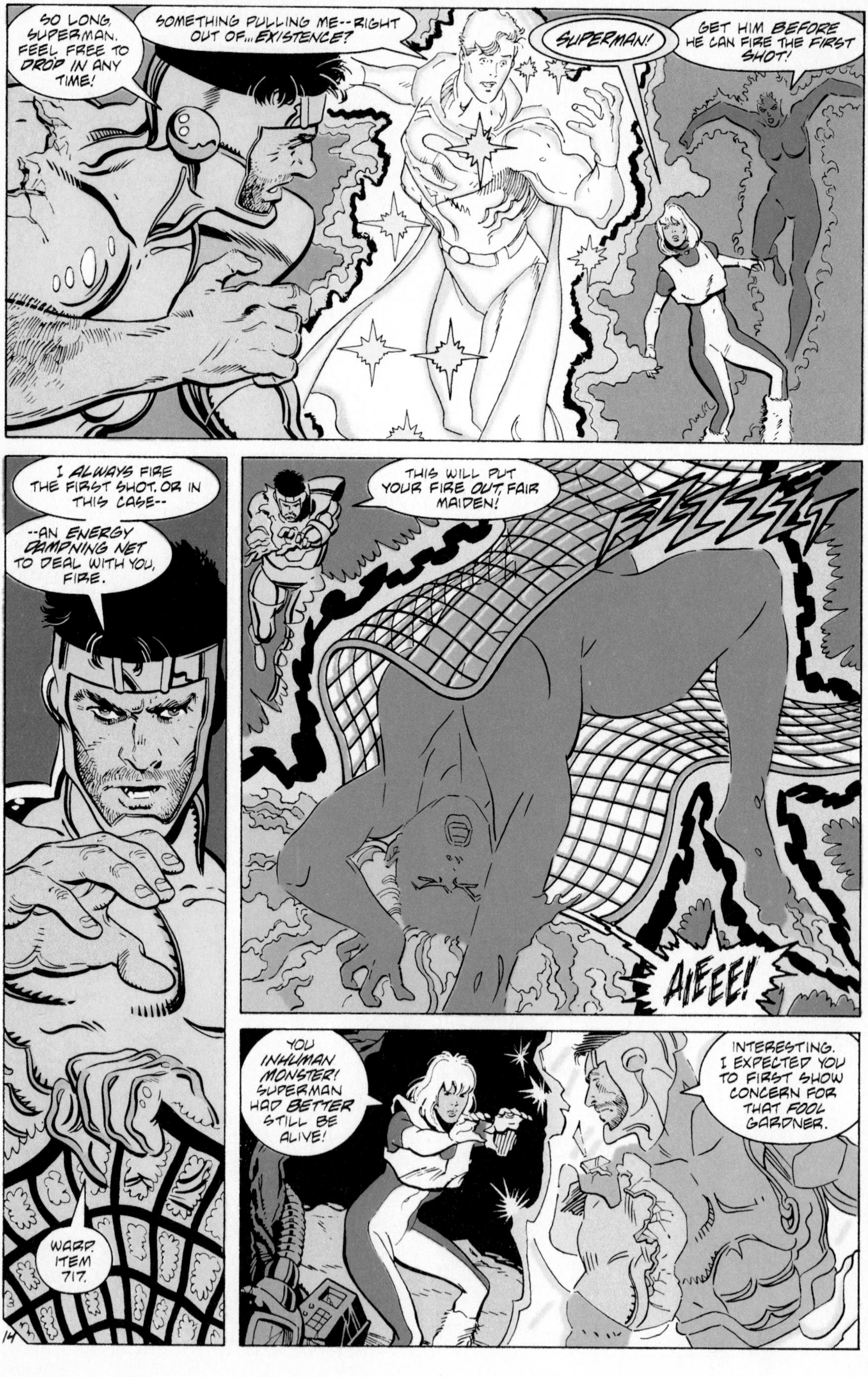
SO LONG, SUPERMAN. FEEL FREE TO DROP IN ANY TIME!
SOMETHING PULLING ME--RIGHT OUT OF... EXISTENCE?
SUPERMAN!
GET HIM BEFORE HE CAN FIRE THE FIRST SHOT!
I ALWAYS FIRE THE FIRST SHOT. OR IN THIS CASE--
--AN ENERGY DAMPNING NET TO DEAL WITH YOU, FIRE.
WARD ITEM 717.
THIS WILL PUT YOUR FIRE OUT, FAIR MAIDEN!
FZZZZT
AIEEE!
YOU INHUMAN MONSTER! SUPERMAN HAD BETTER STILL BE ALIVE!
INTERESTING. I EXPECTED YOU TO FIRST SHOW CONCERN FOR THAT FOOL GARDNER.

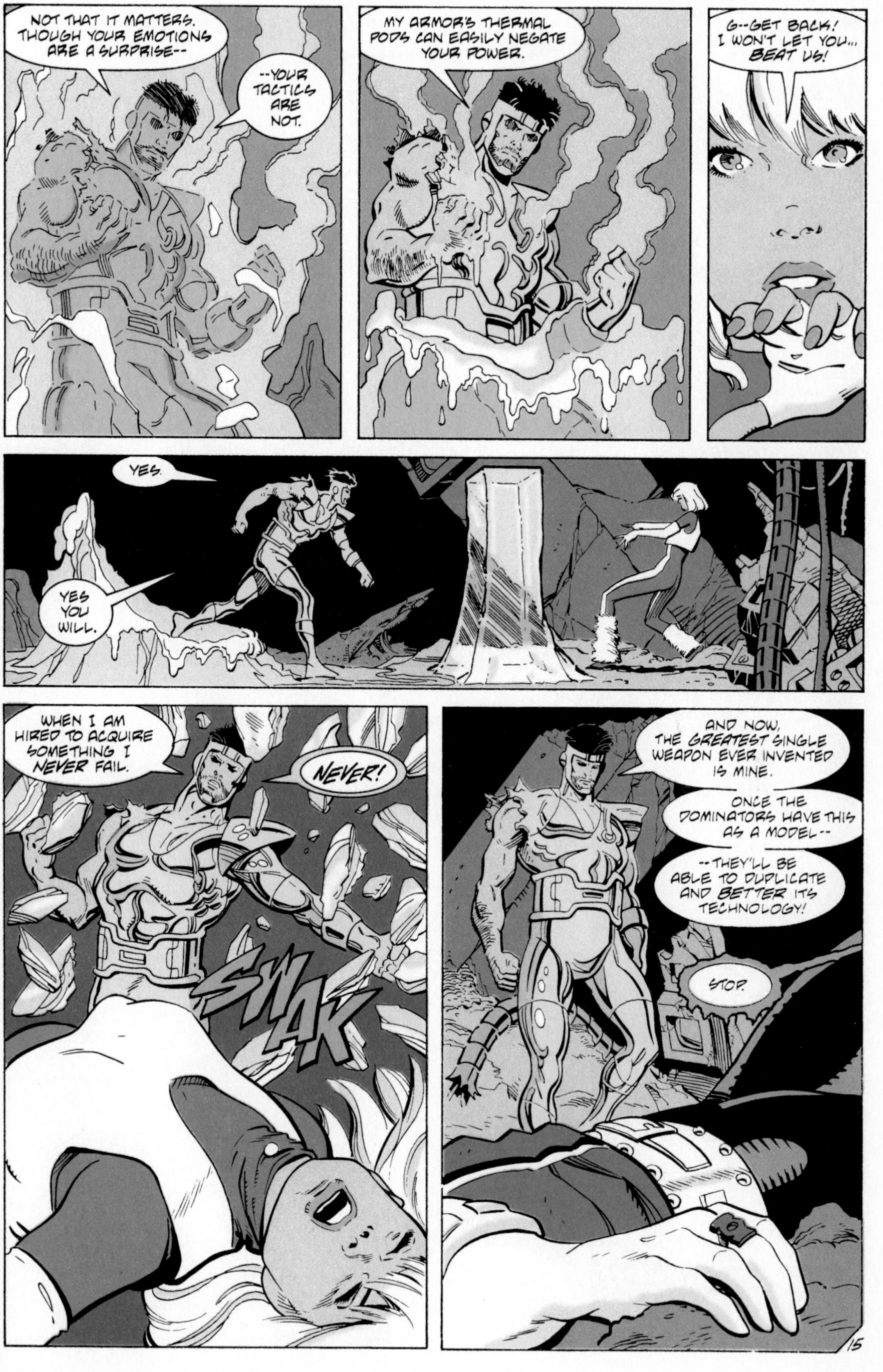
NOT THAT IT MATTERS. THOUGH YOUR EMOTIONS ARE A SURPRISE--
--YOUR TACTICS ARE NOT.
MY ARMOR'S THERMAL PODS CAN EASILY NEGATE YOUR POWER.
G--GET BACK! I WON'T LET YOU... BEAT US!
YES.
YES YOU WILL.
WHEN I AM HIRED TO ACQUIRE SOMETHING I NEVER FAIL.
NEVER!
SNAK
AND NOW, THE GREATEST SINGLE WEAPON EVER INVENTED IS MINE.
ONCE THE DOMINATORS HAVE THIS AS A MODEL--
--THEY'LL BE ABLE TO DUPLICATE AND BETTER ITS TECHNOLOGY!
STOP.
15

ANOTHER INTRUDER? AND ONE I DON'T KNOW?

I SEE. YOU'RE THE SILENT TYPE. A MYSTERY MAN!

WELL, YOU'RE NO JUSTICE LEAGUER. AND IF YOU'RE OUT TO GET GARDNER'S RING FOR YOUR OWN USE IT'S TOO LATE.

IT'S MINE! AND IT'S WORTH MILLIONS!

SO LONG--

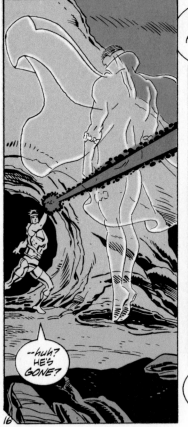

--HUH? HE'S GONE?

I HAVE NO DATA ON THIS MAN-- NO INFORMATION! I MAY HAVE ACCESS TO ANY WEAPONS EVER DEVISED--

--BUT THAT DOES ME LITTLE GOOD IF I DON'T KNOW WHICH ONES TO USE!

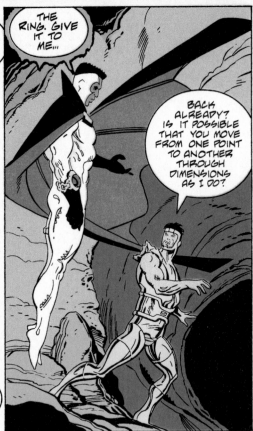

THE RING. GIVE IT TO ME...

BACK ALREADY? IS IT POSSIBLE THAT YOU MOVE FROM ONE POINT TO ANOTHER THROUGH DIMENSIONS AS I DO?

16

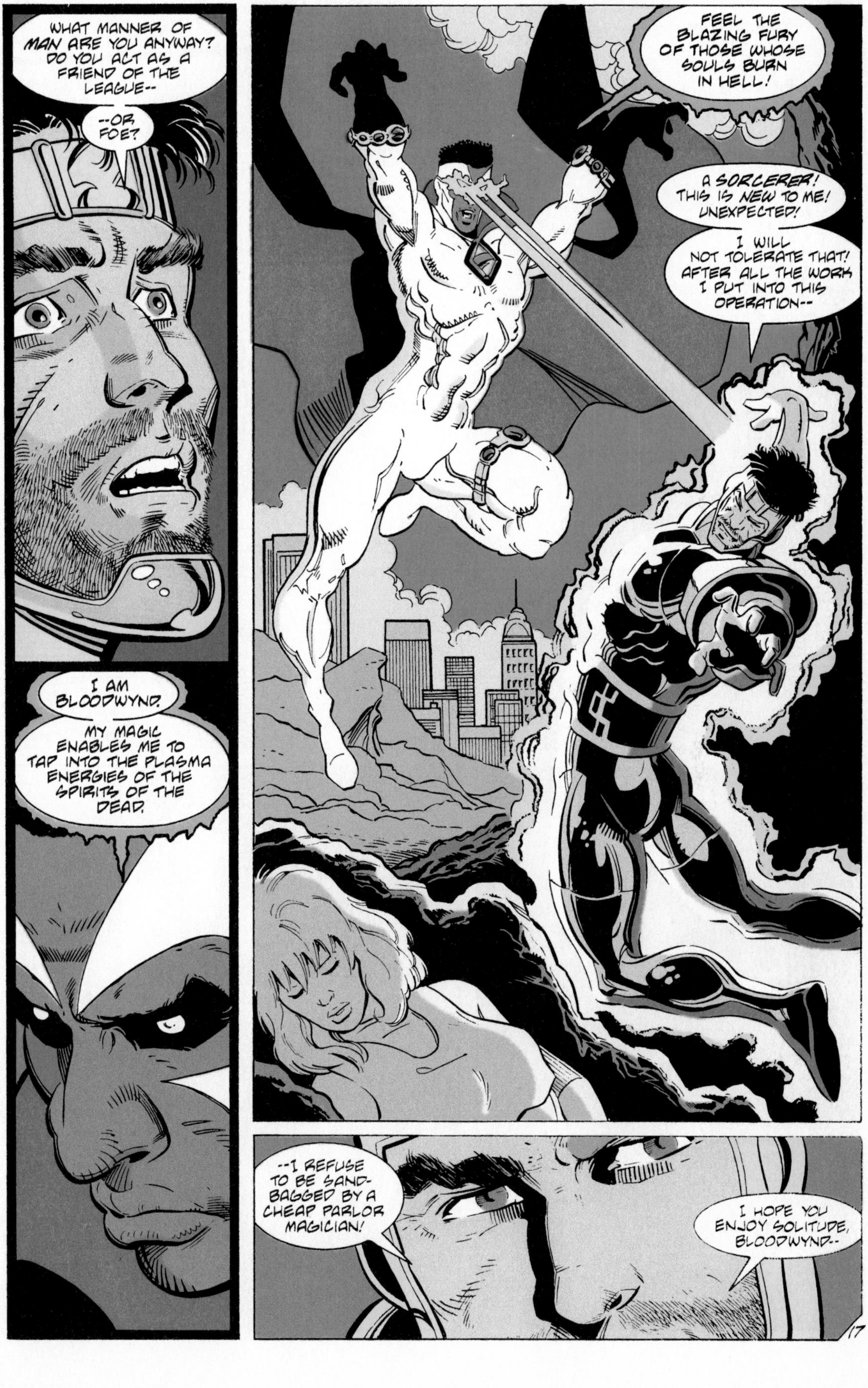
WHAT MANNER OF MAN ARE YOU ANYWAY? DO YOU ACT AS A FRIEND OF THE LEAGUE--
--OR FOE?
I AM BLOODWYND.
MY MAGIC ENABLES ME TO TAP INTO THE PLASMA ENERGIES OF THE SPIRITS OF THE DEAD.
FEEL THE BLAZING FURY OF THOSE WHOSE SOULS BURN IN HELL!
A SORCERER! THIS IS NEW TO ME! UNEXPECTED!
I WILL NOT TOLERATE THAT! AFTER ALL THE WORK I PUT INTO THIS OPERATION--
--I REFUSE TO BE SAND-BAGGED BY A CHEAP PARLOR MAGICIAN!
I HOPE YOU ENJOY SOLITUDE, BLOODWYND--

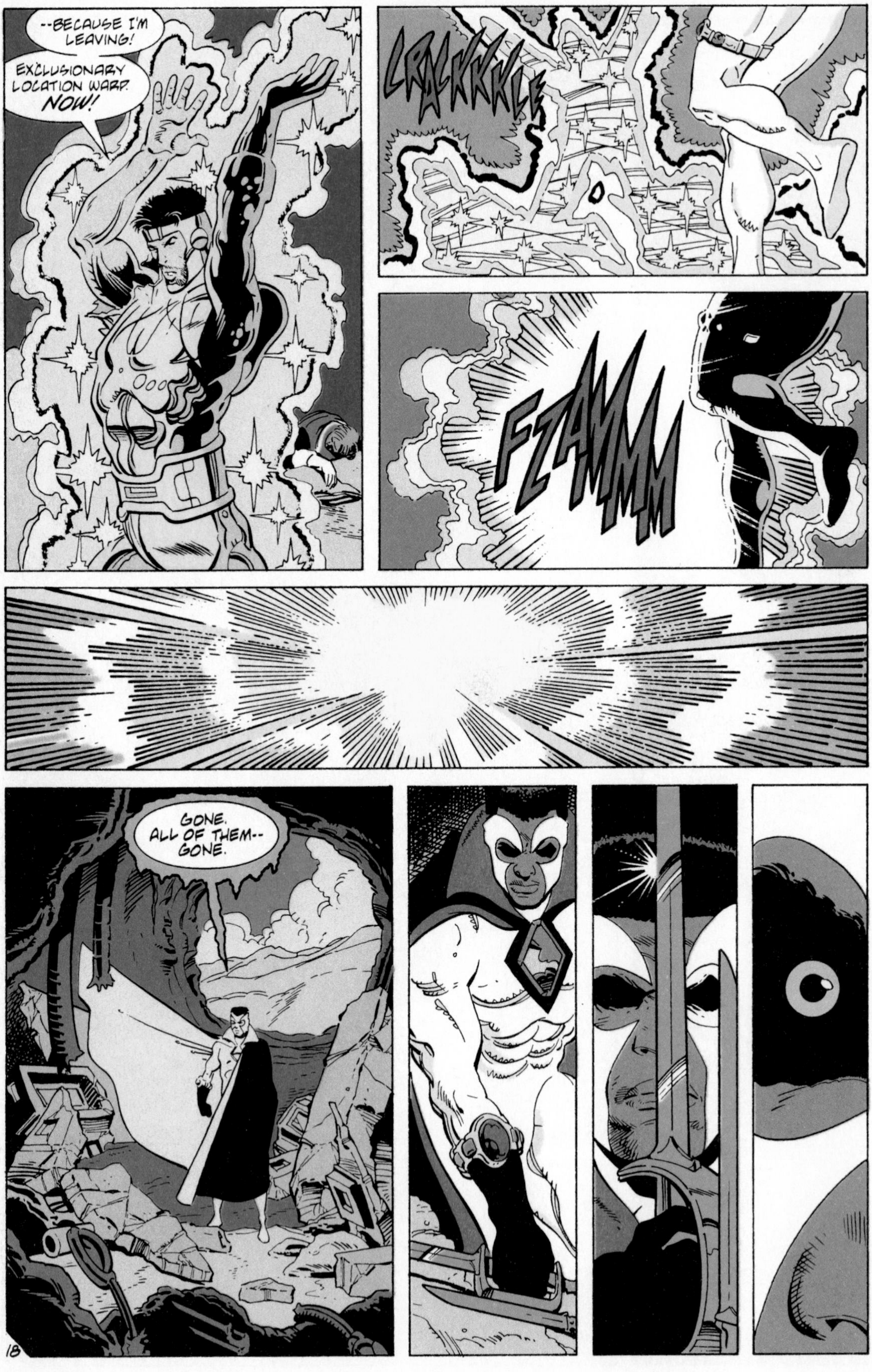
--BECAUSE I'M LEAVING!
EXCLUSIONARY LOCATION WARP. NOW!
CRACKKKLE
FZAMMM
GONE. ALL OF THEM-- GONE.

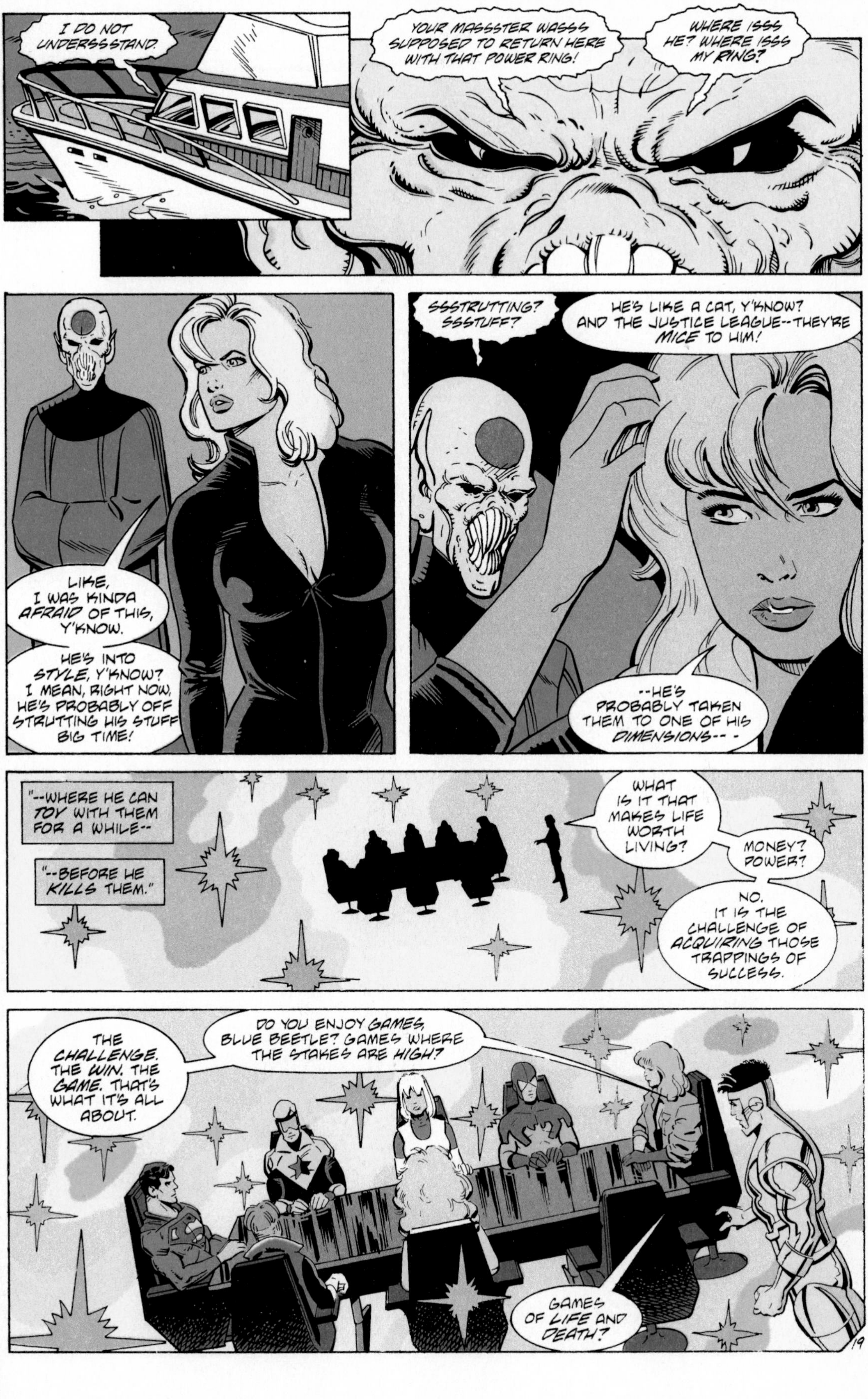
I DO NOT UNDERSSSTAND.
YOUR MASSSTER WASSS SUPPOSED TO RETURN HERE WITH THAT POWER RING!
WHERE ISSS HE? WHERE ISSS MY RING?
LIKE, I WAS KINDA AFRAID OF THIS, Y'KNOW.
HE'S INTO STYLE, Y'KNOW? I MEAN, RIGHT NOW, HE'S PROBABLY OFF STRUTTING HIS STUFF BIG TIME!
SSSTRUTTING? SSSTUFF?
HE'S LIKE A CAT, Y'KNOW? AND THE JUSTICE LEAGUE--THEY'RE MICE TO HIM!
--HE'S PROBABLY TAKEN THEM TO ONE OF HIS DIMENSIONS-- -
"--WHERE HE CAN TOY WITH THEM FOR A WHILE--
"--BEFORE HE KILLS THEM."
WHAT IS IT THAT MAKES LIFE WORTH LIVING?
MONEY? POWER?
NO. IT IS THE CHALLENGE OF ACQUIRING THOSE TRAPPINGS OF SUCCESS.
THE CHALLENGE. THE WIN. THE GAME. THAT'S WHAT IT'S ALL ABOUT.
DO YOU ENJOY GAMES, BLUE BEETLE? GAMES WHERE THE STAKES ARE HIGH?
GAMES OF LIFE AND DEATH?
19

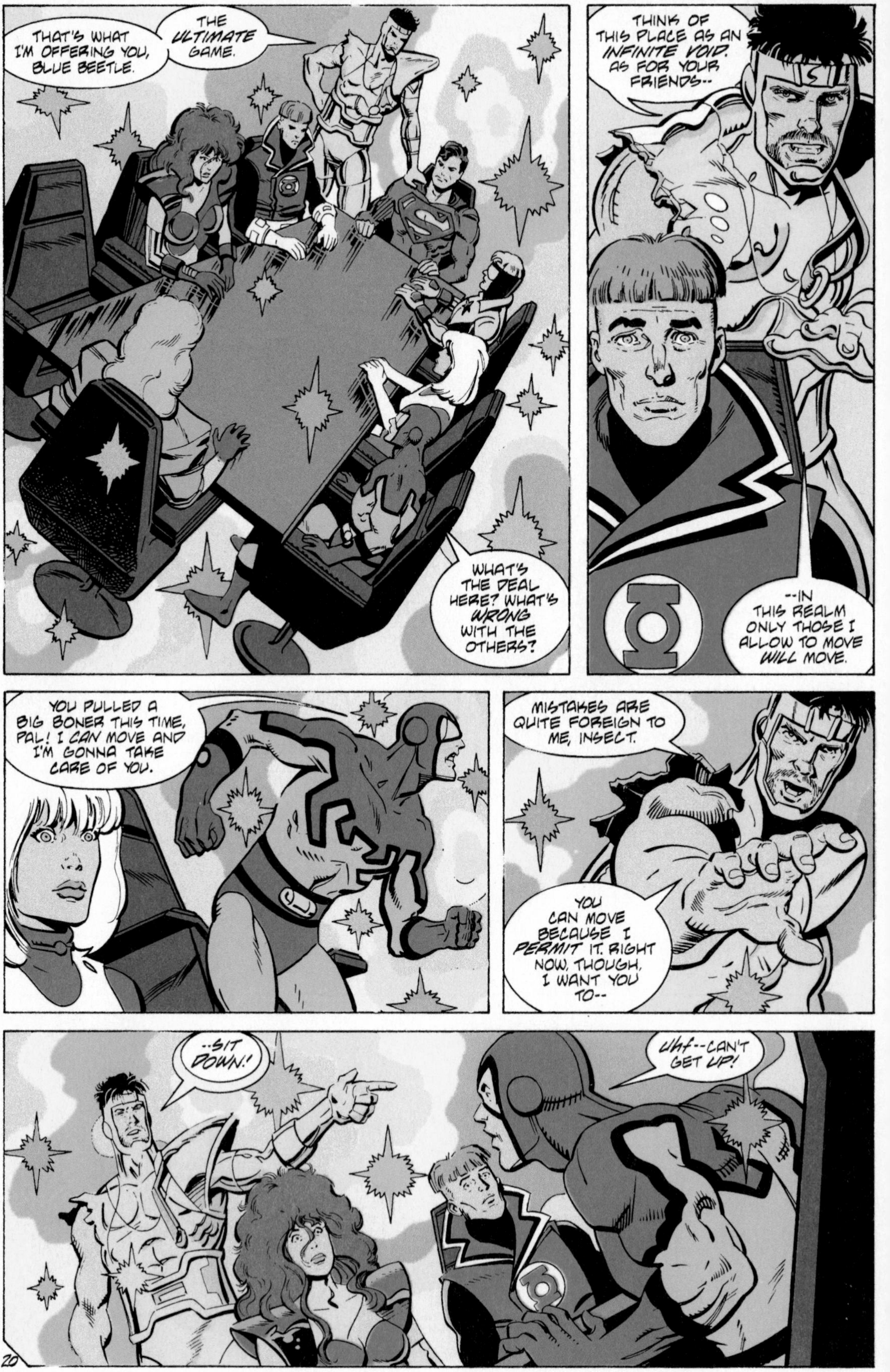
THAT'S WHAT I'M OFFERING YOU, BLUE BEETLE.
THE ULTIMATE GAME.
WHAT'S THE DEAL HERE? WHAT'S WRONG WITH THE OTHERS?
THINK OF THIS PLACE AS AN INFINITE VOID. AS FOR YOUR FRIENDS--
--IN THIS REALM ONLY THOSE I ALLOW TO MOVE WILL MOVE.
YOU PULLED A BIG BONER THIS TIME, PAL! I CAN MOVE AND I'M GONNA TAKE CARE OF YOU.
MISTAKES ARE QUITE FOREIGN TO ME, INSECT.
YOU CAN MOVE BECAUSE I PERMIT IT. RIGHT NOW, THOUGH, I WANT YOU TO--
--SIT DOWN!
UHF--CAN'T GET UP!

NOW, IF YOU'LL CEASE YOUR CHILDISH *OUTBURSTS*, WE CAN GET BACK TO THE *GAME!*

AND MORE IMPORTANT, THE GAME'S *PRIZE*.

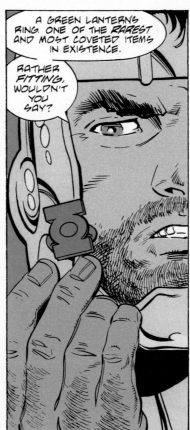

A GREEN LANTERN'S RING. ONE OF THE *RAREST* AND MOST COVETED ITEMS IN EXISTENCE.

RATHER *FITTING*, WOULDN'T YOU SAY?

BIG DEAL. GUY GARDNER WITHOUT A RING IS ACTUALLY KIND OF *APPEALING*.

FAR AS I'M CONCERNED, IT'S YOURS. TAKE IT.

I THOUGHT YOUR SMALL, INSIGNIFICANT MIND MIGHT REACT THAT WAY.

PERHAPS YOU STILL DON'T REALIZE WHAT *ELSE* IS AT STAKE.

ISN'T THIS CHESS BOARD *INTERESTING?* THE MAN WHO SOLD IT TO ME SAID HE GOT IT FROM A RED-SKINNED, THREE-EYED ALIEN.

THIS GAME REPRESENTS THE *LIVES* OF YOUR *FRIENDS.*

PLACE A FIGURE ON A *DANGER* SQUARE, AND THE CORRESPONDING PERSON WILL LIKELY *DIE*.

PLACE THE FIGURE ON A *FREEDOM* SQUARE AND I WILL RETURN THE PERSON TO THE CAVE.

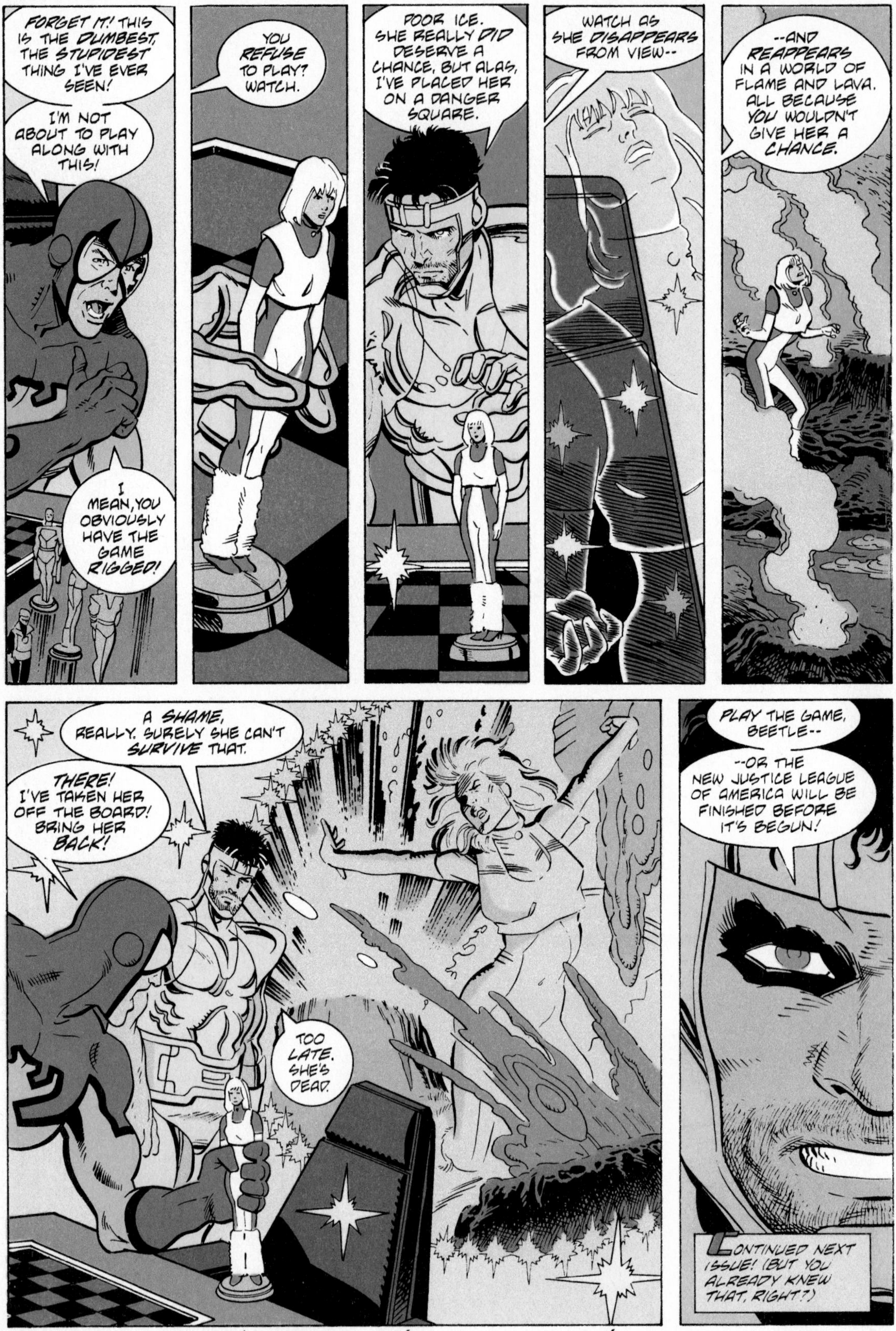
FORGET IT! THIS IS THE DUMBEST, THE STUPIDEST THING I'VE EVER SEEN!
I'M NOT ABOUT TO PLAY ALONG WITH THIS!
I MEAN, YOU OBVIOUSLY HAVE THE GAME RIGGED!
YOU REFUSE TO PLAY? WATCH.
POOR ICE. SHE REALLY DID DESERVE A CHANCE, BUT ALAS, I'VE PLACED HER ON A DANGER SQUARE.
WATCH AS SHE DISAPPEARS FROM VIEW--
--AND REAPPEARS IN A WORLD OF FLAME AND LAVA. ALL BECAUSE YOU WOULDN'T GIVE HER A CHANCE.
A SHAME, REALLY. SURELY SHE CAN'T SURVIVE THAT.
THERE! I'VE TAKEN HER OFF THE BOARD! BRING HER BACK!
TOO LATE. SHE'S DEAD.
PLAY THE GAME, BEETLE--
--OR THE NEW JUSTICE LEAGUE OF AMERICA WILL BE FINISHED BEFORE IT'S BEGUN!
CONTINUED NEXT ISSUE! (BUT YOU ALREADY KNEW THAT, RIGHT?)

story and art **Dan Jurgens** *finished art* **Rick Burchett** *letterer* **Willie Schubert** *colorist* **Gene D'Angelo** *editor* **Brian Augustyn**

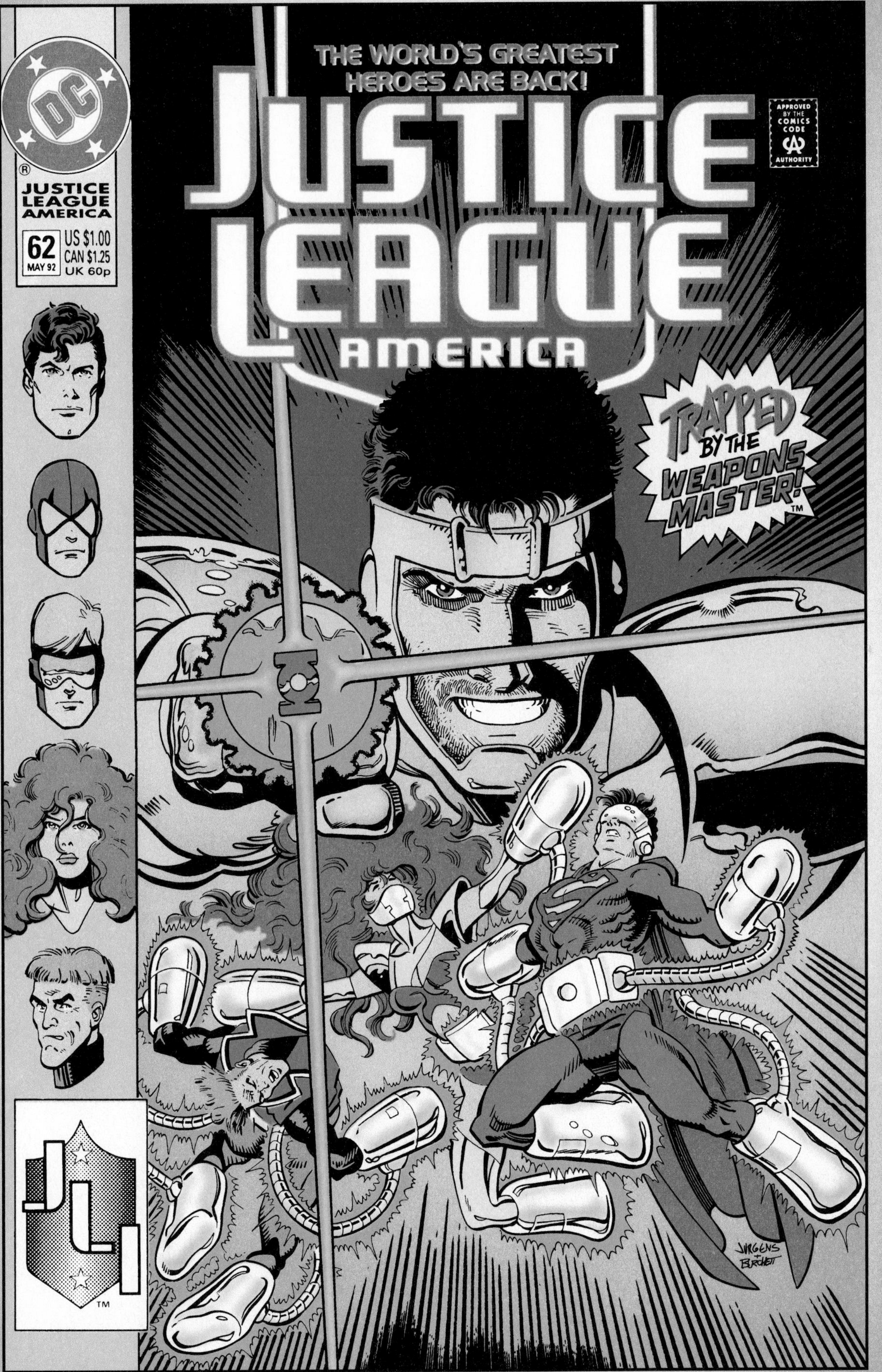

THE WORLD'S GREATEST HEROES ARE BACK!
JUSTICE LEAGUE AMERICA
APPROVED BY THE COMICS CODE AUTHORITY
JUSTICE LEAGUE AMERICA
62
MAY 92
US $1.00
CAN $1.25
UK 60p
TRAPPED BY THE WEAPONS MASTER!™
JURGENS + BURCHETT

Cover art by **DAN JURGENS**
and **RICK BURCHETT**

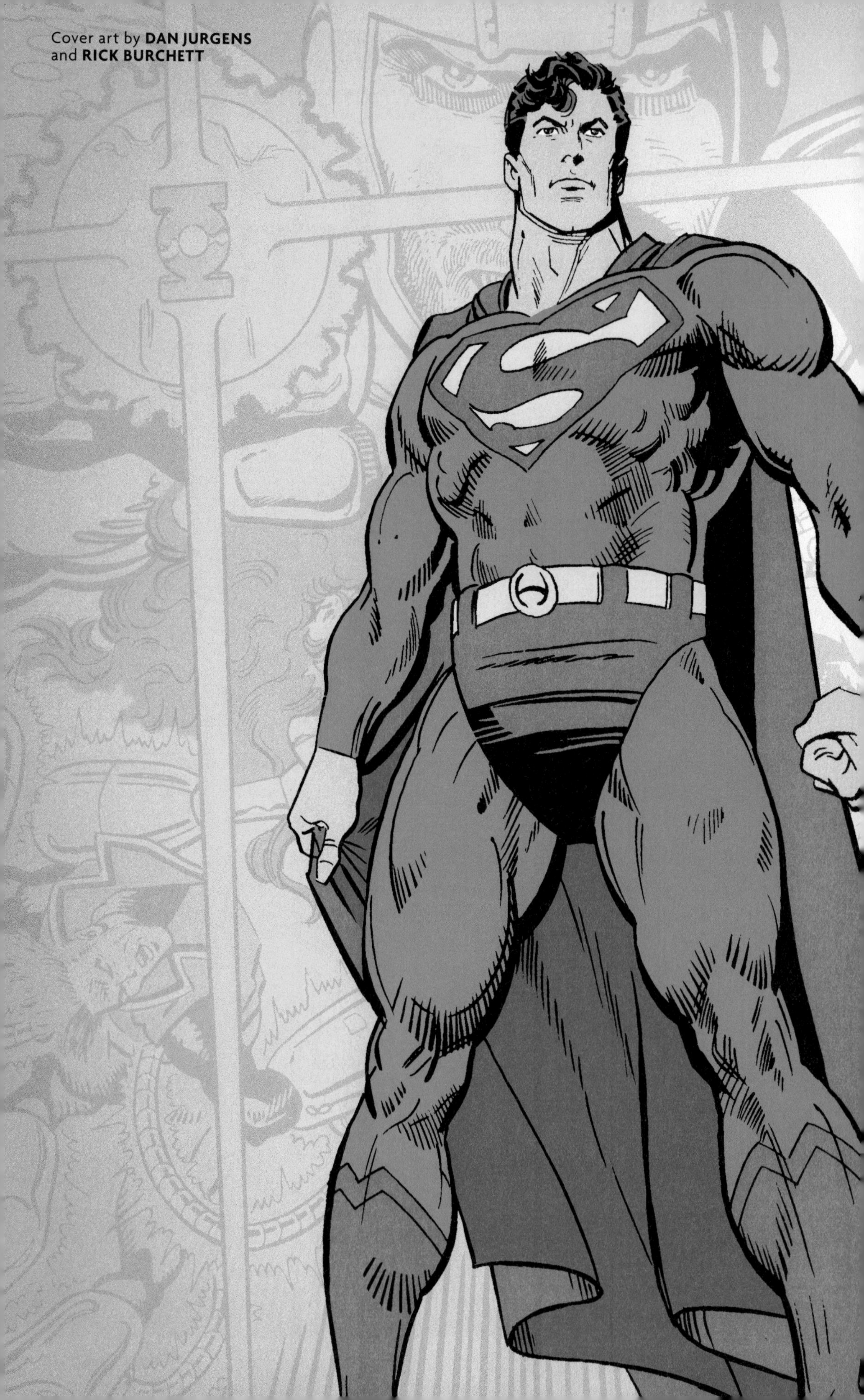

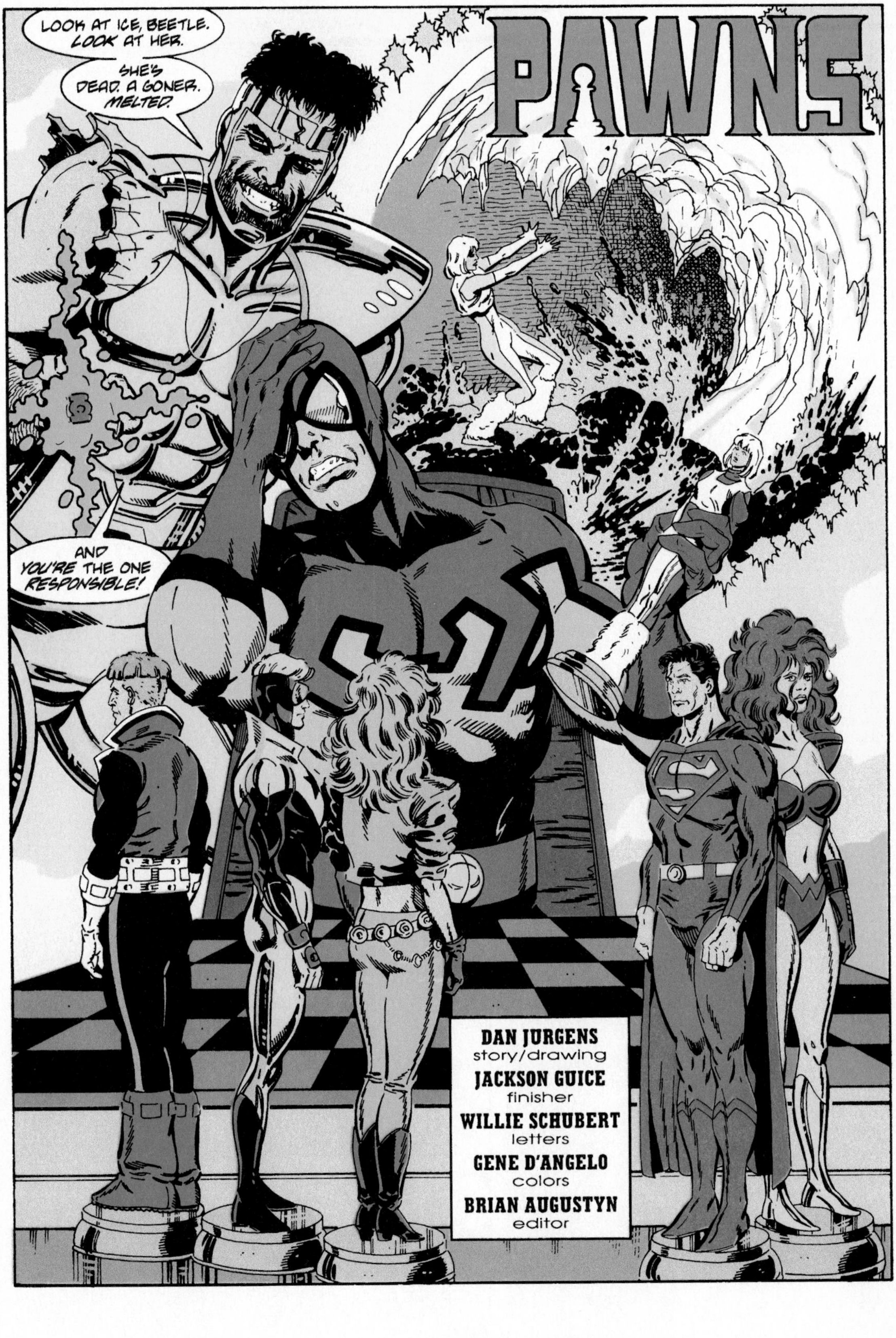
LOOK AT ICE, BEETLE. LOOK AT HER.
SHE'S DEAD. A GONER. MELTED.
PAWNS
AND YOU'RE THE ONE RESPONSIBLE!
DAN JURGENS story/drawing
JACKSON GUICE finisher
WILLIE SCHUBERT letters
GENE D'ANGELO colors
BRIAN AUGUSTYN editor

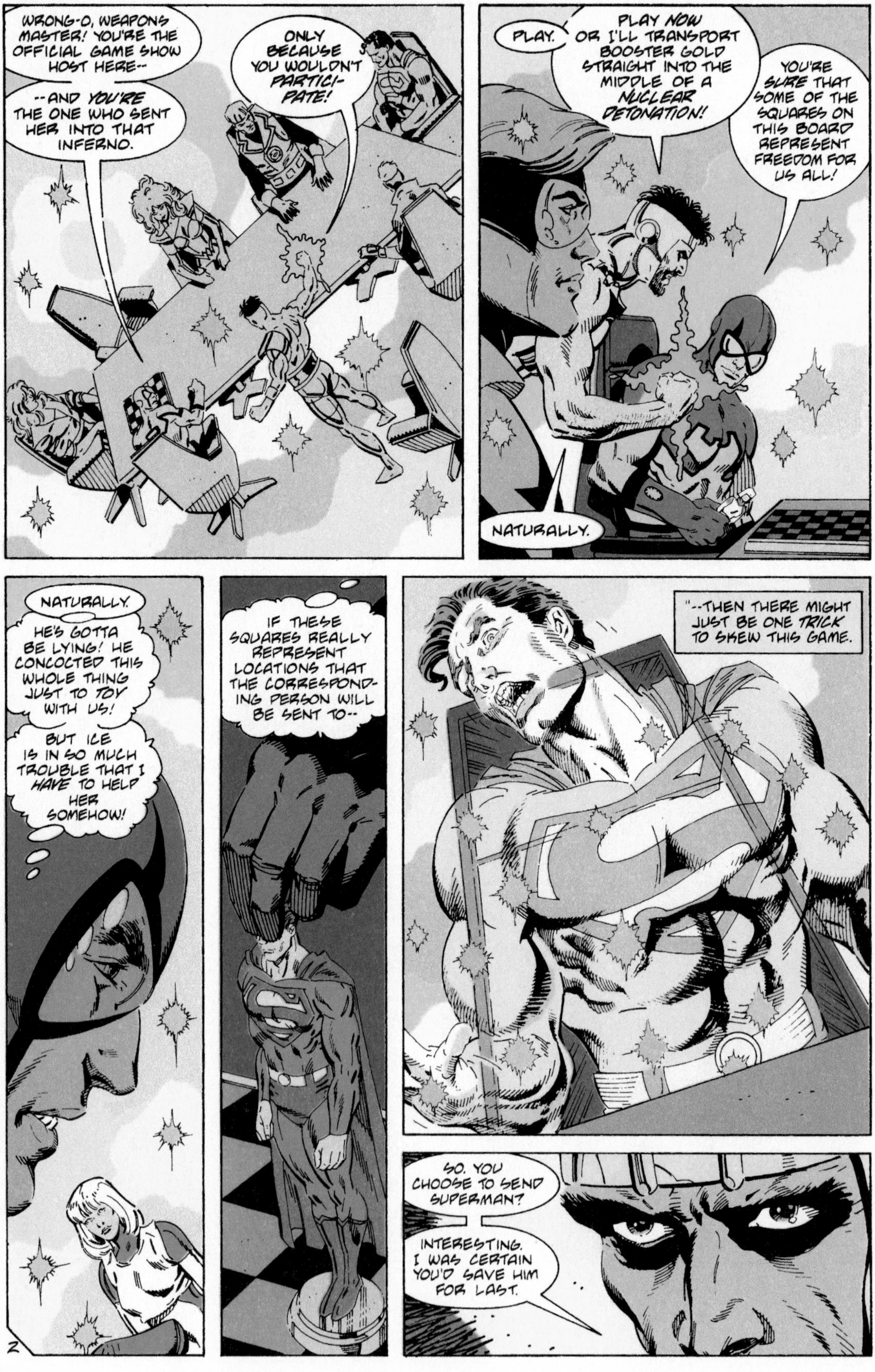
WRONG-O, WEAPONS MASTER! YOU'RE THE OFFICIAL GAME SHOW HOST HERE--
--AND YOU'RE THE ONE WHO SENT HER INTO THAT INFERNO.
ONLY BECAUSE YOU WOULDN'T PARTICI-PATE!
PLAY.
PLAY NOW OR I'LL TRANSPORT BOOSTER GOLD STRAIGHT INTO THE MIDDLE OF A NUCLEAR DETONATION!
YOU'RE SURE THAT SOME OF THE SQUARES ON THIS BOARD REPRESENT FREEDOM FOR US ALL!
NATURALLY.
NATURALLY.
HE'S GOTTA BE LYING! HE CONCOCTED THIS WHOLE THING JUST TO TOY WITH US!
BUT ICE IS IN SO MUCH TROUBLE THAT I HAVE TO HELP HER SOMEHOW!
IF THESE SQUARES REALLY REPRESENT LOCATIONS THAT THE CORRESPOND-ING PERSON WILL BE SENT TO--
"--THEN THERE MIGHT JUST BE ONE TRICK TO SKEW THIS GAME.
SO. YOU CHOOSE TO SEND SUPERMAN?
INTERESTING. I WAS CERTAIN YOU'D SAVE HIM FOR LAST.
2

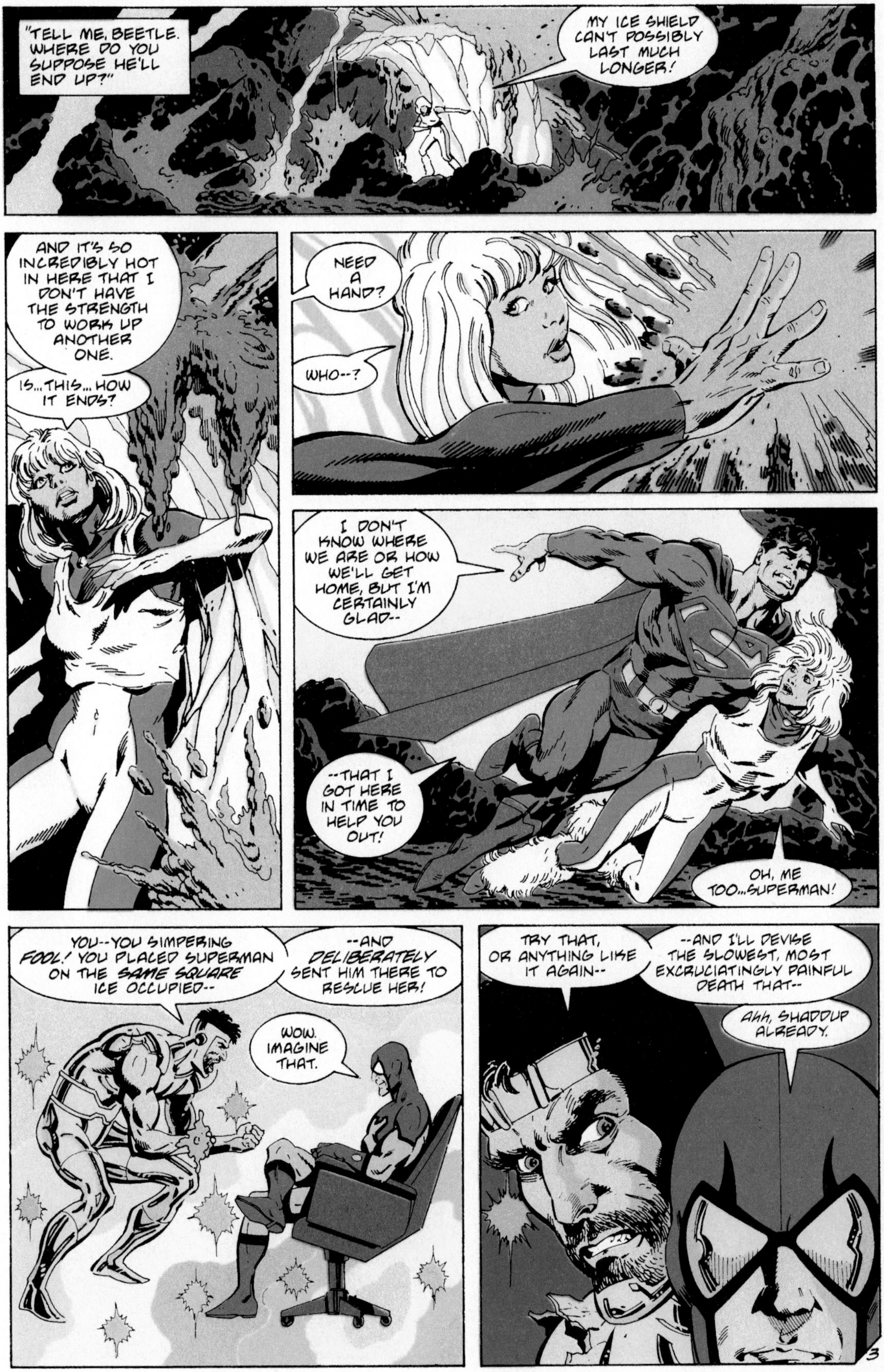
"TELL ME, BEETLE. WHERE DO YOU SUPPOSE HE'LL END UP?"
MY ICE SHIELD CAN'T POSSIBLY LAST MUCH LONGER!
AND IT'S SO INCREDIBLY HOT IN HERE THAT I DON'T HAVE THE STRENGTH TO WORK UP ANOTHER ONE.
IS... THIS... HOW IT ENDS?
NEED A HAND?
WHO--?
I DON'T KNOW WHERE WE ARE OR HOW WE'LL GET HOME, BUT I'M CERTAINLY GLAD--
--THAT I GOT HERE IN TIME TO HELP YOU OUT!
OH, ME TOO... SUPERMAN!
YOU--YOU SIMPERING FOOL! YOU PLACED SUPERMAN ON THE SAME SQUARE ICE OCCUPIED--
--AND DELIBERATELY SENT HIM THERE TO RESCUE HER!
WOW. IMAGINE THAT.
TRY THAT, OR ANYTHING LIKE IT AGAIN--
--AND I'LL DEVISE THE SLOWEST, MOST EXCRUCIATINGLY PAINFUL DEATH THAT--
AHH, SHADDUP ALREADY.

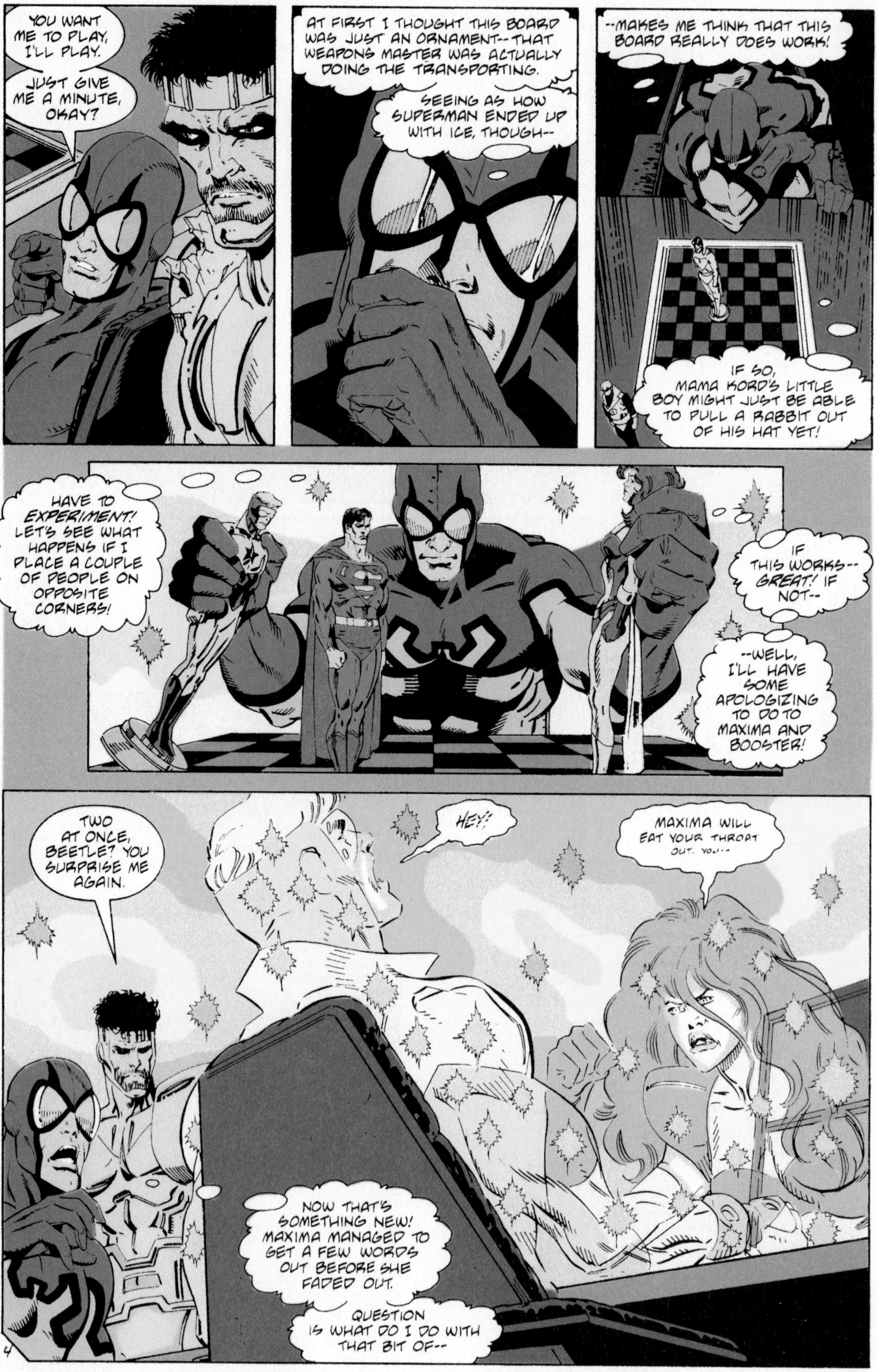
YOU WANT ME TO PLAY, I'LL PLAY.
JUST GIVE ME A MINUTE, OKAY?
AT FIRST I THOUGHT THIS BOARD WAS JUST AN ORNAMENT--THAT WEAPONS MASTER WAS ACTUALLY DOING THE TRANSPORTING.
SEEING AS HOW SUPERMAN ENDED UP WITH ICE, THOUGH--
--MAKES ME THINK THAT THIS BOARD REALLY DOES WORK!
IF SO, MAMA KORD'S LITTLE BOY MIGHT JUST BE ABLE TO PULL A RABBIT OUT OF HIS HAT YET!
HAVE TO EXPERIMENT! LET'S SEE WHAT HAPPENS IF I PLACE A COUPLE OF PEOPLE ON OPPOSITE CORNERS!
IF THIS WORKS--GREAT! IF NOT--
--WELL, I'LL HAVE SOME APOLOGIZING TO DO TO MAXIMA AND BOOSTER!
TWO AT ONCE, BEETLE? YOU SURPRISE ME AGAIN.
HEY!
MAXIMA WILL EAT YOUR THROAT OUT. YOU--
NOW THAT'S SOMETHING NEW! MAXIMA MANAGED TO GET A FEW WORDS OUT BEFORE SHE FADED OUT.
QUESTION IS WHAT DO I DO WITH THAT BIT OF--

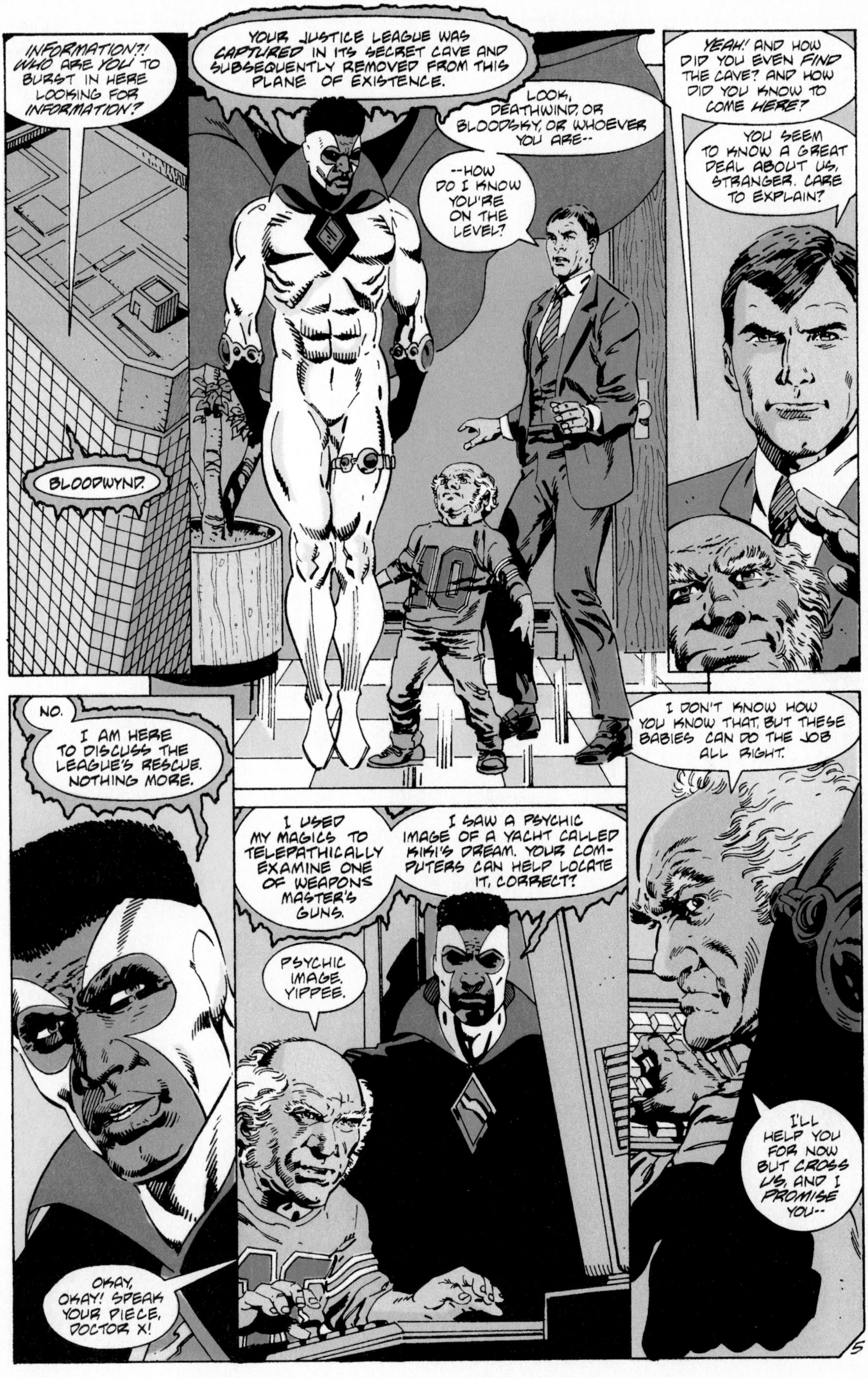

INFORMATION?! WHO ARE YOU TO BURST IN HERE LOOKING FOR INFORMATION?
YOUR JUSTICE LEAGUE WAS CAPTURED IN ITS SECRET CAVE AND SUBSEQUENTLY REMOVED FROM THIS PLANE OF EXISTENCE.
LOOK, DEATHWIND, OR BLOODSKY, OR WHOEVER YOU ARE--
--HOW DO I KNOW YOU'RE ON THE LEVEL?
BLOODWYND.
YEAH! AND HOW DID YOU EVEN FIND THE CAVE? AND HOW DID YOU KNOW TO COME HERE?
YOU SEEM TO KNOW A GREAT DEAL ABOUT US, STRANGER. CARE TO EXPLAIN?
NO.
I AM HERE TO DISCUSS THE LEAGUE'S RESCUE. NOTHING MORE.
OKAY, OKAY! SPEAK YOUR PIECE, DOCTOR X!
I USED MY MAGICS TO TELEPATHICALLY EXAMINE ONE OF WEAPONS MASTER'S GUNS.
I SAW A PSYCHIC IMAGE OF A YACHT CALLED KIKI'S DREAM. YOUR COMPUTERS CAN HELP LOCATE IT, CORRECT?
PSYCHIC IMAGE. YIPPEE.
I DON'T KNOW HOW YOU KNOW THAT, BUT THESE BABIES CAN DO THE JOB ALL RIGHT.
I'LL HELP YOU FOR NOW BUT CROSS US, AND I PROMISE YOU--

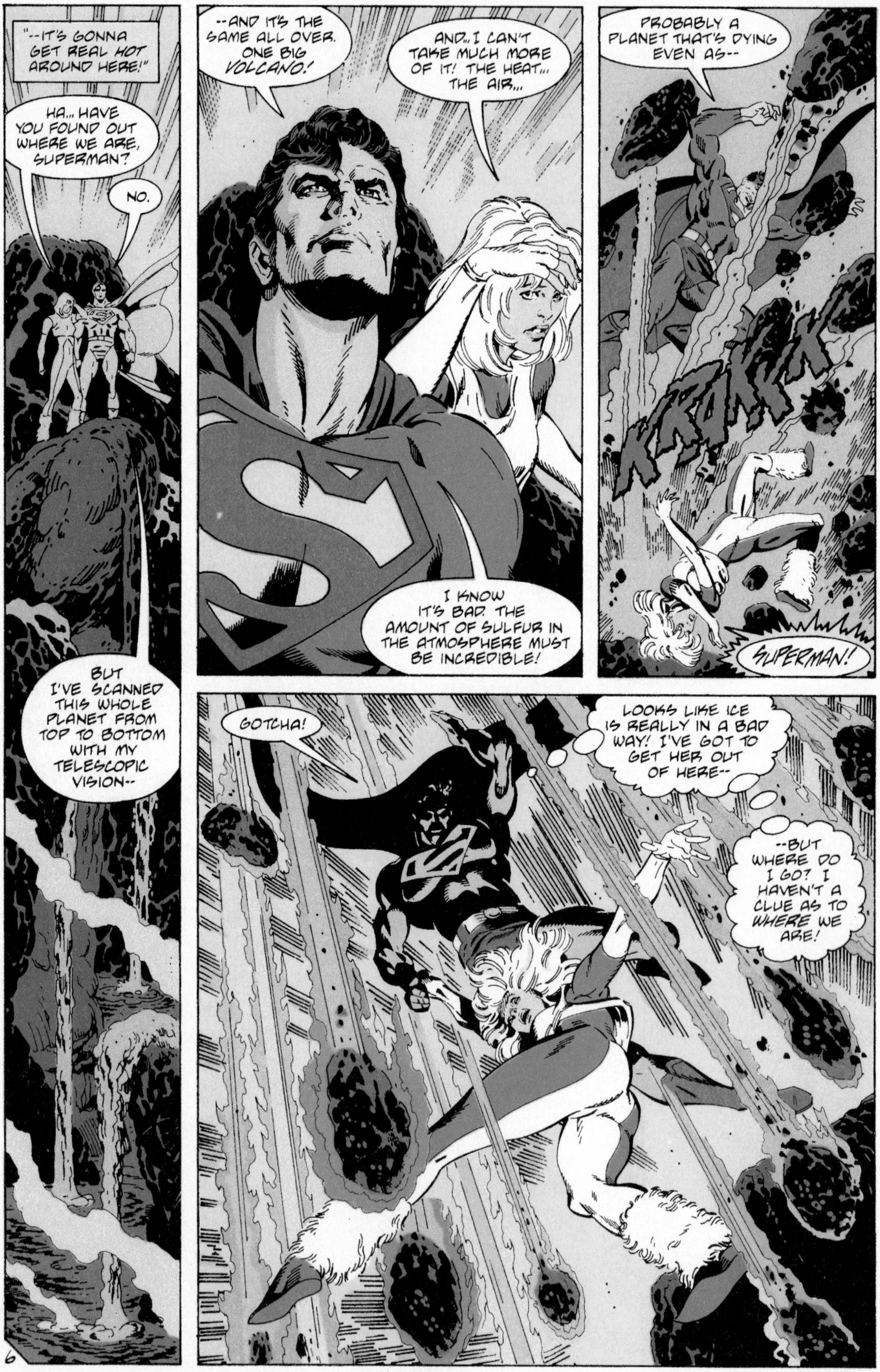
"--IT'S GONNA GET REAL HOT AROUND HERE!"
HA... HAVE YOU FOUND OUT WHERE WE ARE, SUPERMAN?
NO.
BUT I'VE SCANNED THIS WHOLE PLANET FROM TOP TO BOTTOM WITH MY TELESCOPIC VISION--
--AND IT'S THE SAME ALL OVER. ONE BIG VOLCANO!
AND... I CAN'T TAKE MUCH MORE OF IT! THE HEAT... THE AIR...
I KNOW IT'S BAD. THE AMOUNT OF SULFUR IN THE ATMOSPHERE MUST BE INCREDIBLE!
PROBABLY A PLANET THAT'S DYING EVEN AS--
KRAKKK!
SUPERMAN!
GOTCHA!
LOOKS LIKE ICE IS REALLY IN A BAD WAY! I'VE GOT TO GET HER OUT OF HERE--
--BUT WHERE DO I GO? I HAVEN'T A CLUE AS TO WHERE WE ARE!

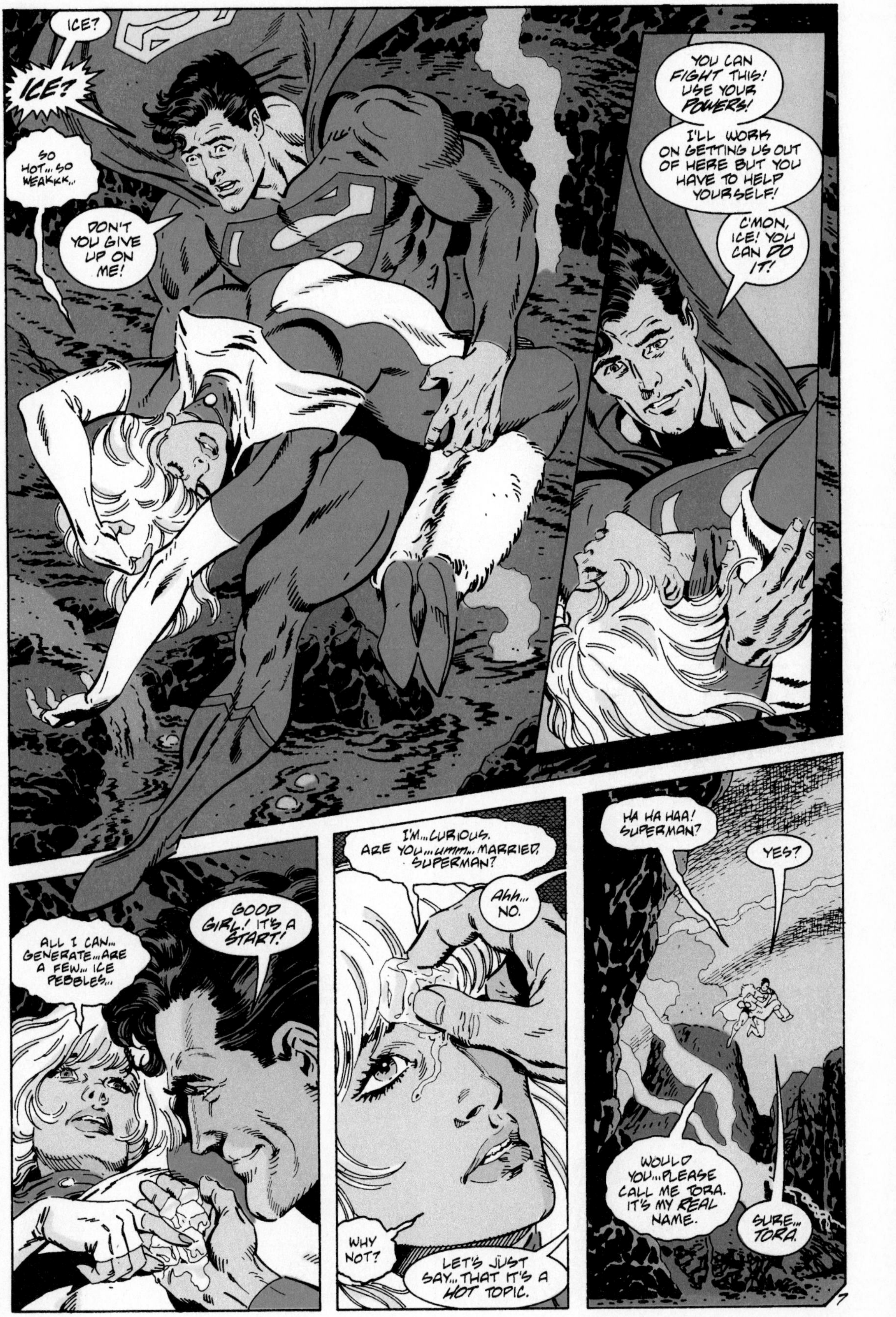
ICE?
ICE?
SO HOT... SO WEAKKK...
DON'T YOU GIVE UP ON ME!
YOU CAN FIGHT THIS! USE YOUR POWERS!
I'LL WORK ON GETTING US OUT OF HERE BUT YOU HAVE TO HELP YOURSELF!
C'MON, ICE! YOU CAN DO IT!
ALL I CAN... GENERATE... ARE A FEW... ICE PEBBLES...
GOOD GIRL! IT'S A START!
I'M... CURIOUS. ARE YOU... UMM... MARRIED, SUPERMAN?
AHH... NO.
WHY NOT?
LET'S JUST SAY... THAT IT'S A HOT TOPIC.
HA HA HAA! SUPERMAN?
YES?
WOULD YOU... PLEASE CALL ME TORA. IT'S MY REAL NAME.
SURE... TORA.

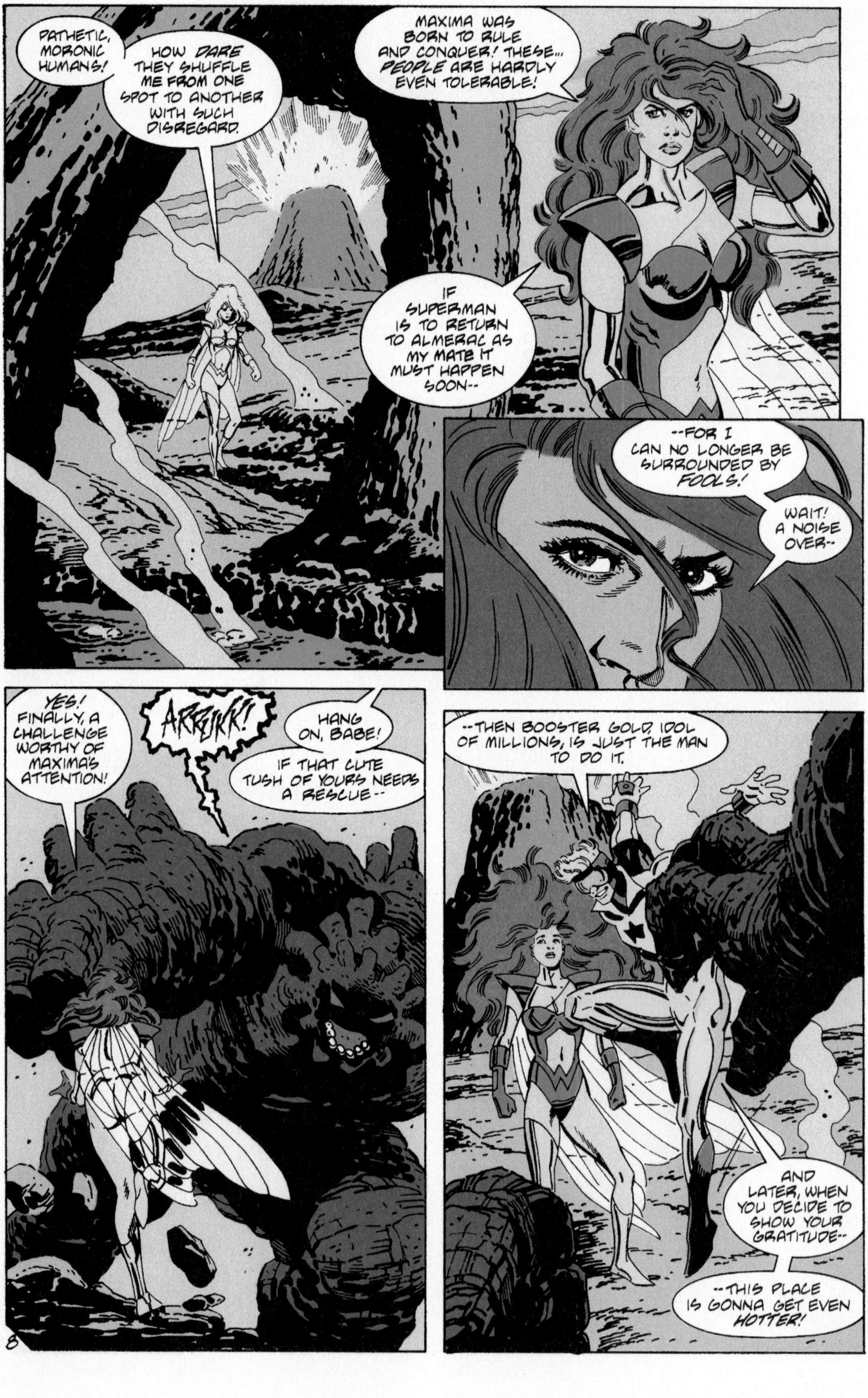
PATHETIC, MORONIC HUMANS!
HOW DARE THEY SHUFFLE ME FROM ONE SPOT TO ANOTHER WITH SUCH DISREGARD.
MAXIMA WAS BORN TO RULE AND CONQUER! THESE... PEOPLE ARE HARDLY EVEN TOLERABLE!
IF SUPERMAN IS TO RETURN TO ALMERAC AS MY MATE IT MUST HAPPEN SOON--
--FOR I CAN NO LONGER BE SURROUNDED BY FOOLS!
WAIT! A NOISE OVER--
YES! FINALLY, A CHALLENGE WORTHY OF MAXIMA'S ATTENTION!
ARRRKK!
HANG ON, BABE!
IF THAT CUTE TUSH OF YOURS NEEDS A RESCUE--
--THEN BOOSTER GOLD, IDOL OF MILLIONS, IS JUST THE MAN TO DO IT.
AND LATER, WHEN YOU DECIDE TO SHOW YOUR GRATITUDE--
--THIS PLACE IS GONNA GET EVEN HOTTER!

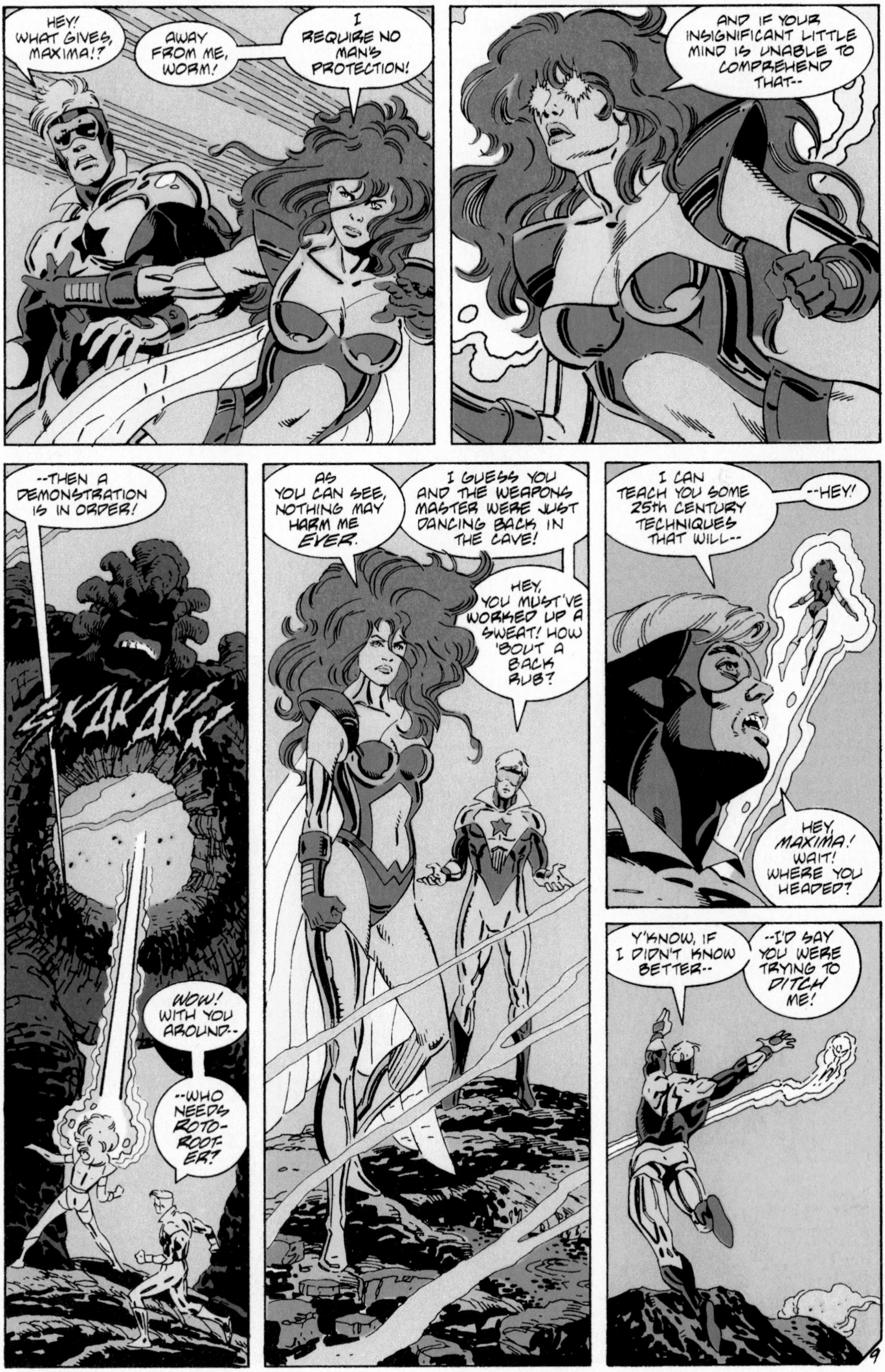
HEY! WHAT GIVES, MAXIMA!?
AWAY FROM ME, WORM!
I REQUIRE NO MAN'S PROTECTION!
AND IF YOUR INSIGNIFICANT LITTLE MIND IS UNABLE TO COMPREHEND THAT--
--THEN A DEMONSTRATION IS IN ORDER!
SKAKAKK!
WOW! WITH YOU AROUND--
--WHO NEEDS ROTO-ROOTER?
AS YOU CAN SEE, NOTHING MAY HARM ME EVER.
I GUESS YOU AND THE WEAPONS MASTER WERE JUST DANCING BACK IN THE CAVE!
HEY, YOU MUST'VE WORKED UP A SWEAT! HOW 'BOUT A BACK RUB?
I CAN TEACH YOU SOME 25th CENTURY TECHNIQUES THAT WILL--
--HEY!
HEY, MAXIMA! WAIT! WHERE YOU HEADED?
Y'KNOW, IF I DIDN'T KNOW BETTER--
--I'D SAY YOU WERE TRYING TO DITCH ME!
9

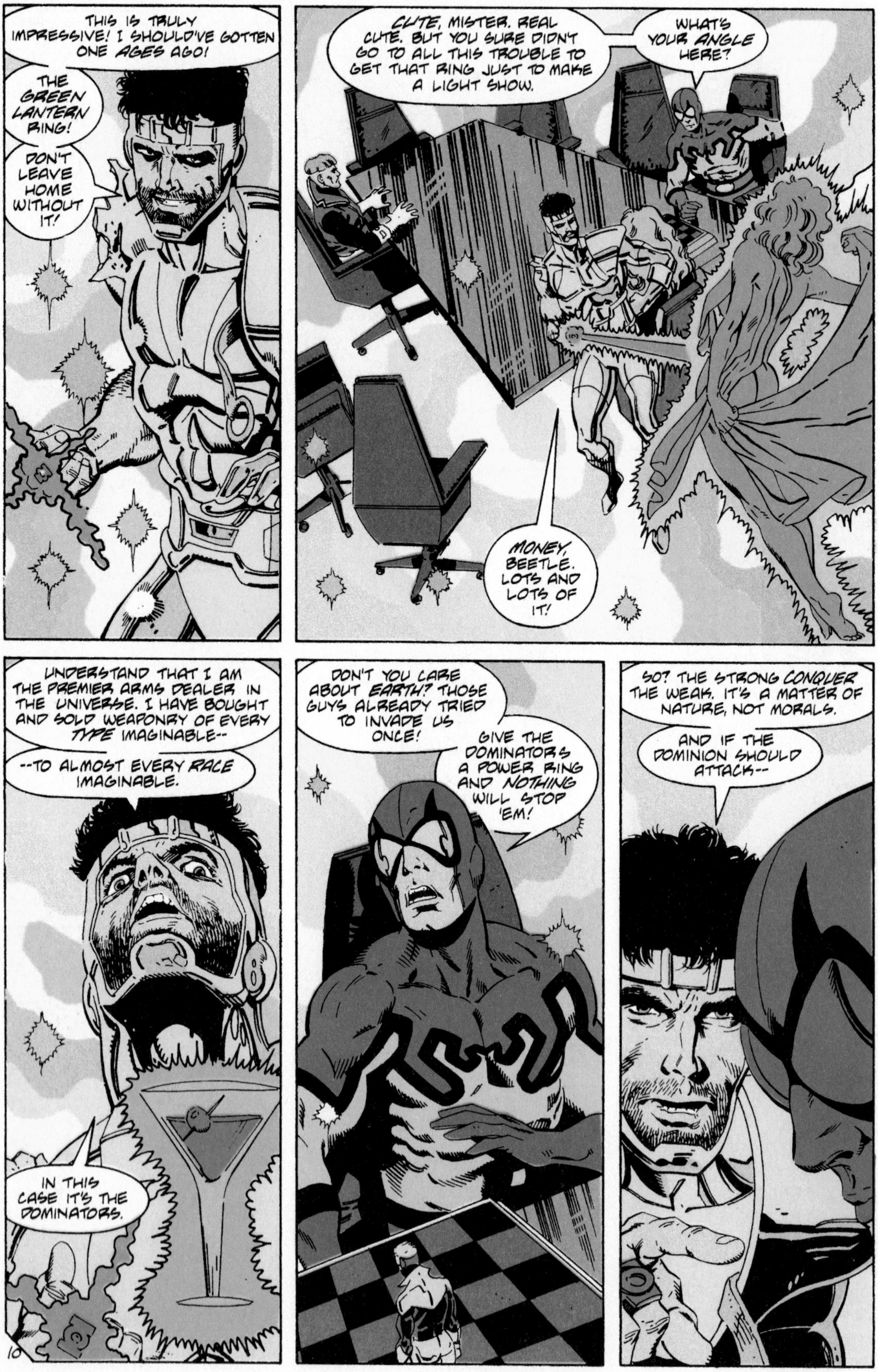
THIS IS TRULY IMPRESSIVE! I SHOULD'VE GOTTEN ONE AGES AGO!
THE GREEN LANTERN RING!
DON'T LEAVE HOME WITHOUT IT!
CUTE, MISTER. REAL CUTE. BUT YOU SURE DIDN'T GO TO ALL THIS TROUBLE TO GET THAT RING JUST TO MAKE A LIGHT SHOW.
WHAT'S YOUR ANGLE HERE?
MONEY, BEETLE. LOTS AND LOTS OF IT!
UNDERSTAND THAT I AM THE PREMIER ARMS DEALER IN THE UNIVERSE. I HAVE BOUGHT AND SOLD WEAPONRY OF EVERY TYPE IMAGINABLE--
--TO ALMOST EVERY RACE IMAGINABLE.
IN THIS CASE IT'S THE DOMINATORS.
DON'T YOU CARE ABOUT EARTH? THOSE GUYS ALREADY TRIED TO INVADE US ONCE!
GIVE THE DOMINATORS A POWER RING AND NOTHING WILL STOP 'EM!
SO? THE STRONG CONQUER THE WEAK. IT'S A MATTER OF NATURE, NOT MORALS.
AND IF THE DOMINION SHOULD ATTACK--

--THEN I'LL BE GLAD TO SELL *EARTH* WEAPONS TO DEFEND ITSELF WITH!

OH, WELL, THAT MAKES IT ALL *BETTER,* DOESN'T IT?

YOU HAVE TWO MORE PIECES, BEETLE. *PLAY.*

HE'S RIGHT, I DO HAVE TO PLAY. I HAVE TO MAKE A PLAY THAT WILL STOP HIM IN HIS TRACKS.

IF I CAN *STALL*-- AND IF GUY IS SMART ENOUGH TO MAKE HIS MOVE--

--AND THAT IS BIG *"IF"--*

--THEN THIS COULD BE THE TICKET!

NICE MOVE, BUG!

HEY, PAL--

"--GIMME MY RING!"

HOW IS THIS POSSIBLE?

"EASY! I SAW THAT YOUR TRANSPORT VICTIMS HAD A BRIEF SECOND OF CONSCIOUS FREEDOM BEFORE THEY DISAPPEARED!

"I FIGURED GUY MIGHT JUST HAVE ENOUGH TIME TO RE-ESTABLISH HIS *LINK* WITH HIS RING--

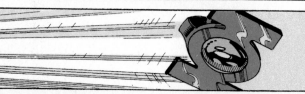

"--AND GET IT BACK!"

BWA-HA-HA HAAA!

KISS YOUR WEAPONS GOOD-BYE, SUCKER!

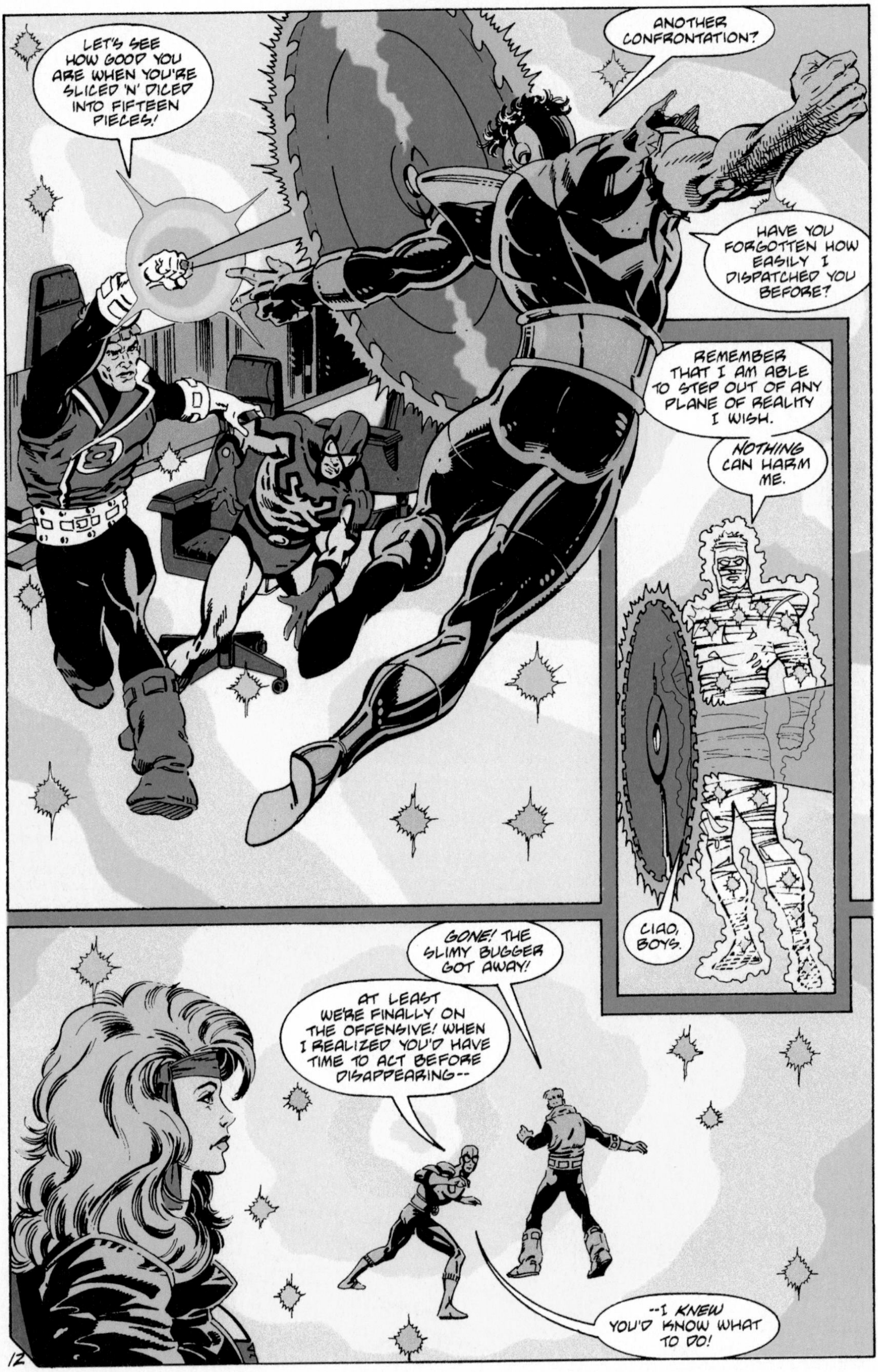
LET'S SEE HOW GOOD YOU ARE WHEN YOU'RE SLICED 'N' DICED INTO FIFTEEN PIECES!
ANOTHER CONFRONTATION?
HAVE YOU FORGOTTEN HOW EASILY I DISPATCHED YOU BEFORE?
REMEMBER THAT I AM ABLE TO STEP OUT OF ANY PLANE OF REALITY I WISH.
NOTHING CAN HARM ME.
CIAO, BOYS.
GONE! THE SLIMY BUGGER GOT AWAY!
AT LEAST WE'RE FINALLY ON THE OFFENSIVE! WHEN I REALIZED YOU'D HAVE TIME TO ACT BEFORE DISAPPEARING--
--I KNEW YOU'D KNOW WHAT TO DO!

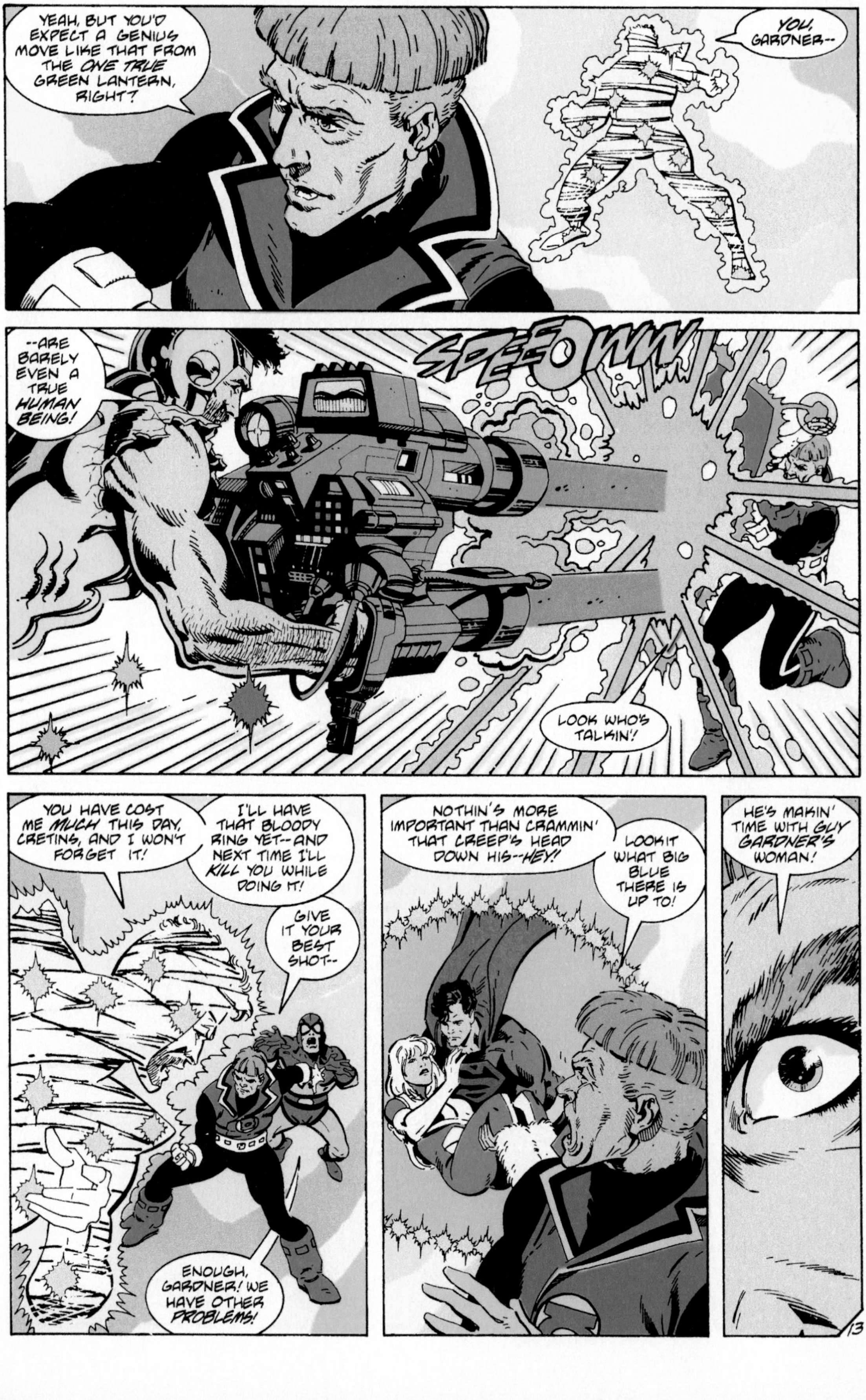
YEAH, BUT YOU'D EXPECT A GENIUS MOVE LIKE THAT FROM THE *ONE TRUE* GREEN LANTERN, RIGHT?
YOU, GARDNER--
--ARE BARELY EVEN A TRUE *HUMAN BEING!*
SPEEOWW
LOOK WHO'S TALKIN'!
YOU HAVE COST ME *MUCH* THIS DAY, CRETINS, AND I WON'T FORGET IT!
I'LL HAVE THAT BLOODY RING YET--AND NEXT TIME I'LL *KILL* YOU WHILE DOING IT!
GIVE IT YOUR BEST SHOT--
ENOUGH, GARDNER! WE HAVE OTHER *PROBLEMS!*
NOTHIN'S MORE IMPORTANT THAN CRAMMIN' THAT CREEP'S HEAD DOWN HIS--*HEY!*
LOOKIT WHAT BIG BLUE THERE IS UP TO!
HE'S MAKIN' TIME WITH *GUY GARDNER'S* WOMAN!

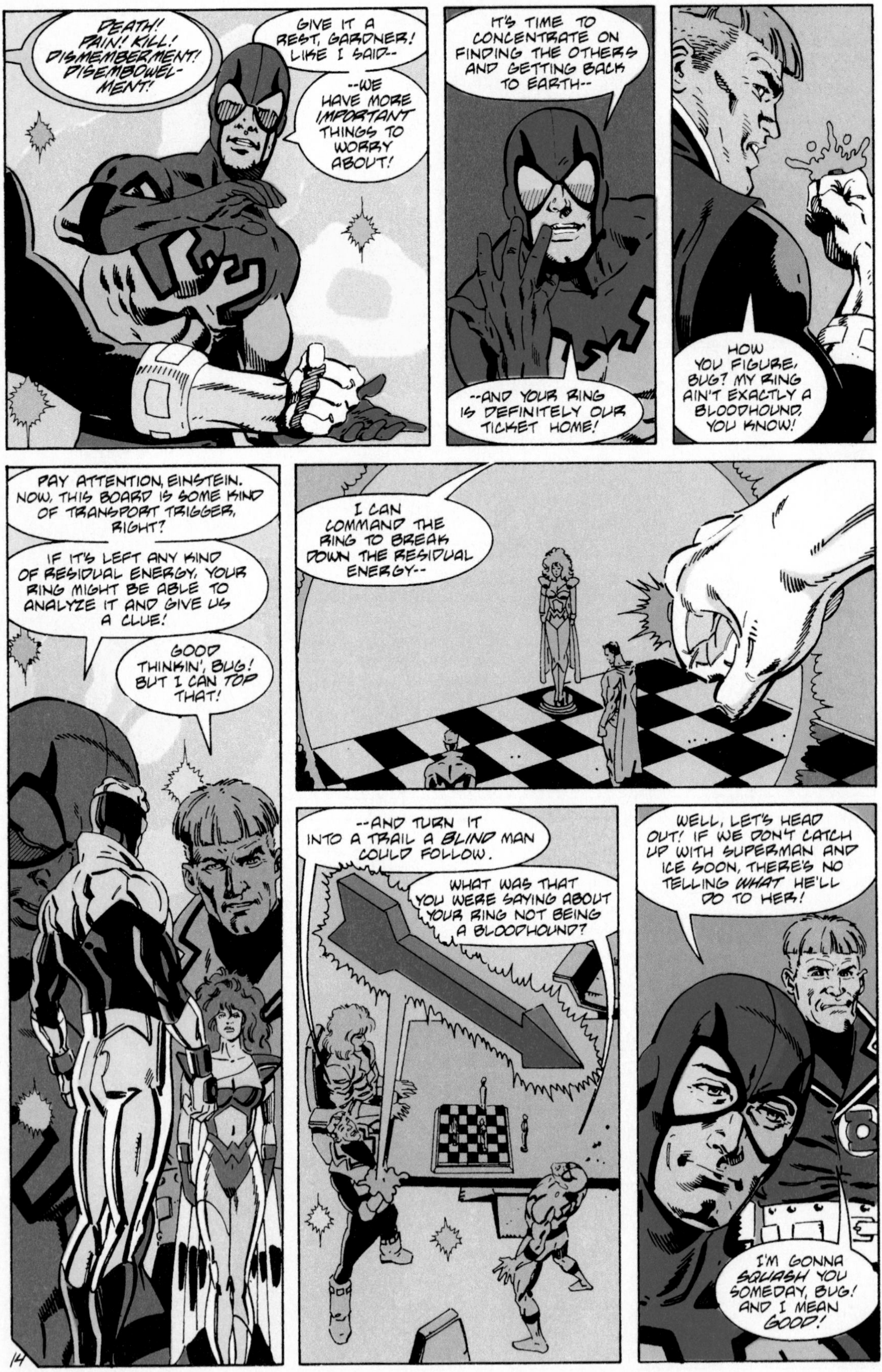
DEATH! PAIN! KILL! DISMEMBERMENT! DISEMBOWELMENT!
GIVE IT A REST, GARDNER! LIKE I SAID--
--WE HAVE MORE IMPORTANT THINGS TO WORRY ABOUT!
IT'S TIME TO CONCENTRATE ON FINDING THE OTHERS AND GETTING BACK TO EARTH--
--AND YOUR RING IS DEFINITELY OUR TICKET HOME!
HOW YOU FIGURE, BUG? MY RING AIN'T EXACTLY A BLOODHOUND, YOU KNOW!
PAY ATTENTION, EINSTEIN. NOW, THIS BOARD IS SOME KIND OF TRANSPORT TRIGGER, RIGHT?
IF IT'S LEFT ANY KIND OF RESIDUAL ENERGY, YOUR RING MIGHT BE ABLE TO ANALYZE IT AND GIVE US A CLUE!
GOOD THINKIN', BUG! BUT I CAN TOP THAT!
I CAN COMMAND THE RING TO BREAK DOWN THE RESIDUAL ENERGY--
--AND TURN IT INTO A TRAIL A BLIND MAN COULD FOLLOW.
WHAT WAS THAT YOU WERE SAYING ABOUT YOUR RING NOT BEING A BLOODHOUND?
WELL, LET'S HEAD OUT! IF WE DON'T CATCH UP WITH SUPERMAN AND ICE SOON, THERE'S NO TELLING WHAT HE'LL DO TO HER!
I'M GONNA SQUASH YOU SOMEDAY, BUG! AND I MEAN GOOD!

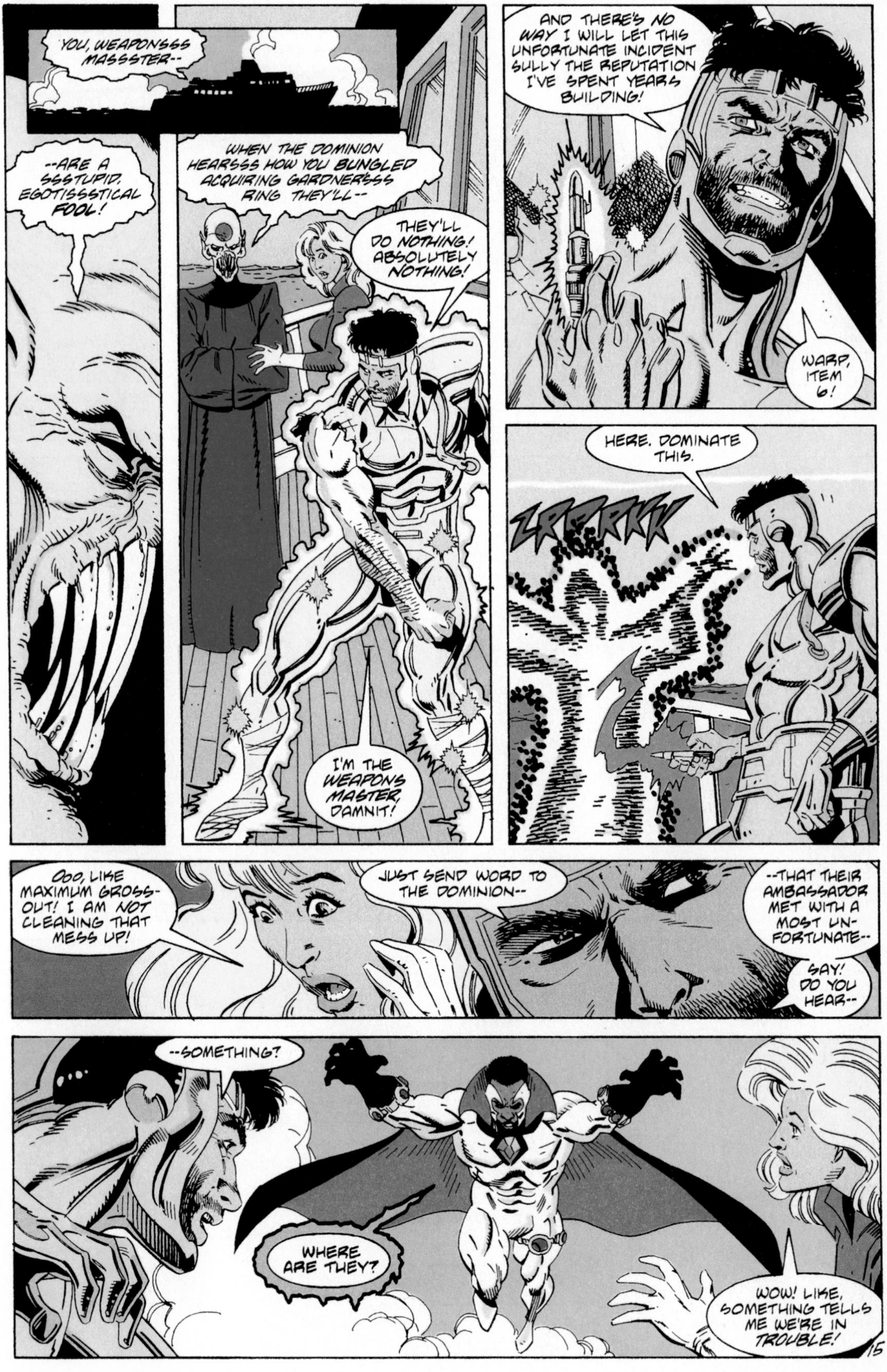
YOU, WEAPONSSS MASSSTER--
--ARE A SSSTUPID, EGOTISSSTICAL FOOL!
WHEN THE DOMINION HEARSSS HOW YOU BUNGLED ACQUIRING GARDNERSSS RING THEY'LL--
THEY'LL DO NOTHING! ABSOLUTELY NOTHING!
I'M THE WEAPONS MASTER, DAMNIT!
AND THERE'S NO WAY I WILL LET THIS UNFORTUNATE INCIDENT SULLY THE REPUTATION I'VE SPENT YEARS BUILDING!
WARP, ITEM 6!
HERE. DOMINATE THIS.
ZRRRKK
OOO, LIKE MAXIMUM GROSS-OUT! I AM NOT CLEANING THAT MESS UP!
JUST SEND WORD TO THE DOMINION--
--THAT THEIR AMBASSADOR MET WITH A MOST UN-FORTUNATE--
SAY! DO YOU HEAR--
--SOMETHING?
WHERE ARE THEY?
WOW! LIKE, SOMETHING TELLS ME WE'RE IN TROUBLE!

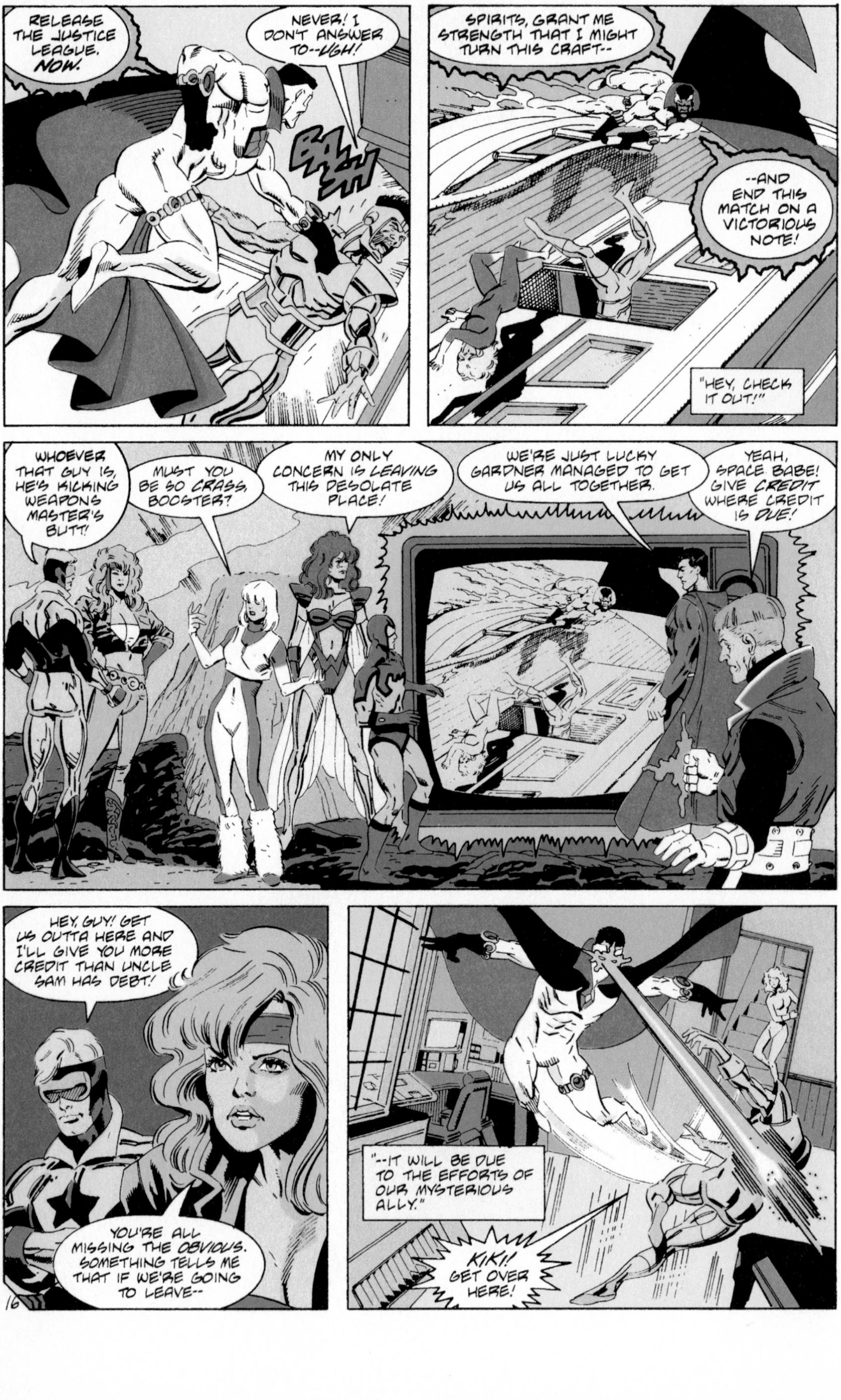
RELEASE THE JUSTICE LEAGUE. NOW.
NEVER! I DON'T ANSWER TO--UGH!
BA-ZAM
SPIRITS, GRANT ME STRENGTH THAT I MIGHT TURN THIS CRAFT--
--AND END THIS MATCH ON A VICTORIOUS NOTE!
"HEY, CHECK IT OUT!"
WHOEVER THAT GUY IS, HE'S KICKING WEAPONS MASTER'S BUTT!
MUST YOU BE SO CRASS, BOOSTER?
MY ONLY CONCERN IS LEAVING THIS DESOLATE PLACE!
WE'RE JUST LUCKY GARDNER MANAGED TO GET US ALL TOGETHER.
YEAH, SPACE BABE! GIVE CREDIT WHERE CREDIT IS DUE!
HEY, GUY! GET US OUTTA HERE AND I'LL GIVE YOU MORE CREDIT THAN UNCLE SAM HAS DEBT!
YOU'RE ALL MISSING THE OBVIOUS. SOMETHING TELLS ME THAT IF WE'RE GOING TO LEAVE--
"--IT WILL BE DUE TO THE EFFORTS OF OUR MYSTERIOUS ALLY."
KIKI! GET OVER HERE!

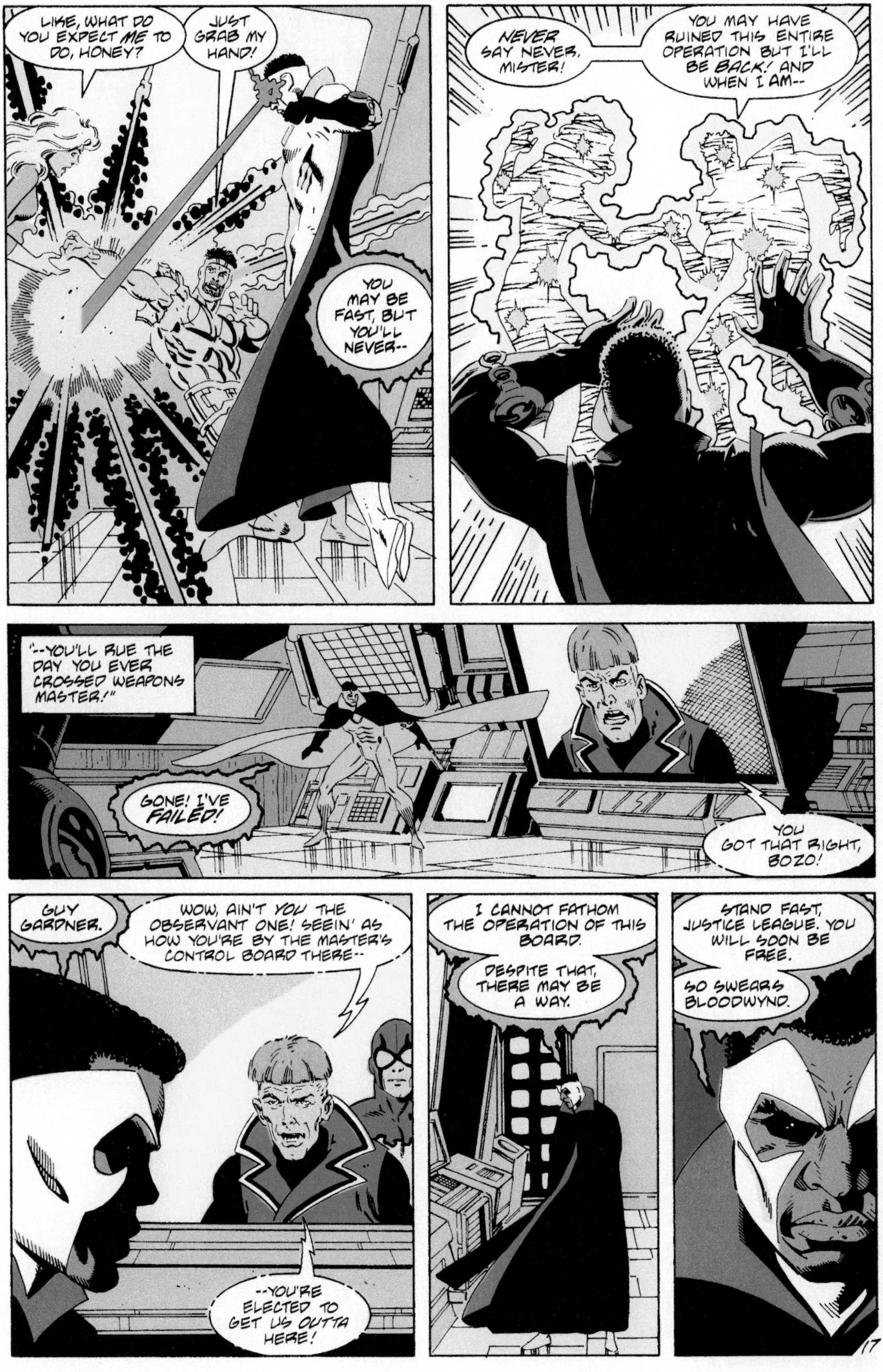
LIKE, WHAT DO YOU EXPECT *ME* TO DO, HONEY?
JUST GRAB MY HAND!
YOU MAY BE FAST, BUT YOU'LL NEVER--
NEVER SAY NEVER, MISTER!
YOU MAY HAVE RUINED THIS ENTIRE OPERATION BUT I'LL BE *BACK!* AND WHEN I AM--
"--YOU'LL RUE THE DAY YOU EVER CROSSED WEAPONS MASTER!"
GONE! I'VE *FAILED!*
YOU GOT THAT RIGHT, BOZO!
GUY GARDNER.
WOW, AIN'T *YOU* THE OBSERVANT ONE! SEEIN' AS HOW YOU'RE BY THE MASTER'S CONTROL BOARD THERE--
--YOU'RE ELECTED TO GET US *OUTTA* HERE!
I CANNOT FATHOM THE OPERATION OF THIS BOARD.
DESPITE THAT, THERE MAY BE A WAY.
STAND FAST, JUSTICE LEAGUE. YOU WILL SOON BE FREE.
SO SWEARS BLOODWYND.

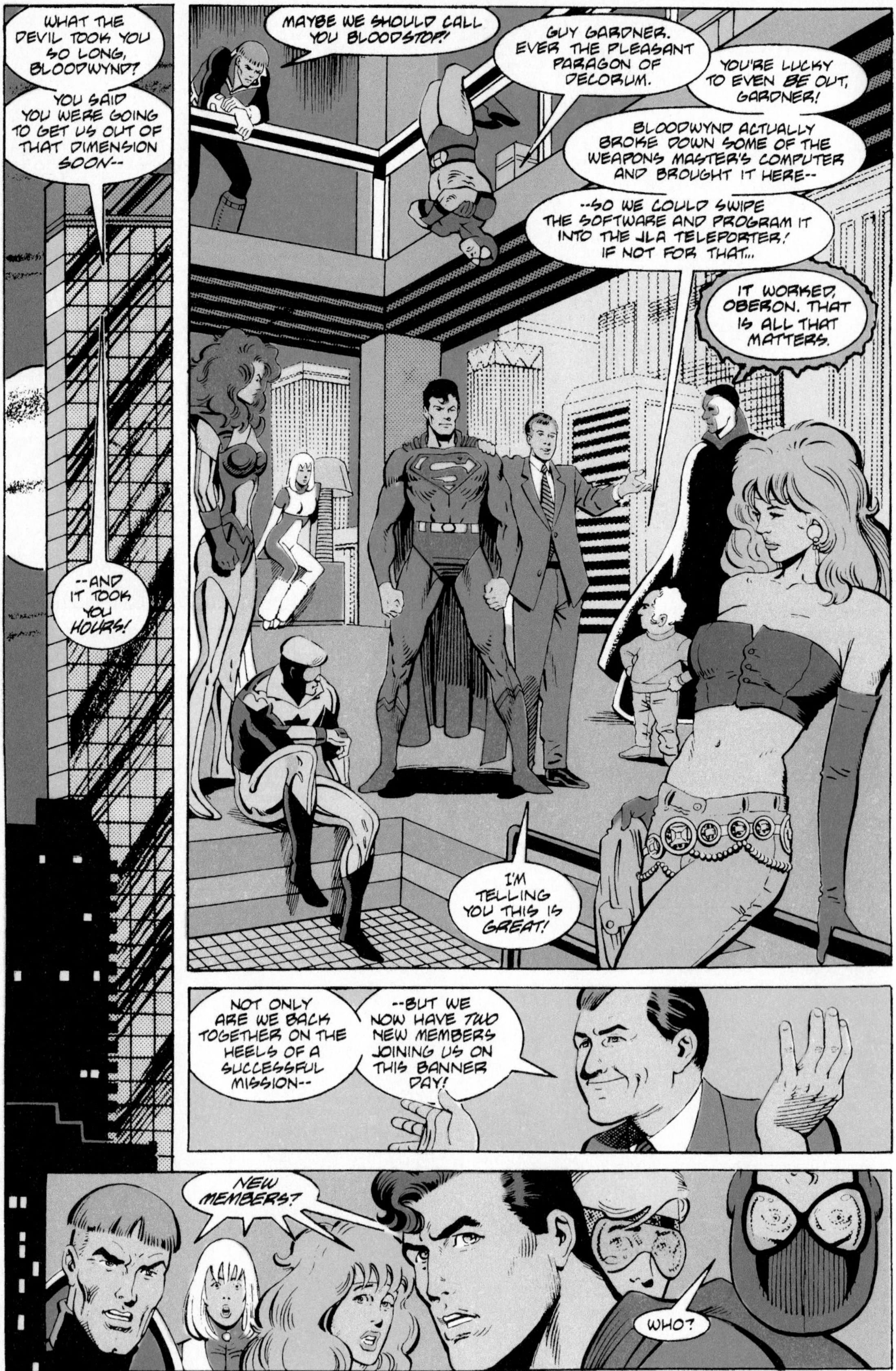

WHAT THE DEVIL TOOK YOU SO LONG, BLOODWYND?
YOU SAID YOU WERE GOING TO GET US OUT OF THAT DIMENSION SOON--
--AND IT TOOK YOU HOURS!
MAYBE WE SHOULD CALL YOU BLOODSTOP!
GUY GARDNER. EVER THE PLEASANT PARAGON OF DECORUM.
YOU'RE LUCKY TO EVEN BE OUT, GARDNER!
BLOODWYND ACTUALLY BROKE DOWN SOME OF THE WEAPONS MASTER'S COMPUTER AND BROUGHT IT HERE--
--SO WE COULD SWIPE THE SOFTWARE AND PROGRAM IT INTO THE JLA TELEPORTER! IF NOT FOR THAT...
IT WORKED, OBERON. THAT IS ALL THAT MATTERS.
I'M TELLING YOU THIS IS GREAT!
NOT ONLY ARE WE BACK TOGETHER ON THE HEELS OF A SUCCESSFUL MISSION--
--BUT WE NOW HAVE TWO NEW MEMBERS JOINING US ON THIS BANNER DAY!
NEW MEMBERS?
WHO?

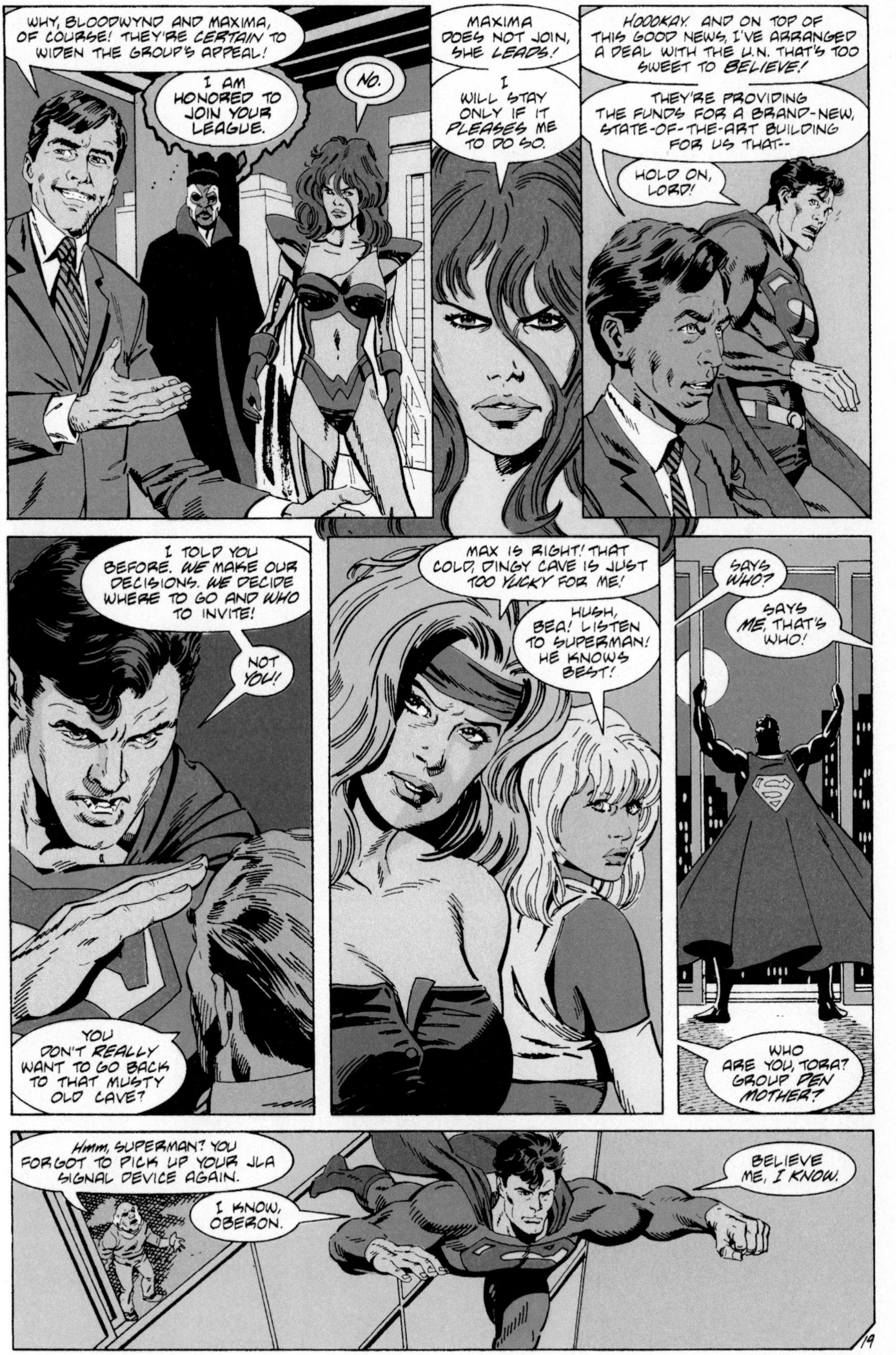
WHY, BLOODWYND AND MAXIMA, OF COURSE! THEY'RE CERTAIN TO WIDEN THE GROUP'S APPEAL!
I AM HONORED TO JOIN YOUR LEAGUE.
NO.
MAXIMA DOES NOT JOIN, SHE LEADS!
I WILL STAY ONLY IF IT PLEASES ME TO DO SO.
HOOOKAY. AND ON TOP OF THIS GOOD NEWS, I'VE ARRANGED A DEAL WITH THE U.N. THAT'S TOO SWEET TO BELIEVE!
THEY'RE PROVIDING THE FUNDS FOR A BRAND-NEW, STATE-OF-THE-ART BUILDING FOR US THAT--
HOLD ON, LORD!
I TOLD YOU BEFORE. WE MAKE OUR DECISIONS. WE DECIDE WHERE TO GO AND WHO TO INVITE!
NOT YOU!
YOU DON'T REALLY WANT TO GO BACK TO THAT MUSTY OLD CAVE?
MAX IS RIGHT! THAT COLD, DINGY CAVE IS JUST TOO YUCKY FOR ME!
HUSH, BEA! LISTEN TO SUPERMAN! HE KNOWS BEST!
SAYS WHO?
SAYS ME, THAT'S WHO!
WHO ARE YOU, TORA? GROUP DEN MOTHER?
HMM, SUPERMAN? YOU FORGOT TO PICK UP YOUR JLA SIGNAL DEVICE AGAIN.
I KNOW, OBERON.
BELIEVE ME, I KNOW.

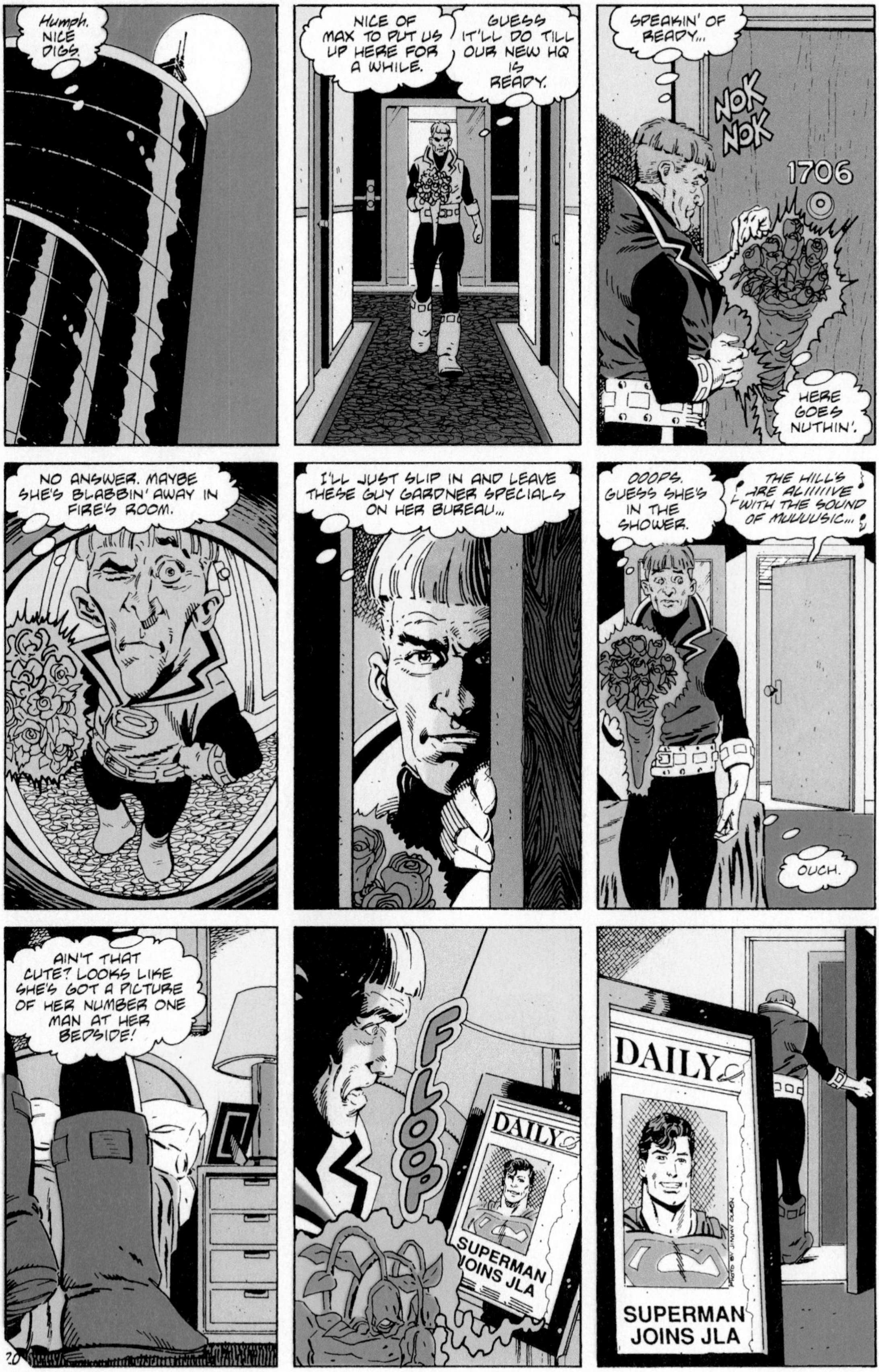
Humph. NICE DIGS.
NICE OF MAX TO PUT US UP HERE FOR A WHILE.
GUESS IT'LL DO TILL OUR NEW HQ IS READY.
SPEAKIN' OF READY...
NOK NOK
1706
HERE GOES NUTHIN'.
NO ANSWER. MAYBE SHE'S BLABBIN' AWAY IN FIRE'S ROOM.
I'LL JUST SLIP IN AND LEAVE THESE GUY GARDNER SPECIALS ON HER BUREAU...
OOOPS. GUESS SHE'S IN THE SHOWER.
THE HILL'S ARE ALIIIIIVE WITH THE SOUND OF MUUUUSIC...
OUCH.
AIN'T THAT CUTE? LOOKS LIKE SHE'S GOT A PICTURE OF HER NUMBER ONE MAN AT HER BEDSIDE!
FLOOP
DAILY
SUPERMAN JOINS JLA
DAILY
SUPERMAN JOINS JLA

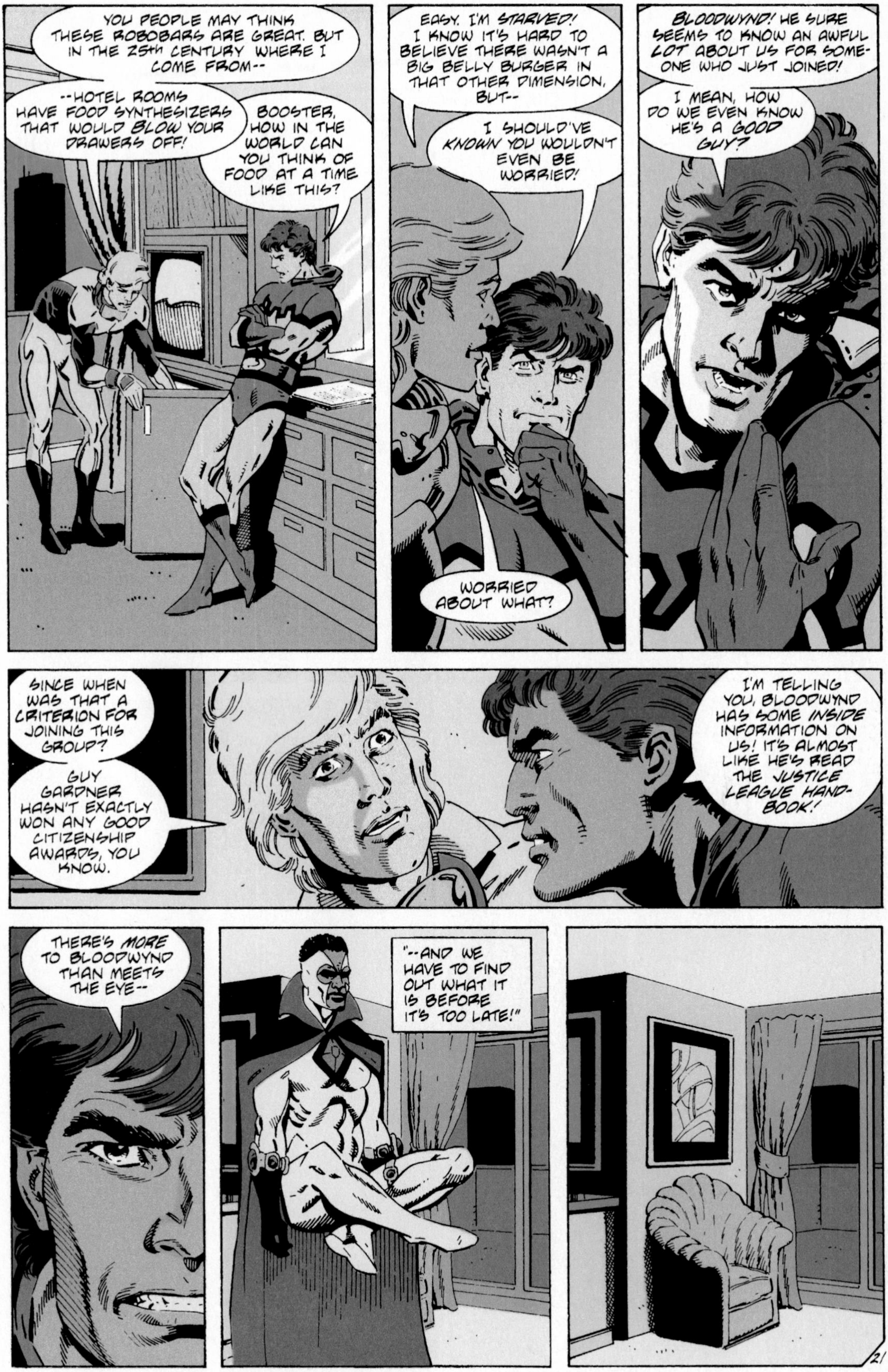
YOU PEOPLE MAY THINK THESE ROBOBARS ARE GREAT. BUT IN THE 25th CENTURY WHERE I COME FROM--
--HOTEL ROOMS HAVE FOOD SYNTHESIZERS THAT WOULD BLOW YOUR DRAWERS OFF!
BOOSTER, HOW IN THE WORLD CAN YOU THINK OF FOOD AT A TIME LIKE THIS?
EASY. I'M STARVED! I KNOW IT'S HARD TO BELIEVE THERE WASN'T A BIG BELLY BURGER IN THAT OTHER DIMENSION, BUT--
I SHOULD'VE KNOWN YOU WOULDN'T EVEN BE WORRIED!
WORRIED ABOUT WHAT?
BLOODWYND! HE SURE SEEMS TO KNOW AN AWFUL LOT ABOUT US FOR SOME-ONE WHO JUST JOINED!
I MEAN, HOW DO WE EVEN KNOW HE'S A GOOD GUY?
SINCE WHEN WAS THAT A CRITERION FOR JOINING THIS GROUP?
GUY GARDNER HASN'T EXACTLY WON ANY GOOD CITIZENSHIP AWARDS, YOU KNOW.
I'M TELLING YOU, BLOODWYND HAS SOME INSIDE INFORMATION ON US! IT'S ALMOST LIKE HE'S READ THE JUSTICE LEAGUE HAND-BOOK!
THERE'S MORE TO BLOODWYND THAN MEETS THE EYE--
"--AND WE HAVE TO FIND OUT WHAT IT IS BEFORE IT'S TOO LATE!"

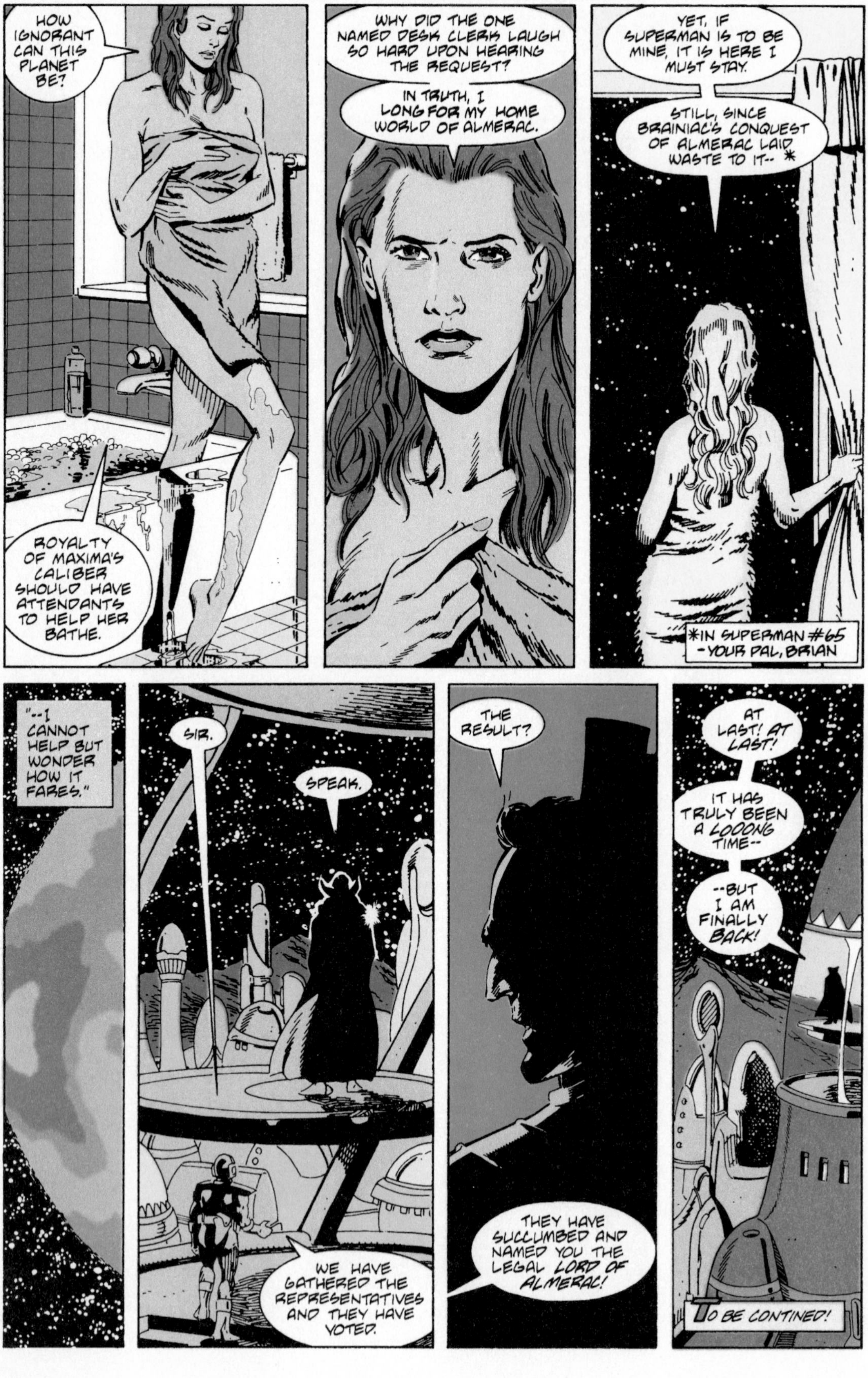
HOW IGNORANT CAN THIS PLANET BE?
ROYALTY OF MAXIMA'S CALIBER SHOULD HAVE ATTENDANTS TO HELP HER BATHE.
WHY DID THE ONE NAMED DESK CLERK LAUGH SO HARD UPON HEARING THE REQUEST?
IN TRUTH, I LONG FOR MY HOME WORLD OF ALMERAC.
YET, IF SUPERMAN IS TO BE MINE, IT IS HERE I MUST STAY.
STILL, SINCE BRAINIAC'S CONQUEST OF ALMERAC LAID WASTE TO IT-- *
*IN SUPERMAN #65 -YOUR PAL, BRIAN
"--I CANNOT HELP BUT WONDER HOW IT FARES."
SIR.
SPEAK.
WE HAVE GATHERED THE REPRESENTATIVES AND THEY HAVE VOTED.
THE RESULT?
THEY HAVE SUCCUMBED AND NAMED YOU THE LEGAL LORD OF ALMERAC!
AT LAST! AT LAST!
IT HAS TRULY BEEN A LOOONG TIME--
--BUT I AM FINALLY BACK!
TO BE CONTINED!

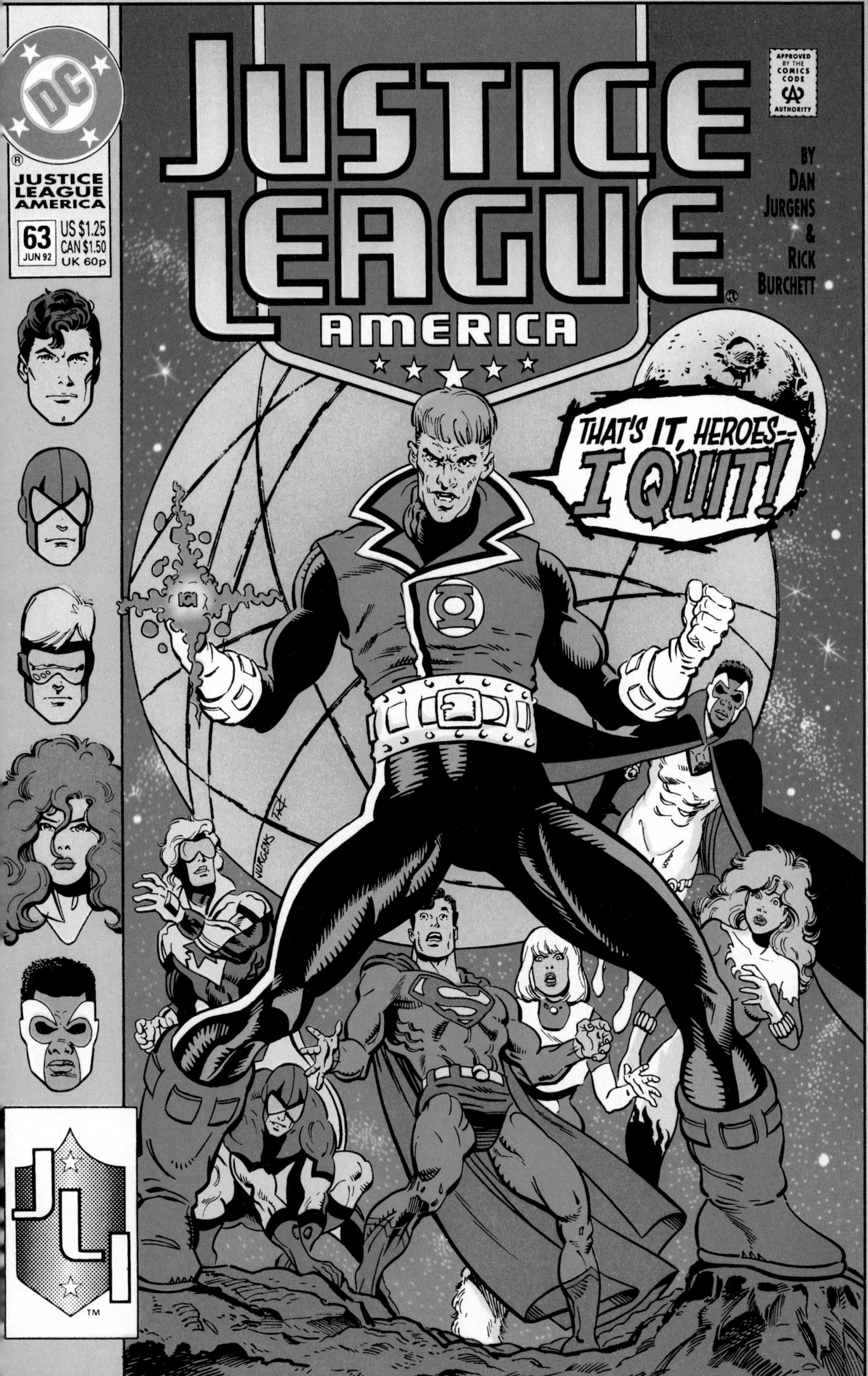
DC
JUSTICE LEAGUE AMERICA
63
JUN 92
US $1.25
CAN $1.50
UK 60p
JUSTICE LEAGUE AMERICA
APPROVED BY THE COMICS CODE AUTHORITY
BY DAN JURGENS & RICK BURCHETT
THAT'S IT, HEROES-- I QUIT!
JURGENS
JLI
TM

Cover art by **DAN JURGENS**
and **RICK BURCHETT**

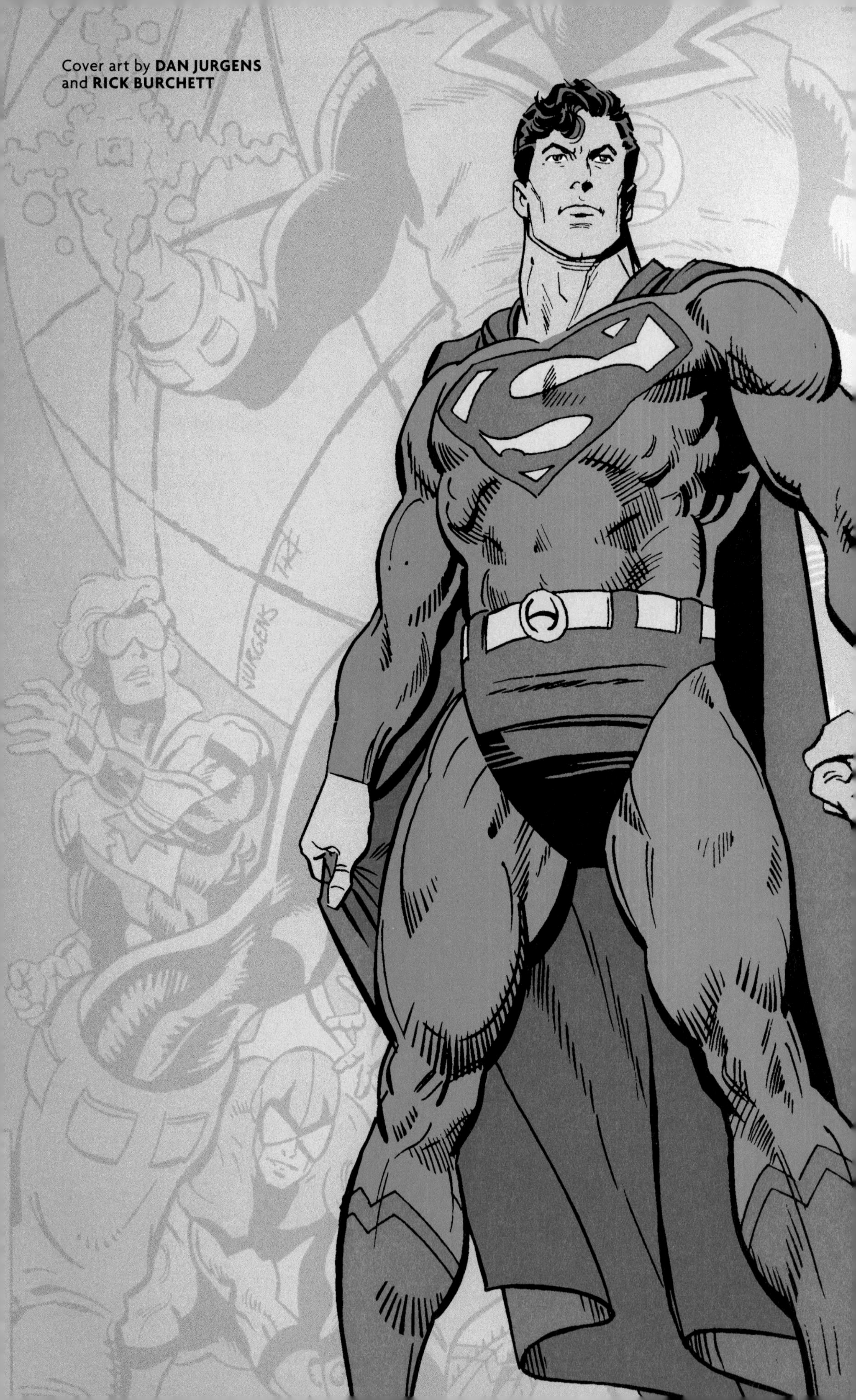
JURGENS

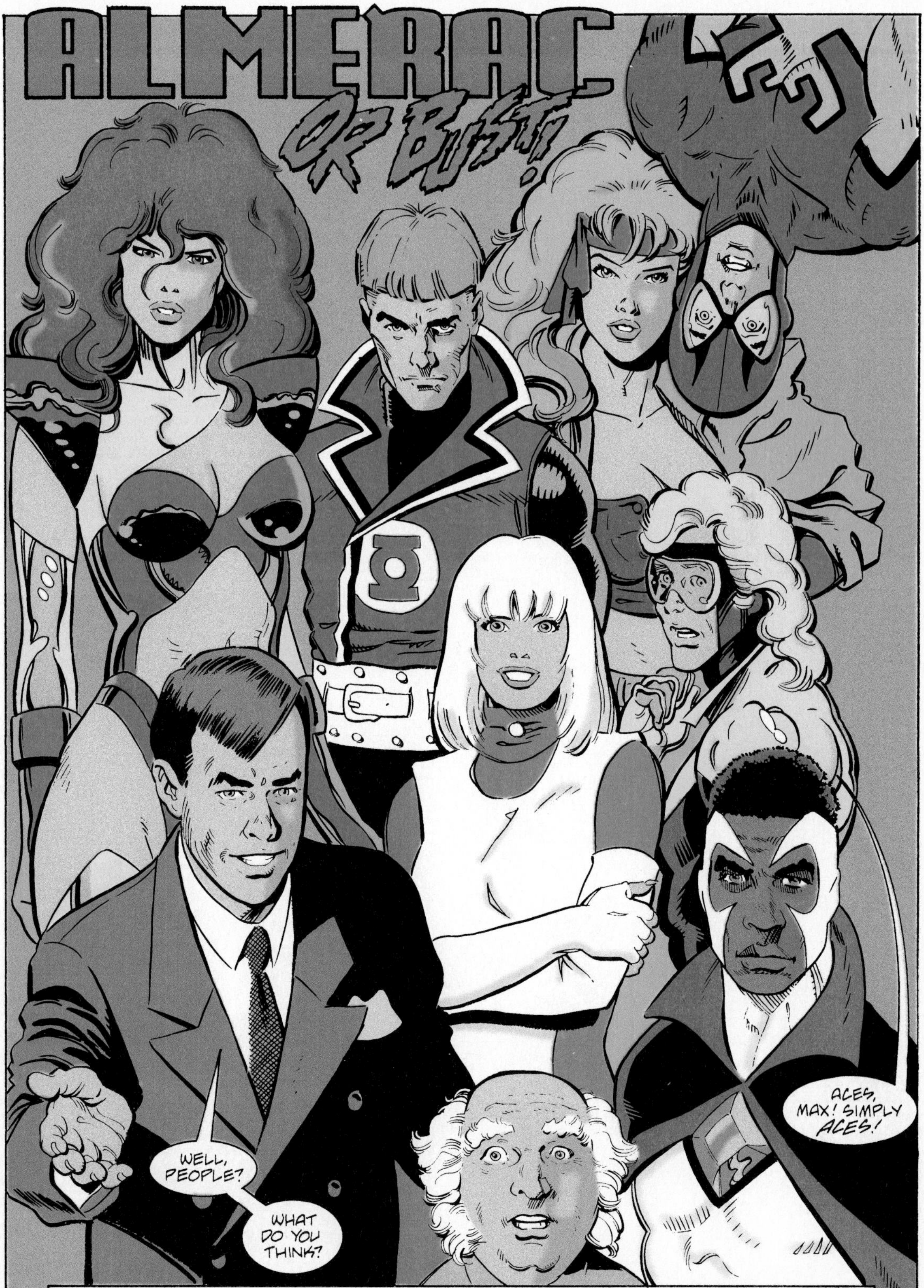
ALMERAC OR BUST!
WELL, PEOPLE?
WHAT DO YOU THINK?
ACES, MAX! SIMPLY ACES!

DAN JURGENS story/drawing RICK BURCHETT finished inks WILLIE SCHUBERT letters GENE D'ANGELO colors BRIAN AUGUSTYN spiritual guide

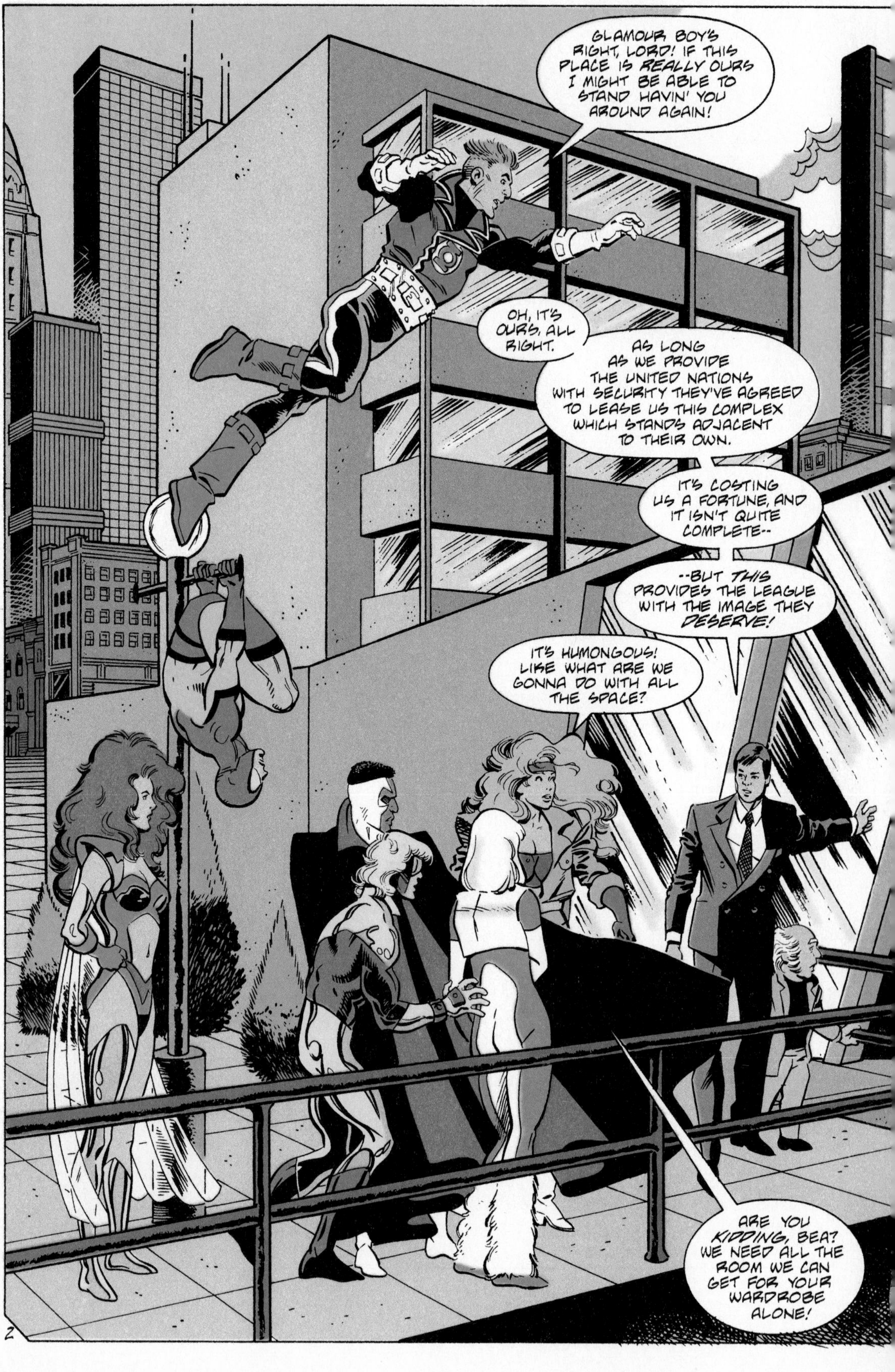
GLAMOUR BOY'S RIGHT, LORD! IF THIS PLACE IS REALLY OURS I MIGHT BE ABLE TO STAND HAVIN' YOU AROUND AGAIN!
OH, IT'S OURS, ALL RIGHT.
AS LONG AS WE PROVIDE THE UNITED NATIONS WITH SECURITY THEY'VE AGREED TO LEASE US THIS COMPLEX WHICH STANDS ADJACENT TO THEIR OWN.
IT'S COSTING US A FORTUNE, AND IT ISN'T QUITE COMPLETE--
--BUT THIS PROVIDES THE LEAGUE WITH THE IMAGE THEY DESERVE!
IT'S HUMONGOUS! LIKE WHAT ARE WE GONNA DO WITH ALL THE SPACE?
ARE YOU KIDDING, BEA? WE NEED ALL THE ROOM WE CAN GET FOR YOUR WARDROBE ALONE!

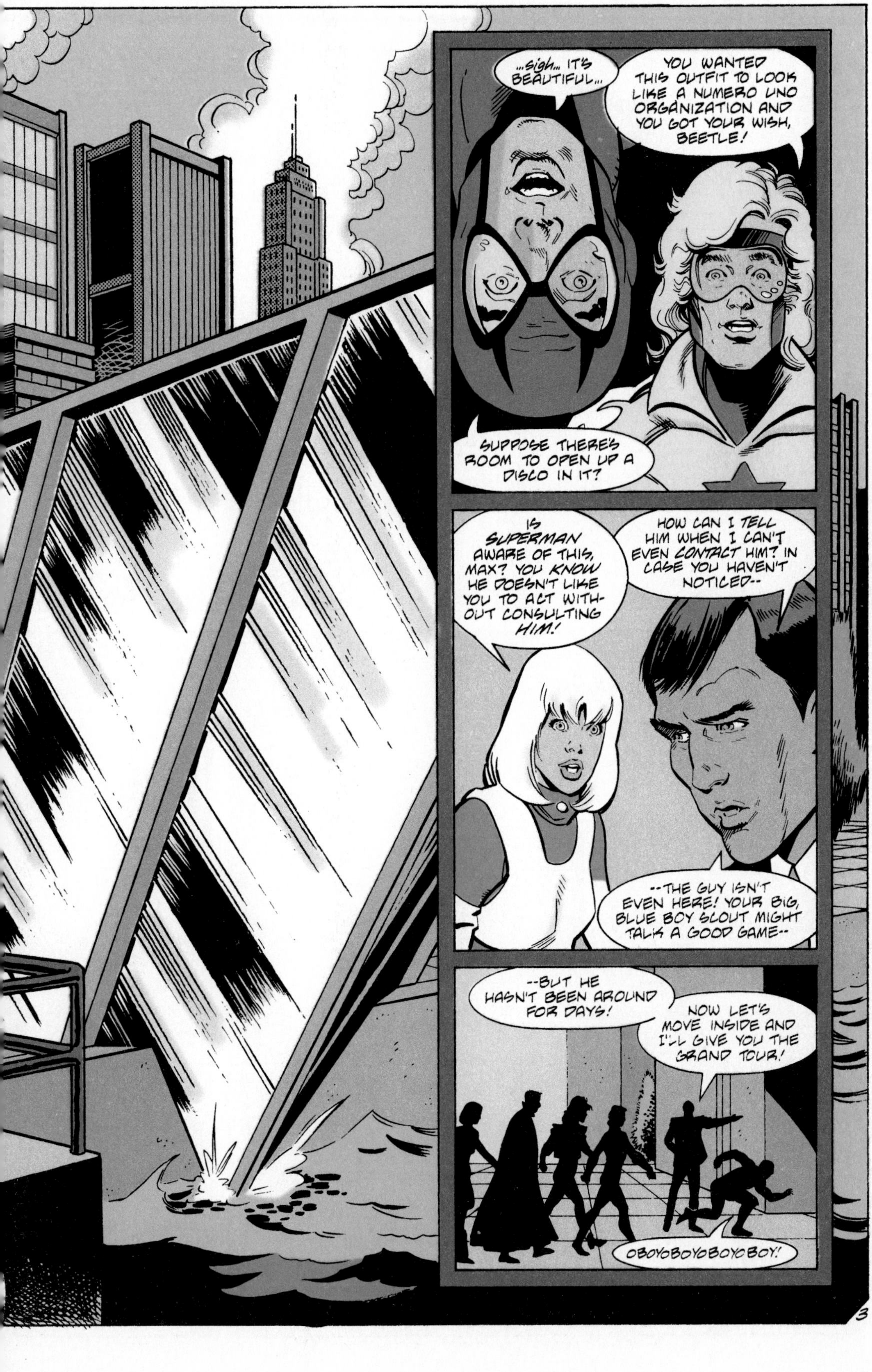

...sigh... IT'S BEAUTIFUL...
YOU WANTED THIS OUTFIT TO LOOK LIKE A NUMERO UNO ORGANIZATION AND YOU GOT YOUR WISH, BEETLE!
SUPPOSE THERE'S ROOM TO OPEN UP A DISCO IN IT?
IS SUPERMAN AWARE OF THIS, MAX? YOU KNOW HE DOESN'T LIKE YOU TO ACT WITH-OUT CONSULTING HIM!
HOW CAN I TELL HIM WHEN I CAN'T EVEN CONTACT HIM? IN CASE YOU HAVEN'T NOTICED--
--THE GUY ISN'T EVEN HERE! YOUR BIG, BLUE BOY SCOUT MIGHT TALK A GOOD GAME--
--BUT HE HASN'T BEEN AROUND FOR DAYS!
NOW LET'S MOVE INSIDE AND I'LL GIVE YOU THE GRAND TOUR!
OBOYOBOYOBOYOBOY!

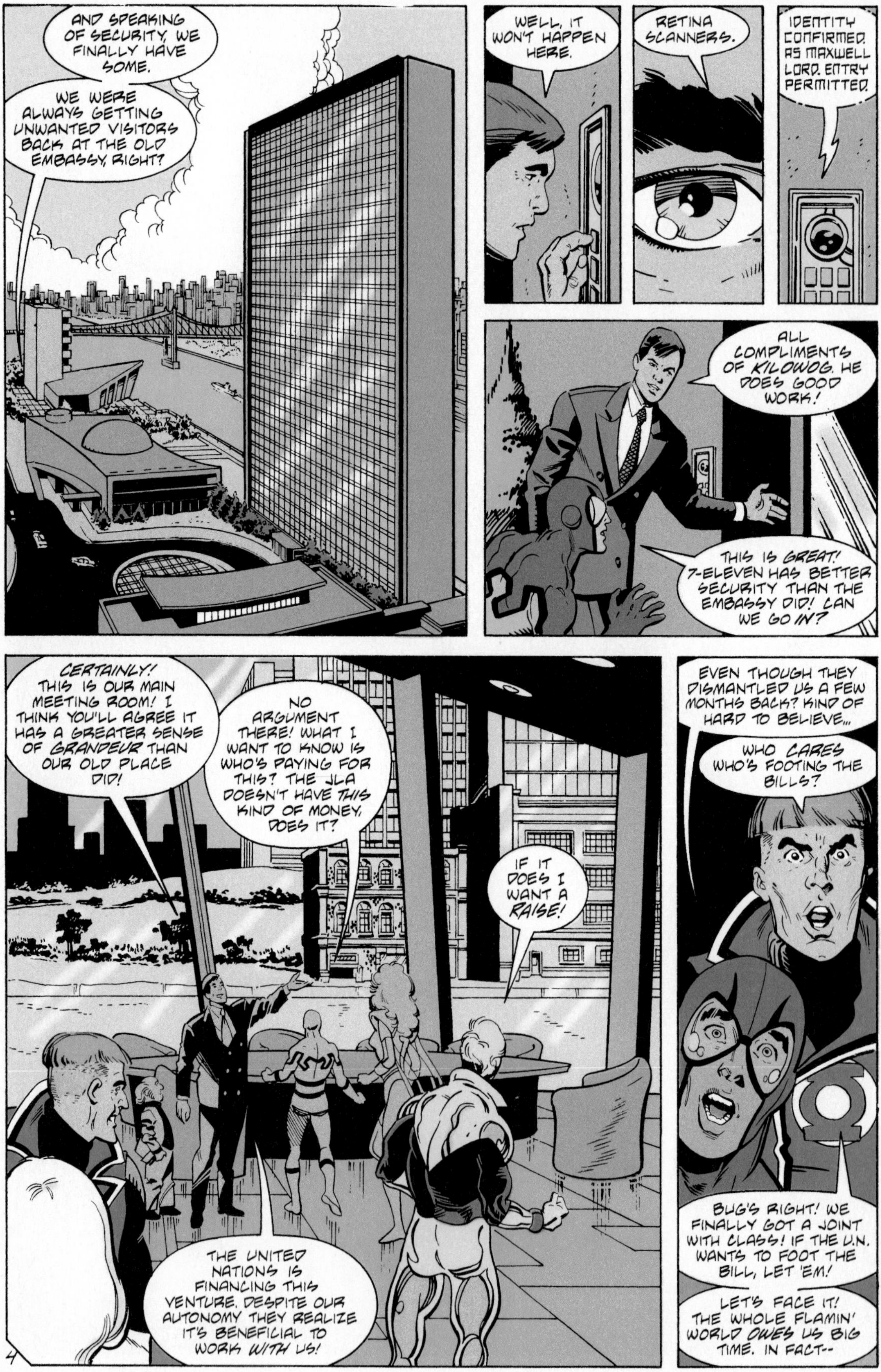

AND SPEAKING OF SECURITY, WE FINALLY HAVE SOME.
WE WERE ALWAYS GETTING UNWANTED VISITORS BACK AT THE OLD EMBASSY, RIGHT?
WELL, IT WON'T HAPPEN HERE.
RETINA SCANNERS.
IDENTITY CONFIRMED. AS MAXWELL LORD. ENTRY PERMITTED.
ALL COMPLIMENTS OF KILOWOG. HE DOES GOOD WORK!
THIS IS GREAT! 7-ELEVEN HAS BETTER SECURITY THAN THE EMBASSY DID! CAN WE GO IN?
CERTAINLY! THIS IS OUR MAIN MEETING ROOM! I THINK YOU'LL AGREE IT HAS A GREATER SENSE OF GRANDEUR THAN OUR OLD PLACE DID!
NO ARGUMENT THERE! WHAT I WANT TO KNOW IS WHO'S PAYING FOR THIS? THE JLA DOESN'T HAVE THIS KIND OF MONEY, DOES IT?
IF IT DOES I WANT A RAISE!
THE UNITED NATIONS IS FINANCING THIS VENTURE. DESPITE OUR AUTONOMY THEY REALIZE IT'S BENEFICIAL TO WORK WITH US!
EVEN THOUGH THEY DISMANTLED US A FEW MONTHS BACK? KIND OF HARD TO BELIEVE...
WHO CARES WHO'S FOOTING THE BILLS?
BUG'S RIGHT! WE FINALLY GOT A JOINT WITH CLASS! IF THE U.N. WANTS TO FOOT THE BILL, LET 'EM!
LET'S FACE IT! THE WHOLE FLAMIN' WORLD OWES US BIG TIME. IN FACT--

"-- THE WHOLE *UNIVERSE* DOES TOO!"

I CAN'T *BELIEVE* I ESCAPED ALL THOSE GUN SHIPS!

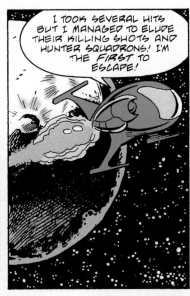

I TOOK SEVERAL HITS BUT I MANAGED TO ELUDE THEIR *KILLING* SHOTS AND HUNTER SQUADRONS! I'M THE *FIRST* TO ESCAPE!

BUT I'VE MADE IT! EARTH IS ONLY *MINUTES* AWAY! IF I CAN ONLY FIND *HER* WE MAY YET BE SAVED!

WHO KNOWS HOW MANY HAVE DIED? TENS -- *HUNDREDS* OF THOUSANDS? MILLIONS, PERHAPS.

ALMERAC IS BEING DESTROYED --

-- AND ONLY *MAXIMA* CAN SAVE US!

SHE IS OUR *QUEEN!* OUR LEADER, BRED TO RULE AND CONQUER! ONLY MAXIMA CAN DELIVER US FROM THE *MADMAN* WHO --

WARNING! WARNING!

COMPUTER? WHAT IS IT? WHAT'S *WRONG?*

A STRAY SHOT DESTROYED THE ATMOSPHERIC ENTRY SYSTEM. THIS CRAFT WILL BE UNABLE TO LAND INTACT.

I DON'T *CARE!* I MUST ALERT *HER HIGHNESS!* IF I CAN LOCATE HER WITH MY SENSORS --

THIS CRAFT IS INCAPABLE OF A SAFE LANDING. THE LIKELIHOOD OF YOUR SURVIVAL --

DOESN'T MATTER! I *HAVE* TO TRY!

ALL SYSTEMS HAVE FAILED.

ABORT LANDING. REPEAT. ABORT --

SPLASSH

5

BOOSTER, BEETLE, COME WITH ME, PLEASE. WHILE THE OTHERS EXPLORE ON THEIR OWN--

--I WANT TO SHOW YOU SOMETHING OF PARTICULAR INTEREST.

FSSS

WE'RE GOING *DOWN*?

NATURALLY. WE ADDED SUBTERRANEAN LEVELS FOR SEVERAL REASONS.

ONE: WE NEEDED THE ROOM.

TWO: IT PROVIDES AN ADDED SAFETY FACTOR FOR OUR WEAPONS DEVELOPMENT, SECURITY AND LABORATORY STATIONS.

LAB? WE HAVE A LAB? I THINK I'M IN *HEAVEN*!

IT'S ALL YOURS, BEETLE! RIGHT DOWN AT THE END OF THE HALL! AND IF YOU LOOK OUT THE WINDOW--

--I THINK YOU'LL SEE SOMETHING THAT WILL *REALLY* MAKE YOU HAPPY!

SEXY, PROVOCATIVE MERMAIDS SWIMMING BEFORE OUR VERY EYES?

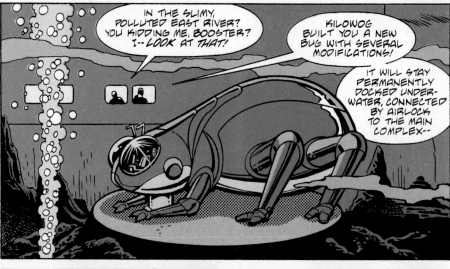

IN THE SLIMY, POLLUTED EAST RIVER? YOU KIDDING ME, BOOSTER? I--LOOK AT THAT!

KILOWOG BUILT YOU A NEW BUG WITH SEVERAL MODIFICATIONS!

IT WILL STAY PERMANENTLY DOCKED UNDER-WATER, CONNECTED BY AIRLOCK TO THE MAIN COMPLEX--

THAT'S IT! I *KNOW* I'M IN HEAVEN!

OF COURSE. WE BUILT THE COMPLEX WITH *EVERYBODY'S* WISHES IN MIND.

YOU TWO, FIRE, ICE, BLOODWYND. EVEN--

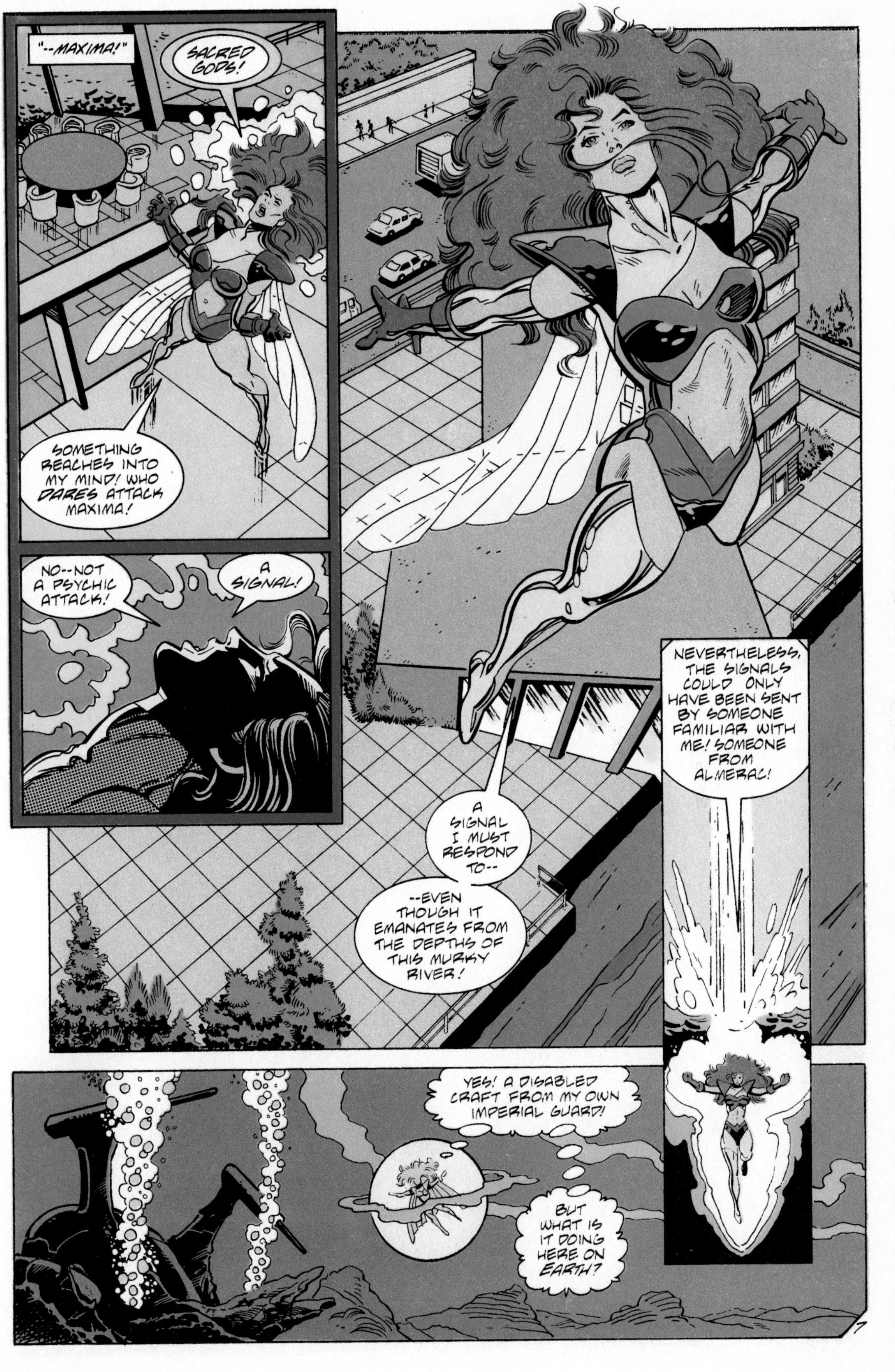

"--MAXIMA!"
SACRED GODS!
SOMETHING REACHES INTO MY MIND! WHO DARES ATTACK MAXIMA!
NO--NOT A PSYCHIC ATTACK!
A SIGNAL!
A SIGNAL I MUST RESPOND TO--
--EVEN THOUGH IT EMANATES FROM THE DEPTHS OF THIS MURKY RIVER!
NEVERTHELESS, THE SIGNALS COULD ONLY HAVE BEEN SENT BY SOMEONE FAMILIAR WITH ME! SOMEONE FROM ALMERAC!
YES! A DISABLED CRAFT FROM MY OWN IMPERIAL GUARD!
BUT WHAT IS IT DOING HERE ON EARTH?

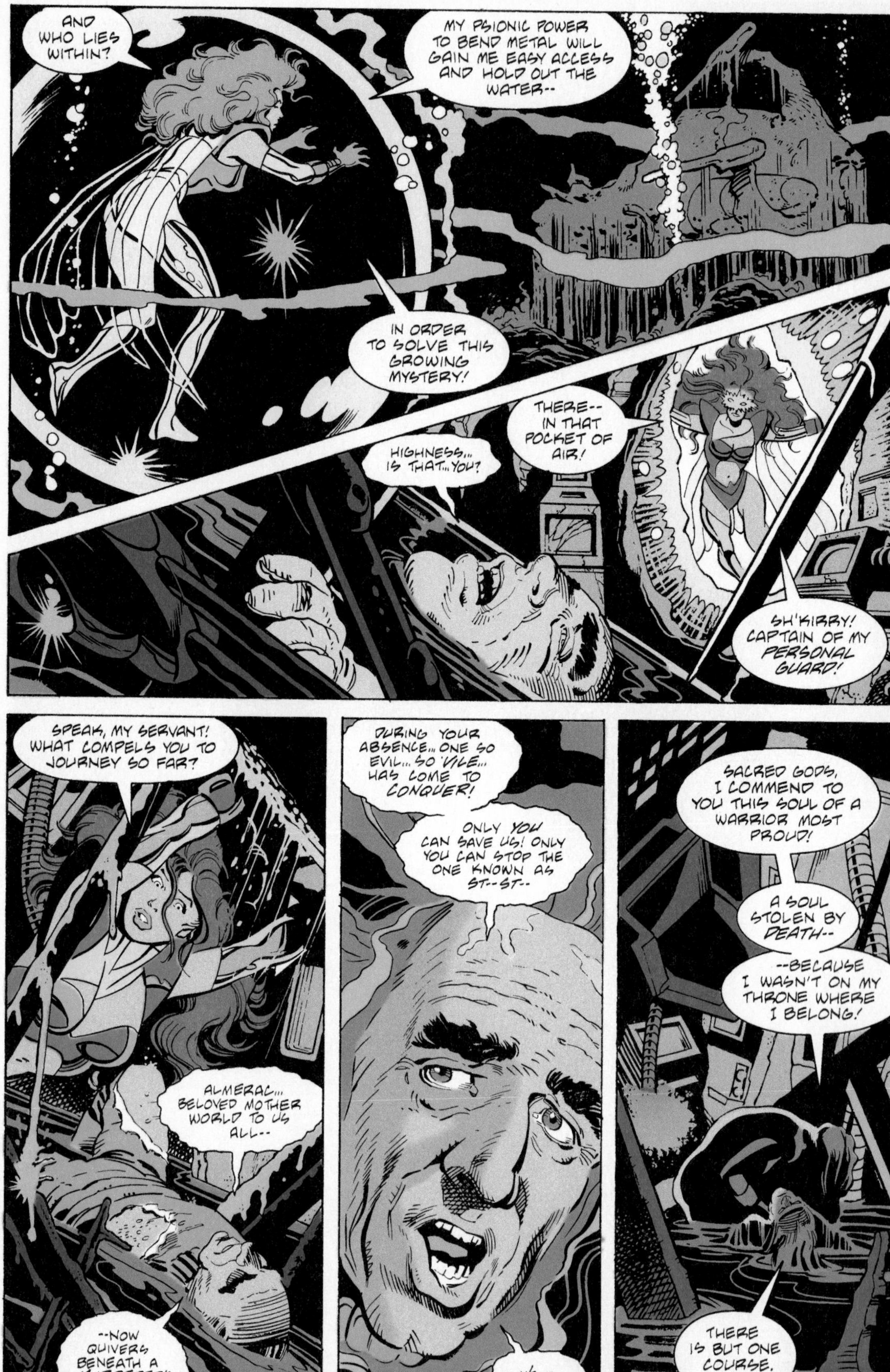
AND WHO LIES WITHIN?
MY PSIONIC POWER TO BEND METAL WILL GAIN ME EASY ACCESS AND HOLD OUT THE WATER--
IN ORDER TO SOLVE THIS GROWING MYSTERY!
THERE-- IN THAT POCKET OF AIR!
HIGHNESS... IS THAT... YOU?
SH'KIRRY! CAPTAIN OF MY PERSONAL GUARD!
SPEAK, MY SERVANT! WHAT COMPELS YOU TO JOURNEY SO FAR?
ALMERAC... BELOVED MOTHER WORLD TO US ALL--
--NOW QUIVERS BENEATH A MURDERER'S BOOT HEEL!
DURING YOUR ABSENCE... ONE SO EVIL... SO VILE... HAS COME TO CONQUER!
ONLY YOU CAN SAVE US! ONLY YOU CAN STOP THE ONE KNOWN AS ST--ST--
--uhnnn.
SACRED GODS, I COMMEND TO YOU THIS SOUL OF A WARRIOR MOST PROUD!
A SOUL STOLEN BY DEATH--
--BECAUSE I WASN'T ON MY THRONE WHERE I BELONG!
THERE IS BUT ONE COURSE. I--

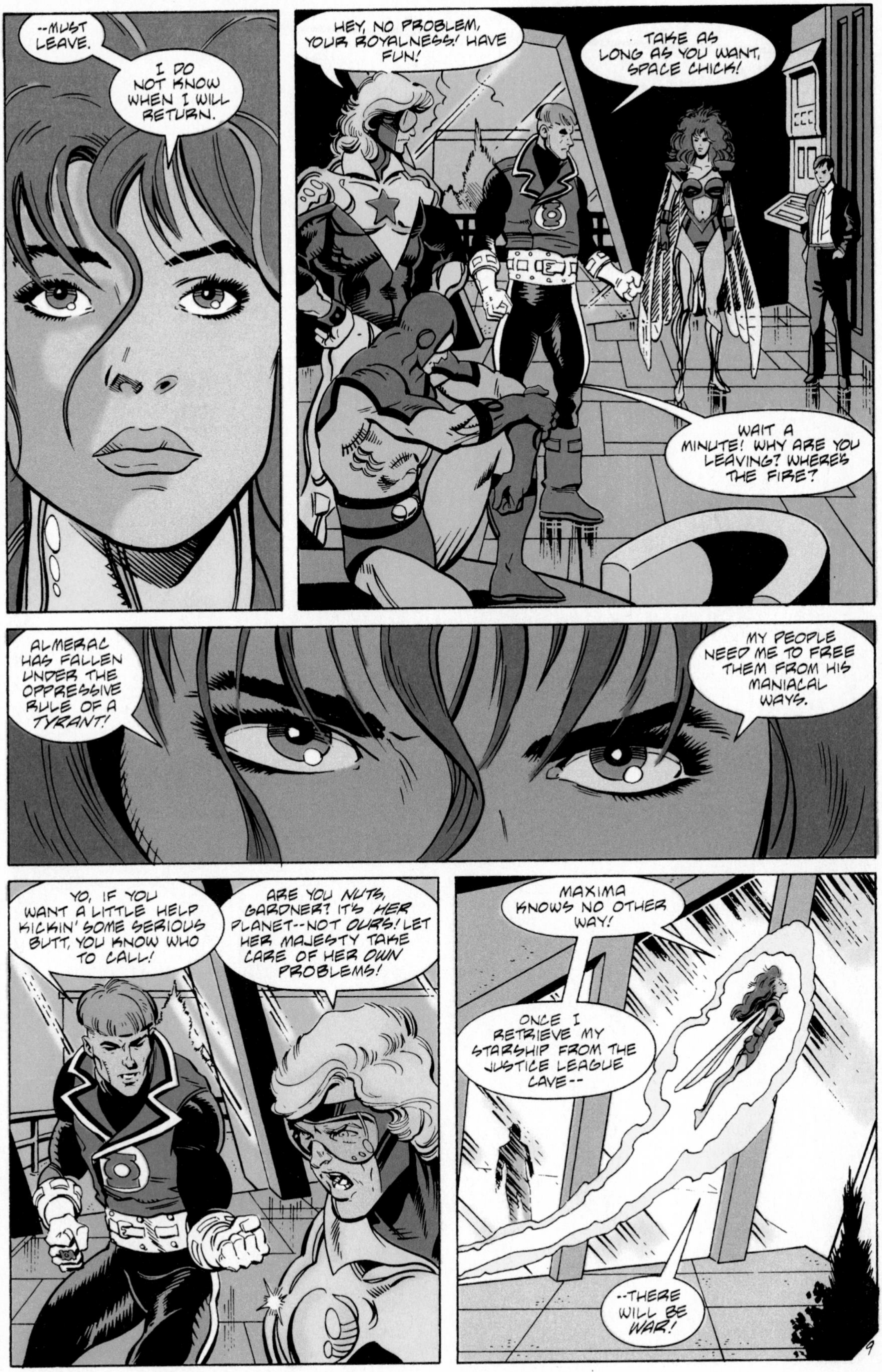
--MUST LEAVE.
I DO NOT KNOW WHEN I WILL RETURN.
HEY, NO PROBLEM, YOUR ROYALNESS! HAVE FUN!
TAKE AS LONG AS YOU WANT, SPACE CHICK!
WAIT A MINUTE! WHY ARE YOU LEAVING? WHERE'S THE FIRE?
ALMERAC HAS FALLEN UNDER THE OPPRESSIVE RULE OF A TYRANT!
MY PEOPLE NEED ME TO FREE THEM FROM HIS MANIACAL WAYS.
YO, IF YOU WANT A LITTLE HELP KICKIN' SOME SERIOUS BUTT, YOU KNOW WHO TO CALL!
ARE YOU NUTS, GARDNER? IT'S HER PLANET--NOT OURS! LET HER MAJESTY TAKE CARE OF HER OWN PROBLEMS!
MAXIMA KNOWS NO OTHER WAY!
ONCE I RETRIEVE MY STARSHIP FROM THE JUSTICE LEAGUE CAVE--
--THERE WILL BE WAR!
9

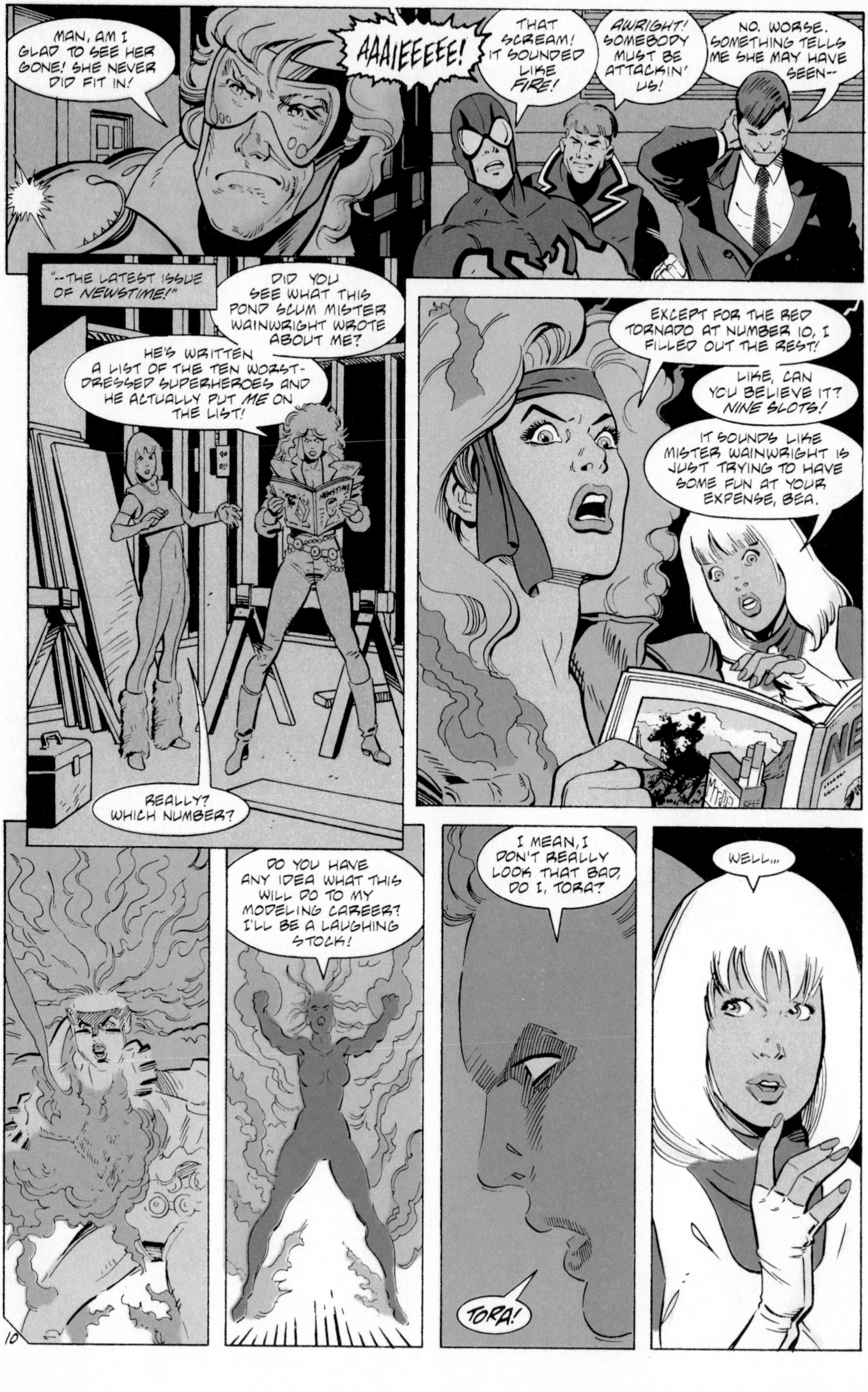

MAN, AM I GLAD TO SEE HER GONE! SHE NEVER DID FIT IN!
AAAIEEEEEE!
THAT SCREAM! IT SOUNDED LIKE FIRE!
AWRIGHT! SOMEBODY MUST BE ATTACKIN' US!
NO. WORSE. SOMETHING TELLS ME SHE MAY HAVE SEEN--
"--THE LATEST ISSUE OF NEWSTIME!"
DID YOU SEE WHAT THIS POND SCUM MISTER WAINWRIGHT WROTE ABOUT ME?
HE'S WRITTEN A LIST OF THE TEN WORST-DRESSED SUPERHEROES AND HE ACTUALLY PUT ME ON THE LIST!
NEWSTIME
REALLY? WHICH NUMBER?
EXCEPT FOR THE RED TORNADO AT NUMBER 10, I FILLED OUT THE REST!
LIKE, CAN YOU BELIEVE IT? NINE SLOTS!
IT SOUNDS LIKE MISTER WAINWRIGHT IS JUST TRYING TO HAVE SOME FUN AT YOUR EXPENSE, BEA.
DO YOU HAVE ANY IDEA WHAT THIS WILL DO TO MY MODELING CAREER? I'LL BE A LAUGHING STOCK!
I MEAN, I DON'T REALLY LOOK THAT BAD, DO I, TORA?
TORA!
WELL...

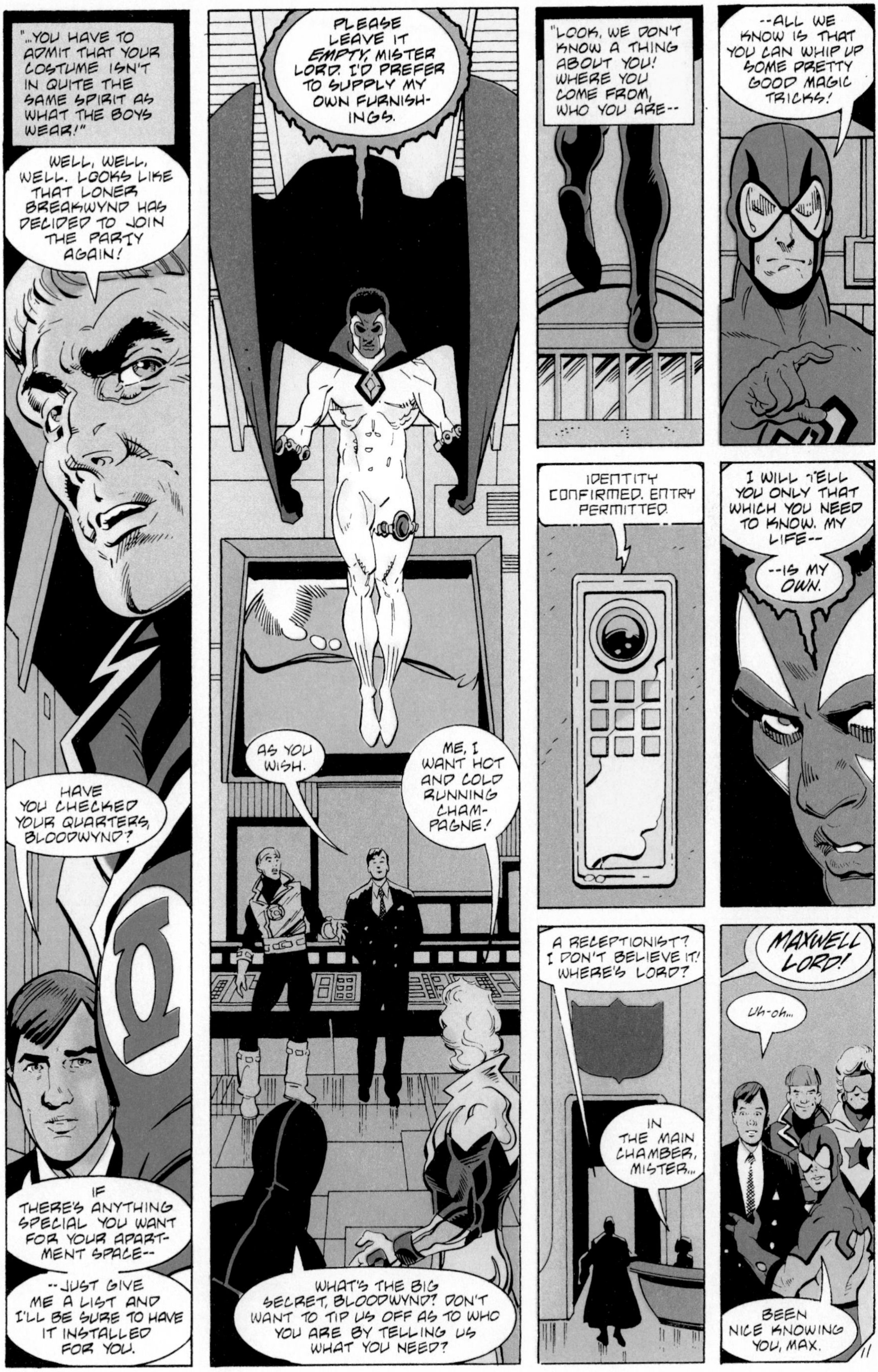

"...YOU HAVE TO ADMIT THAT YOUR COSTUME ISN'T IN QUITE THE SAME SPIRIT AS WHAT THE BOYS WEAR!"
WELL, WELL, WELL. LOOKS LIKE THAT LONER BREAKWYND HAS DECIDED TO JOIN THE PARTY AGAIN!
HAVE YOU CHECKED YOUR QUARTERS, BLOODWYND?
IF THERE'S ANYTHING SPECIAL YOU WANT FOR YOUR APARTMENT SPACE--
--JUST GIVE ME A LIST AND I'LL BE SURE TO HAVE IT INSTALLED FOR YOU.
PLEASE LEAVE IT EMPTY, MISTER LORD. I'D PREFER TO SUPPLY MY OWN FURNISHINGS.
AS YOU WISH.
ME, I WANT HOT AND COLD RUNNING CHAMPAGNE!
WHAT'S THE BIG SECRET, BLOODWYND? DON'T WANT TO TIP US OFF AS TO WHO YOU ARE BY TELLING US WHAT YOU NEED?
"LOOK, WE DON'T KNOW A THING ABOUT YOU! WHERE YOU COME FROM, WHO YOU ARE--
--ALL WE KNOW IS THAT YOU CAN WHIP UP SOME PRETTY GOOD MAGIC TRICKS!
IDENTITY CONFIRMED. ENTRY PERMITTED.
I WILL TELL YOU ONLY THAT WHICH YOU NEED TO KNOW. MY LIFE--
--IS MY OWN.
A RECEPTIONIST? I DON'T BELIEVE IT! WHERE'S LORD?
IN THE MAIN CHAMBER, MISTER...
MAXWELL LORD!
Uh-oh...
BEEN NICE KNOWING YOU, MAX.

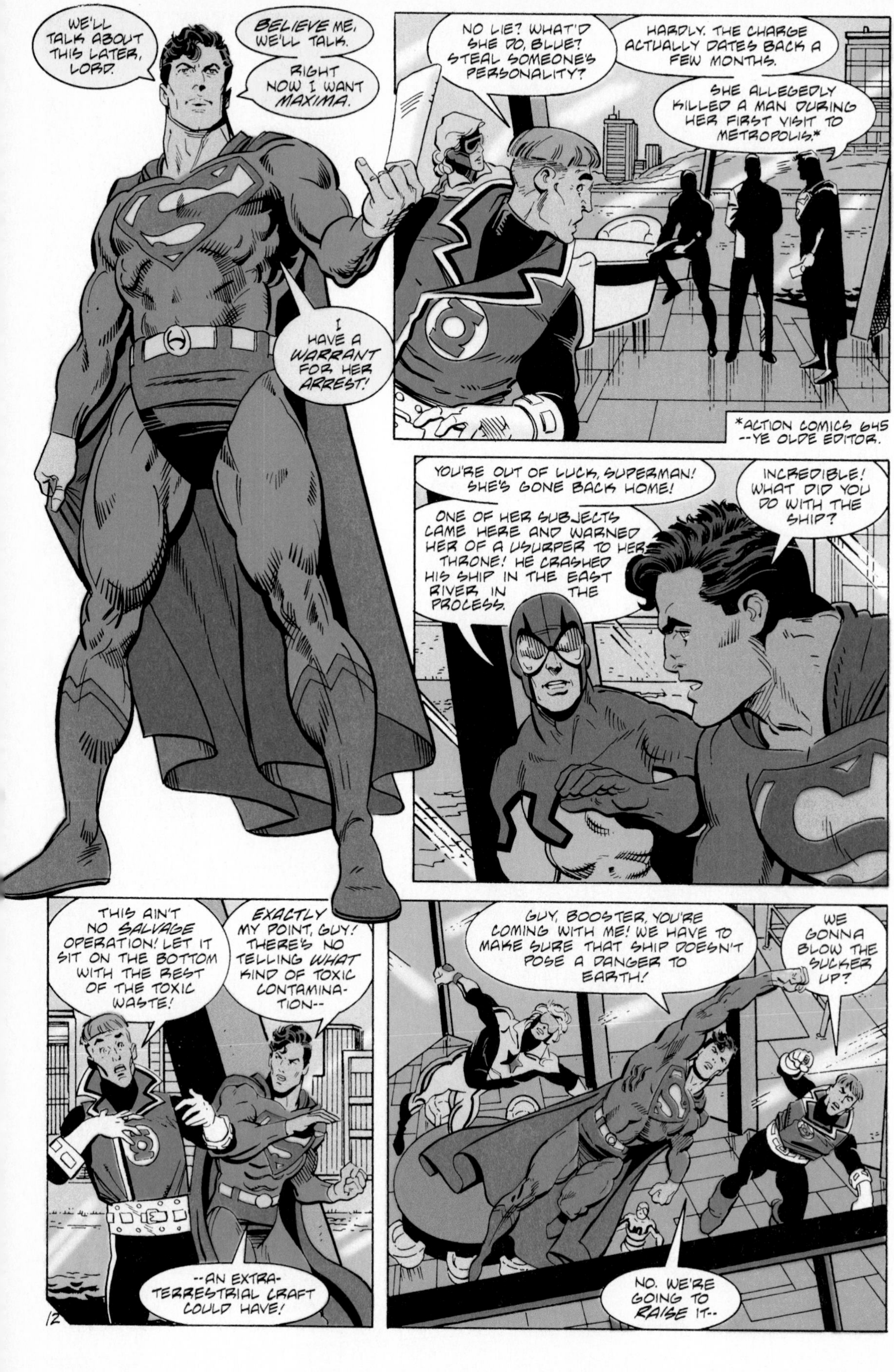
WE'LL TALK ABOUT THIS LATER, LORD.
BELIEVE ME, WE'LL TALK.
RIGHT NOW I WANT MAXIMA.
I HAVE A WARRANT FOR HER ARREST!
NO LIE? WHAT'D SHE DO, BLUE? STEAL SOMEONE'S PERSONALITY?
HARDLY. THE CHARGE ACTUALLY DATES BACK A FEW MONTHS.
SHE ALLEGEDLY KILLED A MAN DURING HER FIRST VISIT TO METROPOLIS.*
*ACTION COMICS 645 --YE OLDE EDITOR.
YOU'RE OUT OF LUCK, SUPERMAN! SHE'S GONE BACK HOME!
ONE OF HER SUBJECTS CAME HERE AND WARNED HER OF A USURPER TO HER THRONE! HE CRASHED HIS SHIP IN THE EAST RIVER IN THE PROCESS.
INCREDIBLE! WHAT DID YOU DO WITH THE SHIP?
THIS AIN'T NO SALVAGE OPERATION! LET IT SIT ON THE BOTTOM WITH THE REST OF THE TOXIC WASTE!
EXACTLY MY POINT, GUY! THERE'S NO TELLING WHAT KIND OF TOXIC CONTAMINATION--
--AN EXTRA-TERRESTRIAL CRAFT COULD HAVE!
GUY, BOOSTER, YOU'RE COMING WITH ME! WE HAVE TO MAKE SURE THAT SHIP DOESN'T POSE A DANGER TO EARTH!
WE GONNA BLOW THE SUCKER UP?
NO. WE'RE GOING TO RAISE IT--

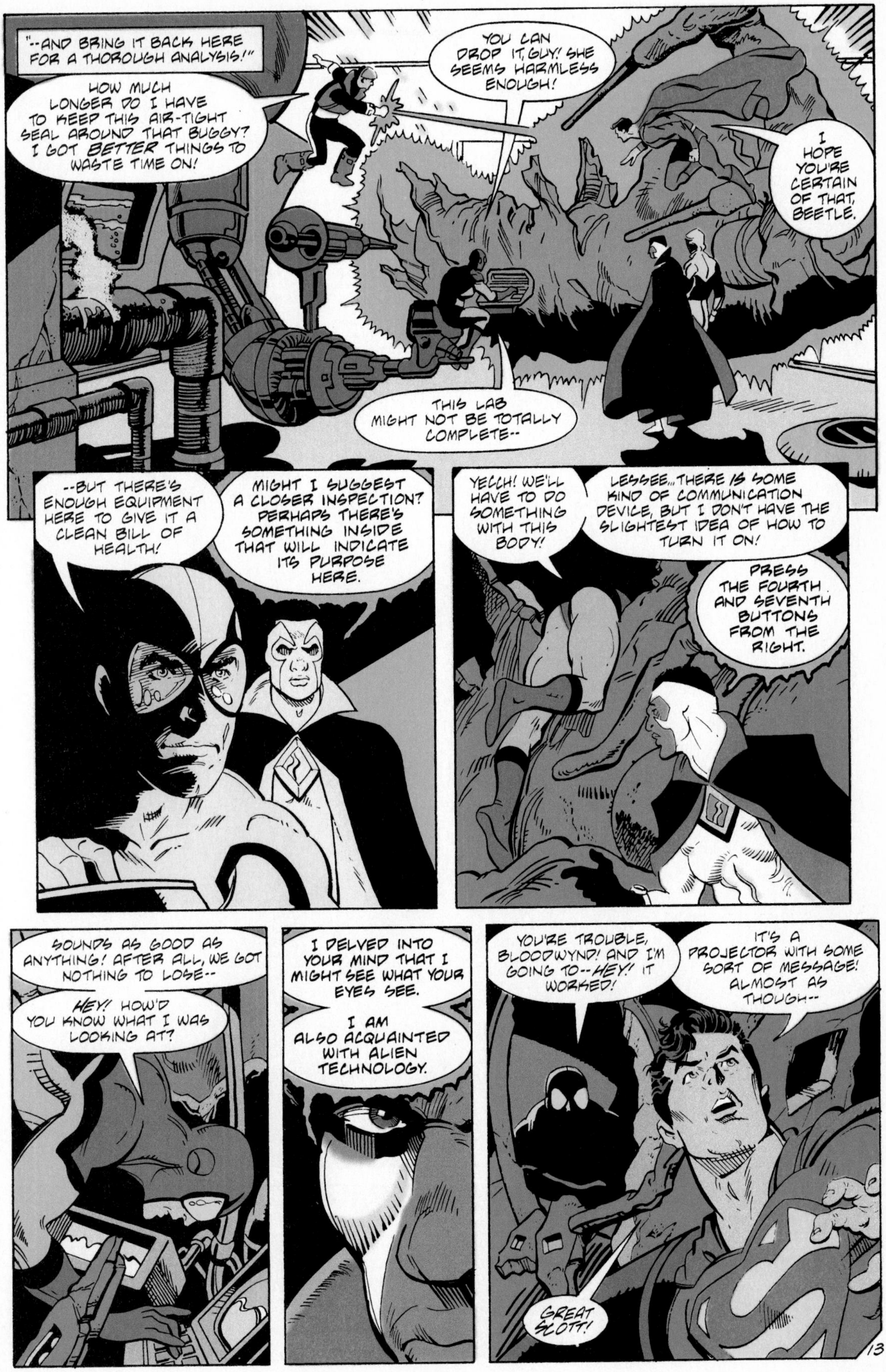
"--AND BRING IT BACK HERE FOR A THOROUGH ANALYSIS!"
HOW MUCH LONGER DO I HAVE TO KEEP THIS AIR-TIGHT SEAL AROUND THAT BUGGY? I GOT BETTER THINGS TO WASTE TIME ON!
YOU CAN DROP IT, GUY! SHE SEEMS HARMLESS ENOUGH!
I HOPE YOU'RE CERTAIN OF THAT, BEETLE.
THIS LAB MIGHT NOT BE TOTALLY COMPLETE--
--BUT THERE'S ENOUGH EQUIPMENT HERE TO GIVE IT A CLEAN BILL OF HEALTH!
MIGHT I SUGGEST A CLOSER INSPECTION? PERHAPS THERE'S SOMETHING INSIDE THAT WILL INDICATE ITS PURPOSE HERE.
YECCH! WE'LL HAVE TO DO SOMETHING WITH THIS BODY!
LESSEE... THERE IS SOME KIND OF COMMUNICATION DEVICE, BUT I DON'T HAVE THE SLIGHTEST IDEA OF HOW TO TURN IT ON!
PRESS THE FOURTH AND SEVENTH BUTTONS FROM THE RIGHT.
SOUNDS AS GOOD AS ANYTHING! AFTER ALL, WE GOT NOTHING TO LOSE--
HEY! HOW'D YOU KNOW WHAT I WAS LOOKING AT?
I DELVED INTO YOUR MIND THAT I MIGHT SEE WHAT YOUR EYES SEE.
I AM ALSO ACQUAINTED WITH ALIEN TECHNOLOGY.
YOU'RE TROUBLE, BLOODWYND! AND I'M GOING TO--HEY! IT WORKED!
IT'S A PROJECTOR WITH SOME SORT OF MESSAGE! ALMOST AS THOUGH--
GREAT SCOTT!

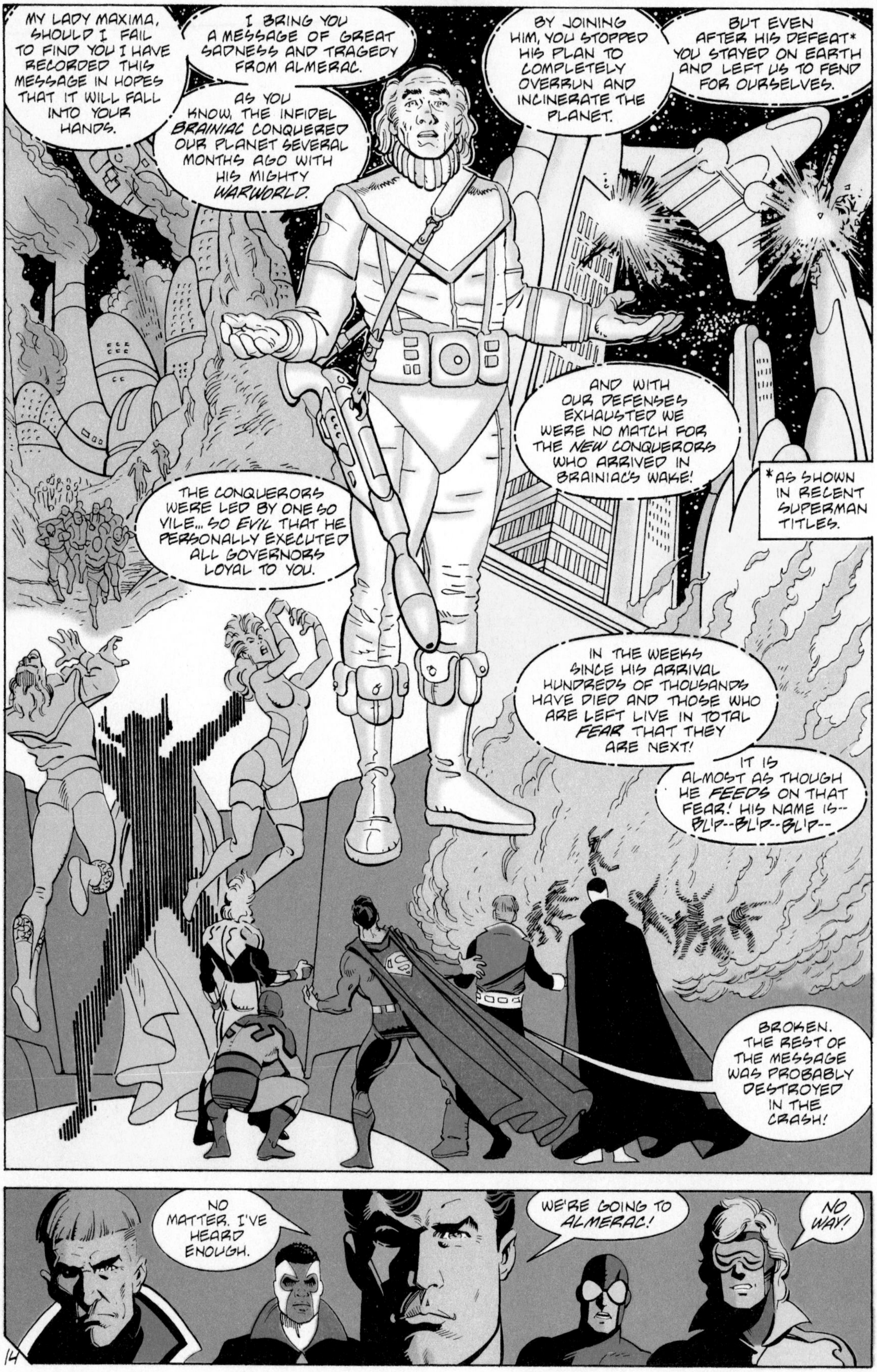
MY LADY MAXIMA, SHOULD I FAIL TO FIND YOU I HAVE RECORDED THIS MESSAGE IN HOPES THAT IT WILL FALL INTO YOUR HANDS.
I BRING YOU A MESSAGE OF GREAT SADNESS AND TRAGEDY FROM ALMERAC.
AS YOU KNOW, THE INFIDEL BRAINIAC CONQUERED OUR PLANET SEVERAL MONTHS AGO WITH HIS MIGHTY WARWORLD.
BY JOINING HIM, YOU STOPPED HIS PLAN TO COMPLETELY OVERRUN AND INCINERATE THE PLANET.
BUT EVEN AFTER HIS DEFEAT* YOU STAYED ON EARTH AND LEFT US TO FEND FOR OURSELVES.
AND WITH OUR DEFENSES EXHAUSTED WE WERE NO MATCH FOR THE NEW CONQUERORS WHO ARRIVED IN BRAINIAC'S WAKE!
*AS SHOWN IN RECENT SUPERMAN TITLES.
THE CONQUERORS WERE LED BY ONE SO VILE... SO EVIL THAT HE PERSONALLY EXECUTED ALL GOVERNORS LOYAL TO YOU.
IN THE WEEKS SINCE HIS ARRIVAL HUNDREDS OF THOUSANDS HAVE DIED AND THOSE WHO ARE LEFT LIVE IN TOTAL FEAR THAT THEY ARE NEXT!
IT IS ALMOST AS THOUGH HE FEEDS ON THAT FEAR! HIS NAME IS-- BLIP--BLIP--BLIP--
BROKEN. THE REST OF THE MESSAGE WAS PROBABLY DESTROYED IN THE CRASH!

NO MATTER. I'VE HEARD ENOUGH.
WE'RE GOING TO ALMERAC!
NO WAY!

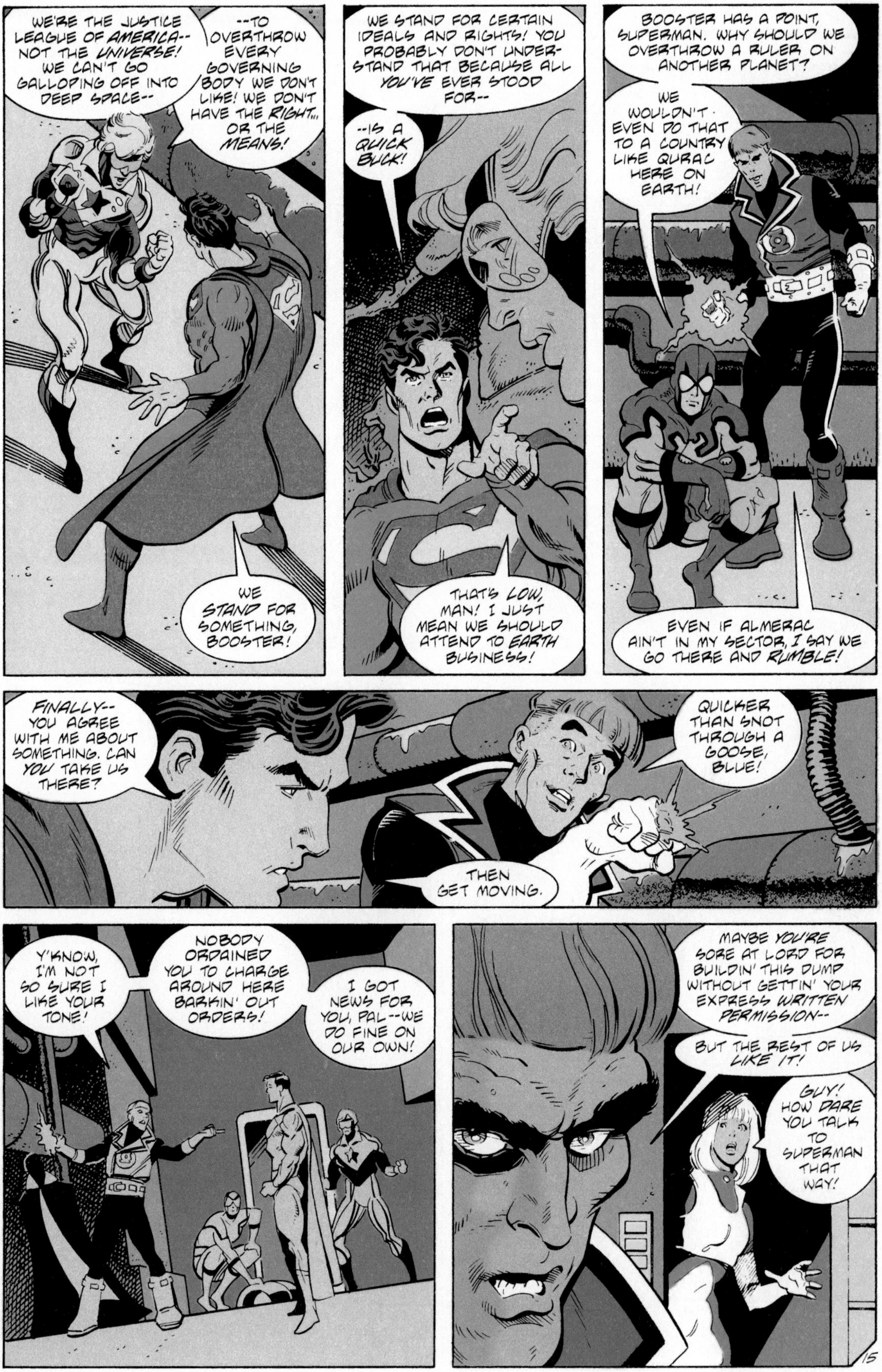
WE'RE THE JUSTICE LEAGUE OF AMERICA-- NOT THE UNIVERSE! WE CAN'T GO GALLOPING OFF INTO DEEP SPACE--
--TO OVERTHROW EVERY GOVERNING BODY WE DON'T LIKE! WE DON'T HAVE THE RIGHT... OR THE MEANS!
WE STAND FOR SOMETHING, BOOSTER!
WE STAND FOR CERTAIN IDEALS AND RIGHTS! YOU PROBABLY DON'T UNDERSTAND THAT BECAUSE ALL YOU'VE EVER STOOD FOR--
--IS A QUICK BUCK!
THAT'S LOW, MAN! I JUST MEAN WE SHOULD ATTEND TO EARTH BUSINESS!
BOOSTER HAS A POINT, SUPERMAN. WHY SHOULD WE OVERTHROW A RULER ON ANOTHER PLANET?
WE WOULDN'T EVEN DO THAT TO A COUNTRY LIKE QURAC HERE ON EARTH!
EVEN IF ALMERAC AIN'T IN MY SECTOR, I SAY WE GO THERE AND RUMBLE!
FINALLY-- YOU AGREE WITH ME ABOUT SOMETHING. CAN YOU TAKE US THERE?
QUICKER THAN SNOT THROUGH A GOOSE, BLUE!
THEN GET MOVING.
Y'KNOW, I'M NOT SO SURE I LIKE YOUR TONE!
NOBODY ORDAINED YOU TO CHARGE AROUND HERE BARKIN' OUT ORDERS!
I GOT NEWS FOR YOU, PAL--WE DO FINE ON OUR OWN!
MAYBE YOU'RE SORE AT LORD FOR BUILDIN' THIS DUMP WITHOUT GETTIN' YOUR EXPRESS WRITTEN PERMISSION--
BUT THE REST OF US LIKE IT!
GUY! HOW DARE YOU TALK TO SUPERMAN THAT WAY!
15

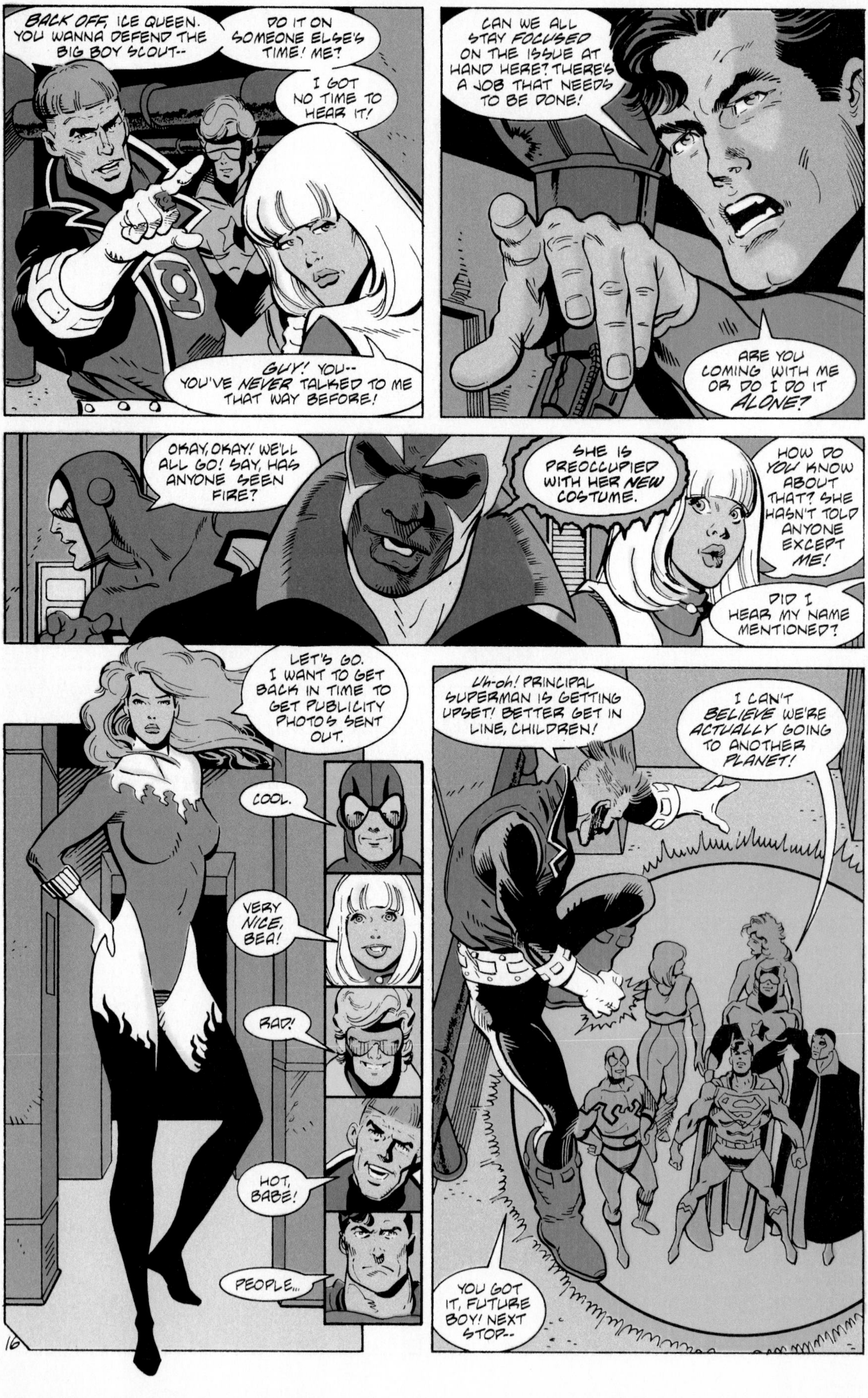
BACK OFF, ICE QUEEN. YOU WANNA DEFEND THE BIG BOY SCOUT--
DO IT ON SOMEONE ELSE'S TIME! ME?
I GOT NO TIME TO HEAR IT!
GUY! YOU-- YOU'VE NEVER TALKED TO ME THAT WAY BEFORE!
CAN WE ALL STAY FOCUSED ON THE ISSUE AT HAND HERE? THERE'S A JOB THAT NEEDS TO BE DONE!
ARE YOU COMING WITH ME OR DO I DO IT ALONE?
OKAY, OKAY! WE'LL ALL GO! SAY, HAS ANYONE SEEN FIRE?
SHE IS PREOCCUPIED WITH HER NEW COSTUME.
HOW DO YOU KNOW ABOUT THAT? SHE HASN'T TOLD ANYONE EXCEPT ME!
DID I HEAR MY NAME MENTIONED?
LET'S GO. I WANT TO GET BACK IN TIME TO GET PUBLICITY PHOTOS SENT OUT.
COOL.
VERY NICE, BEA!
RAD!
HOT, BABE!
PEOPLE...
Uh-oh! PRINCIPAL SUPERMAN IS GETTING UPSET! BETTER GET IN LINE, CHILDREN!
I CAN'T BELIEVE WE'RE ACTUALLY GOING TO ANOTHER PLANET!
YOU GOT IT, FUTURE BOY! NEXT STOP--

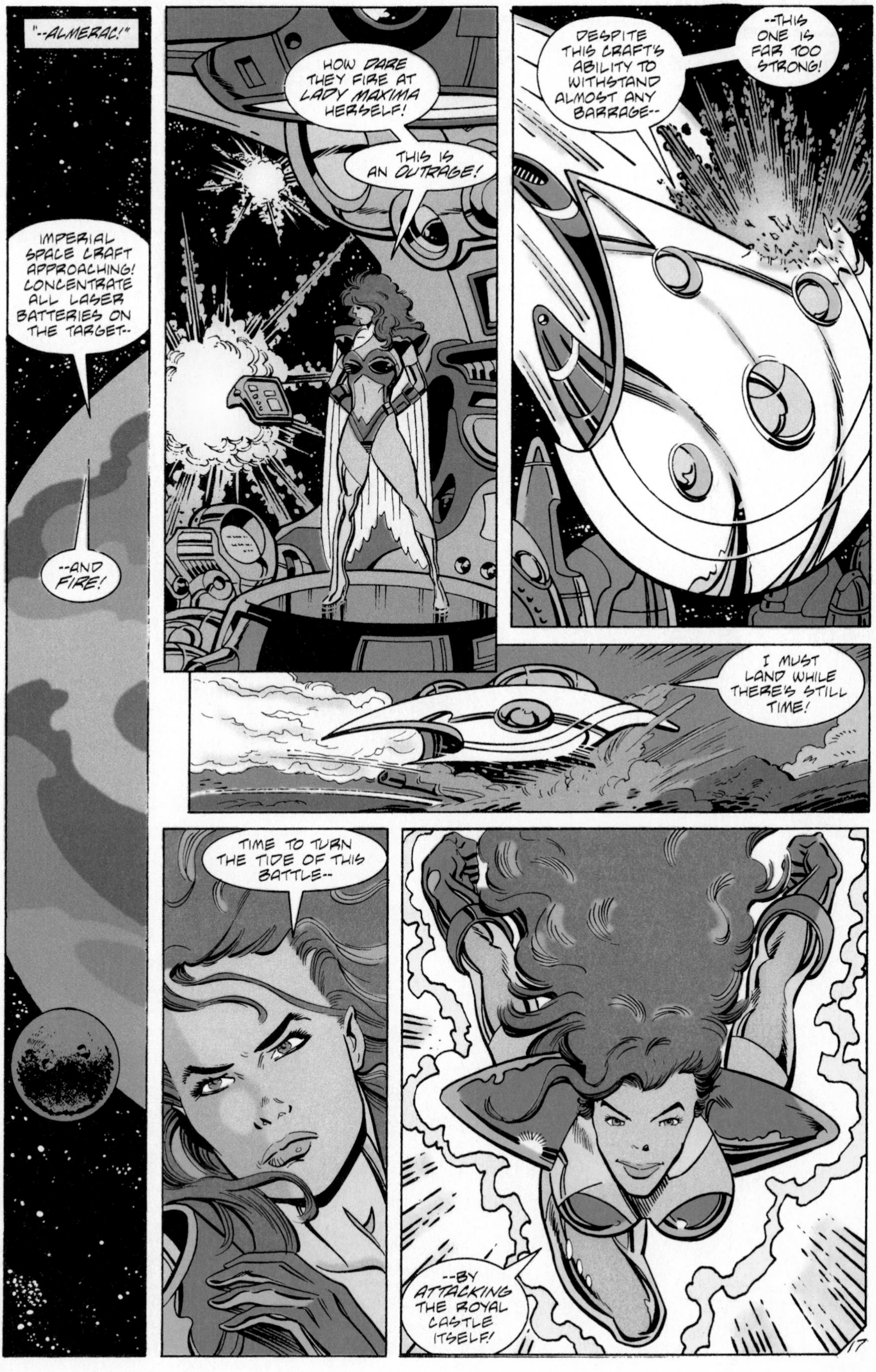

"--ALMERAC!"
HOW DARE THEY FIRE AT LADY MAXIMA HERSELF!
THIS IS AN OUTRAGE!
DESPITE THIS CRAFT'S ABILITY TO WITHSTAND ALMOST ANY BARRAGE--
--THIS ONE IS FAR TOO STRONG!
IMPERIAL SPACE CRAFT APPROACHING! CONCENTRATE ALL LASER BATTERIES ON THE TARGET--
--AND FIRE!
I MUST LAND WHILE THERE'S STILL TIME!
TIME TO TURN THE TIDE OF THIS BATTLE--
--BY ATTACKING THE ROYAL CASTLE ITSELF!

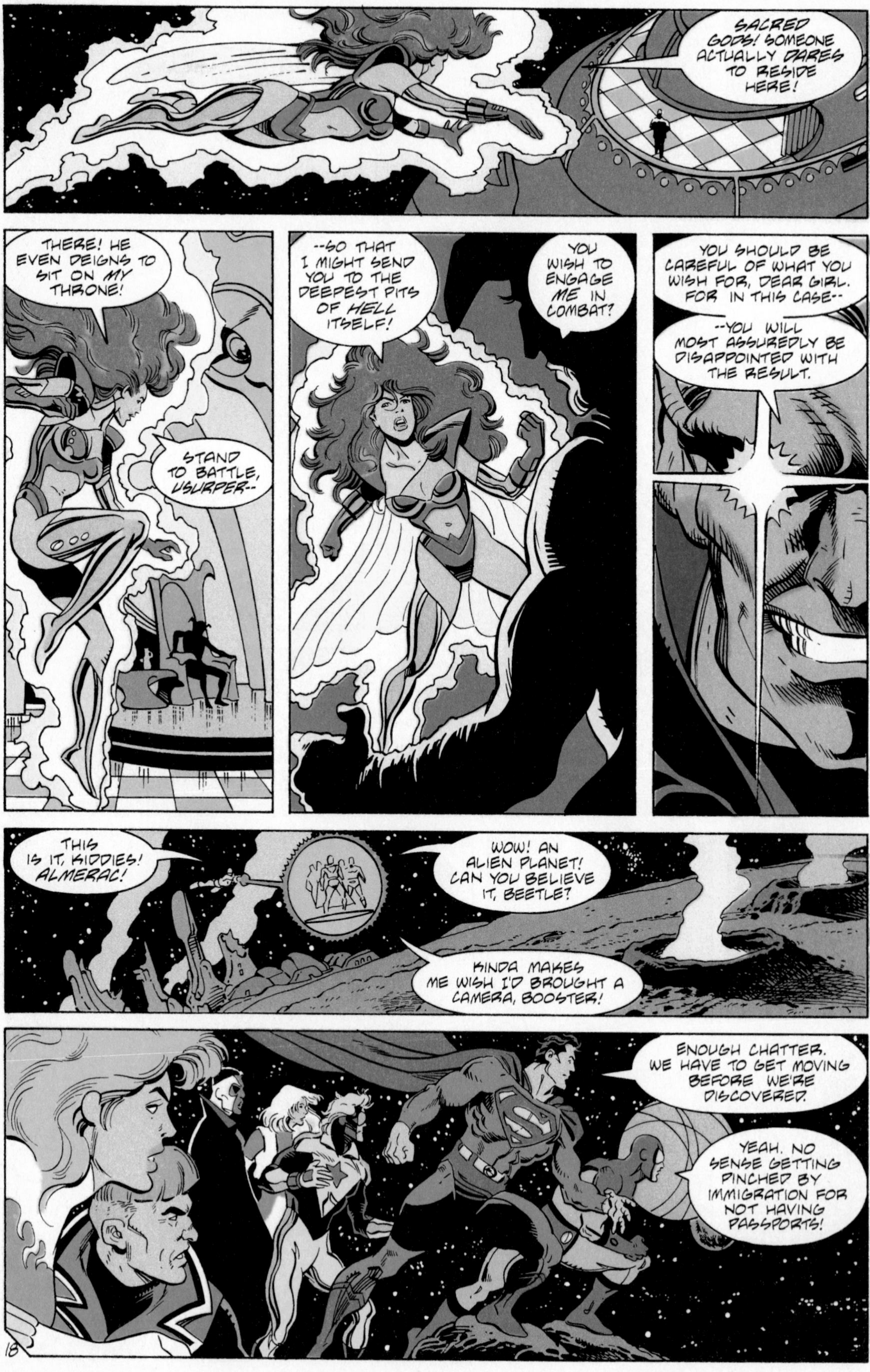
SACRED GODS! SOMEONE ACTUALLY DARES TO RESIDE HERE!
THERE! HE EVEN DEIGNS TO SIT ON MY THRONE!
STAND TO BATTLE, USURPER--
--SO THAT I MIGHT SEND YOU TO THE DEEPEST PITS OF HELL ITSELF!
YOU WISH TO ENGAGE ME IN COMBAT?
YOU SHOULD BE CAREFUL OF WHAT YOU WISH FOR, DEAR GIRL. FOR IN THIS CASE--
--YOU WILL MOST ASSUREDLY BE DISAPPOINTED WITH THE RESULT.
THIS IS IT, KIDDIES! ALMERAC!
WOW! AN ALIEN PLANET! CAN YOU BELIEVE IT, BEETLE?
KINDA MAKES ME WISH I'D BROUGHT A CAMERA, BOOSTER!
ENOUGH CHATTER. WE HAVE TO GET MOVING BEFORE WE'RE DISCOVERED.
YEAH. NO SENSE GETTING PINCHED BY IMMIGRATION FOR NOT HAVING PASSPORTS!

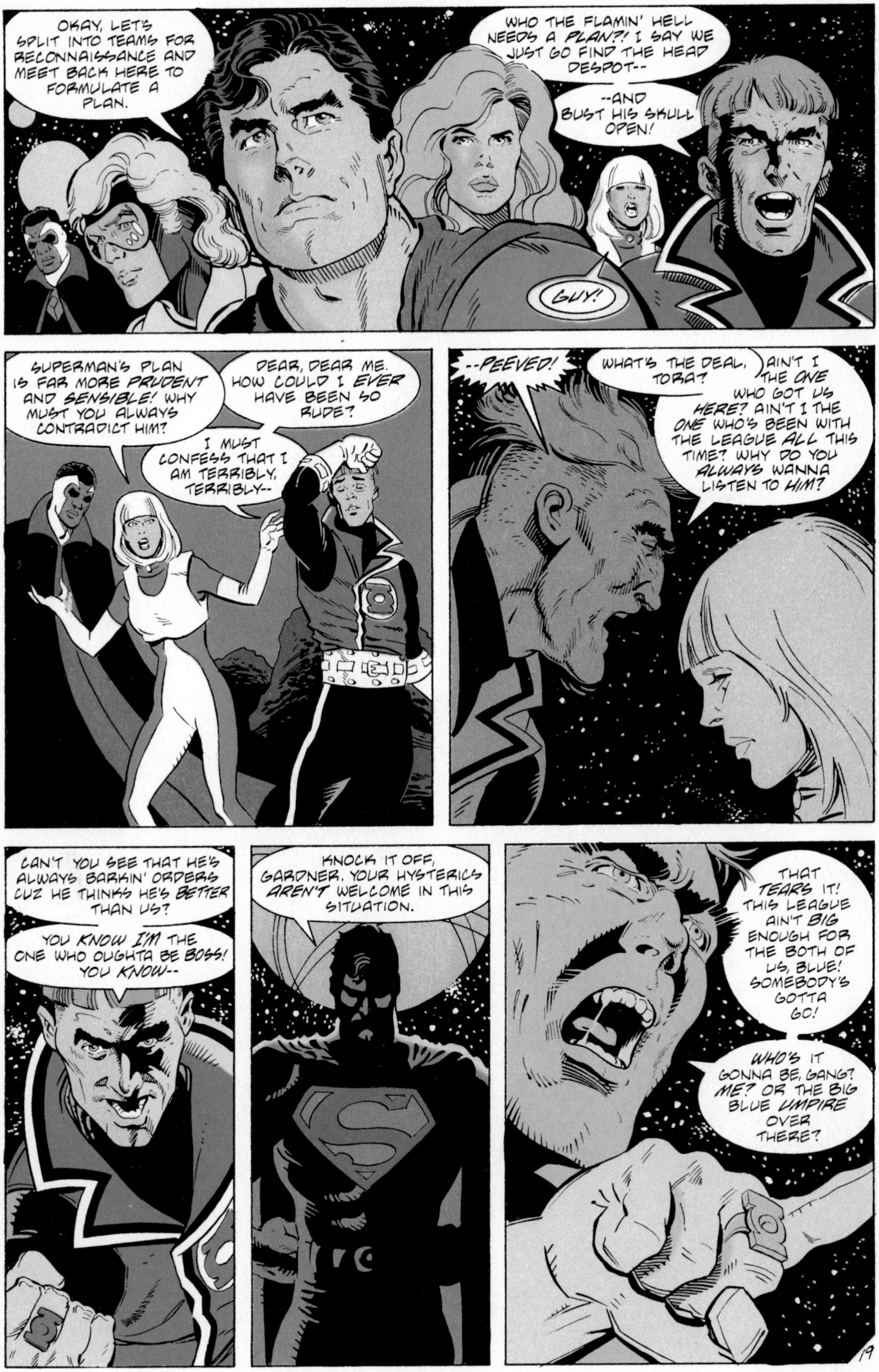
OKAY, LET'S SPLIT INTO TEAMS FOR RECONNAISSANCE AND MEET BACK HERE TO FORMULATE A PLAN.
WHO THE FLAMIN' HELL NEEDS A PLAN?! I SAY WE JUST GO FIND THE HEAD DESPOT--
--AND BUST HIS SKULL OPEN!
GUY!
SUPERMAN'S PLAN IS FAR MORE PRUDENT AND SENSIBLE! WHY MUST YOU ALWAYS CONTRADICT HIM?
DEAR, DEAR ME. HOW COULD I EVER HAVE BEEN SO RUDE?
I MUST CONFESS THAT I AM TERRIBLY, TERRIBLY--
--PEEVED!
WHAT'S THE DEAL, TORA?
AIN'T I THE ONE WHO GOT US HERE? AIN'T I THE ONE WHO'S BEEN WITH THE LEAGUE ALL THIS TIME? WHY DO YOU ALWAYS WANNA LISTEN TO HIM?
CAN'T YOU SEE THAT HE'S ALWAYS BARKIN' ORDERS CUZ HE THINKS HE'S BETTER THAN US?
YOU KNOW I'M THE ONE WHO OUGHTA BE BOSS! YOU KNOW--
KNOCK IT OFF, GARDNER. YOUR HYSTERICS AREN'T WELCOME IN THIS SITUATION.
THAT TEARS IT! THIS LEAGUE AIN'T BIG ENOUGH FOR THE BOTH OF US, BLUE! SOMEBODY'S GOTTA GO!
WHO'S IT GONNA BE, GANG? ME? OR THE BIG BLUE UMPIRE OVER THERE?

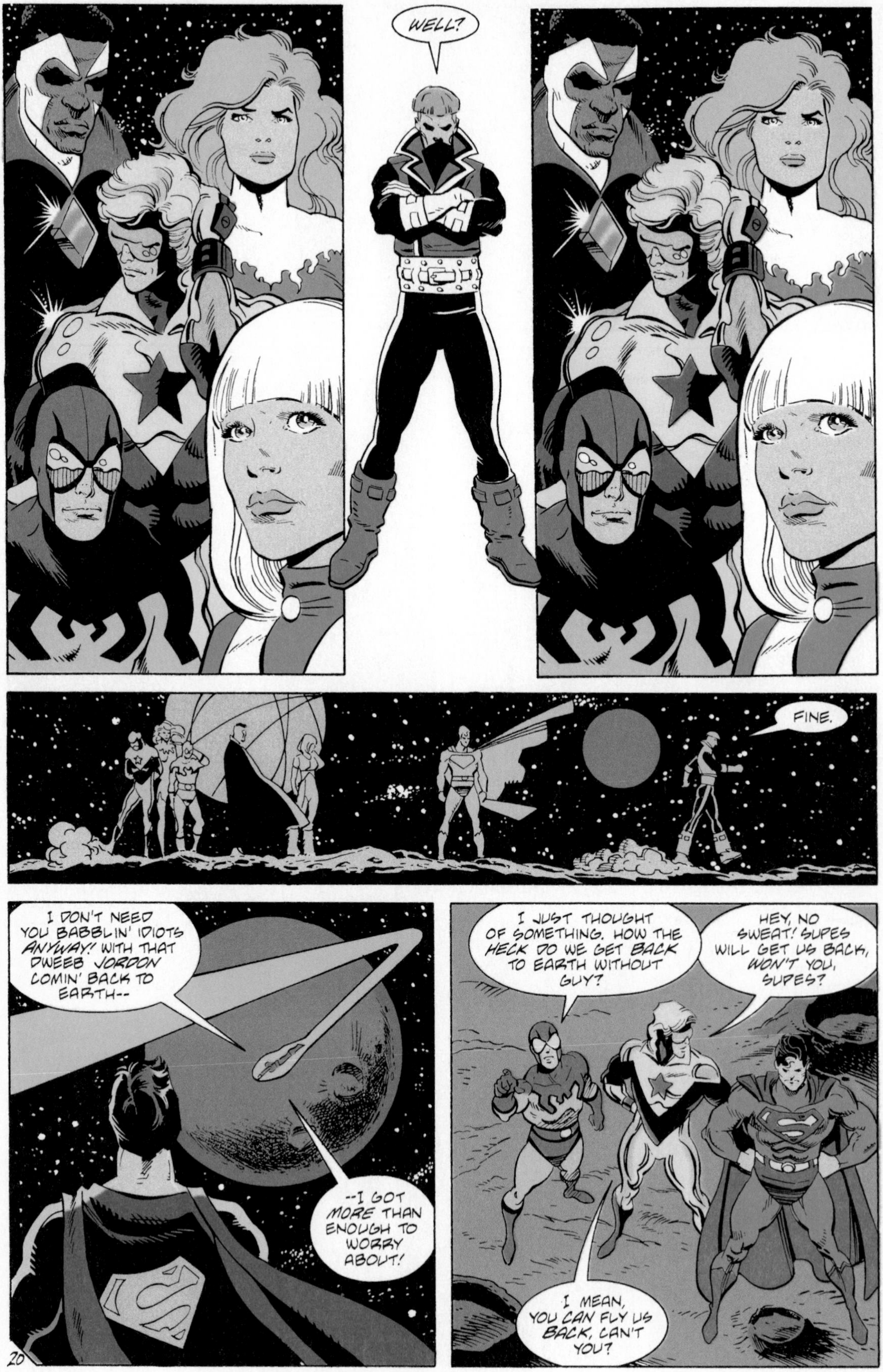

WELL?
FINE.
I DON'T NEED YOU BABBLIN' IDIOTS ANYWAY! WITH THAT DWEEB JORDON COMIN' BACK TO EARTH--
--I GOT MORE THAN ENOUGH TO WORRY ABOUT!
I JUST THOUGHT OF SOMETHING. HOW THE HECK DO WE GET BACK TO EARTH WITHOUT GUY?
HEY, NO SWEAT! SUPES WILL GET US BACK, WON'T YOU, SUPES?
I MEAN, YOU CAN FLY US BACK, CAN'T YOU?
20

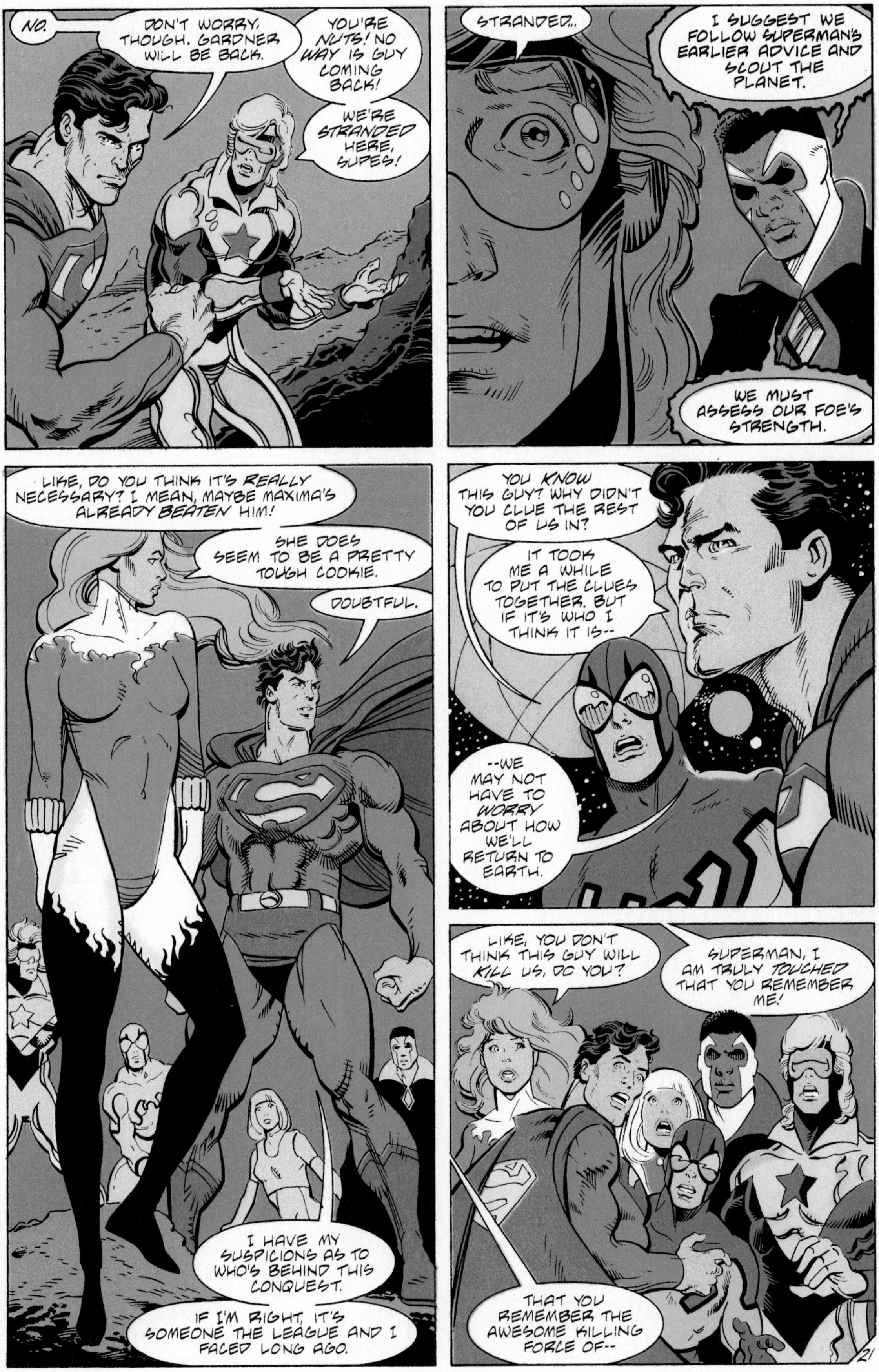
NO.
DON'T WORRY, THOUGH. GARDNER WILL BE BACK.
YOU'RE NUTS! NO WAY IS GUY COMING BACK!
WE'RE STRANDED HERE, SUPES!
STRANDED...
I SUGGEST WE FOLLOW SUPERMAN'S EARLIER ADVICE AND SCOUT THE PLANET.
WE MUST ASSESS OUR FOE'S STRENGTH.
LIKE, DO YOU THINK IT'S REALLY NECESSARY? I MEAN, MAYBE MAXIMA'S ALREADY BEATEN HIM!
SHE DOES SEEM TO BE A PRETTY TOUGH COOKIE.
DOUBTFUL.
I HAVE MY SUSPICIONS AS TO WHO'S BEHIND THIS CONQUEST.
IF I'M RIGHT, IT'S SOMEONE THE LEAGUE AND I FACED LONG AGO.
YOU KNOW THIS GUY? WHY DIDN'T YOU CLUE THE REST OF US IN?
IT TOOK ME A WHILE TO PUT THE CLUES TOGETHER. BUT IF IT'S WHO I THINK IT IS--
--WE MAY NOT HAVE TO WORRY ABOUT HOW WE'LL RETURN TO EARTH.
LIKE, YOU DON'T THINK THIS GUY WILL KILL US, DO YOU?
SUPERMAN, I AM TRULY TOUCHED THAT YOU REMEMBER ME!
THAT YOU REMEMBER THE AWESOME KILLING FORCE OF--
21

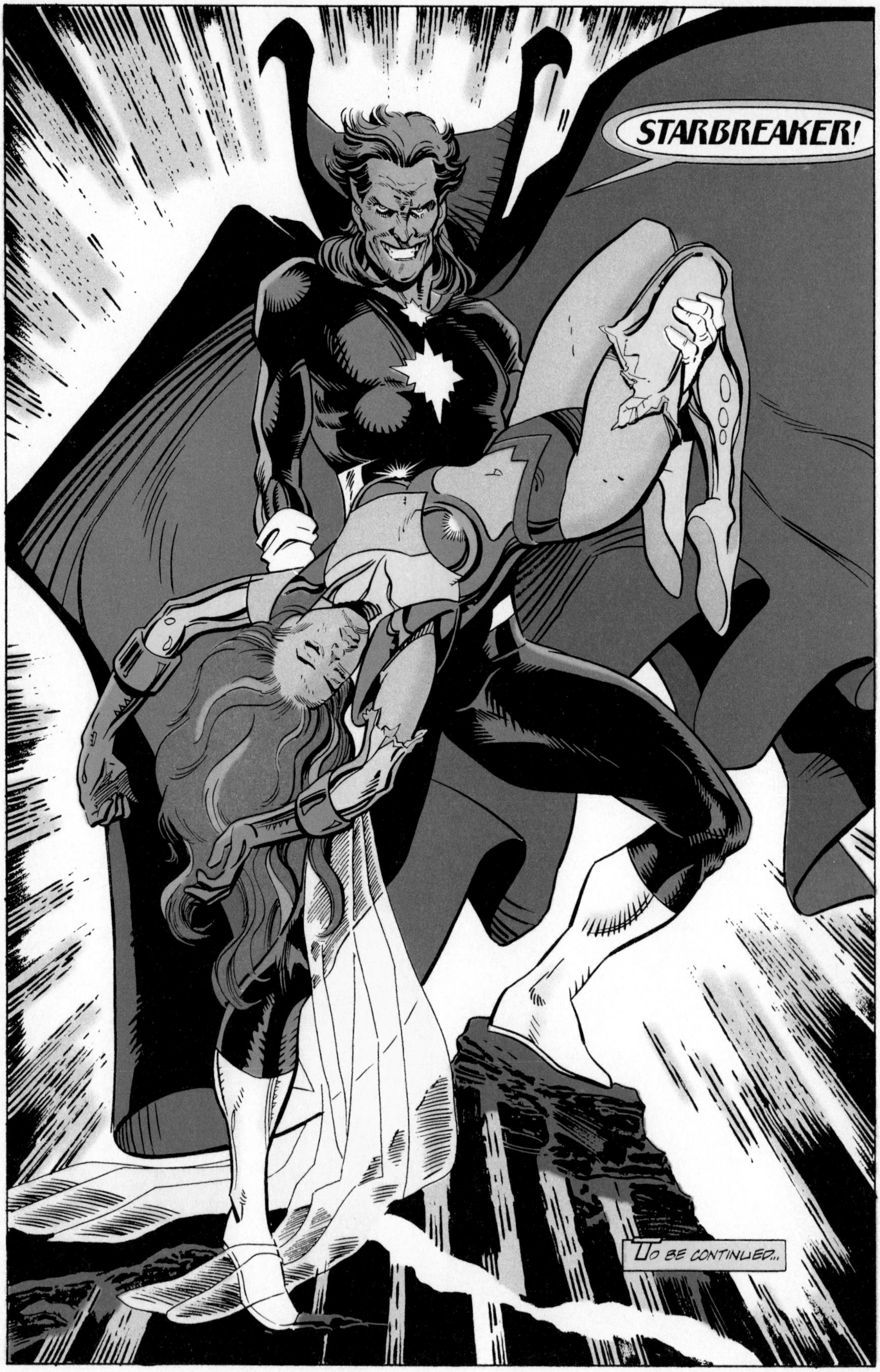
STARBREAKER!
TO BE CONTINUED...

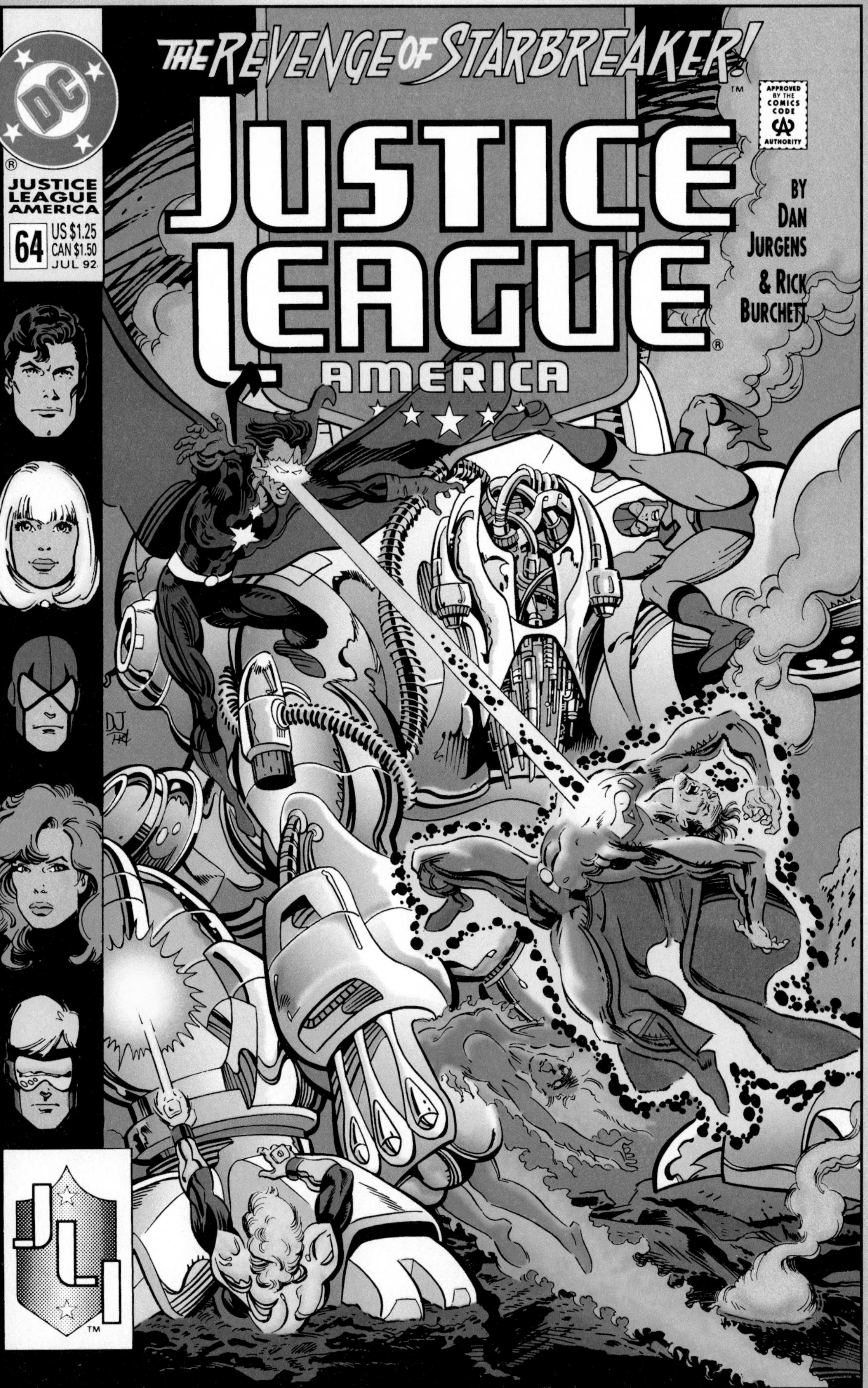
THE REVENGE OF STARBREAKER!
JUSTICE LEAGUE AMERICA
BY DAN JURGENS & RICK BURCHETT
JUSTICE LEAGUE AMERICA
64
US $1.25
CAN $1.50
JUL 92
APPROVED BY THE COMICS CODE AUTHORITY
DJ

Cover art by **DAN JURGENS**
and **RICK BURCHETT**

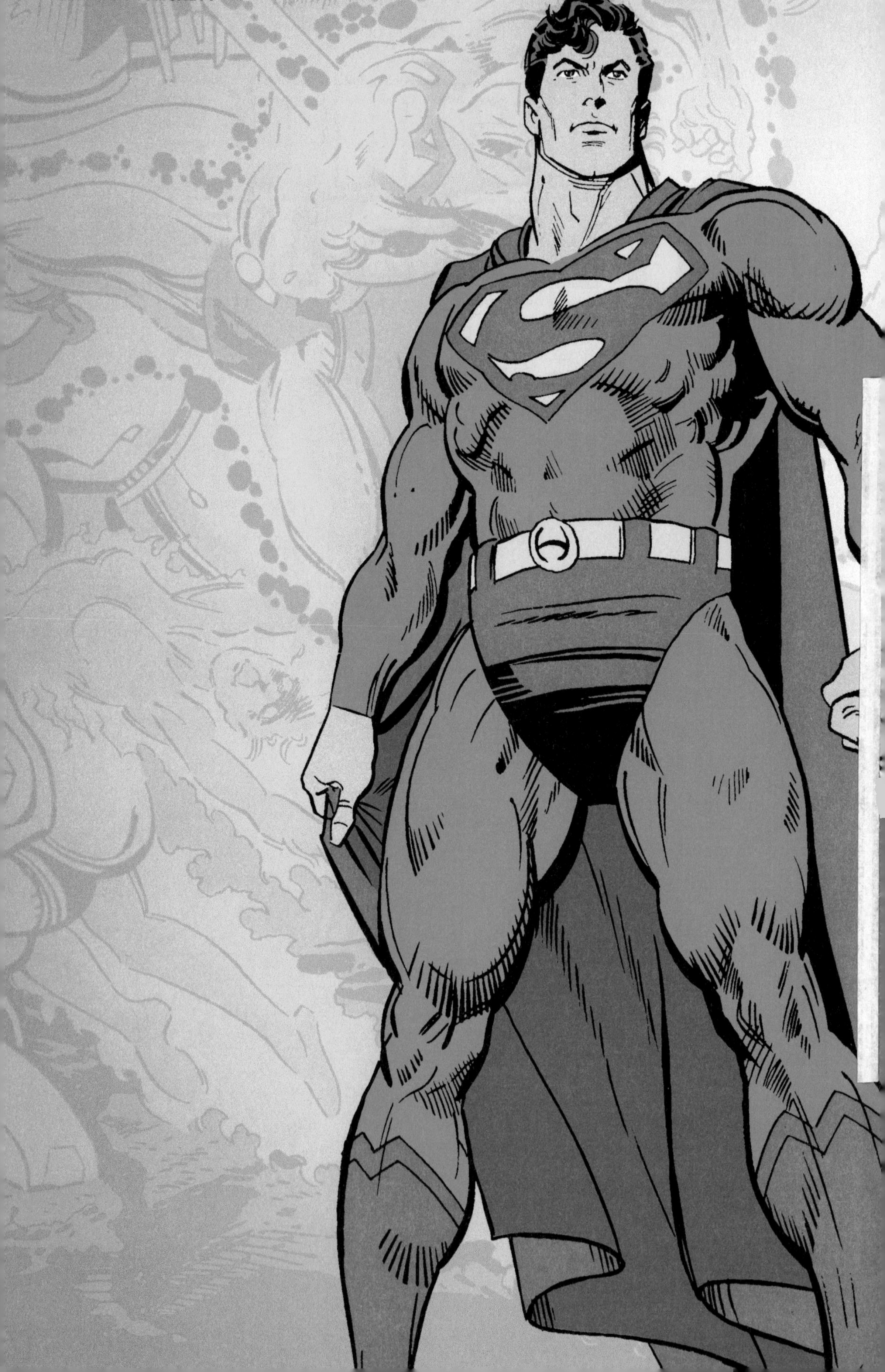

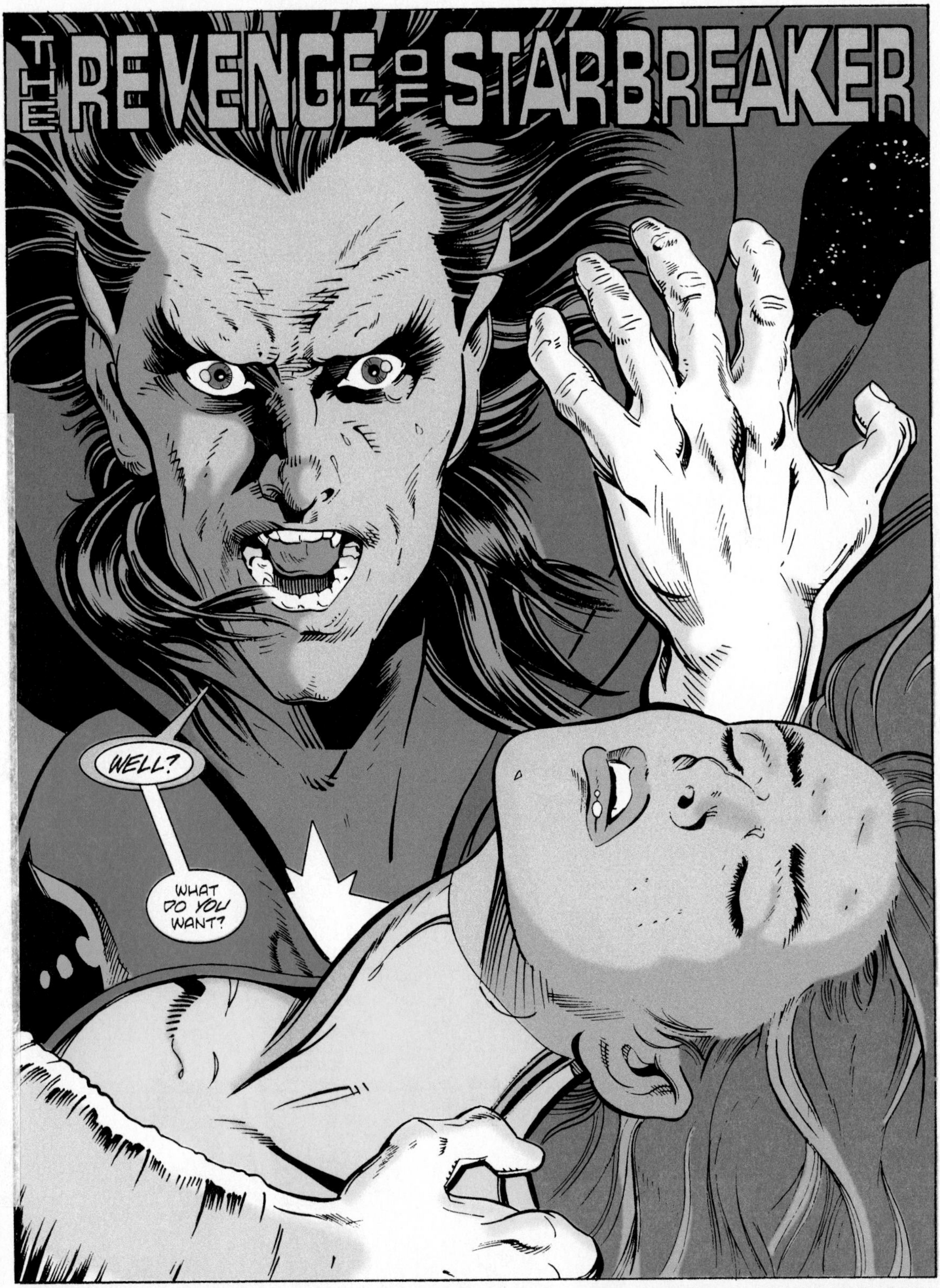
THE REVENGE OF STARBREAKER
WELL?
WHAT DO YOU WANT?

DAN JURGENS *story and art* **RICK BURCHETT** *finished art* **WILLIE SCHUBERT** *letters* **GENE D'ANGELO** *colors* **BRIAN AUGUSTYN** *editor*

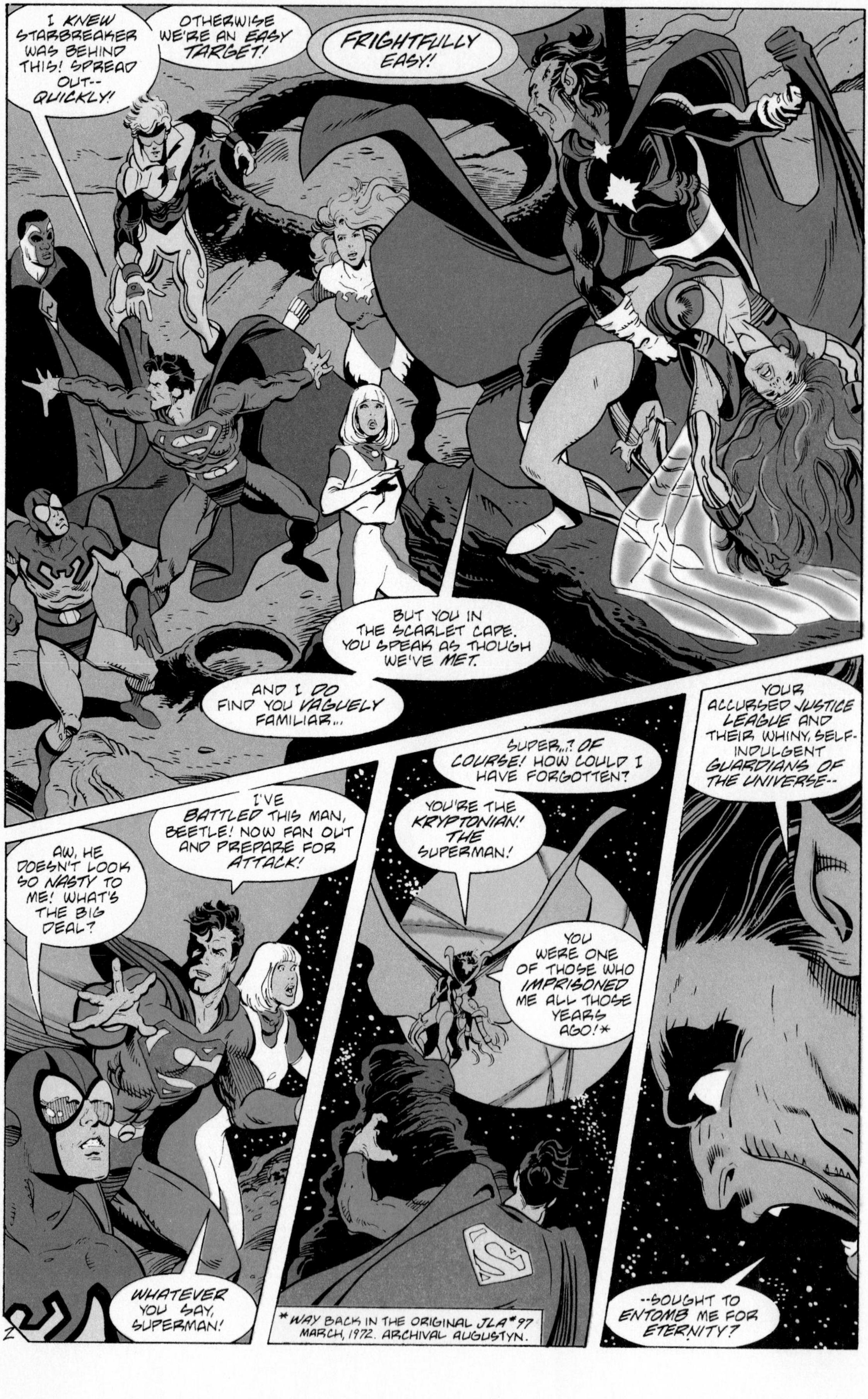
I KNEW STARBREAKER WAS BEHIND THIS! SPREAD OUT-- QUICKLY!
OTHERWISE WE'RE AN EASY TARGET!
FRIGHTFULLY EASY!
BUT YOU IN THE SCARLET CAPE. YOU SPEAK AS THOUGH WE'VE MET.
AND I DO FIND YOU VAGUELY FAMILIAR...
I'VE BATTLED THIS MAN, BEETLE! NOW FAN OUT AND PREPARE FOR ATTACK!
AW, HE DOESN'T LOOK SO NASTY TO ME! WHAT'S THE BIG DEAL?
WHATEVER YOU SAY, SUPERMAN!
SUPER...? OF COURSE! HOW COULD I HAVE FORGOTTEN?
YOU'RE THE KRYPTONIAN! THE SUPERMAN!
YOU WERE ONE OF THOSE WHO IMPRISONED ME ALL THOSE YEARS AGO!*
* WAY BACK IN THE ORIGINAL JLA #97 MARCH, 1972. ARCHIVAL AUGUSTYN.
YOUR ACCURSED JUSTICE LEAGUE AND THEIR WHINY, SELF-INDULGENT GUARDIANS OF THE UNIVERSE--
--SOUGHT TO ENTOMB ME FOR ETERNITY?

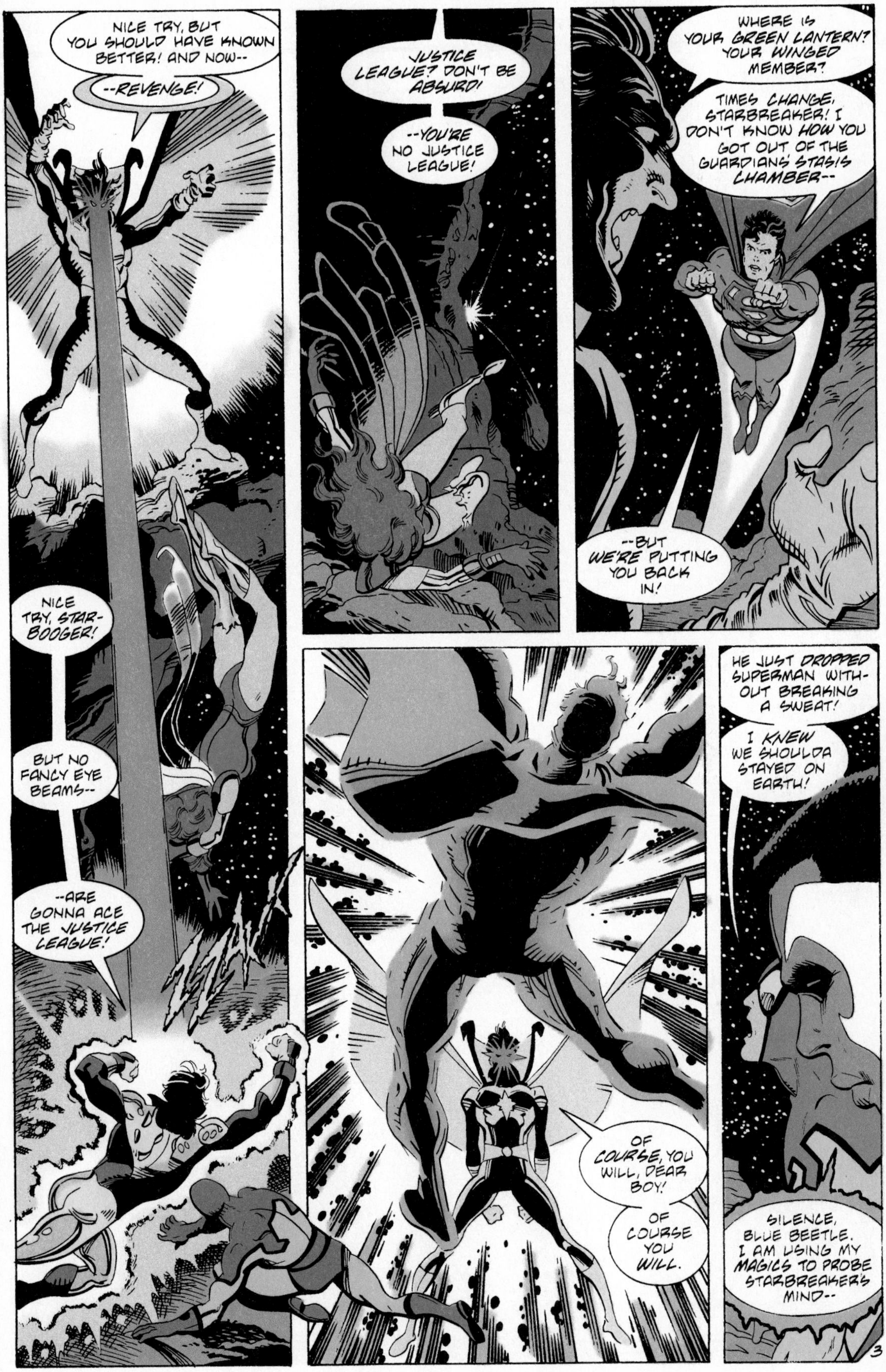
NICE TRY, BUT YOU SHOULD HAVE KNOWN BETTER! AND NOW--
--REVENGE!
NICE TRY, STAR-BOOGER!
BUT NO FANCY EYE BEAMS--
--ARE GONNA ACE THE JUSTICE LEAGUE!
JUSTICE LEAGUE? DON'T BE ABSURD!
--YOU'RE NO JUSTICE LEAGUE!
WHERE IS YOUR GREEN LANTERN? YOUR WINGED MEMBER?
TIMES CHANGE, STARBREAKER! I DON'T KNOW HOW YOU GOT OUT OF THE GUARDIANS' STASIS CHAMBER--
--BUT WE'RE PUTTING YOU BACK IN!
OF COURSE, YOU WILL, DEAR BOY!
OF COURSE YOU WILL.
HE JUST DROPPED SUPERMAN WITHOUT BREAKING A SWEAT!
I KNEW WE SHOULDA STAYED ON EARTH!
SILENCE, BLUE BEETLE. I AM USING MY MAGICS TO PROBE STARBREAKER'S MIND--

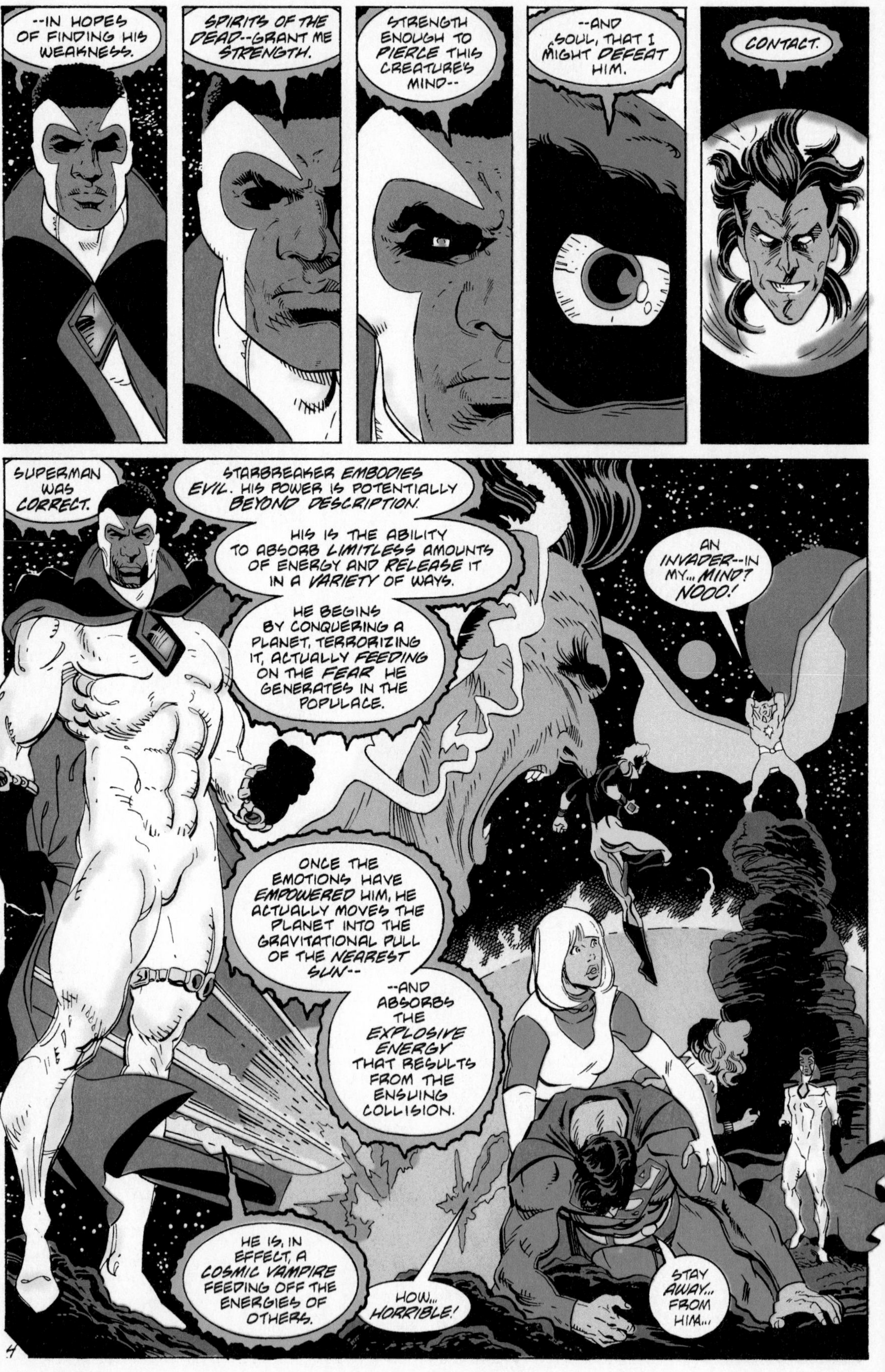
--IN HOPES OF FINDING HIS WEAKNESS.
SPIRITS OF THE DEAD--GRANT ME STRENGTH.
STRENGTH ENOUGH TO PIERCE THIS CREATURE'S MIND--
--AND SOUL, THAT I MIGHT DEFEAT HIM.
CONTACT.
SUPERMAN WAS CORRECT.
STARBREAKER EMBODIES EVIL. HIS POWER IS POTENTIALLY BEYOND DESCRIPTION.
HIS IS THE ABILITY TO ABSORB LIMITLESS AMOUNTS OF ENERGY AND RELEASE IT IN A VARIETY OF WAYS.
HE BEGINS BY CONQUERING A PLANET, TERRORIZING IT, ACTUALLY FEEDING ON THE FEAR HE GENERATES IN THE POPULACE.
AN INVADER--IN MY... MIND? NOOO!
ONCE THE EMOTIONS HAVE EMPOWERED HIM, HE ACTUALLY MOVES THE PLANET INTO THE GRAVITATIONAL PULL OF THE NEAREST SUN--
--AND ABSORBS THE EXPLOSIVE ENERGY THAT RESULTS FROM THE ENSUING COLLISION.
HE IS, IN EFFECT, A COSMIC VAMPIRE FEEDING OFF THE ENERGIES OF OTHERS.
HOW... HORRIBLE!
STAY AWAY... FROM HIM...

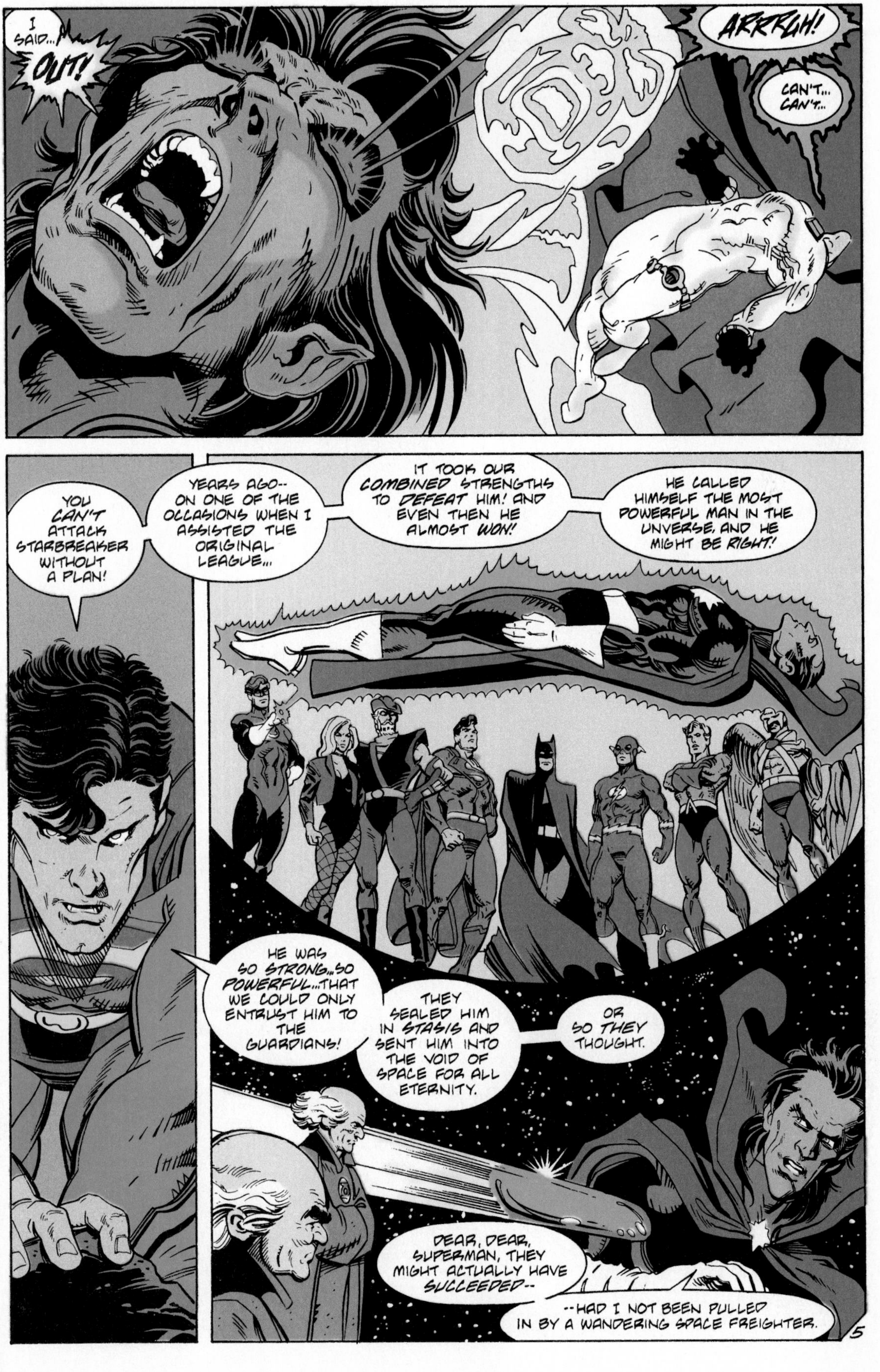

I SAID... OUT!
ARRRGH!
CAN'T... CAN'T...
YOU CAN'T ATTACK STARBREAKER WITHOUT A PLAN!
YEARS AGO-- ON ONE OF THE OCCASIONS WHEN I ASSISTED THE ORIGINAL LEAGUE...
IT TOOK OUR COMBINED STRENGTHS TO DEFEAT HIM! AND EVEN THEN HE ALMOST WON!
HE CALLED HIMSELF THE MOST POWERFUL MAN IN THE UNVERSE, AND HE MIGHT BE RIGHT!
HE WAS SO STRONG...SO POWERFUL...THAT WE COULD ONLY ENTRUST HIM TO THE GUARDIANS!
THEY SEALED HIM IN STASIS AND SENT HIM INTO THE VOID OF SPACE FOR ALL ETERNITY.
OR SO THEY THOUGHT.
DEAR, DEAR, SUPERMAN, THEY MIGHT ACTUALLY HAVE SUCCEEDED--
--HAD I NOT BEEN PULLED IN BY A WANDERING SPACE FREIGHTER.

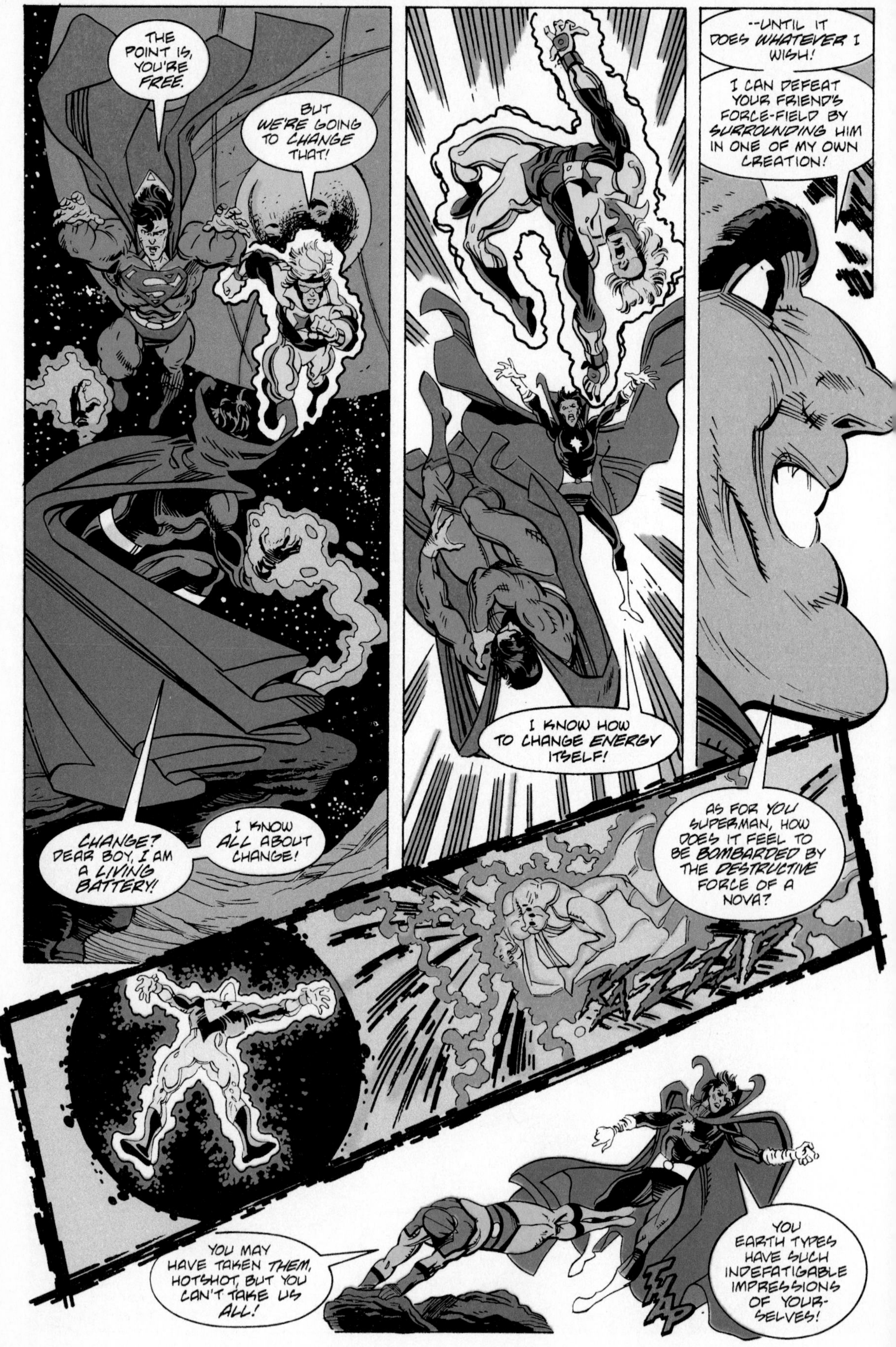
THE POINT IS, YOU'RE FREE.
BUT WE'RE GOING TO CHANGE THAT!
CHANGE? DEAR BOY, I AM A LIVING BATTERY!
I KNOW ALL ABOUT CHANGE!
I KNOW HOW TO CHANGE ENERGY ITSELF!
--UNTIL IT DOES WHATEVER I WISH!
I CAN DEFEAT YOUR FRIEND'S FORCE-FIELD BY SURROUNDING HIM IN ONE OF MY OWN CREATION!
AS FOR YOU SUPERMAN, HOW DOES IT FEEL TO BE BOMBARDED BY THE DESTRUCTIVE FORCE OF A NOVA?
KA-ZZAP
YOU MAY HAVE TAKEN THEM, HOTSHOT, BUT YOU CAN'T TAKE US ALL!
THAP
YOU EARTH TYPES HAVE SUCH INDEFATIGABLE IMPRESSIONS OF YOUR-SELVES!

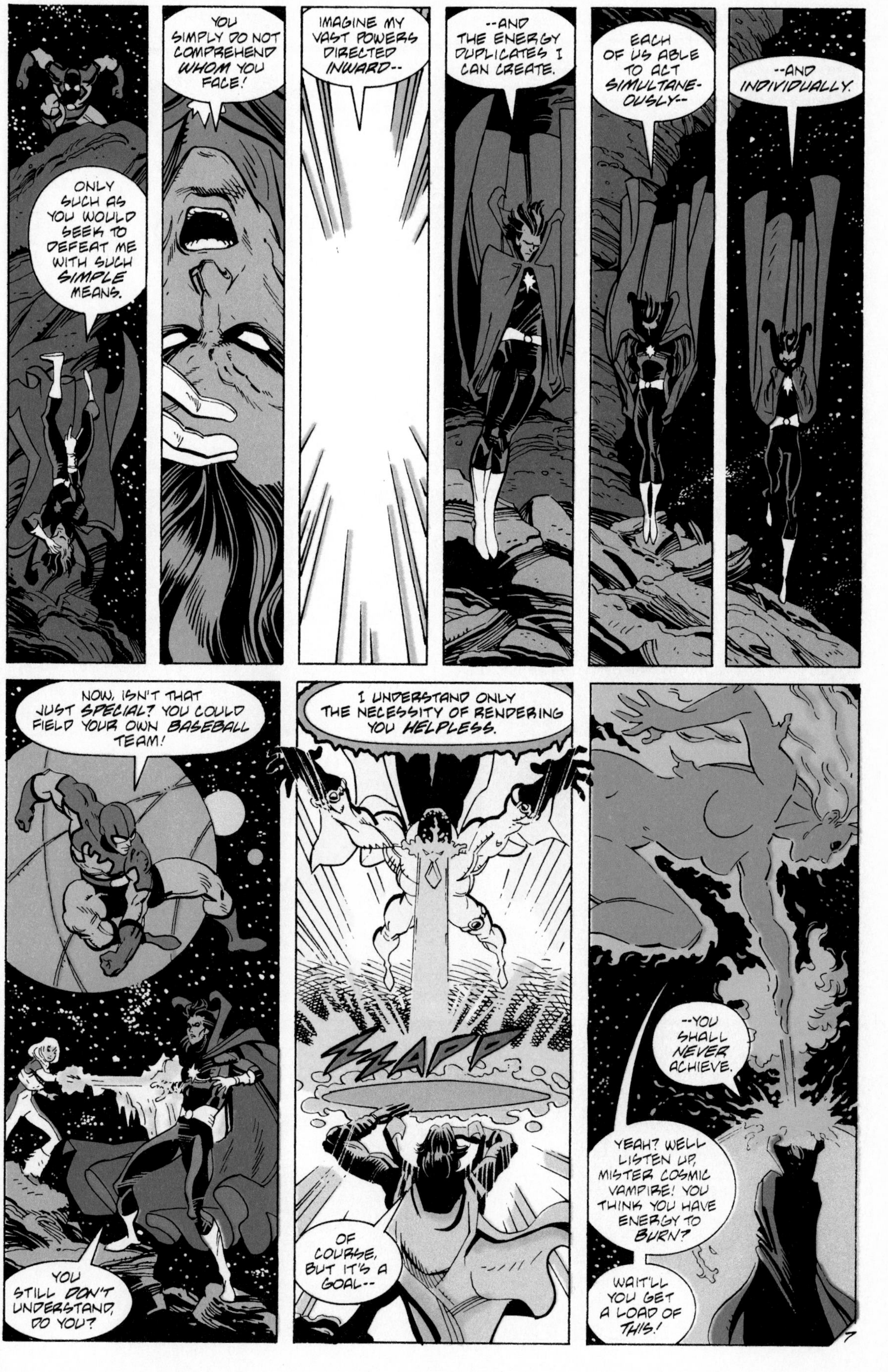
ONLY SUCH AS YOU WOULD SEEK TO DEFEAT ME WITH SUCH SIMPLE MEANS.
YOU SIMPLY DO NOT COMPREHEND WHOM YOU FACE!
IMAGINE MY VAST POWERS DIRECTED INWARD--
--AND THE ENERGY DUPLICATES I CAN CREATE.
EACH OF US ABLE TO ACT SIMULTANE-OUSLY--
--AND INDIVIDUALLY.
NOW, ISN'T THAT JUST SPECIAL? YOU COULD FIELD YOUR OWN BASEBALL TEAM!
YOU STILL DON'T UNDERSTAND, DO YOU?
I UNDERSTAND ONLY THE NECESSITY OF RENDERING YOU HELPLESS.
ZZAPP
OF COURSE, BUT IT'S A GOAL--
--YOU SHALL NEVER ACHIEVE.
YEAH? WELL LISTEN UP, MISTER COSMIC VAMPIRE! YOU THINK YOU HAVE ENERGY TO BURN?
WAIT'LL YOU GET A LOAD OF THIS!

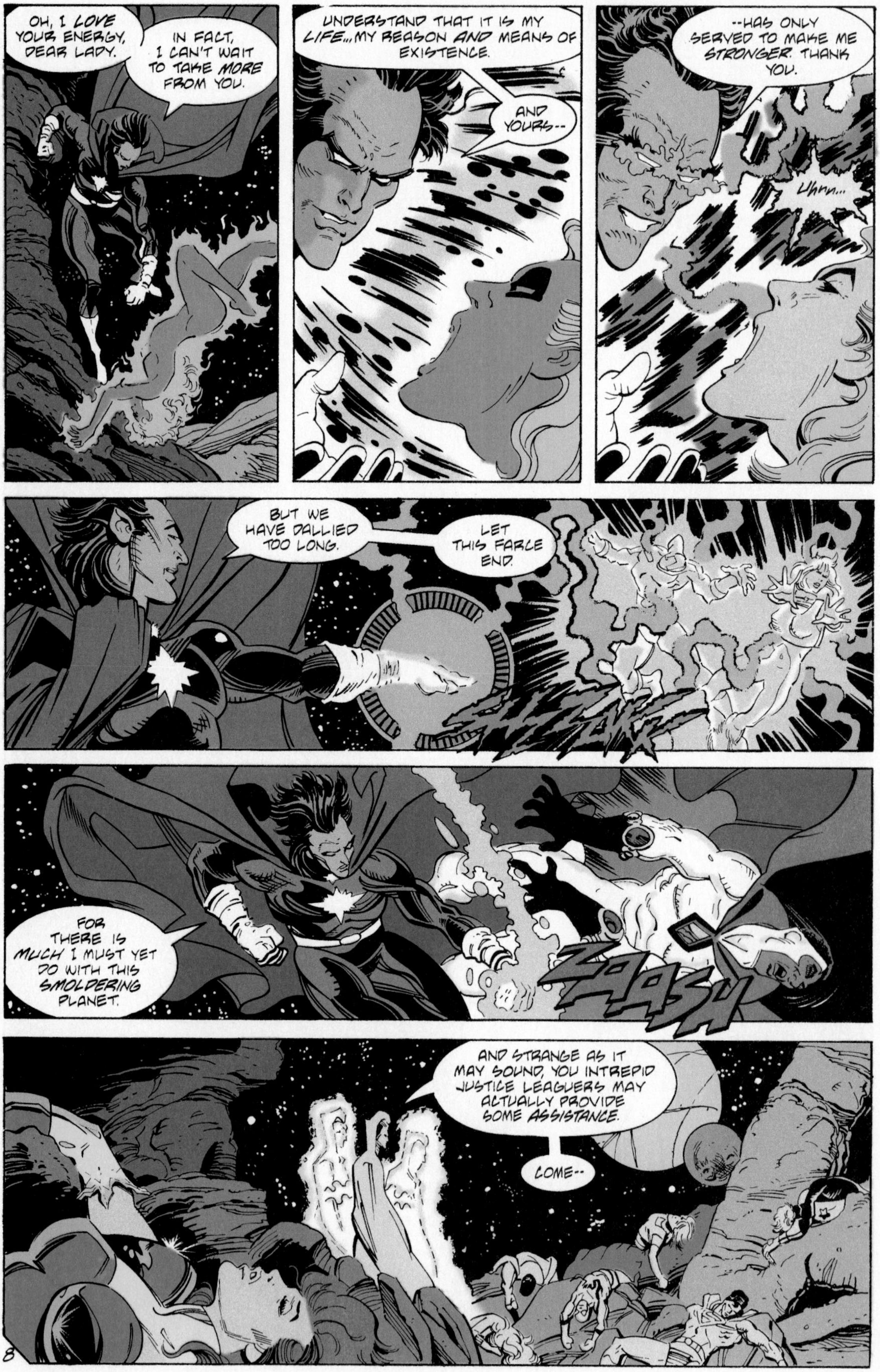
OH, I LOVE YOUR ENERGY, DEAR LADY.
IN FACT, I CAN'T WAIT TO TAKE MORE FROM YOU.
UNDERSTAND THAT IT IS MY LIFE... MY REASON AND MEANS OF EXISTENCE.
AND YOURS--
--HAS ONLY SERVED TO MAKE ME STRONGER. THANK YOU.
Uhnn...
BUT WE HAVE DALLIED TOO LONG.
LET THIS FARCE END.
FOR THERE IS MUCH I MUST YET DO WITH THIS SMOLDERING PLANET.
AND STRANGE AS IT MAY SOUND, YOU INTREPID JUSTICE LEAGUERS MAY ACTUALLY PROVIDE SOME ASSISTANCE.
COME--

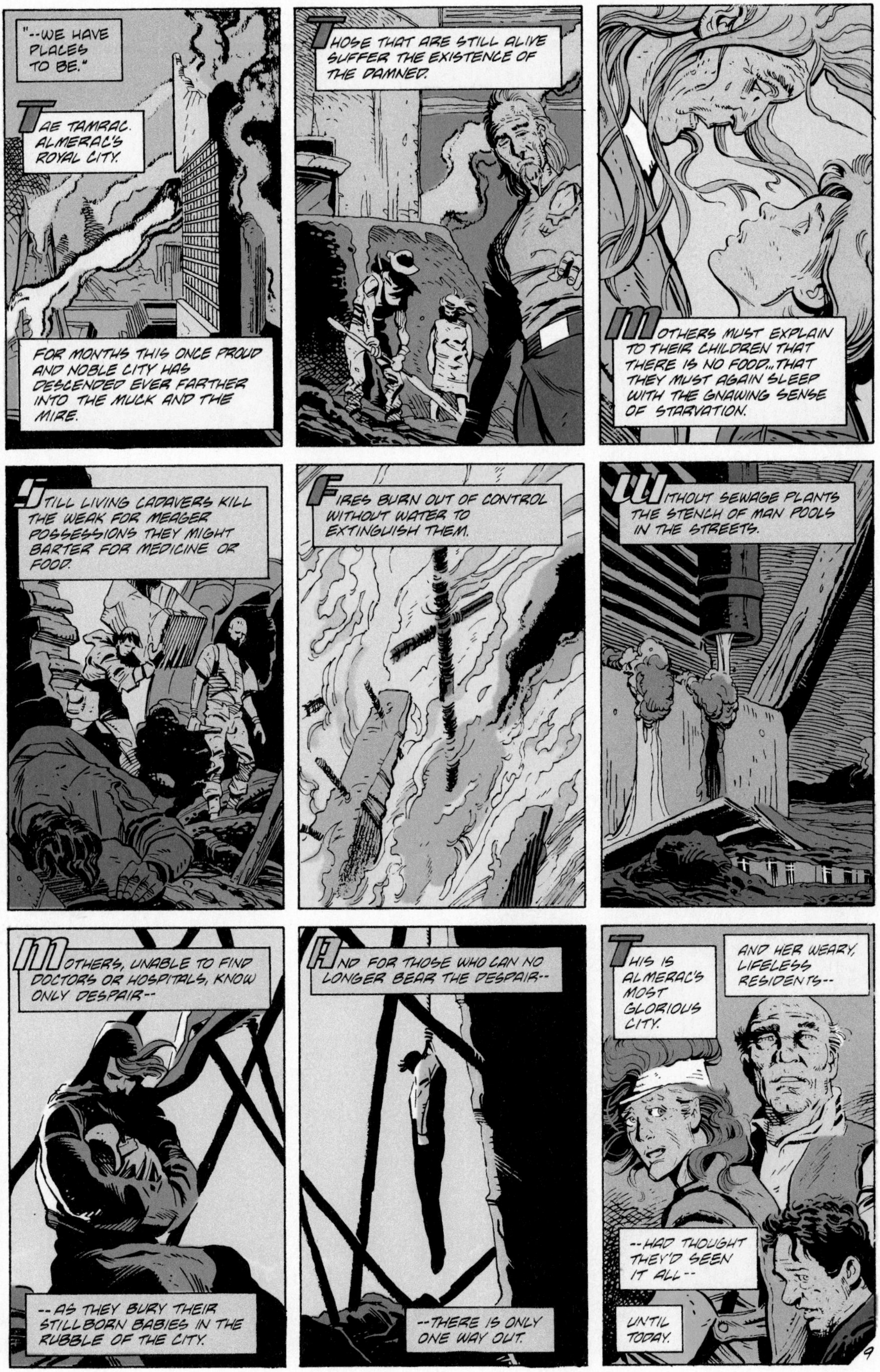
"--WE HAVE PLACES TO BE."
THE TAMRAC. ALMERAC'S ROYAL CITY.
FOR MONTHS THIS ONCE PROUD AND NOBLE CITY HAS DESCENDED EVER FARTHER INTO THE MUCK AND THE MIRE.
THOSE THAT ARE STILL ALIVE SUFFER THE EXISTENCE OF THE DAMNED.
MOTHERS MUST EXPLAIN TO THEIR CHILDREN THAT THERE IS NO FOOD...THAT THEY MUST AGAIN SLEEP WITH THE GNAWING SENSE OF STARVATION.
STILL LIVING CADAVERS KILL THE WEAK FOR MEAGER POSSESSIONS THEY MIGHT BARTER FOR MEDICINE OR FOOD.
FIRES BURN OUT OF CONTROL WITHOUT WATER TO EXTINGUISH THEM.
WITHOUT SEWAGE PLANTS THE STENCH OF MAN POOLS IN THE STREETS.
MOTHERS, UNABLE TO FIND DOCTORS OR HOSPITALS, KNOW ONLY DESPAIR--
--AS THEY BURY THEIR STILLBORN BABIES IN THE RUBBLE OF THE CITY.
AND FOR THOSE WHO CAN NO LONGER BEAR THE DESPAIR--
--THERE IS ONLY ONE WAY OUT.
THIS IS ALMERAC'S MOST GLORIOUS CITY.
AND HER WEARY, LIFELESS RESIDENTS--
--HAD THOUGHT THEY'D SEEN IT ALL--
UNTIL TODAY.

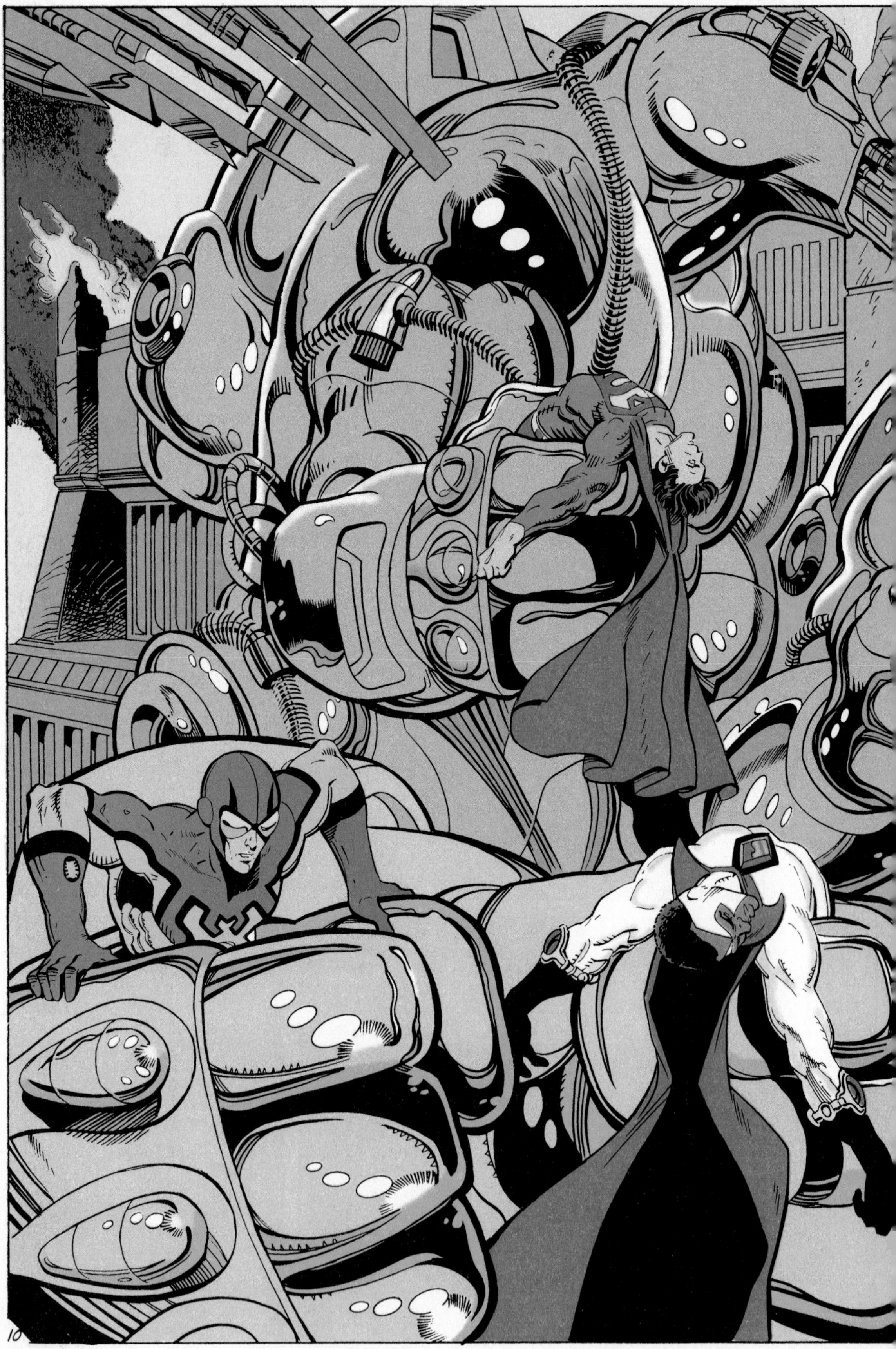

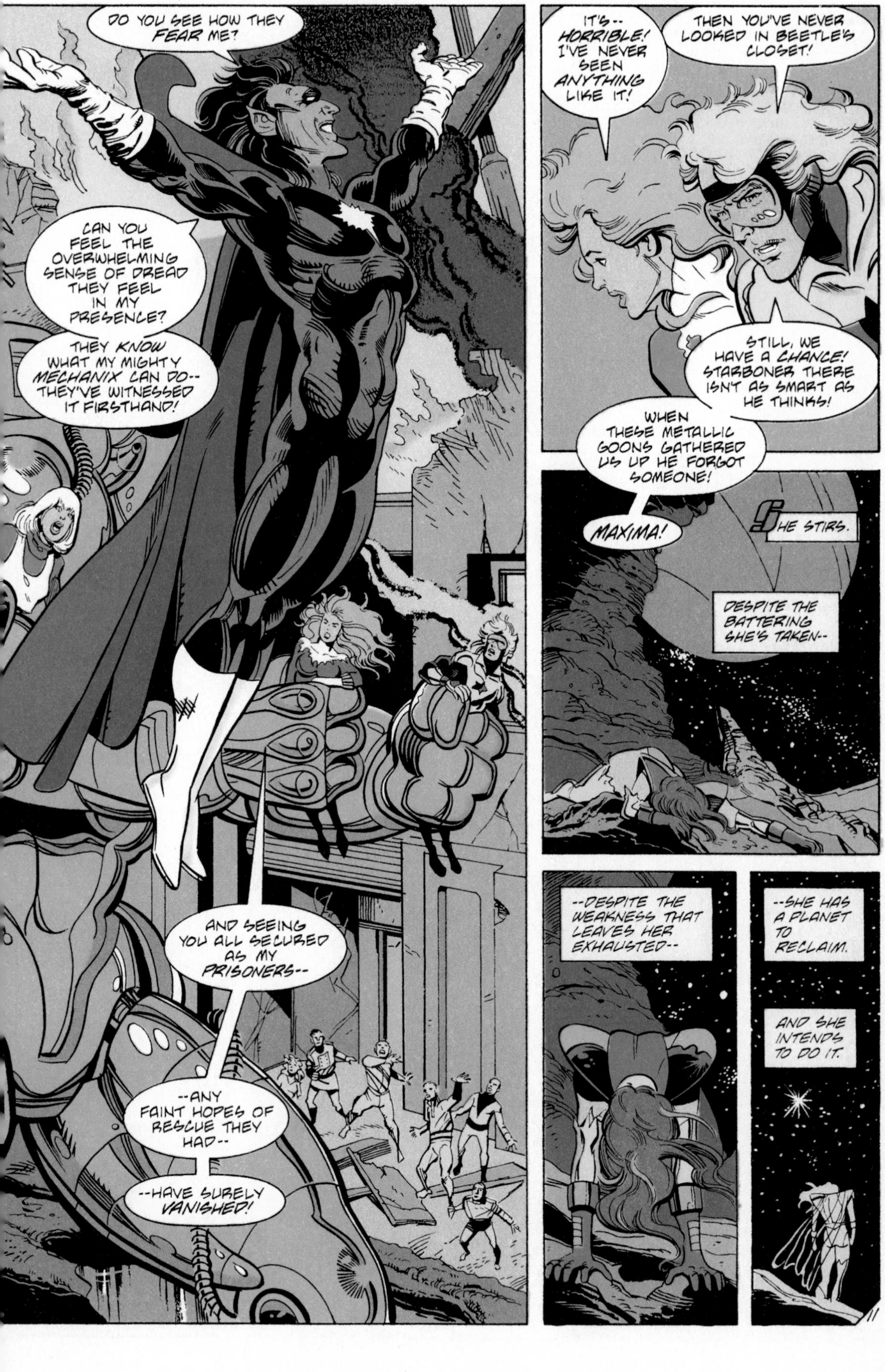
DO YOU SEE HOW THEY FEAR ME?
CAN YOU FEEL THE OVERWHELMING SENSE OF DREAD THEY FEEL IN MY PRESENCE?
THEY KNOW WHAT MY MIGHTY MECHANIX CAN DO-- THEY'VE WITNESSED IT FIRSTHAND!
AND SEEING YOU ALL SECURED AS MY PRISONERS--
--ANY FAINT HOPES OF RESCUE THEY HAD--
--HAVE SURELY VANISHED!
IT'S--HORRIBLE! I'VE NEVER SEEN ANYTHING LIKE IT!
THEN YOU'VE NEVER LOOKED IN BEETLE'S CLOSET!
STILL, WE HAVE A CHANCE! STARBONER THERE ISN'T AS SMART AS HE THINKS!
WHEN THESE METALLIC GOONS GATHERED US UP HE FORGOT SOMEONE!
MAXIMA!
SHE STIRS.
DESPITE THE BATTERING SHE'S TAKEN--
--DESPITE THE WEAKNESS THAT LEAVES HER EXHAUSTED--
--SHE HAS A PLANET TO RECLAIM.
AND SHE INTENDS TO DO IT.

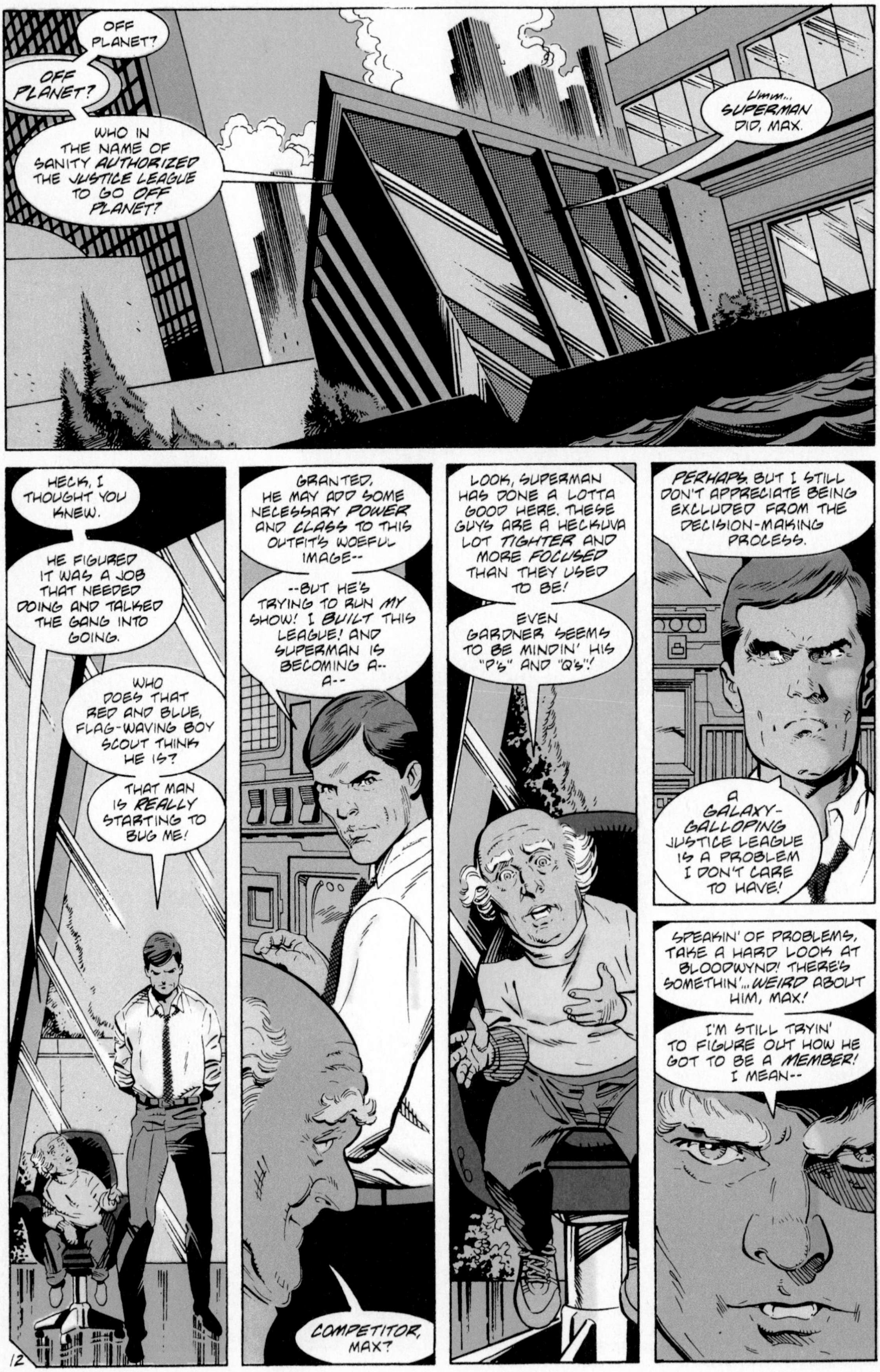
OFF PLANET?
OFF PLANET?
WHO IN THE NAME OF SANITY AUTHORIZED THE JUSTICE LEAGUE TO GO OFF PLANET?
Umm... SUPERMAN DID, MAX.
HECK, I THOUGHT YOU KNEW.
HE FIGURED IT WAS A JOB THAT NEEDED DOING AND TALKED THE GANG INTO GOING.
WHO DOES THAT RED AND BLUE, FLAG-WAVING BOY SCOUT THINK HE IS?
THAT MAN IS REALLY STARTING TO BUG ME!
GRANTED, HE MAY ADD SOME NECESSARY POWER AND CLASS TO THIS OUTFIT'S WOEFUL IMAGE--
--BUT HE'S TRYING TO RUN MY SHOW! I BUILT THIS LEAGUE! AND SUPERMAN IS BECOMING A-- A--
COMPETITOR, MAX?
LOOK, SUPERMAN HAS DONE A LOTTA GOOD HERE. THESE GUYS ARE A HECKUVA LOT TIGHTER AND MORE FOCUSED THAN THEY USED TO BE!
EVEN GARDNER SEEMS TO BE MINDIN' HIS "P's" AND "Q's"!
PERHAPS. BUT I STILL DON'T APPRECIATE BEING EXCLUDED FROM THE DECISION-MAKING PROCESS.
A GALAXY-GALLOPING JUSTICE LEAGUE IS A PROBLEM I DON'T CARE TO HAVE!
SPEAKIN' OF PROBLEMS, TAKE A HARD LOOK AT BLOODWYND! THERE'S SOMETHIN'... WEIRD ABOUT HIM, MAX!
I'M STILL TRYIN' TO FIGURE OUT HOW HE GOT TO BE A MEMBER! I MEAN--

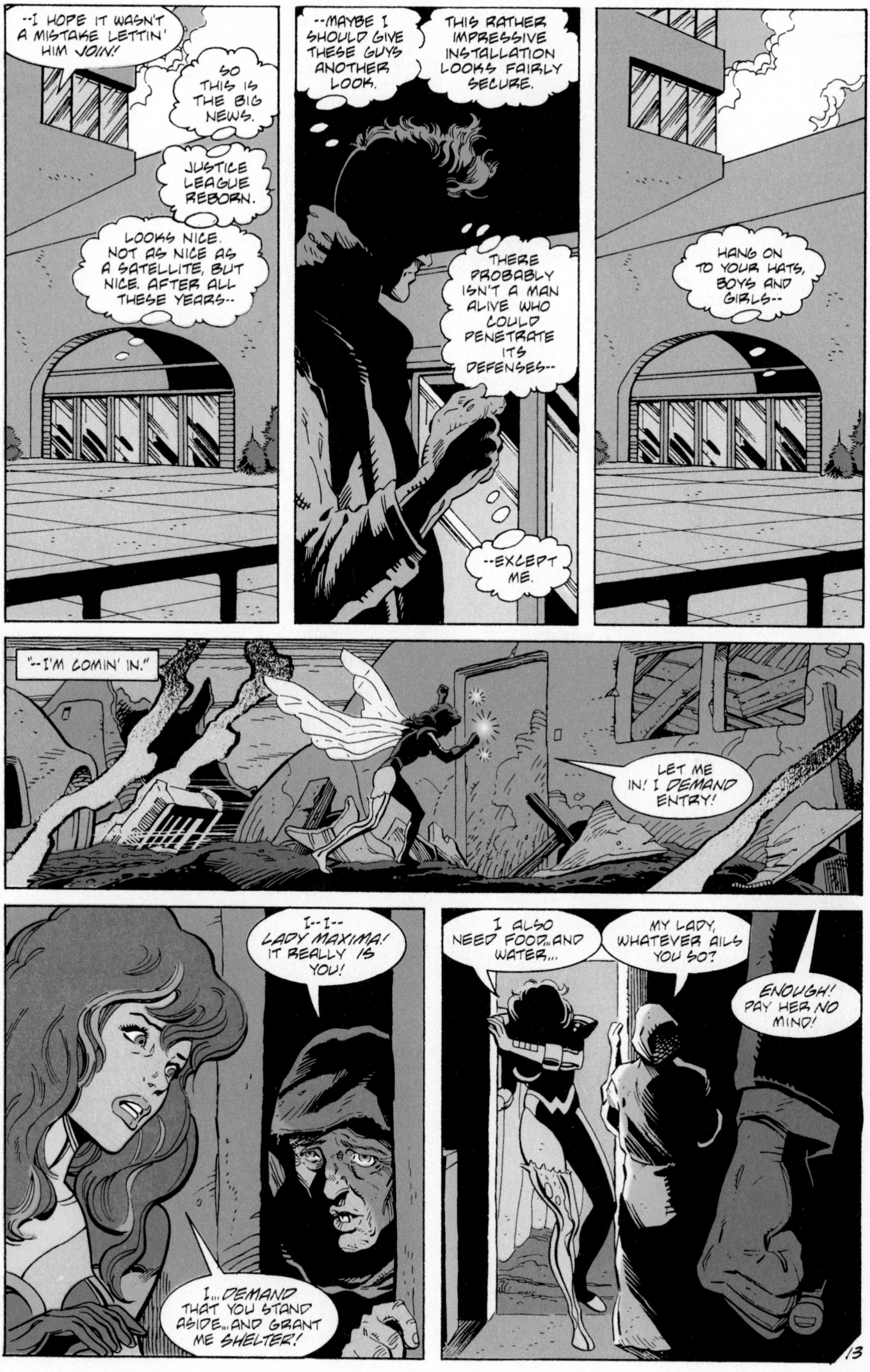
--I HOPE IT WASN'T A MISTAKE LETTIN' HIM JOIN!
SO THIS IS THE BIG NEWS.
JUSTICE LEAGUE REBORN.
LOOKS NICE. NOT AS NICE AS A SATELLITE, BUT NICE. AFTER ALL THESE YEARS--
--MAYBE I SHOULD GIVE THESE GUYS ANOTHER LOOK.
THIS RATHER IMPRESSIVE INSTALLATION LOOKS FAIRLY SECURE.
THERE PROBABLY ISN'T A MAN ALIVE WHO COULD PENETRATE ITS DEFENSES--
--EXCEPT ME.
HANG ON TO YOUR HATS, BOYS AND GIRLS--
"--I'M COMIN' IN."
LET ME IN! I DEMAND ENTRY!
I-- I-- LADY MAXIMA! IT REALLY IS YOU!
I... DEMAND THAT YOU STAND ASIDE... AND GRANT ME SHELTER!
I ALSO NEED FOOD... AND WATER...
MY LADY, WHATEVER AILS YOU SO?
ENOUGH! PAY HER NO MIND!

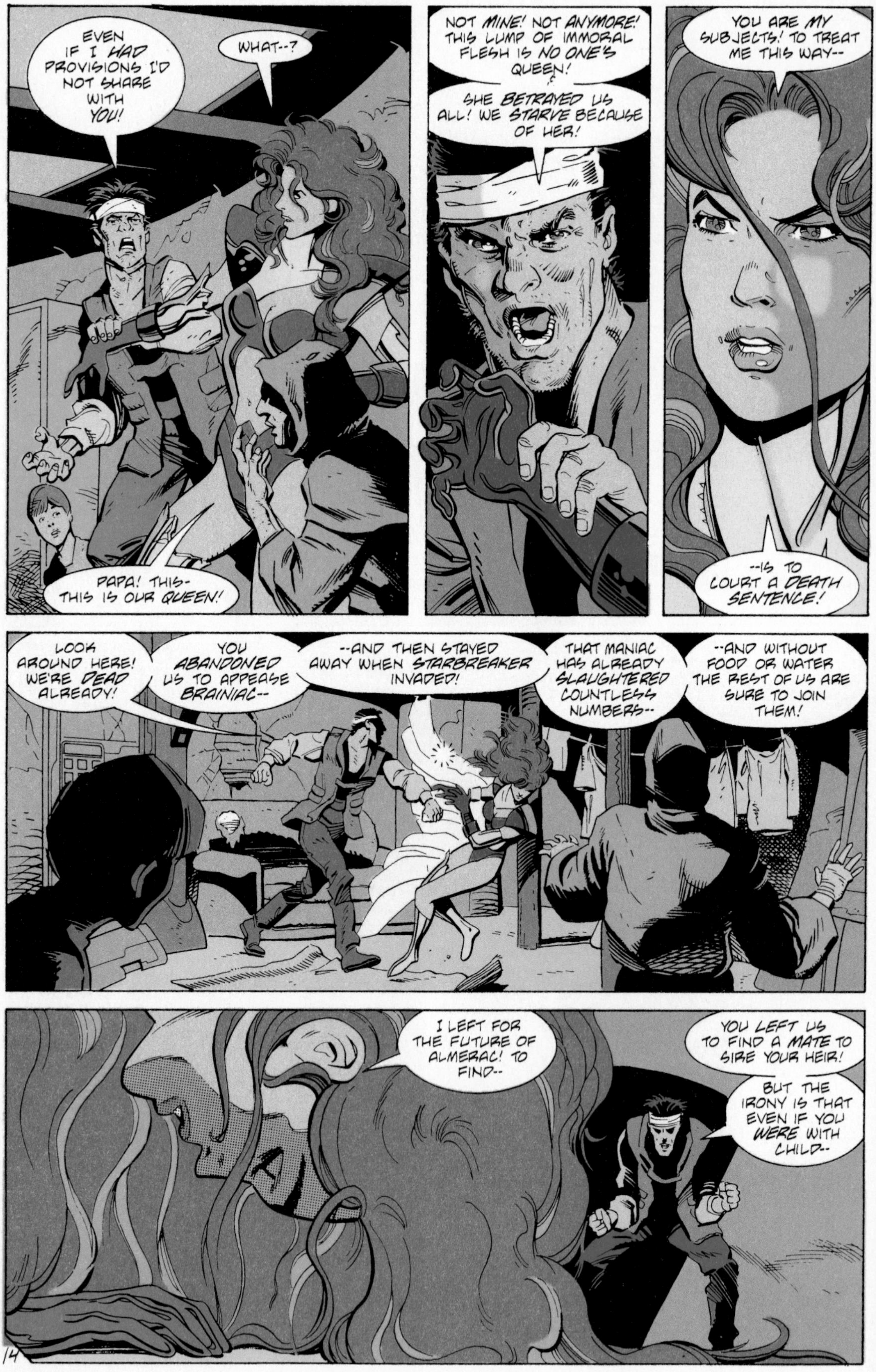
EVEN IF I HAD PROVISIONS I'D NOT SHARE WITH YOU!
WHAT--?
PAPA! THIS-THIS IS OUR QUEEN!
NOT MINE! NOT ANYMORE! THIS LUMP OF IMMORAL FLESH IS NO ONE'S QUEEN!
SHE BETRAYED US ALL! WE STARVE BECAUSE OF HER!
YOU ARE MY SUBJECTS! TO TREAT ME THIS WAY--
--IS TO COURT A DEATH SENTENCE!
LOOK AROUND HERE! WE'RE DEAD ALREADY!
YOU ABANDONED US TO APPEASE BRAINIAC--
--AND THEN STAYED AWAY WHEN STARBREAKER INVADED!
THAT MANIAC HAS ALREADY SLAUGHTERED COUNTLESS NUMBERS--
--AND WITHOUT FOOD OR WATER THE REST OF US ARE SURE TO JOIN THEM!
I LEFT FOR THE FUTURE OF ALMERAC! TO FIND--
YOU LEFT US TO FIND A MATE TO SIRE YOUR HEIR!
BUT THE IRONY IS THAT EVEN IF YOU WERE WITH CHILD--

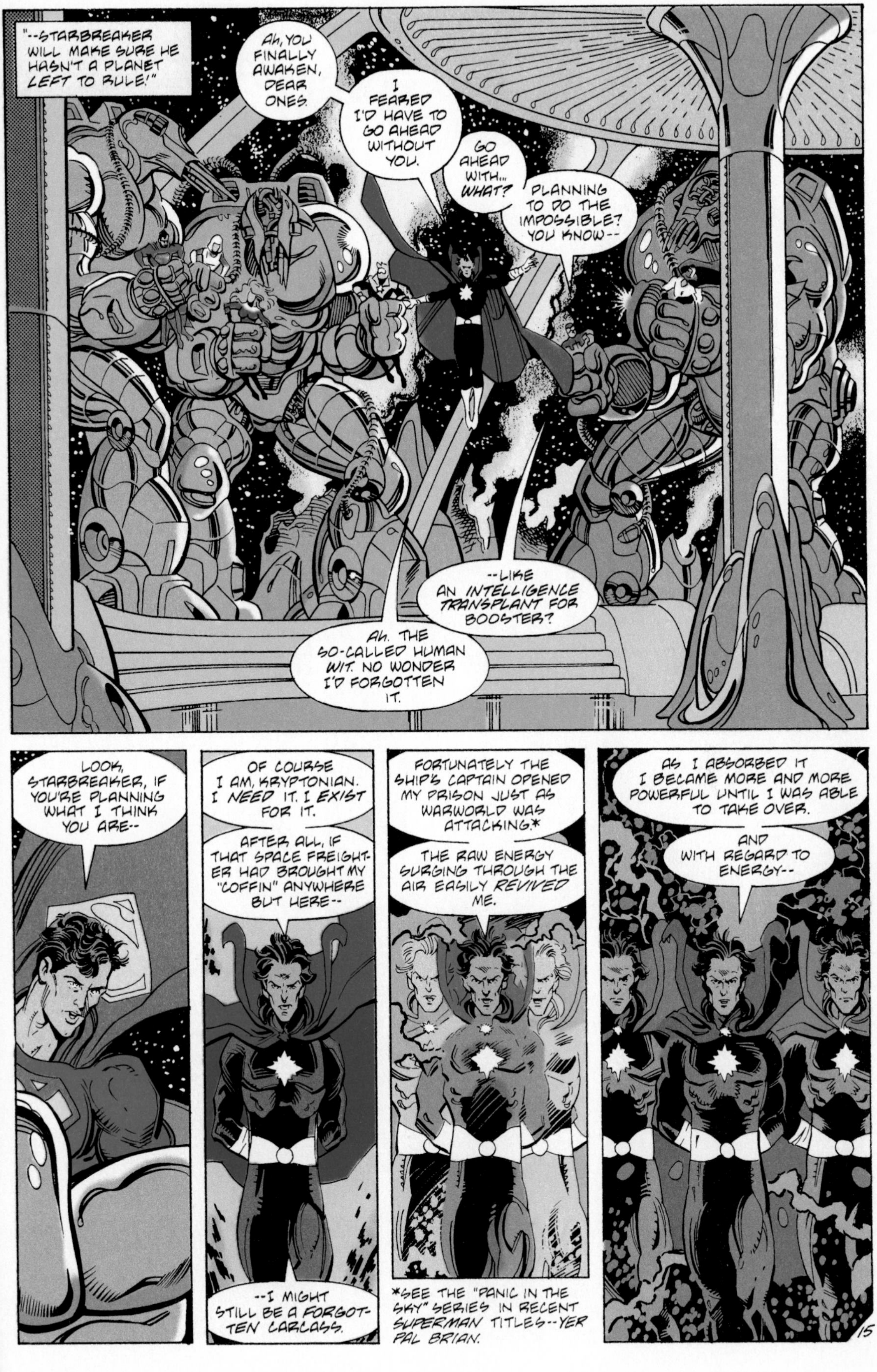
"--STARBREAKER WILL MAKE SURE HE HASN'T A PLANET LEFT TO RULE!"
AH, YOU FINALLY AWAKEN, DEAR ONES.
I FEARED I'D HAVE TO GO AHEAD WITHOUT YOU.
GO AHEAD WITH... WHAT?
PLANNING TO DO THE IMPOSSIBLE? YOU KNOW--
--LIKE AN INTELLIGENCE TRANSPLANT FOR BOOSTER?
AH. THE SO-CALLED HUMAN WIT. NO WONDER I'D FORGOTTEN IT.
LOOK, STARBREAKER, IF YOU'RE PLANNING WHAT I THINK YOU ARE--
OF COURSE I AM, KRYPTONIAN. I NEED IT. I EXIST FOR IT.
AFTER ALL, IF THAT SPACE FREIGHTER HAD BROUGHT MY "COFFIN" ANYWHERE BUT HERE--
--I MIGHT STILL BE A FORGOTTEN CARCASS.
FORTUNATELY THE SHIP'S CAPTAIN OPENED MY PRISON JUST AS WARWORLD WAS ATTACKING.*
THE RAW ENERGY SURGING THROUGH THE AIR EASILY REVIVED ME.
*SEE THE "PANIC IN THE SKY" SERIES IN RECENT SUPERMAN TITLES--YER PAL BRIAN.
AS I ABSORBED IT I BECAME MORE AND MORE POWERFUL UNTIL I WAS ABLE TO TAKE OVER.
AND WITH REGARD TO ENERGY--

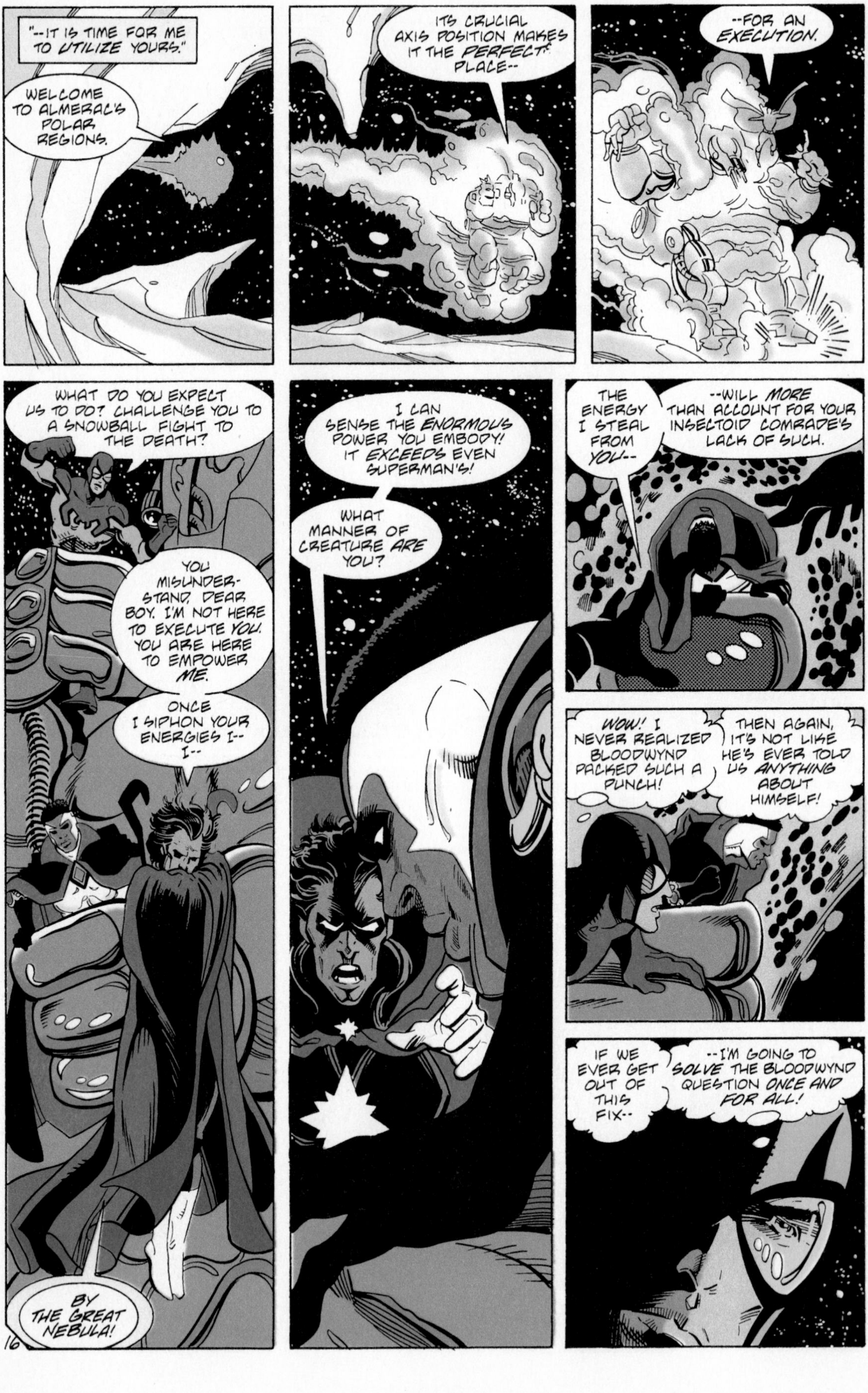
"--IT IS TIME FOR ME TO UTILIZE YOURS."
WELCOME TO ALMERAC'S POLAR REGIONS.
ITS CRUCIAL AXIS POSITION MAKES IT THE PERFECT PLACE--
--FOR AN EXECUTION.
WHAT DO YOU EXPECT US TO DO? CHALLENGE YOU TO A SNOWBALL FIGHT TO THE DEATH?
YOU MISUNDER-STAND, DEAR BOY. I'M NOT HERE TO EXECUTE YOU. YOU ARE HERE TO EMPOWER ME.
ONCE I SIPHON YOUR ENERGIES I-- I--
BY THE GREAT NEBULA!
I CAN SENSE THE ENORMOUS POWER YOU EMBODY! IT EXCEEDS EVEN SUPERMAN'S!
WHAT MANNER OF CREATURE ARE YOU?
THE ENERGY I STEAL FROM YOU--
--WILL MORE THAN ACCOUNT FOR YOUR INSECTOID COMRADE'S LACK OF SUCH.
WOW! I NEVER REALIZED BLOODWYND PACKED SUCH A PUNCH!
THEN AGAIN, IT'S NOT LIKE HE'S EVER TOLD US ANYTHING ABOUT HIMSELF!
IF WE EVER GET OUT OF THIS FIX--
--I'M GOING TO SOLVE THE BLOODWYND QUESTION ONCE AND FOR ALL!

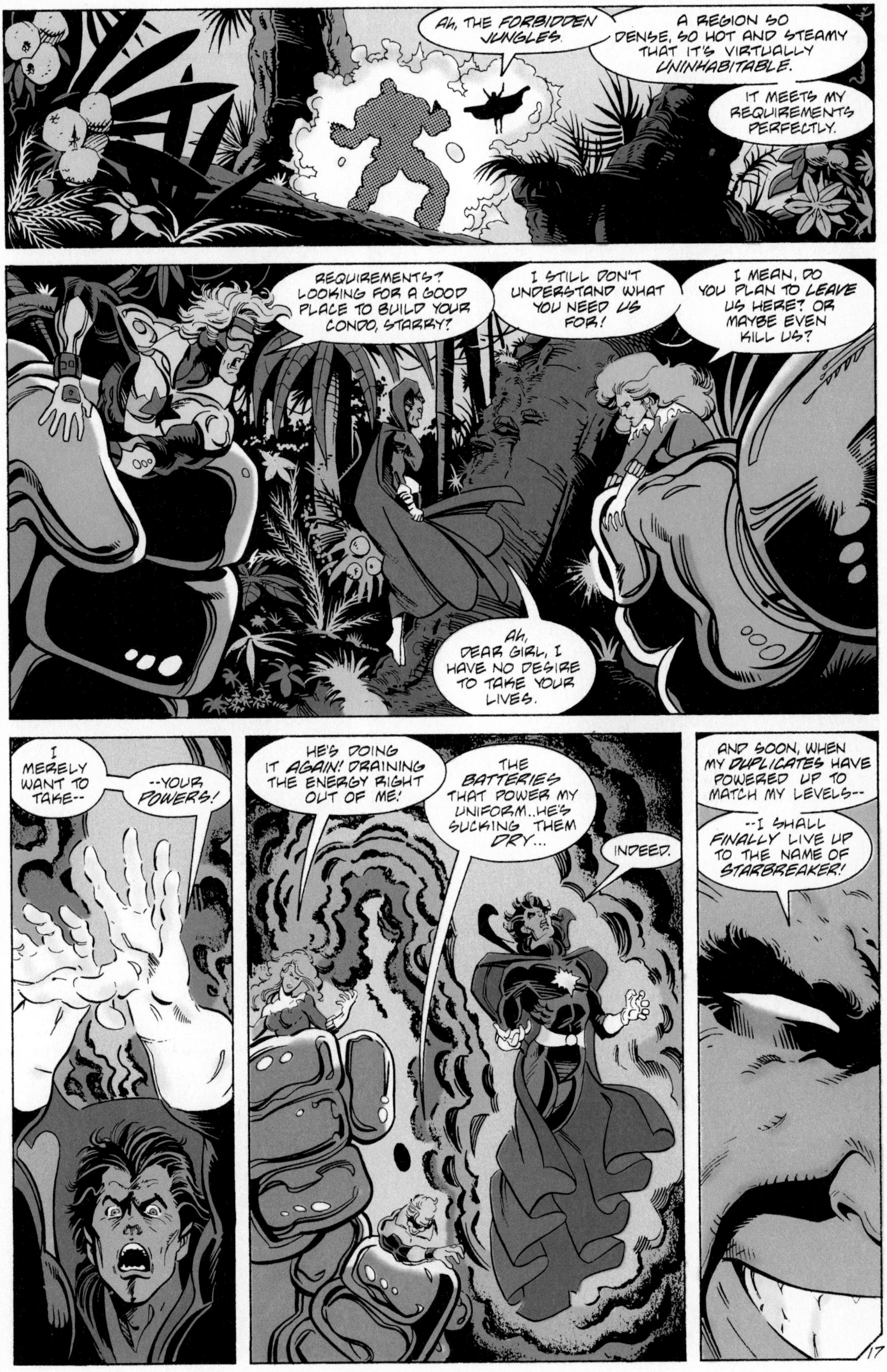

AH, THE FORBIDDEN JUNGLES.
A REGION SO DENSE, SO HOT AND STEAMY THAT IT'S VIRTUALLY UNINHABITABLE.
IT MEETS MY REQUIREMENTS PERFECTLY.
REQUIREMENTS? LOOKING FOR A GOOD PLACE TO BUILD YOUR CONDO, STARRY?
I STILL DON'T UNDERSTAND WHAT YOU NEED US FOR!
I MEAN, DO YOU PLAN TO LEAVE US HERE? OR MAYBE EVEN KILL US?
AH, DEAR GIRL, I HAVE NO DESIRE TO TAKE YOUR LIVES.
I MERELY WANT TO TAKE--
--YOUR POWERS!
HE'S DOING IT AGAIN! DRAINING THE ENERGY RIGHT OUT OF ME!
THE BATTERIES THAT POWER MY UNIFORM..HE'S SUCKING THEM DRY...
INDEED.
AND SOON, WHEN MY DUPLICATES HAVE POWERED UP TO MATCH MY LEVELS--
--I SHALL FINALLY LIVE UP TO THE NAME OF STARBREAKER!

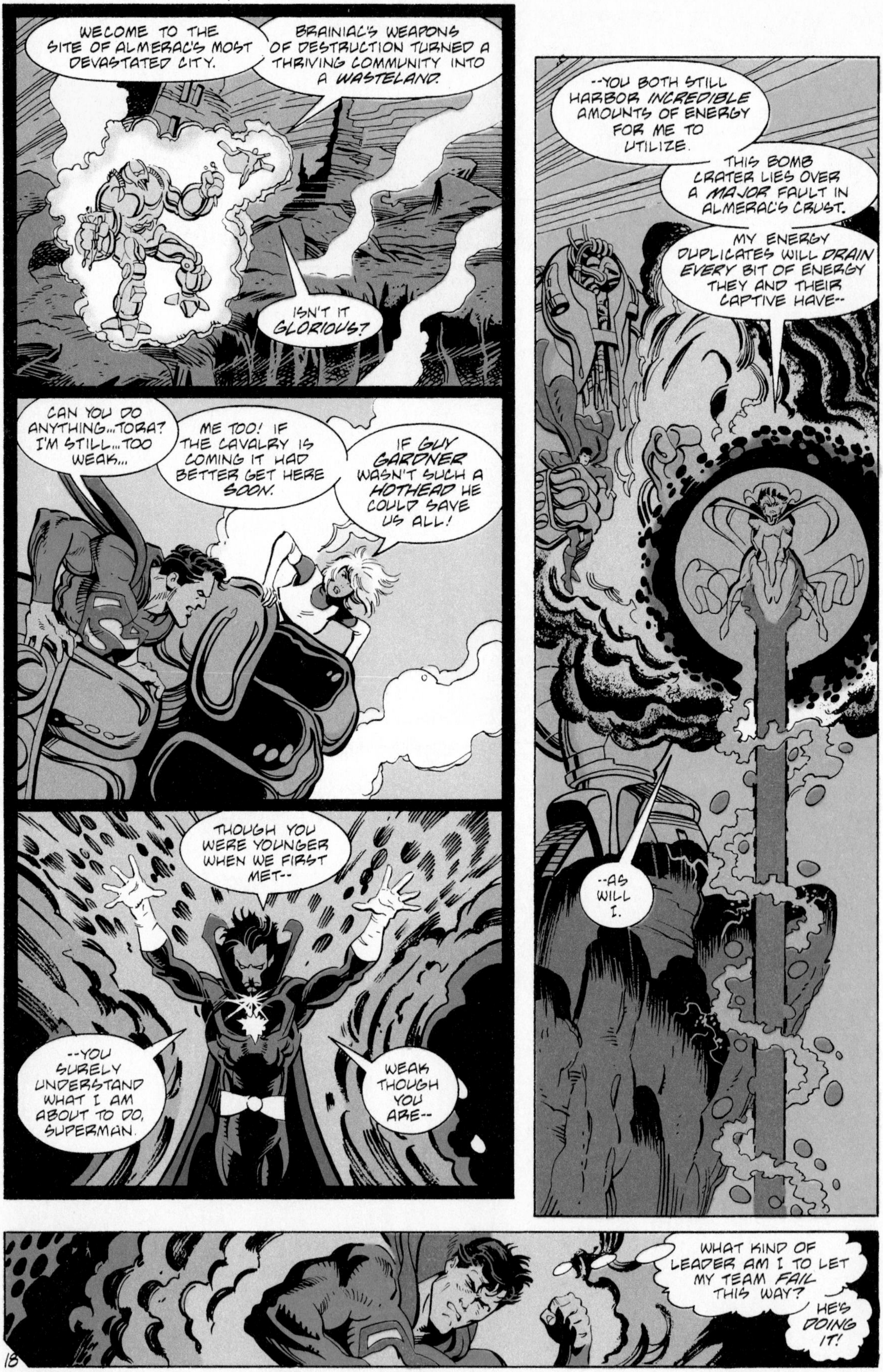
WELCOME TO THE SITE OF ALMERAC'S MOST DEVASTATED CITY.
BRAINIAC'S WEAPONS OF DESTRUCTION TURNED A THRIVING COMMUNITY INTO A WASTELAND.
ISN'T IT GLORIOUS?
CAN YOU DO ANYTHING...TORA? I'M STILL...TOO WEAK...
ME TOO! IF THE CAVALRY IS COMING IT HAD BETTER GET HERE SOON.
IF GUY GARDNER WASN'T SUCH A HOTHEAD HE COULD SAVE US ALL!
THOUGH YOU WERE YOUNGER WHEN WE FIRST MET--
--YOU SURELY UNDERSTAND WHAT I AM ABOUT TO DO, SUPERMAN.
WEAK THOUGH YOU ARE--
--YOU BOTH STILL HARBOR INCREDIBLE AMOUNTS OF ENERGY FOR ME TO UTILIZE.
THIS BOMB CRATER LIES OVER A MAJOR FAULT IN ALMERAC'S CRUST.
MY ENERGY DUPLICATES WILL DRAIN EVERY BIT OF ENERGY THEY AND THEIR CAPTIVE HAVE--
--AS WILL I.
WHAT KIND OF LEADER AM I TO LET MY TEAM FAIL THIS WAY?
HE'S DOING IT!

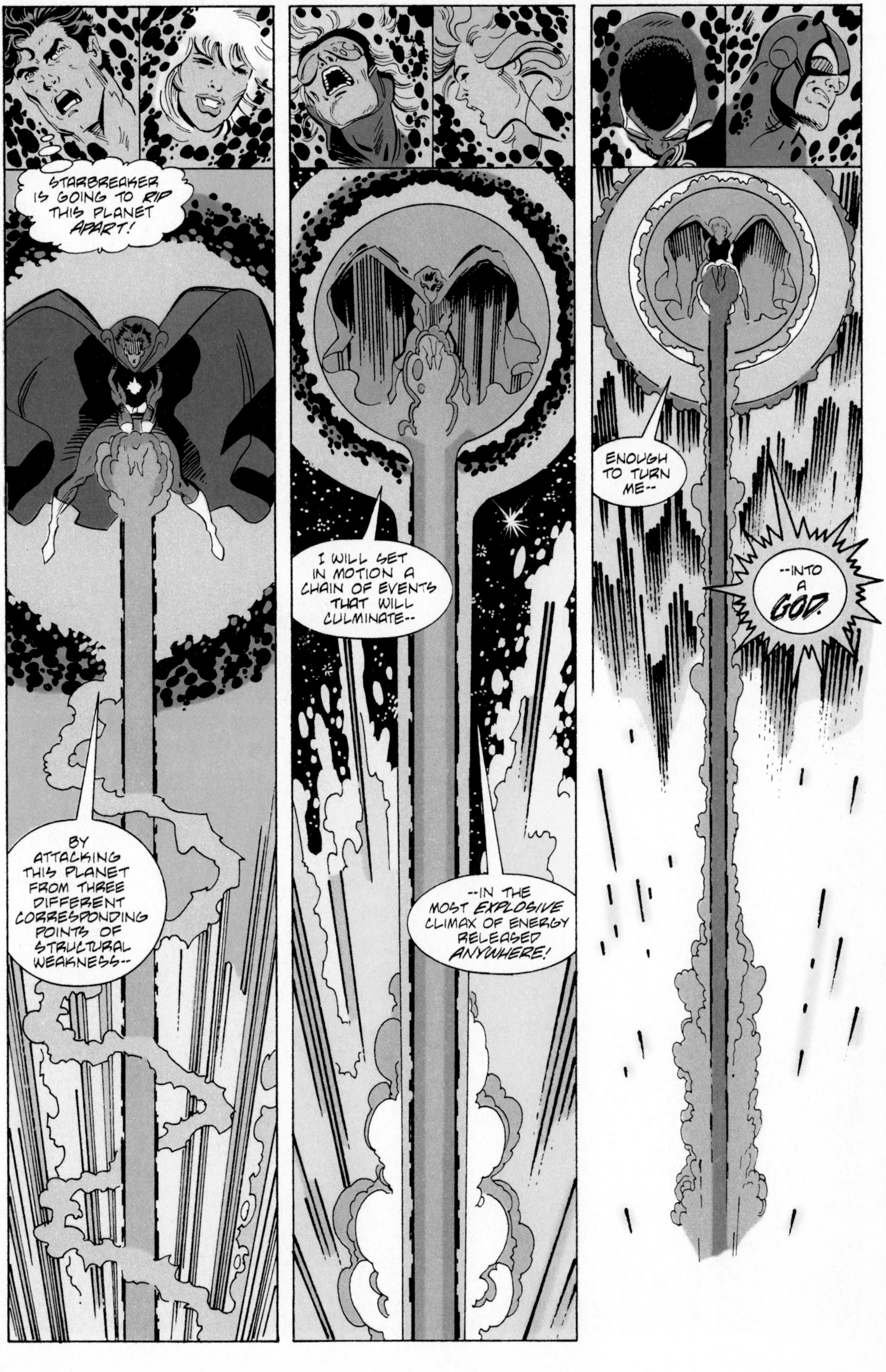
STARBREAKER IS GOING TO RIP THIS PLANET APART!
BY ATTACKING THIS PLANET FROM THREE DIFFERENT CORRESPONDING POINTS OF STRUCTURAL WEAKNESS--
I WILL SET IN MOTION A CHAIN OF EVENTS THAT WILL CULMINATE--
--IN THE MOST EXPLOSIVE CLIMAX OF ENERGY RELEASED ANYWHERE!
ENOUGH TO TURN ME--
--INTO A GOD.

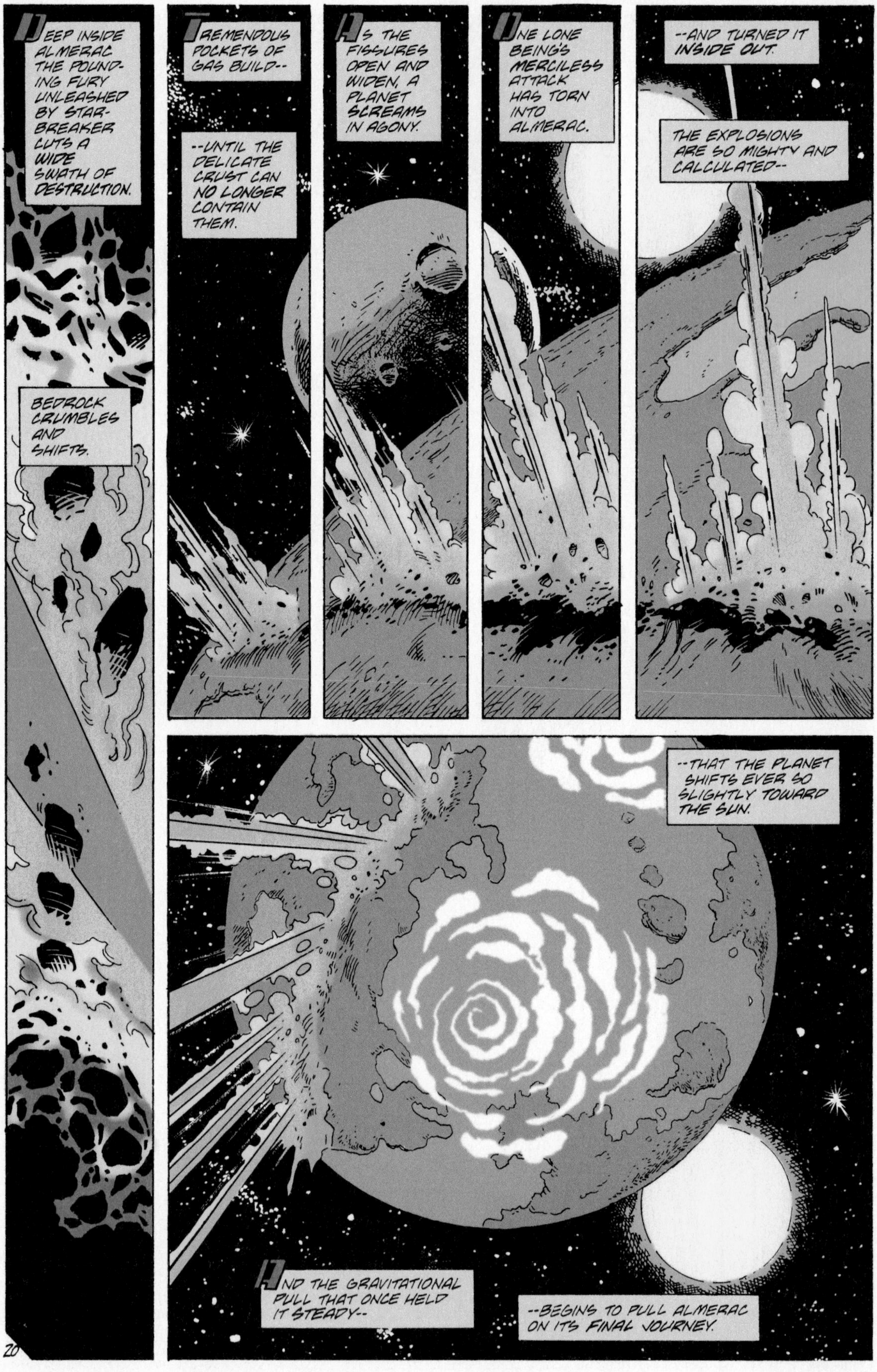
DEEP INSIDE ALMERAC THE POUNDING FURY UNLEASHED BY STARBREAKER CUTS A WIDE SWATH OF DESTRUCTION.
BEDROCK CRUMBLES AND SHIFTS.
TREMENDOUS POCKETS OF GAS BUILD--
--UNTIL THE DELICATE CRUST CAN NO LONGER CONTAIN THEM.
AS THE FISSURES OPEN AND WIDEN, A PLANET SCREAMS IN AGONY.
ONE LONE BEING'S MERCILESS ATTACK HAS TORN INTO ALMERAC.
--AND TURNED IT INSIDE OUT.
THE EXPLOSIONS ARE SO MIGHTY AND CALCULATED--
--THAT THE PLANET SHIFTS EVER SO SLIGHTLY TOWARD THE SUN.
AND THE GRAVITATIONAL PULL THAT ONCE HELD IT STEADY--
--BEGINS TO PULL ALMERAC ON ITS FINAL JOURNEY.

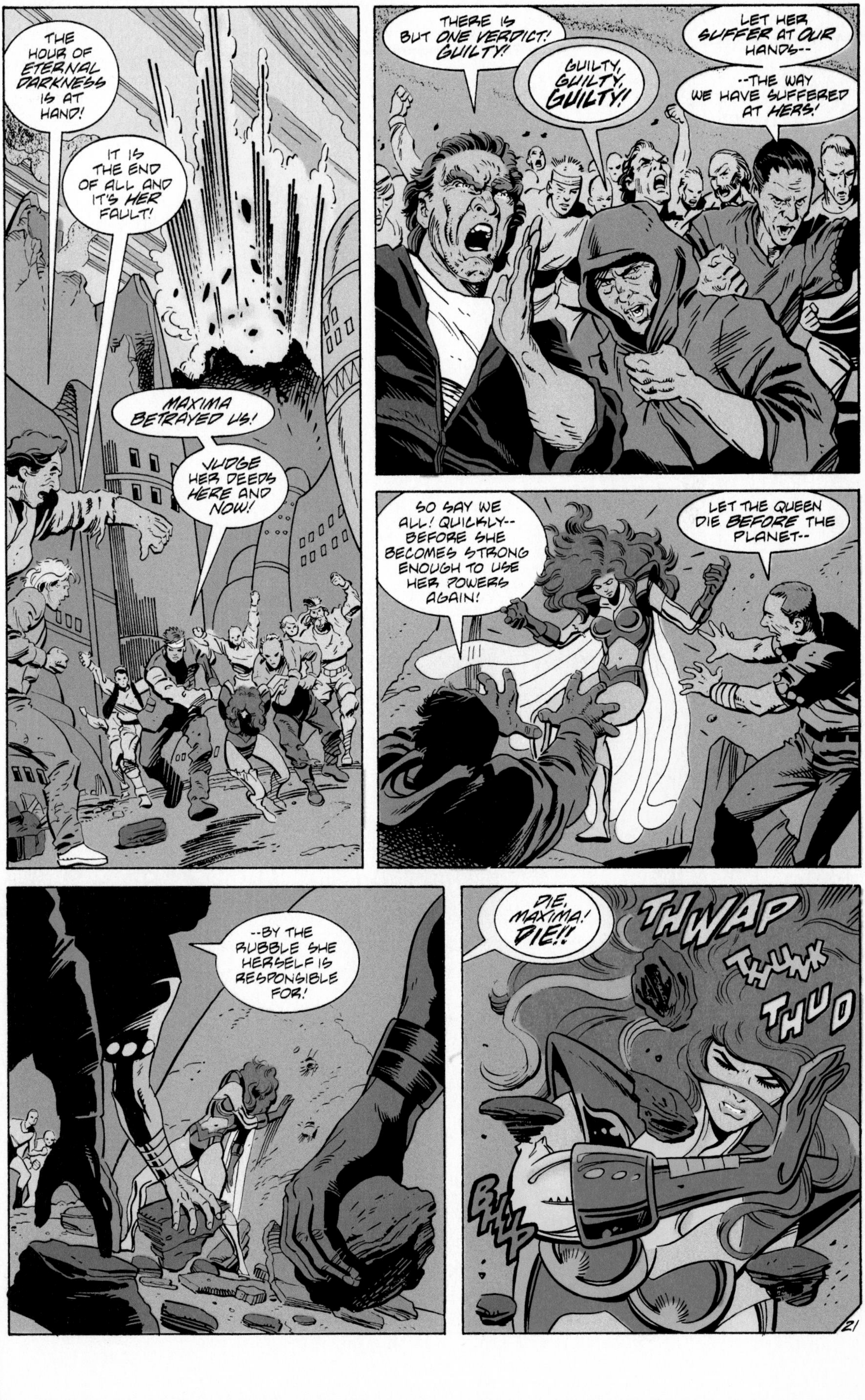
THE HOUR OF ETERNAL DARKNESS IS AT HAND!
IT IS THE END OF ALL AND IT'S HER FAULT!
MAXIMA BETRAYED US!
JUDGE HER DEEDS HERE AND NOW!
THERE IS BUT ONE VERDICT! GUILTY!
GUILTY, GUILTY, GUILTY!
LET HER SUFFER AT OUR HANDS--
--THE WAY WE HAVE SUFFERED AT HERS!
SO SAY WE ALL! QUICKLY-- BEFORE SHE BECOMES STRONG ENOUGH TO USE HER POWERS AGAIN!
LET THE QUEEN DIE BEFORE THE PLANET--
--BY THE RUBBLE SHE HERSELF IS RESPONSIBLE FOR!
DIE, MAXIMA! DIE!!
THWAP
THUNK
THUD
BLAP

AND SO IT ENDS.

ONLY ONE TASK REMAINS.

WHAT DO YOU WANT WITH SUPERMAN?

HE'S *UNCONSCIOUS!* HE CAN'T POSSIBLY *HURT* YOU ANYMORE!

TRUE ENOUGH, *DEAR GIRL.* I HAVE TAKEN *ALL* HE HAS.

YET THIS KRYPTONIAN *BESTED* ME ONCE BEFORE. ONLY A *FOOL* WOULD LET HIM LIVE TO TRY *AGAIN.*

NO....

NOOO!

IN HIS WEAKENED CONDITION HE CANNOT POSSIBLY SURVIVE THE MOLTEN CORE OF ALMERAC.

DIE-- AS THIS PLANET DIES, SUPERMAN.

ONCE IT COLLIDES WITH THE SUN--

--I BECOME THE MOST *POWERFUL* BEING IN ALL OF *CREATION!*

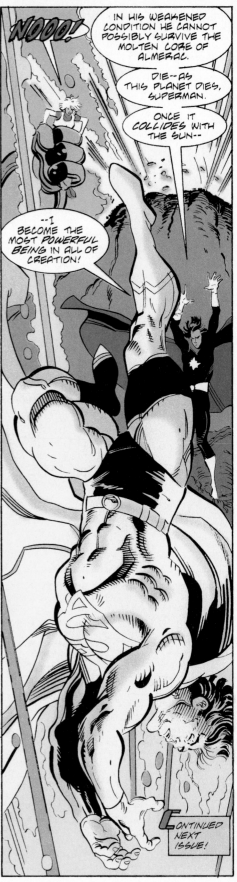

CONTINUED NEXT ISSUE!

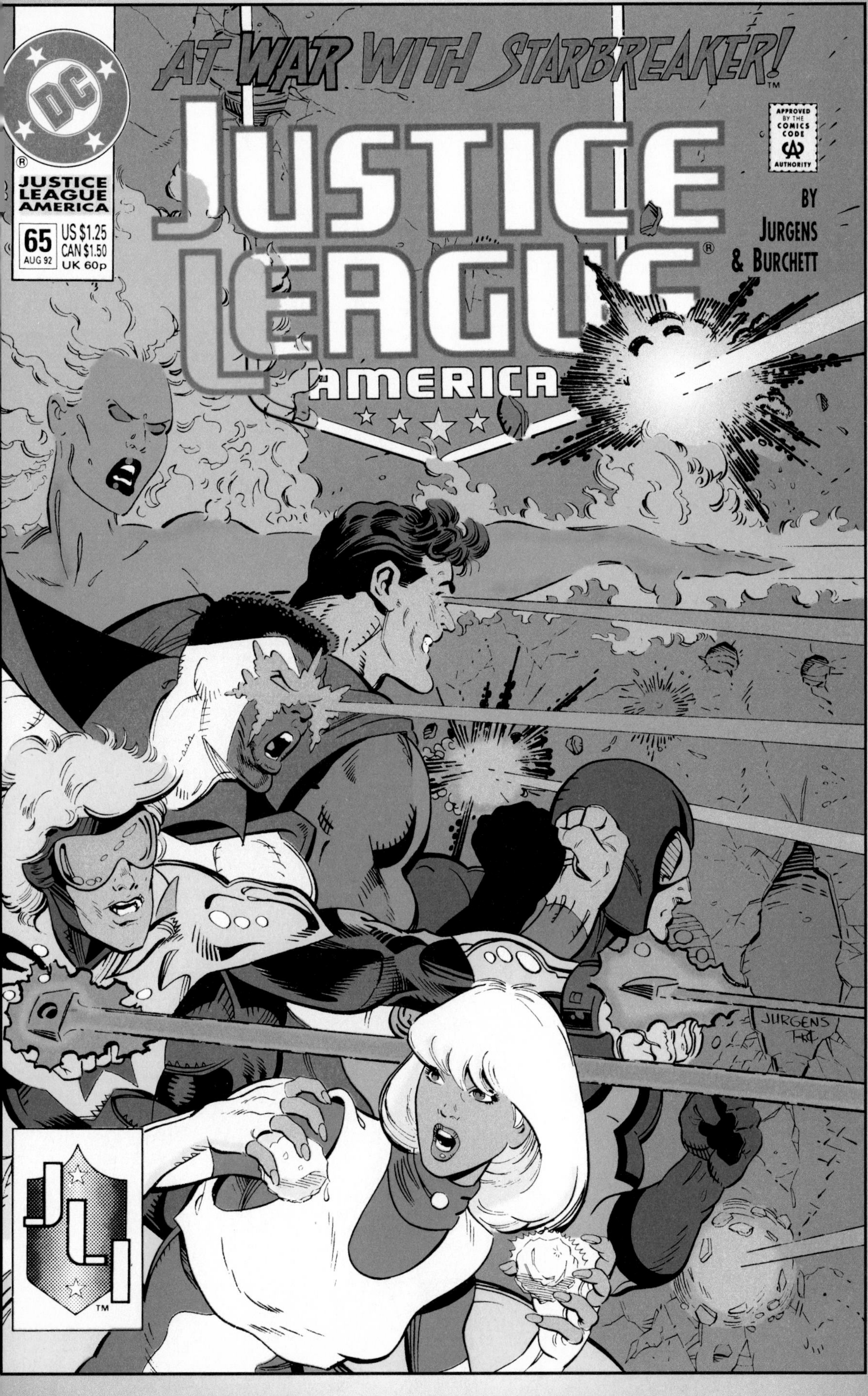

AT WAR WITH STARBREAKER!
JUSTICE LEAGUE AMERICA
DC
JUSTICE LEAGUE AMERICA
65
AUG 92
US $1.25
CAN $1.50
UK 60p
APPROVED BY THE COMICS CODE AUTHORITY
BY JURGENS & BURCHETT
JURGENS

Cover art by **DAN JURGENS** and **RICK BURCHETT**

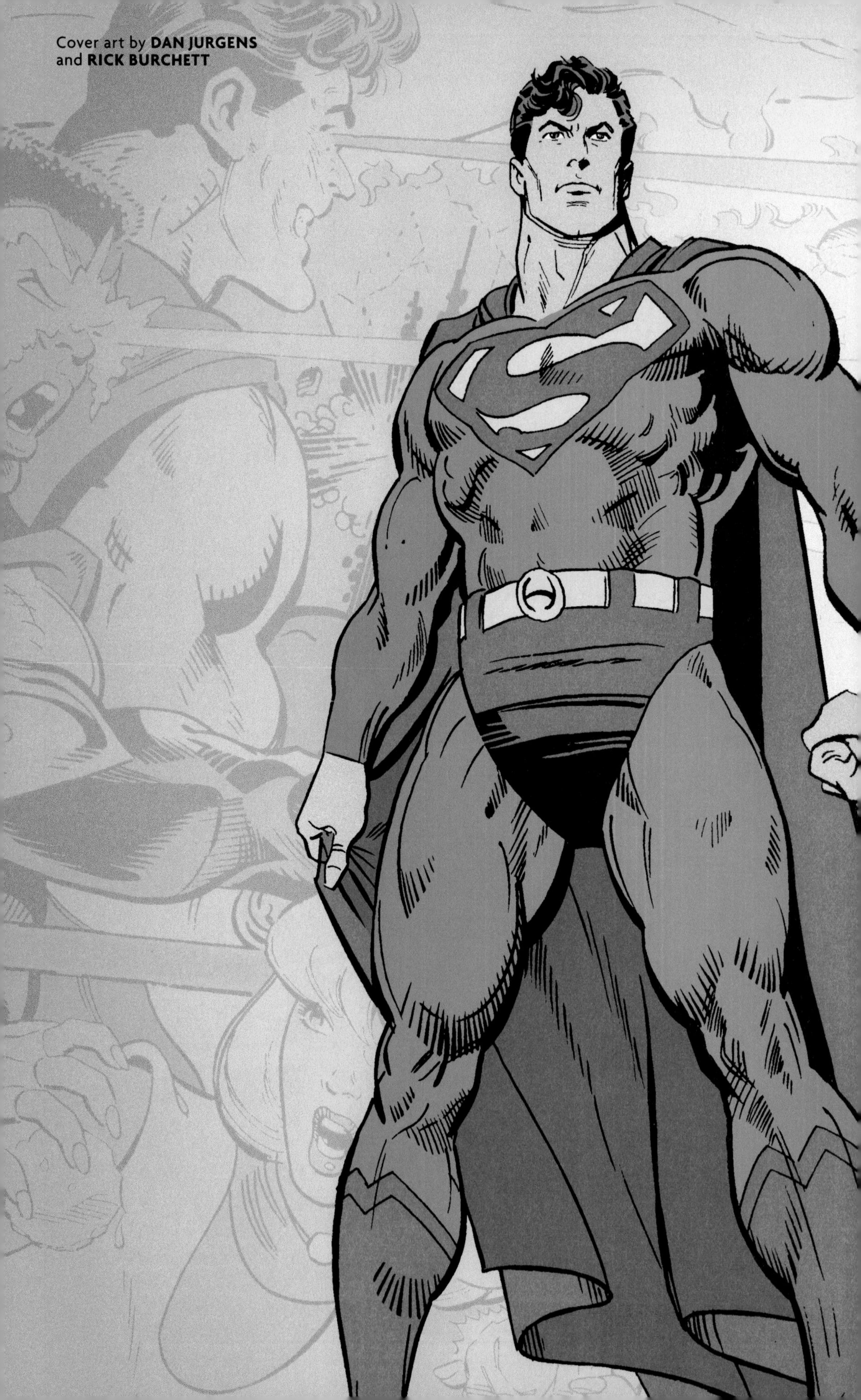

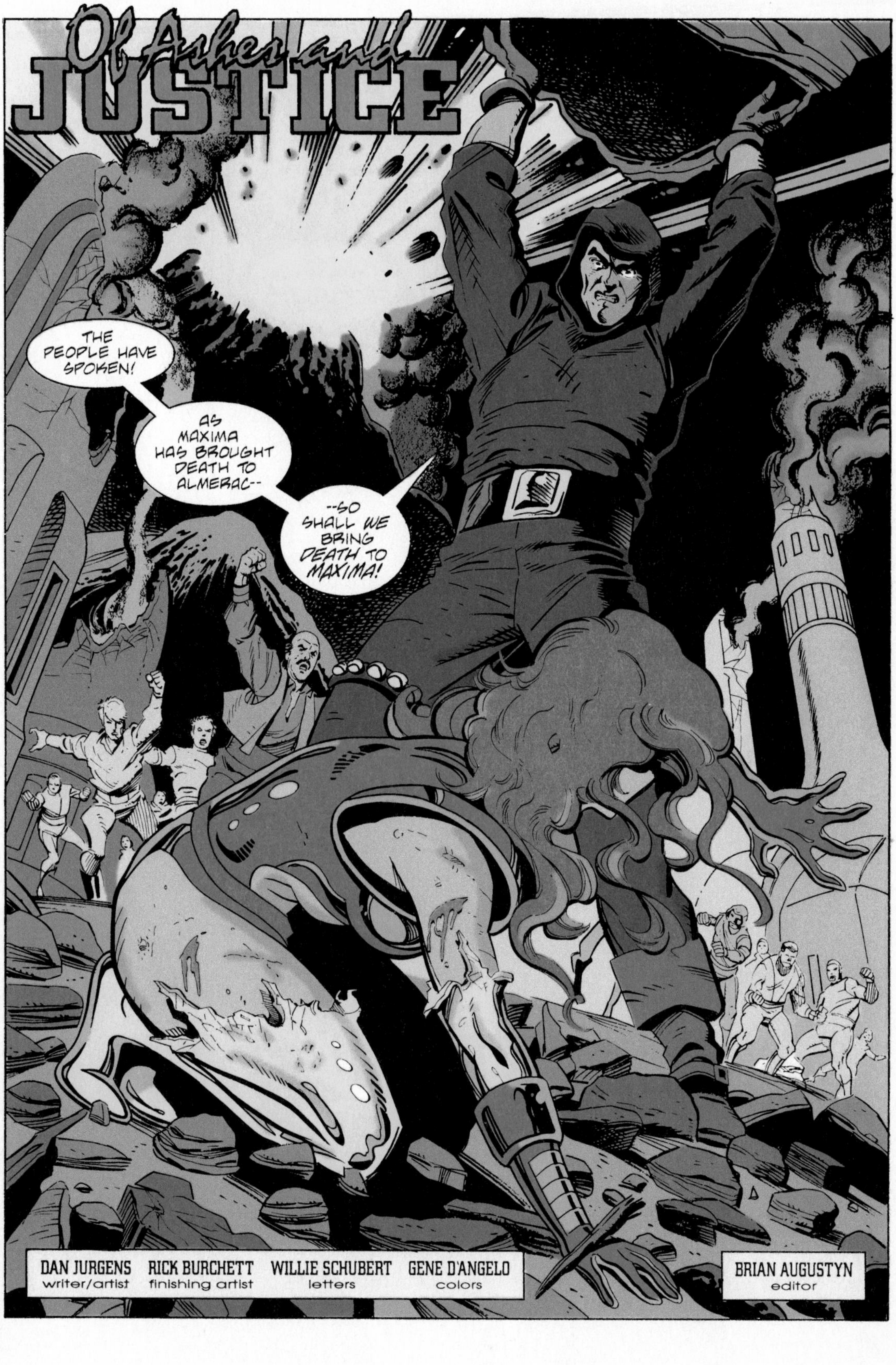

Of Ashes and JUSTICE
THE PEOPLE HAVE SPOKEN!
AS MAXIMA HAS BROUGHT DEATH TO ALMERAC--
--SO SHALL WE BRING DEATH TO MAXIMA!
DAN JURGENS writer/artist
RICK BURCHETT finishing artist
WILLIE SCHUBERT letters
GENE D'ANGELO colors
BRIAN AUGUSTYN editor

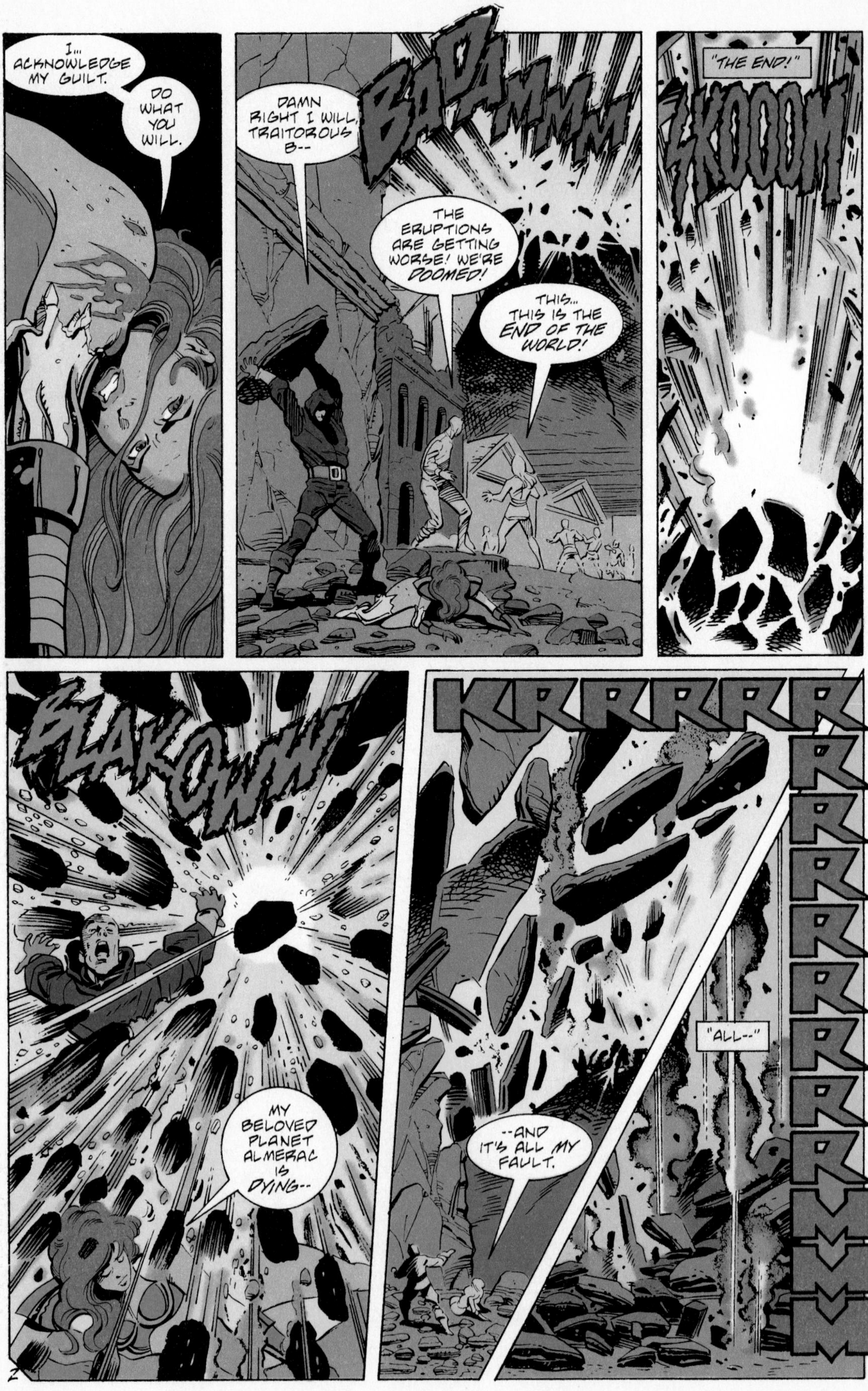

I... ACKNOWLEDGE MY GUILT.
DO WHAT YOU WILL.
DAMN RIGHT I WILL, TRAITOROUS B--
BADAMMMM
THE ERUPTIONS ARE GETTING WORSE! WE'RE DOOMED!
THIS... THIS IS THE END OF THE WORLD!
"THE END!"
SKOOOM
BLAKOWW
MY BELOVED PLANET ALMERAC IS DYING--
KRRRRRRRRRRRRRRRRUMMM
"ALL--"
--AND IT'S ALL MY FAULT.

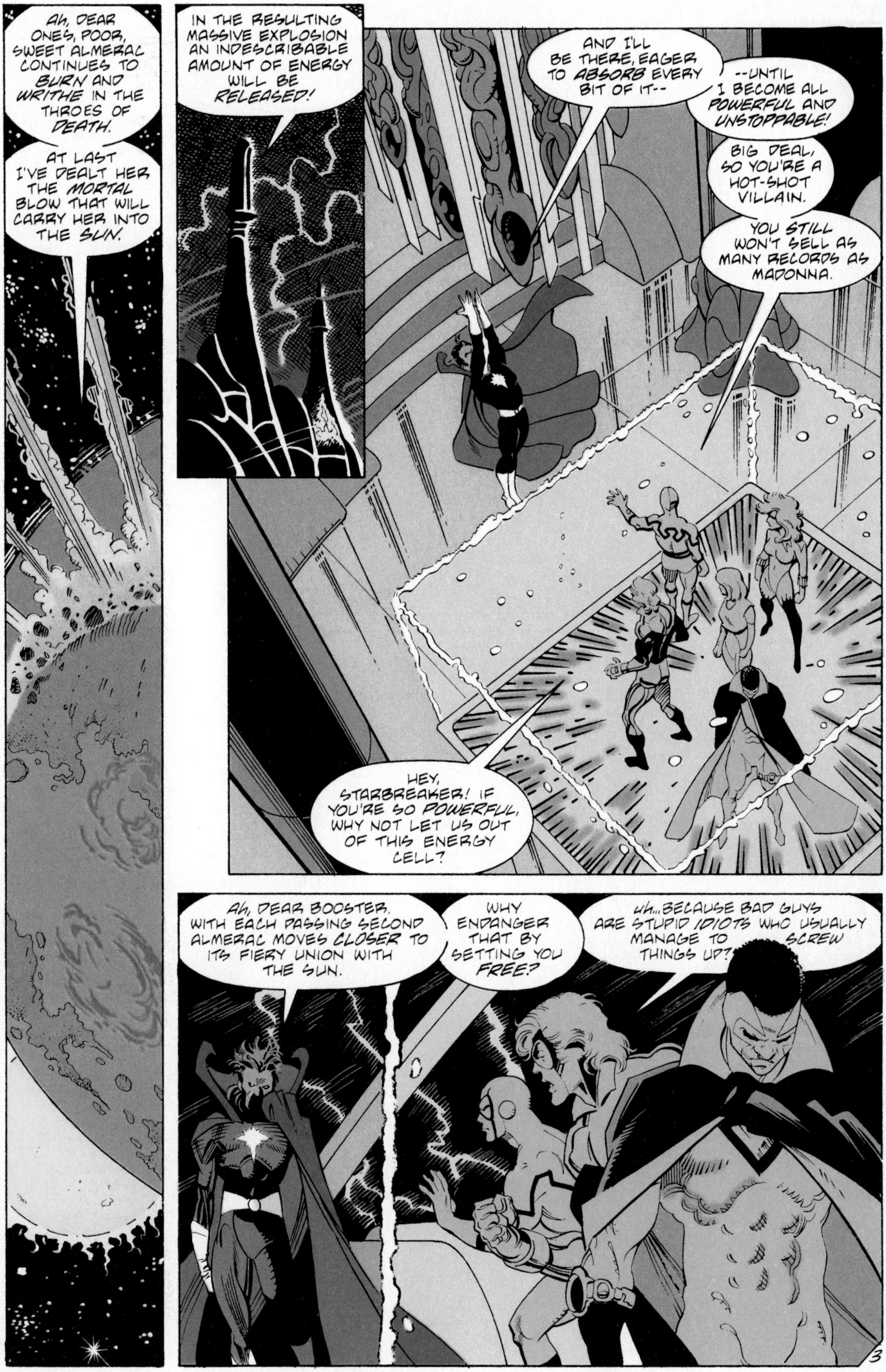
AH, DEAR ONES, POOR, SWEET ALMERAC CONTINUES TO BURN AND WRITHE IN THE THROES OF DEATH.
AT LAST I'VE DEALT HER THE MORTAL BLOW THAT WILL CARRY HER INTO THE SUN.
IN THE RESULTING MASSIVE EXPLOSION AN INDESCRIBABLE AMOUNT OF ENERGY WILL BE RELEASED!
AND I'LL BE THERE, EAGER TO ABSORB EVERY BIT OF IT--
--UNTIL I BECOME ALL POWERFUL AND UNSTOPPABLE!
BIG DEAL, SO YOU'RE A HOT-SHOT VILLAIN.
YOU STILL WON'T SELL AS MANY RECORDS AS MADONNA.
HEY, STARBREAKER! IF YOU'RE SO POWERFUL, WHY NOT LET US OUT OF THIS ENERGY CELL?
AH, DEAR BOOSTER. WITH EACH PASSING SECOND ALMERAC MOVES CLOSER TO ITS FIERY UNION WITH THE SUN.
WHY ENDANGER THAT BY SETTING YOU FREE?
UH...BECAUSE BAD GUYS ARE STUPID IDIOTS WHO USUALLY MANAGE TO SCREW THINGS UP?

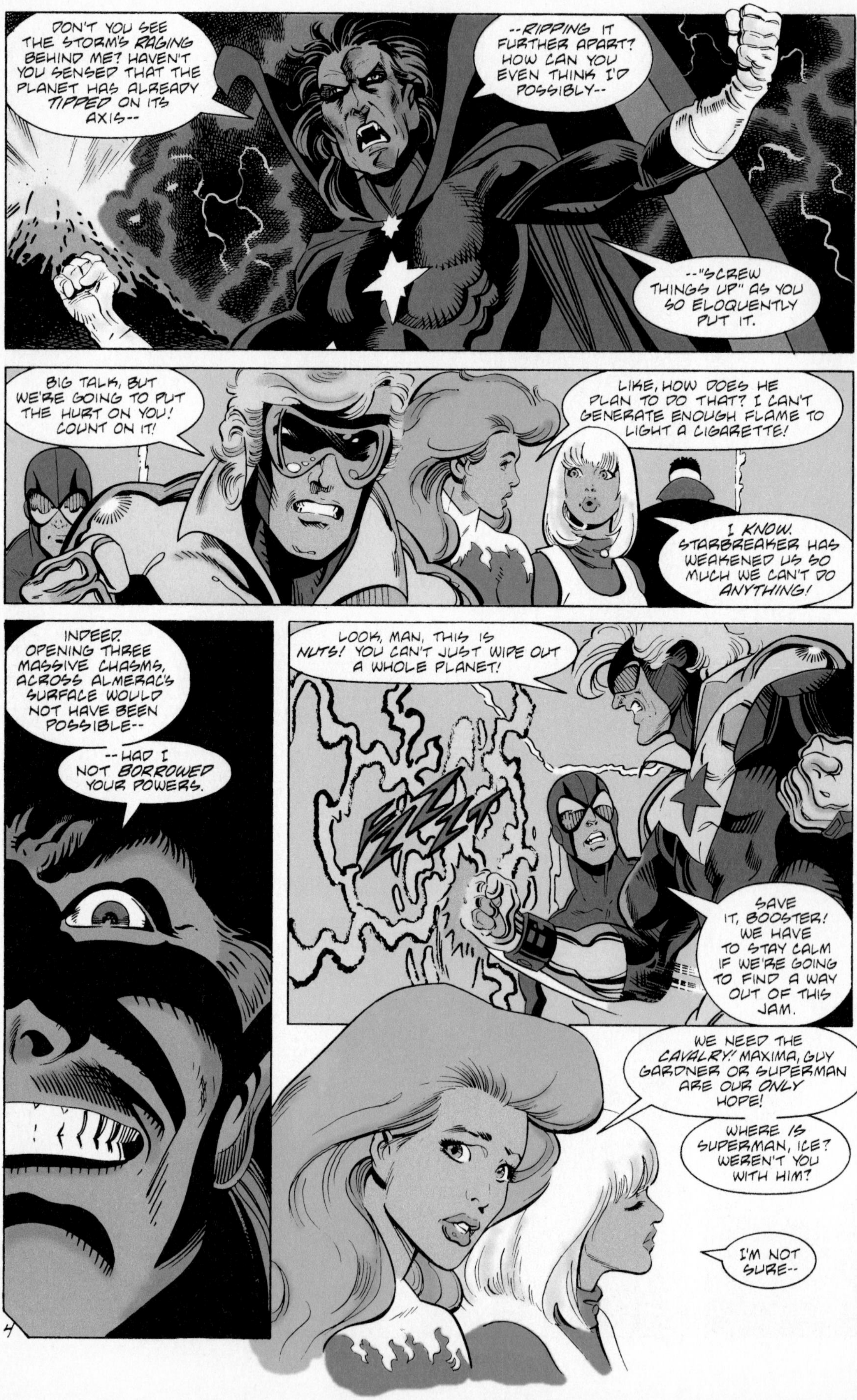
DON'T YOU SEE THE STORM'S RAGING BEHIND ME? HAVEN'T YOU SENSED THAT THE PLANET HAS ALREADY TIPPED ON ITS AXIS--
--RIPPING IT FURTHER APART? HOW CAN YOU EVEN THINK I'D POSSIBLY--
--"SCREW THINGS UP" AS YOU SO ELOQUENTLY PUT IT.
BIG TALK, BUT WE'RE GOING TO PUT THE HURT ON YOU! COUNT ON IT!
LIKE, HOW DOES HE PLAN TO DO THAT? I CAN'T GENERATE ENOUGH FLAME TO LIGHT A CIGARETTE!
I KNOW. STARBREAKER HAS WEAKENED US SO MUCH WE CAN'T DO ANYTHING!
INDEED. OPENING THREE MASSIVE CHASMS ACROSS ALMERAC'S SURFACE WOULD NOT HAVE BEEN POSSIBLE--
--HAD I NOT BORROWED YOUR POWERS.
LOOK, MAN, THIS IS NUTS! YOU CAN'T JUST WIPE OUT A WHOLE PLANET!
SAVE IT, BOOSTER! WE HAVE TO STAY CALM IF WE'RE GOING TO FIND A WAY OUT OF THIS JAM.
WE NEED THE CAVALRY! MAXIMA, GUY GARDNER OR SUPERMAN ARE OUR ONLY HOPE!
WHERE IS SUPERMAN, ICE? WEREN'T YOU WITH HIM?
I'M NOT SURE--
4

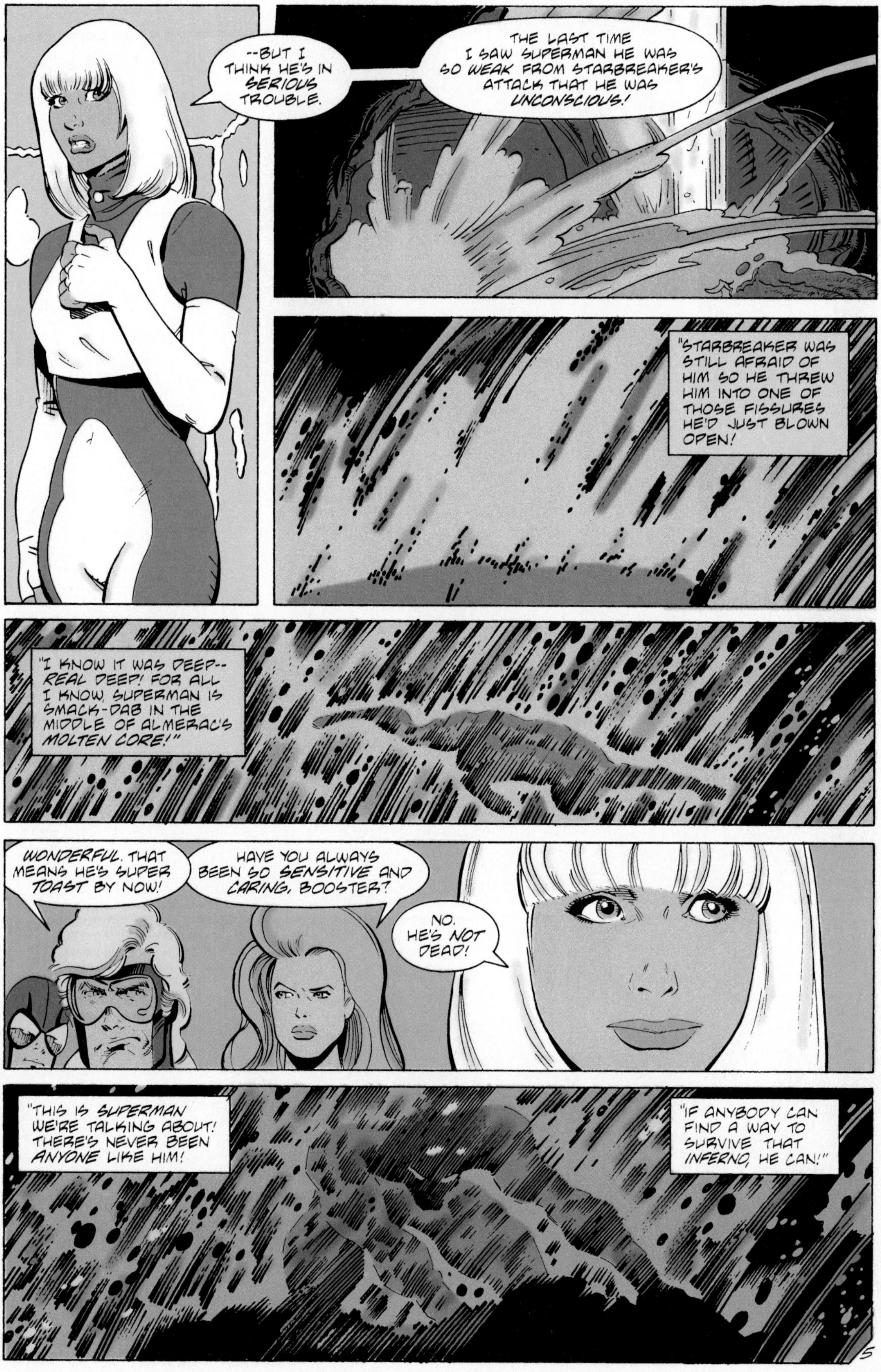
--BUT I THINK HE'S IN SERIOUS TROUBLE.
THE LAST TIME I SAW SUPERMAN HE WAS SO WEAK FROM STARBREAKER'S ATTACK THAT HE WAS UNCONSCIOUS!
"STARBREAKER WAS STILL AFRAID OF HIM SO HE THREW HIM INTO ONE OF THOSE FISSURES HE'D JUST BLOWN OPEN!
"I KNOW IT WAS DEEP--REAL DEEP! FOR ALL I KNOW, SUPERMAN IS SMACK-DAB IN THE MIDDLE OF ALMERAC'S MOLTEN CORE!"
WONDERFUL. THAT MEANS HE'S SUPER TOAST BY NOW!
HAVE YOU ALWAYS BEEN SO SENSITIVE AND CARING, BOOSTER?
NO. HE'S NOT DEAD!
"THIS IS SUPERMAN WE'RE TALKING ABOUT! THERE'S NEVER BEEN ANYONE LIKE HIM!
"IF ANYBODY CAN FIND A WAY TO SURVIVE THAT INFERNO, HE CAN!"
5

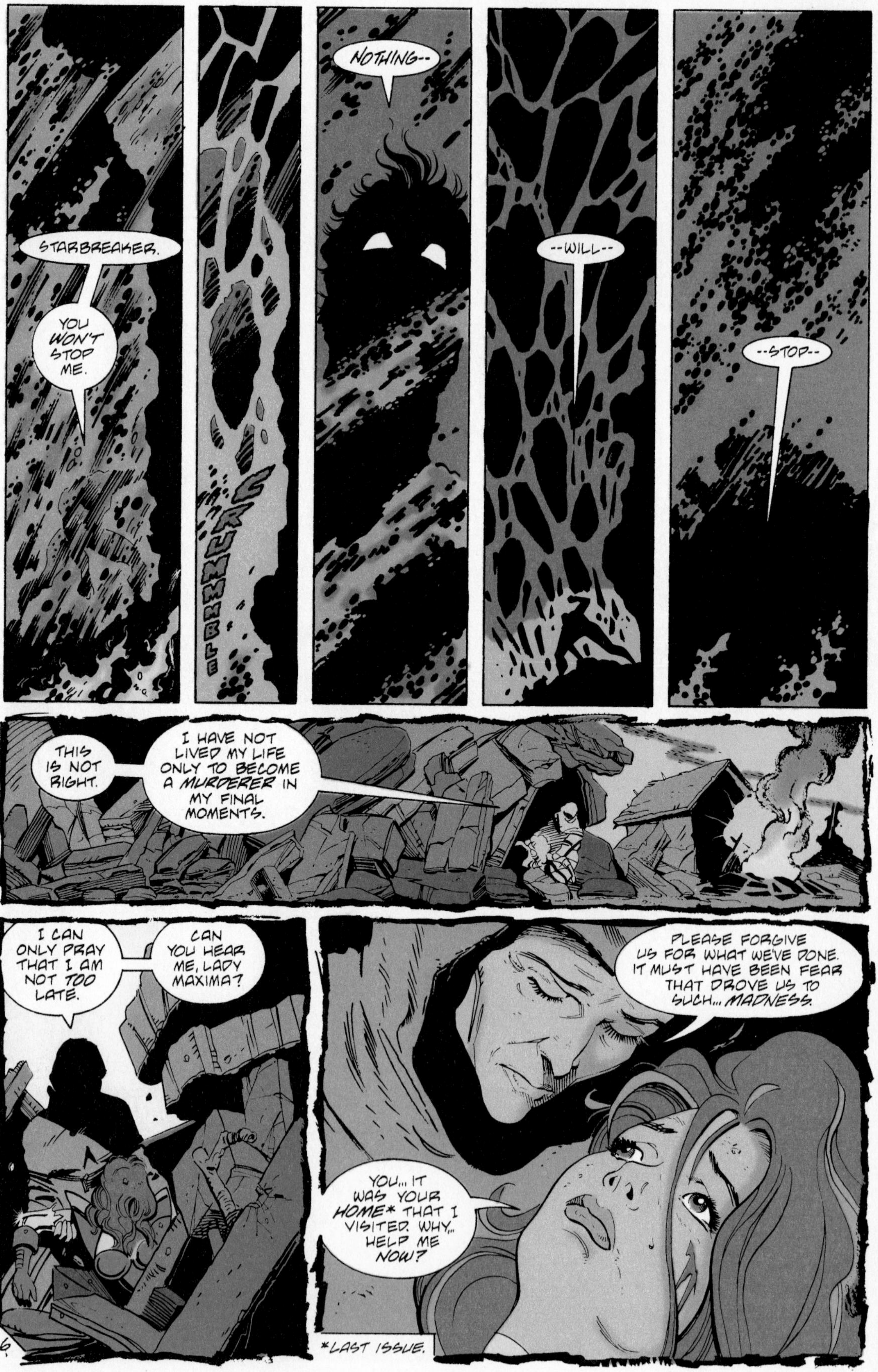
STARBREAKER.
YOU WON'T STOP ME.
NOTHING--
--WILL--
--STOP--
THIS IS NOT RIGHT.
I HAVE NOT LIVED MY LIFE ONLY TO BECOME A MURDERER IN MY FINAL MOMENTS.
I CAN ONLY PRAY THAT I AM NOT TOO LATE.
CAN YOU HEAR ME, LADY MAXIMA?
PLEASE FORGIVE US FOR WHAT WE'VE DONE. IT MUST HAVE BEEN FEAR THAT DROVE US TO SUCH... MADNESS.
YOU... IT WAS YOUR HOME* THAT I VISITED. WHY... HELP ME NOW?
*LAST ISSUE.

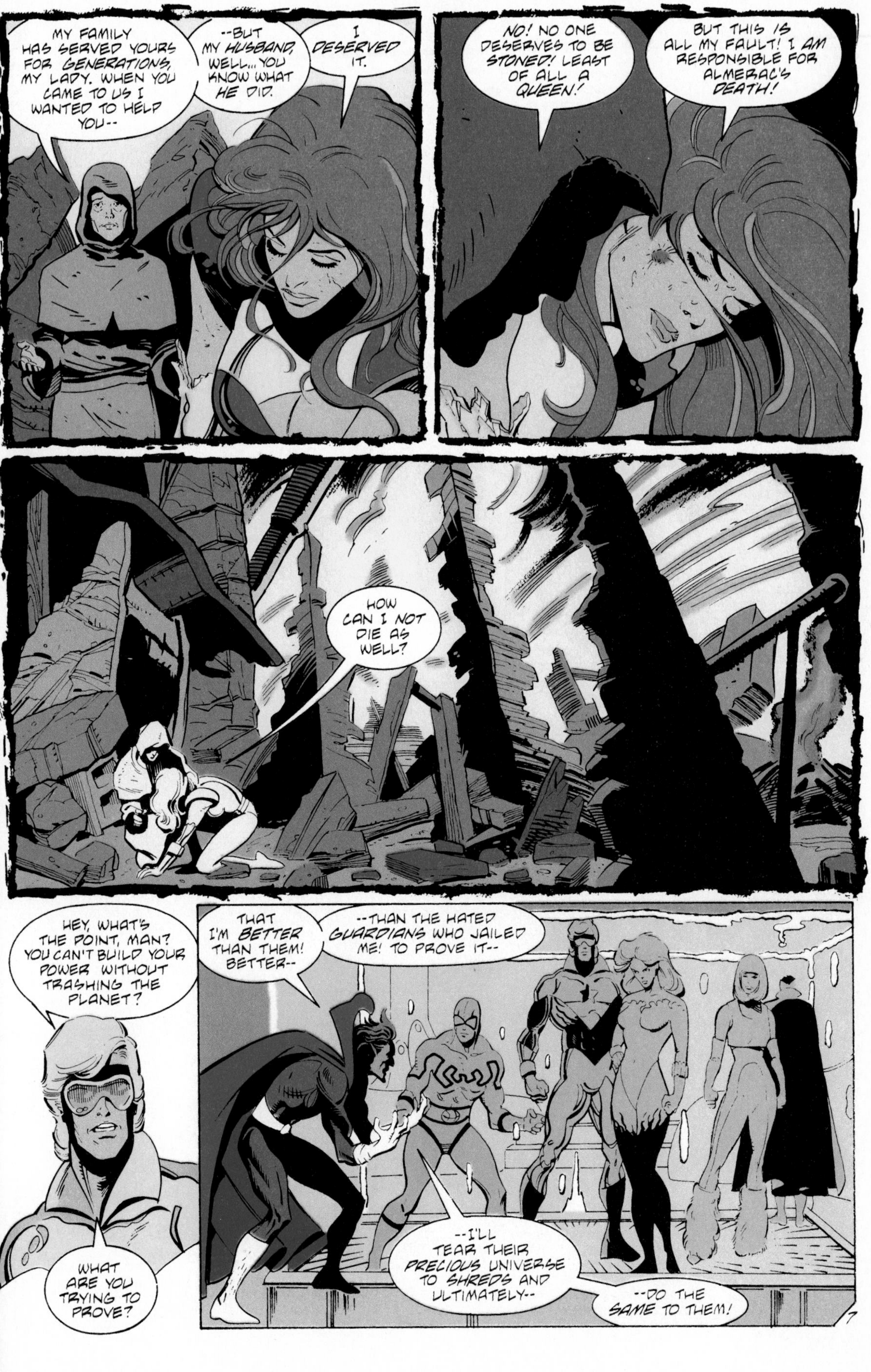
MY FAMILY HAS SERVED YOURS FOR GENERATIONS, MY LADY. WHEN YOU CAME TO US I WANTED TO HELP YOU--
--BUT MY HUSBAND, WELL... YOU KNOW WHAT HE DID.
I DESERVED IT.
NO! NO ONE DESERVES TO BE STONED! LEAST OF ALL A QUEEN!
BUT THIS IS ALL MY FAULT! I AM RESPONSIBLE FOR ALMERAC'S DEATH!
HOW CAN I NOT DIE AS WELL?
HEY, WHAT'S THE POINT, MAN? YOU CAN'T BUILD YOUR POWER WITHOUT TRASHING THE PLANET?
WHAT ARE YOU TRYING TO PROVE?
THAT I'M BETTER THAN THEM! BETTER--
--THAN THE HATED GUARDIANS WHO JAILED ME! TO PROVE IT--
--I'LL TEAR THEIR PRECIOUS UNIVERSE TO SHREDS AND ULTIMATELY--
--DO THE SAME TO THEM!

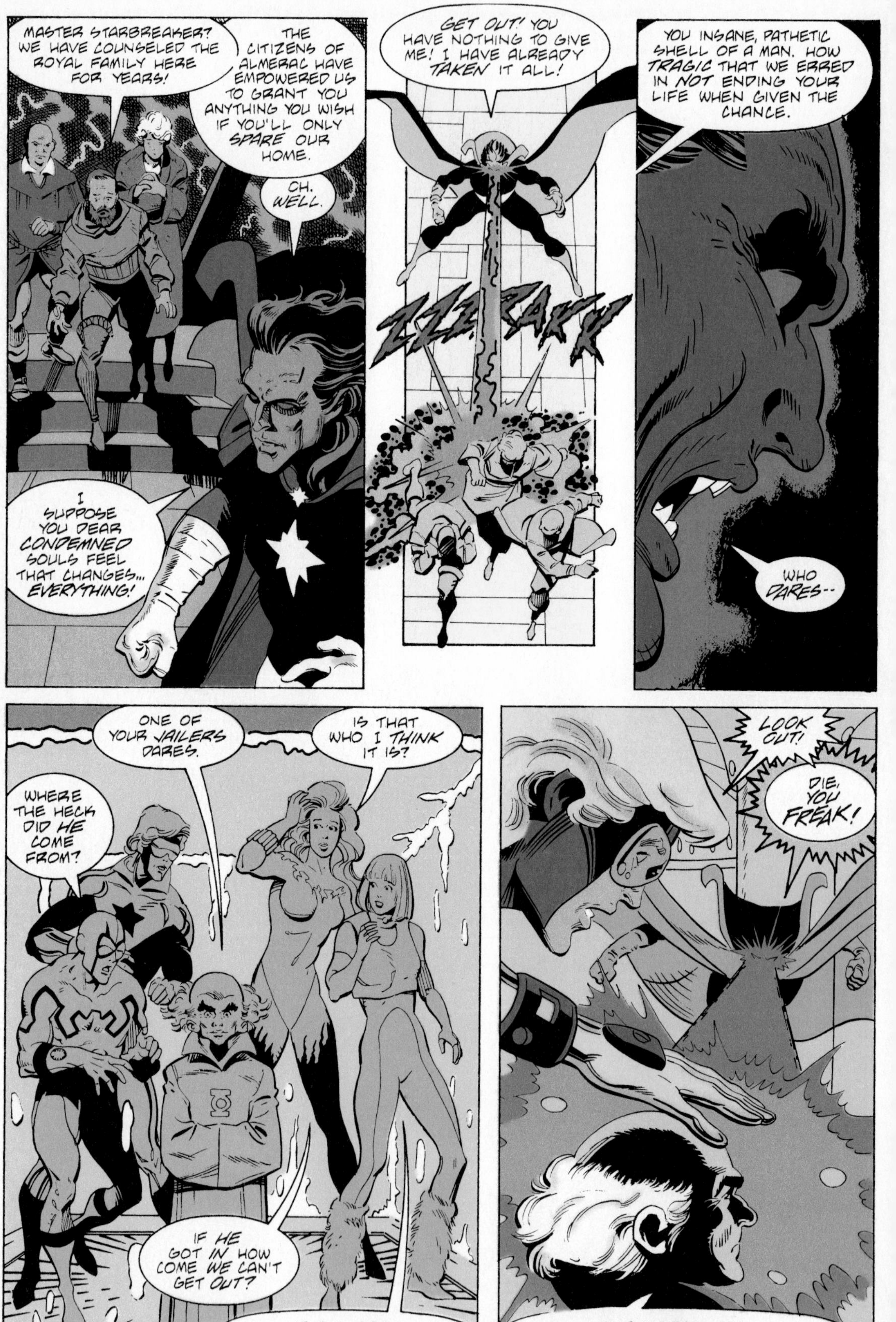
MASTER STARBREAKER? WE HAVE COUNSELED THE ROYAL FAMILY HERE FOR YEARS!
THE CITIZENS OF ALMERAC HAVE EMPOWERED US TO GRANT YOU ANYTHING YOU WISH IF YOU'LL ONLY SPARE OUR HOME.
OH. WELL.
I SUPPOSE YOU DEAR CONDEMNED SOULS FEEL THAT CHANGES... EVERYTHING!
GET OUT! YOU HAVE NOTHING TO GIVE ME! I HAVE ALREADY TAKEN IT ALL!
ZZZRAKK
YOU INSANE, PATHETIC SHELL OF A MAN. HOW TRAGIC THAT WE ERRED IN NOT ENDING YOUR LIFE WHEN GIVEN THE CHANCE.
WHO DARES--
ONE OF YOUR JAILERS DARES.
IS THAT WHO I THINK IT IS?
WHERE THE HECK DID HE COME FROM?
IF HE GOT IN HOW COME WE CAN'T GET OUT?
IF A GUARDIAN IS HERE THEN GUY MUST BE NEARBY! HE HAS TO BE!
LOOK OUT!
DIE, YOU FREAK!
YOUR INADEQUATE POWER CANNOT POSSIBLY PIERCE YOUR OWN FORCE FIELD CELL.

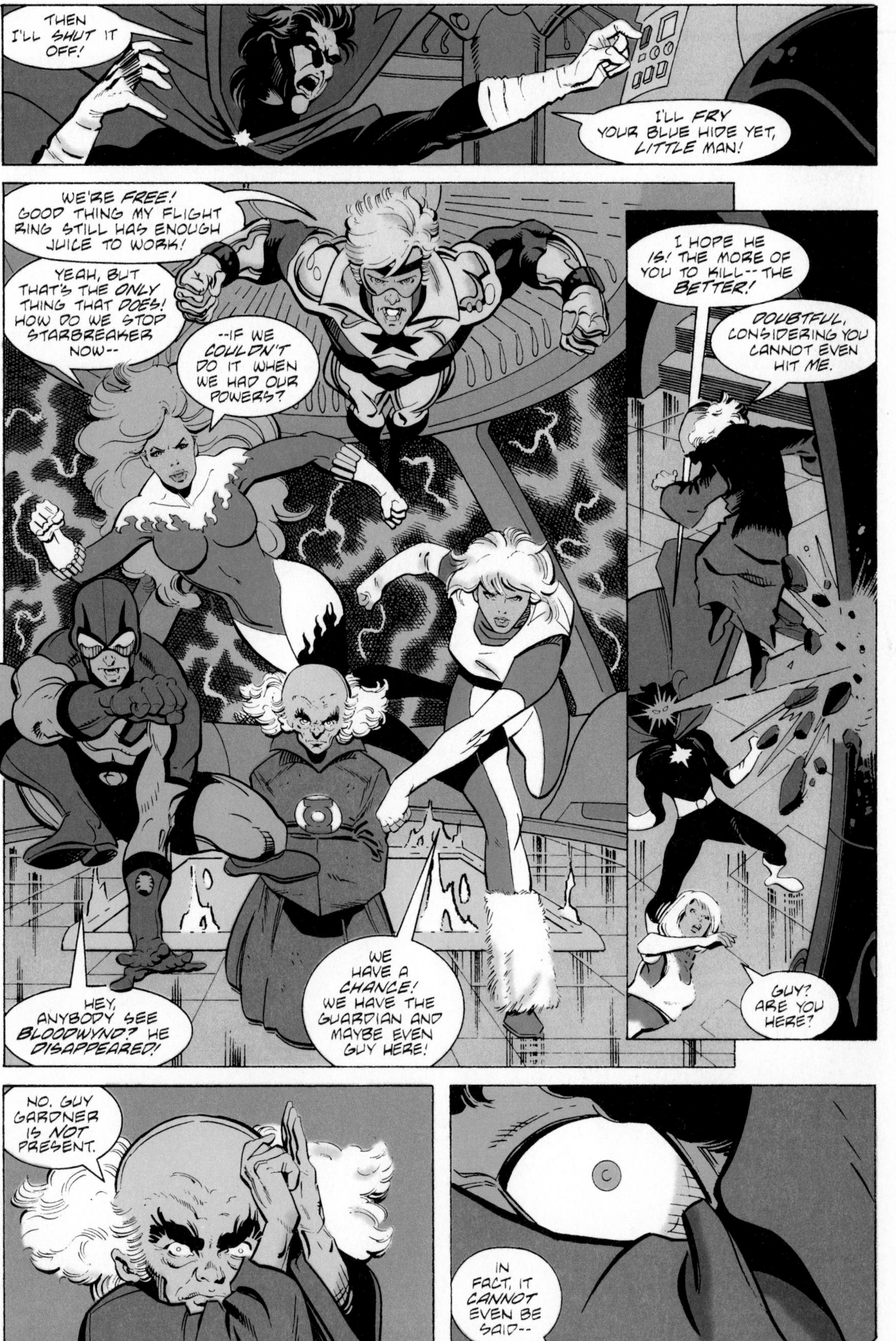
THEN I'LL SHUT IT OFF!
I'LL FRY YOUR BLUE HIDE YET, LITTLE MAN!
WE'RE FREE! GOOD THING MY FLIGHT RING STILL HAS ENOUGH JUICE TO WORK!
YEAH, BUT THAT'S THE ONLY THING THAT DOES! HOW DO WE STOP STARBREAKER NOW--
--IF WE COULDN'T DO IT WHEN WE HAD OUR POWERS?
HEY, ANYBODY SEE BLOODWYND? HE DISAPPEARED!
WE HAVE A CHANCE! WE HAVE THE GUARDIAN AND MAYBE EVEN GUY HERE!
I HOPE HE IS! THE MORE OF YOU TO KILL-- THE BETTER!
DOUBTFUL, CONSIDERING YOU CANNOT EVEN HIT ME.
GUY? ARE YOU HERE?
NO. GUY GARDNER IS NOT PRESENT.
IN FACT, IT CANNOT EVEN BE SAID--

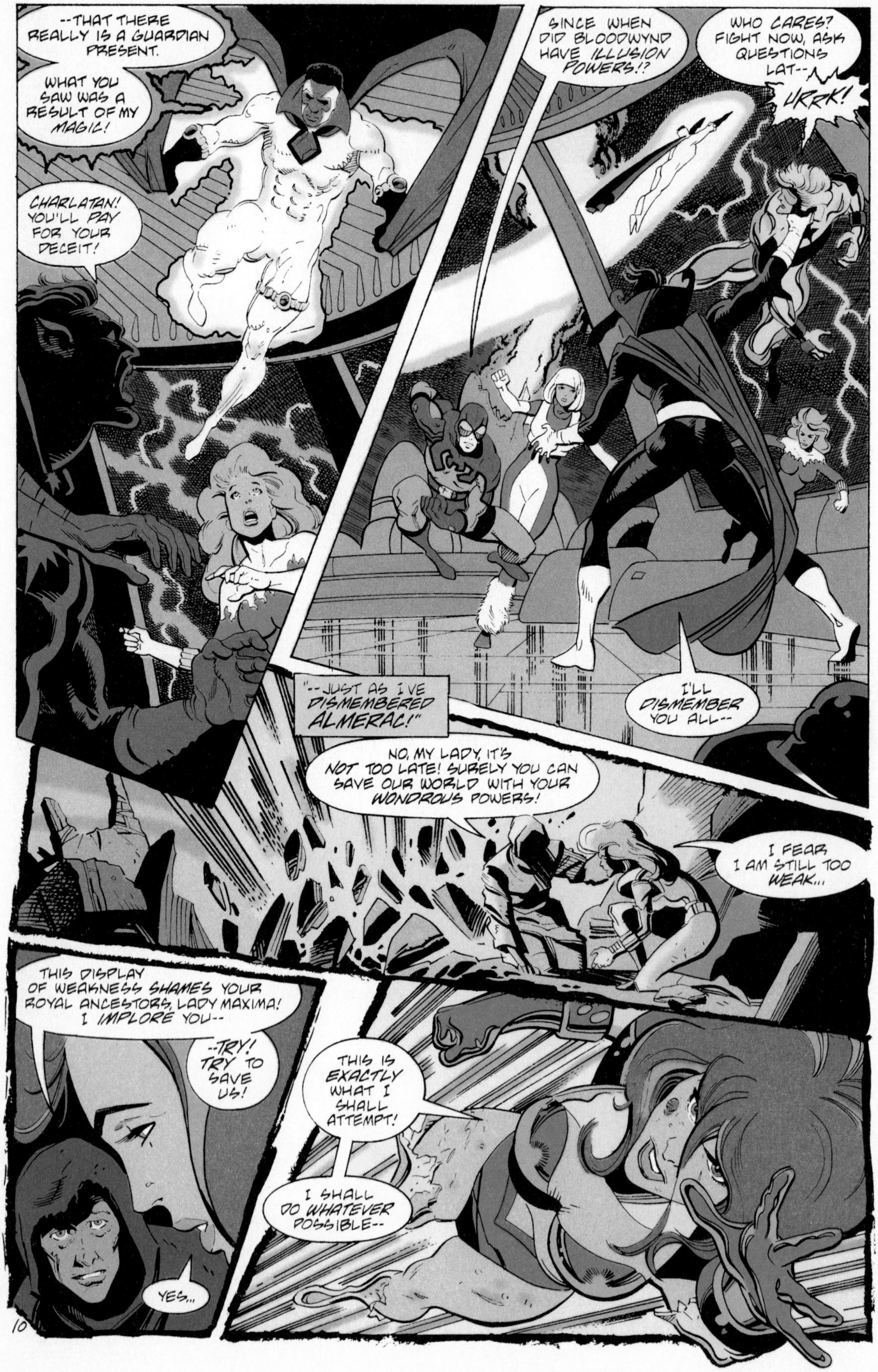
--THAT THERE REALLY IS A GUARDIAN PRESENT.
WHAT YOU SAW WAS A RESULT OF MY MAGIC!
CHARLATAN! YOU'LL PAY FOR YOUR DECEIT!
SINCE WHEN DID BLOODWYND HAVE ILLUSION POWERS!?
WHO CARES? FIGHT NOW, ASK QUESTIONS LAT--
URRK!
I'LL DISMEMBER YOU ALL--
"--JUST AS I'VE DISMEMBERED ALMERAC!"
NO, MY LADY, IT'S NOT TOO LATE! SURELY YOU CAN SAVE OUR WORLD WITH YOUR WONDROUS POWERS!
I FEAR I AM STILL TOO WEAK...
THIS DISPLAY OF WEAKNESS SHAMES YOUR ROYAL ANCESTORS, LADY MAXIMA! I IMPLORE YOU--
--TRY! TRY TO SAVE US!
THIS IS EXACTLY WHAT I SHALL ATTEMPT!
I SHALL DO WHATEVER POSSIBLE--
YES...

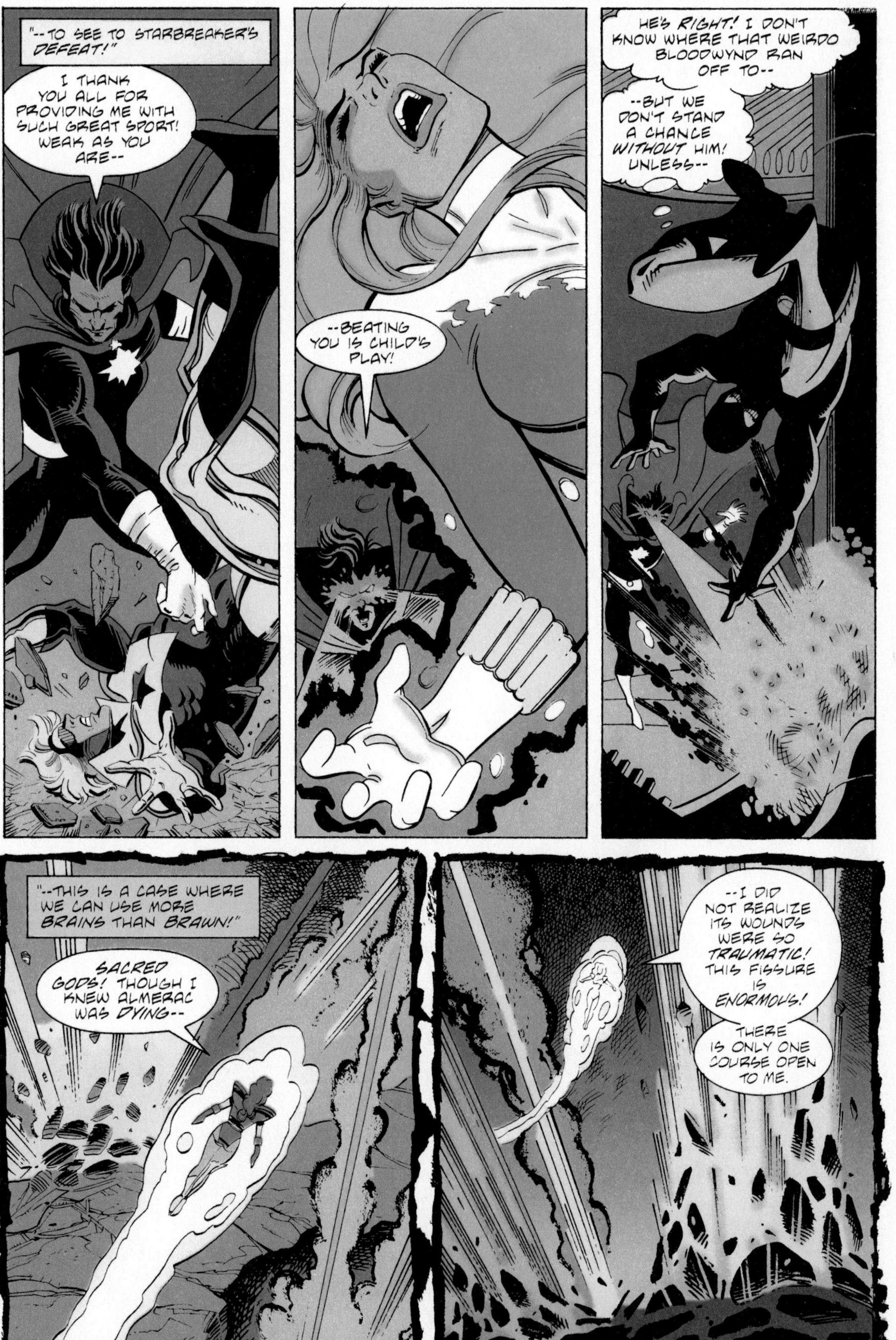
"--TO SEE TO STARBREAKER'S DEFEAT!"
I THANK YOU ALL FOR PROVIDING ME WITH SUCH GREAT SPORT! WEAK AS YOU ARE--
--BEATING YOU IS CHILD'S PLAY!
HE'S RIGHT! I DON'T KNOW WHERE THAT WEIRDO BLOODWYND RAN OFF TO--
--BUT WE DON'T STAND A CHANCE WITHOUT HIM! UNLESS--
"--THIS IS A CASE WHERE WE CAN USE MORE BRAINS THAN BRAWN!"
SACRED GODS! THOUGH I KNEW ALMERAC WAS DYING--
--I DID NOT REALIZE ITS WOUNDS WERE SO TRAUMATIC! THIS FISSURE IS ENORMOUS!
THERE IS ONLY ONE COURSE OPEN TO ME.

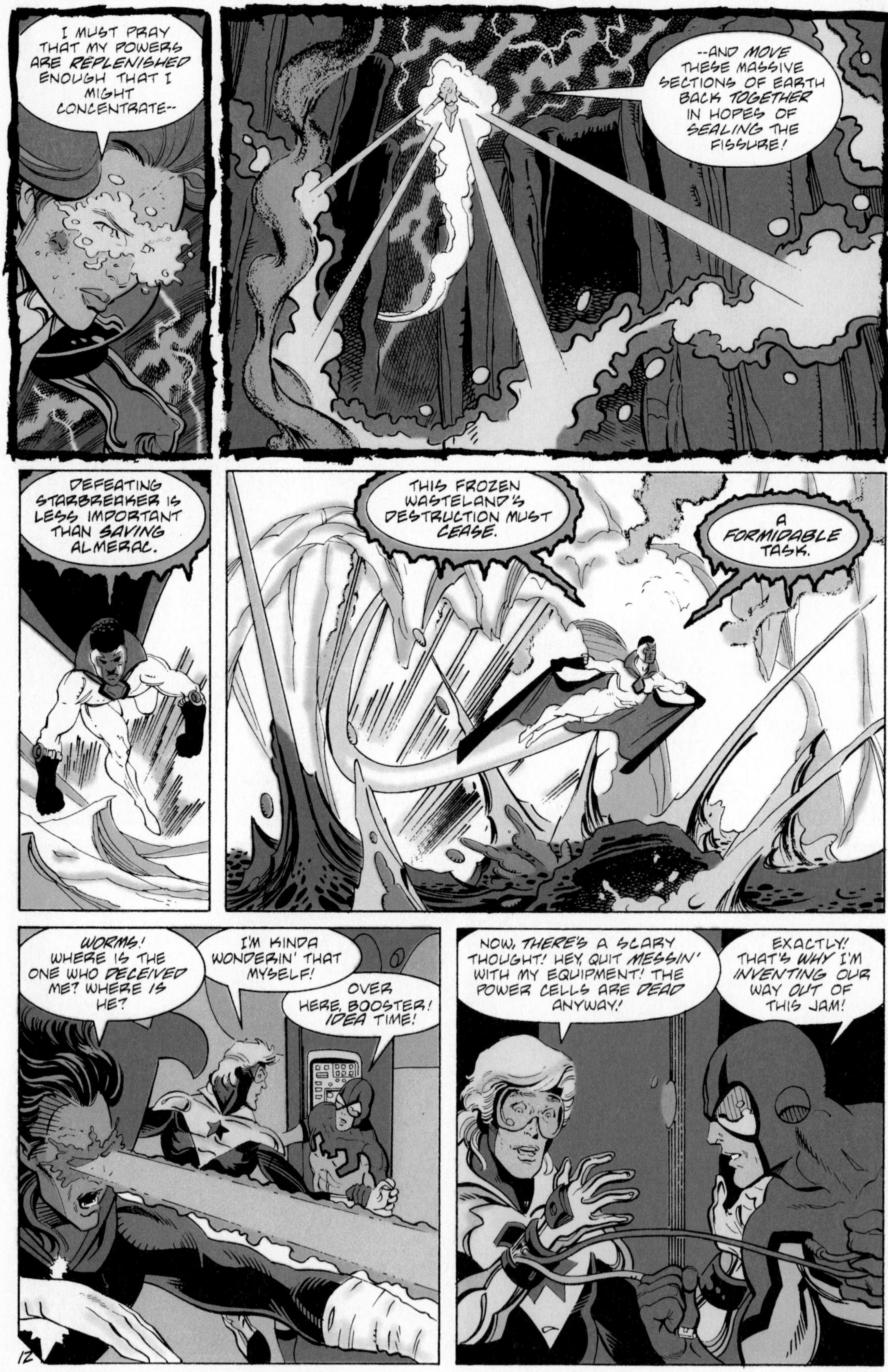
I MUST PRAY THAT MY POWERS ARE REPLENISHED ENOUGH THAT I MIGHT CONCENTRATE--
--AND MOVE THESE MASSIVE SECTIONS OF EARTH BACK TOGETHER IN HOPES OF SEALING THE FISSURE!
DEFEATING STARBREAKER IS LESS IMPORTANT THAN SAVING ALMERAC.
THIS FROZEN WASTELAND'S DESTRUCTION MUST CEASE.
A FORMIDABLE TASK.
WORMS! WHERE IS THE ONE WHO DECEIVED ME? WHERE IS HE?
I'M KINDA WONDERIN' THAT MYSELF!
OVER HERE, BOOSTER! IDEA TIME!
NOW, THERE'S A SCARY THOUGHT! HEY, QUIT MESSIN' WITH MY EQUIPMENT! THE POWER CELLS ARE DEAD ANYWAY!
EXACTLY! THAT'S WHY I'M INVENTING OUR WAY OUT OF THIS JAM!

I'VE EXAMINED THESE *FUTURISTIC GIZMOS* OF YOURS ENOUGH TO KNOW WHAT MAKES THEM TICK.

THEORETICALLY, WE CAN DO SOME *SERIOUS* DAMAGE BY PLUGGING YOU INTO THIS FORCE FIELD GENERATOR!

HEY...

YOU *TWO!* WHAT *MISCHIEF* ARE YOU DEAR BOYS *PLOTTING?*

HEY! YOU'RE MAKING ME A *TARGET!* YOU'RE GONNA GET ME *FRIED!*

IF THIS DOESN'T WORK, WE *ALL* GET FRIED!

AT LEAST *YOU* GET TO GO *FIRST!*

SOUNDS FINE TO ME.

FZZZAM

SPOWWW

I'M... STILL *HERE?*

WHAT HAPPENS WHEN HE *STOPS* PUTTING OUT THE JUICE?

HE *CAN'T.* IT'S LIKE SIPHONING GAS. ONCE YOU GET IT STARTED, IT JUST KEEPS ON POURING!

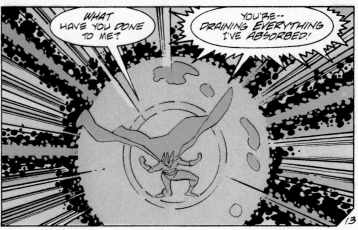

WHAT HAVE YOU *DONE* TO ME?

YOU'RE-- *DRAINING* EVERYTHING I'VE ABSORBED!

13

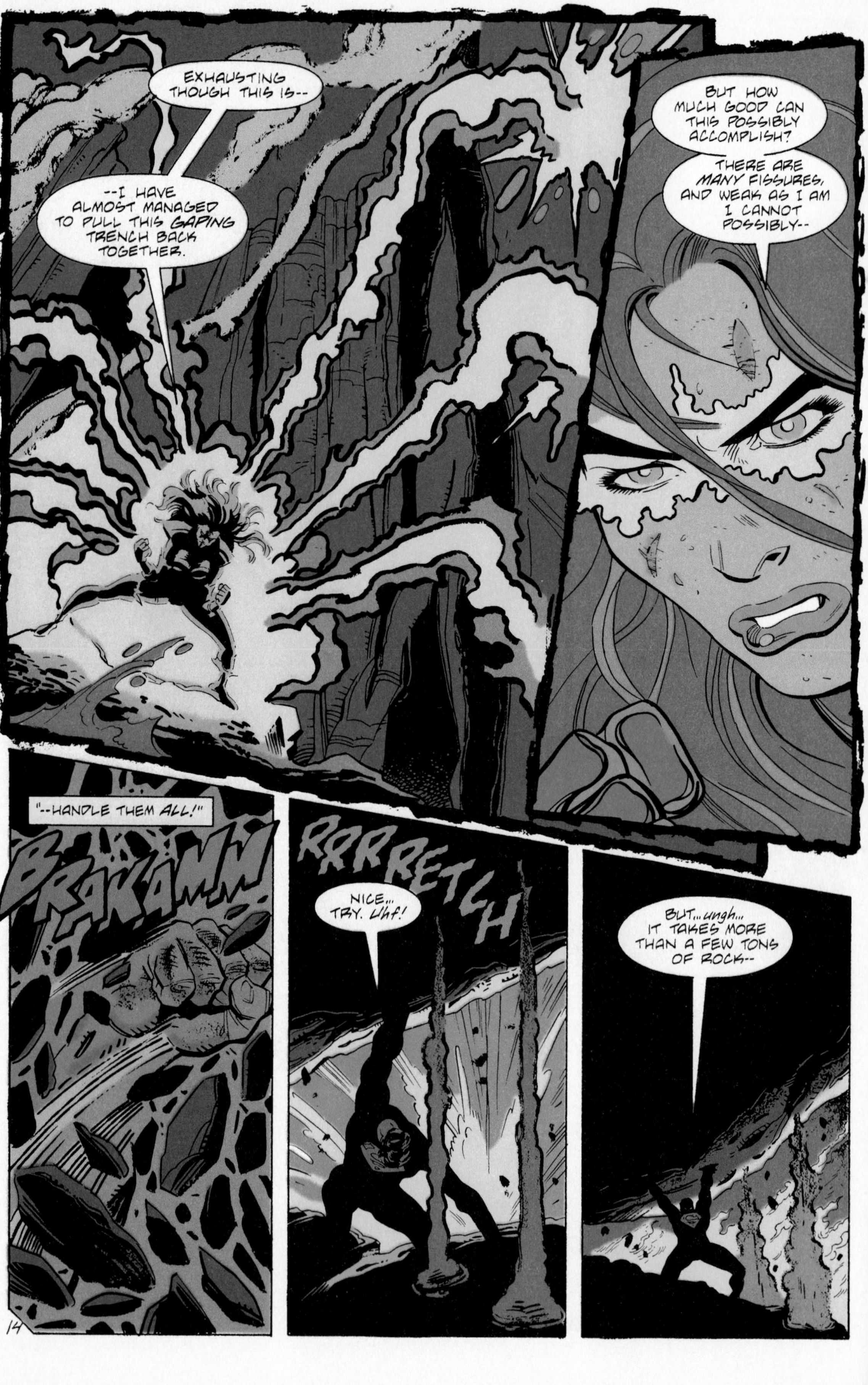
EXHAUSTING THOUGH THIS IS--
--I HAVE ALMOST MANAGED TO PULL THIS *GAPING* TRENCH BACK TOGETHER.
BUT HOW MUCH GOOD CAN THIS POSSIBLY ACCOMPLISH?
THERE ARE *MANY* FISSURES, AND WEAK AS I AM I CANNOT POSSIBLY--
"--HANDLE THEM *ALL!*"
BRAKAMM
RRRRETCH
NICE... TRY. *UHF!*
BUT... *UNGH*... IT TAKES MORE THAN A FEW TONS OF ROCK--

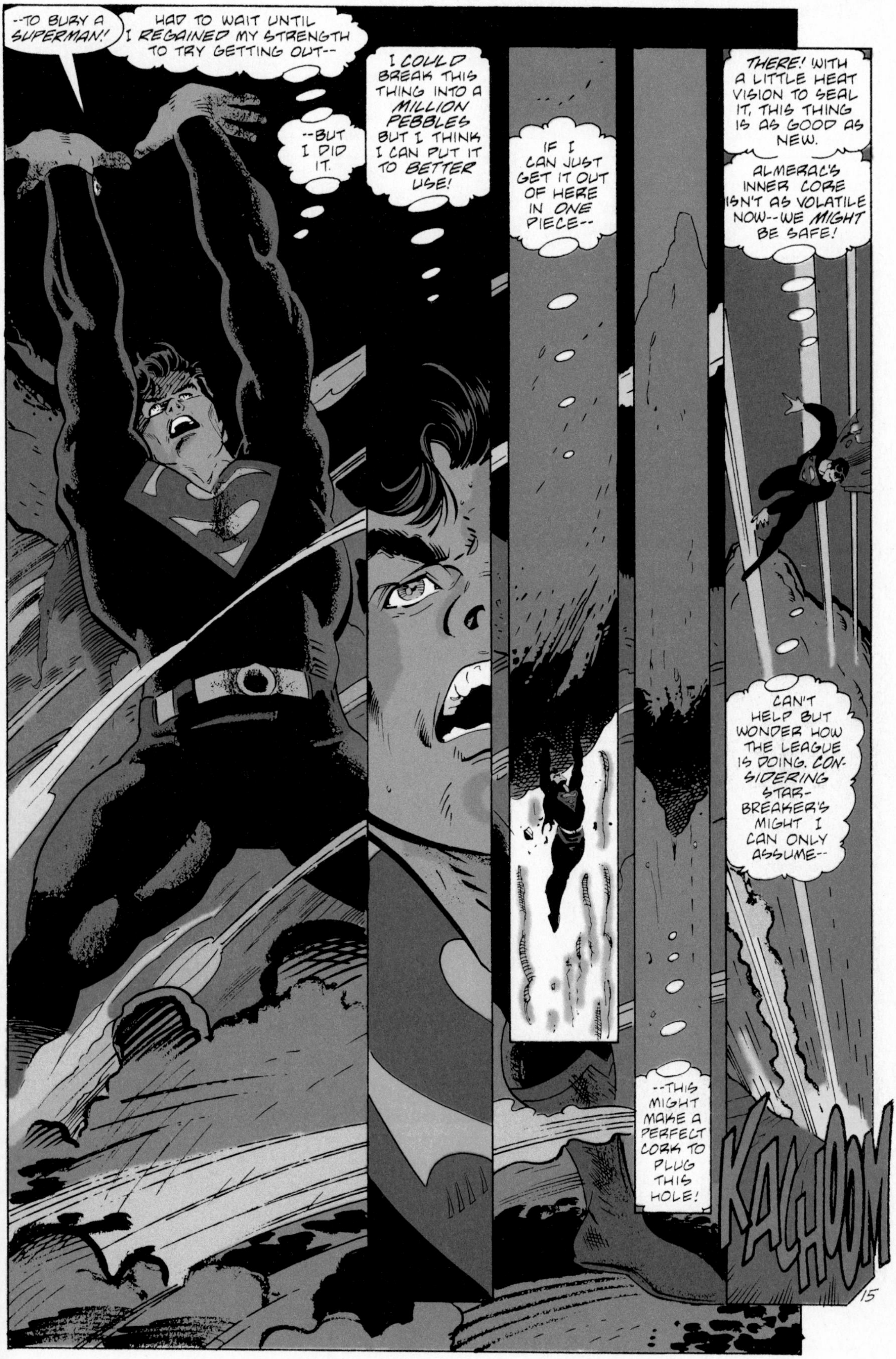

--TO BURY A SUPERMAN!
HAD TO WAIT UNTIL I REGAINED MY STRENGTH TO TRY GETTING OUT--
--BUT I DID IT.
I COULD BREAK THIS THING INTO A MILLION PEBBLES BUT I THINK I CAN PUT IT TO BETTER USE!
IF I CAN JUST GET IT OUT OF HERE IN ONE PIECE--
--THIS MIGHT MAKE A PERFECT CORK TO PLUG THIS HOLE!
THERE! WITH A LITTLE HEAT VISION TO SEAL IT, THIS THING IS AS GOOD AS NEW.
ALMERAC'S INNER CORE ISN'T AS VOLATILE NOW--WE MIGHT BE SAFE!
CAN'T HELP BUT WONDER HOW THE LEAGUE IS DOING. CONSIDERING STAR-BREAKER'S MIGHT I CAN ONLY ASSUME--
KACHOOM

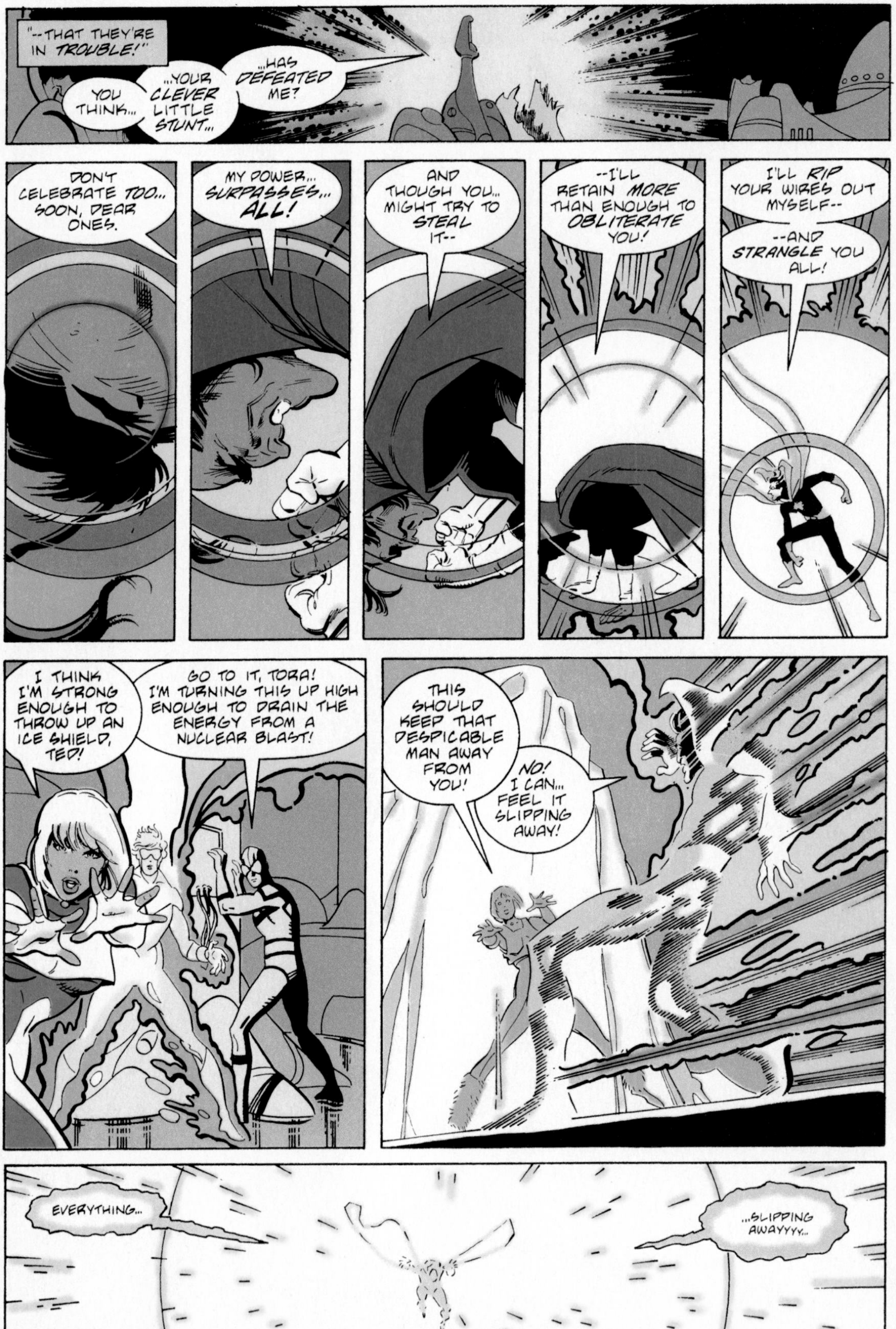
"--THAT THEY'RE IN TROUBLE!"
YOU THINK...
...YOUR CLEVER LITTLE STUNT...
...HAS DEFEATED ME?
DON'T CELEBRATE TOO... SOON, DEAR ONES.
MY POWER... SURPASSES... ALL!
AND THOUGH YOU... MIGHT TRY TO STEAL IT--
--I'LL RETAIN MORE THAN ENOUGH TO OBLITERATE YOU!
I'LL RIP YOUR WIRES OUT MYSELF--
--AND STRANGLE YOU ALL!
I THINK I'M STRONG ENOUGH TO THROW UP AN ICE SHIELD, TED!
GO TO IT, TORA! I'M TURNING THIS UP HIGH ENOUGH TO DRAIN THE ENERGY FROM A NUCLEAR BLAST!
THIS SHOULD KEEP THAT DESPICABLE MAN AWAY FROM YOU!
NO! I CAN... FEEL IT SLIPPING AWAY!
EVERYTHING...
...SLIPPING AWAYYYY...

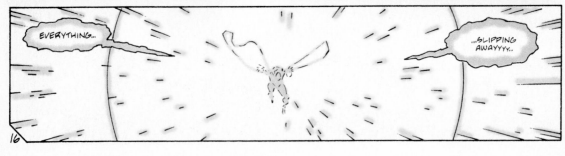

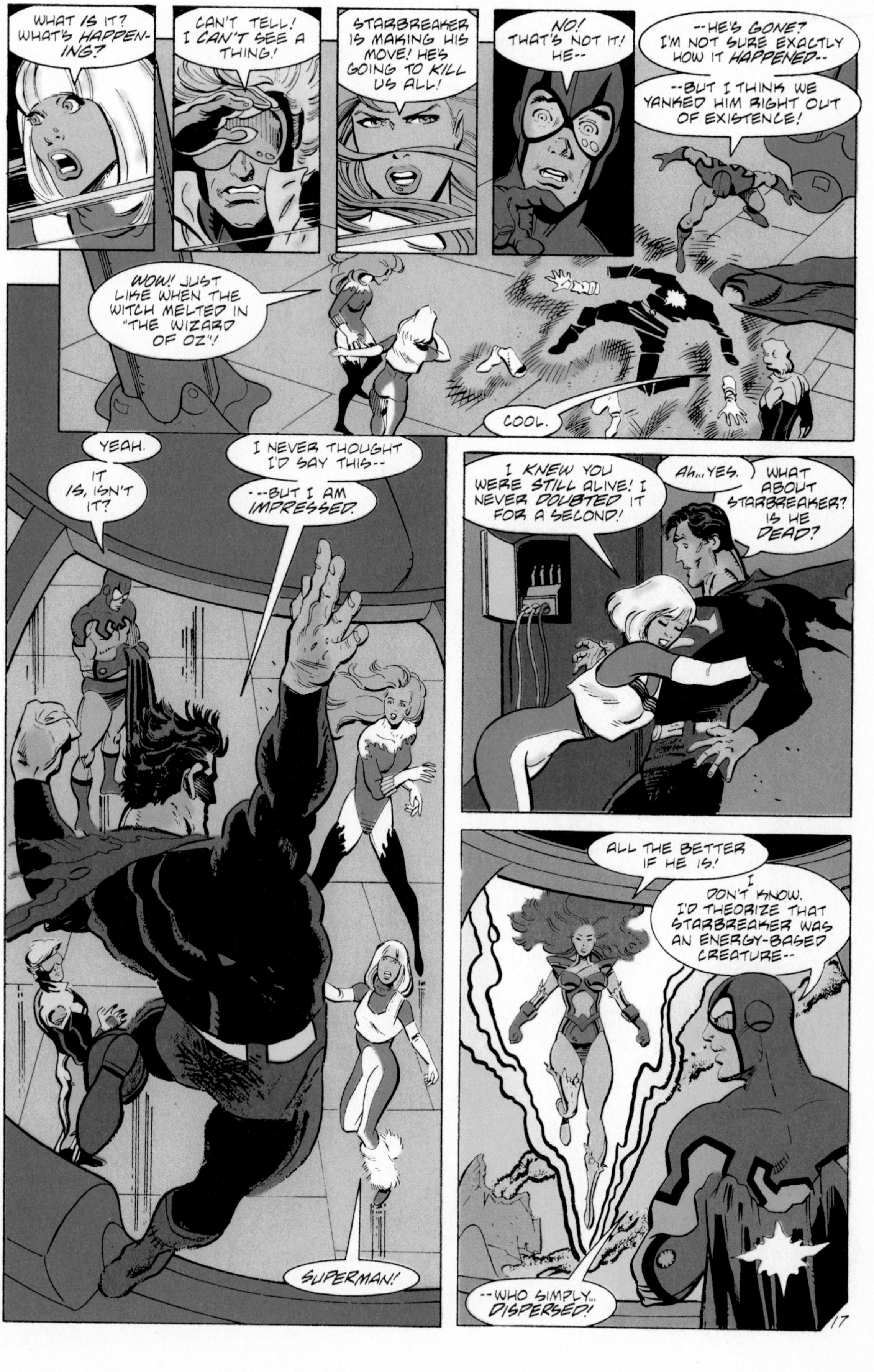
WHAT IS IT? WHAT'S HAPPEN-ING?
CAN'T TELL! I CAN'T SEE A THING!
STARBREAKER IS MAKING HIS MOVE! HE'S GOING TO KILL US ALL!
NO! THAT'S NOT IT! HE--
--HE'S GONE? I'M NOT SURE EXACTLY HOW IT HAPPENED--
--BUT I THINK WE YANKED HIM RIGHT OUT OF EXISTENCE!
WOW! JUST LIKE WHEN THE WITCH MELTED IN "THE WIZARD OF OZ"!
COOL.
YEAH.
IT IS, ISN'T IT?
I NEVER THOUGHT I'D SAY THIS--
--BUT I AM IMPRESSED.
SUPERMAN!
I KNEW YOU WERE STILL ALIVE! I NEVER DOUBTED IT FOR A SECOND!
Ah...YES.
WHAT ABOUT STARBREAKER? IS HE DEAD?
ALL THE BETTER IF HE IS!
I DON'T KNOW. I'D THEORIZE THAT STARBREAKER WAS AN ENERGY-BASED CREATURE--
--WHO SIMPLY... DISPERSED!

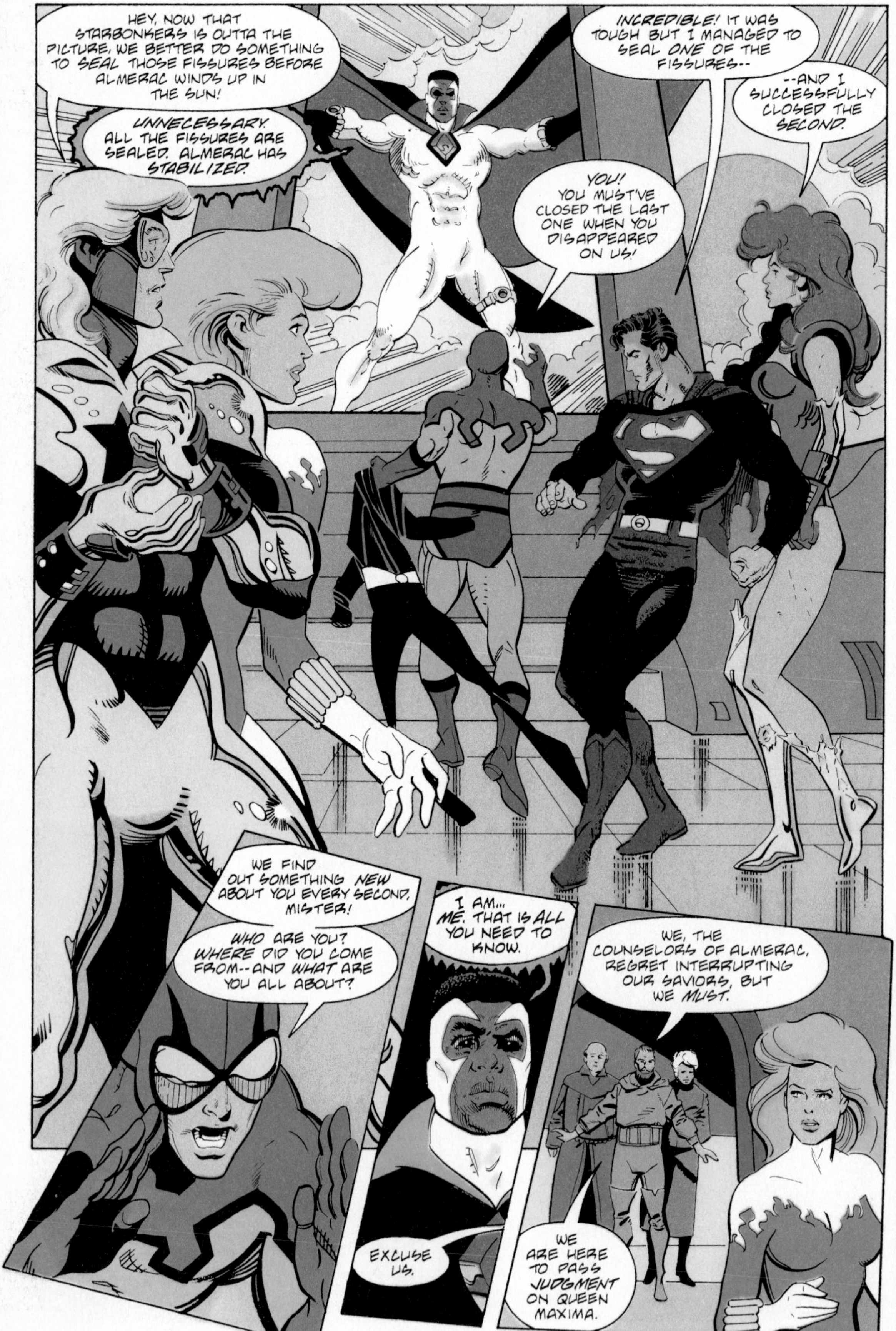
HEY, NOW THAT STARBONKERS IS OUTTA THE PICTURE, WE BETTER DO SOMETHING TO SEAL THOSE FISSURES BEFORE ALMERAC WINDS UP IN THE SUN!
UNNECESSARY. ALL THE FISSURES ARE SEALED. ALMERAC HAS STABILIZED.
INCREDIBLE! IT WAS TOUGH BUT I MANAGED TO SEAL ONE OF THE FISSURES--
--AND I SUCCESSFULLY CLOSED THE SECOND.
YOU! YOU MUST'VE CLOSED THE LAST ONE WHEN YOU DISAPPEARED ON US!
WE FIND OUT SOMETHING NEW ABOUT YOU EVERY SECOND, MISTER!
WHO ARE YOU? WHERE DID YOU COME FROM--AND WHAT ARE YOU ALL ABOUT?
I AM... ME. THAT IS ALL YOU NEED TO KNOW.
EXCUSE US.
WE, THE COUNSELORS OF ALMERAC, REGRET INTERRUPTING OUR SAVIORS, BUT WE MUST.
WE ARE HERE TO PASS JUDGMENT ON QUEEN MAXIMA.

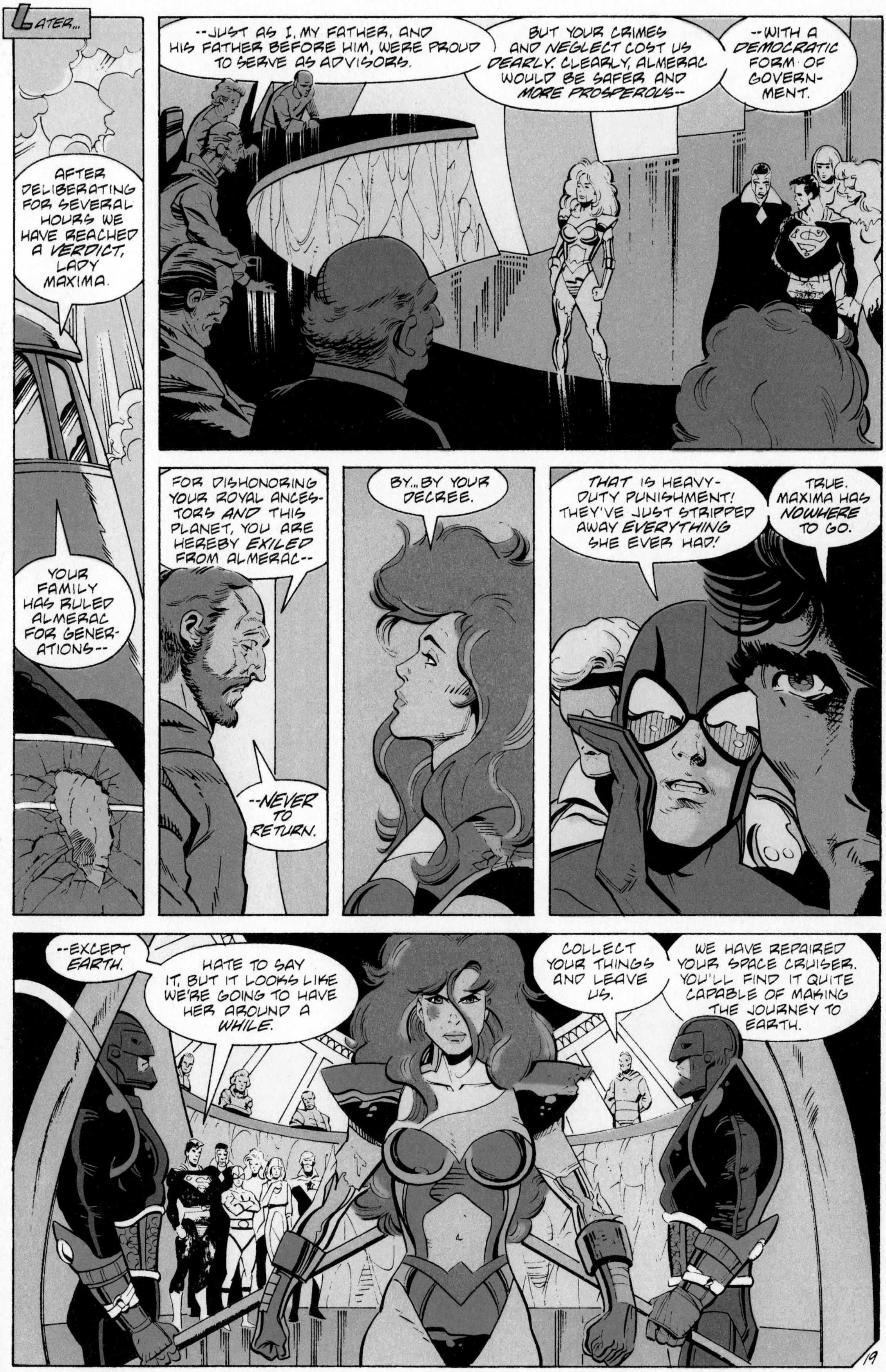
LATER...
AFTER DELIBERATING FOR SEVERAL HOURS WE HAVE REACHED A VERDICT, LADY MAXIMA.
--JUST AS I, MY FATHER, AND HIS FATHER BEFORE HIM, WERE PROUD TO SERVE AS ADVISORS.
BUT YOUR CRIMES AND NEGLECT COST US DEARLY. CLEARLY, ALMERAC WOULD BE SAFER AND MORE PROSPEROUS--
--WITH A DEMOCRATIC FORM OF GOVERNMENT.
YOUR FAMILY HAS RULED ALMERAC FOR GENERATIONS--
FOR DISHONORING YOUR ROYAL ANCESTORS AND THIS PLANET, YOU ARE HEREBY EXILED FROM ALMERAC--
--NEVER TO RETURN.
BY...BY YOUR DECREE.
THAT IS HEAVY-DUTY PUNISHMENT! THEY'VE JUST STRIPPED AWAY EVERYTHING SHE EVER HAD!
TRUE. MAXIMA HAS NOWHERE TO GO.
--EXCEPT EARTH.
HATE TO SAY IT, BUT IT LOOKS LIKE WE'RE GOING TO HAVE HER AROUND A WHILE.
COLLECT YOUR THINGS AND LEAVE US.
WE HAVE REPAIRED YOUR SPACE CRUISER. YOU'LL FIND IT QUITE CAPABLE OF MAKING THE JOURNEY TO EARTH.

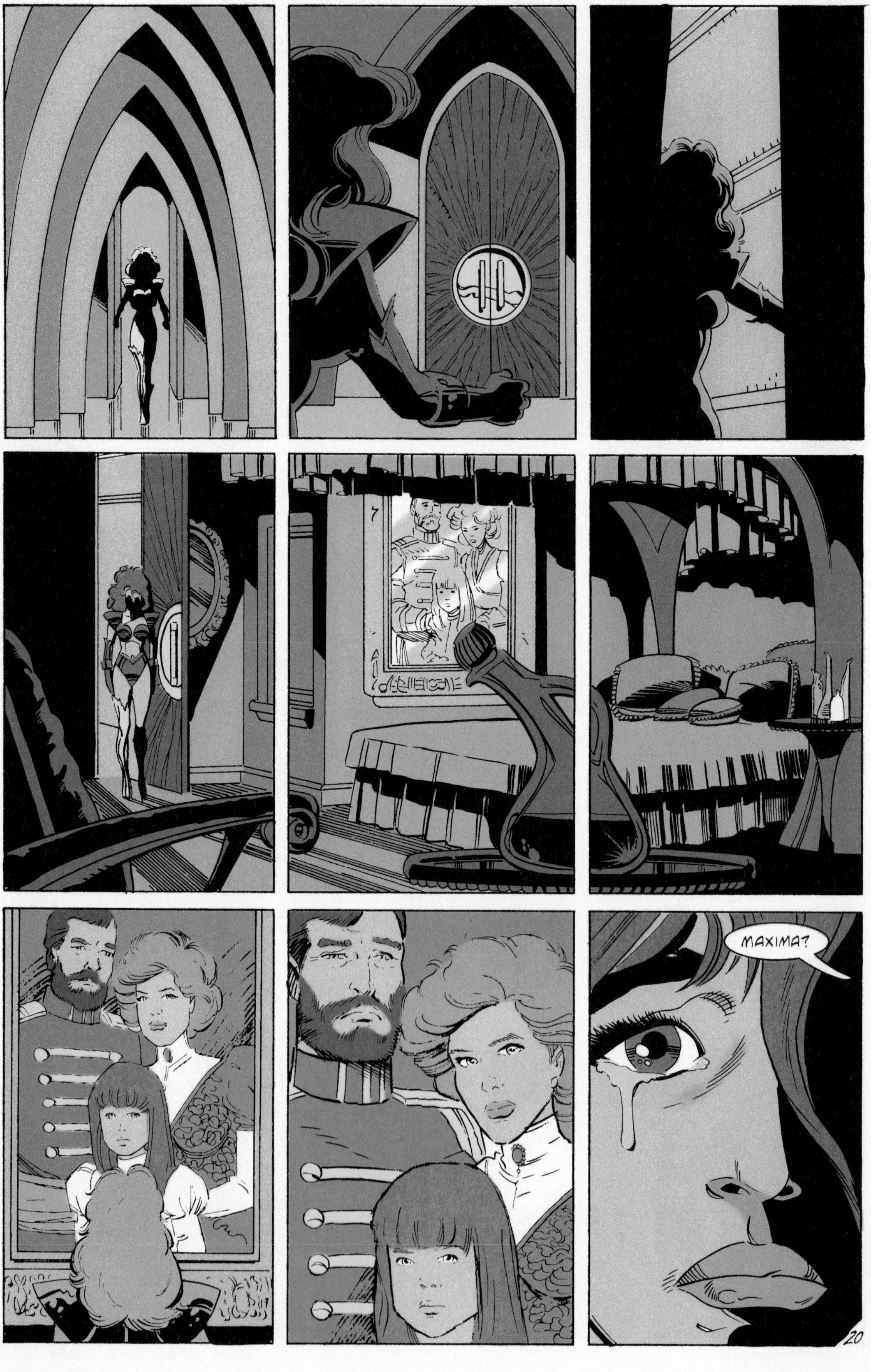
MAXIMA?

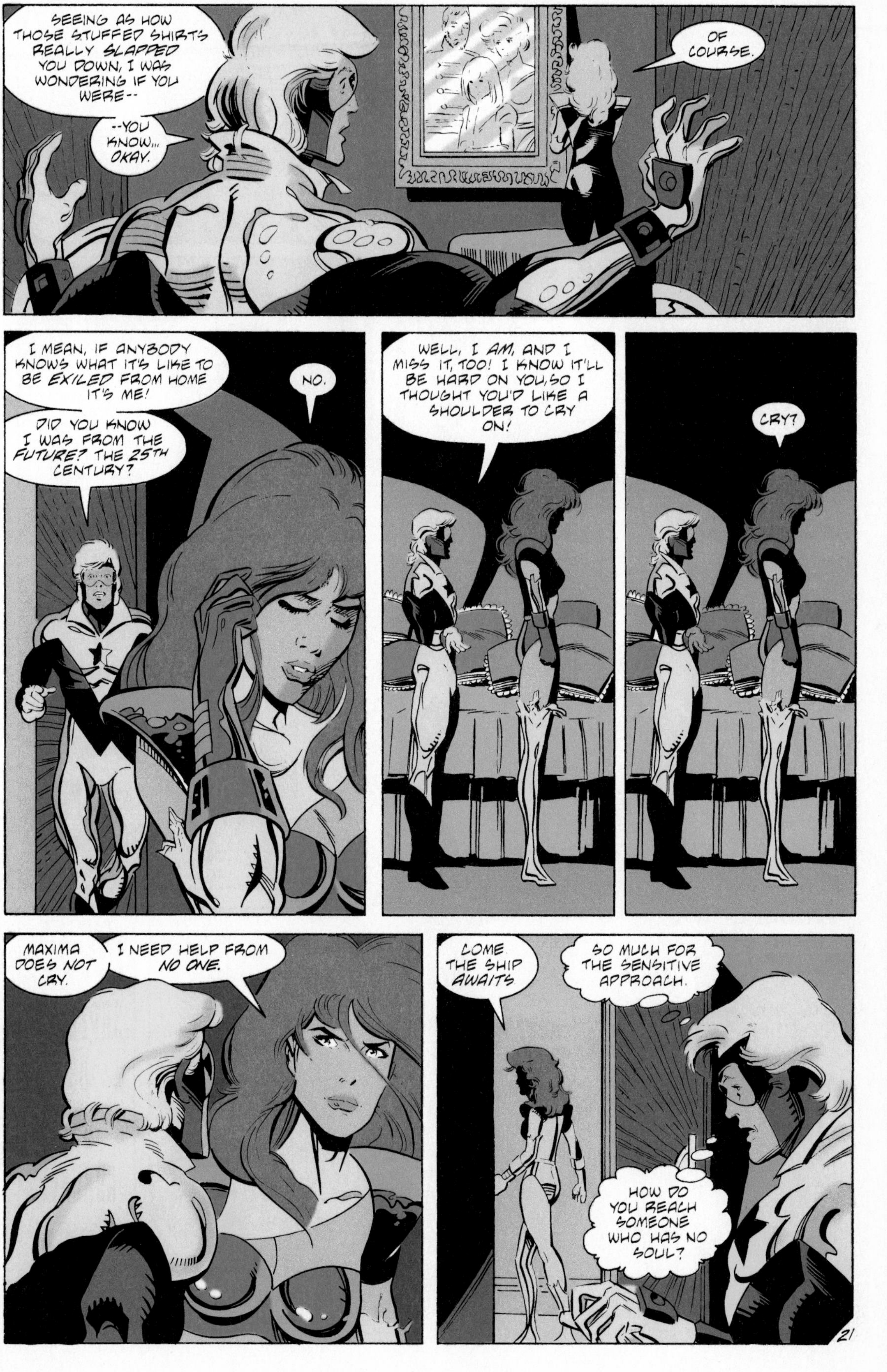
SEEING AS HOW THOSE STUFFED SHIRTS REALLY SLAPPED YOU DOWN, I WAS WONDERING IF YOU WERE--
--YOU KNOW... OKAY.
OF COURSE.
I MEAN, IF ANYBODY KNOWS WHAT IT'S LIKE TO BE EXILED FROM HOME IT'S ME!
DID YOU KNOW I WAS FROM THE FUTURE? THE 25TH CENTURY?
NO.
WELL, I AM, AND I MISS IT, TOO! I KNOW IT'LL BE HARD ON YOU, SO I THOUGHT YOU'D LIKE A SHOULDER TO CRY ON!
CRY?
MAXIMA DOES NOT CRY.
I NEED HELP FROM NO ONE.
COME. THE SHIP AWAITS.
SO MUCH FOR THE SENSITIVE APPROACH.
HOW DO YOU REACH SOMEONE WHO HAS NO SOUL?
21

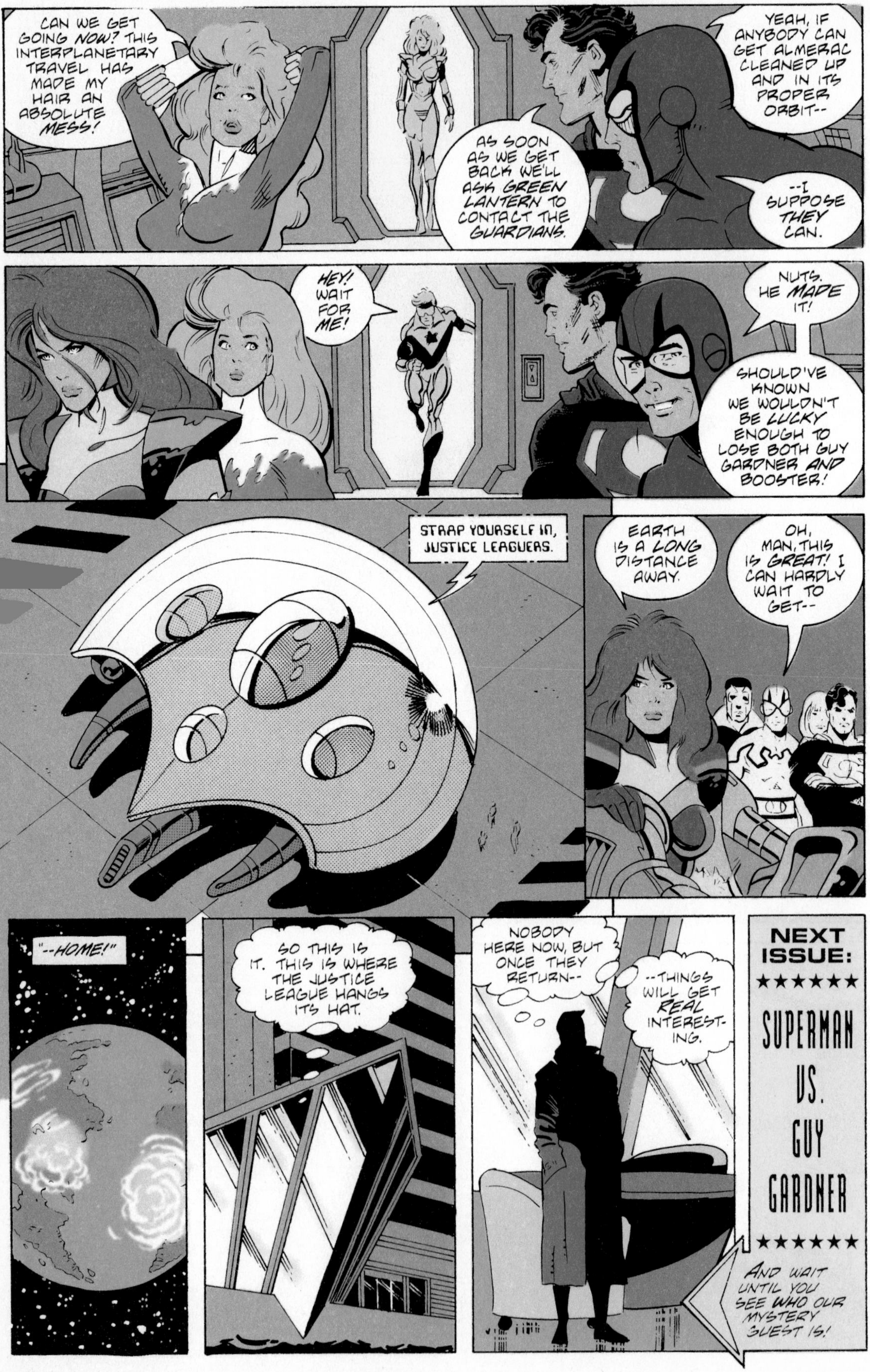
CAN WE GET GOING NOW? THIS INTERPLANETARY TRAVEL HAS MADE MY HAIR AN ABSOLUTE MESS!
AS SOON AS WE GET BACK WE'LL ASK GREEN LANTERN TO CONTACT THE GUARDIANS.
YEAH, IF ANYBODY CAN GET ALMERAC CLEANED UP AND IN ITS PROPER ORBIT--
--I SUPPOSE THEY CAN.
HEY! WAIT FOR ME!
NUTS. HE MADE IT!
SHOULD'VE KNOWN WE WOULDN'T BE LUCKY ENOUGH TO LOSE BOTH GUY GARDNER AND BOOSTER!
STRAP YOURSELF IN, JUSTICE LEAGUERS.
EARTH IS A LONG DISTANCE AWAY.
OH, MAN, THIS IS GREAT! I CAN HARDLY WAIT TO GET--
"--HOME!"
SO THIS IS IT. THIS IS WHERE THE JUSTICE LEAGUE HANGS ITS HAT.
NOBODY HERE NOW, BUT ONCE THEY RETURN--
--THINGS WILL GET REAL INTERESTING.
NEXT ISSUE:
★★★★★★
SUPERMAN VS. GUY GARDNER
★★★★★★
AND WAIT UNTIL YOU SEE WHO OUR MYSTERY GUEST IS!

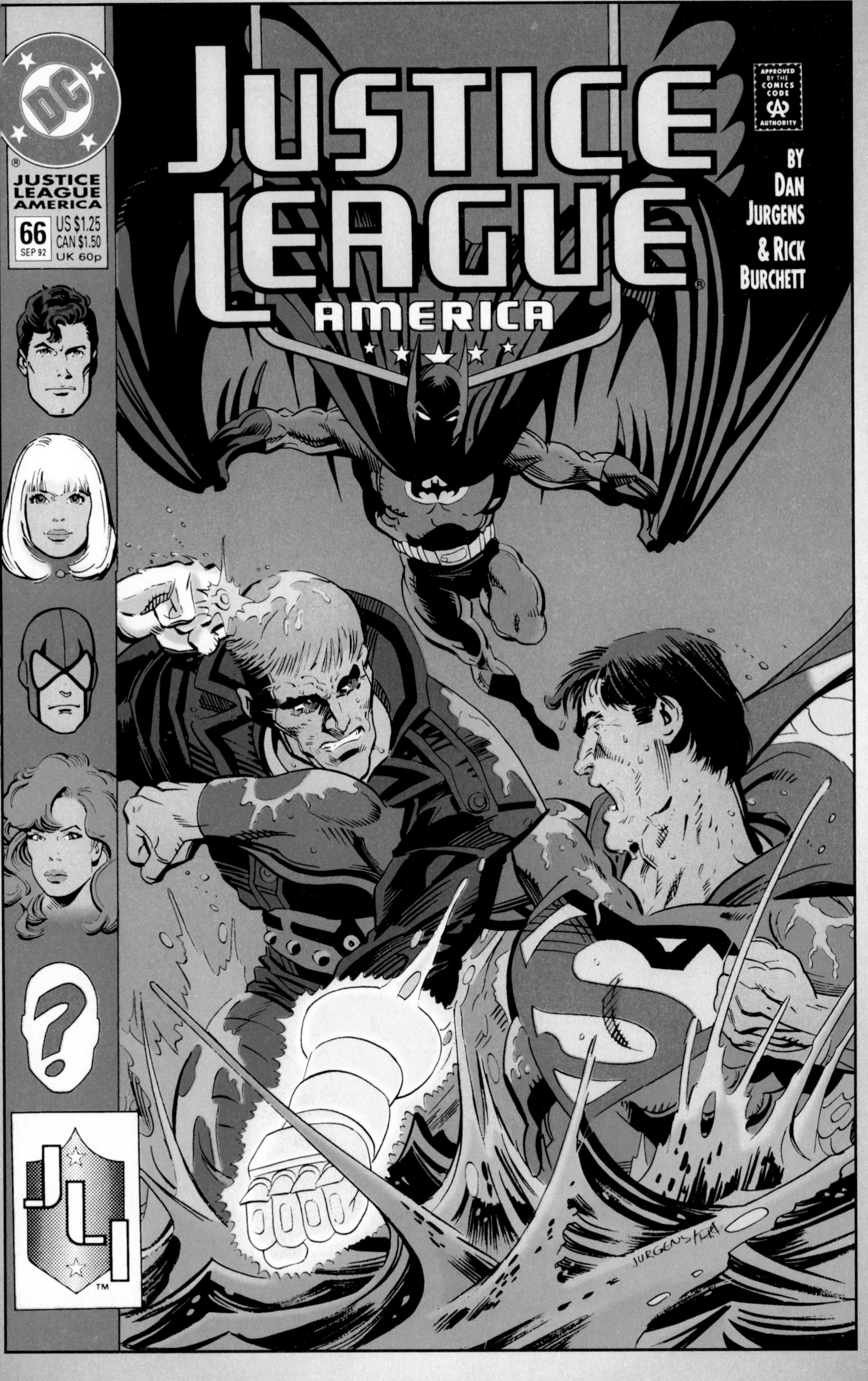

JUSTICE LEAGUE AMERICA
JUSTICE LEAGUE AMERICA
66
SEP 92
US $1.25
CAN $1.50
UK 60p
APPROVED BY THE COMICS CODE AUTHORITY
BY DAN JURGENS & RICK BURCHETT
JLI
JURGENS/RB

Cover art by **DAN JURGENS**
and **RICK BURCHETT**

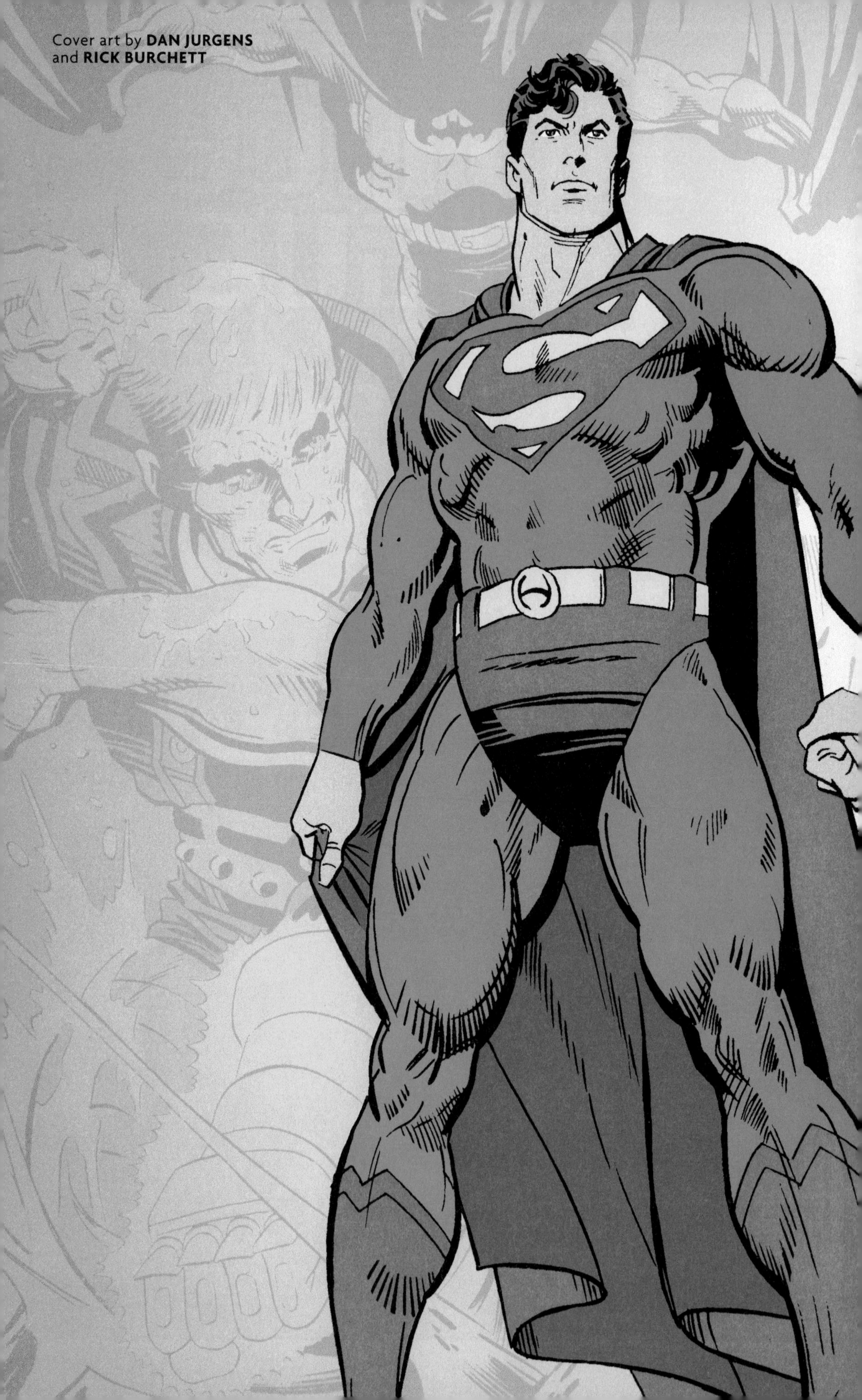

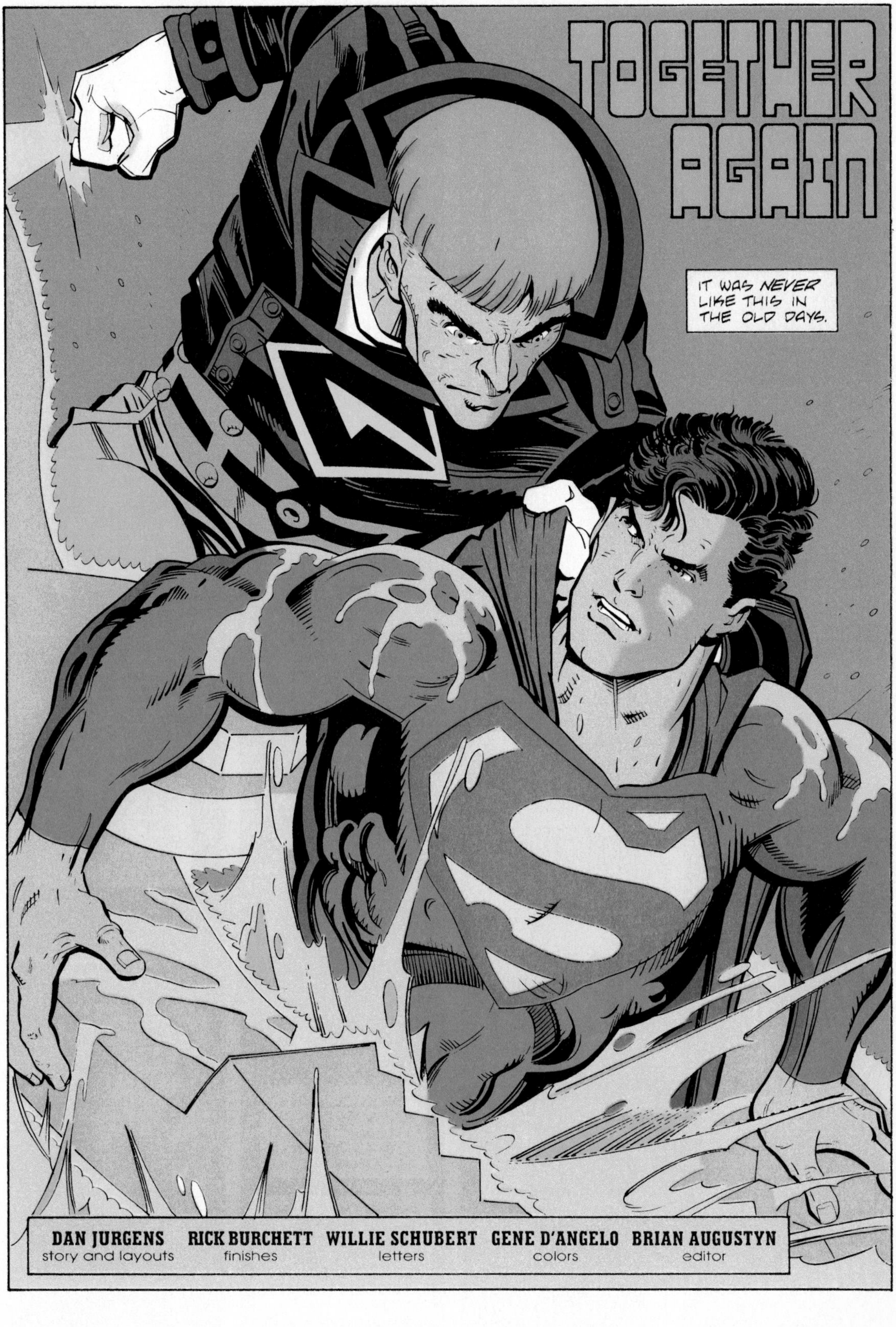
TOGETHER AGAIN
IT WAS NEVER LIKE THIS IN THE OLD DAYS.
DAN JURGENS story and layouts
RICK BURCHETT finishes
WILLIE SCHUBERT letters
GENE D'ANGELO colors
BRIAN AUGUSTYN editor

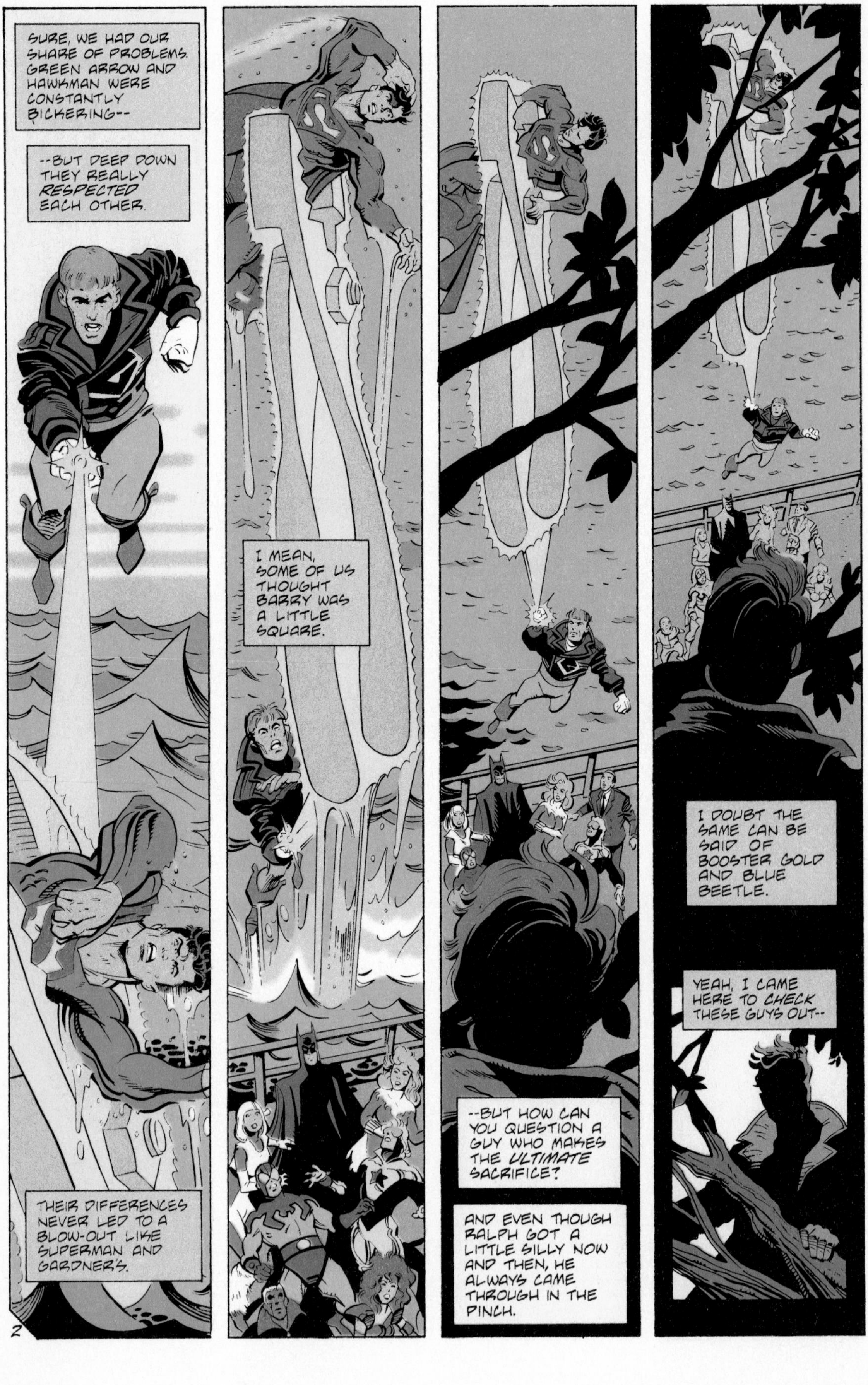

SURE, WE HAD OUR SHARE OF PROBLEMS. GREEN ARROW AND HAWKMAN WERE CONSTANTLY BICKERING--
--BUT DEEP DOWN THEY REALLY *RESPECTED* EACH OTHER.
THEIR DIFFERENCES NEVER LED TO A BLOW-OUT LIKE SUPERMAN AND GARDNER'S.
I MEAN, SOME OF US THOUGHT BARRY WAS A LITTLE SQUARE.
--BUT HOW CAN YOU QUESTION A GUY WHO MAKES THE *ULTIMATE* SACRIFICE?
AND EVEN THOUGH RALPH GOT A LITTLE SILLY NOW AND THEN, HE ALWAYS CAME THROUGH IN THE PINCH.
I DOUBT THE SAME CAN BE SAID OF BOOSTER GOLD AND BLUE BEETLE.
YEAH, I CAME HERE TO *CHECK* THESE GUYS OUT--

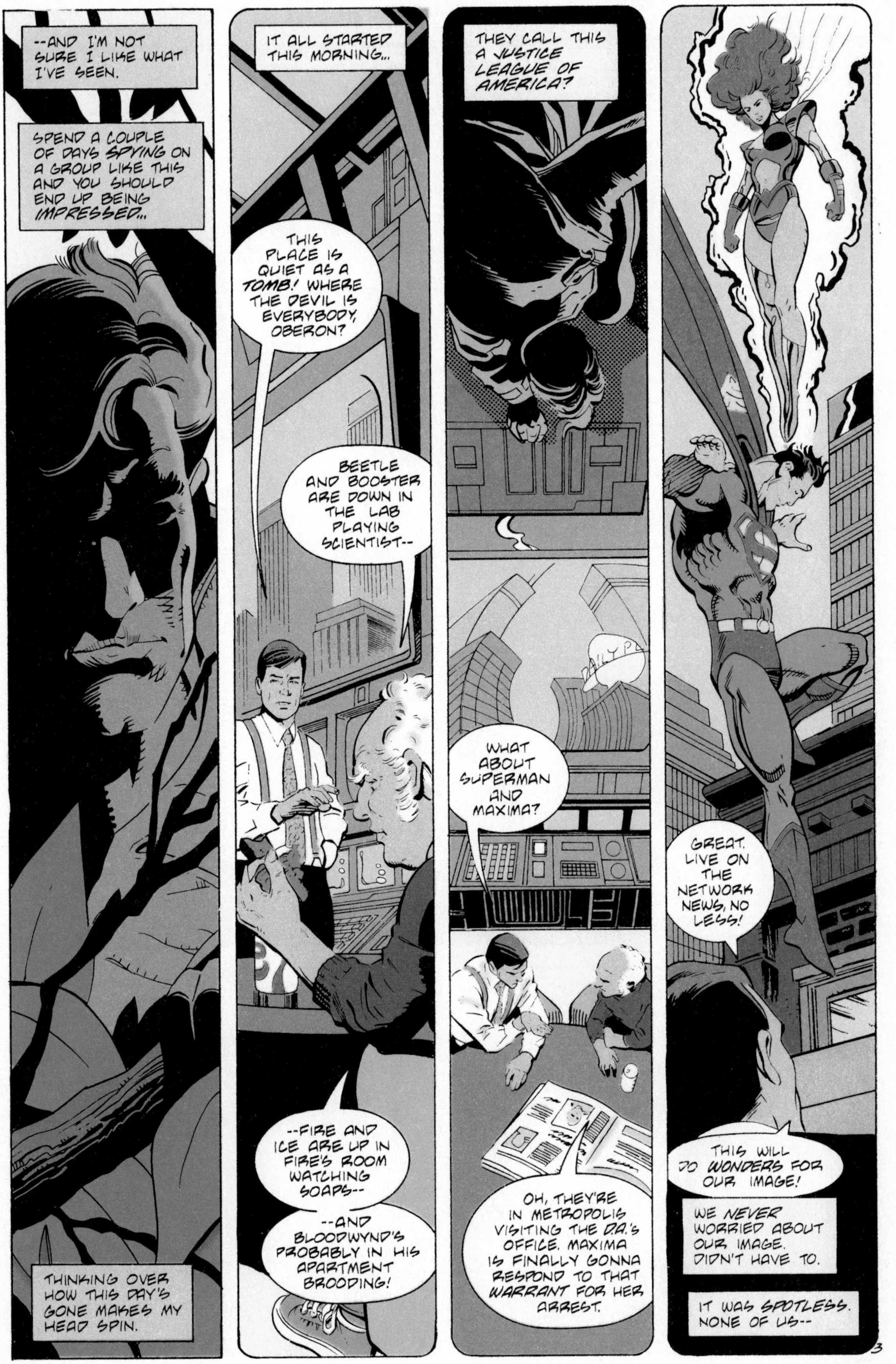

--AND I'M NOT SURE I LIKE WHAT I'VE SEEN.
SPEND A COUPLE OF DAYS SPYING ON A GROUP LIKE THIS AND YOU SHOULD END UP BEING IMPRESSED...
THINKING OVER HOW THIS DAY'S GONE MAKES MY HEAD SPIN.
IT ALL STARTED THIS MORNING...
THIS PLACE IS QUIET AS A TOMB! WHERE THE DEVIL IS EVERYBODY, OBERON?
BEETLE AND BOOSTER ARE DOWN IN THE LAB PLAYING SCIENTIST--
--FIRE AND ICE ARE UP IN FIRE'S ROOM WATCHING SOAPS--
--AND BLOODWYND'S PROBABLY IN HIS APARTMENT BROODING!
THEY CALL THIS A JUSTICE LEAGUE OF AMERICA?
WHAT ABOUT SUPERMAN AND MAXIMA?
OH, THEY'RE IN METROPOLIS VISITING THE D.A.'S OFFICE. MAXIMA IS FINALLY GONNA RESPOND TO THAT WARRANT FOR HER ARREST.
GREAT. LIVE ON THE NETWORK NEWS, NO LESS!
THIS WILL DO WONDERS FOR OUR IMAGE!
WE NEVER WORRIED ABOUT OUR IMAGE. DIDN'T HAVE TO.
IT WAS SPOTLESS. NONE OF US--

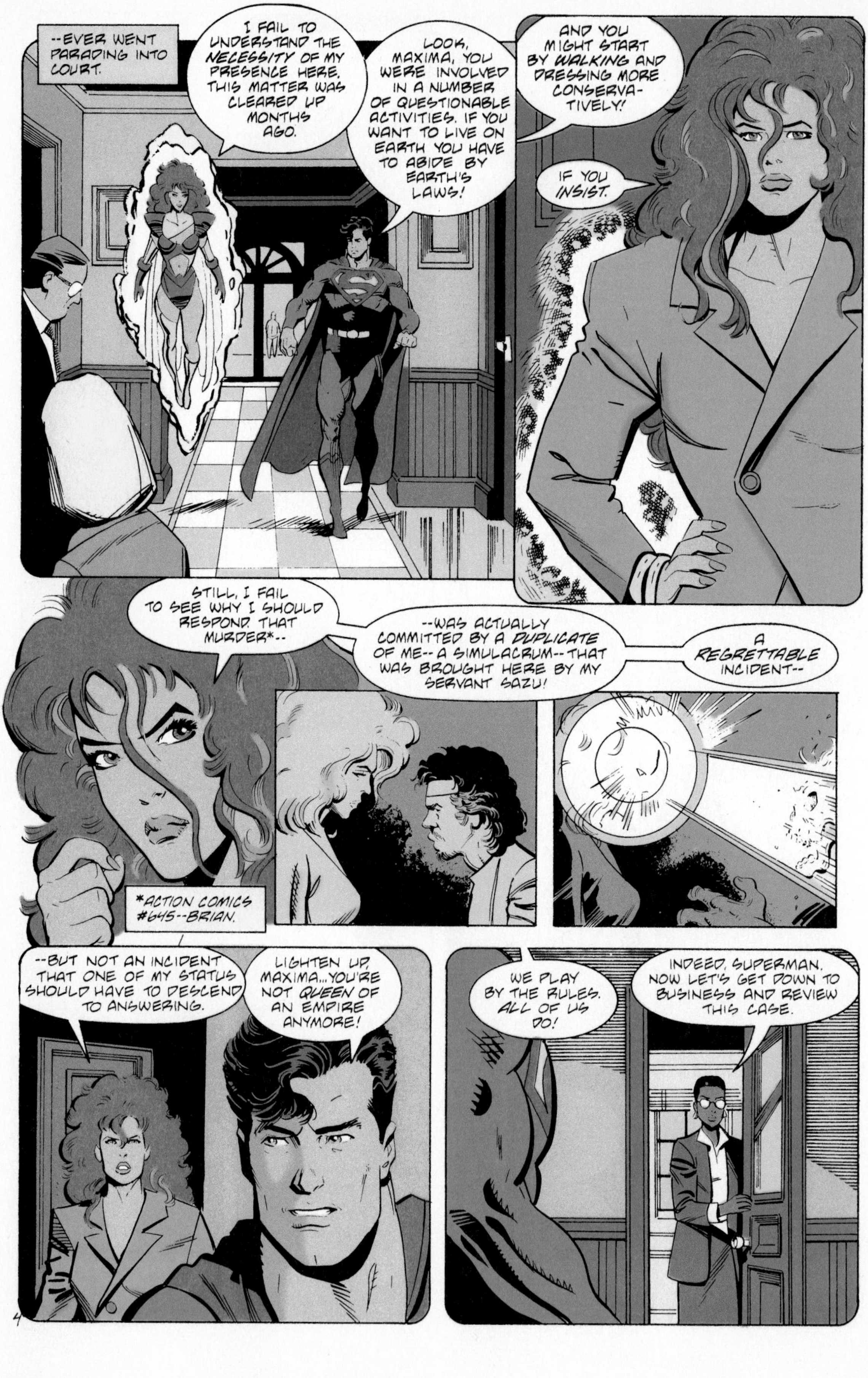
--EVER WENT PARADING INTO COURT.
I FAIL TO UNDERSTAND THE NECESSITY OF MY PRESENCE HERE. THIS MATTER WAS CLEARED UP MONTHS AGO.
LOOK, MAXIMA, YOU WERE INVOLVED IN A NUMBER OF QUESTIONABLE ACTIVITIES. IF YOU WANT TO LIVE ON EARTH YOU HAVE TO ABIDE BY EARTH'S LAWS!
AND YOU MIGHT START BY WALKING AND DRESSING MORE CONSERVATIVELY!
IF YOU INSIST.
STILL, I FAIL TO SEE WHY I SHOULD RESPOND. THAT MURDER*--
*ACTION COMICS #645--BRIAN.
--WAS ACTUALLY COMMITTED BY A DUPLICATE OF ME-- A SIMULACRUM--THAT WAS BROUGHT HERE BY MY SERVANT SAZU!
A REGRETTABLE INCIDENT--
--BUT NOT AN INCIDENT THAT ONE OF MY STATUS SHOULD HAVE TO DESCEND TO ANSWERING.
LIGHTEN UP, MAXIMA...YOU'RE NOT QUEEN OF AN EMPIRE ANYMORE!
WE PLAY BY THE RULES. ALL OF US DO!
INDEED, SUPERMAN. NOW LET'S GET DOWN TO BUSINESS AND REVIEW THIS CASE.

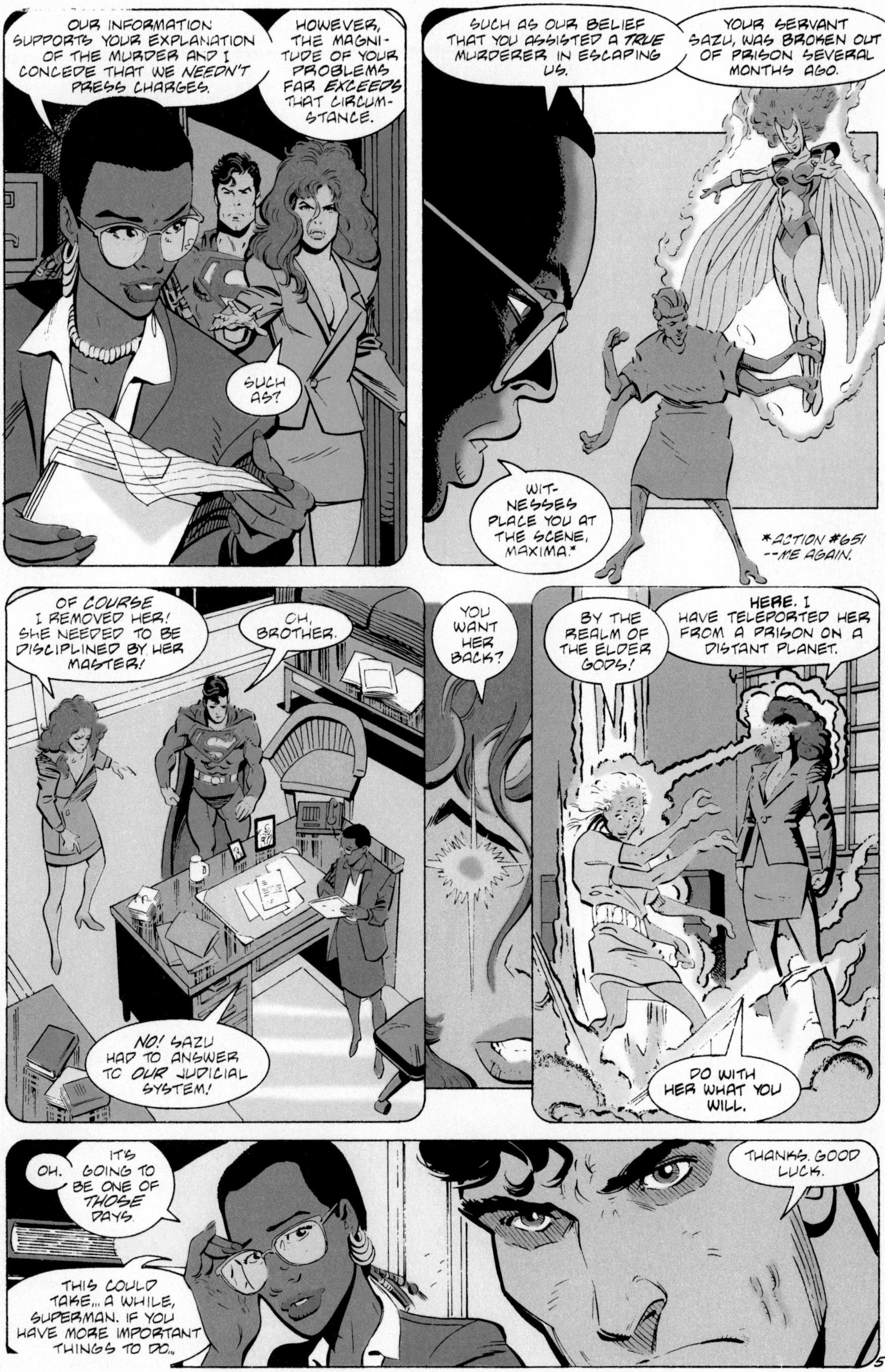

OUR INFORMATION SUPPORTS YOUR EXPLANATION OF THE MURDER AND I CONCEDE THAT WE NEEDN'T PRESS CHARGES.
HOWEVER, THE MAGNITUDE OF YOUR PROBLEMS FAR EXCEEDS THAT CIRCUMSTANCE.
SUCH AS?
SUCH AS OUR BELIEF THAT YOU ASSISTED A TRUE MURDERER IN ESCAPING US.
YOUR SERVANT SAZU, WAS BROKEN OUT OF PRISON SEVERAL MONTHS AGO.
WITNESSES PLACE YOU AT THE SCENE, MAXIMA.*
*ACTION #651 --ME AGAIN.
OF COURSE I REMOVED HER! SHE NEEDED TO BE DISCIPLINED BY HER MASTER!
OH, BROTHER.
NO! SAZU HAD TO ANSWER TO OUR JUDICIAL SYSTEM!
YOU WANT HER BACK?
BY THE REALM OF THE ELDER GODS!
HERE. I HAVE TELEPORTED HER FROM A PRISON ON A DISTANT PLANET.
DO WITH HER WHAT YOU WILL.
OH.
IT'S GOING TO BE ONE OF THOSE DAYS.
THIS COULD TAKE... A WHILE, SUPERMAN. IF YOU HAVE MORE IMPORTANT THINGS TO DO...
THANKS. GOOD LUCK.

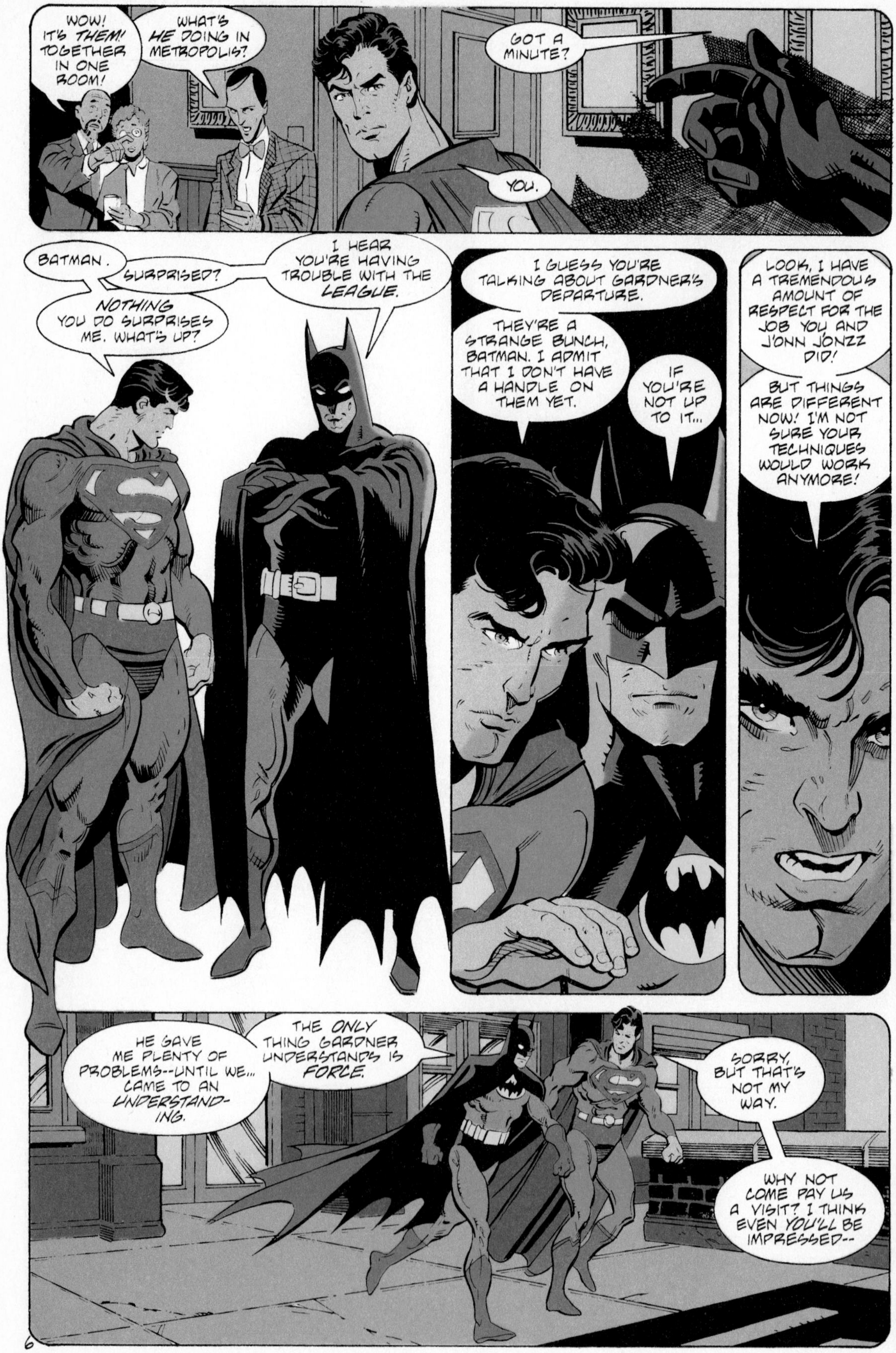
WOW! IT'S THEM! TOGETHER IN ONE ROOM!
WHAT'S HE DOING IN METROPOLIS?
GOT A MINUTE?
YOU.
BATMAN.
SURPRISED?
I HEAR YOU'RE HAVING TROUBLE WITH THE LEAGUE.
NOTHING YOU DO SURPRISES ME. WHAT'S UP?
I GUESS YOU'RE TALKING ABOUT GARDNER'S DEPARTURE.
THEY'RE A STRANGE BUNCH, BATMAN. I ADMIT THAT I DON'T HAVE A HANDLE ON THEM YET.
IF YOU'RE NOT UP TO IT...
LOOK, I HAVE A TREMENDOUS AMOUNT OF RESPECT FOR THE JOB YOU AND J'ONN J'ONZZ DID!
BUT THINGS ARE DIFFERENT NOW! I'M NOT SURE YOUR TECHNIQUES WOULD WORK ANYMORE!
HE GAVE ME PLENTY OF PROBLEMS--UNTIL WE... CAME TO AN UNDERSTANDING.
THE ONLY THING GARDNER UNDERSTANDS IS FORCE.
SORRY, BUT THAT'S NOT MY WAY.
WHY NOT COME PAY US A VISIT? I THINK EVEN YOU'LL BE IMPRESSED--

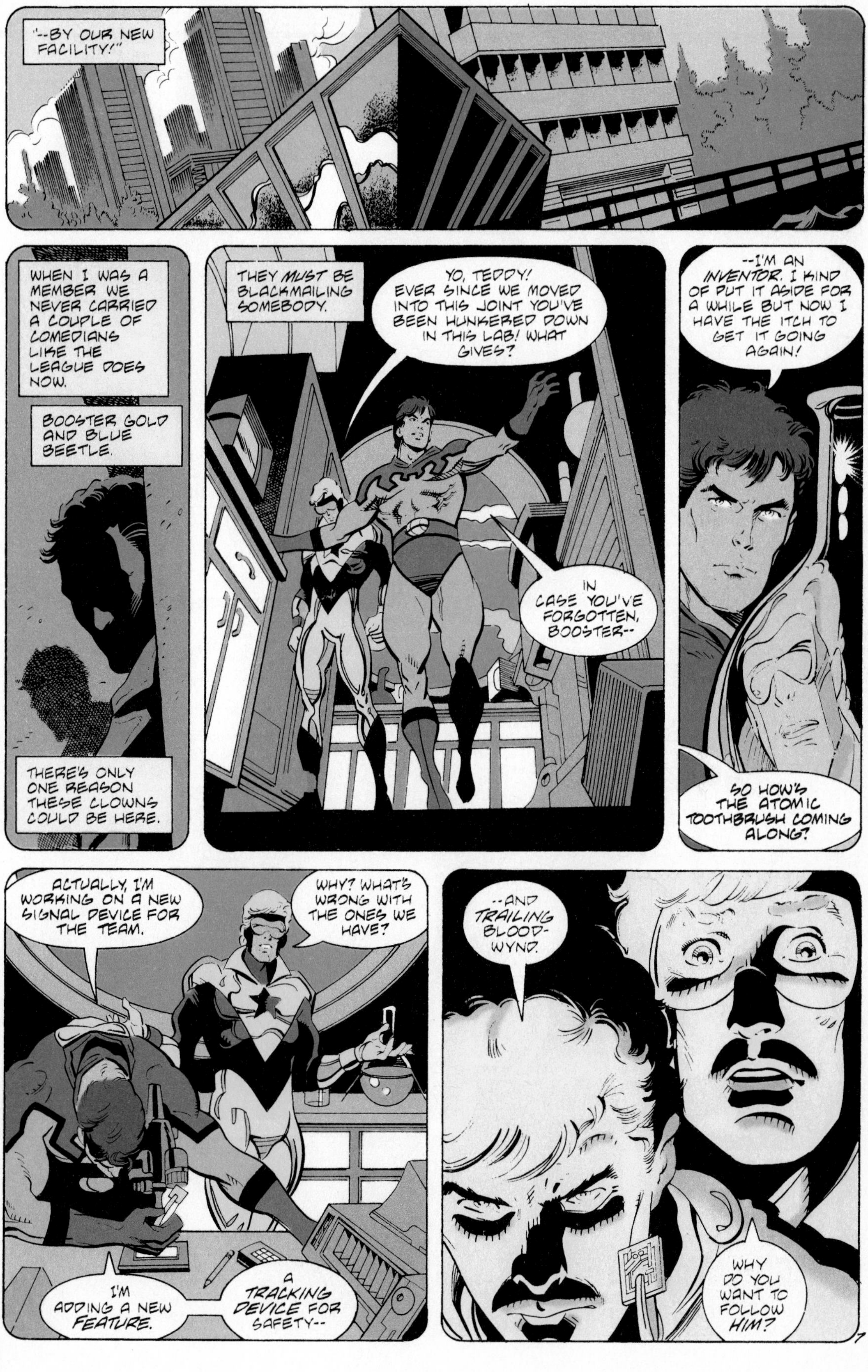

"--BY OUR NEW FACILITY!"
WHEN I WAS A MEMBER WE NEVER CARRIED A COUPLE OF COMEDIANS LIKE THE LEAGUE DOES NOW.
BOOSTER GOLD AND BLUE BEETLE.
THERE'S ONLY ONE REASON THESE CLOWNS COULD BE HERE.
THEY *MUST* BE BLACKMAILING SOMEBODY.
YO, TEDDY! EVER SINCE WE MOVED INTO THIS JOINT YOU'VE BEEN HUNKERED DOWN IN THIS LAB! WHAT GIVES?
IN CASE YOU'VE FORGOTTEN, BOOSTER--
--I'M AN *INVENTOR*. I KIND OF PUT IT ASIDE FOR A WHILE BUT NOW I HAVE THE ITCH TO GET IT GOING AGAIN!
SO HOW'S THE ATOMIC TOOTHBRUSH COMING ALONG?
ACTUALLY, I'M WORKING ON A NEW SIGNAL DEVICE FOR THE TEAM.
WHY? WHAT'S WRONG WITH THE ONES WE HAVE?
I'M ADDING A NEW *FEATURE*.
A *TRACKING DEVICE* FOR SAFETY--
--AND *TRAILING* BLOOD-WYND.
WHY DO YOU WANT TO FOLLOW *HIM*?

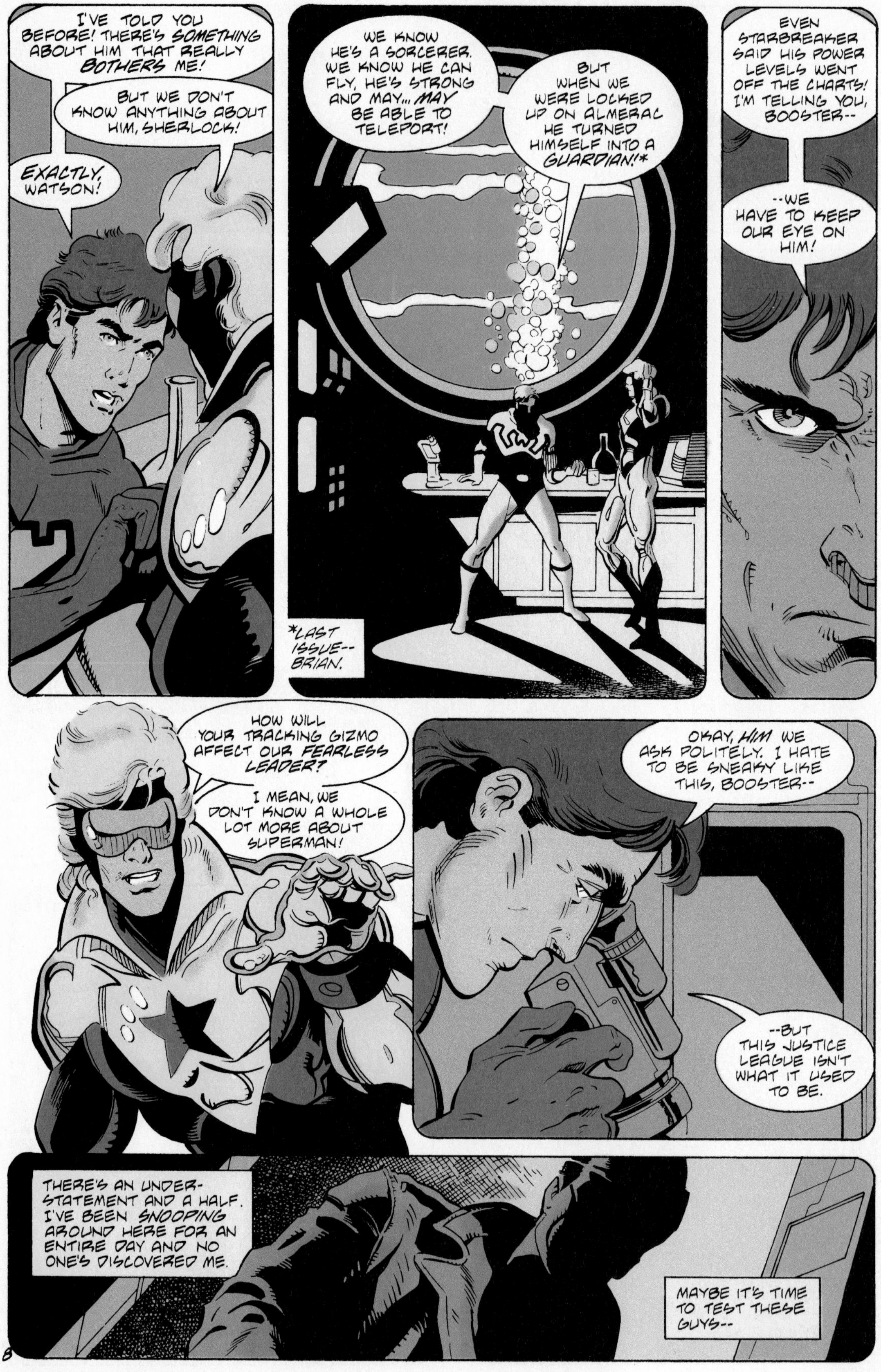
I'VE TOLD YOU BEFORE! THERE'S SOMETHING ABOUT HIM THAT REALLY BOTHERS ME!
BUT WE DON'T KNOW ANYTHING ABOUT HIM, SHERLOCK!
EXACTLY, WATSON!
WE KNOW HE'S A SORCERER. WE KNOW HE CAN FLY, HE'S STRONG AND MAY... MAY BE ABLE TO TELEPORT!
BUT WHEN WE WERE LOCKED UP ON ALMERAC HE TURNED HIMSELF INTO A GUARDIAN!*
*LAST ISSUE--BRIAN.
EVEN STARBREAKER SAID HIS POWER LEVELS WENT OFF THE CHARTS! I'M TELLING YOU, BOOSTER--
--WE HAVE TO KEEP OUR EYE ON HIM!
HOW WILL YOUR TRACKING GIZMO AFFECT OUR FEARLESS LEADER?
I MEAN, WE DON'T KNOW A WHOLE LOT MORE ABOUT SUPERMAN!
OKAY, HIM WE ASK POLITELY. I HATE TO BE SNEAKY LIKE THIS, BOOSTER--
--BUT THIS JUSTICE LEAGUE ISN'T WHAT IT USED TO BE.
THERE'S AN UNDER-STATEMENT AND A HALF. I'VE BEEN SNOOPING AROUND HERE FOR AN ENTIRE DAY AND NO ONE'S DISCOVERED ME.
MAYBE IT'S TIME TO TEST THESE GUYS--

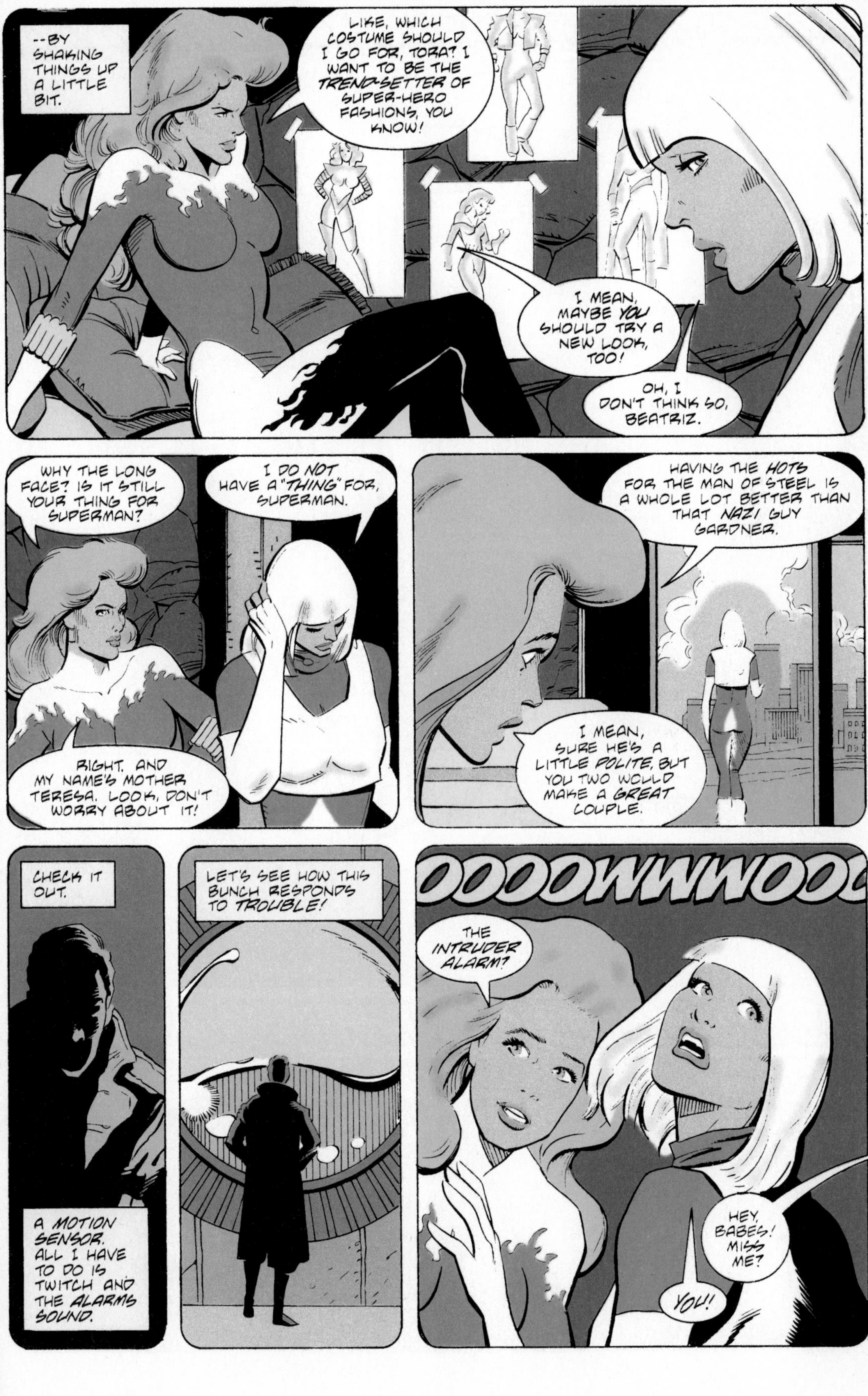
--BY SHAKING THINGS UP A LITTLE BIT.
LIKE, WHICH COSTUME SHOULD I GO FOR, TORA? I WANT TO BE THE TREND-SETTER OF SUPER-HERO FASHIONS, YOU KNOW!
I MEAN, MAYBE YOU SHOULD TRY A NEW LOOK, TOO!
OH, I DON'T THINK SO, BEATRIZ.
WHY THE LONG FACE? IS IT STILL YOUR THING FOR SUPERMAN?
I DO NOT HAVE A "THING" FOR, SUPERMAN.
RIGHT. AND MY NAME'S MOTHER TERESA. LOOK, DON'T WORRY ABOUT IT!
HAVING THE HOTS FOR THE MAN OF STEEL IS A WHOLE LOT BETTER THAN THAT NAZI GUY GARDNER.
I MEAN, SURE HE'S A LITTLE POLITE, BUT YOU TWO WOULD MAKE A GREAT COUPLE.
CHECK IT OUT.
A MOTION SENSOR. ALL I HAVE TO DO IS TWITCH AND THE ALARMS SOUND.
LET'S SEE HOW THIS BUNCH RESPONDS TO TROUBLE!
OOOOOWWWOOO
THE INTRUDER ALARM?
HEY, BABES! MISS ME?
YOU!

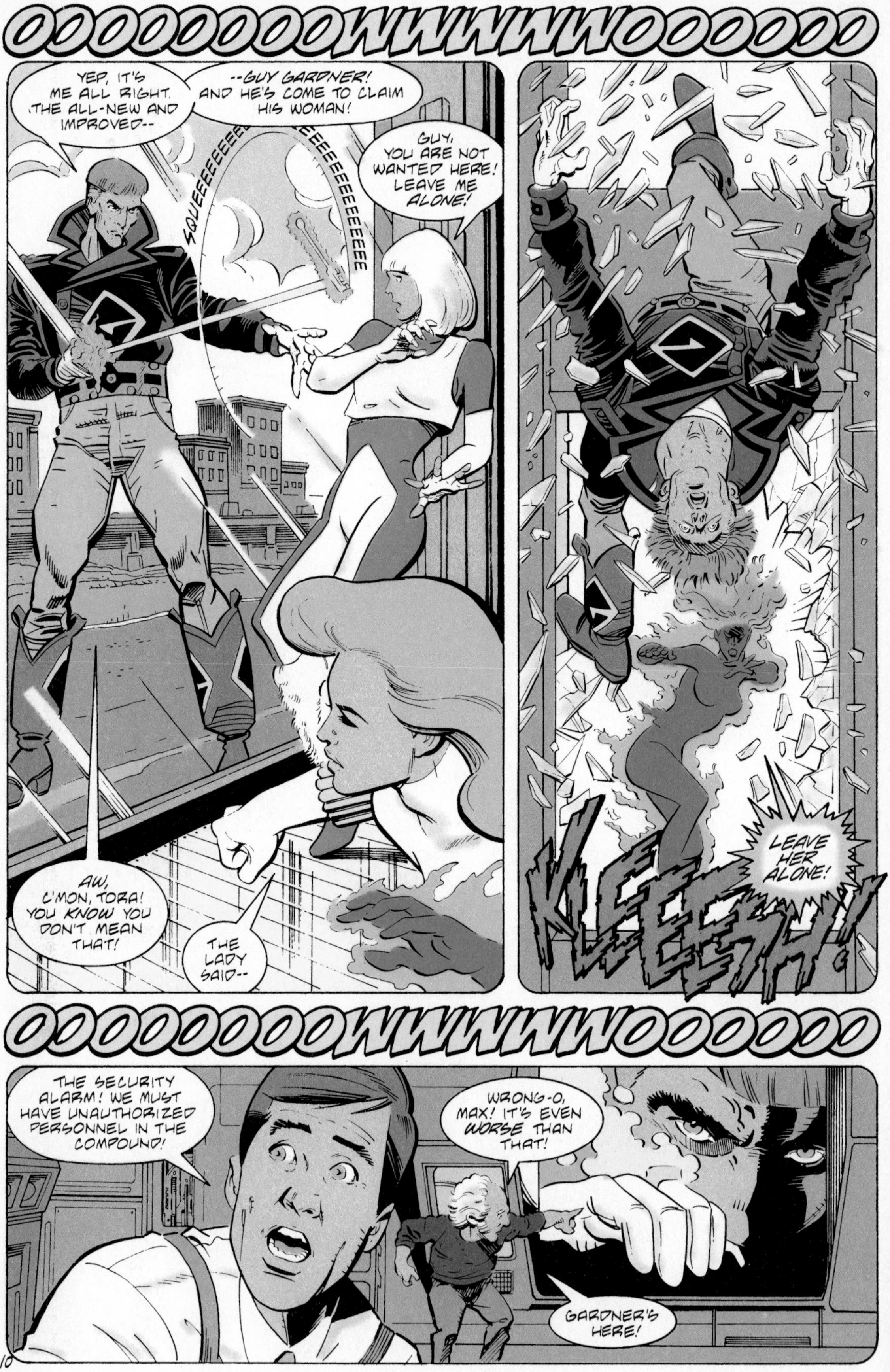
OOOOOOOOOWWWWWWOOOOOOO
YEP, IT'S ME ALL RIGHT. THE ALL-NEW AND IMPROVED--
--GUY GARDNER! AND HE'S COME TO CLAIM HIS WOMAN!
GUY, YOU ARE NOT WANTED HERE! LEAVE ME ALONE!
SQUEEEEEEEEEEEEEEEEEEEEEEEEE
AW, C'MON, TORA! YOU KNOW YOU DON'T MEAN THAT!
THE LADY SAID--
LEAVE HER ALONE!
KLEEEESH!
OOOOOOOOOWWWWWWOOOOOOO
THE SECURITY ALARM! WE MUST HAVE UNAUTHORIZED PERSONNEL IN THE COMPOUND!
WRONG-O, MAX! IT'S EVEN WORSE THAN THAT!
GARDNER'S HERE!

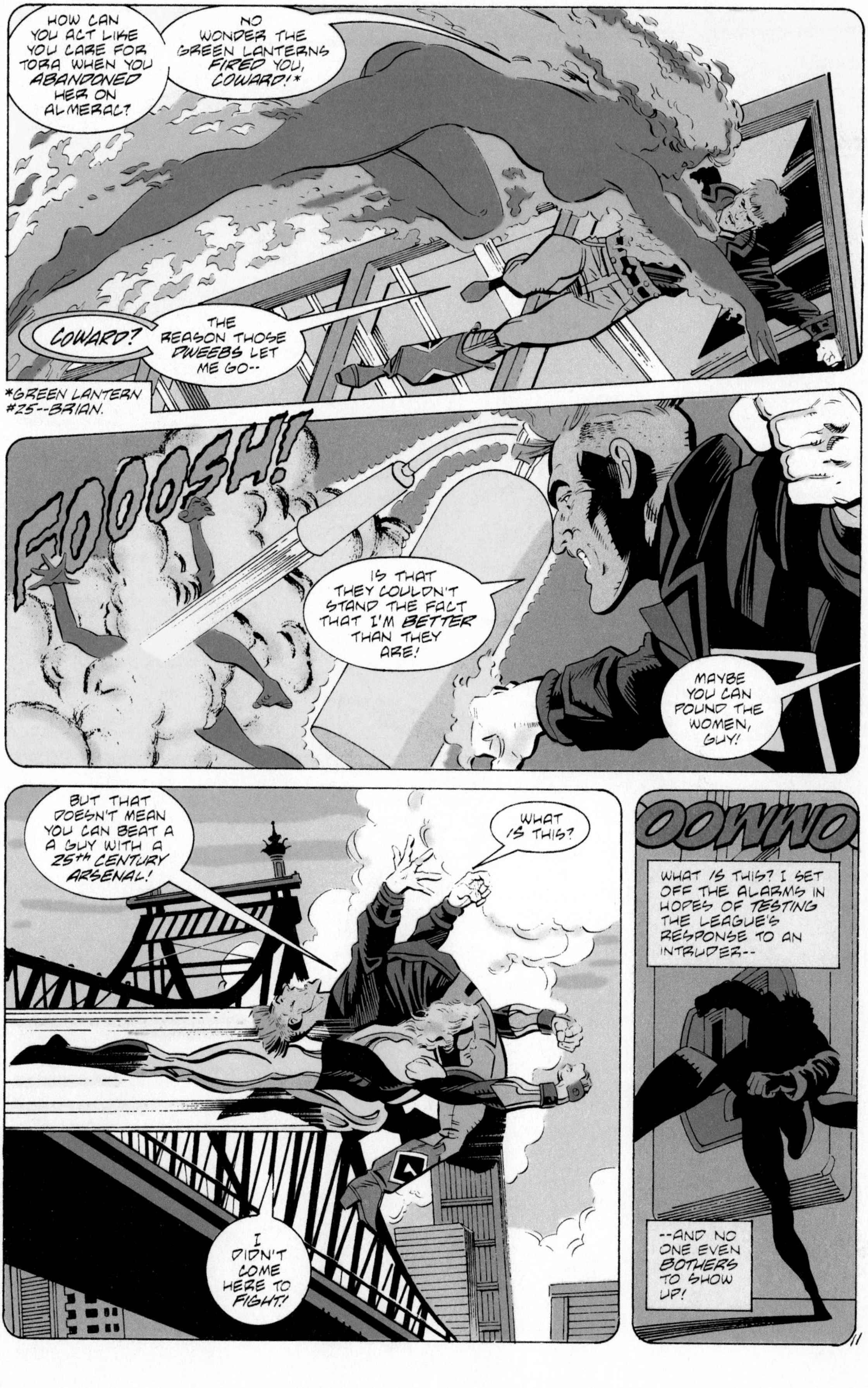
HOW CAN YOU ACT LIKE YOU CARE FOR TORA WHEN YOU ABANDONED HER ON ALMERAC?
NO WONDER THE GREEN LANTERNS FIRED YOU, COWARD!*
COWARD?
THE REASON THOSE DWEEBS LET ME GO--
*GREEN LANTERN #25--BRIAN.
FOOOSH!
IS THAT THEY COULDN'T STAND THE FACT THAT I'M BETTER THAN THEY ARE!
MAYBE YOU CAN FOUND THE WOMEN, GUY!
BUT THAT DOESN'T MEAN YOU CAN BEAT A A GUY WITH A 25th CENTURY ARSENAL!
WHAT IS THIS?
I DIDN'T COME HERE TO FIGHT!
OOWNNO
WHAT IS THIS? I SET OFF THE ALARMS IN HOPES OF TESTING THE LEAGUE'S RESPONSE TO AN INTRUDER--
--AND NO ONE EVEN BOTHERS TO SHOW UP!

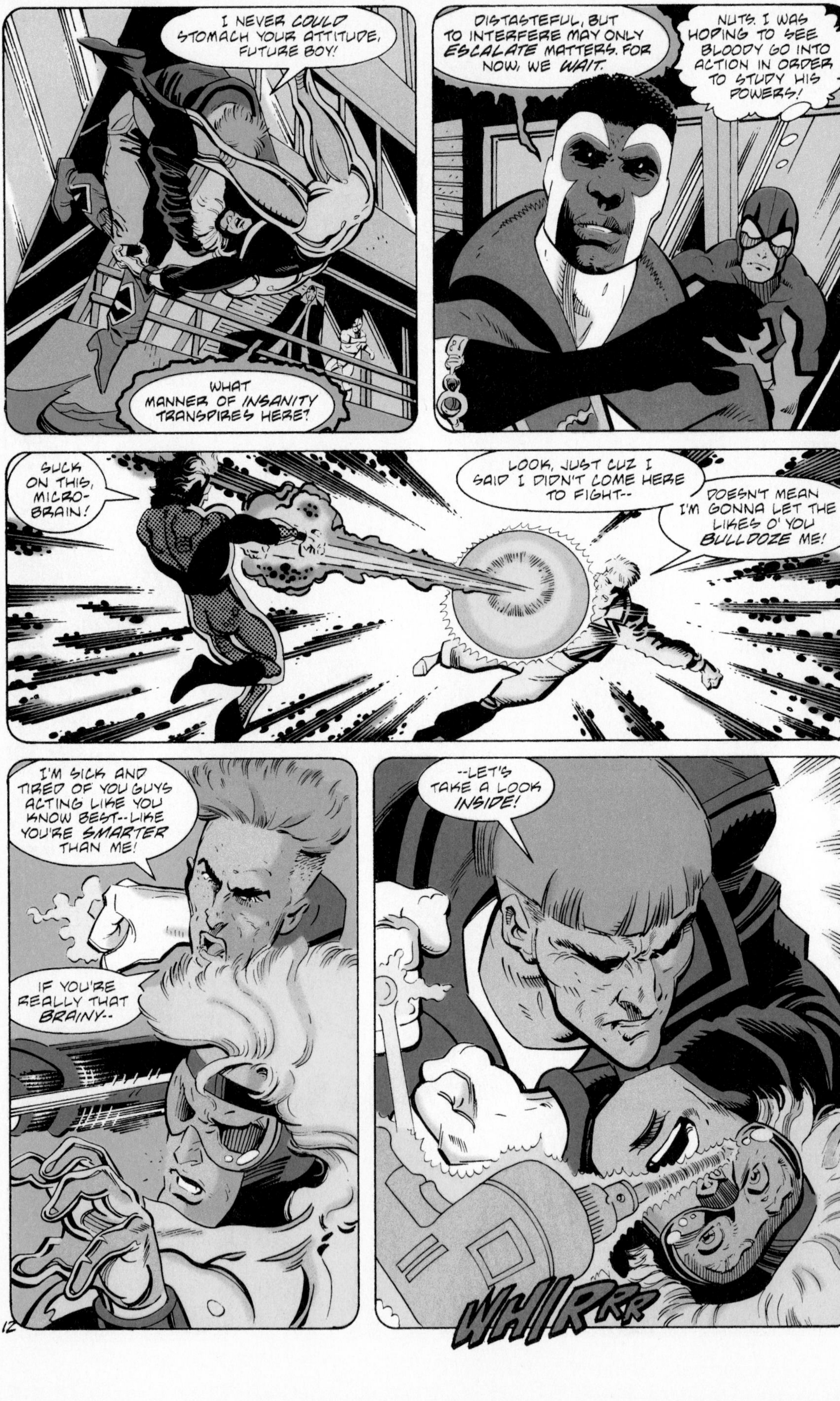

I NEVER COULD STOMACH YOUR ATTITUDE, FUTURE BOY!
WHAT MANNER OF INSANITY TRANSPIRES HERE?
DISTASTEFUL, BUT TO INTERFERE MAY ONLY ESCALATE MATTERS. FOR NOW, WE WAIT.
NUTS. I WAS HOPING TO SEE BLOODY GO INTO ACTION IN ORDER TO STUDY HIS POWERS!
SUCK ON THIS, MICRO-BRAIN!
LOOK, JUST CUZ I SAID I DIDN'T COME HERE TO FIGHT--
DOESN'T MEAN I'M GONNA LET THE LIKES O' YOU BULLDOZE ME!
I'M SICK AND TIRED OF YOU GUYS ACTING LIKE YOU KNOW BEST--LIKE YOU'RE SMARTER THAN ME!
IF YOU'RE REALLY THAT BRAINY--
--LET'S TAKE A LOOK INSIDE!
WHIRRR

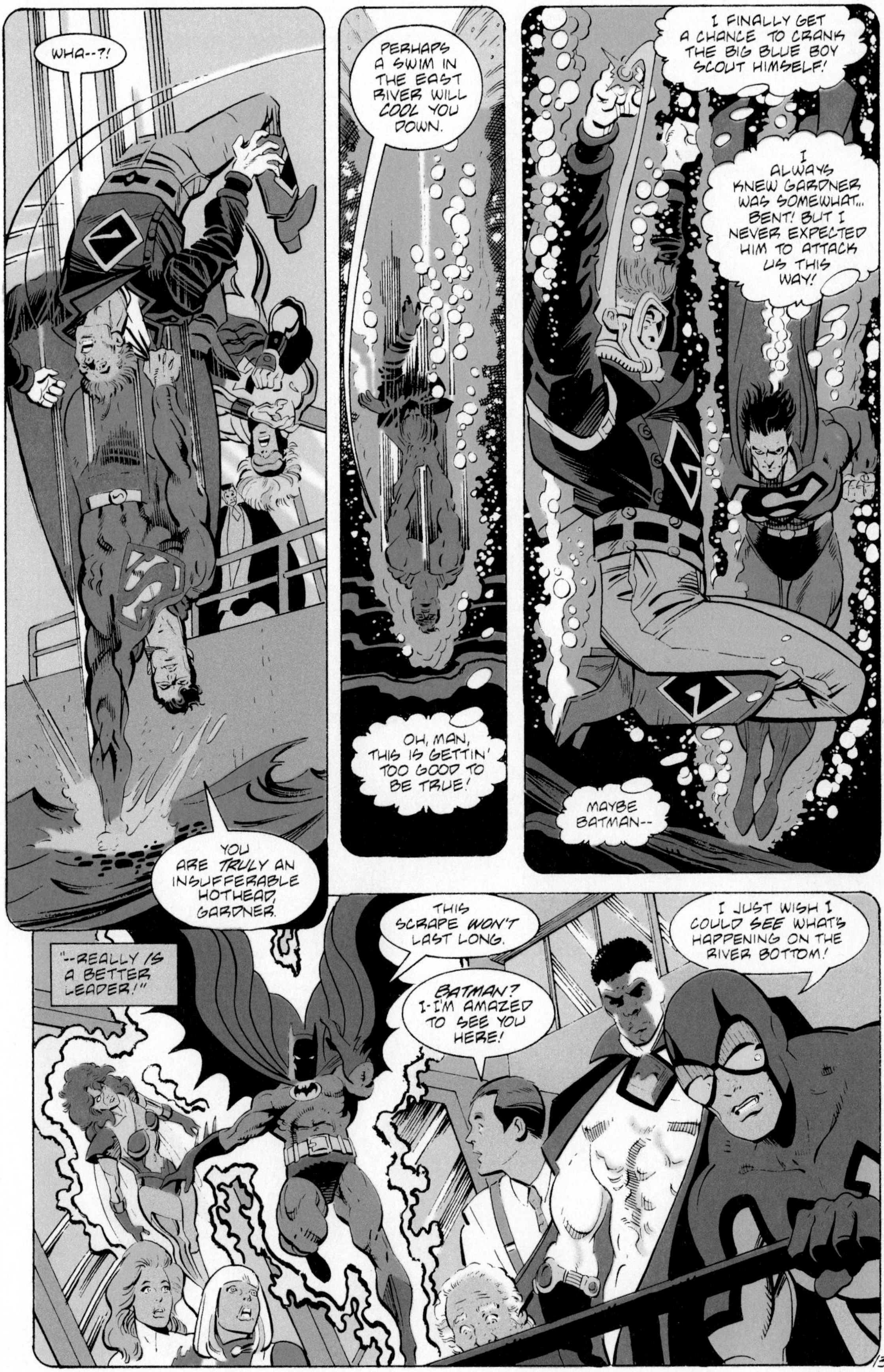

WHA--?!
PERHAPS A SWIM IN THE EAST RIVER WILL COOL YOU DOWN.
YOU ARE TRULY AN INSUFFERABLE HOTHEAD, GARDNER.
OH, MAN, THIS IS GETTIN' TOO GOOD TO BE TRUE!
I FINALLY GET A CHANCE TO CRANK THE BIG BLUE BOY SCOUT HIMSELF!
I ALWAYS KNEW GARDNER WAS SOMEWHAT... BENT! BUT I NEVER EXPECTED HIM TO ATTACK US THIS WAY!
MAYBE BATMAN--
"--REALLY IS A BETTER LEADER!"
THIS SCRAPE WON'T LAST LONG.
BATMAN? I-I'M AMAZED TO SEE YOU HERE!
I JUST WISH I COULD SEE WHAT'S HAPPENING ON THE RIVER BOTTOM!

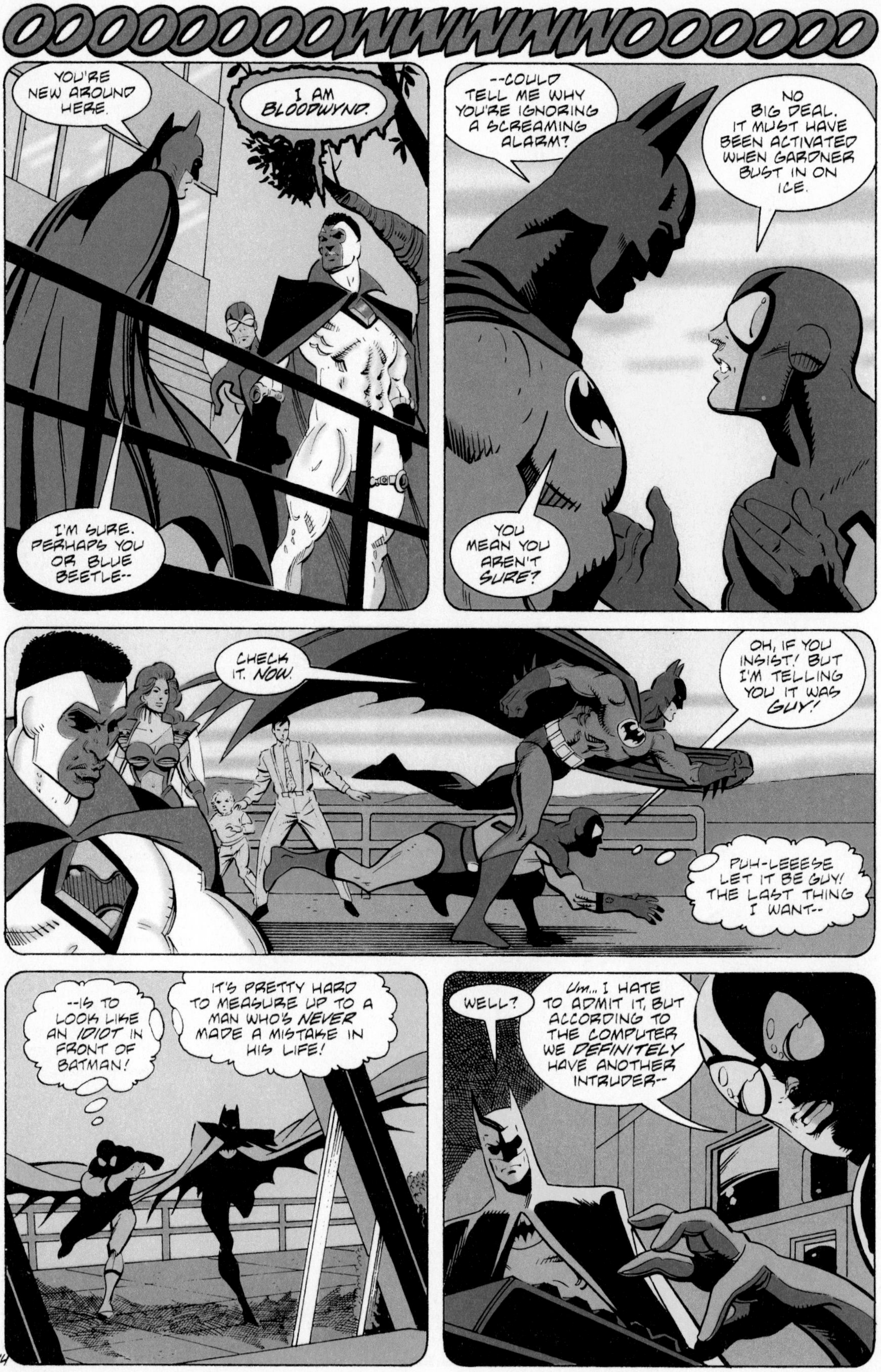

OOOOOOOOOWWWWWWOOOOOOO
YOU'RE NEW AROUND HERE.
I AM BLOODWYND.
I'M SURE. PERHAPS YOU OR BLUE BEETLE--
--COULD TELL ME WHY YOU'RE IGNORING A SCREAMING ALARM?
NO BIG DEAL. IT MUST HAVE BEEN ACTIVATED WHEN GARDNER BUST IN ON ICE.
YOU MEAN YOU AREN'T SURE?
CHECK IT. NOW.
OH, IF YOU INSIST! BUT I'M TELLING YOU IT WAS GUY!
PUH-LEEESE LET IT BE GUY! THE LAST THING I WANT--
--IS TO LOOK LIKE AN IDIOT IN FRONT OF BATMAN!
IT'S PRETTY HARD TO MEASURE UP TO A MAN WHO'S NEVER MADE A MISTAKE IN HIS LIFE!
WELL?
Um... I HATE TO ADMIT IT, BUT ACCORDING TO THE COMPUTER WE DEFINITELY HAVE ANOTHER INTRUDER--

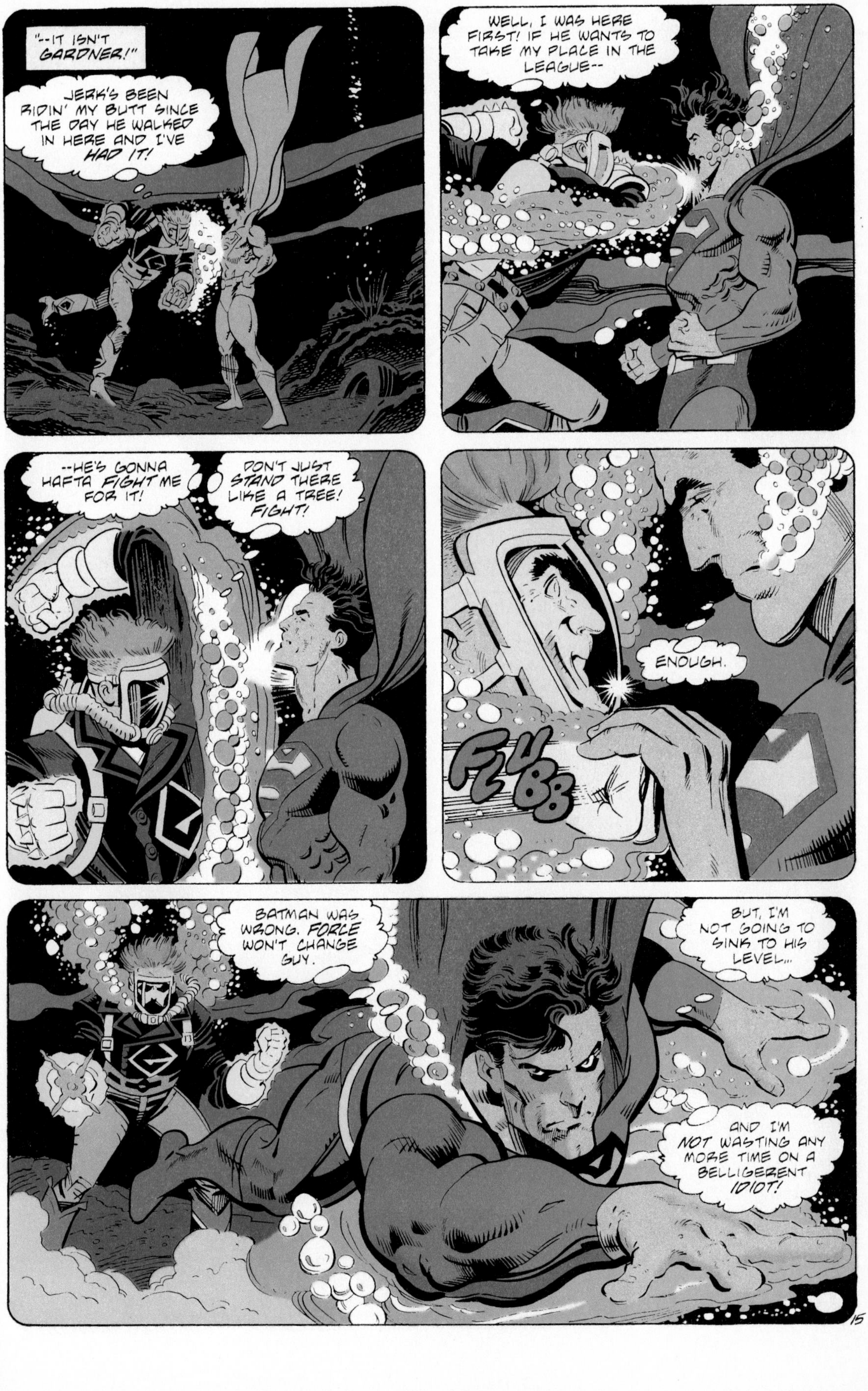
"--IT ISN'T GARDNER!"
JERK'S BEEN RIDIN' MY BUTT SINCE THE DAY HE WALKED IN HERE AND I'VE HAD IT!
WELL, I WAS HERE FIRST! IF HE WANTS TO TAKE MY PLACE IN THE LEAGUE--
--HE'S GONNA HAFTA FIGHT ME FOR IT!
DON'T JUST STAND THERE LIKE A TREE! FIGHT!
ENOUGH.
FLUBB
BATMAN WAS WRONG. FORCE WON'T CHANGE GUY.
BUT, I'M NOT GOING TO SINK TO HIS LEVEL...
AND I'M NOT WASTING ANY MORE TIME ON A BELLIGERENT IDIOT!

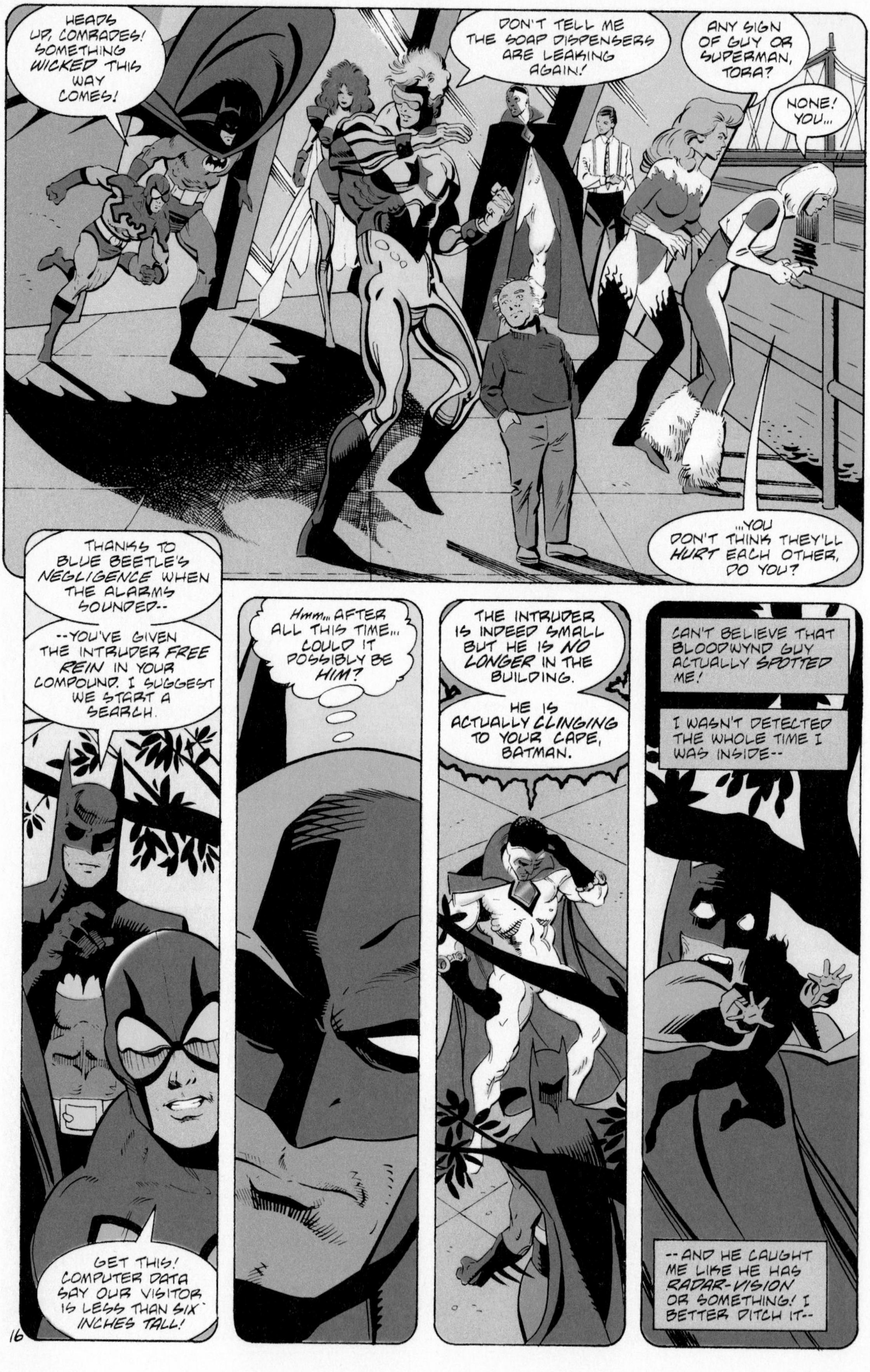

HEADS UP, COMRADES! SOMETHING WICKED THIS WAY COMES!
DON'T TELL ME THE SOAP DISPENSERS ARE LEAKING AGAIN!
ANY SIGN OF GUY OR SUPERMAN, TORA?
NONE! YOU...
...YOU DON'T THINK THEY'LL HURT EACH OTHER, DO YOU?
THANKS TO BLUE BEETLE'S NEGLIGENCE WHEN THE ALARMS SOUNDED--
--YOU'VE GIVEN THE INTRUDER FREE REIN IN YOUR COMPOUND. I SUGGEST WE START A SEARCH.
GET THIS! COMPUTER DATA SAY OUR VISITOR IS LESS THAN SIX INCHES TALL!
Hmm... AFTER ALL THIS TIME... COULD IT POSSIBLY BE HIM?
THE INTRUDER IS INDEED SMALL BUT HE IS NO LONGER IN THE BUILDING.
HE IS ACTUALLY CLINGING TO YOUR CAPE, BATMAN.
CAN'T BELIEVE THAT BLOODWYND GUY ACTUALLY SPOTTED ME!
I WASN'T DETECTED THE WHOLE TIME I WAS INSIDE--
--AND HE CAUGHT ME LIKE HE HAS RADAR-VISION OR SOMETHING! I BETTER DITCH IT--

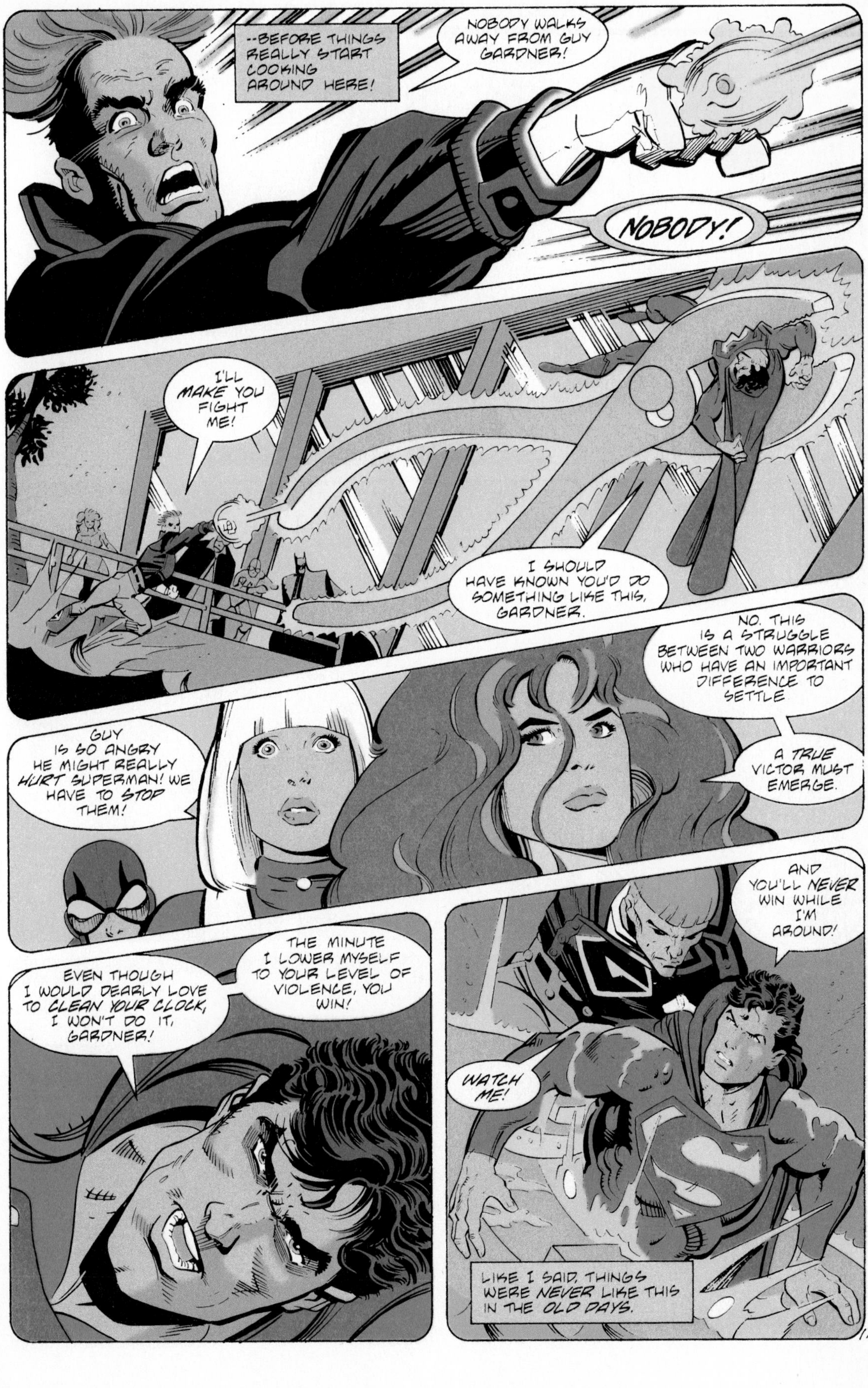

--BEFORE THINGS REALLY START COOKING AROUND HERE!
NOBODY WALKS AWAY FROM GUY GARDNER!
NOBODY!
I'LL MAKE YOU FIGHT ME!
I SHOULD HAVE KNOWN YOU'D DO SOMETHING LIKE THIS, GARDNER.
GUY IS SO ANGRY HE MIGHT REALLY HURT SUPERMAN! WE HAVE TO STOP THEM!
NO. THIS IS A STRUGGLE BETWEEN TWO WARRIORS WHO HAVE AN IMPORTANT DIFFERENCE TO SETTLE.
A TRUE VICTOR MUST EMERGE.
EVEN THOUGH I WOULD DEARLY LOVE TO CLEAN YOUR CLOCK, I WON'T DO IT, GARDNER!
THE MINUTE I LOWER MYSELF TO YOUR LEVEL OF VIOLENCE, YOU WIN!
AND YOU'LL NEVER WIN WHILE I'M AROUND!
WATCH ME!
LIKE I SAID, THINGS WERE NEVER LIKE THIS IN THE OLD DAYS.

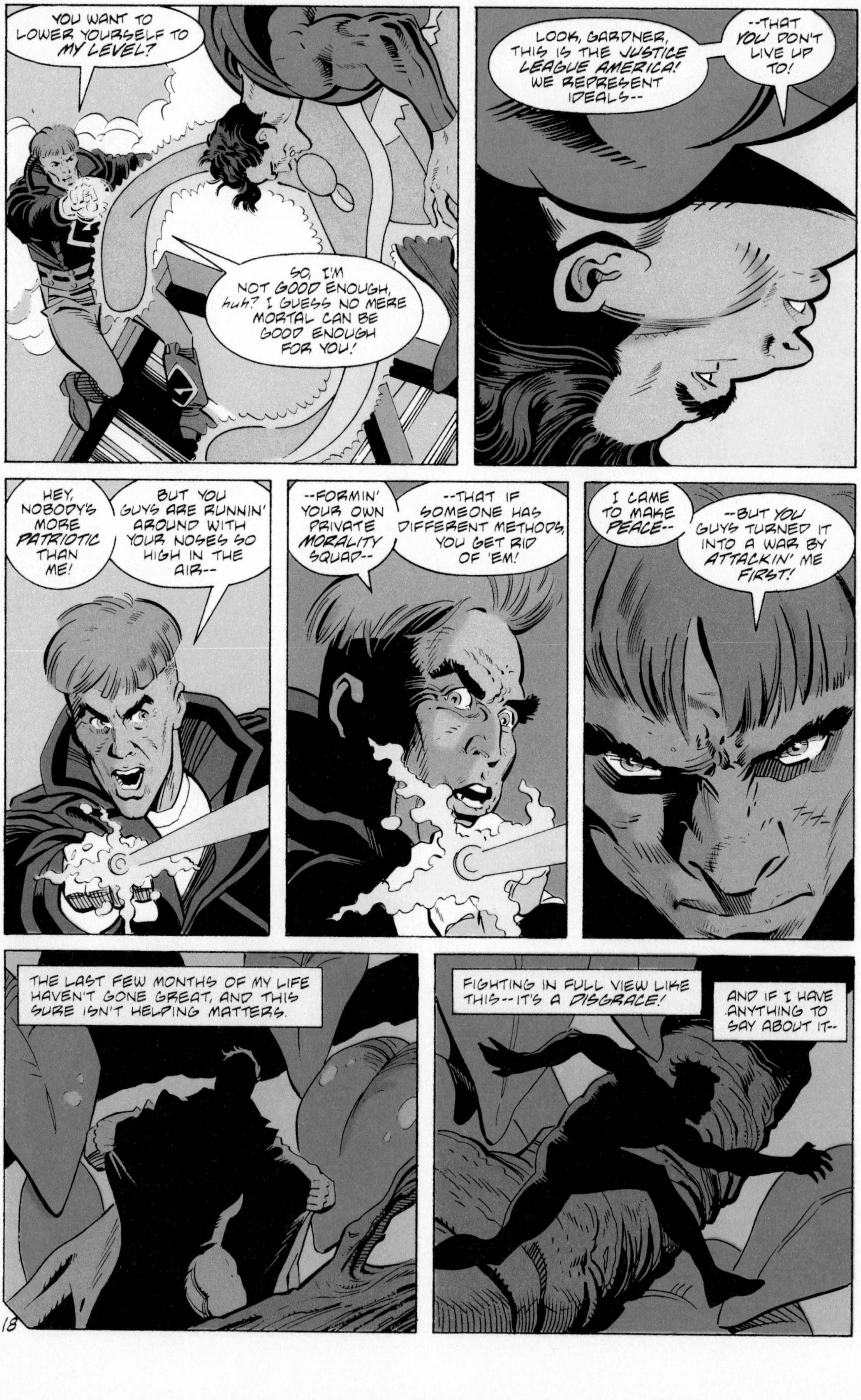
YOU WANT TO LOWER YOURSELF TO MY LEVEL?
SO, I'M NOT GOOD ENOUGH, huh? I GUESS NO MERE MORTAL CAN BE GOOD ENOUGH FOR YOU!
LOOK, GARDNER, THIS IS THE JUSTICE LEAGUE AMERICA! WE REPRESENT IDEALS--
--THAT YOU DON'T LIVE UP TO!
HEY, NOBODY'S MORE PATRIOTIC THAN ME!
BUT YOU GUYS ARE RUNNIN' AROUND WITH YOUR NOSES SO HIGH IN THE AIR--
--FORMIN' YOUR OWN PRIVATE MORALITY SQUAD--
--THAT IF SOMEONE HAS DIFFERENT METHODS, YOU GET RID OF 'EM!
I CAME TO MAKE PEACE--
--BUT YOU GUYS TURNED IT INTO A WAR BY ATTACKIN' ME FIRST!
THE LAST FEW MONTHS OF MY LIFE HAVEN'T GONE GREAT, AND THIS SURE ISN'T HELPING MATTERS.
FIGHTING IN FULL VIEW LIKE THIS--IT'S A DISGRACE!
AND IF I HAVE ANYTHING TO SAY ABOUT IT--

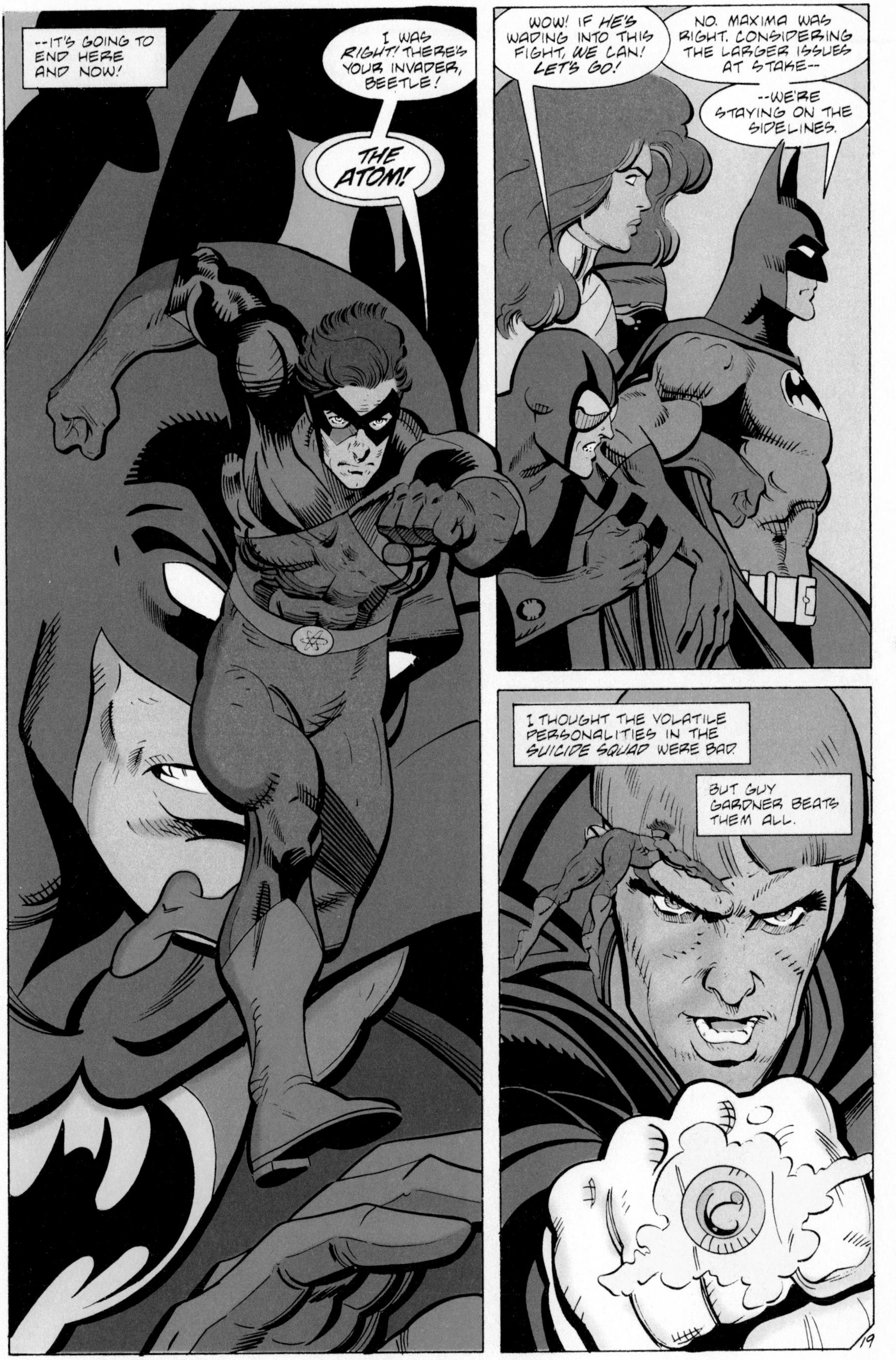
--IT'S GOING TO END HERE AND NOW!
I WAS RIGHT! THERE'S YOUR INVADER, BEETLE!
THE ATOM!
WOW! IF HE'S WADING INTO THIS FIGHT, WE CAN! LET'S GO!
NO. MAXIMA WAS RIGHT. CONSIDERING THE LARGER ISSUES AT STAKE--
--WE'RE STAYING ON THE SIDELINES.
I THOUGHT THE VOLATILE PERSONALITIES IN THE SUICIDE SQUAD WERE BAD.
BUT GUY GARDNER BEATS THEM ALL.

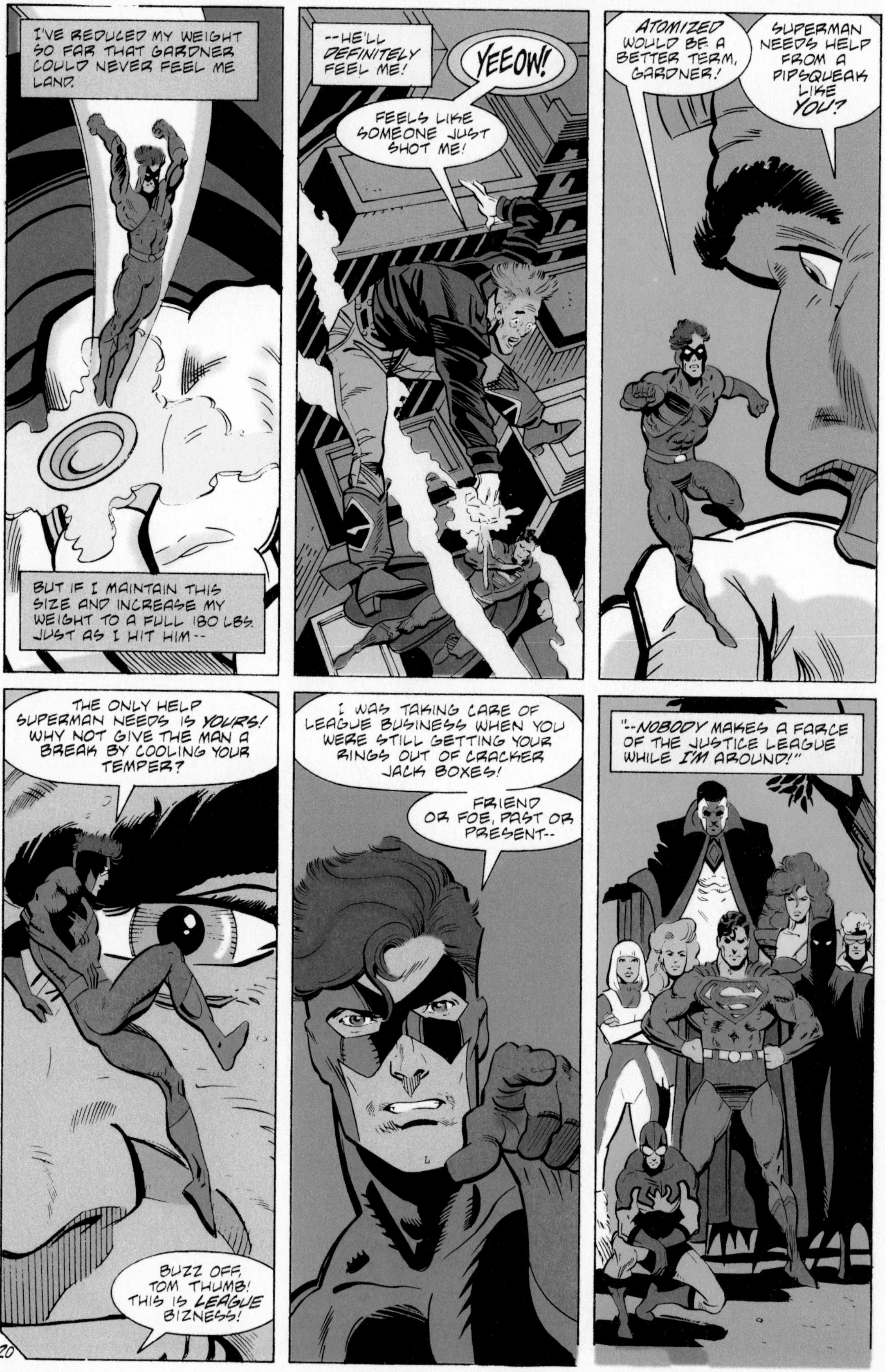
I'VE REDUCED MY WEIGHT SO FAR THAT GARDNER COULD NEVER FEEL ME LAND.
BUT IF I MAINTAIN THIS SIZE AND INCREASE MY WEIGHT TO A FULL 180 LBS. JUST AS I HIT HIM--
--HE'LL DEFINITELY FEEL ME!
YEEOW!
FEELS LIKE SOMEONE JUST SHOT ME!
ATOMIZED WOULD BE A BETTER TERM, GARDNER!
SUPERMAN NEEDS HELP FROM A PIPSQUEAK LIKE YOU?
THE ONLY HELP SUPERMAN NEEDS IS YOURS! WHY NOT GIVE THE MAN A BREAK BY COOLING YOUR TEMPER?
BUZZ OFF, TOM THUMB! THIS IS LEAGUE BIZNESS!
I WAS TAKING CARE OF LEAGUE BUSINESS WHEN YOU WERE STILL GETTING YOUR RINGS OUT OF CRACKER JACK BOXES!
FRIEND OR FOE, PAST OR PRESENT--
"--NOBODY MAKES A FARCE OF THE JUSTICE LEAGUE WHILE I'M AROUND!"

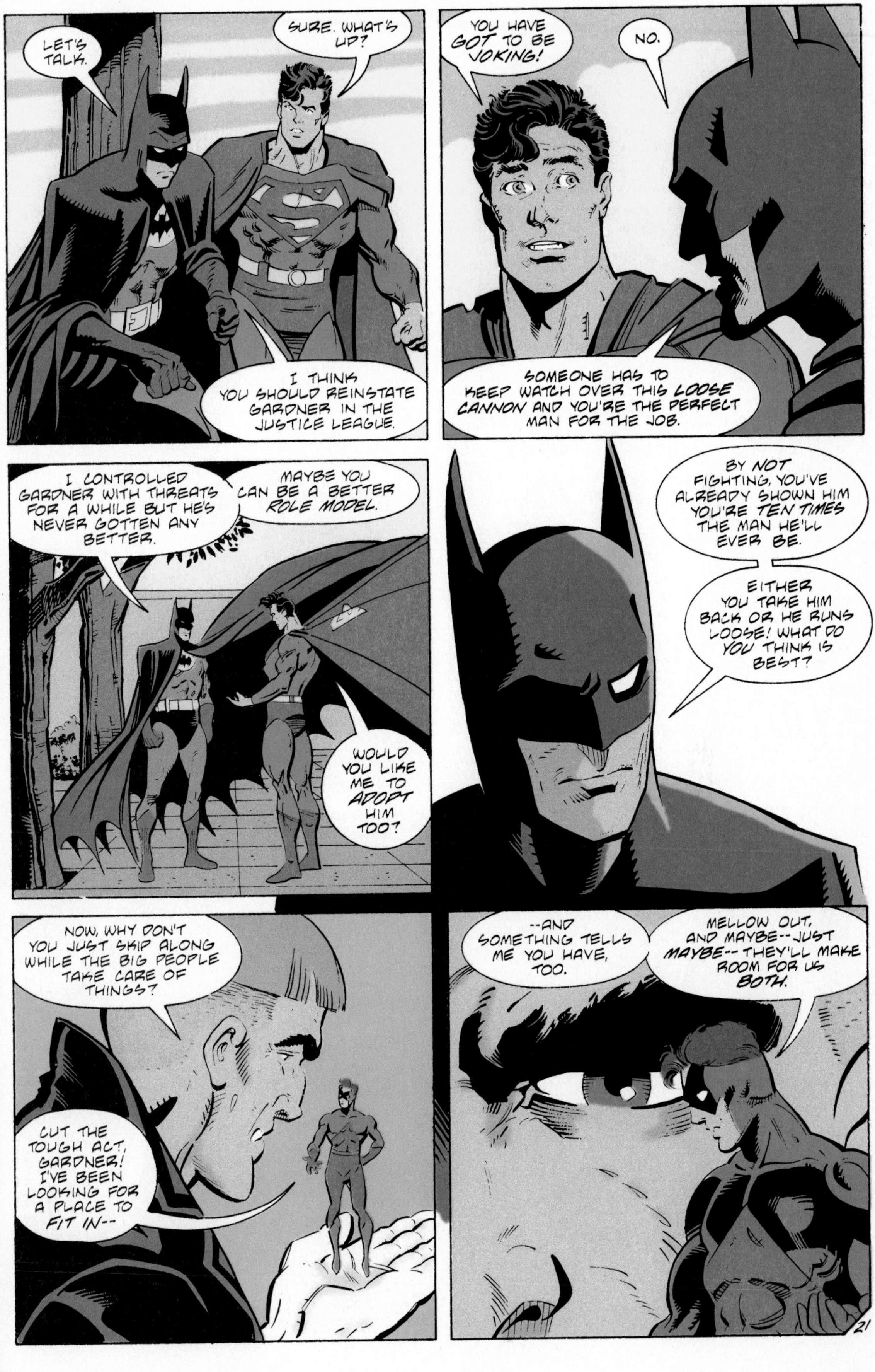
LET'S TALK.
SURE. WHAT'S UP?
I THINK YOU SHOULD REINSTATE GARDNER IN THE JUSTICE LEAGUE.
YOU HAVE GOT TO BE JOKING!
NO.
SOMEONE HAS TO KEEP WATCH OVER THIS LOOSE CANNON AND YOU'RE THE PERFECT MAN FOR THE JOB.
I CONTROLLED GARDNER WITH THREATS FOR A WHILE BUT HE'S NEVER GOTTEN ANY BETTER.
MAYBE YOU CAN BE A BETTER ROLE MODEL.
WOULD YOU LIKE ME TO ADOPT HIM TOO?
BY NOT FIGHTING, YOU'VE ALREADY SHOWN HIM YOU'RE TEN TIMES THE MAN HE'LL EVER BE.
EITHER YOU TAKE HIM BACK OR HE RUNS LOOSE! WHAT DO YOU THINK IS BEST?
NOW, WHY DON'T YOU JUST SKIP ALONG WHILE THE BIG PEOPLE TAKE CARE OF THINGS?
CUT THE TOUGH ACT, GARDNER! I'VE BEEN LOOKING FOR A PLACE TO FIT IN--
--AND SOMETHING TELLS ME YOU HAVE, TOO.
MELLOW OUT, AND MAYBE-- JUST MAYBE-- THEY'LL MAKE ROOM FOR US BOTH.
21

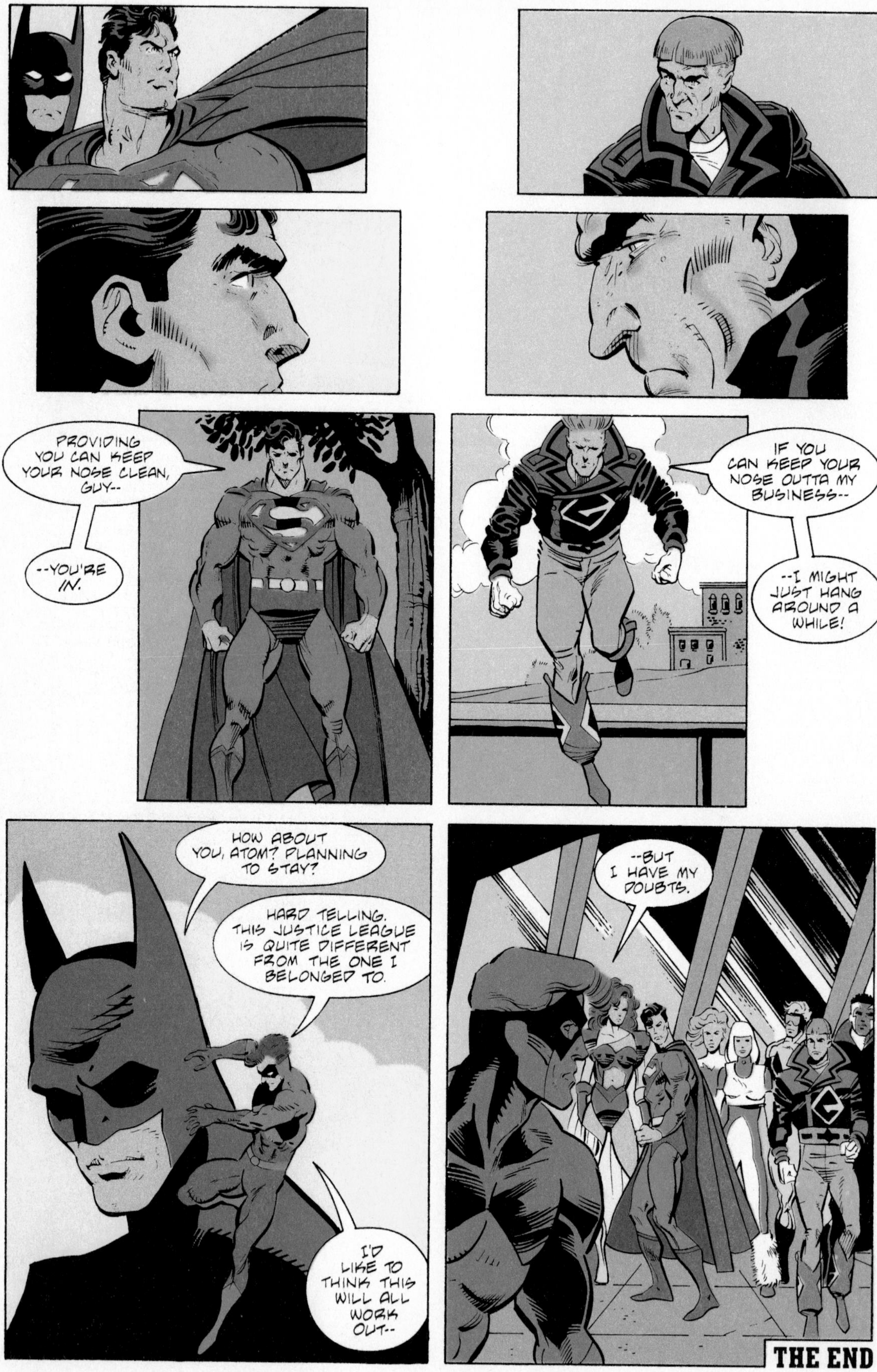
PROVIDING YOU CAN KEEP YOUR NOSE CLEAN, GUY--
--YOU'RE IN.
IF YOU CAN KEEP YOUR NOSE OUTTA MY BUSINESS--
--I MIGHT JUST HANG AROUND A WHILE!
HOW ABOUT YOU, ATOM? PLANNING TO STAY?
HARD TELLING. THIS JUSTICE LEAGUE IS QUITE DIFFERENT FROM THE ONE I BELONGED TO.
I'D LIKE TO THINK THIS WILL ALL WORK OUT--
--BUT I HAVE MY DOUBTS.
THE END

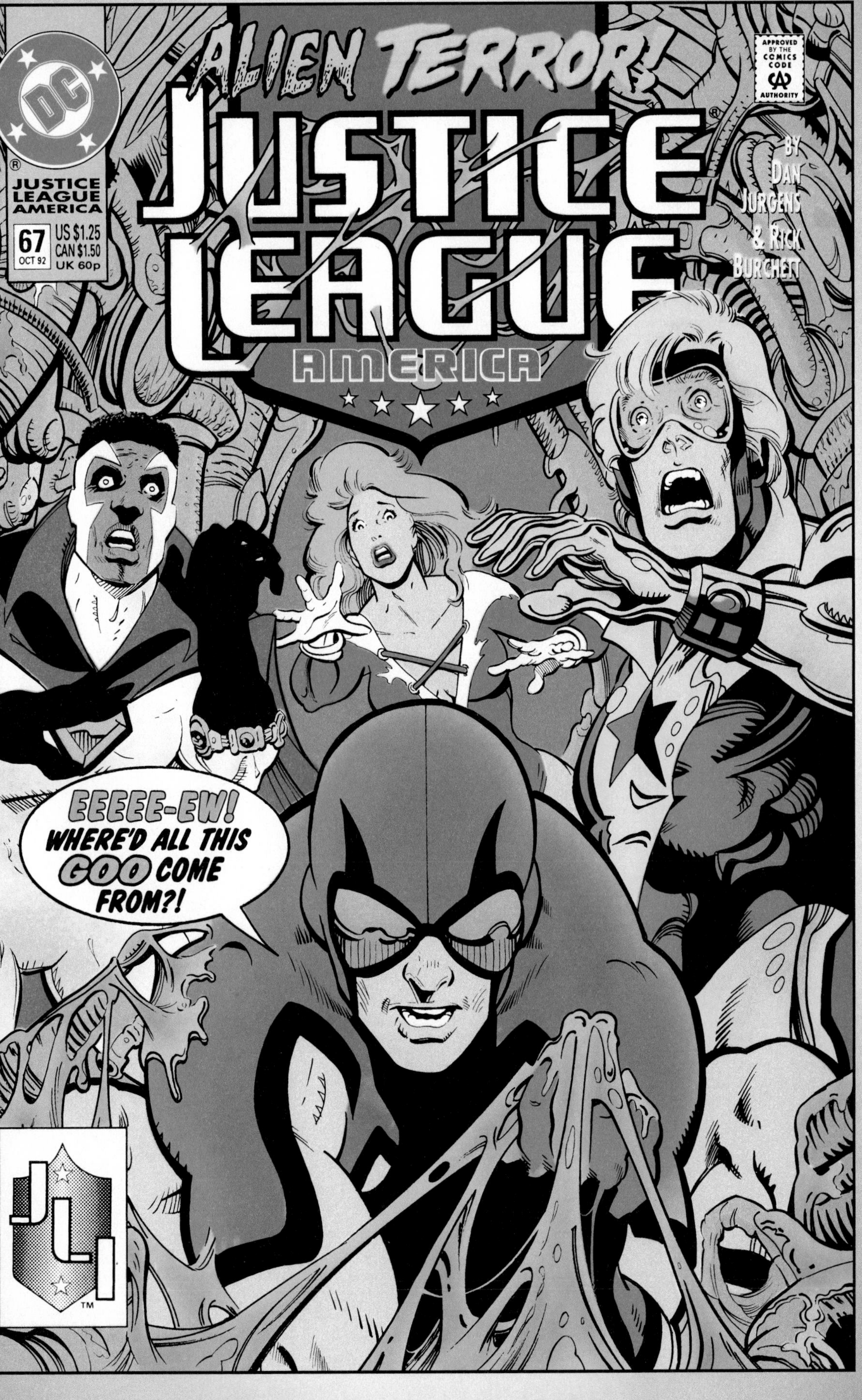
ALIEN TERROR!
JUSTICE LEAGUE AMERICA
JUSTICE LEAGUE AMERICA
67
OCT 92
US $1.25
CAN $1.50
UK 60p
APPROVED BY THE COMICS CODE AUTHORITY
BY DAN JURGENS & RICK BURCHETT
EEEEE-EW! WHERE'D ALL THIS GOO COME FROM?!

Cover art by **DAN JURGENS**
and **RICK BURCHETT**

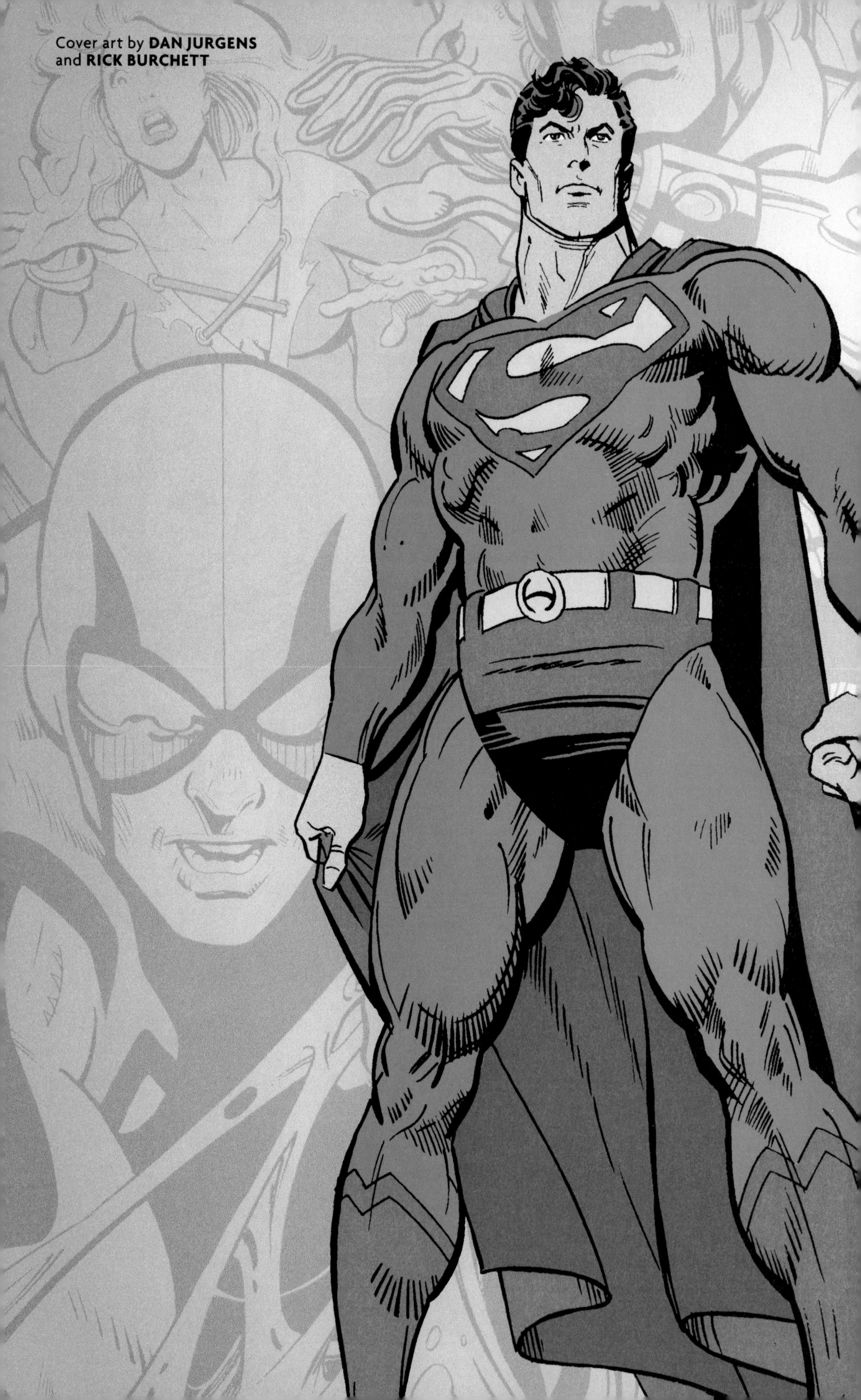

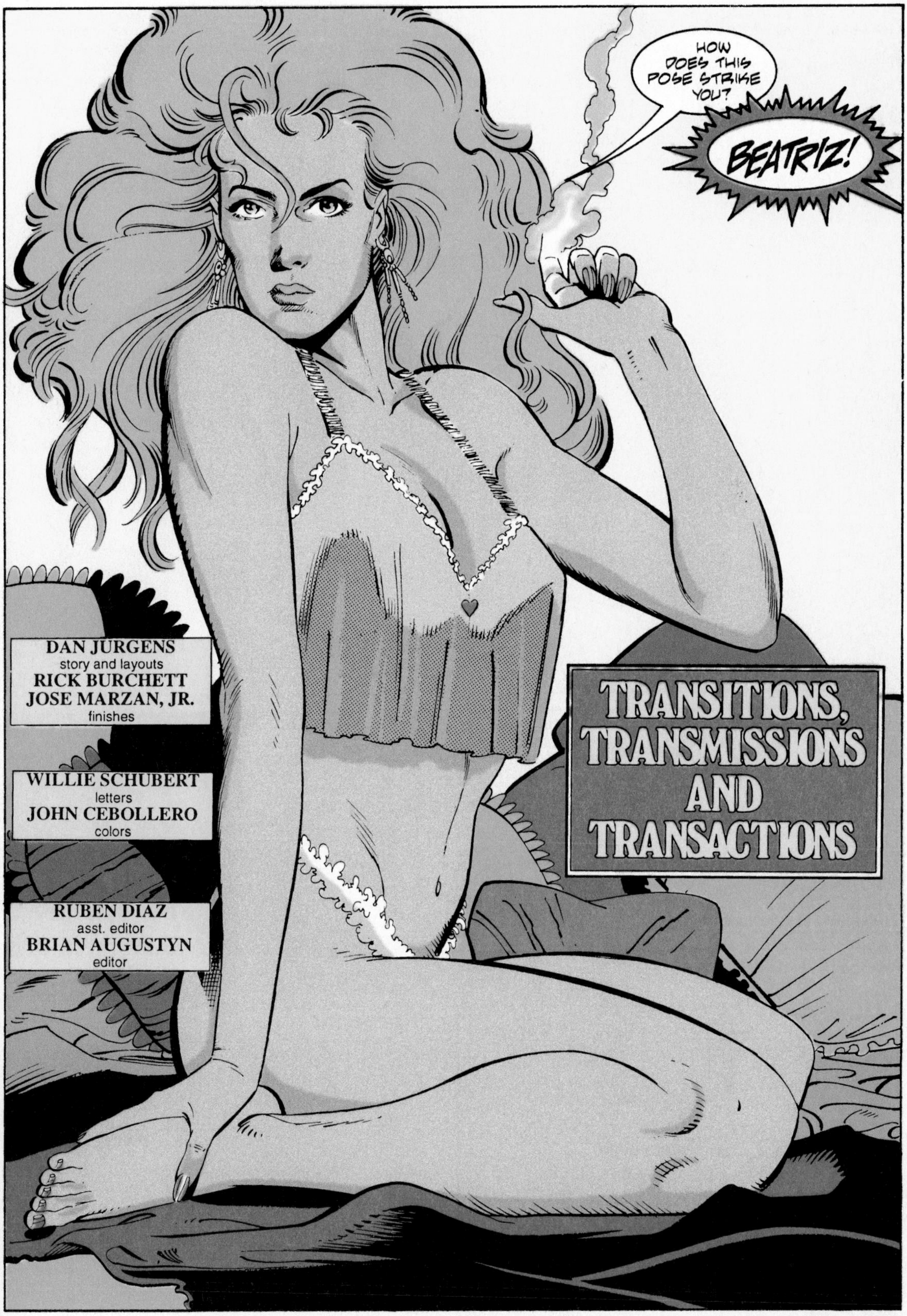
HOW DOES THIS POSE STRIKE YOU?
BEATRIZ!
DAN JURGENS
story and layouts
RICK BURCHETT
JOSE MARZAN, JR.
finishes
WILLIE SCHUBERT
letters
JOHN CEBOLLERO
colors
RUBEN DIAZ
asst. editor
BRIAN AUGUSTYN
editor
TRANSITIONS, TRANSMISSIONS AND TRANSACTIONS

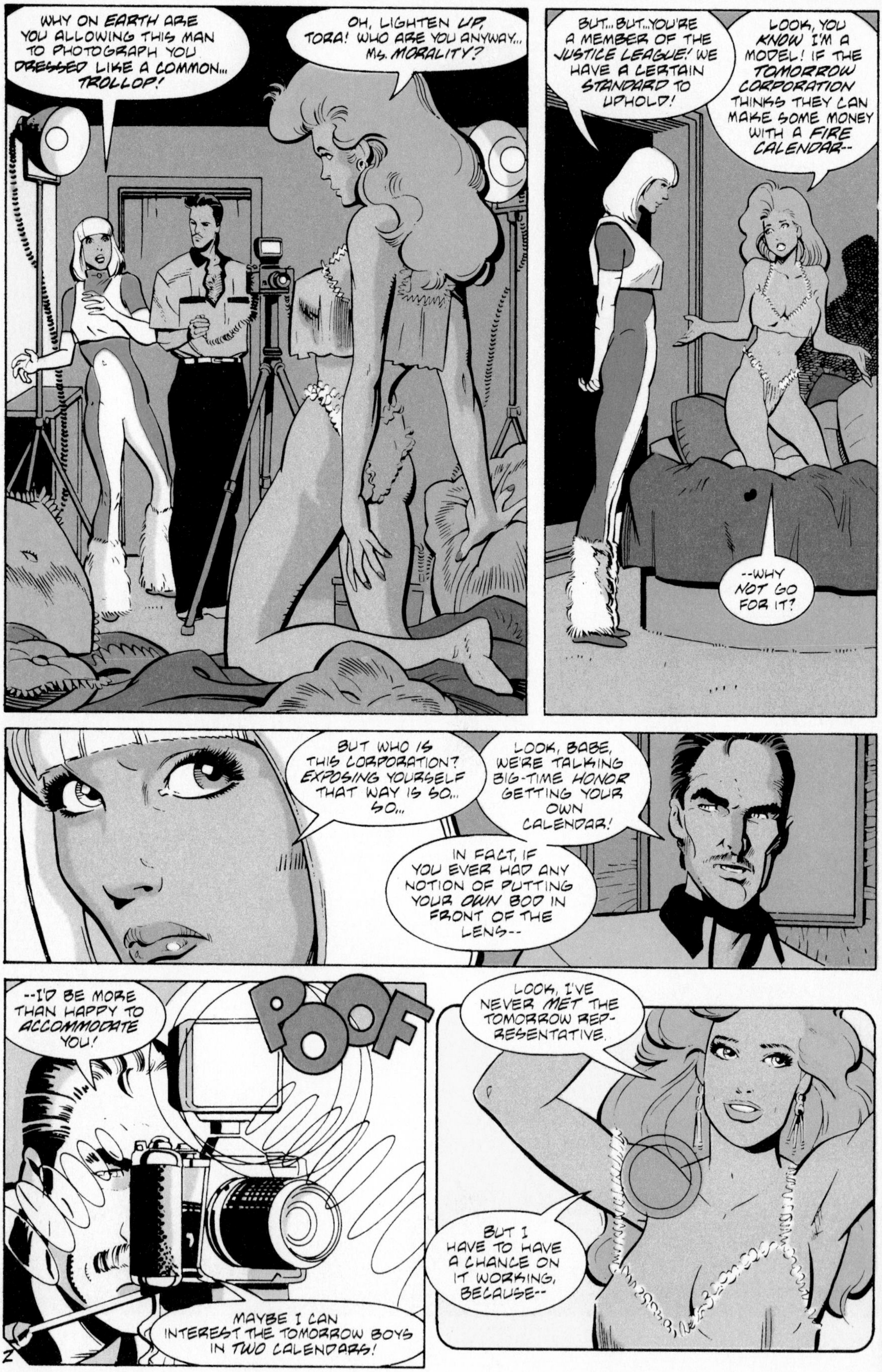

WHY ON EARTH ARE YOU ALLOWING THIS MAN TO PHOTOGRAPH YOU DRESSED LIKE A COMMON... TROLLOP!
OH, LIGHTEN UP, TORA! WHO ARE YOU ANYWAY... Ms. MORALITY?
BUT... BUT... YOU'RE A MEMBER OF THE JUSTICE LEAGUE! WE HAVE A CERTAIN STANDARD TO UPHOLD!
LOOK, YOU KNOW I'M A MODEL! IF THE TOMORROW CORPORATION THINKS THEY CAN MAKE SOME MONEY WITH A FIRE CALENDAR--
--WHY NOT GO FOR IT?
BUT WHO IS THIS CORPORATION? EXPOSING YOURSELF THAT WAY IS SO... SO...
LOOK, BABE, WE'RE TALKING BIG-TIME HONOR GETTING YOUR OWN CALENDAR!
IN FACT, IF YOU EVER HAD ANY NOTION OF PUTTING YOUR OWN BOD IN FRONT OF THE LENS--
--I'D BE MORE THAN HAPPY TO ACCOMMODATE YOU!
POOF
MAYBE I CAN INTEREST THE TOMORROW BOYS IN TWO CALENDARS!
LOOK, I'VE NEVER MET THE TOMORROW REP-RESENTATIVE.
BUT I HAVE TO HAVE A CHANCE ON IT WORKING, BECAUSE--

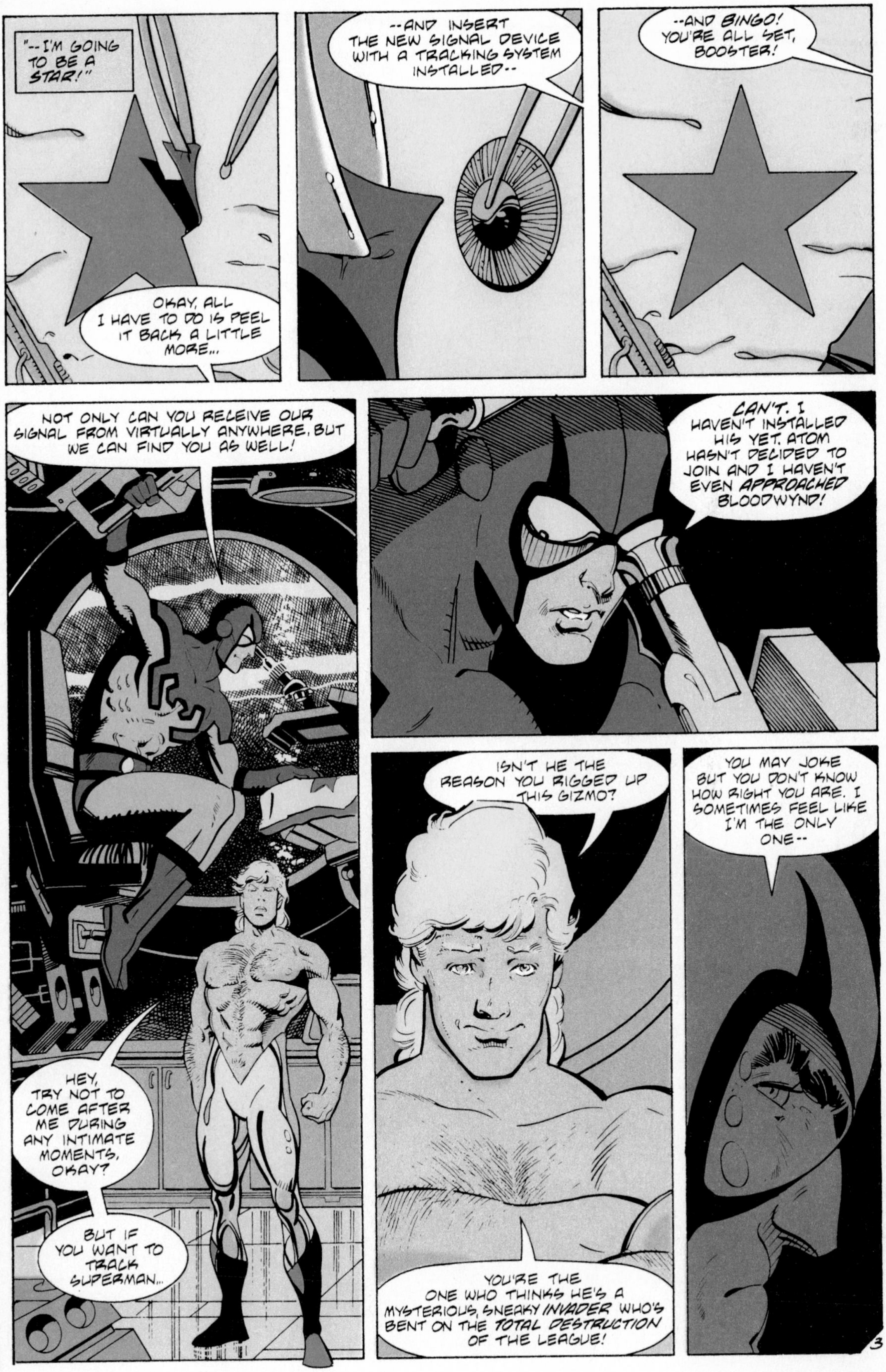
"--I'M GOING TO BE A STAR!"
OKAY, ALL I HAVE TO DO IS PEEL IT BACK A LITTLE MORE...
--AND INSERT THE NEW SIGNAL DEVICE WITH A TRACKING SYSTEM INSTALLED--
--AND BINGO! YOU'RE ALL SET, BOOSTER!
NOT ONLY CAN YOU RECEIVE OUR SIGNAL FROM VIRTUALLY ANYWHERE, BUT WE CAN FIND YOU AS WELL!
HEY, TRY NOT TO COME AFTER ME DURING ANY INTIMATE MOMENTS, OKAY?
BUT IF YOU WANT TO TRACK SUPERMAN...
CAN'T. I HAVEN'T INSTALLED HIS YET. ATOM HASN'T DECIDED TO JOIN AND I HAVEN'T EVEN APPROACHED BLOODWYND!
ISN'T HE THE REASON YOU RIGGED UP THIS GIZMO?
YOU'RE THE ONE WHO THINKS HE'S A MYSTERIOUS, SNEAKY INVADER WHO'S BENT ON THE TOTAL DESTRUCTION OF THE LEAGUE!
YOU MAY JOKE BUT YOU DON'T KNOW HOW RIGHT YOU ARE. I SOMETIMES FEEL LIKE I'M THE ONLY ONE--
3

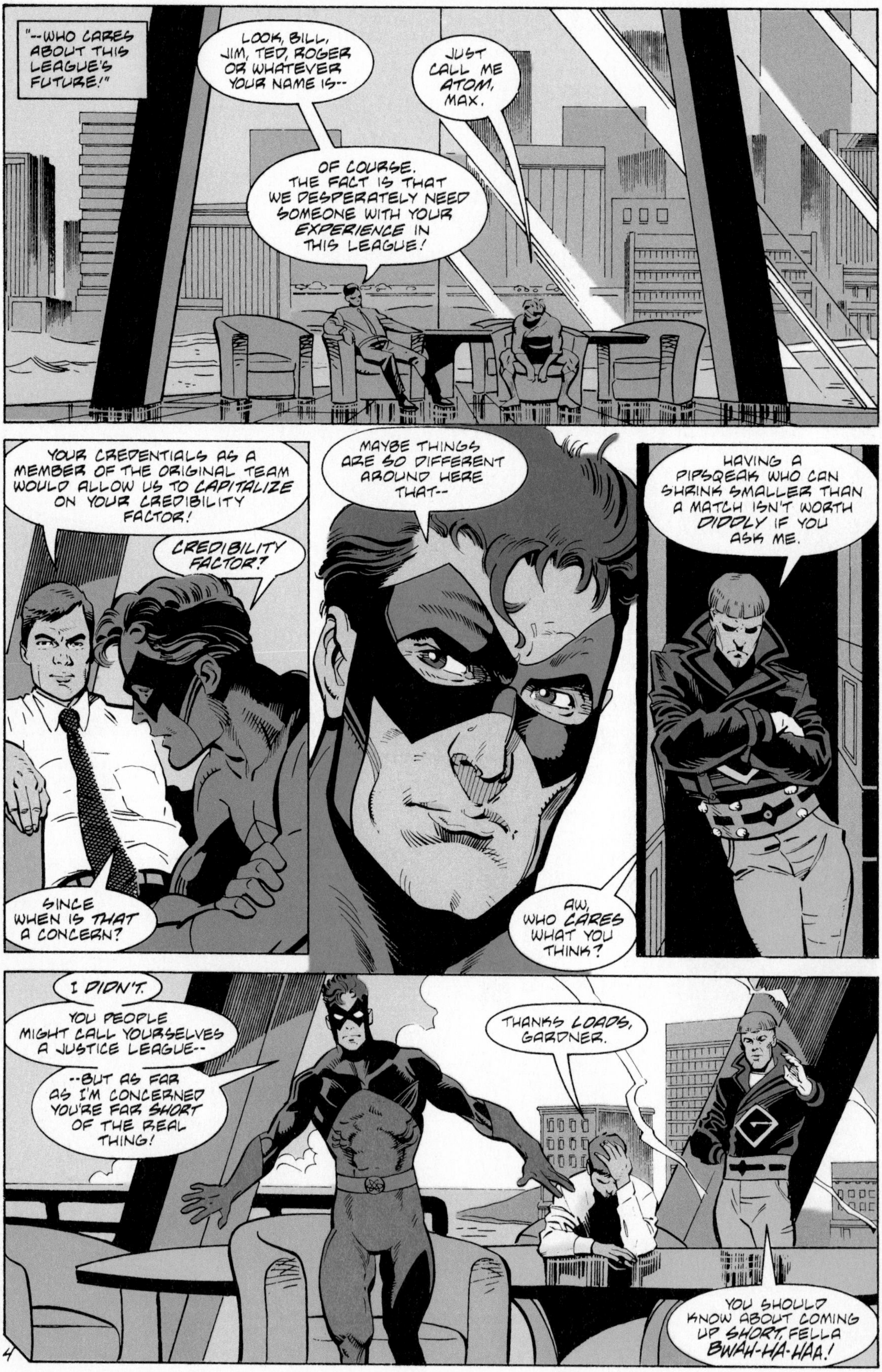
"--WHO CARES ABOUT THIS LEAGUE'S FUTURE!"
LOOK, BILL, JIM, TED, ROGER OR WHATEVER YOUR NAME IS--
JUST CALL ME ATOM, MAX.
OF COURSE. THE FACT IS THAT WE DESPERATELY NEED SOMEONE WITH YOUR EXPERIENCE IN THIS LEAGUE!
YOUR CREDENTIALS AS A MEMBER OF THE ORIGINAL TEAM WOULD ALLOW US TO CAPITALIZE ON YOUR CREDIBILITY FACTOR!
CREDIBILITY FACTOR?
SINCE WHEN IS THAT A CONCERN?
MAYBE THINGS ARE SO DIFFERENT AROUND HERE THAT--
HAVING A PIPSQEAK WHO CAN SHRINK SMALLER THAN A MATCH ISN'T WORTH DIDDLY IF YOU ASK ME.
AW, WHO CARES WHAT YOU THINK?
I DIDN'T.
YOU PEOPLE MIGHT CALL YOURSELVES A JUSTICE LEAGUE--
--BUT AS FAR AS I'M CONCERNED YOU'RE FAR SHORT OF THE REAL THING!
THANKS LOADS, GARDNER.
YOU SHOULD KNOW ABOUT COMING UP SHORT, FELLA BWAH-HA-HAA!

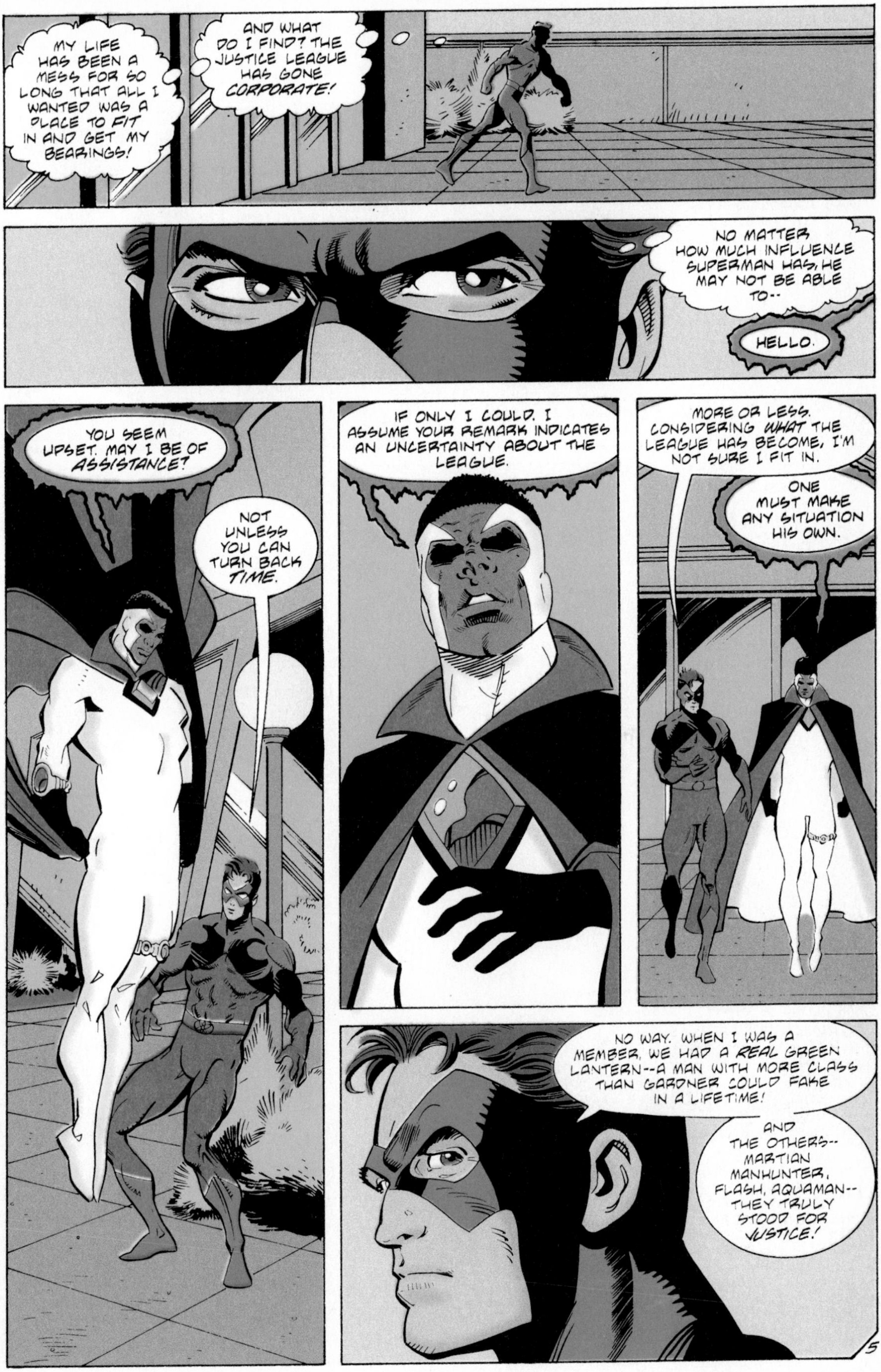
MY LIFE HAS BEEN A MESS FOR SO LONG THAT ALL I WANTED WAS A PLACE TO FIT IN AND GET MY BEARINGS!
AND WHAT DO I FIND? THE JUSTICE LEAGUE HAS GONE CORPORATE!
NO MATTER HOW MUCH INFLUENCE SUPERMAN HAS, HE MAY NOT BE ABLE TO--
HELLO.
YOU SEEM UPSET. MAY I BE OF ASSISTANCE?
NOT UNLESS YOU CAN TURN BACK TIME.
IF ONLY I COULD. I ASSUME YOUR REMARK INDICATES AN UNCERTAINTY ABOUT THE LEAGUE.
MORE OR LESS. CONSIDERING WHAT THE LEAGUE HAS BECOME, I'M NOT SURE I FIT IN.
ONE MUST MAKE ANY SITUATION HIS OWN.
NO WAY. WHEN I WAS A MEMBER, WE HAD A REAL GREEN LANTERN--A MAN WITH MORE CLASS THAN GARDNER COULD FAKE IN A LIFETIME!
AND THE OTHERS-- MARTIAN MANHUNTER, FLASH, AQUAMAN-- THEY TRULY STOOD FOR JUSTICE!

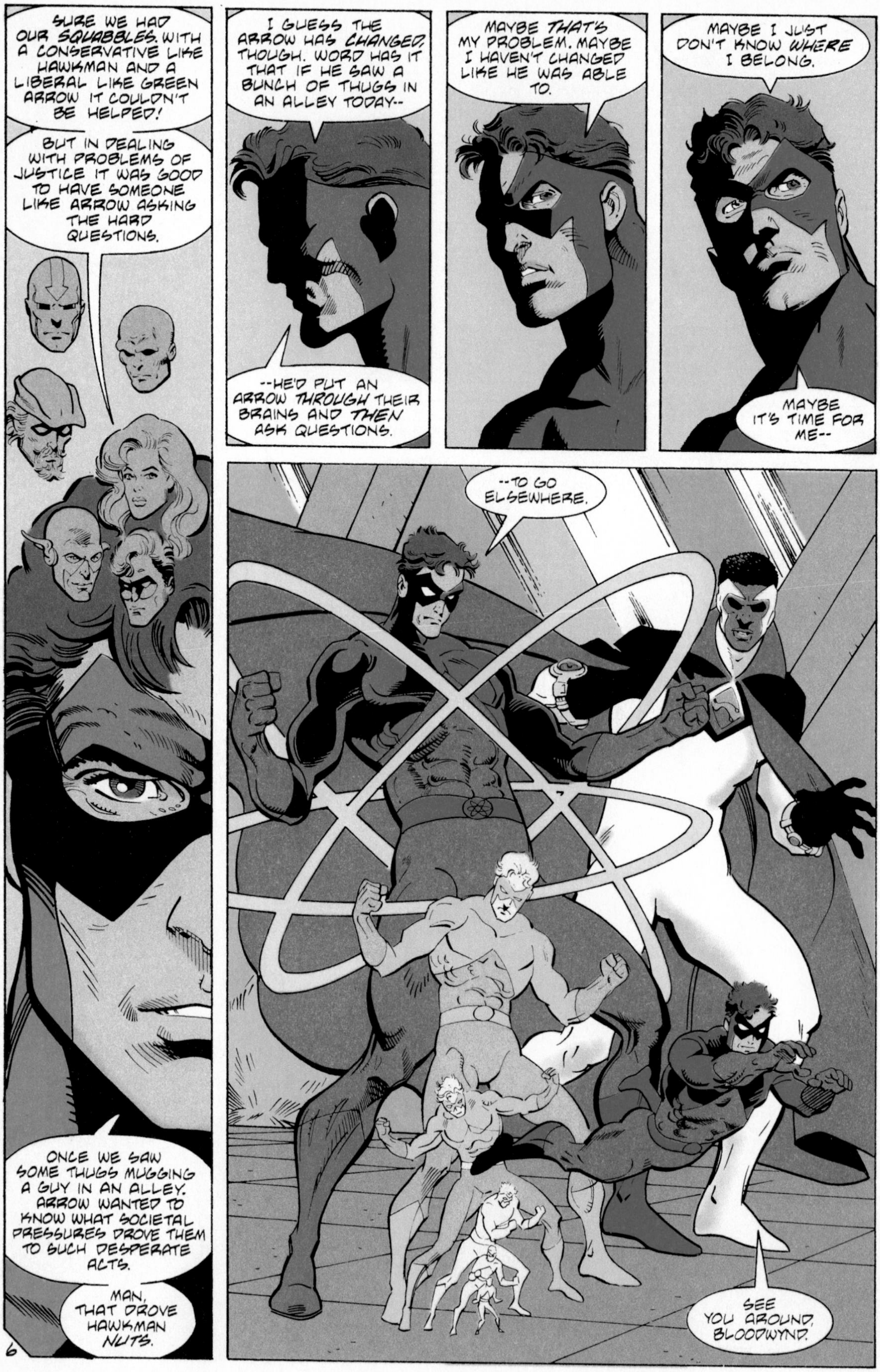
SURE WE HAD OUR SQUABBLES. WITH A CONSERVATIVE LIKE HAWKMAN AND A LIBERAL LIKE GREEN ARROW IT COULDN'T BE HELPED!
BUT IN DEALING WITH PROBLEMS OF JUSTICE IT WAS GOOD TO HAVE SOMEONE LIKE ARROW ASKING THE HARD QUESTIONS.
ONCE WE SAW SOME THUGS MUGGING A GUY IN AN ALLEY. ARROW WANTED TO KNOW WHAT SOCIETAL PRESSURES DROVE THEM TO SUCH DESPERATE ACTS.
MAN, THAT DROVE HAWKMAN NUTS.
I GUESS THE ARROW HAS CHANGED, THOUGH. WORD HAS IT THAT IF HE SAW A BUNCH OF THUGS IN AN ALLEY TODAY--
--HE'D PUT AN ARROW THROUGH THEIR BRAINS AND THEN ASK QUESTIONS.
MAYBE THAT'S MY PROBLEM. MAYBE I HAVEN'T CHANGED LIKE HE WAS ABLE TO.
MAYBE I JUST DON'T KNOW WHERE I BELONG.
MAYBE IT'S TIME FOR ME--
--TO GO ELSEWHERE.
SEE YOU AROUND, BLOODWYND.
6

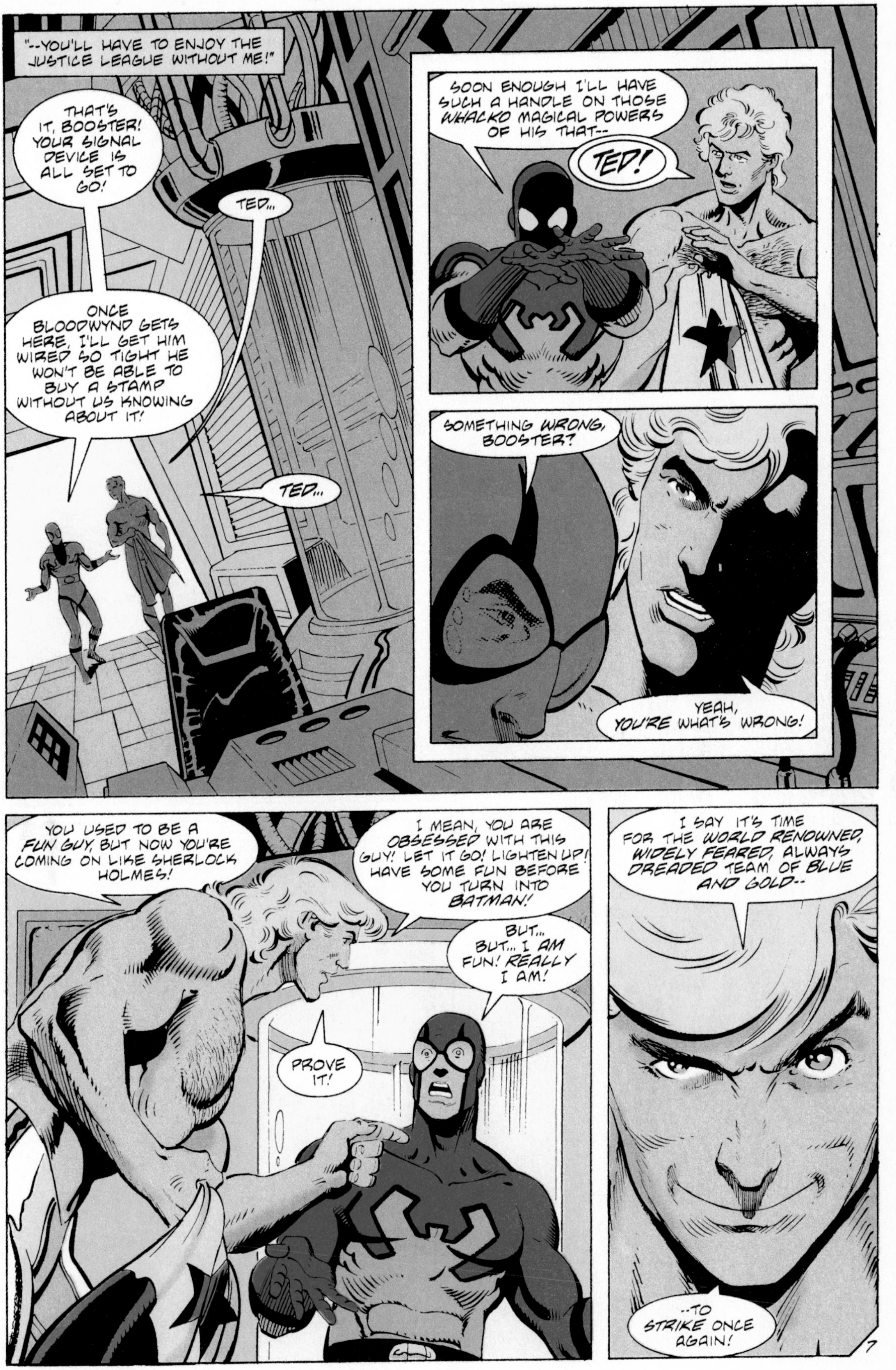
"--YOU'LL HAVE TO ENJOY THE JUSTICE LEAGUE WITHOUT ME!"
THAT'S IT, BOOSTER! YOUR SIGNAL DEVICE IS ALL SET TO GO!
TED...
ONCE BLOODWYND GETS HERE, I'LL GET HIM WIRED SO TIGHT HE WON'T BE ABLE TO BUY A STAMP WITHOUT US KNOWING ABOUT IT!
TED...
SOON ENOUGH I'LL HAVE SUCH A HANDLE ON THOSE WHACKO MAGICAL POWERS OF HIS THAT--
TED!
SOMETHING WRONG, BOOSTER?
YEAH, YOU'RE WHAT'S WRONG!
YOU USED TO BE A FUN GUY, BUT NOW YOU'RE COMING ON LIKE SHERLOCK HOLMES!
I MEAN, YOU ARE OBSESSED WITH THIS GUY! LET IT GO! LIGHTEN UP! HAVE SOME FUN BEFORE YOU TURN INTO BATMAN!
BUT... BUT... I AM FUN! REALLY I AM!
PROVE IT!
I SAY IT'S TIME FOR THE WORLD RENOWNED, WIDELY FEARED, ALWAYS DREADED TEAM OF BLUE AND GOLD--
--TO STRIKE ONCE AGAIN!

YO, JLE LONDON! THIS IS THE U.S.A. CALLING!

OH, GREAT. *BOOSTER.*

BEETLE AND I THOUGHT WE'D TRANSPORT OVER TO SIT AROUND AND SHOOT THE BREEZE ABOUT THE GOOD OLD DAYS!

ROLL OUT THE RED CARPET AND CRACK OPEN THE *CHAMPAGNE!*

REPROGRAM THE TRANSPORTER. DO WHATEVER IS NECESSARY--

--TO SEE THAT THEY WIND UP IN THE *ARCTIC.* OR *TIMBUKTU.* PERHAPS EVEN THE *BOWELS* OF HELL.

C'MON, THEY'RE NOT *THAT* BAD. DEEP DOWN THEY'RE...

...*TOLERABLE* SOMETIMES!

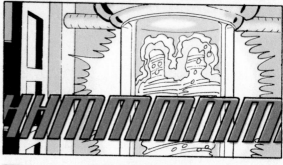

AND BE SURE TO *MONITOR* THE TRANSPORTER SIGNAL. WE'VE HAD SOME *TROUBLES* LATELY.

NO PROBLEM, BOOSTEROO.

HMMMMMMMM

AIEEE! THE PAIN! THE *PAIN!*

OH, MAN! SOMETHING WENT *WRONG!*

LORD.

8

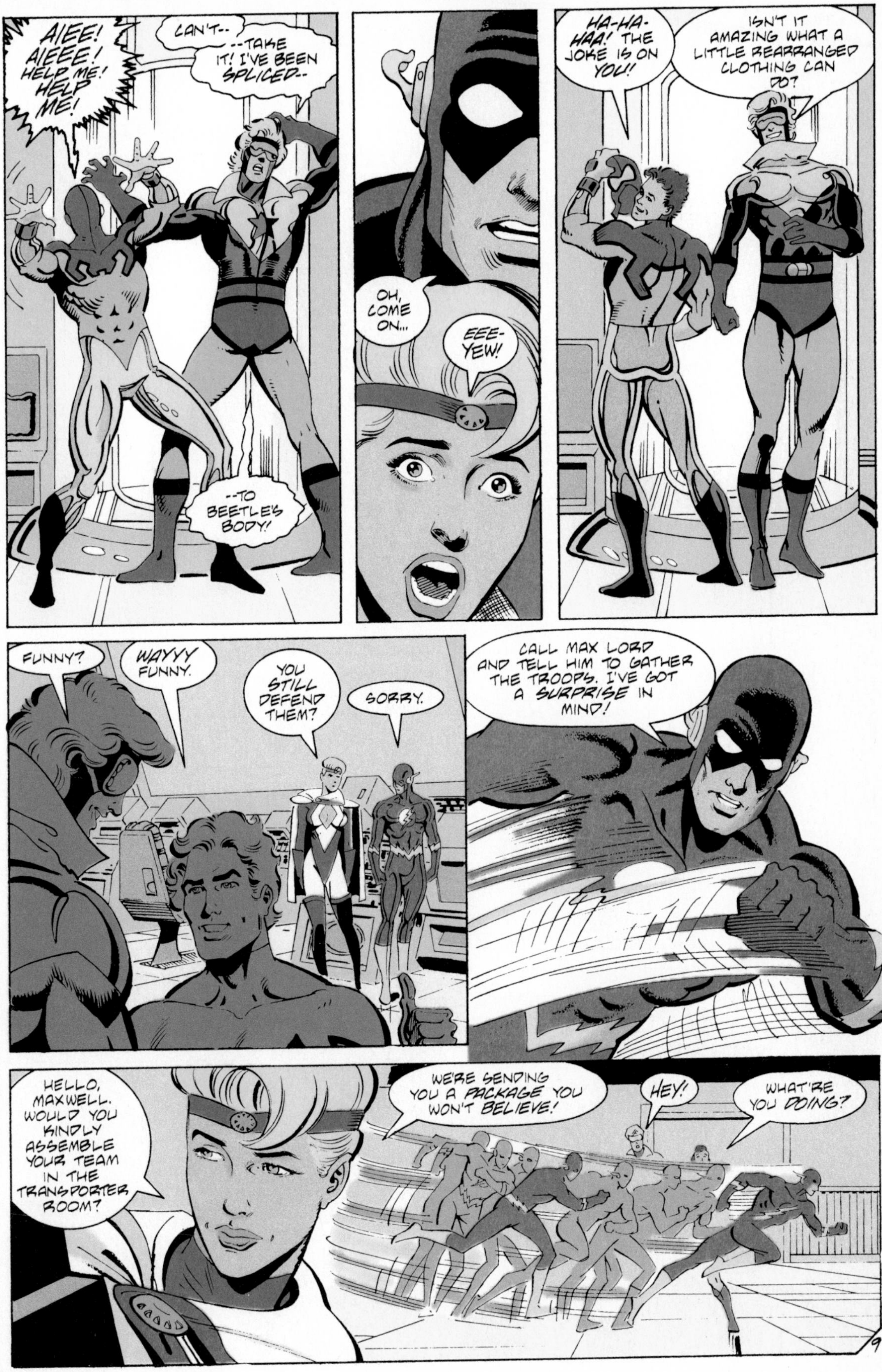
AIEE! AIEEE! HELP ME! HELP ME!
CAN'T--
--TAKE IT! I'VE BEEN SPLICED--
--TO BEETLE'S BODY!
OH, COME ON...
EEE-YEW!
HA-HA-HAA! THE JOKE IS ON YOU!
ISN'T IT AMAZING WHAT A LITTLE REARRANGED CLOTHING CAN DO?
FUNNY?
WAYYY FUNNY.
YOU STILL DEFEND THEM?
SORRY.
CALL MAX LORD AND TELL HIM TO GATHER THE TROOPS. I'VE GOT A SURPRISE IN MIND!
HELLO, MAXWELL. WOULD YOU KINDLY ASSEMBLE YOUR TEAM IN THE TRANSPORTER ROOM?
WE'RE SENDING YOU A PACKAGE YOU WON'T BELIEVE!
HEY!
WHAT'RE YOU DOING?
9

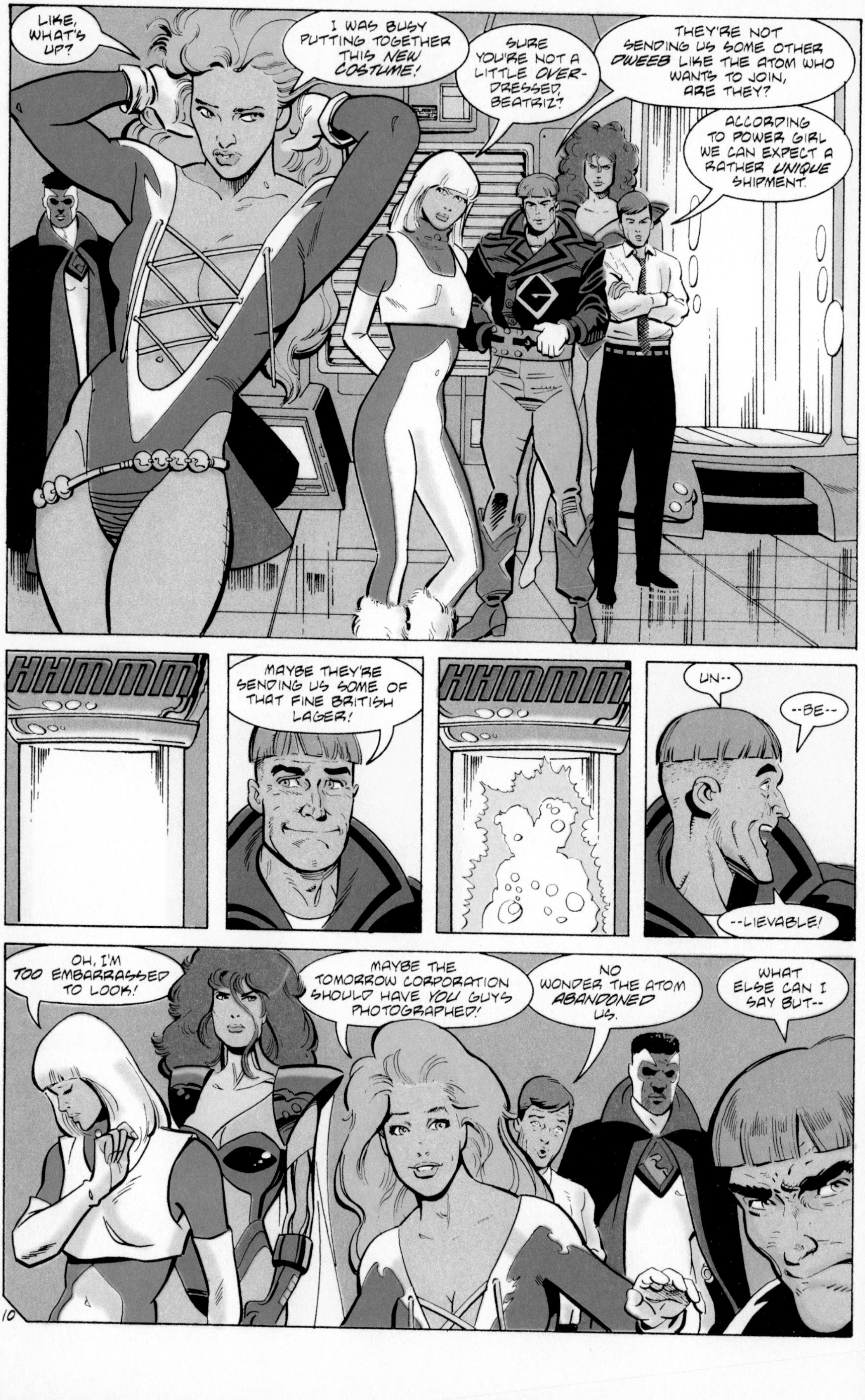
LIKE, WHAT'S UP?
I WAS BUSY PUTTING TOGETHER THIS NEW COSTUME!
SURE YOU'RE NOT A LITTLE OVER-DRESSED, BEATRIZ?
THEY'RE NOT SENDING US SOME OTHER DWEEB LIKE THE ATOM WHO WANTS TO JOIN, ARE THEY?
ACCORDING TO POWER GIRL WE CAN EXPECT A RATHER UNIQUE SHIPMENT.
HHMMMM
MAYBE THEY'RE SENDING US SOME OF THAT FINE BRITISH LAGER!
HHMMMM
UN--
--BE--
--LIEVABLE!
OH, I'M TOO EMBARRASSED TO LOOK!
MAYBE THE TOMORROW CORPORATION SHOULD HAVE YOU GUYS PHOTOGRAPHED!
NO WONDER THE ATOM ABANDONED US.
WHAT ELSE CAN I SAY BUT--

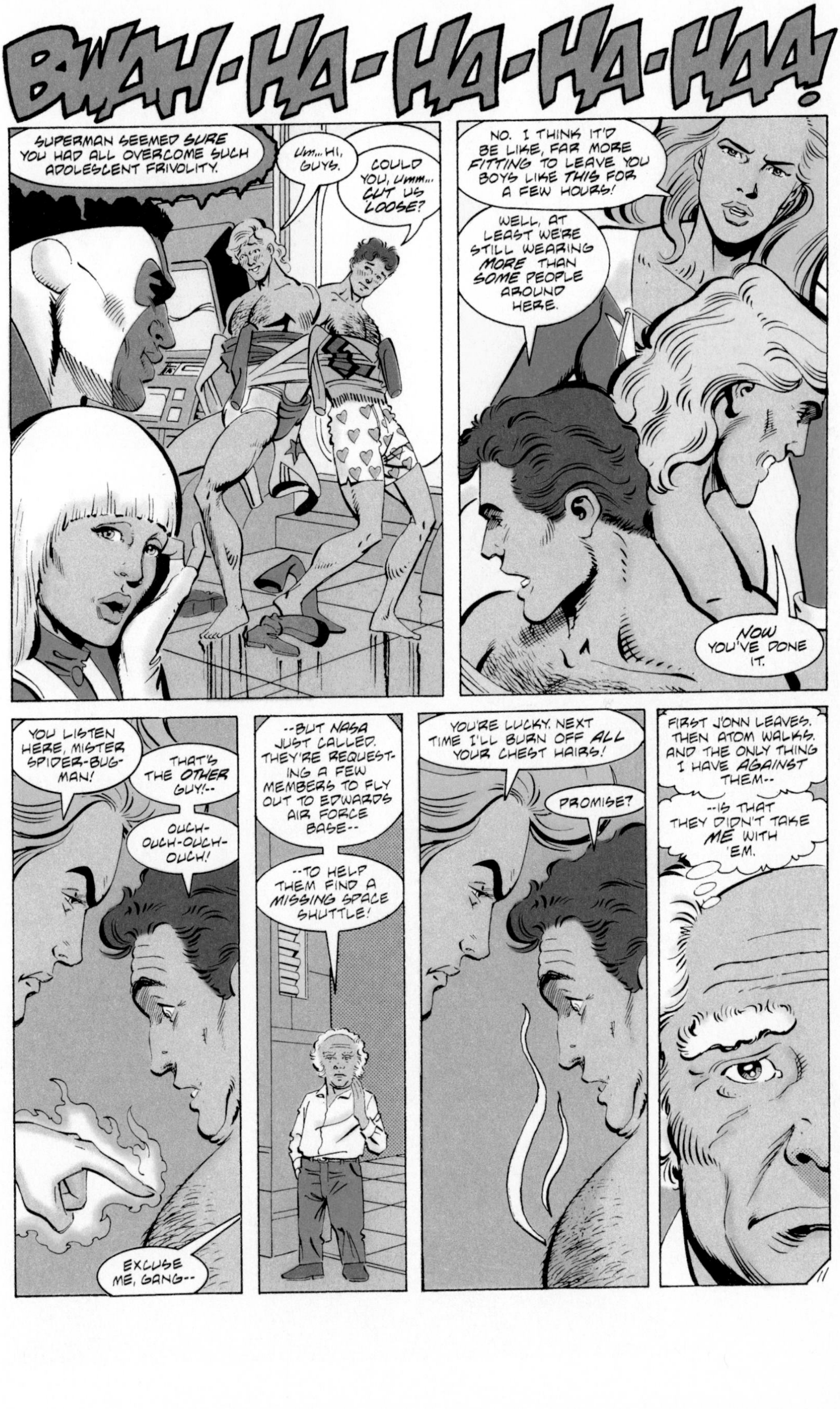
BWAH-HA-HA-HA-HAA!
SUPERMAN SEEMED SURE YOU HAD ALL OVERCOME SUCH ADOLESCENT FRIVOLITY.
UM...HI, GUYS.
COULD YOU, UMM... CUT US LOOSE?
NO. I THINK IT'D BE LIKE, FAR MORE FITTING TO LEAVE YOU BOYS LIKE THIS FOR A FEW HOURS!
WELL, AT LEAST WE'RE STILL WEARING MORE THAN SOME PEOPLE AROUND HERE.
NOW YOU'VE DONE IT.
YOU LISTEN HERE, MISTER SPIDER-BUG-MAN!
THAT'S THE OTHER GUY!--
OUCH-OUCH-OUCH-OUCH!
EXCUSE ME, GANG--
--BUT NASA JUST CALLED. THEY'RE REQUESTING A FEW MEMBERS TO FLY OUT TO EDWARDS AIR FORCE BASE--
--TO HELP THEM FIND A MISSING SPACE SHUTTLE!
YOU'RE LUCKY. NEXT TIME I'LL BURN OFF ALL YOUR CHEST HAIRS!
PROMISE?
FIRST J'ONN LEAVES. THEN ATOM WALKS. AND THE ONLY THING I HAVE AGAINST THEM--
--IS THAT THEY DIDN'T TAKE ME WITH 'EM.

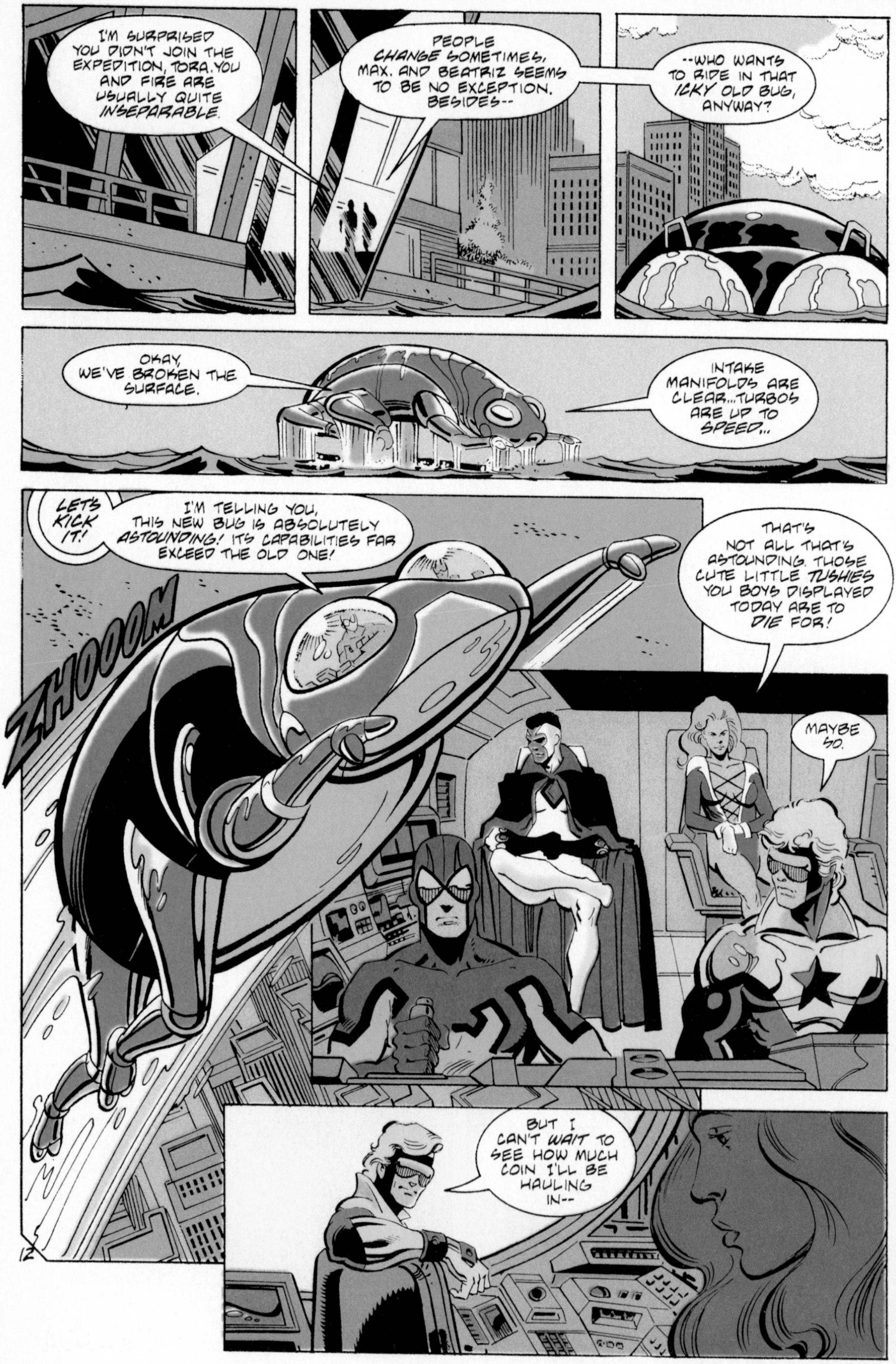

I'M SURPRISED YOU DIDN'T JOIN THE EXPEDITION, TORA. YOU AND FIRE ARE USUALLY QUITE INSEPARABLE.
PEOPLE CHANGE SOMETIMES, MAX. AND BEATRIZ SEEMS TO BE NO EXCEPTION. BESIDES--
--WHO WANTS TO RIDE IN THAT ICKY OLD BUG, ANYWAY?
OKAY, WE'VE BROKEN THE SURFACE.
INTAKE MANIFOLDS ARE CLEAR...TURBOS ARE UP TO SPEED...
LET'S KICK IT!
ZHOOOM
I'M TELLING YOU, THIS NEW BUG IS ABSOLUTELY ASTOUNDING! ITS CAPABILITIES FAR EXCEED THE OLD ONE!
THAT'S NOT ALL THAT'S ASTOUNDING. THOSE CUTE LITTLE TUSHIES YOU BOYS DISPLAYED TODAY ARE TO DIE FOR!
MAYBE SO.
BUT I CAN'T WAIT TO SEE HOW MUCH COIN I'LL BE HAULING IN--

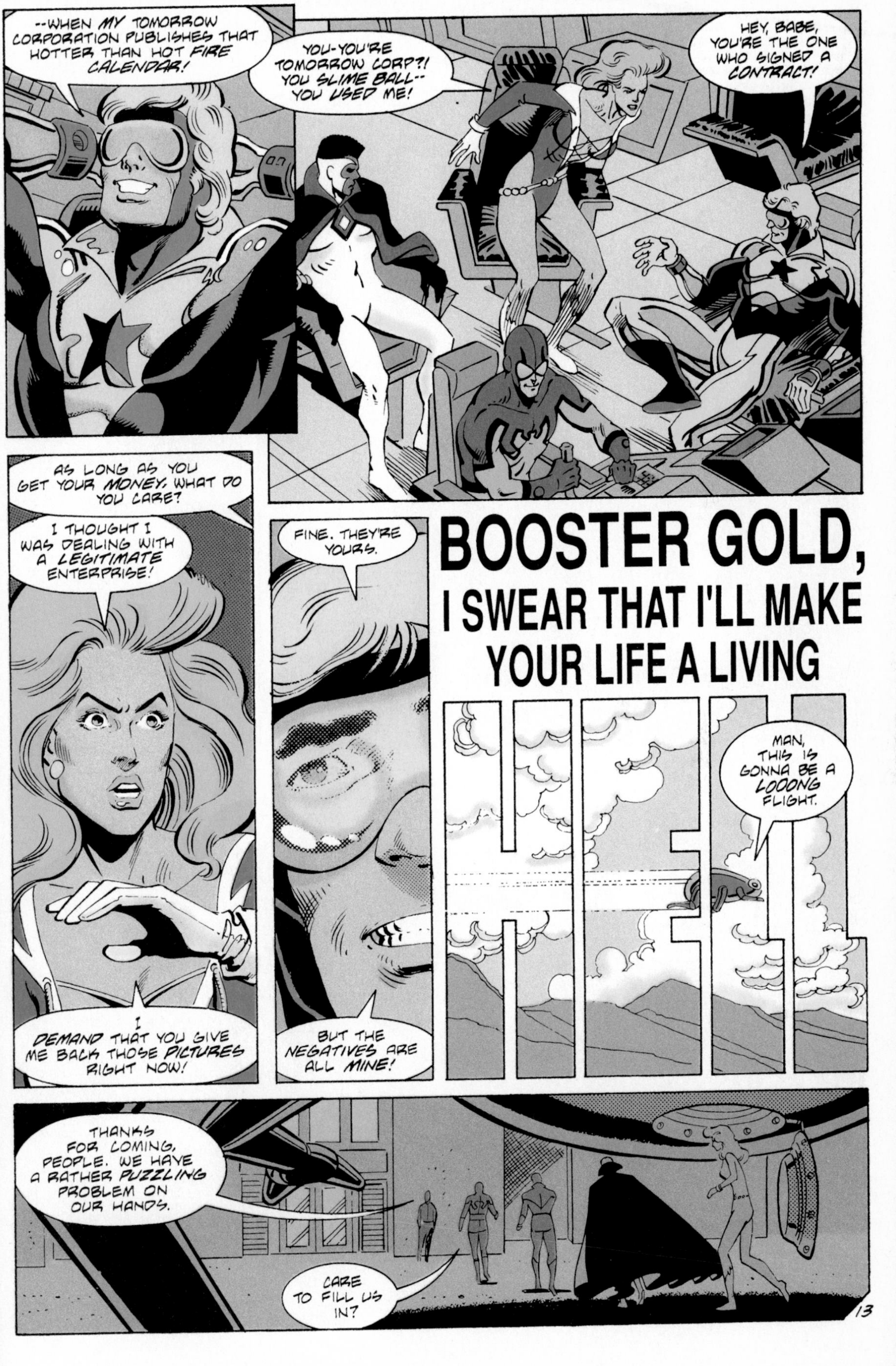
--WHEN MY TOMORROW CORPORATION PUBLISHES THAT HOTTER THAN HOT FIRE CALENDAR!
YOU-YOU'RE TOMORROW CORP?! YOU SLIME BALL-- YOU USED ME!
HEY, BABE, YOU'RE THE ONE WHO SIGNED A CONTRACT!
AS LONG AS YOU GET YOUR MONEY, WHAT DO YOU CARE?
I THOUGHT I WAS DEALING WITH A LEGITIMATE ENTERPRISE!
I DEMAND THAT YOU GIVE ME BACK THOSE PICTURES RIGHT NOW!
FINE. THEY'RE YOURS.
BUT THE NEGATIVES ARE ALL MINE!
BOOSTER GOLD,
I SWEAR THAT I'LL MAKE
YOUR LIFE A LIVING
HELL
MAN, THIS IS GONNA BE A LOOONG FLIGHT.
THANKS FOR COMING, PEOPLE. WE HAVE A RATHER PUZZLING PROBLEM ON OUR HANDS.
CARE TO FILL US IN?
13

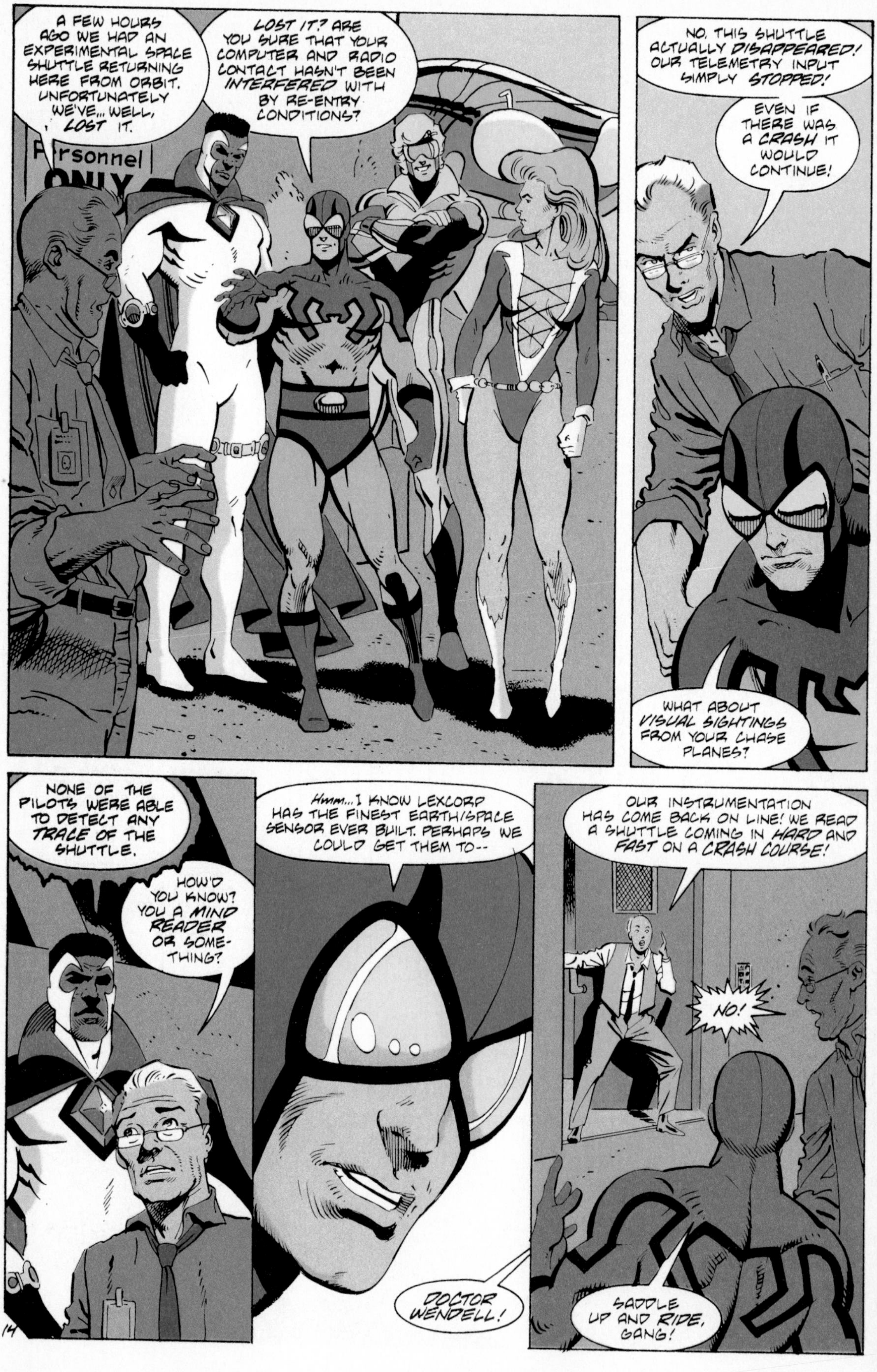
A FEW HOURS AGO WE HAD AN EXPERIMENTAL SPACE SHUTTLE RETURNING HERE FROM ORBIT. UNFORTUNATELY WE'VE... WELL, *LOST* IT.
LOST IT? ARE YOU SURE THAT YOUR COMPUTER AND RADIO CONTACT HASN'T BEEN *INTERFERED* WITH BY RE-ENTRY CONDITIONS?
Personnel ONLY
NO, THIS SHUTTLE ACTUALLY *DISAPPEARED!* OUR TELEMETRY INPUT SIMPLY *STOPPED!*
EVEN IF THERE WAS A *CRASH* IT WOULD CONTINUE!
WHAT ABOUT *VISUAL SIGHTINGS* FROM YOUR CHASE PLANES?
NONE OF THE PILOTS WERE ABLE TO DETECT ANY *TRACE* OF THE SHUTTLE.
HOW'D YOU KNOW? YOU A *MIND READER* OR SOME-THING?
Hmm... I KNOW LEXCORP HAS THE FINEST EARTH/SPACE SENSOR EVER BUILT. PERHAPS WE COULD GET THEM TO--
DOCTOR WENDELL!
OUR INSTRUMENTATION HAS COME BACK ON LINE! WE READ A SHUTTLE COMING IN *HARD* AND *FAST* ON A *CRASH COURSE!*
NO!
SADDLE UP AND *RIDE*, GANG!

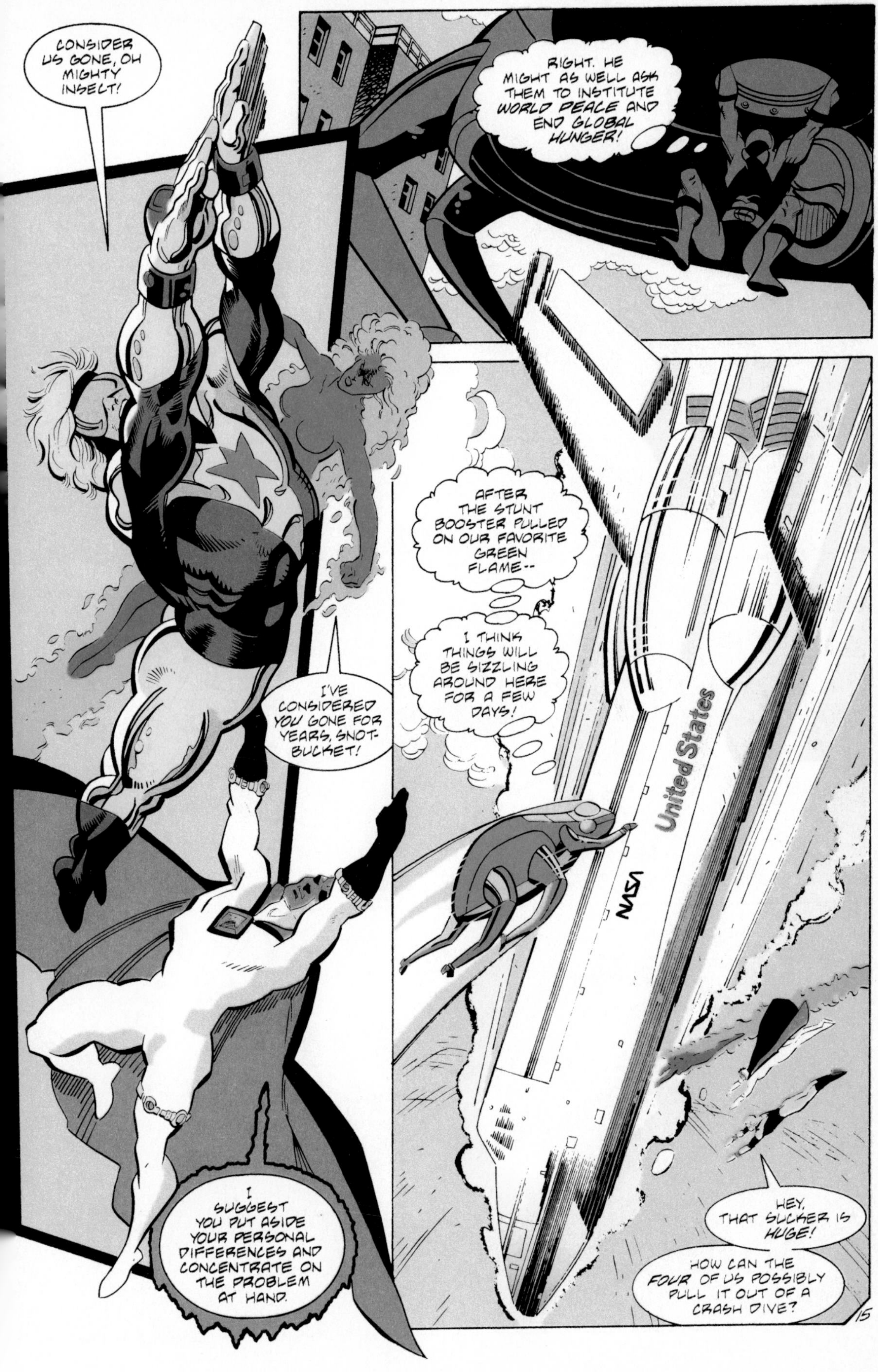
CONSIDER US GONE, OH MIGHTY INSECT!
RIGHT. HE MIGHT AS WELL ASK THEM TO INSTITUTE WORLD PEACE AND END GLOBAL HUNGER!
I'VE CONSIDERED YOU GONE FOR YEARS, SNOT-BUCKET!
I SUGGEST YOU PUT ASIDE YOUR PERSONAL DIFFERENCES AND CONCENTRATE ON THE PROBLEM AT HAND.
AFTER THE STUNT BOOSTER PULLED ON OUR FAVORITE GREEN FLAME--
I THINK THINGS WILL BE SIZZLING AROUND HERE FOR A FEW DAYS!
United States
NASA
HEY, THAT SUCKER IS HUGE!
HOW CAN THE FOUR OF US POSSIBLY PULL IT OUT OF A CRASH DIVE?

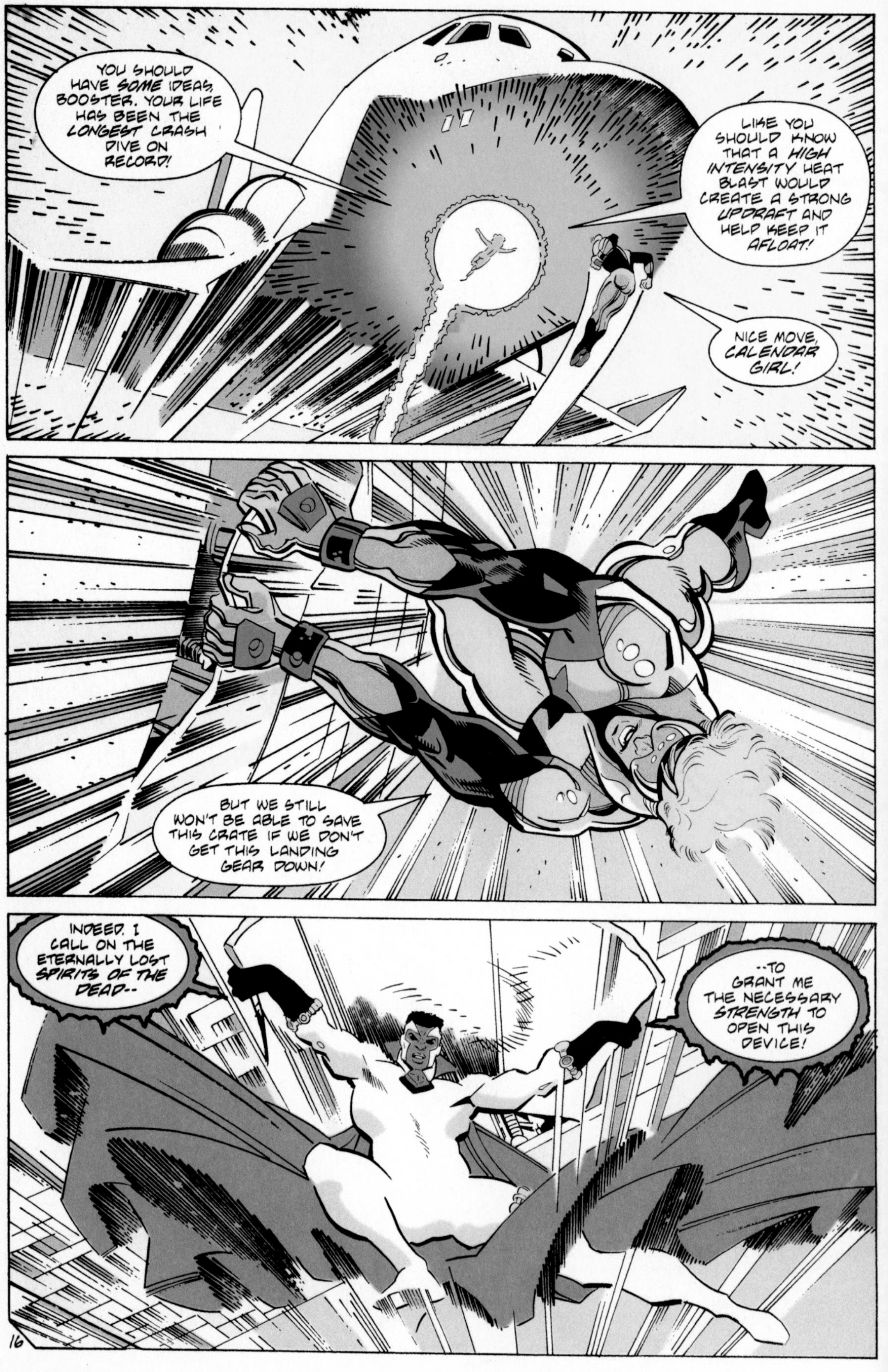
YOU SHOULD HAVE SOME IDEAS, BOOSTER. YOUR LIFE HAS BEEN THE LONGEST CRASH DIVE ON RECORD!
LIKE YOU SHOULD KNOW THAT A HIGH INTENSITY HEAT BLAST WOULD CREATE A STRONG UPDRAFT AND HELP KEEP IT AFLOAT!
NICE MOVE, CALENDAR GIRL!
BUT WE STILL WON'T BE ABLE TO SAVE THIS CRATE IF WE DON'T GET THIS LANDING GEAR DOWN!
INDEED. I CALL ON THE ETERNALLY LOST SPIRITS OF THE DEAD--
--TO GRANT ME THE NECESSARY STRENGTH TO OPEN THIS DEVICE!

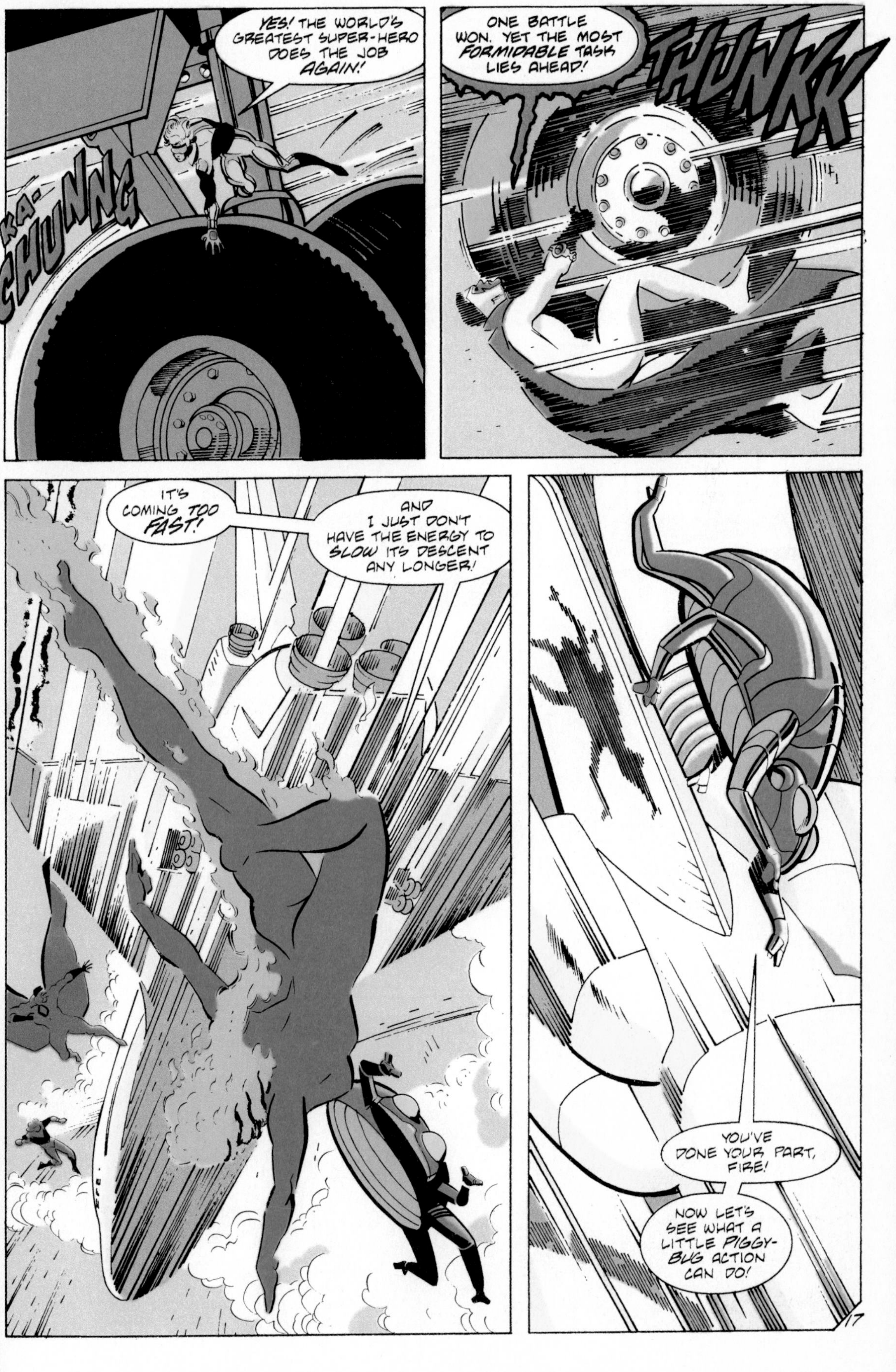
YES! THE WORLD'S GREATEST SUPER-HERO DOES THE JOB AGAIN!
KA-CHUNNG
ONE BATTLE WON. YET THE MOST FORMIDABLE TASK LIES AHEAD!
THUNKK
IT'S COMING TOO FAST!
AND I JUST DON'T HAVE THE ENERGY TO SLOW ITS DESCENT ANY LONGER!
YOU'VE DONE YOUR PART, FIRE!
NOW LET'S SEE WHAT A LITTLE PIGGY-BUG ACTION CAN DO!

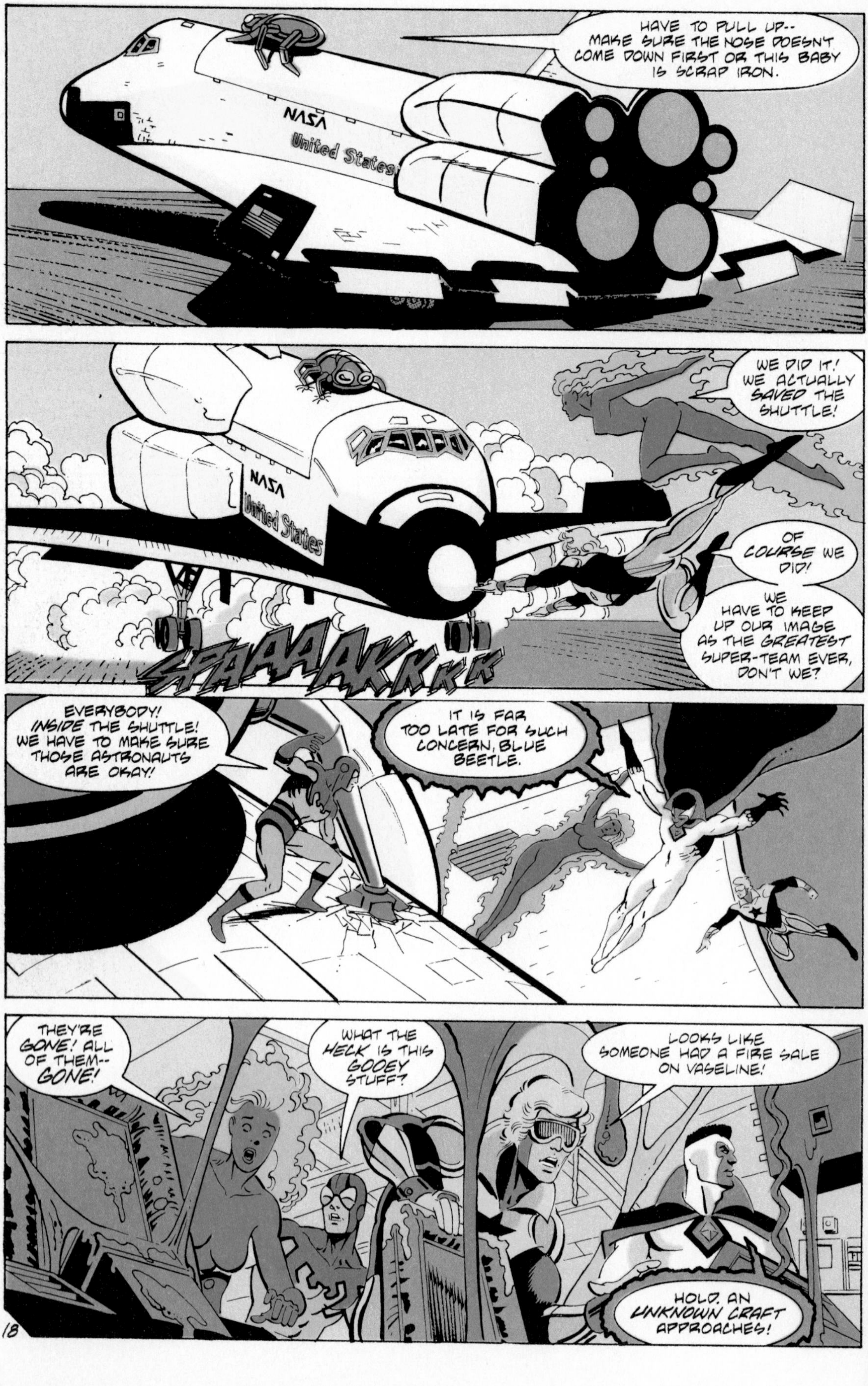
HAVE TO PULL UP-- MAKE SURE THE NOSE DOESN'T COME DOWN FIRST OR THIS BABY IS SCRAP IRON.
NASA
United States
WE DID IT! WE ACTUALLY SAVED THE SHUTTLE!
NASA
United States
OF COURSE WE DID!
WE HAVE TO KEEP UP OUR IMAGE AS THE GREATEST SUPER-TEAM EVER, DON'T WE?
SPAAAAKKKK
EVERYBODY! INSIDE THE SHUTTLE! WE HAVE TO MAKE SURE THOSE ASTRONAUTS ARE OKAY!
IT IS FAR TOO LATE FOR SUCH CONCERN, BLUE BEETLE.
THEY'RE GONE! ALL OF THEM-- GONE!
WHAT THE HECK IS THIS GOOEY STUFF?
LOOKS LIKE SOMEONE HAD A FIRE SALE ON VASELINE!
HOLD. AN UNKNOWN CRAFT APPROACHES!

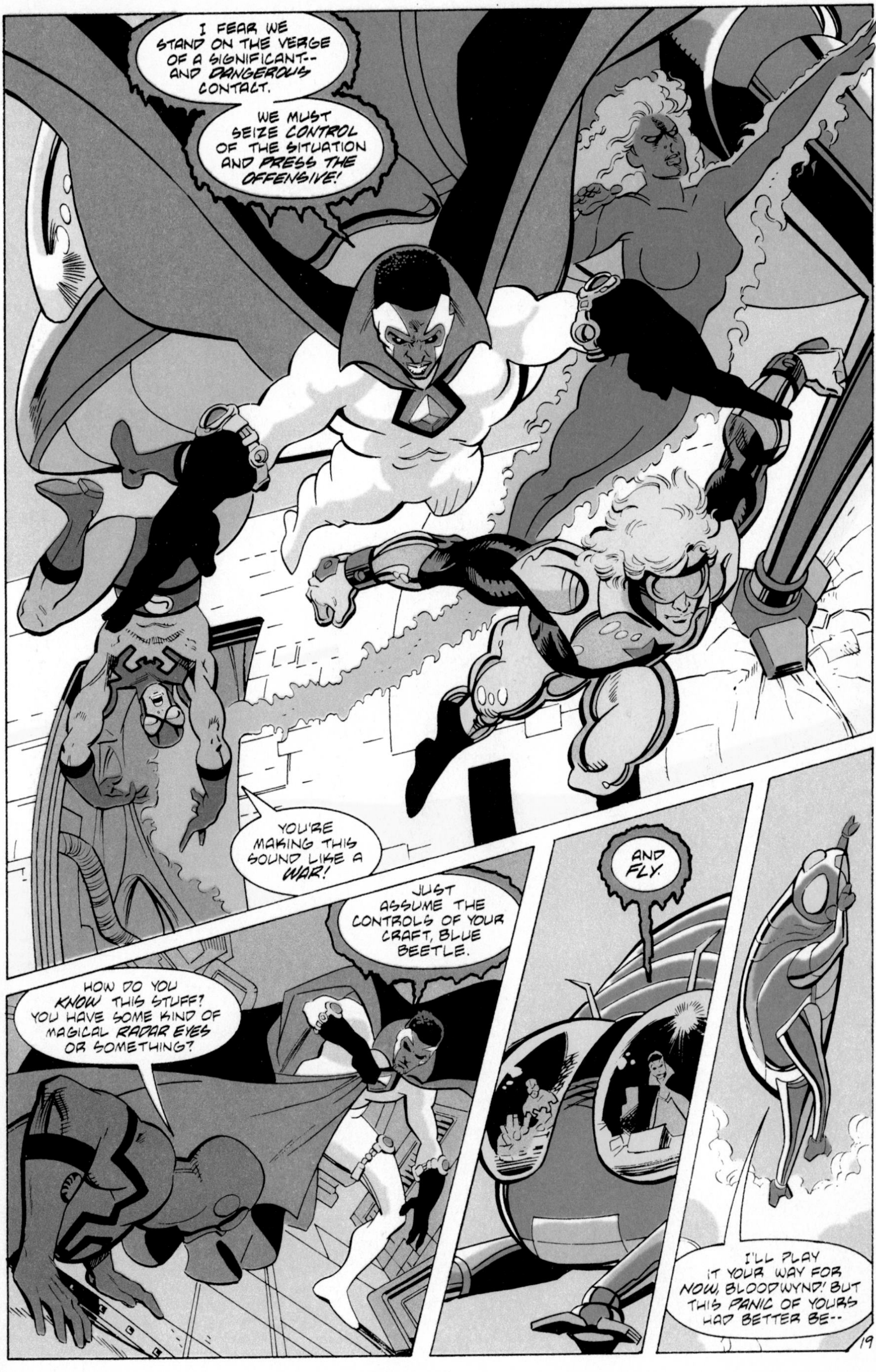

I FEAR WE STAND ON THE VERGE OF A SIGNIFICANT-- AND DANGEROUS CONTACT.
WE MUST SEIZE CONTROL OF THE SITUATION AND PRESS THE OFFENSIVE!
YOU'RE MAKING THIS SOUND LIKE A WAR!
JUST ASSUME THE CONTROLS OF YOUR CRAFT, BLUE BEETLE.
HOW DO YOU KNOW THIS STUFF? YOU HAVE SOME KIND OF MAGICAL RADAR EYES OR SOMETHING?
AND FLY.
I'LL PLAY IT YOUR WAY FOR NOW, BLOODWYND! BUT THIS PANIC OF YOURS HAD BETTER BE--

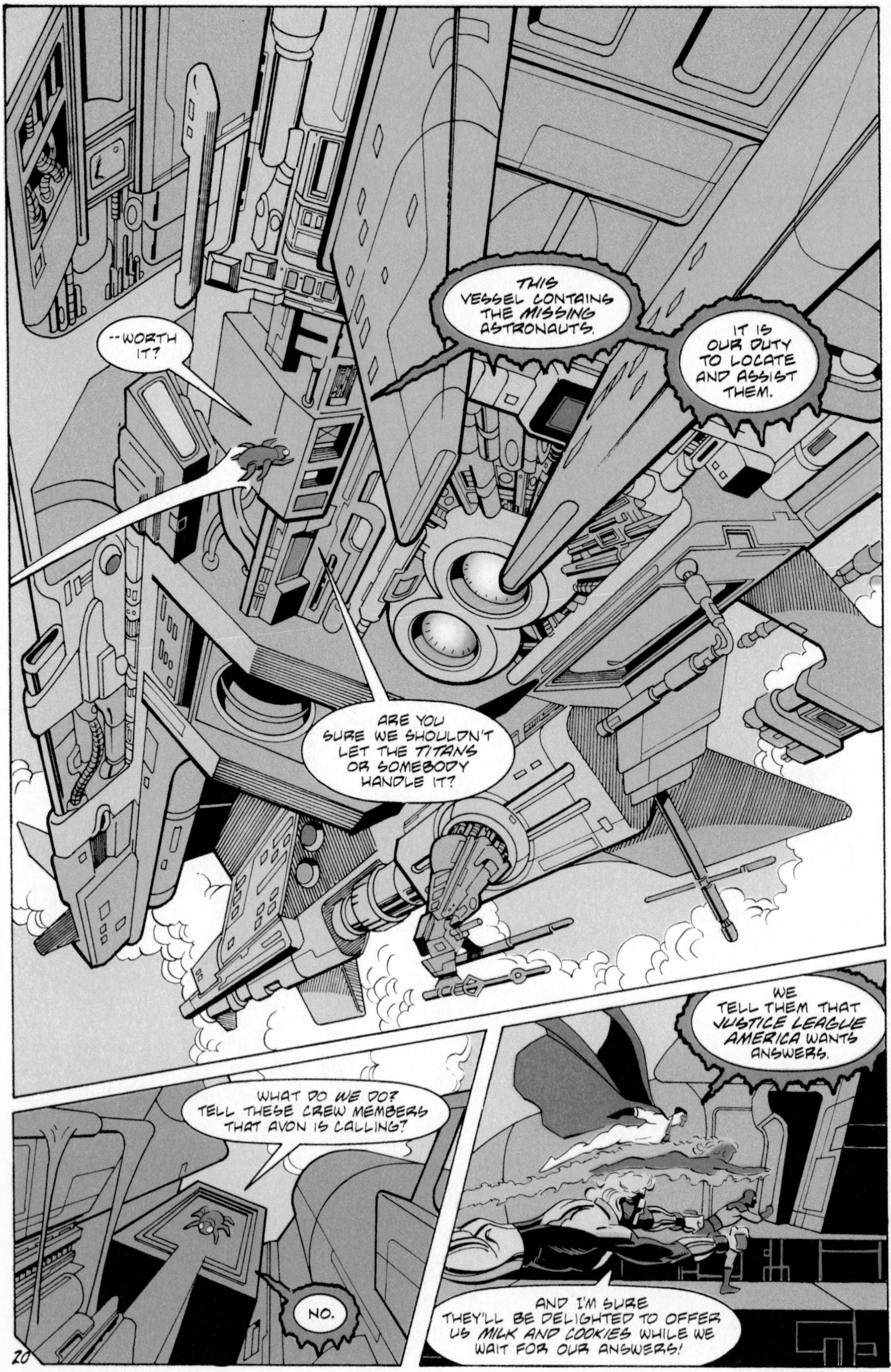
--WORTH IT?
THIS VESSEL CONTAINS THE MISSING ASTRONAUTS.
IT IS OUR DUTY TO LOCATE AND ASSIST THEM.
ARE YOU SURE WE SHOULDN'T LET THE TITANS OR SOMEBODY HANDLE IT?
WHAT DO WE DO? TELL THESE CREW MEMBERS THAT AVON IS CALLING?
NO.
WE TELL THEM THAT JUSTICE LEAGUE AMERICA WANTS ANSWERS.
AND I'M SURE THEY'LL BE DELIGHTED TO OFFER US MILK AND COOKIES WHILE WE WAIT FOR OUR ANSWERS!

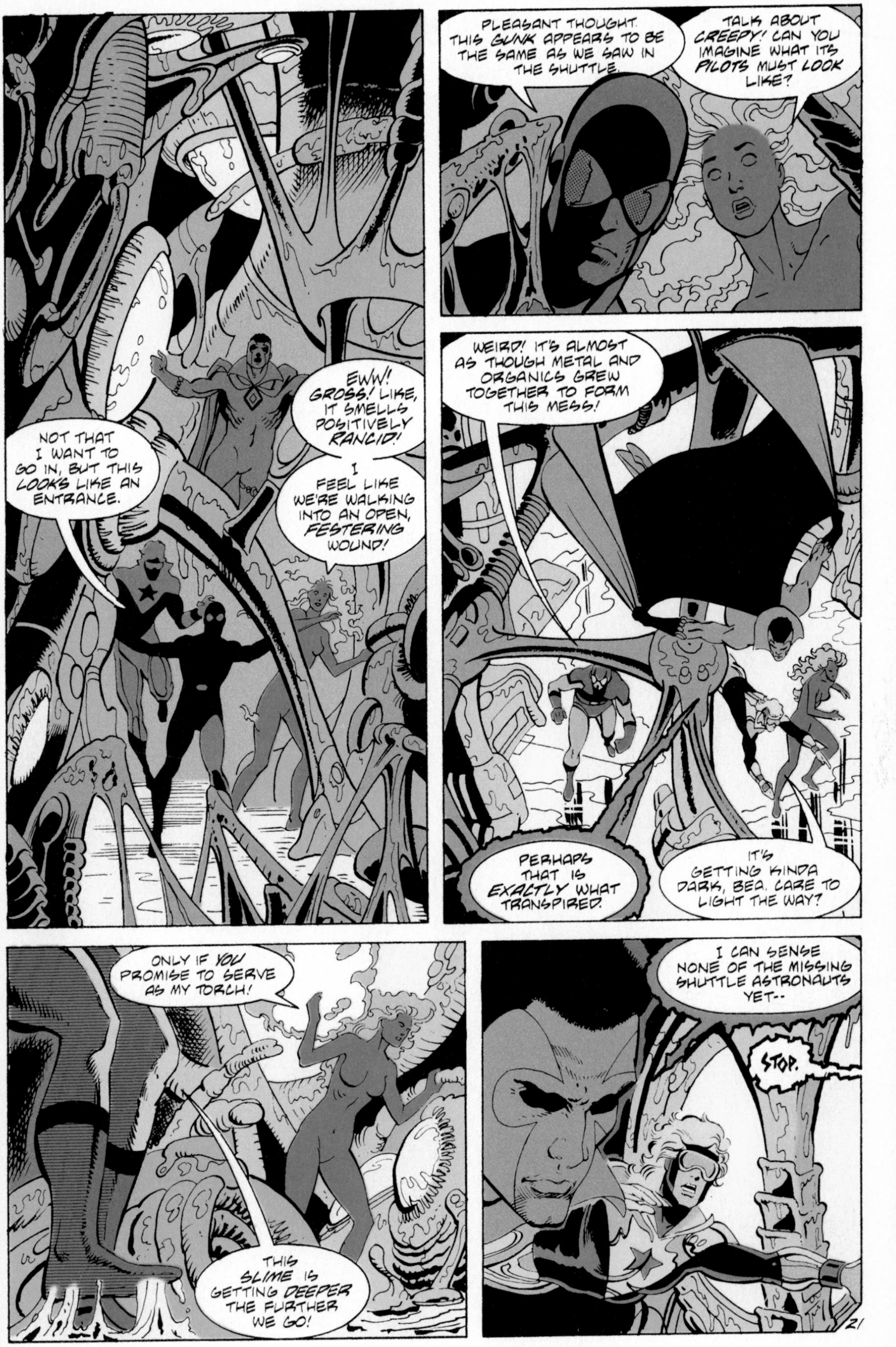

NOT THAT I WANT TO GO IN, BUT THIS LOOKS LIKE AN ENTRANCE.
EWW! GROSS! LIKE, IT SMELLS POSITIVELY RANCID!
I FEEL LIKE WE'RE WALKING INTO AN OPEN, FESTERING WOUND!
PLEASANT THOUGHT. THIS GUNK APPEARS TO BE THE SAME AS WE SAW IN THE SHUTTLE.
TALK ABOUT CREEPY! CAN YOU IMAGINE WHAT ITS PILOTS MUST LOOK LIKE?
WEIRD! IT'S ALMOST AS THOUGH METAL AND ORGANICS GREW TOGETHER TO FORM THIS MESS!
PERHAPS THAT IS EXACTLY WHAT TRANSPIRED.
IT'S GETTING KINDA DARK, BEA. CARE TO LIGHT THE WAY?
ONLY IF YOU PROMISE TO SERVE AS MY TORCH!
THIS SLIME IS GETTING DEEPER THE FURTHER WE GO!
I CAN SENSE NONE OF THE MISSING SHUTTLE ASTRONAUTS YET--
STOP.

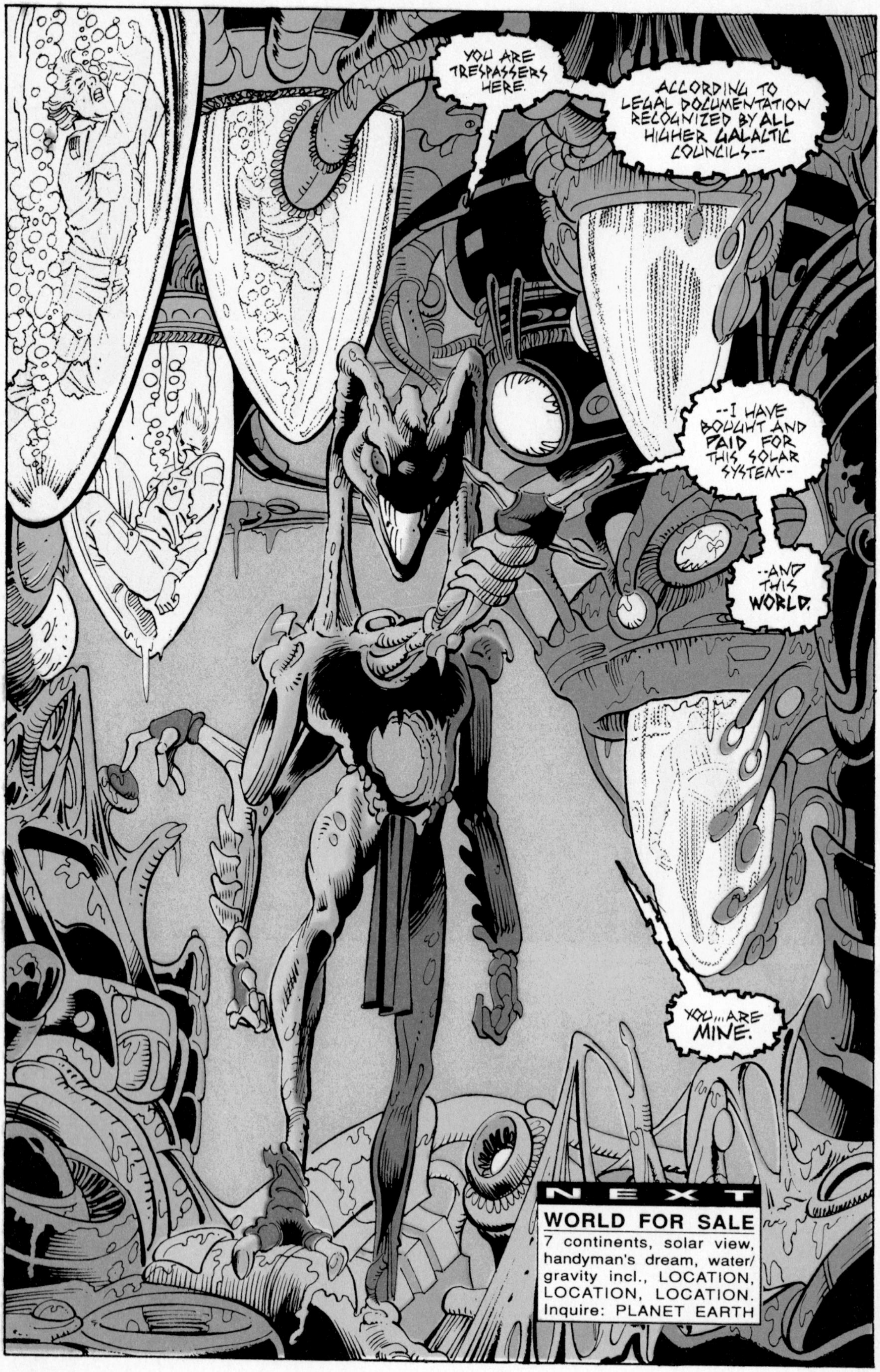
YOU ARE TRESPASSERS HERE.
ACCORDING TO LEGAL DOCUMENTATION RECOGNIZED BY ALL HIGHER GALACTIC COUNCILS--
--I HAVE BOUGHT AND PAID FOR THIS SOLAR SYSTEM--
--AND THIS WORLD.
YOU... ARE MINE.
NEXT
WORLD FOR SALE
7 continents, solar view, handyman's dream, water/gravity incl., LOCATION, LOCATION, LOCATION. Inquire: PLANET EARTH

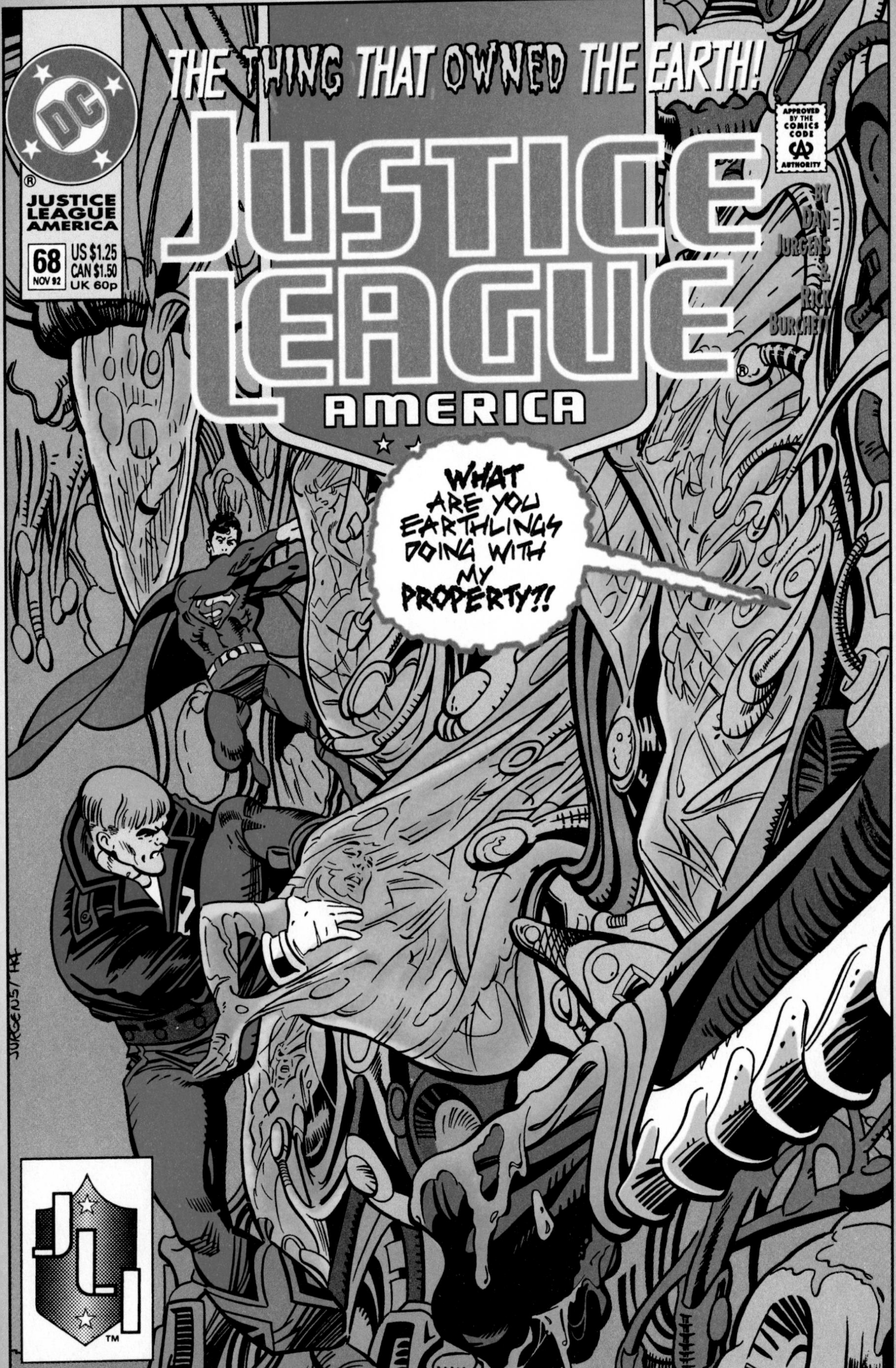
THE THING THAT OWNED THE EARTH!
DC
JUSTICE LEAGUE AMERICA
68 NOV 92
US $1.25
CAN $1.50
UK 60p
APPROVED BY THE COMICS CODE AUTHORITY
JUSTICE LEAGUE AMERICA
BY DAN JURGENS & RICK BURCHETT
WHAT ARE YOU EARTHLINGS DOING WITH MY PROPERTY?!
JURGENS/RB
JLA

Cover art by **DAN JURGENS**
and **RICK BURCHETT**

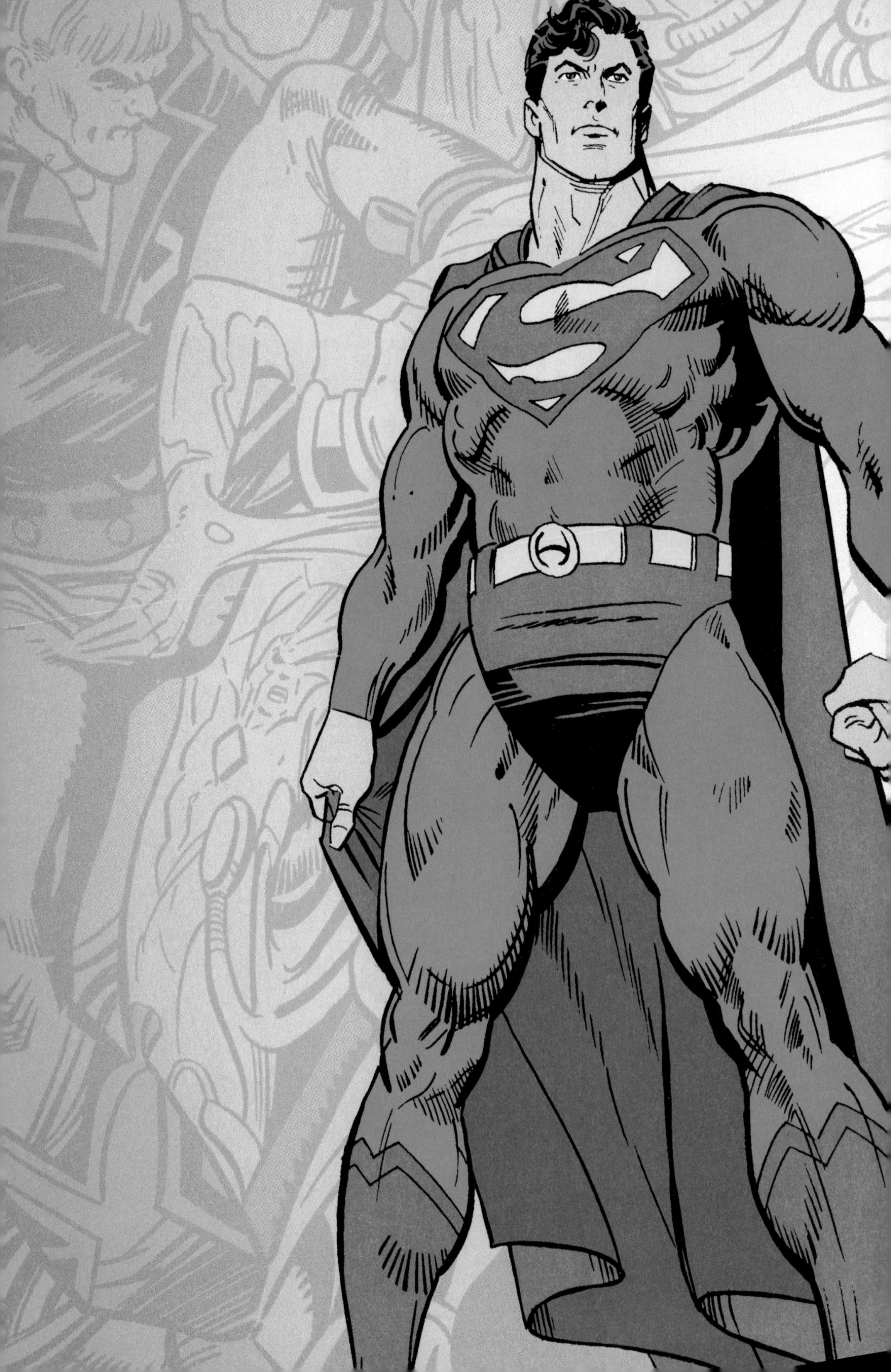

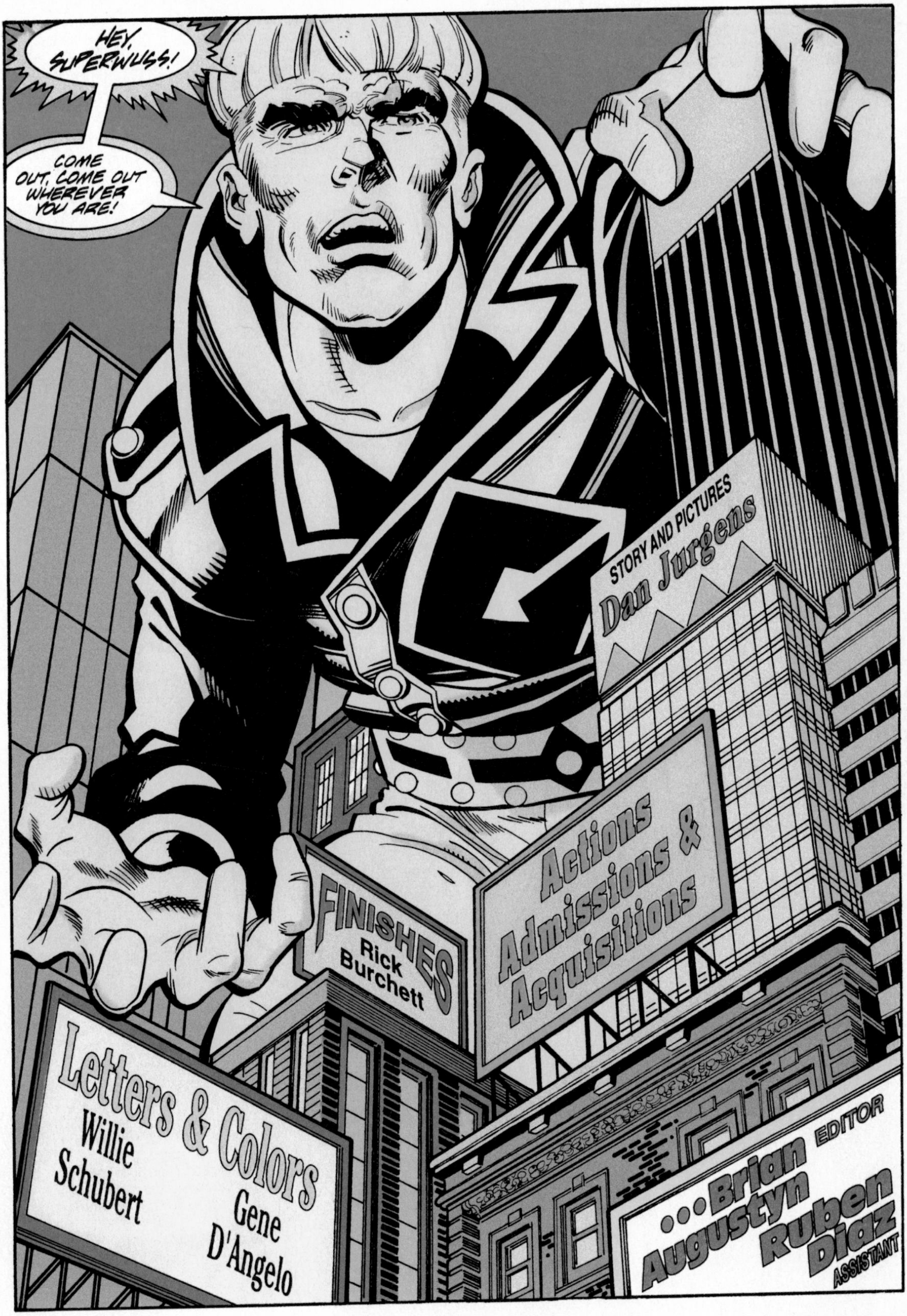
HEY, SUPERWUSS!
COME OUT, COME OUT WHEREVER YOU ARE!
STORY AND PICTURES Dan Jurgens
Actions Admissions & Acquisitions
FINISHES Rick Burchett
Letters & Colors Willie Schubert Gene D'Angelo
...Brian Augustyn EDITOR
Ruben Diaz ASSISTANT

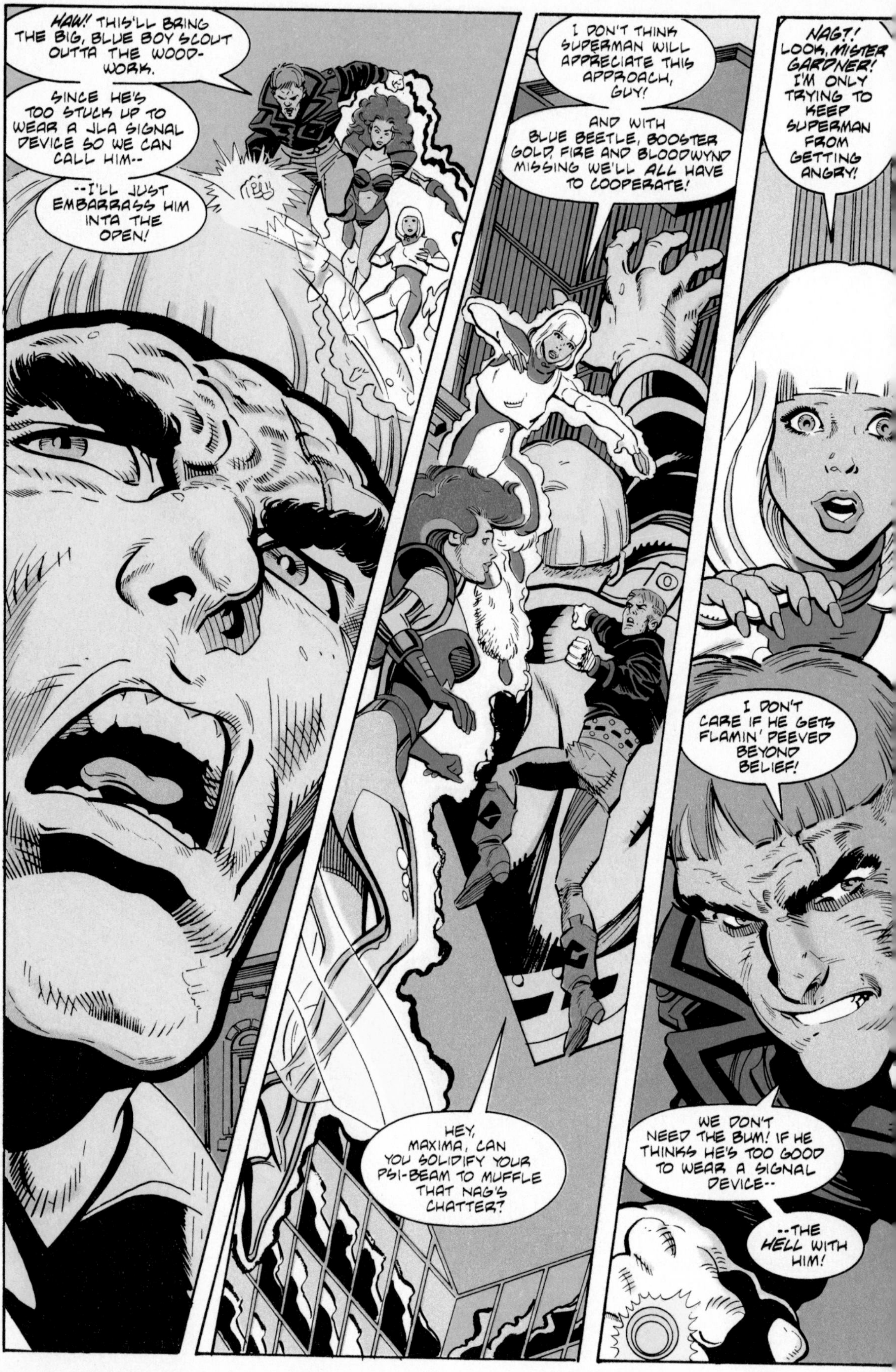
HAW! THIS'LL BRING THE BIG, BLUE BOY SCOUT OUTTA THE WOOD-WORK.
SINCE HE'S TOO STUCK UP TO WEAR A JLA SIGNAL DEVICE SO WE CAN CALL HIM--
--I'LL JUST EMBARRASS HIM INTA THE OPEN!
I DON'T THINK SUPERMAN WILL APPRECIATE THIS APPROACH, GUY!
AND WITH BLUE BEETLE, BOOSTER GOLD, FIRE AND BLOODWYND MISSING WE'LL ALL HAVE TO COOPERATE!
HEY, MAXIMA, CAN YOU SOLIDIFY YOUR PSI-BEAM TO MUFFLE THAT NAG'S CHATTER?
NAG?! LOOK, MISTER GARDNER! I'M ONLY TRYING TO KEEP SUPERMAN FROM GETTING ANGRY!
I DON'T CARE IF HE GETS FLAMIN' PEEVED BEYOND BELIEF!
WE DON'T NEED THE BUM! IF HE THINKS HE'S TOO GOOD TO WEAR A SIGNAL DEVICE--
--THE HELL WITH HIM!

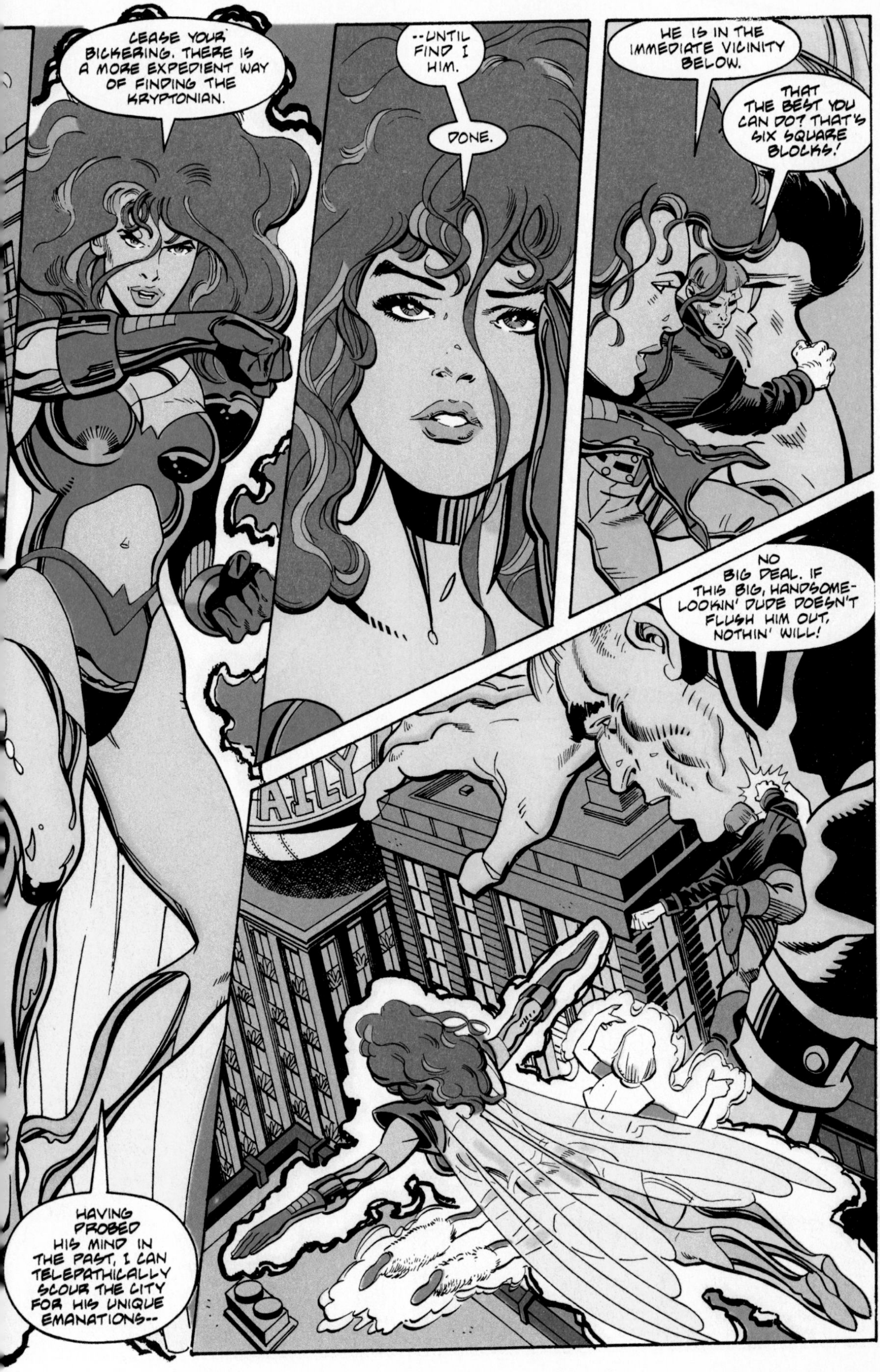
CEASE YOUR BICKERING. THERE IS A MORE EXPEDIENT WAY OF FINDING THE KRYPTONIAN.
HAVING PROBED HIS MIND IN THE PAST, I CAN TELEPATHICALLY SCOUR THE CITY FOR HIS UNIQUE EMANATIONS--
--UNTIL FIND I HIM.
DONE.
HE IS IN THE IMMEDIATE VICINITY BELOW.
THAT THE BEST YOU CAN DO? THAT'S SIX SQUARE BLOCKS!
NO BIG DEAL. IF THIS BIG, HANDSOME-LOOKIN' DUDE DOESN'T FLUSH HIM OUT, NOTHIN' WILL!
AILY

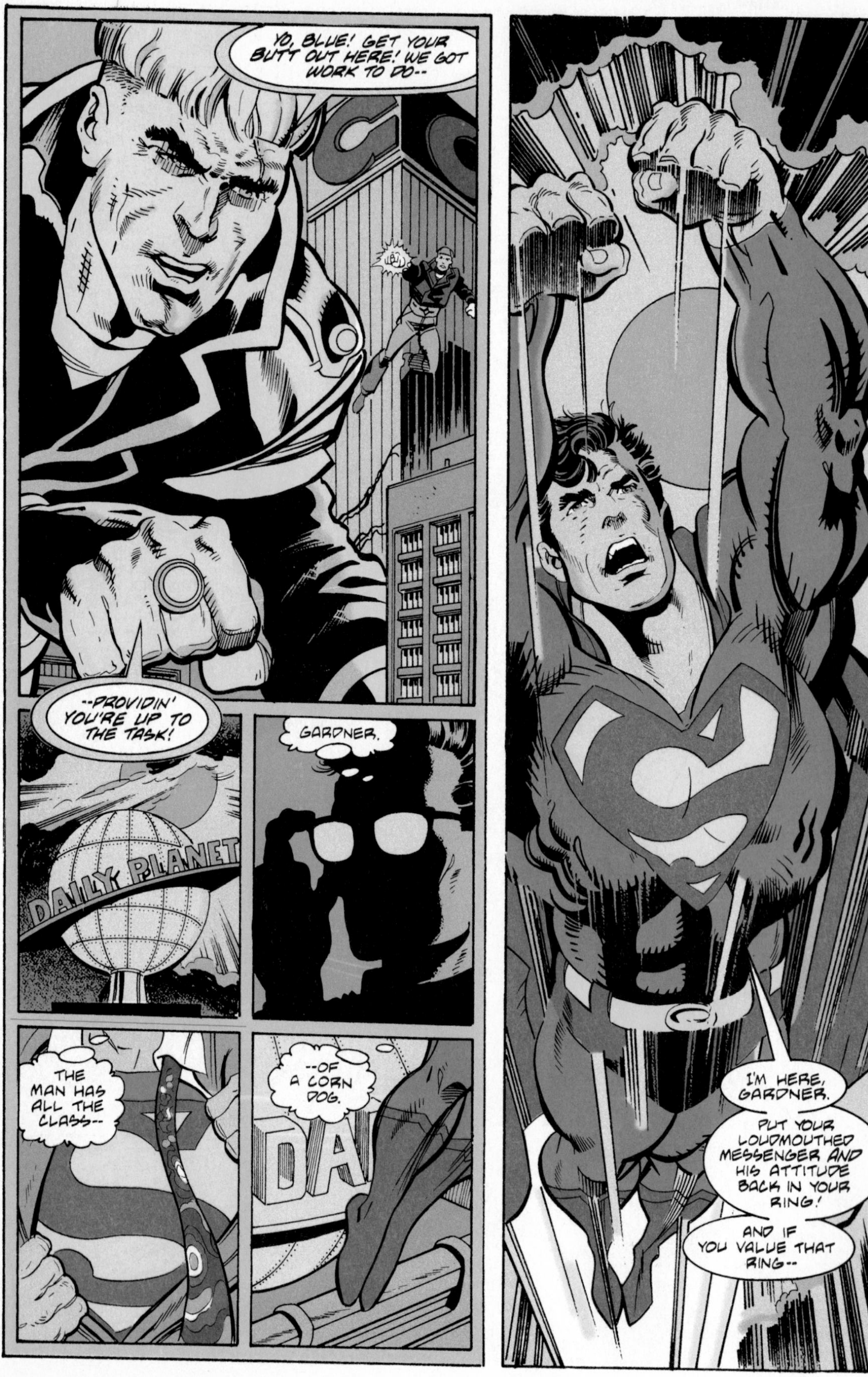
YO, BLUE! GET YOUR BUTT OUT HERE! WE GOT WORK TO DO--
--PROVIDIN' YOU'RE UP TO THE TASK!
GARDNER.
DAILY PLANET
THE MAN HAS ALL THE CLASS--
--OF A CORN DOG.
I'M HERE, GARDNER.
PUT YOUR LOUDMOUTHED MESSENGER AND HIS ATTITUDE BACK IN YOUR RING!
AND IF YOU VALUE THAT RING--

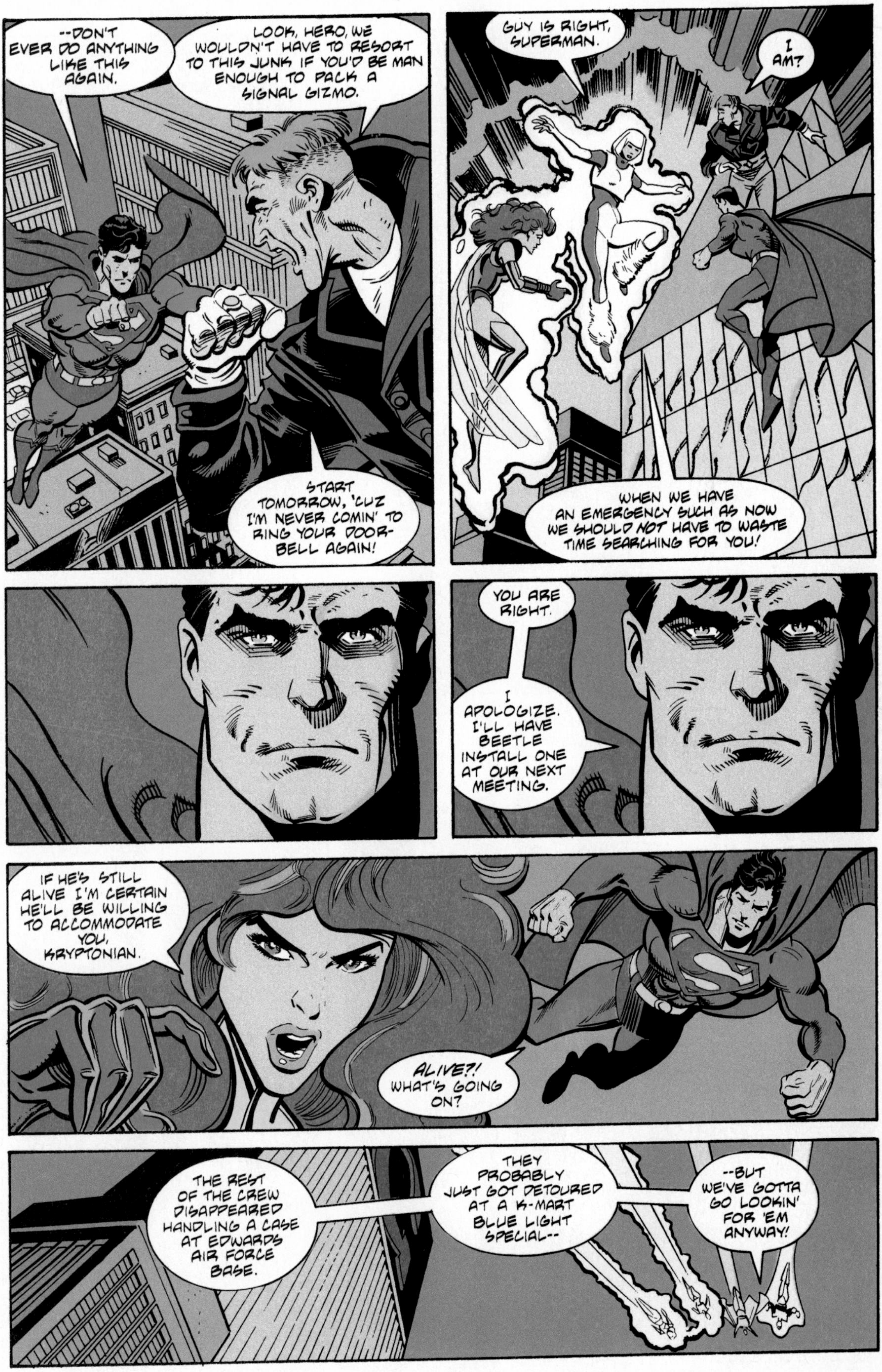
--DON'T EVER DO ANYTHING LIKE THIS AGAIN.
LOOK, HERO, WE WOULDN'T HAVE TO RESORT TO THIS JUNK IF YOU'D BE MAN ENOUGH TO PACK A SIGNAL GIZMO.
START TOMORROW, 'CUZ I'M NEVER COMIN' TO RING YOUR DOOR-BELL AGAIN!
GUY IS RIGHT, SUPERMAN.
I AM?
WHEN WE HAVE AN EMERGENCY SUCH AS NOW WE SHOULD NOT HAVE TO WASTE TIME SEARCHING FOR YOU!
YOU ARE RIGHT.
I APOLOGIZE. I'LL HAVE BEETLE INSTALL ONE AT OUR NEXT MEETING.
IF HE'S STILL ALIVE I'M CERTAIN HE'LL BE WILLING TO ACCOMMODATE YOU, KRYPTONIAN.
ALIVE?! WHAT'S GOING ON?
THE REST OF THE CREW DISAPPEARED HANDLING A CASE AT EDWARDS AIR FORCE BASE.
THEY PROBABLY JUST GOT DETOURED AT A K-MART BLUE LIGHT SPECIAL--
--BUT WE'VE GOTTA GO LOOKIN' FOR 'EM ANYWAY!

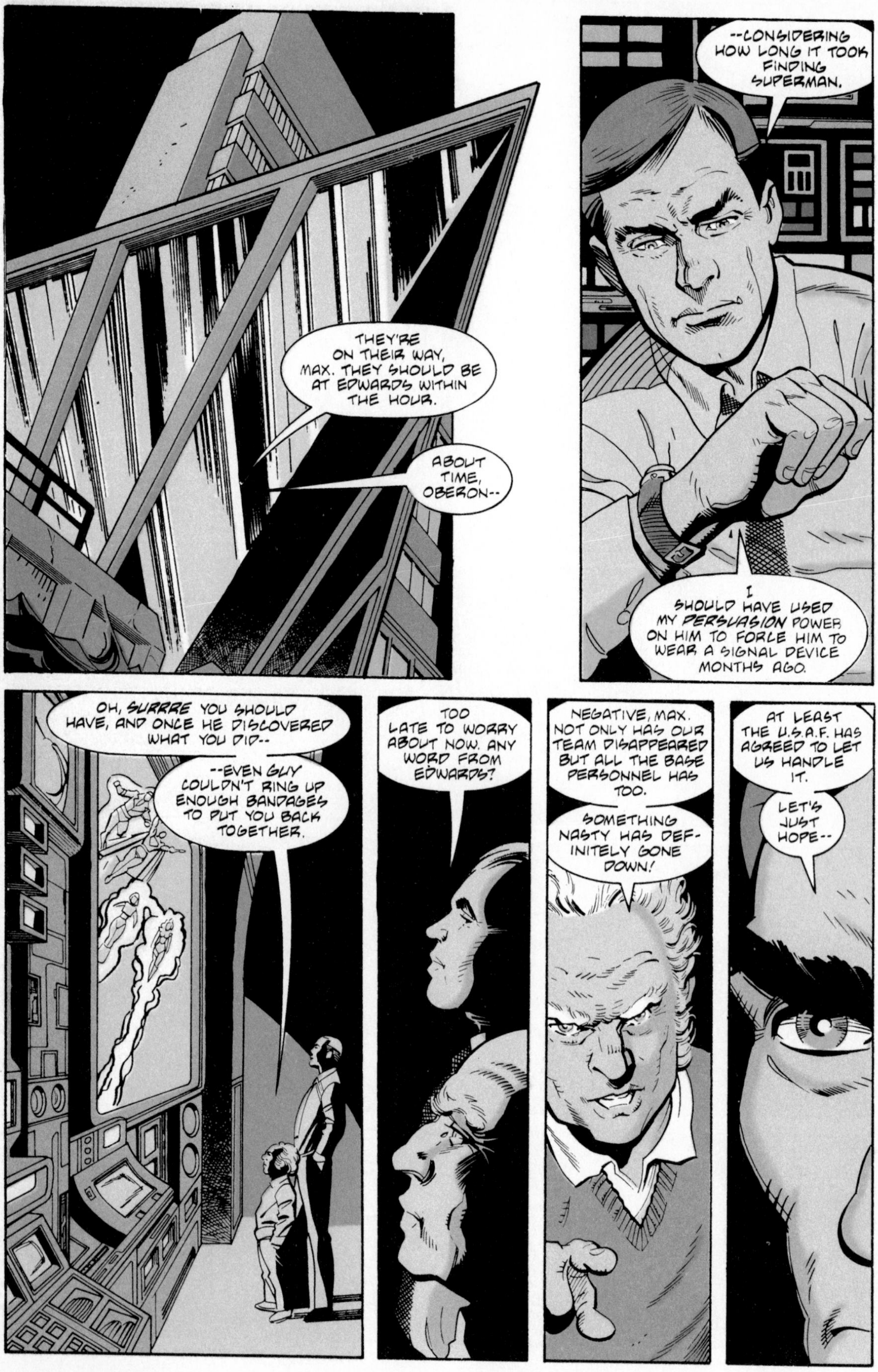
THEY'RE ON THEIR WAY, MAX. THEY SHOULD BE AT EDWARDS WITHIN THE HOUR.
ABOUT TIME, OBERON--
--CONSIDERING HOW LONG IT TOOK FINDING SUPERMAN.
I SHOULD HAVE USED MY PERSUASION POWER ON HIM TO FORCE HIM TO WEAR A SIGNAL DEVICE MONTHS AGO.
OH, SURRRE YOU SHOULD HAVE, AND ONCE HE DISCOVERED WHAT YOU DID--
--EVEN GUY COULDN'T RING UP ENOUGH BANDAGES TO PUT YOU BACK TOGETHER.
TOO LATE TO WORRY ABOUT NOW. ANY WORD FROM EDWARDS?
NEGATIVE, MAX. NOT ONLY HAS OUR TEAM DISAPPEARED BUT ALL THE BASE PERSONNEL HAS TOO.
SOMETHING NASTY HAS DEFINITELY GONE DOWN!
AT LEAST THE U.S.A.F. HAS AGREED TO LET US HANDLE IT.
LET'S JUST HOPE--

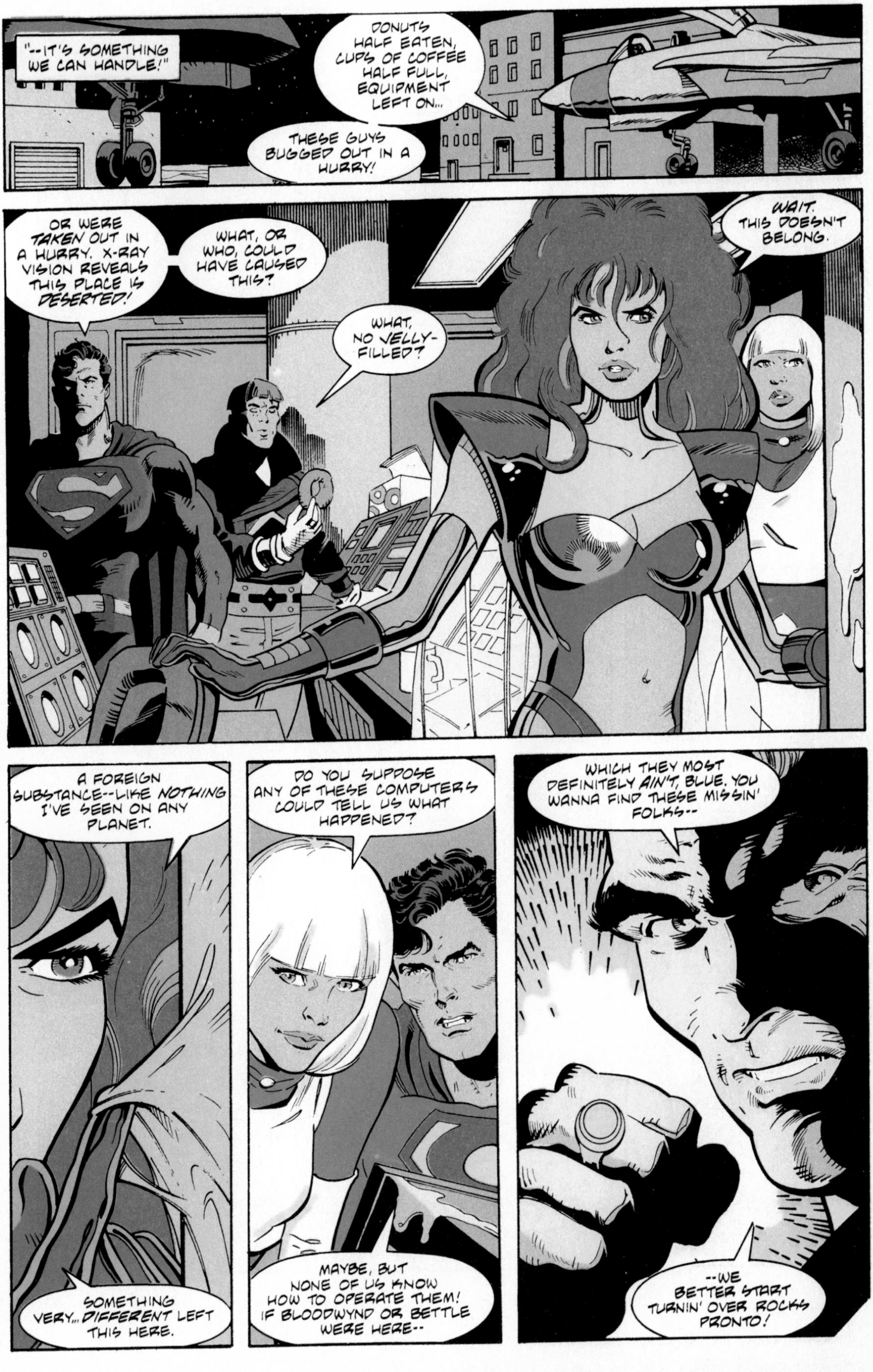
"--IT'S SOMETHING WE CAN HANDLE!"
DONUTS HALF EATEN, CUPS OF COFFEE HALF FULL, EQUIPMENT LEFT ON...
THESE GUYS BUGGED OUT IN A HURRY!
OR WERE TAKEN OUT IN A HURRY. X-RAY VISION REVEALS THIS PLACE IS DESERTED!
WHAT, OR WHO, COULD HAVE CAUSED THIS?
WHAT, NO JELLY-FILLED?
WAIT. THIS DOESN'T BELONG.
A FOREIGN SUBSTANCE--LIKE NOTHING I'VE SEEN ON ANY PLANET.
SOMETHING VERY... DIFFERENT LEFT THIS HERE.
DO YOU SUPPOSE ANY OF THESE COMPUTERS COULD TELL US WHAT HAPPENED?
MAYBE, BUT NONE OF US KNOW HOW TO OPERATE THEM! IF BLOODWYND OR BETTLE WERE HERE--
WHICH THEY MOST DEFINITELY AIN'T, BLUE. YOU WANNA FIND THESE MISSIN' FOLKS--
--WE BETTER START TURNIN' OVER ROCKS PRONTO!

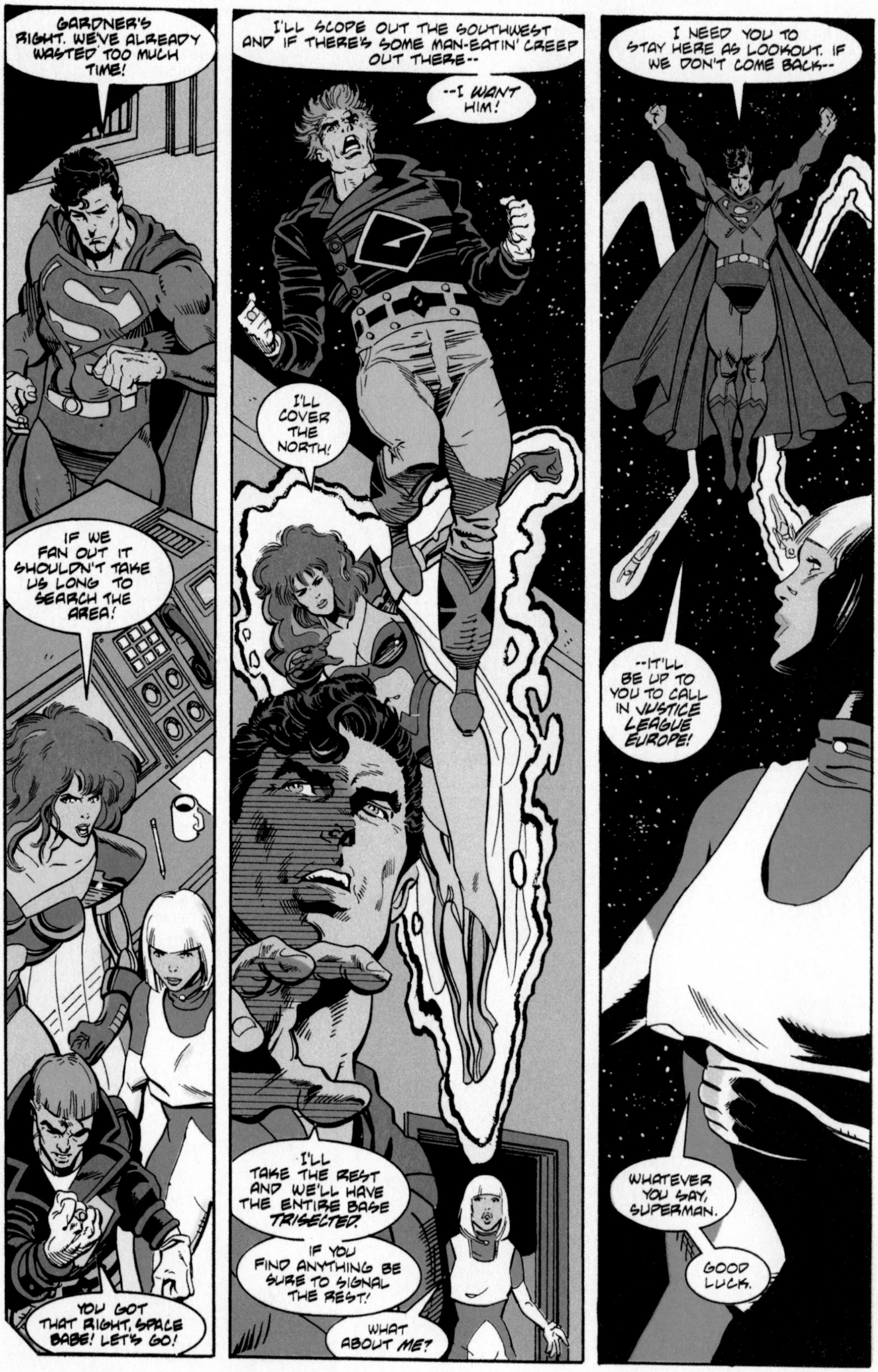
GARDNER'S RIGHT. WE'VE ALREADY WASTED TOO MUCH TIME!
IF WE FAN OUT IT SHOULDN'T TAKE US LONG TO SEARCH THE AREA!
YOU GOT THAT RIGHT, SPACE BABE! LET'S GO!
I'LL SCOPE OUT THE SOUTHWEST AND IF THERE'S SOME MAN-EATIN' CREEP OUT THERE--
--I WANT HIM!
I'LL COVER THE NORTH!
I'LL TAKE THE REST AND WE'LL HAVE THE ENTIRE BASE TRISECTED.
IF YOU FIND ANYTHING BE SURE TO SIGNAL THE REST!
WHAT ABOUT ME?
I NEED YOU TO STAY HERE AS LOOKOUT. IF WE DON'T COME BACK--
--IT'LL BE UP TO YOU TO CALL IN JUSTICE LEAGUE EUROPE!
WHATEVER YOU SAY, SUPERMAN.
GOOD LUCK.

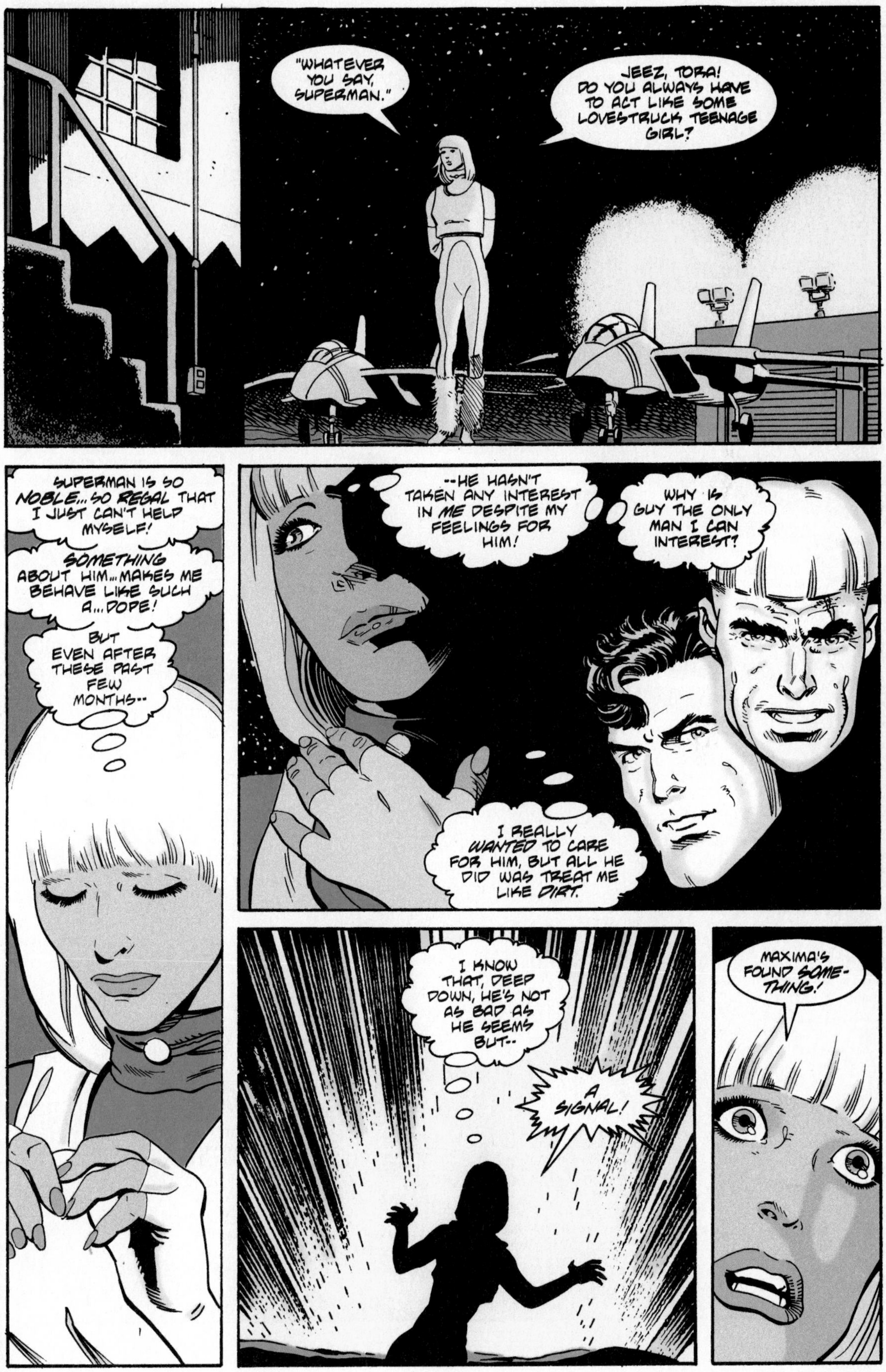
"WHATEVER YOU SAY, SUPERMAN."
JEEZ, TORA! DO YOU ALWAYS HAVE TO ACT LIKE SOME LOVESTRUCK TEENAGE GIRL?
SUPERMAN IS SO NOBLE... SO REGAL THAT I JUST CAN'T HELP MYSELF!
SOMETHING ABOUT HIM... MAKES ME BEHAVE LIKE SUCH A... DOPE!
BUT EVEN AFTER THESE PAST FEW MONTHS--
--HE HASN'T TAKEN ANY INTEREST IN ME DESPITE MY FEELINGS FOR HIM!
WHY IS GUY THE ONLY MAN I CAN INTEREST?
I REALLY WANTED TO CARE FOR HIM, BUT ALL HE DID WAS TREAT ME LIKE DIRT.
I KNOW THAT, DEEP DOWN, HE'S NOT AS BAD AS HE SEEMS BUT--
A SIGNAL!
MAXIMA'S FOUND SOME-THING!

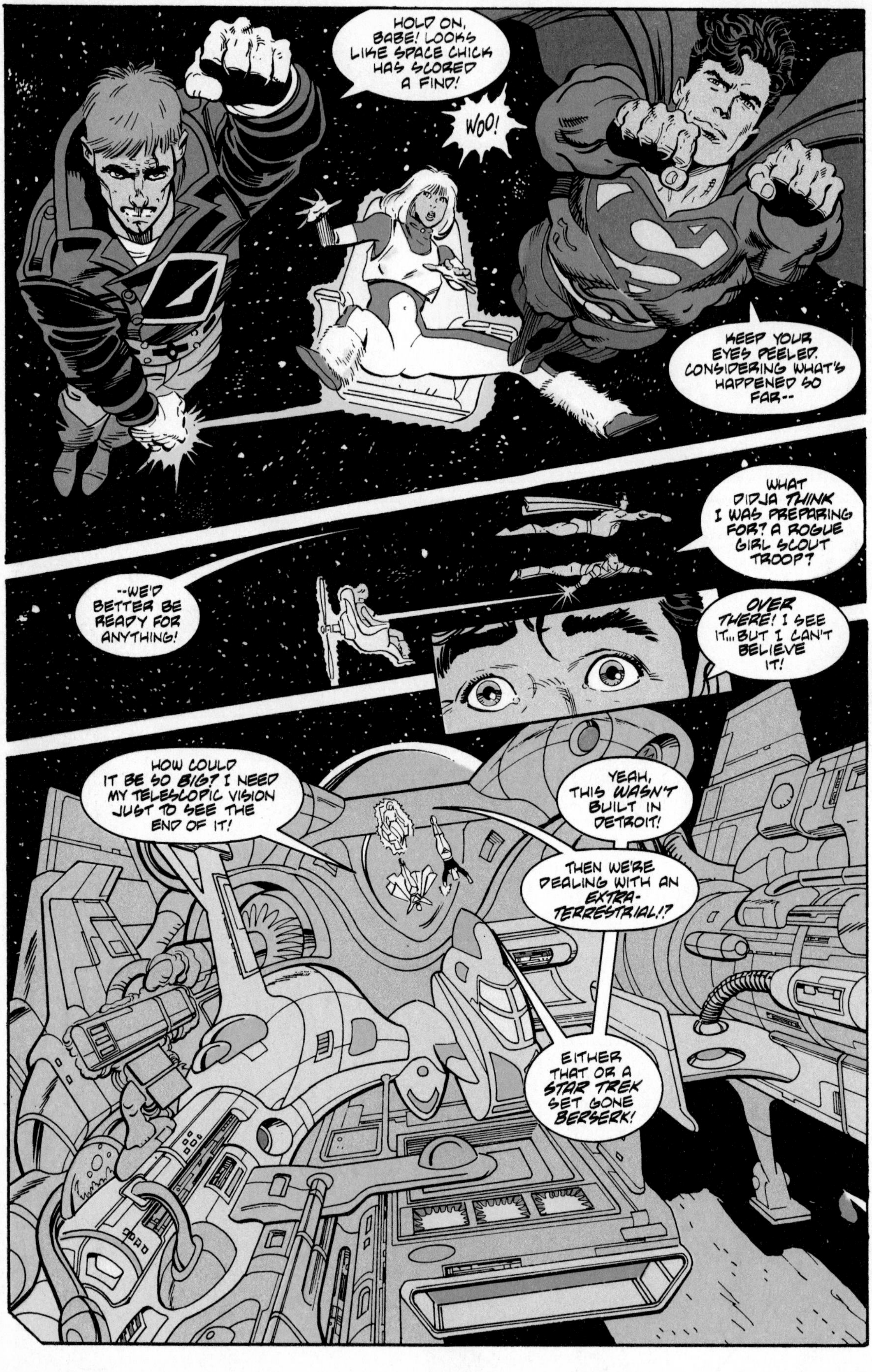
HOLD ON, BABE! LOOKS LIKE SPACE CHICK HAS SCORED A FIND!
WOO!
KEEP YOUR EYES PEELED. CONSIDERING WHAT'S HAPPENED SO FAR--
WHAT DIDJA THINK I WAS PREPARING FOR? A ROGUE GIRL SCOUT TROOP?
--WE'D BETTER BE READY FOR ANYTHING!
OVER THERE! I SEE IT... BUT I CAN'T BELIEVE IT!
HOW COULD IT BE SO BIG? I NEED MY TELESCOPIC VISION JUST TO SEE THE END OF IT!
YEAH, THIS WASN'T BUILT IN DETROIT!
THEN WE'RE DEALING WITH AN EXTRA-TERRESTRIAL!?
EITHER THAT OR A STAR TREK SET GONE BERSERK!

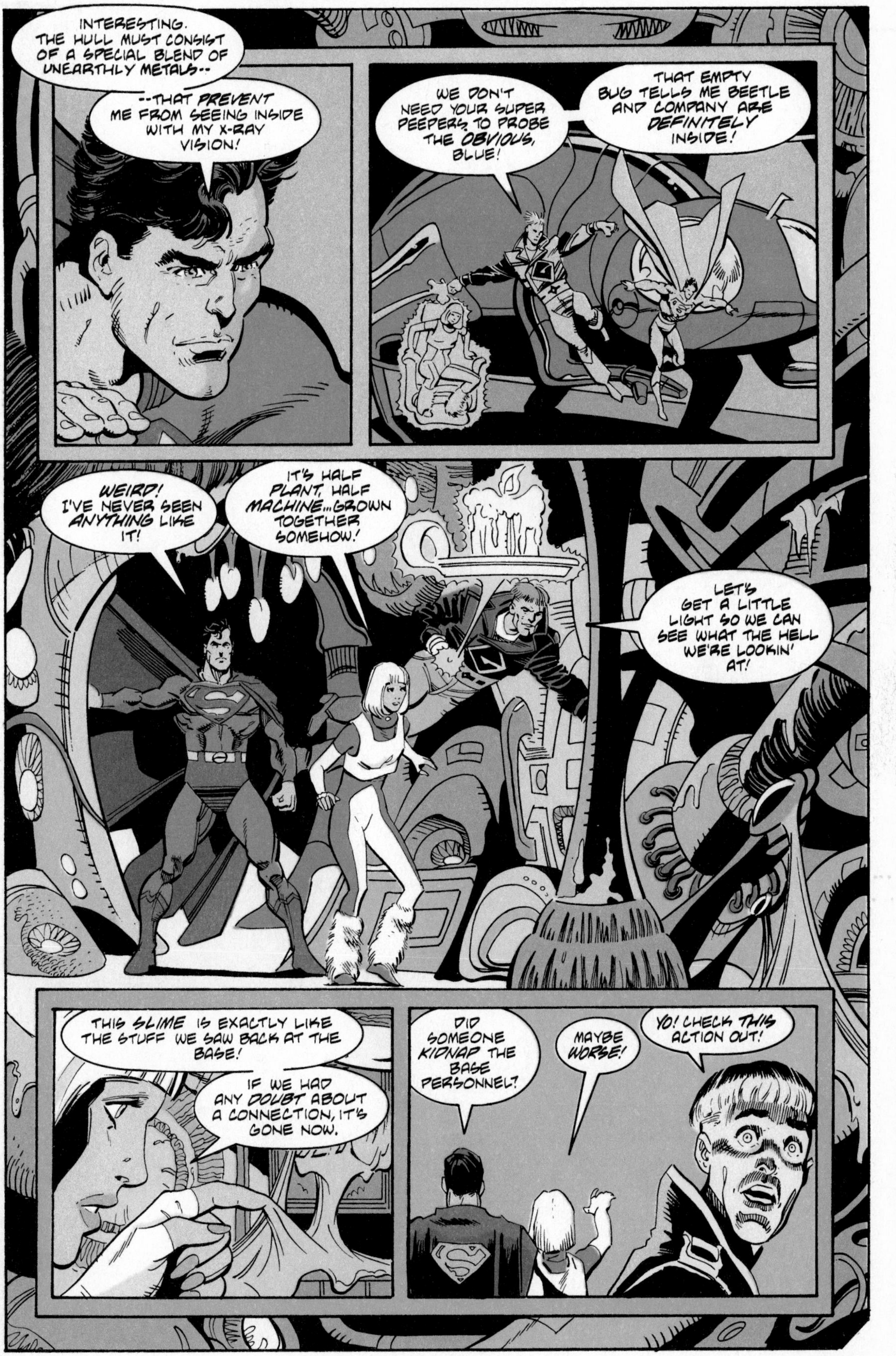
INTERESTING. THE HULL MUST CONSIST OF A SPECIAL BLEND OF UNEARTHLY METALS--
--THAT PREVENT ME FROM SEEING INSIDE WITH MY X-RAY VISION!
WE DON'T NEED YOUR SUPER PEEPERS TO PROBE THE OBVIOUS, BLUE!
THAT EMPTY BUG TELLS ME BEETLE AND COMPANY ARE DEFINITELY INSIDE!
WEIRD! I'VE NEVER SEEN ANYTHING LIKE IT!
IT'S HALF PLANT, HALF MACHINE...GROWN TOGETHER SOMEHOW!
LET'S GET A LITTLE LIGHT SO WE CAN SEE WHAT THE HELL WE'RE LOOKIN' AT!
THIS SLIME IS EXACTLY LIKE THE STUFF WE SAW BACK AT THE BASE!
IF WE HAD ANY DOUBT ABOUT A CONNECTION, IT'S GONE NOW.
DID SOMEONE KIDNAP THE BASE PERSONNEL?
MAYBE WORSE!
YO! CHECK THIS ACTION OUT!

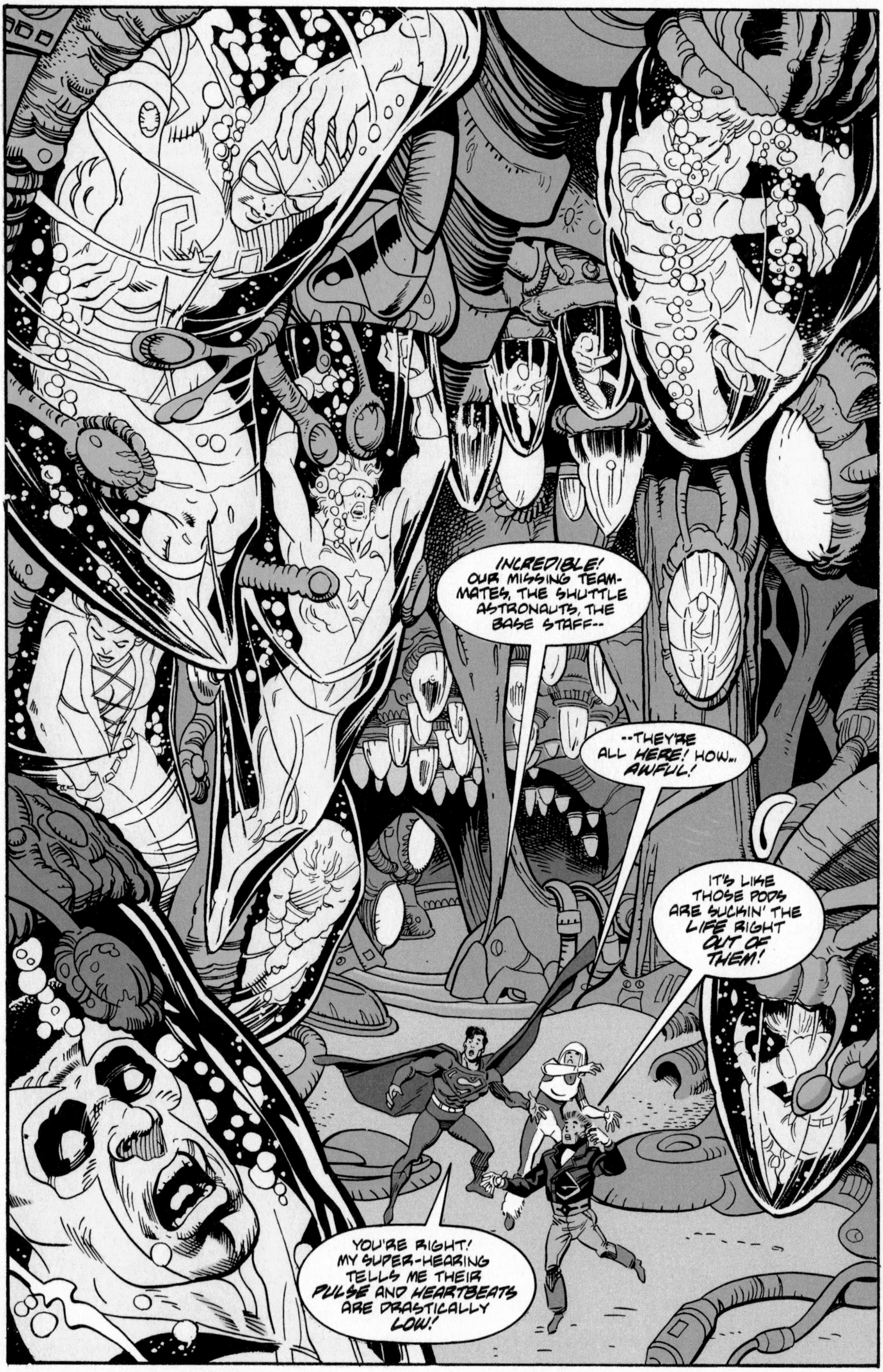
INCREDIBLE! OUR MISSING TEAM-MATES, THE SHUTTLE ASTRONAUTS, THE BASE STAFF--
--THEY'RE ALL HERE! HOW... AWFUL!
IT'S LIKE THOSE PODS ARE SUCKIN' THE LIFE RIGHT OUT OF THEM!
YOU'RE RIGHT! MY SUPER-HEARING TELLS ME THEIR PULSE AND HEARTBEATS ARE DRASTICALLY LOW!

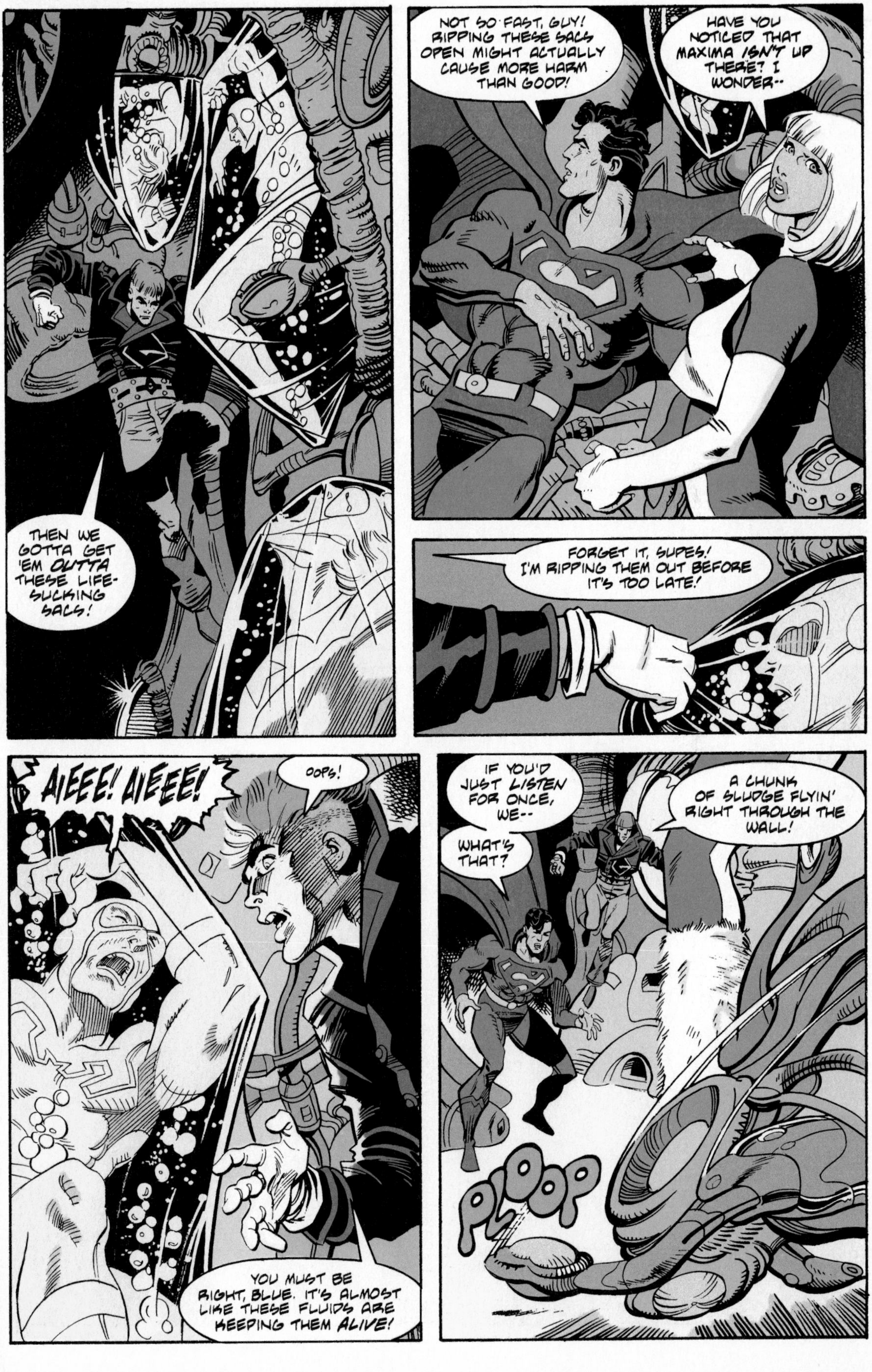
THEN WE GOTTA GET 'EM OUTTA THESE LIFE-SUCKING SACS!
NOT SO FAST, GUY! RIPPING THESE SACS OPEN MIGHT ACTUALLY CAUSE MORE HARM THAN GOOD!
HAVE YOU NOTICED THAT MAXIMA ISN'T UP THERE? I WONDER--
FORGET IT, SUPES! I'M RIPPING THEM OUT BEFORE IT'S TOO LATE!
AIEEE! AIEEE!
OOPS!
YOU MUST BE RIGHT, BLUE. IT'S ALMOST LIKE THESE FLUIDS ARE KEEPING THEM ALIVE!
IF YOU'D JUST LISTEN FOR ONCE, WE--
WHAT'S THAT?
A CHUNK OF SLUDGE FLYIN' RIGHT THROUGH THE WALL!
PLOOP

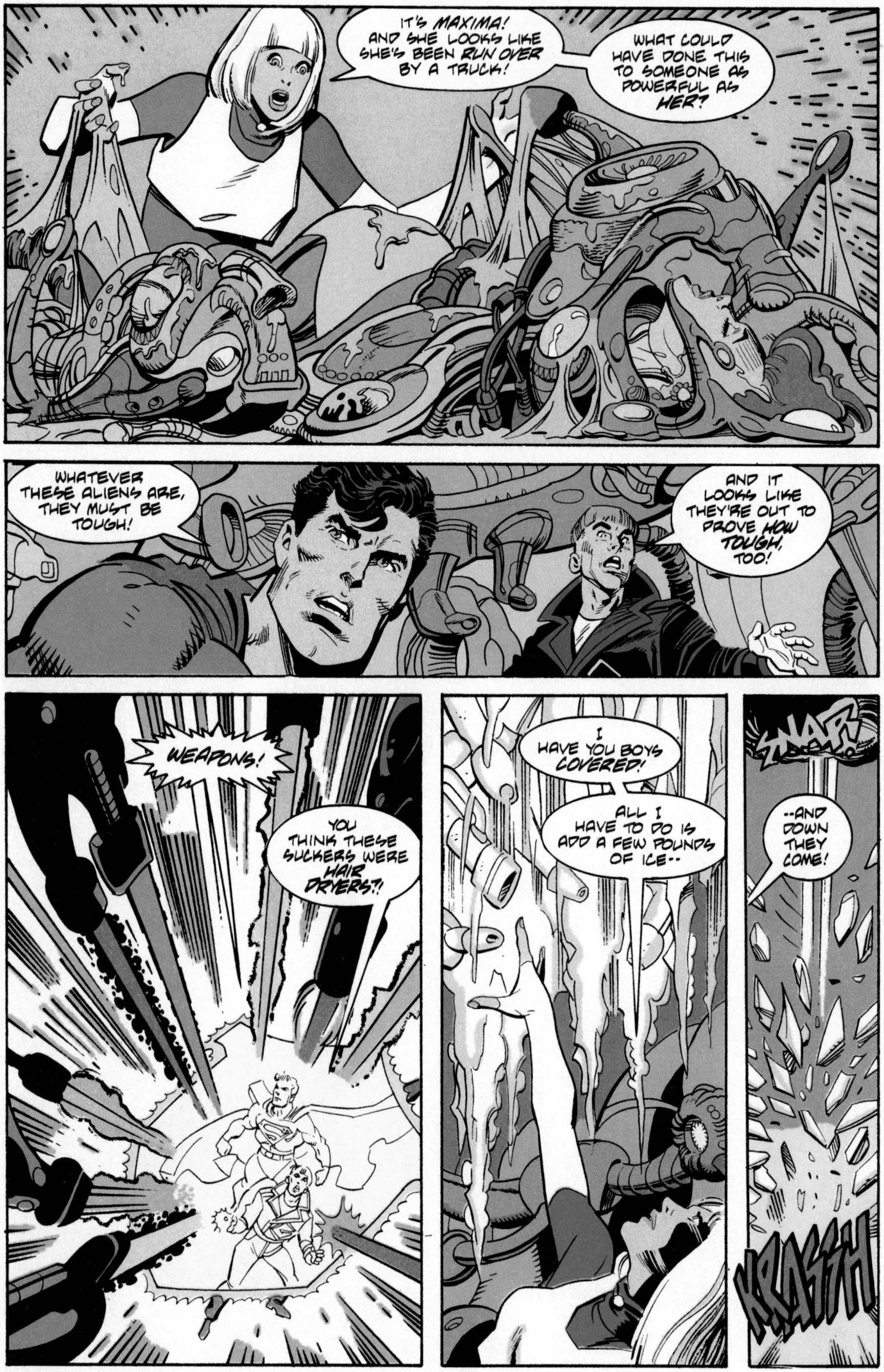
IT'S MAXIMA! AND SHE LOOKS LIKE SHE'S BEEN RUN OVER BY A TRUCK!
WHAT COULD HAVE DONE THIS TO SOMEONE AS POWERFUL AS HER?
WHATEVER THESE ALIENS ARE, THEY MUST BE TOUGH!
AND IT LOOKS LIKE THEY'RE OUT TO PROVE HOW TOUGH, TOO!
WEAPONS!
YOU THINK THESE SUCKERS WERE HAIR DRYERS?!
I HAVE YOU BOYS COVERED!
ALL I HAVE TO DO IS ADD A FEW POUNDS OF ICE--
SNAP!
--AND DOWN THEY COME!
KRASSH

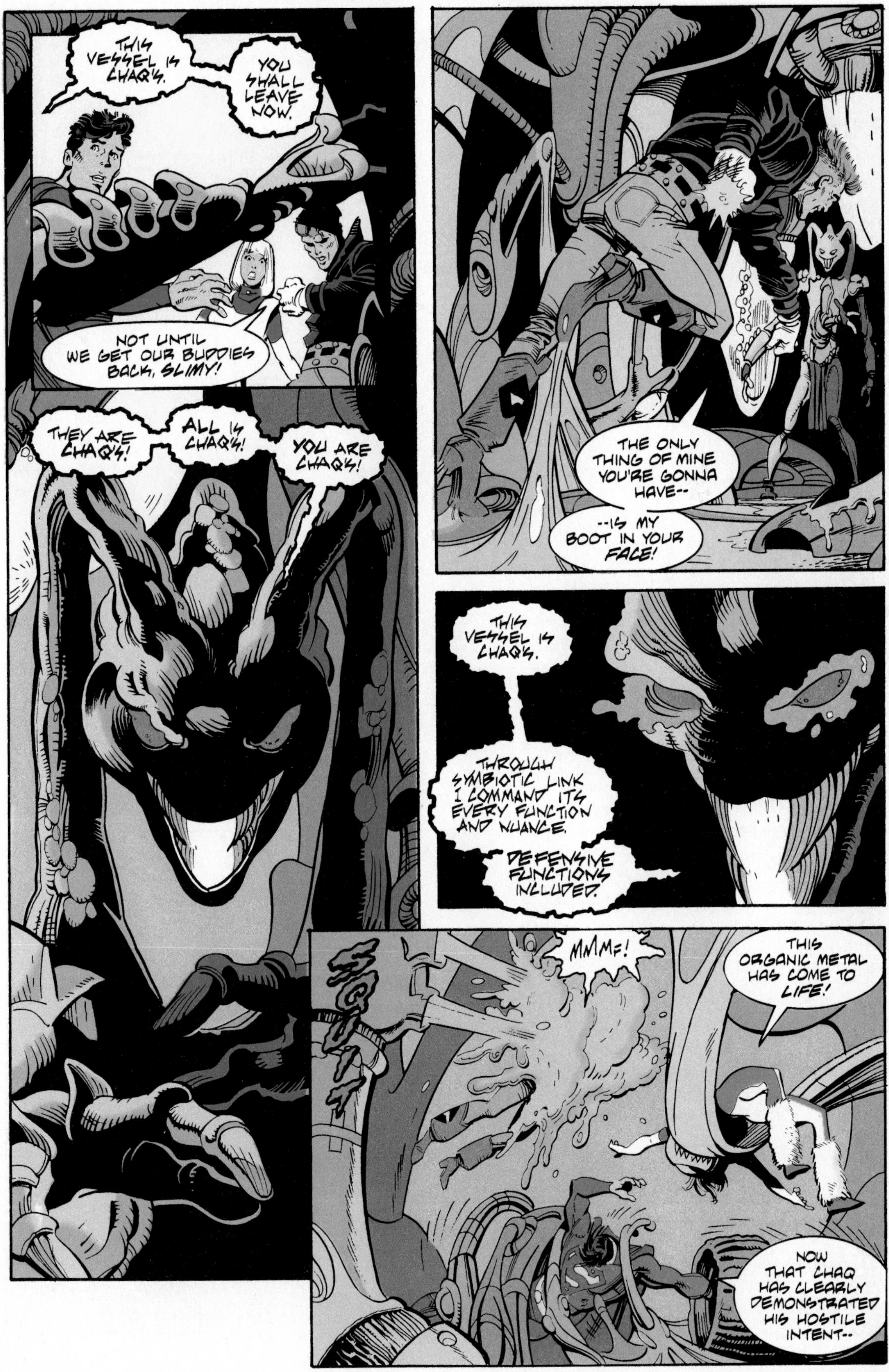
THIS VESSEL IS CHAQ'S.
YOU SHALL LEAVE NOW.
NOT UNTIL WE GET OUR BUDDIES BACK, SLIMY!
THE ONLY THING OF MINE YOU'RE GONNA HAVE--
--IS MY BOOT IN YOUR FACE!
THEY ARE CHAQ'S!
ALL IS CHAQ'S!
YOU ARE CHAQ'S!
THIS VESSEL IS CHAQ'S.
THROUGH SYMBIOTIC LINK I COMMAND ITS EVERY FUNCTION AND NUANCE.
DEFENSIVE FUNCTIONS INCLUDED.
MMMF!
THIS ORGANIC METAL HAS COME TO LIFE!
NOW THAT CHAQ HAS CLEARLY DEMONSTRATED HIS HOSTILE INTENT--

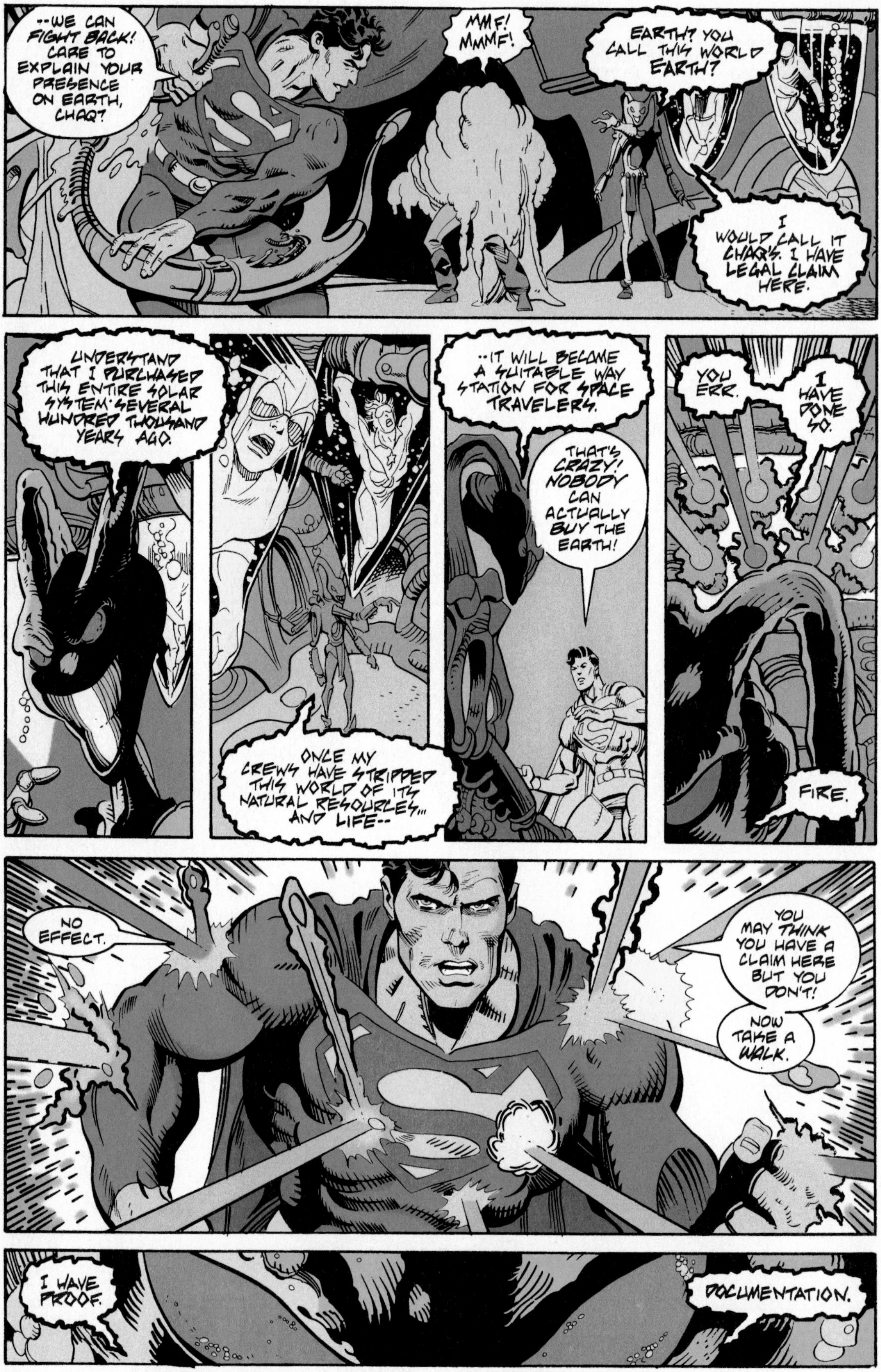
--WE CAN FIGHT BACK! CARE TO EXPLAIN YOUR PRESENCE ON EARTH, CHAQ?
MMF! MMMF!
EARTH? YOU CALL THIS WORLD EARTH?
I WOULD CALL IT CHAQ'S. I HAVE LEGAL CLAIM HERE.
UNDERSTAND THAT I PURCHASED THIS ENTIRE SOLAR SYSTEM SEVERAL HUNDRED THOUSAND YEARS AGO.
ONCE MY CREWS HAVE STRIPPED THIS WORLD OF ITS NATURAL RESOURCES... AND LIFE--
--IT WILL BECOME A SUITABLE WAY STATION FOR SPACE TRAVELERS.
THAT'S CRAZY! NOBODY CAN ACTUALLY BUY THE EARTH!
YOU ERR.
I HAVE DONE SO.
FIRE.
NO EFFECT.
YOU MAY THINK YOU HAVE A CLAIM HERE BUT YOU DON'T!
NOW TAKE A WALK.
I HAVE PROOF.
DOCUMENTATION.

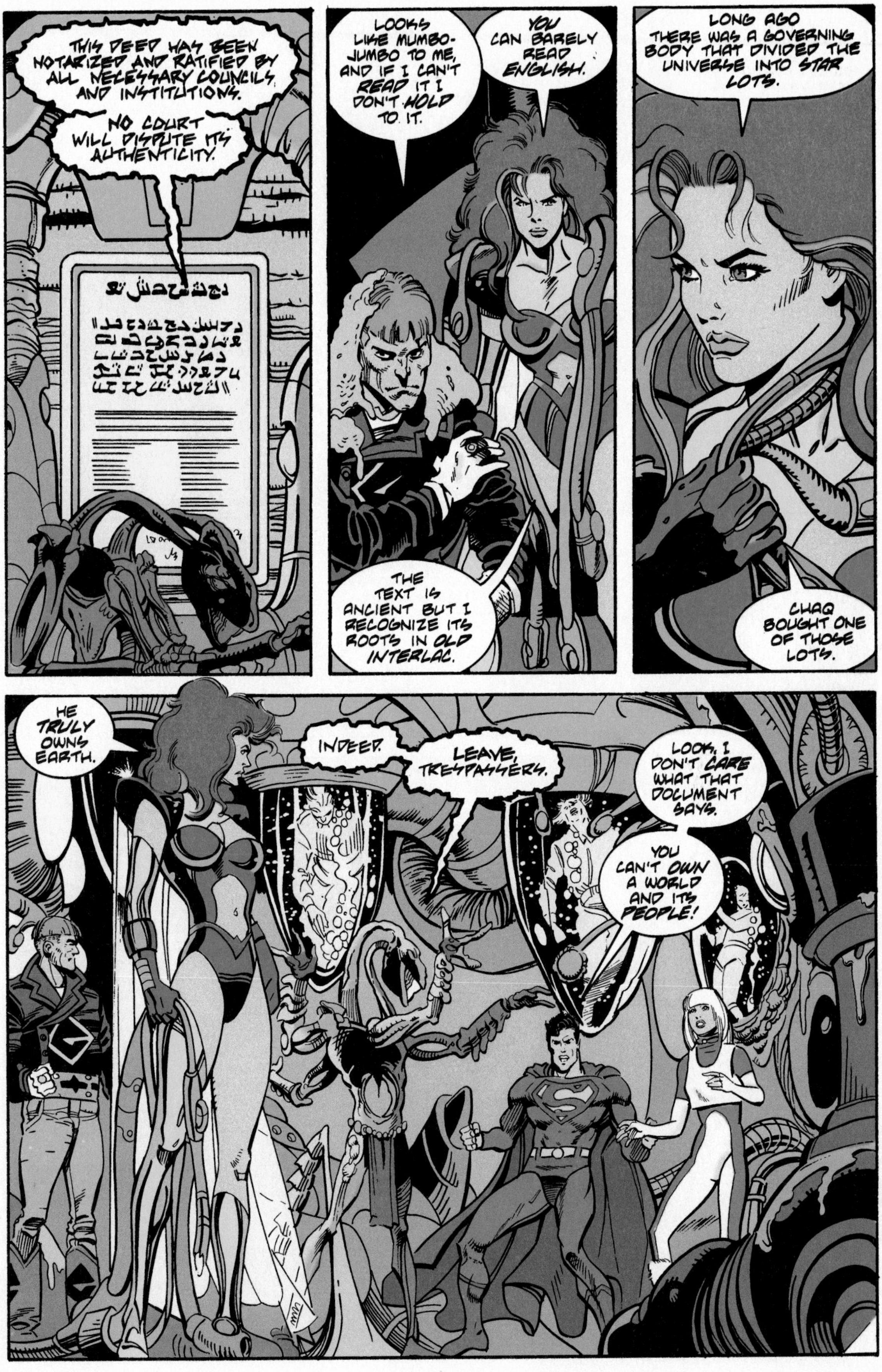
THIS DEED HAS BEEN NOTARIZED AND RATIFIED BY ALL NECESSARY COUNCILS AND INSTITUTIONS.
NO COURT WILL DISPUTE ITS AUTHENTICITY.
LOOKS LIKE MUMBO-JUMBO TO ME, AND IF I CAN'T READ IT I DON'T HOLD TO IT.
YOU CAN BARELY READ ENGLISH.
THE TEXT IS ANCIENT BUT I RECOGNIZE ITS ROOTS IN OLD INTERLAC.
LONG AGO THERE WAS A GOVERNING BODY THAT DIVIDED THE UNIVERSE INTO STAR LOTS.
CHAQ BOUGHT ONE OF THOSE LOTS.
HE TRULY OWNS EARTH.
INDEED.
LEAVE, TRESPASSERS.
LOOK, I DON'T CARE WHAT THAT DOCUMENT SAYS.
YOU CAN'T OWN A WORLD AND ITS PEOPLE!

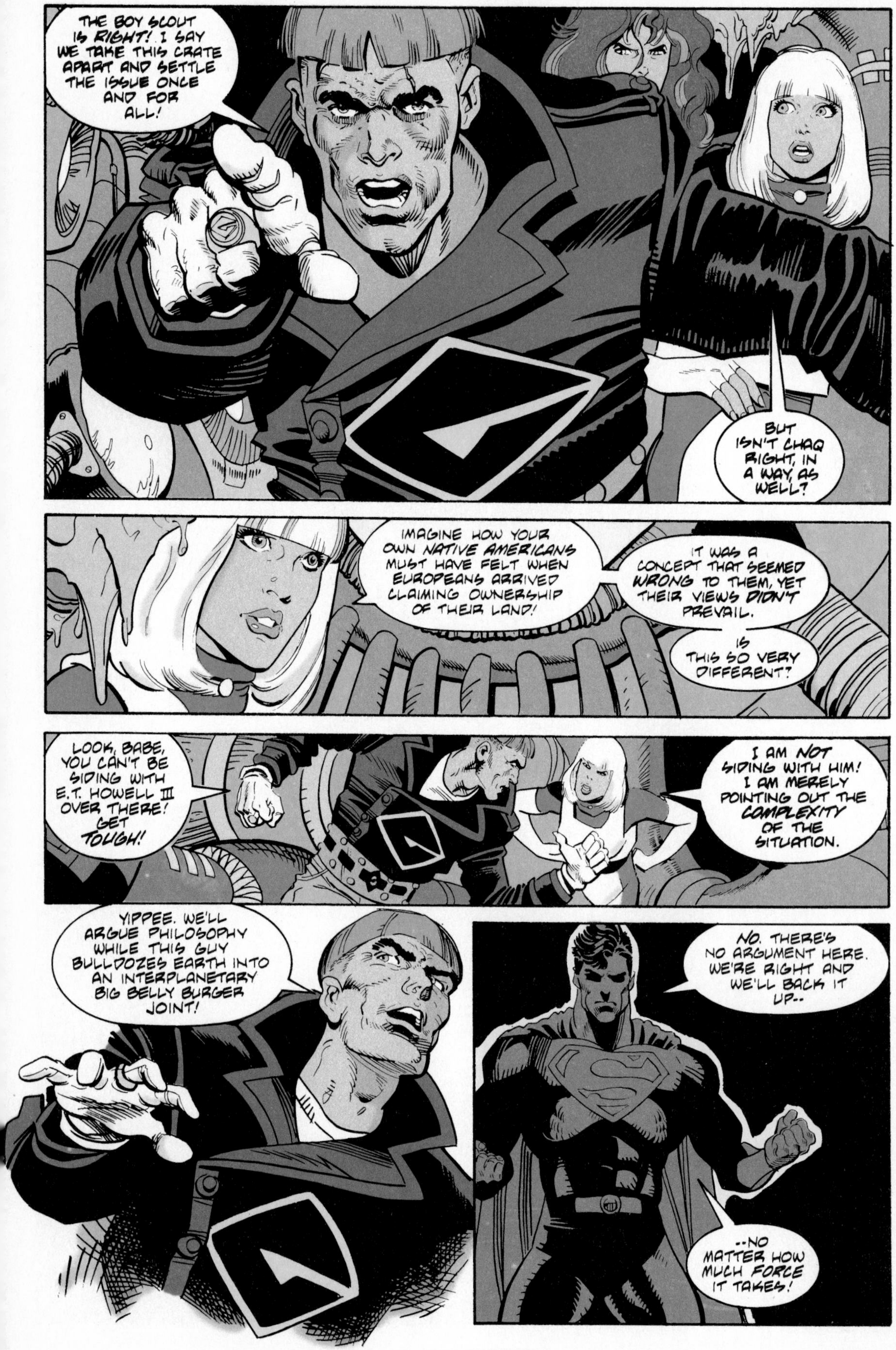
THE BOY SCOUT IS RIGHT! I SAY WE TAKE THIS CRATE APART AND SETTLE THE ISSUE ONCE AND FOR ALL!
BUT ISN'T CHAQ RIGHT, IN A WAY, AS WELL?
IMAGINE HOW YOUR OWN NATIVE AMERICANS MUST HAVE FELT WHEN EUROPEANS ARRIVED CLAIMING OWNERSHIP OF THEIR LAND!
IT WAS A CONCEPT THAT SEEMED WRONG TO THEM, YET THEIR VIEWS DIDN'T PREVAIL.
IS THIS SO VERY DIFFERENT?
LOOK, BABE, YOU CAN'T BE SIDING WITH E.T. HOWELL III OVER THERE! GET TOUGH!
I AM NOT SIDING WITH HIM! I AM MERELY POINTING OUT THE COMPLEXITY OF THE SITUATION.
YIPPEE. WE'LL ARGUE PHILOSOPHY WHILE THIS GUY BULLDOZES EARTH INTO AN INTERPLANETARY BIG BELLY BURGER JOINT!
NO. THERE'S NO ARGUMENT HERE. WE'RE RIGHT AND WE'LL BACK IT UP--
--NO MATTER HOW MUCH FORCE IT TAKES!

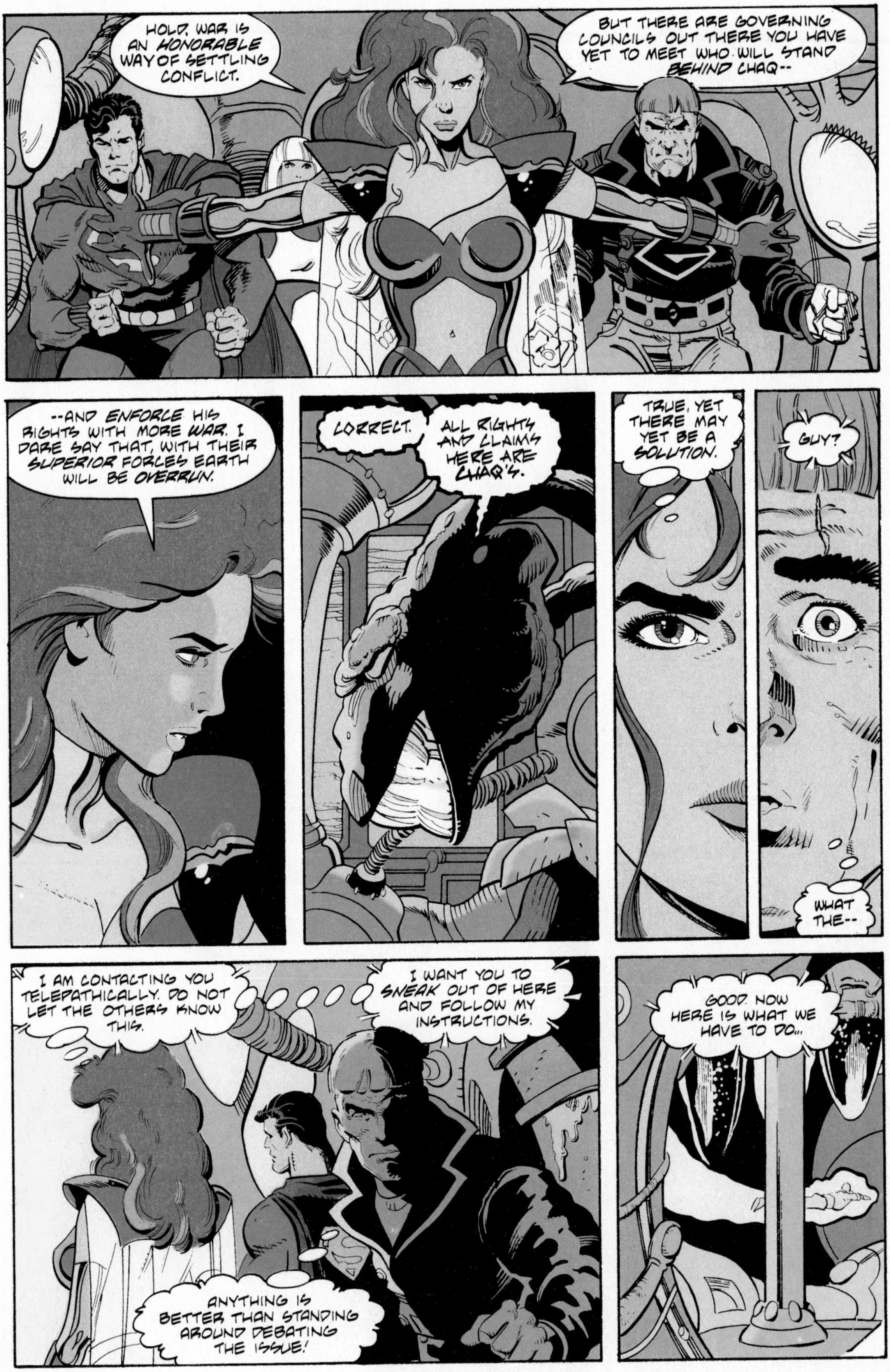
HOLD. WAR IS AN HONORABLE WAY OF SETTLING CONFLICT.
BUT THERE ARE GOVERNING COUNCILS OUT THERE YOU HAVE YET TO MEET WHO WILL STAND BEHIND CHAQ--
--AND ENFORCE HIS RIGHTS WITH MORE WAR. I DARE SAY THAT, WITH THEIR SUPERIOR FORCES EARTH WILL BE OVERRUN.
CORRECT.
ALL RIGHTS AND CLAIMS HERE ARE CHAQ'S.
TRUE, YET THERE MAY YET BE A SOLUTION.
GUY?
WHAT THE--
I AM CONTACTING YOU TELEPATHICALLY. DO NOT LET THE OTHERS KNOW THIS.
I WANT YOU TO SNEAK OUT OF HERE AND FOLLOW MY INSTRUCTIONS.
ANYTHING IS BETTER THAN STANDING AROUND DEBATING THE ISSUE!
GOOD. NOW HERE IS WHAT WE HAVE TO DO...

BEFORE WE LEAVE MAXIMA WOULD ASK CHAQ A QUESTION.

YOU AREN'T INTENTIONALLY MALEVOLENT...YOU ONLY WANT TO PROFIT HERE!

YES, OF COURSE...THE MORE THE BETTER.

THEN I OFFER YOU 800 TRILLION SENTEES FOR YOUR RIGHTS TO EARTH!

YOU...YOU HAVE ALLESS TO FUNDS SO GREAT?

YES, IT IS THE WELL-KNOWN CURRENCY OF OVER TWO HUNDRED WORLDS!

YES! AND THE COMBINED WEALTH OF AT LEAST HALF THAT NUMBER!

WHAT IS SHE UP TO?

I THINK I'M BEGINNING TO UNDERSTAND...

CHECK YOUR SHIP'S CARGO HOLDS, CHAQ, AND YOU'LL FIND THE SENTEES WAITING AS PROOF. DO WE HAVE A DEAL?

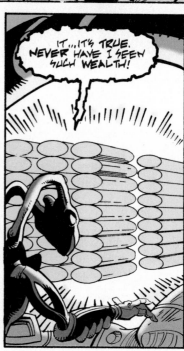

IT...IT'S TRUE. NEVER HAVE I SEEN SUCH WEALTH!

NO KIDDIN'. AND I'M THE ONE WHO MADE THE DEPOSIT, PAL!

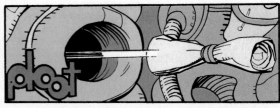

FAR GREATER PROFIT THAN I PLANNED!

EARTH IS *YOURS*!

BREEP BREEP

THE *DEED.* YOU ARE NOW *RIGHTFUL OWNER* OF *SOL,* THE *NINE PLANETS* THAT ORBIT IT AND ALL THEY CONTAIN.

THEN... I *ACTUALLY OWN EARTH?* AND *ALL* THE PEOPLE ON IT?!

BWAH HA HA HAHH!

I SHALL RELEASE ALL CAPTIVES INTO YOUR CUSTODY SIR. DO WITH THEM AS YOU WISH.

WE'VE WON WITH *SMARTS* SOMETIMES AND *BRAWN* THE OTHERS.

BUT THIS IS THE *FIRST* TIME WE'VE EVER *SCAMMED* OUR WAY TO VICTORY!

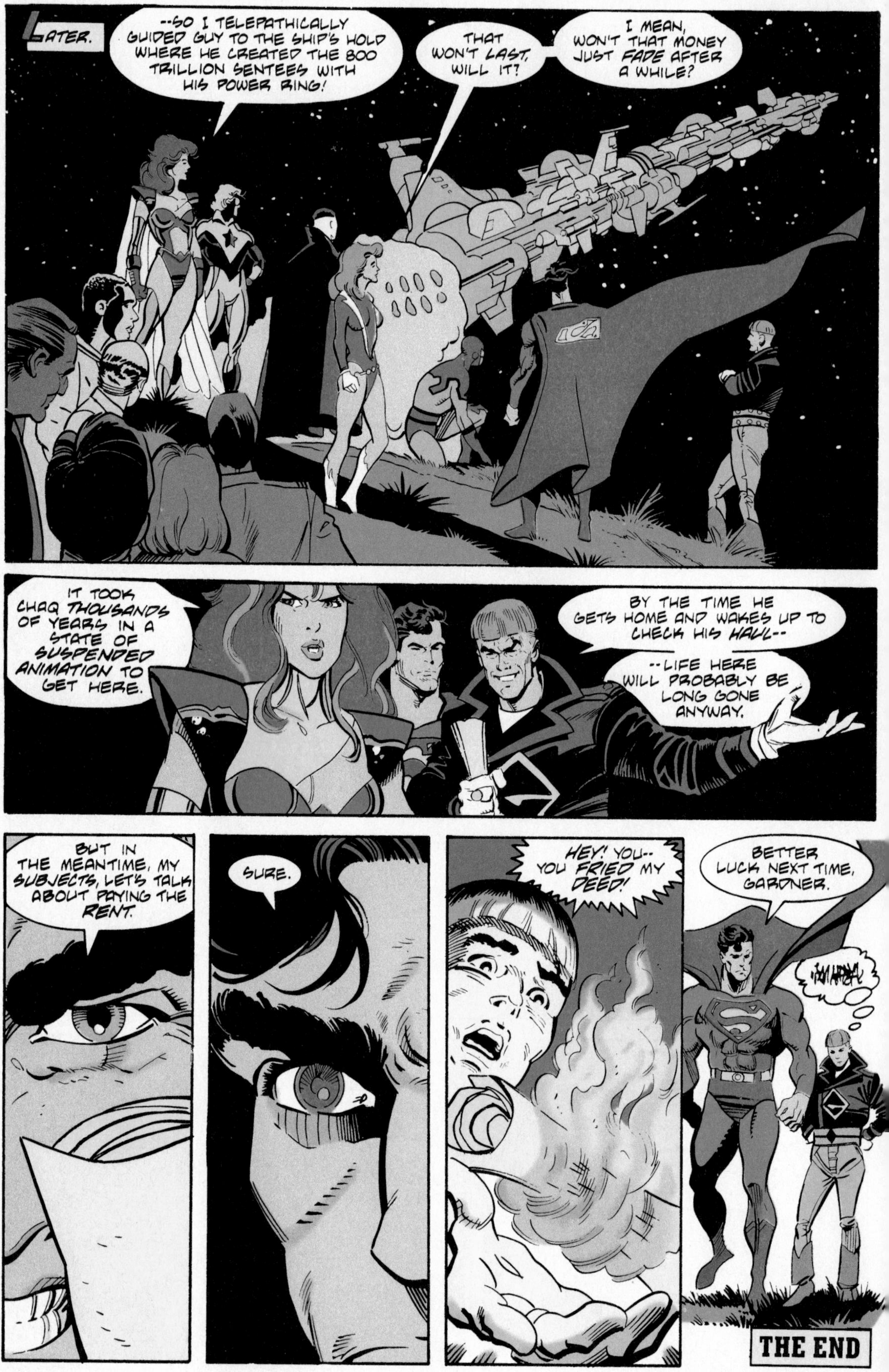
LATER.
--SO I TELEPATHICALLY GUIDED GUY TO THE SHIP'S HOLD WHERE HE CREATED THE 800 TRILLION SENTEES WITH HIS POWER RING!
THAT WON'T LAST, WILL IT?
I MEAN, WON'T THAT MONEY JUST FADE AFTER A WHILE?
IT TOOK CHAQ THOUSANDS OF YEARS IN A STATE OF SUSPENDED ANIMATION TO GET HERE.
BY THE TIME HE GETS HOME AND WAKES UP TO CHECK HIS HAUL--
--LIFE HERE WILL PROBABLY BE LONG GONE ANYWAY.
BUT IN THE MEANTIME, MY SUBJECTS, LET'S TALK ABOUT PAYING THE RENT.
SURE.
HEY! YOU-- YOU FRIED MY DEED!
BETTER LUCK NEXT TIME, GARDNER.
THE END

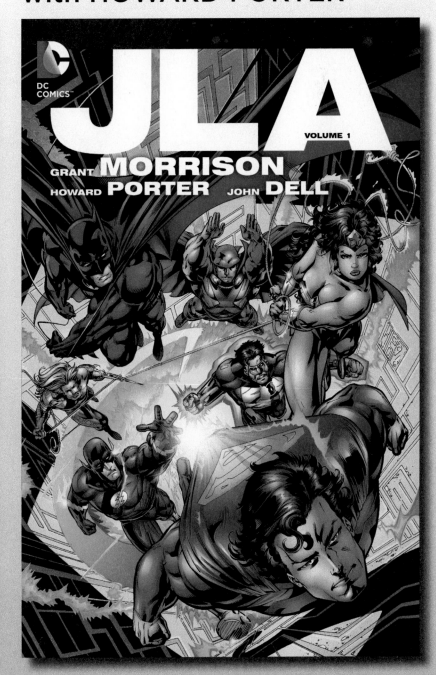

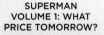

DC COMICS™

START AT THE BEGINNING!

SUPERMAN: ACTION COMICS VOLUME 1: SUPERMAN AND THE MEN OF STEEL

SUPERMAN VOLUME 1: WHAT PRICE TOMORROW?

GEORGE *PEREZ* JESÚS *MERINO* NICOLA *SCOTT*

SUPERGIRL VOLUME 1: THE LAST DAUGHTER OF KRYPTON

MICHAEL *GREEN* MIKE *JOHNSON* MAHMUD *ASRAR*

SUPERBOY VOLUME 1: INCUBATION

SCOTT *LOBDELL* R.B. *SILVA* ROB *LEAN*

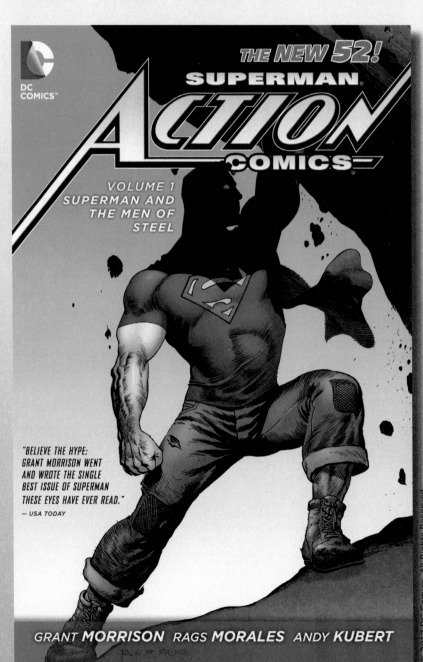

GRANT *MORRISON* RAGS *MORALES* ANDY *KUBERT*